GREAT C

The Nob

CW00968003

Daniel Green shares with Cobbett the experience of having been, at various times, lawyer, soldier, farmer, journalist, and author. He has published several books on subjects as various as the politics of food and Jefferson's Utopian concept of a farming and landowning democracy. Before becoming a full-time author he contributed to several journals and was, for a time, an agricultural correspondent and columnist for the *Daily Telegraph*.

GREAT COBBETT
The Noblest Agitator

DANIEL GREEN

'I saw great Cobbett riding
The Horseman of the shires;
And his face was red with judgement
And the light of Luddite fires.'
    G. K. Chesterton, *The Old Song*

Oxford   New York
OXFORD UNIVERSITY PRESS
1985

Oxford University Press, Walton Street, Oxford OX2 6DP

London New York Toronto
Delhi Bombay Calcutta Madras Karachi
Kuala Lumpur Singapore Hong Kong Tokyo
Nairobi Dar es Salaam Cape Town
Melbourne Auckland

and associated companies in
Beirut Berlin Ibadan Mexico City Nicosia

Oxford is a trade mark of Oxford University Press

First published 1983 by Hodder and Stoughton
First published as an Oxford University Press paperback 1985

British Library Cataloguing in Publication Data
Green, Daniel
Great Cobbett: the noblest agitator.—
(Oxford paperbacks)
1. Cobbett, William   2. Politicians—Great
Britain—Biography   3. Journalists—Great
Britain—Biography   4. Reformers—Great
Britain—Biography
I. Title
828'.608   DA522.C5
ISBN 0-19-281865-1

Library of Congress Cataloging in Publication Data
Green, Daniel.
Great Cobbett.
Reprint. Originally published: London: Hodder and
Stoughton, 1983.
Includes bibliographical references and index.
Bibliography: p.
Includes index.
1. Cobbett, William, 1763–1835.   2. Politicians—
Great Britain—Biography.   3. Authors, English—19th
century—Biography.   4. Great Britain—Politics and
government—1789–1820.   I. Title
DA522.C5G73 1985   941.07'3'0924[B]   84–22770
ISBN 0-19-281-865-1 (pbk.)

Printed in Great Britain by
Richard Clay (The Chaucer Press) Ltd
Bungay, Suffolk

To E.D.J.G.
Who
May grow up to enjoy Cobbett's
Company
And
To my Bankers
Who
Although not themselves in the
Book Trade
Made this Book Possible

AUTHOR'S ACKNOWLEDGMENTS

Anyone who lives as I do, in pleasant isolation, has to depend for much of his research material on the long-term loan of books from central and University libraries. I have, therefore, to thank Mr. Gall and all his staff at the East Lothian Library, Haddington, for so patiently arranging such loans. I have also to thank the staff at the Scottish National Library, the British Museum, the National Central Library and the Library of the National Army Museum for the help they have given me at various times. Whenever I have needed advice on bibliographical matters and the location of research material I have turned to Mr. M. W. Grose of Leicester University Library, and I acknowledge the help he has so constantly given me with great gratitude.

Mr. K. H. Grose, formerly of the English Department at Winchester College, has spent rather too much of his retirement reading this work in its various drafts and I have to thank him for undertaking a task many would gladly have avoided. Mr. J. R. Grey of the Cobbett Society has been an unsparing and encouraging correspondent over the years and I must record my gratitude to that most knowledgeable and constant of Cobbett enthusiasts. I have also to thank those other members of the Cobbett Society and the Cobbett family who have so kindly answered the queries I have put to them.

Many professional writers must, when undertaking a work such as this, look these days for financial help to tide them over the years that must elapse between preliminary draft and completed text. The most important assistance afforded me I have acknowledged in the dedication. The work would never, perhaps, have been started without generous help by way of a research grant from the Scottish Arts Council whose assistance in this and other matters I gratefully acknowledge. I have also to thank various publishers of previous works of mine who, wittingly or otherwise, provided some of the money which has gone into financing what can only be described as an obstinate and quite unprofessional labour of love. The only one of these it would be ungrateful not to name is Mr. M. D. J. Chesterman.

AUTHOR'S ACKNOWLEDGEMENTS

I have also to thank Mr. Rivers Scott, formerly of Hodder & Stoughton, who originally commissioned this work. If his successors have felt, from time to time, that they have, by inheritance, got an unexpected and awkward pig by the tail, I apologise to them and thank them for having chosen Mr. John Bright-Holmes as the out-of-house editor with whom I should work. No author could hope to have a more sympathetic or skilful partner in the Procrustean task of making Cobbett fit into a single volume when several would still be too small to contain him. If the cuts and lacunae are obvious, the fault is entirely mine. Where the stitching together has been achieved without post-operational shock the skill has always been the editor's.

Most of all, however, must I thank my wife Barbara, who has had to live for far too many years in Cobbett's company, and has had, as a consequence, to endure a Cottage Economy.

CONTENTS

Author's Introduction

AUTHOR'S INTRODUCTION

There are two things I am confident I can do very well; one is an introduction to any literary work, stating what it is to contain, and how it should be executed in the most perfect manner; the other is a conclusion, shewing from various causes, why the execution has not been equal to what the author promised to himself and to the public.

Dr. Samuel Johnson: *Boswell's Life of Johnson*

When William Cobbett died on 18 June 1835 all the newspapers and journals, including those most persistently opposed to him, insisted that a great and extraordinary Englishman had disappeared from a scene over which he had, for the past thirty years, cast an increasingly large shadow. It was, perhaps, the last occasion on which so much greatness would be conceded to him by so many. Subsequent generations soon forgot what the obituarists had claimed for him. If members of the general public remember him at all today, it is not because he may or may not have been a great man or a noble one, but because he was the author of *Rural Rides* and a few other frequently mentioned but infrequently read minor classics.

But if the public has come close to forgetting him, the biographers never have. An anonymous *Life of William Cobbett Esq, Late M.P. for Oldham* was in the bookshops within a few months of his death. Robert Huish's two-volume *Memoirs of the Late William Cobbett* appeared the following year, and these have been followed, at decent intervals, by such a steady flow of Biographies, Memoirs, Lives and Letters, Works, Thoughts and Extracts as to make it probable that Cobbett is, by now, more written about than read.

If, as a consequence, something that might be described as a Cobbett industry has grown up around him, it is primarily because it is difficult for any student of that period to overlook him. He played too vigorous a part in the history of his times to be safely ignored, although how effective he was can still be argued about. More important than what he may or may not have achieved is what he left behind him in the vast body of his writings. These, quite apart from whatever other values they might have, provide

1

what is by far the most comprehensive, if prejudiced, blow by blow and day by day account of those times. This would still be the case if one ignored all his other published works together with all his letters, lectures and speeches, and relied solely on the twelve volumes of *The Collected Works of Peter Porcupine* (his pseudonym when in America, 1792–1800) and the 40,000-odd pages of his *Political Register*.

He is not, however, solely for the historians. Other writers have been equally attracted to him. Literary critics ought to consider him, and generally do, whenever they consider the writing of English prose, for he was something of a literary phenomenon – an acknowledged master of the language who had few stylistic ancestors and has had even fewer heirs. Those interested in English humour or in the now decaying art of the political polemic find it difficult to ignore him. Countrymen studying the countryside and the way of life they have inherited have to pay him particular attention, if only in order to understand why, and how greatly, their heritage has changed.

He has been made the subject of books by writers who are primarily interested in some aspect or other of human nature or the English character, for few writers have ever exposed themselves so entirely and so unselfconsciously to their readers as Cobbett, and few have ever been more obviously – and more insistently – English. What Pepys confided to a cipher Cobbett, confident that he had nothing to conceal, presented, week by week, to the British public. He was, in short, a rare example of the complete and completely unashamed egotist, a quality which eventually obliged even his enemies to admit that he was indisputably 'a character'. This meant, as it always has in England, that the public took more notice of him than it did of any mere statesman or national hero. Most writers would agree that any one of these attributes is reason enough for a biography.

Taken all in all, however, they are attributes which make it almost impossible to describe Cobbett whole. There is altogether too much of him, as his career demonstrated. He was, at one time or another and sometimes concurrently, ploughboy, attorney's clerk, professional soldier, autodidact, pamphleteer, journalist, translator, author, publisher, bookseller, farmer, landowner, business man, bankrupt, litigant, prisoner, fugitive, exile, traveller, arboriculturalist and gardener. He wrote alternately as a polemicist, an expert on foreign and military affairs, an historian, a grammarian, an educationalist, an economist, an agronomist, a somewhat homespun philosopher, and a decidedly lay preacher. He was, as a consequence, the most prolific, widely-read, all-purpose literary hack of his day and the author of at least half a dozen classics. He was a High Tory for more than ten years (1789–1800), a potential Whig for two or three (1801–4), and a Radical for the remainder of his life, yet there was never a time when he was not, in the truest sense of the word, an Independent. He was one of the greatest of all political agitators, a fine if histrionic orator, a disappointing Member of Parliament and one of the very few English journalists ever to graduate from writing political leaders to leading a political party.

It would take a remarkable biographer to do equal justice to every aspect of such a many-sided and versatile man. If few have attempted the task it is because of the obvious danger of producing a work as crowded as a railway timetable and not greatly more entertaining. Most have, instead, sketched in as much of Cobbett's character and career as they considered essential; thereafter they have concentrated on those aspects of him they felt best qualified to discuss and most likely to enjoy. There is, as a consequence, a certain element of the autobiographical in almost every Cobbett biography.

One would, for example, expect the political writers to concentrate on Cobbett's politics to the exclusion of almost everything else. Many of them, however, have been even more selective, have concentrated on the years when his political views approximated to their own and have skated over those other years when he was preaching an opposite doctrine. This was especially the case with the late G. D. H. Cole, who was certainly the most informed of all Cobbett biographers. Even he came very close to disregarding what he obviously thought of as Cobbett's aberrant Tory years in order to concentrate on the Radical ones. Only two chapters in his magisterial biography are devoted to Cobbett the High Tory whilst no fewer than eleven are devoted to the Radical who, as a consequence, and in the face of much evidence to the contrary, emerges as a proto-Socialist who has some right to be recognised as the precursor to Keir Hardie.

On the other hand G. K. Chesterton, in a much slighter biography, was happy to present Cobbett as a precursor to G. K. Chesterton. That is, he saw him as a mediaevalist who looked backwards towards pre-Reformation England, who appreciated the sad paradox inherent in the belief that the new industries and the new capitalism represented progress, and who followed paths of thought that must have led him, had he not died, along the path to Rome. Here, then, are two out of a large number of biographies, each in its own way excellent, and each presenting with equal conviction a quite different version of Cobbett. Anyone whose first approach to Cobbett has led him to read both is entitled tó feel puzzled. When he is offered yet another version he has some right to be told how its author arrived at it.

I have, whether by choice or force of circumstance, been variously a lawyer, a farmer, a soldier, a journalist and an author. This may or may not have given me a better understanding of certain aspects of Cobbett, who also followed those callings a century and a half earlier. What is certain, however, is that the balance of this work and, as a consequence, the version of Cobbett it advances have been influenced by that odd coincidence of experiences. I have stayed longer with Cobbett when he was on his farms, or in the Army, or in Fleet Street, or defending himself in court than other biographers may have done. This has meant that, in so far as it was possible with such a completely political animal as Cobbett, I have spent less time on his politics than others and may, indeed, have approached that subject in a slightly different manner.

It is, of course, right that most of his biographers should have paid more attention to Cobbett's Radical period, which lasted for thirty years, than to his earlier Tory one which lasted about ten years; and it was as a Radical that Cobbett entered British political history. If I have discussed his Tory period at greater length than is customary, it may be because I believe that its importance in relation to his political development and to the politics of the time has too often been overlooked, as has that innate and peasant conservatism which made him the particular sort of Radical he eventually became. I cannot, however, ignore the possibility that it may also be because, whenever I remember to have any political opinions, they are usually closer to those Cobbett held when he was a High Tory than to those he ought to have held when he was a Radical.

On the whole, however, I prefer to believe that it is because most of us feel that a man's ultimate political convictions are always less interesting than the manner by which he arrived at them. In this respect Cobbett is unique amongst politicians. The progress of his politicisation can be followed in his writings from the time when he first found himself to be a Tory to his ultimate conversion to Radicalism. Few other politicians have written about their political careers before they have reached the end of them. Most of them have, by then, forgotten the early years and many of them have more to conceal or explain away in the later ones than they have to reveal. It was the opposite with Cobbett. From the start he published such a regular account of his political education that one can almost name the week in which he first acquired a political conviction and the one in which he finally abandoned it. He was never ashamed of changing his opinions in public.

The history of the part Cobbett played in the struggle for Reform has been frequently and very adequately explored: the history of his political education has not. I have chosen, therefore, to concentrate on what has been comparatively underexplored and to treat the whole of the Reform period as the culmination of a political pilgrimage which, if for nothing else, was remarkable for its transparency. I have, in short, chosen to study *how* Cobbett became 'the father of Reform' rather than add to the many studies of what he actually did in that capacity.

The reader should be warned that no attempt has been made in this work to correct Cobbett's version of the history of his times. He was, it should be said, a most perceptive man and a remarkably honest one in his own way. If there is an apparent element of humbug about him it is because he had successfully humbugged himself before attempting to do as much with his readers. No one can be a truly successful polemicist and agitator unless he can do the same. It is the duty of the biographer to look at life, in so far as that is possible, through his hero's eyes. Cobbett, almost of necessity, suffered from tunnel vision and generally saw no more than he wanted to see. His version of history, therefore, differs, not only from accepted versions but also from that of the most partisan historians. Jefferson was not the dangerous fool Porcupine depicted, any more than William Pitt was the ogre Cobbett wrote about. Nevertheless, it is still one of the joys of reading Cobbett that he so frequently jolts us out of our accepted positions and tempts us, however much we allow for his prejudices, to consider the possibility that there may be more in history than the historians have agreed upon.

Hazlitt, rather puzzlingly, maintained that 'there is not a single *bon-mot*, not a single sentence in Cobbett that has ever been quoted again'. If he meant that nothing in Cobbett was quotable, he was wrong. But if he meant that Cobbett has to be quoted at length or not at all, his remark was justified. Cobbett, never an epigrammatic writer, built up his effects passage by passage and even paragraph by paragraph. To epitomise him is to lose him; to paraphrase him is an act of presumption and an insult to a man who was a master of English prose.

Wherever I have quoted him, therefore, I have usually done so at length. There are two reasons for this. I am very conscious that it is difficult, if not impossible, to put a thing better than he put it and one of the main aims of this work is to give the newcomer to Cobbett something of the authentic flavour of the man. Wherever the quotation could be shortened by putting parts of sentences or passages together without losing that flavour I have done so, marking the omission where what was left out was irrelevant, but running the quotation on when the loss was merely one of repetition.

The number after each quotation refers to the work from which it is taken, and these sources are listed at the end of the book. Since most of Cobbett's books went into several editions during his lifetime and some have been republished since, page numbers are of little use to the reader. Cobbett, however, generally numbered his paragraphs and those numbers have been given wherever possible. When the quotation is taken from one of Cobbett's newspapers, copies of which are normally available only in the statute libraries, I have used the date of publication as a guide.

Although Cobbett was a grammarian who prided himself on the correctness of his writing and was more than ready to point out that his opponents were as weak in their syntax as they were in their logic, his own orthography is sometimes at fault, and his punctuation, by modern standards, unusual. I have followed the texts as they were first printed, with not a single (*sic*) to emphasise the fact that even the author of three different grammars in two different languages could make an occasional mistake. Cobbett's lavish use of italics may irritate the modern reader, but it was a necessary part of his style and the passages read more flatly if that old-fashioned typographical device is omitted.

This Introduction, which began with a quotation from Dr. Johnson, has not entirely complied with its epigraph. It has attempted to tell the reader what the work will *not* contain and to explain why it has not, and probably cannot be 'executed in the most perfect manner'. As for any conclusions, they are best left to the reader. The author is very conscious that the execution 'has not been equal to what he promised himself'; nor, perhaps, could it ever be. His first hope is that it might induce the reader to turn to what Cobbett wrote instead of to what others have written about him. This it can only do if it has persuaded him that Cobbett is still a man worth keeping company with; a man who speaks to us across the centuries about matters that still concern us and in language we can still understand; a man to be listened to with pleasure and irritation, to be laughed with, argued with and, on occasion, laughed at; a man who is, above all other things, a great 'character', and to be enjoyed as such. If the reader can be persuaded of any of these things the author will have achieved more than he has dared promise, and a great deal more than he dares to expect.

PART ONE

THE MAKING OF AN AGITATOR

William Cobbett is the noblest English example of the noble
calling of an agitator.
        G. K. Chesterton: Introduction to *Cottage Economy*

CHAPTER ONE

Arcadia Lost

Say not thou, 'What is the cause that the former days were better than these', for thou dost not enquire wisely concerning this.

Ecclesiastes 7:10

William Cobbett was born, in 1763, into a middling-poor peasant* family in West Surrey. He cannot be said to have attracted any public attention until he was in his mid-thirties, or to have taken any noteworthy part in English public life until he was in his mid-forties. All that we know of his early years, therefore, is what he himself saw fit to record. Fortunately, however, Cobbett, who developed into one of the most autobiographical of writers, scattered references to his childhood, upbringing and early adventures over the vast body of his writings. He was at once so self-centred and so self-regarding that he always found it difficult to discuss any subject without reference to himself. This compulsion to use himself as a reference point may have been what prevented him from ultimately writing the Autobiography he had always planned, for which he had already selected as a sub-title, *The Progress of a Plough-Boy to a Seat in Parliament*. In fact, the nearest he ever came to a detailed and chronological description of his early life was contained in *The Life and Adventures of Peter Porcupine*, which he wrote at the age of thirty-three during his first sojourn in the United States. That work, however, contained no more autobiographical detail than he thought would rebut the lies then being circulated about him by his many enemies in Philadelphia. It never amounted to a detailed description of the period and the manner in which his adult character was formed.

Consequently, although Cobbett has to be described as an autobiographical writer, one never feels that he is a wholly self-

---

* The word 'peasant' means even less in English than it does in other languages, perhaps because England was the first European country to dispense with its peasantry. I use the word here loosely to refer to all those at the lower end of the economic scale who had to make their livings from the land, whether they worked it for themselves or for others.

revealing one. He never felt compelled, like St. Augustine or Jean-Jacques Rousseau, to expose himself to his readers in all his frailties and shortcomings. He never, indeed, seemed to feel conscious of possessing any. Almost the only failings he would ever confess to were omniscience, infallibility and the most absolute rectitude. This had always, of course, some bearing on the amount of credulity his readers could bring to him. When a writer so obviously feels it essential, on so many different occasions, to be his own best hero, his reader is obliged to wonder whether, on at least some of those occasions, he felt it equally essential to be absolutely honest with himself or with them.

Nevertheless, as his is almost the only evidence we have about his early life, I have, like other biographers before me, accepted it *au pied de la lettre.* Since it was only the second half of his life that was of any literary or historical importance, and since that half has been amply, and more than amply recorded by his contemporaries and by later biographers, the absence of any evidence but his own about the early years might seem unimportant. There is, however, this to consider. Cobbett was pre-eminently a man in whom character, for want of a better word, always prevailed. He was a reasoning, but seldom a reasonable, man. Those qualities of temperament, instinct, emotion – in a word, character – determined what he thought and what he did. He was also, from all that we know about him, a man whose character was fully formed and fixed at an unusually early age. That is not to say that he was impervious to change. Indeed, in the course of his long life, he changed his positions, his professions, his politics and his friends more frequently than most, but he always did so in reponse to the dictates of a character that never changed. The plough-boy who, on an impulse, ran away to London, the youthful sergeant-major who risked transportation or worse in pursuit of what he conceived to be justice obeyed precisely the same imperatives as the older man who, whatever the risk, thought it necessary, at various times, to attack the Revolutionary, the Democratic and the Conservative establishments of his day.

If one accepts, as I do, that with him, character was all, and if one also accepts that his character was determined in the first twenty years of his life, then it must be right to consider the factors that, in those early years, can be accepted as character-forming. Experts on such matters usually agree that these include heredity, family background and education, even though they seldom agree which of these is the most important. I would also, however, seek for one particular reason to include in the discussion the countryside he was born into.

10

There is much to support the view that the mature Cobbett's political thinking was increasingly coloured by the memories he had constructed for himself of the agrarian civilisation of his childhood. He eventually persuaded himself, reasonably or otherwise, that he had been born into the last decades of an ancient, almost-unchanging, English Arcadia, an Arcadia that had, in the course of a very few years, been wilfully and wickedly destroyed by the new and evil forces and the new and evil men let loose in England.

The myth and reality of that Arcadia, together with the inevitability or otherwise of its loss, do far more than the politics of the day to explain Cobbett to posterity. It would be genetical heresy to believe that his character was entirely or even largely determined by the environment he was born, or believed he was born, into. But it would be far from heresy to believe that his childhood environment provided him, to an unusual degree, with his adult frame of reference. It was because he lamented Arcadia and sought, fruitlessly, to reconstruct it that he ultimately developed into the most backward-looking of all the great early English Radicals. It was because he judged contemporary conditions against all the folk memories he had inherited that he became increasingly contentious, prejudiced and vindictive. It was because he looked back to a lost and improbable Arcadia that he was, in spite of all his down-to-earth, damn-your-eyes, plain-John-Bull-and-no-nonsense attitudes, an unworldly romantic. And it was because of all these things that he can never sit congruously in the Pantheon the progressives have built for their heroes.

When we examine the various factors that went to the making of William Cobbett, therefore, we should also examine the reality and the nature of the Surrey Arcadia in which he was made. We are then in better-charted country. When we discuss Cobbett's family and education, we have only Cobbett himself to rely on. But we have more than Cobbett to guide us when we attempt to discover what was significant about life in Surrey and the South Country and rural England in the middle of the eighteenth century.

One of the lesser problems of relying on Cobbett himself is the question of his age. He persistently under-estimated it by no less than three years. Only in 1904 did E. I. Carlyle finally establish that William Cobbett had been born on 9 March 1763, and not, as he always maintained, on the same date in 1766. He was baptised, according to the register of the Farnham parish church of St. Andrew's, on 1 April 1763: an apt day, perhaps, for a man who would make fools of so many of his contemporaries.

His birthplace was a small public house called, at that time, The Jolly Farmer, situated in Bridge Square on the outskirts of the small West Surrey town of Farnham, opposite the bridge over the River Wey. It is still there, and still a public house. Although it is no longer thatched, it is still clearly recognisable as the building that Gillray put into the first of a series of cartoons which, with some fairly garbled text, went to make one of the many anti-Cobbett lampoons published some forty years later. The cellars still flood, as they did in Cobbett's day, whenever the Wey overflows its banks. The sand-cliff out of which the infant Cobbett scraped his first garden still looms over the back of the house. Indeed, apart from the nature and density of the traffic flowing into Farnham, little has changed here except the name of the house. It is now called The William Cobbett: and it has, in its small way, become a place of pilgrimage.

William was the third of four children, all sons, born to George and Ann Cobbett in the space of four years:

> The exact age of my brothers I have forgotten, but I remember having heard my mother say, that there was but three years and three quarters difference between the age of the eldest and that of the youngest.[1]

All four sons, born though they were on each other's heels, survived into manhood. In most families of that period there would probably have been one stillbirth or one death in infancy to record in any four years of childbearing. William, as his contemporaries observed, was unusually strong, healthy and active. The records of his numerous descendants, down to the present day, reveal that there is, in the Cobbett strain, a predisposition to longevity.

There is little known about that strain, however, prior to William. The common families of our country may well be the mortar of our history but, like mortar, they remain for the most part hidden. All that we know about his parents or grandparents, apart from the bare records in the parish register and the mute testimony of the gravestones, is contained in a few passages in *Life and Adventures*:

> To be descended from an illustrious family certainly reflects honour on any man, in spite of the sans-culotte principles of the present day. This is, however, an honour that I have no pretensions to. All that I can boast of in my birth is that I was born in Old England . . . With respect to my ancestors, I shall go no further back than my grandfather, and for this very plain reason,

that I never heard of any prior to him. He was a day-labourer;
and I have heard my father say, that he worked for one farmer
from the day of his marriage to that of his death, upwards of forty
years.[2]

Here, then, was William's connection with the farm labourers,
the 'chopsticks'* he was to defend, instruct and encourage so
lovingly in the later years of his life. A gravestone in the parish
churchyard records that this particular George Cobbett, the father
of a second George who was, in his turn, the father of William, died
on 15 December 1760, aged fifty-nine. He would, in the course of
his lifetime, have seen little change, for change had not, as yet,
come to the rural communities. He had probably spent the whole
of his working life on the one farm, for before being married he
would likely have lived in and have fed at the farmer's table, where
the farmer 'Used . . . to sit at the head of the oak table along with
his men, say grace to them, and cut up the meat and the pudding.
He might take a cup of *strong beer* to himself, when they had none;
but that was pretty nearly all the difference in their manner of
living.'[3] He would, at that stage in his life, have been what his
grandson would lovingly describe, eighty years later, as a 'Knife-
and-fork chopstick . . . used to sit around the fire with the master
and the mistress, and to pull about and tickle the laughing
maids . . .'[4]
   More important, living-in would have allowed him to save
almost all of his small money wage against the day when he got
married and was obliged to buy a cottage and garden of his own
because the farmhouse could no longer accommodate him. This
probably allowed him to acquire, in addition, rights on the common with such attendant advantages as keeping a cow and finding
his own fuel. William used to remember, in later years, the days he
had spent as a boy in that same cottage with his widowed grandmother:

It was a little thatched cottage, with a garden before the door. It
had but two windows; a damson tree shaded one, and a clump of
filberts the other. Here I and my brothers went every Christmas
and Whitsuntide to spend a week or two, and torment the poor
old woman with our noise and our dilapidations. She used to give

* The dictionaries give neither a definition nor a derivation for a word that
Cobbett used frequently when talking of the farm labourers of Sussex and
Hampshire. These were still, in his day, well-wooded counties in which the rural
poor would, by custom or right, have access to underwood for their fuel. 'Sticking'
is still used to describe the gathering of fallen wood for fuel. The 'chopping' would
come from the need to cut and bind the wood into faggots.

us milk and bread for breakfast, an apple pudding for our dinner, and a piece of bread and cheese for supper. Her fire was made of turf, cut from the neighbouring heath, and her evening light was a rush dipped in grease.[5]

It was a self-sufficient and unchanging society his forebears inhabited, but it was also a more open one than it ever would be in the future. The poor still had some rights of access to the land, and for those who were willing to work and save for it, further access was not impossible. William's father may have inherited no more than a cottage, a 'scythe, reap-hook and flail' from his own father; but this never prevented him moving out of the labouring and more or less landless class into the farming and more or less landed one. William, in short, was born into what was then the largest section of the English middle-class, but he could always, when he chose, claim kin with the labourers. In an age when Marx had not, as yet, formalised the class war, and where class itself meant far less than rank, William's connections and sympathies, placing him as they did in a sector of the community that stretched in economic terms from the poorest to the most important, made him, in later years, one of the most classless of men:

My father, when I was born, was a farmer. The reader will easily believe, from the poverty of his parents, that he had received no very brilliant education: he was, however, learned for a man in his rank of life. When a little boy, he drove the plough for two pence a-day; and these his earnings were appropriated to the expenses of an evening school. What a village schoolmaster could be expected to teach he had learnt; and had besides considerably improved himself in several branches of the mathematics. He understood land-surveying well, and was often chosen to draw the plans of a disputed territory: in short, he had the reputation of possessing experience and understanding, which never fails, in England, to give a man in a country place some little weight with his neighbours. He was honest, industrious and frugal: it was not, therefore, wonderful that he should be situated in a good farm, and happy in a wife of his own rank, like him beloved and respected. So much for my ancestors, from whom, if I derive no honour, I derive no shame.[6]

What, in fact, he derived from his father was an example, for, in describing his parent, William came close to describing himself in his maturity. If the father was industrious, William was even more so. He was, in one way at least, quite as frugal, for he was never

14

inclined to spend much on himself, however much he may have improvidently spent on acquiring new farms or new publishing ventures. He was, like his father, honest: brutally so when it came to voicing his opinions, though perhaps slightly less than candid when it came to reversing them. Where the father had an appetite for education and struggled to acquire it, the son developed into one of the most successful of autodidacts. If the father enjoyed a happy marriage, the son was triumphantly uxorious, and valued the domestic virtues above all others. Finally there was, on his own admission, another characteristic which they shared: 'If my father had any fault, it was not being submissive enough, and I am afraid my acquaintances but too often discovered the same fault in the son.'[7]

The 'good farm' George Cobbett eventually acquired was situated at some distance from The Jolly Farmer, on the edge of what is now the Alice Holt Forest. We do not know how large it was, but internal evidence suggests that it was large enough to support a four-course rotation and a hop-garden of some size, and prosperous enough to have allowed George to acquire The Jolly Farmer. All that is known about 'the wife of his own rank' is that when, in 1759, she was married to George Cobbett, she, being illiterate, signed the register with a cross. Among country people in her station of life this was not unusual, indeed her illiteracy was less surprising than her husband's painfully acquired literacy; and when William came, in his turn, to marry another Ann, she was, so far as can be ascertained, as illiterate as her mother-in-law.

William's three brothers completed the family. These were named, in order of seniority, George, Thomas and Anthony. He wrote of them in 1796, that is, some thirteen years after he had left the family home: 'I had (and hope I yet have) three brothers: the eldest is a shopkeeper; the second a farmer; and the youngest, if alive, is in the service of the Honourable East India Company, a private soldier, perhaps, as I have been in the service of the king.'[8]

Some four years later, when William had just returned to England from the United States, he wrote about his brothers to his friend and patron, Edward Thornton, who had stayed on in Philadelphia as Chargé d'Affaires at the British Legation to the United States:

I have been to see my brothers (those who are in England). My father is dead, and my brothers I found with very large families, and, though not miserable, far from being in easy circumstances; indeed, I may call them *poor*; for, though one has the little paternal estate, and though both of them pay poor rates, they are obliged to work very hard, and their children are not kept constantly at school.[9]

William rejoiced in being able to help his brothers, just as he took pleasure in helping members of his wife's family. Nothing more is known about the oldest brother, who was a shopkeeper. It was, however, characteristic of the times that the 'good farm' their father had possessed had, by 1800, shrunk to 'a little paternal estate' that could only keep Thomas and his family in poverty. Things had changed considerably in farming in the course of that particular half century. The heavy taxes and the soaring inflation brought about by the French wars had made it increasingly difficult for the smaller farms to remain viable. Engrossment had become almost as much an economic necessity as enclosure. The destruction of a landed English peasantry was, as a consequence, already well advanced. The last we hear of Thomas is twenty-eight years later. By then he is working as farm bailiff for his brother William, and William has to advertise, in his *Political Register*, for a youth who will do the running around Thomas is incapable of doing.

As for the youngest brother, Anthony, nothing is known about him after he left India apart from Melville's* comment that he then acquired 'some notoriety as a pugilist'. No doubt he was deploying as a professional talents which his older brother William used to employ as an amateur. William may not have been mentioned by Pierce Egan in *Boxiana,* but he was always, in an *ad hoc* and entirely practical manner, a man of his fists. He stood, according to different accounts, either one inch over or one inch under six feet, and in his maturity rode, according to his own account, at 'Just the weight of a four-bushel sack of good wheat',[10] that is to say, at eighteen stone or 252 lbs. Even those whom he had done most to provoke seemed to realise that wisdom in their dealings with him would always lie this side of fisticuffs.

So it was that, even in the Republican and Jacobinical city of Philadelphia – where duels, horsewhippings, cudgellings and mobbings seemed to be normal aspects of political controversy – no man or mob dared, when it came to it, to face him, even though he spent so many years libelling their heroes and ridiculing their fondly-held beliefs. So far as is known, the only time he ever had to use his fists in Philadelphia was when, meeting Benjamin Franklin Bache, a rival newspaper proprietor, in the street, he promptly knocked him down, so putting an end to a personal and political argument that had gone on for months in their respective journals.

* See Bibliographical Note.

16

He did as much, some years later in London, to Heriot, editor of *The True Briton*. As often as not, however, his mere physical appearance was enough to spare him the necessity for physical violence. In Philadelphia, Beckley, then Clerk to the House of Representatives considered that Cobbett had libelled him, which was almost certainly the case:

> [Beckley] had the assurance to tell me that if I took any more liberties with his name he would horsewhip me! This he accompanied with a posture as menacing as his poor emaciated frame could possibly assume. I replied, that I was resolved to take just what liberties with his name I thought proper, and invited him to come immediately into the street, and put his threat of chastisement into execution. Finding him hang back, it struck me that he might be ashamed to show his bare bones to the populace . . . I therefore proposed to him to go back into my garden and bring his friend with him. He now bethought himself (for the first time) that I was 'a scoundrel beneath his notice' . . .[11]

So it always was with Cobbett, even when he was advanced in age. Men always drew back, in the end, from a physical encounter with him.

He was not, however, a mere bully-boy rejoicing in the advantages of size and strength. He had the sort of courage that is proverbially denied to bullies, and was fearless in facing up to that most frightening of forces, a street mob. He defied one to break his windows and burn his house in Philadelphia, and nothing happened. He did the same, later, to a London mob and had his windows broken as a consequence, for which he promptly secured the arrest and trial of the ringleaders. His was the sort of courage that went beyond defiance, for it could fire him with what was obviously the joy of battle. He was nearly sixty when he fought the Coventry seat in the 1820 election, at a time when gangs of bullies were still hired to keep electors from the polling booth:

> On my way to the polling booth I had to pass through the band of savages; and I was scarcely among them, when they began to endeavour to *press me down*. I got many blows in the sides, and, if I had been either a short or a weak man, I would have been pressed under foot, and inevitably killed . . . I had to fight with my right hand. I had to strike back-handed. One of the sharp corners of my snuff-box, which stuck out beyond the bottom of my little finger, did good service. It cut noses and eyes at a famous rate . . . Just at this time, one of the savages exclaimed,

'Damn him, I'll rip him up!' He was running his hand into his breeches pocket, apparently to take out his knife, but I drew back my right leg, armed with a new and sharp gallashe over my boot, and dealt the ripping savage so delightful a blow . . . that he fell back upon his followers.[12]

No other English man of letters, except perhaps George Borrow, so enjoyed a set-to, or was quite as efficient with his fists, his snuff-box or his gallashes.

Cobbett received no schooling and, indeed, no formal education of any description, even though 'I have some faint recollection of going to school to an old woman who, I believe, did not succeed in teaching me my letters'.[13] His father, however, helped, at intermittent intervals, to educate him and, what is even more important, to reveal the possibilities that lie in self-education: 'In the winter evenings my father taught me to read and write, and gave me a pretty tolerable knowledge of arithmetic. Grammar he did not perfectly understand himself, and therefore his endeavours to teach that failed, for though he made us get the rules by heart, we learnt nothing at all of the principles.'[14]

But more important was the fact that Cobbett, the future 'Rural Rider', was brought up, from his earliest days, at the plough-tail:

To a taste for farming, produced in me by a desire to imitate a father whom I ardently loved and to whose every word I listened with admiration, I owe no small part of my happiness . . . Early habits and affections seldom quit us while we have vigour of mind left. I was brought up under a father, whose talk was chiefly about his garden and his fields, with regard to which he was famed for his skill and exemplary neatness . . .[15]

Farmers are no longer necessarily gardeners, and gardeners are even less necessarily farmers. In the mid-eighteenth century, however, the distinction could not always be made, especially where the smaller farmers and commoners were concerned. For them the garden would often serve as a nursery-bed for the field, and the field would often amount to little more than an extension of the garden. The woods, copses and even the hedgerows could, in many cases, be thought of as an extension of both, for wood in all its various forms was both a cash crop and an essential raw material for smallholder, farmer and landowner. It was used in the garden, the farm and the farmhouse for a multitude of purposes from fencing to firing, from machinery to transport. Forestry and wood-using skills were as important then as gardening and farming ones.

The future author of *The American Gardener*, *The Woodlands*, *Cottage Economy* and *The English Gardener* acquired all these skills unknowingly, for he had to practise them almost as soon as he could walk:

> I do not remember a time when I did not earn my living. My first occupation was, driving small birds from the turnip seed, and the rooks from the peas. When I trudged afield with my wooden bottle* and my satchel over my shoulders, I was hardly able to climb the gates and stiles, and, at the close of day, to reach home was an infinite labour. My next employment was weeding wheat, and leading a single horse at harrowing barley. Hoeing peas followed, and hence I arrived at the honour of joining the reapers in harvest, driving the team and holding the plough. We were all strong and laborious, and my father used to boast that he had four boys, the eldest of whom was but fifteen years old, and who did as much work as any three men in the parish of Farnham.[16]

There were to be long intervals in his life when he could not indulge in his passion for farming, but there would be far fewer when he did not contrive, in some fashion or other, to have a garden to care for. 'From my very infancy . . . when I climbed up the sides of a steep sand rock and there scooped me out a plot of four feet square to make me a garden, and the soil for which I carried up in the bosom of my little blue smock-frock, I have never lost one particle of my passion for those healthy and rational and heart-cheering pursuits . . . I have never, for any months together, been without a garden.'[17]

But there was more, of course, to his education than an introduction to the three Rs and to the arts of gardening and husbandry. There were also those extra-curricular activities that old-fashioned pedagogues thought of as 'character-forming' and modern ones classify as 'physical education'. Cobbett had all the country boy's fondness for cricket, for bird's-nesting and for such entertainments as were to be found at country fairs and markets. He made much,

---

* The crook, the blue smock-frock, the satchel and the wooden bottle recur, time and again, in Cobbett's recollections of childhood, becoming for him convenient symbols of his lost Arcadia. I am indebted to an article by Martin Orme in the Cobbett Society's *New Register* for the information that the wooden bottle was not a bottle at all, but rather a miniature oak barrel with a projecting mouthpiece to drink from, and a cord, usually of plaited horsehair, by which it could be slung.

also, in later life, of an unusual and rather pointless pastime he and his brothers had engaged in as children. Each would, in his turn, be rolled up inside his smock-frock and then tumbled down a particular sand-hill near Farnham that was 'steeper than the roof of a house'. The exertion of climbing back up that hill, the buffeting involved in rolling down it, the small amount of danger and the vast amount of laughter involved furnished, Cobbett would insist, the best preparation for life that any future Member of Parliament could wish for:

I am perfectly satisfied that if I had not received such an education, or something very much like it; and that if I had been brought up a milksop, with a nursery-maid everlastingly at my heels, I should have been at this day as great a fool, as inefficient a mortal, as any of those frivolous idiots that are turned out from Winchester or Westminster School, or from those dens of dunces called Colleges and Universities . . .[18]

For he had developed, as most country boys do, a passion for the true sports, rather than the games and pastimes, of the countryside; and he would, in later life, be a most vocal and staunch supporter of such ancient and robust sports as bull-baiting, bare-knuckle fighting and single-stick play, and show nothing but contempt for those who, in his view, sought to destroy the manly qualities of the race by making the first two illegal and neglecting the third. Of bull-baiting he would write in 1802:

Of all the bull-baiting in England one half is carried on in Staffordshire and Lancashire. The best soldiers in the kingdom . . . come out of those counties . . . The Staffordshire Regiment of Militia is not only the finest but the best-behaved regiment of militia in the kingdom. Wherever this regiment goes it is followed by a score or two of bull-dogs . . .[19]

As for boxing, he reprobated the Bill, presented by Bowles and Spencer Perceval in 1802, which sought to make bare-knuckle fighting illegal, while allowing gloves, or 'mufflers' to be used. Once this was passed, he maintained, Englishmen would no longer settle matters with their fists, but would, like cowardly Frenchmen and Italians, take to stabbing each other. The entire Bill, he said, 'goes to the rearing of puritanism into a system'.[20]

Single-stick play, which was falling into neglect, he attempted to revive when he became the 'Squire' of Botley in Hampshire. He described it, in a letter to his patron William Windham, as:

> An exercise that requires great strength and very great fortitude. The players use a stick three-quarters of an inch in diameter, 2½ feet long, and having a basket hilt to defend the hand. They are stripped to the shirt; and the object is to break the antagonist's head in such a way that the *blood may run an inch* . . . The arms, shoulders and ribs are beaten black and blue, and the contest between two men frequently lasts for more than an hour. Last Whitsuntide there was a match at Bishop's Waltham where one of the players, feeling that he had a tooth knocked out, and knowing that if he opened his mouth the blood would be perceived, *swallowed both blood and tooth*, and continued the combat (with two others driven from their places in his gums) till he obtained the victory.[21]

All of these were sports he first came across in his Farnham days. In later life, he became an enthusiastic shooting man, though it is doubtful whether, as the son of a small farmer, he had much opportunity to shoot when young. His innate, country conservatism made him deplore the new fashion of rearing pheasants for battues. Such barnyard sport, and the new Game Laws devised to protect it, could, he thought, be left to the new men and the new ways they had brought into the countryside. But to shoot the grey partridge, that most native of all the English gamebirds, over dogs was something he prized only slightly less than hunting the hare either on foot or on horse. He was never so fond of the comparatively new sport of fox hunting, but 'I ran after the hare-hounds at the age of *nine or ten*. I have many and many a day left the rooks to dig up the wheat and the peas, while I followed the hounds, and have returned home at dark-night with my legs full of thorns and my belly empty, to go supperless to bed and to congratulate myself if I had escaped a flogging. I was sure of these consequences; but they had not the smallest effect in restraining me. All the lectures, all the threats vanished from my mind in a moment upon hearing the first cry of the hounds, at which my heart used to be ready to bound out of my body.'[22]

It is not only modern, liberal-minded readers who might deplore such an appetite for 'blood sports'. There were many of Cobbett's contemporaries who considered his liking for such robust and antique pursuits unseemly. Mary Russell Mitford, writing of her stay with the Cobbetts at Botley, recorded what took place when a

21

fellow guest, a Mrs. Blamire, firmly told her host that his tastes in sport were barbarous:

> In my life I never saw two people in a greater passion. Each was thoroughly persuaded of being in the right; either would have gone to the stake upon it; and of course the longer they argued the more determined became their conviction. They said all manner of uncivil things; they called each other very unpretty names; she got very near to saying, 'Sir, you're a savage'; he did say, 'Ma'am, you're a fine lady'; they talked both at once, until they could talk no longer; and I have always considered it as one of the greatest pieces of Christian forgiveness that I ever met with when Mr. Cobbett, after they had both cooled down a little, invited Mrs. Blamire to dine at his house the next day. She, less charitable, declined the invitation, and we parted.[23]

Those sporting tastes were, however, part of Cobbett's inheritance and of his education, and they were reflected, therefore, in his character. In such matters as sex, pudor and sobriety the mature Cobbett was, perhaps, a premature Victorian. In almost everything else, however – in his instincts, tastes and preferred mode of living – he remained what he had been born, an eighteenth-century countryman. The squeamishness that went with the heightened sensibilities of the early nineteenth century was never for him.

Cocooned as he was in the right little, tight little rustic world of The Jolly Farmer and the family farm, the young Cobbett had few opportunities and little need to keep in touch with the world outside. It is difficult to believe that the boy who was to become one of the greatest of all political journalists could have been brought up without either politics or newspapers, but such, indeed, was the case:

> I do not remember ever having seen a newspaper in the house; and most certainly that privation did not render us less industrious, happy or free . . . As to politics, we were like the rest of the country people in England; that is to say, we neither knew nor thought anything about the matter.[24]

Politics impinged eventually, however, if only because of George Cobbett's attitude to the war then being fought against the American colonists. Whatever attitude the average Englishman adopted towards that struggle was intrinsically political, however apolitical he might otherwise consider himself to be. To those who, however unthinkingly, were legitimists and monarchists, it was a rebellion. To those who, with no more thought given to the matter, were instinctively levellers and republicans, it was a revolution. Cobbett's father, whether he had considered it rationally or not, was among the latter: 'It is well known that the people were, as to numbers, nearly equally divided in their opinions concerning the war, and their wishes respecting the result of it. My father was a partisan of the Americans . . .'[25]

George Cobbett not only argued about the war in private with his neighbours but, unusually, and perhaps unwisely for a publican, he made his views known in public:

> My father used to take one of us with him every year, to the great hop-fair at Wey-hill . . . and the journey was, to us, a sort of reward for the labours of the summer. It happened to be my turn to go thither, the very year that Long Island was taken by the British. A great company of hop-merchants and farmers were just sitting down to supper as the post arrived, bringing in the Extraordinary Gazette which announced the victory. A hop-factor from London took the paper, placed his chair upon the table, and began to read with an audible voice. He was opposed, a dispute ensued, and my father retired, taking me by the hand, to another apartment, where we supped with about a dozen others of the same sentiment. Here Washington's health and success to the Americans were repeatedly toasted, and this was the first time, so far as I can recollect, that I ever heard the General's name mentioned.[26]

What one has to ask is whether this suggests that more thought was given to politics in The Jolly Farmer than Cobbett claimed, and whether, if there was, this had any influence on the young Cobbett. It would be wrong to claim that merely being pro-American proved that George Cobbett was, knowingly or otherwise, a Radical. But Radicalism, in its old, agrarian form, had always been strong in Surrey and the South Country, and George, it should be remembered, was a Surrey man who had come up in the world. It is not uncommon to find that self-made men are either excessively in favour of the system that allowed them to better themselves or radical critics of it for having made betterment so difficult. He was also an intelligent, literate and stubborn man. It is not improbable therefore that, however little he indulged in politics, such political sympathies as he possessed inclined him towards the left rather than towards the right.

Would this have had any influence on young William? If one accepts that to be brought up to sympathise with the American colonists was to be brought up to sympathise with the republican and radical cause, then, according to his own evidence, given when he was still a High Tory, it had. In the private arguments his father had with 'the gardener of a nobleman who lived near us . . . my father was worsted, without doubt, as he had for antagonist, a shrewd and sensible old Scotchman, far his superior in political knowledge; but he pleaded before a partial audience; we thought that there was but one wise man in the world, and that was our father. He who pleaded the cause of the Americans had an advantage, too, with our young minds; he had only to represent the king's troops as sent to cut the throats of a people, our friends and relations, merely because they would not submit to oppression, and his cause was gained.'[27]

We are dealing, here, with opinions which may never have been formulated and were certainly never recorded. However the only political opinions the young Cobbett ever expressed before he emigrated to the United States and found himself, almost to his surprise, to be a Tory, were anti-monarchical, republican and almost revolutionary in tone. It may well be, therefore, that a certain long-established peasant radicalism was part of his inheritance as a Surrey peasant. The Surrey countryside was also a part of that inheritance.

In the eighteenth century the Bagshot Heaths, which run down close to Farnham, were some of the most unproductive land in lowland England. 'There is barrenness indeed,' he wrote towards the end of his life; 'there it is that you see sterling sterility.'[28] The heaths did not, however, present an uninterrupted scene of agricultural desolation:

In so immense a tract of land . . . there are certainly numerous very pretty dips, and in these the land is generally extraordinarily good; and in cases where the sterility is not so complete, where the commons are greenish, and studded round with cottages and little gardens and fields, most assuredly the sight is the prettiest, and the life the happiest in the world; because the soil is warm, the spring and the singing birds come early, the ground is dry, the air is excellent . . . but, as to produce of food, acre for acre, taking in the whole space that I have described, and leaving out the valley of the Wey, I am very certain that this spot is inferior to the HIGHLANDS of Scotland.[29]

In the south of the county lie the heavy clay lands of the Weald. Its soils would not, in those days, easily give up their fertility, for the practice of thorough draining was not, as yet, widespread and the bullock was only slowly giving way to the horse as a source of plough-power: 'This Weald is a bed of clay, in which nothing grows well but oak trees . . . The fields are small, and about a third of the land is covered with oak-woods and coppice-woods.'[30]

Between the Heaths and the Weald run those ridges of green-sand and chalk that form the North and South Downs:

> I have often mentioned, in describing the parts of the country over which I have travelled . . . the *chalk-ridge* and also the *sand-ridge*, which I had traced, running parallel with each other, from about Farnham in Surrey to Sevenoaks in Kent . . . I was always desirous to ascertain whether these ridges continued on thus *to the sea*. I have now found that they do. And if you go out into the Channel at Folkestone, there you see a sand-cliff and a chalk-cliff.[31]

These chalk and sand ridges, and the valleys and combes between them, provided fertile soils that, being more easily worked than the Weald and very much more productive than the Heaths, constituted what were, at that time, the most important agricultural parts of the county. Nowhere in Surrey, however, was more fertile than the limited area of the Wey Valley, at whose eastern end Farnham stands:

> I was born at FARNHAM in Surrey; and Arthur Young, in his survey of England, says, that from FARNHAM in Surrey to ALTON in Hampshire is 'a space containing the finest ten miles in the kingdom'.[32]

This was one of those limited oases of particular fertility that the happily variegated English countryside can, quite unexpectedly, produce. The rich river-meadows of the narrow valley bottom gave way, on the slopes, to 'the finest hop-gardens in the world', interspersed by highly productive corn fields and orchards and 'very pretty woods'. It was an area made all the more attractive by the poor lands that surrounded it:

> If he [Young] went from London to Chertsey and did not put his spectacles on (he was very weak-sighted all his life and blind several years before he died) . . . his unmixed praises of the vale of FARNHAM are perfectly accountable. He was not bound to

know that the town of FARNHAM and the little valley there was a mere *little strip*; and that, if, when he was in the middle of the town, he had gone off due north or due south, he would have traversed, in either direction, full *twelve miles*, compared to which the HIGHLANDS of Scotland are the land of CANAAN.[33]

There are, from even so brief a description of the topography of Surrey, certain historical inferences to be drawn. What Cobbett wrote at the beginning of the nineteenth century remained very largely true for the next hundred years. At the end of that century, in spite of the tide of suburbs that was beginning to flood over Surrey, almost half of its total area of some half a million acres was still accounted for by wastes, heaths and woodlands. Much of this was still probably unenclosed land, and the woodlands were mainly found on the heavy soils of the Weald, and the other uncultivated lands on the Bagshot Heaths.

This high proportion of land that was, in terms of the art as it was then practised, either difficult to farm or only worth farming in times of shortage, meant that the pressure to enclose came later to Surrey than to many other counties. It remained, in agricultural terms, 'unprogressive' until the French wars forced change. Villeinage, for example, survived there into the sixteenth century, and open-field farming was common throughout the eighteenth century.

As a consequence, the small farmer and those below him in the rural hierarchy – cottagers, commoners and squatters – were seldom disturbed by the enclosers and engrossers. They continued to enjoy as much access to the land as their ancestors had, over the centuries, painfully acquired. This meant that, even at cottager level, rights to pasture, turbary and estover would, respectively, provide grazing for a cow or a few goats or a flock of geese on the commons, and wastes and fuel in the form of turfs or underwood. Cottage gardens large enough to keep a family in vegetables and fruit would be customary, and those who had access to an acre or two of arable land could expect to keep their households in bread and malt for much of the year, with something over, perhaps, for fattening the pig in the sty.

The poorest, in short, could still, if they wished, enjoy a degree of self-sufficiency that ensured a more or less adequate diet for themselves and their families and a less than absolute dependence on a wage and money economy. Cobbett, in later life, fully appreciated the paradox that the rural poor would fare better in the poorer areas:

Invariably have I observed, that the richer the soil, and the more destitute of woods; that is to say, the more purely a corn country, the more miserable the labourers. The cause is this, the great big bull frog grasps all . . . and the wretched labourer has not a stick of wood, and has no place for a pig or a cow to graze, or even to lie down upon. The rabbit countries are the countries for the labouring men. There the ground is not so valuable. There it is not so easily appropriated by the few.[34]

If the heaths were typically rabbit country, the weald was typically forest country, and here, also, there were benefits for the poor that could not be found in the purely corn counties. At a time when, in so many other areas, the farm labourer had been denied access to the land and had, in many cases, had both cottage and cottage garden swept away, Cobbett wrote of the forest-dwellers:

Their cottages are very neat and the people look hearty and well . . . Every cottage has a pig or two. These graze in the forest, and, in the fall, eat acorns and beech-nuts . . . Some of these foresters keep cows, and all of them have bits of ground, cribbed, of course, at different times from the forest, and to what better use can the ground be put?[35]

When Cobbett was young, the southern counties constituted what was probably the most productive, and therefore the most important region in the country. England was then not only self-sufficient in food and raw materials, but was also an exporter of agricultural produce. The South Country produced a large proportion of those things on which the country's economy depended. In 1785, according to Macpherson's *Annals of Commerce*, there were still only three industries in Britain whose annual output was valued at more than ten million pounds. Of these the wool industry, with an output worth more than seventeen million pounds a year, was not only the largest, but also by far the most important, because of the large amount of employment it also gave to the weavers, who were still, for the most part, cottage workers.

Sheep, as a consequence, were more important to the farmer and the nation than either corn or beef, and the as-yet unploughed Downs supported vast flocks of sheep in almost ideal conditions. Their chalk sub-soils made them both free-draining and drought-proof, and so provided a long grazing season. The acquifers held deep in the chalk give up their moisture in summer and keep the pastures of even the upper Downs from burning. Those pastures,

27

with their undisturbed turf full of fine, sweet grasses and chalk-loving clovers, provide the best of all summer grazing for sheep. The deeper soils of the valleys and lower slopes furnish the water meadows and arable land that will produce all the winter keep they will need, and still leave broad acres for corn and other cash crops. England, it should be remembered, was still the most important corn-exporting country in Western Europe. As late as 1750, when her population was already beginning to increase at a hitherto unprecedented rate, she exported half a million tons of corn to the Continent, much of it grown in the southern counties. Half a century later she was already dependent on imports of no less than three quarters of a million tons.

If sheep supported the country's most important industry, the next most important was connected with the production and working of iron. This was still done in small units scattered over those areas where iron ores could be found in close proximity to the woodlands that would produce the charcoal needed for the smelting. Kent and Sussex had, for centuries, been the most suitable of those areas, and their iron-masters had been, perhaps, the first of England's industrial magnates. The Darbys of Coalbrookdale, however, were already experimenting with the use of coal for smelting, largely because deforestation in Sussex and Kent had made charcoal increasingly expensive. Once they had succeeded in their experiments, the metal-producing and the metal-using industries would become increasingly concentrated around the coal-fields, and the Black Country, symbol of England's industrial rise and ultimate decay, would be born. Until then, however, the southern counties were as essential to the metal-using industries as they were to the textile ones.

Wood was still in more common use than iron, however, when Cobbett was born, and so timber constituted a far more important domestic crop than it does today. But, for the shipwright, the millwright, the wheelwright and all engaged in the other timber-using trades, wood, in those days, meant hardwoods. Cobbett, who became one of the leading arboriculturalists of his day, despised the conifers that monopolise forestry today: 'These plantations are of fir, or at least, I could see nothing else, and they can never be of any more use to the nation than the sprigs of heather which cover the rest of the forest.'[36]

Hardwoods, however, whether grown for timber or coppice, require soils that are deep and strong enough to allow timber trees to reach optimum growth and coppice to renew itself rapidly. They require, in short, such soils as are to be found in the Wealds, and in the valleys and lower slopes of the Downs. Here again, Cobbett's

28

country was the leading producer of a raw material essential to the national economy.

Wool, mutton, beef, corn, iron and timber ensured the economic importance of the South Country. It was, not to put it too finely, the heartland of England. It also, so far as Cobbett was concerned, produced the best hops, a secondary crop but one that was considerably more important than it is today. Beer was not only a national drink, as perhaps it still is, but it was also an almost essential ingredient in the production of what was a most valuable part of the working man's diet. Most beer was then home-brewed, and almost every farmhouse and cottage had a continuing need for hops to give flavour and keeping quality to the very large amounts of small and strong ale produced domestically. Cobbett calculated that when tea replaced beer in the worker's diet, each man lost some 500 lb of what he called 'sweet', and we would call carbohydrates, in the course of a year. Although he constantly preached and ostentatiously practised sobriety in what was still a hard-drinking age, he none the less thought it essential to the well-being of any farm labourer that something approaching three hundred gallons of beer should be brewed and drunk in his cottage in the course of a year.

We have come close, these days, to accepting the theory that the only aspect of his environment that has any important influence on a child is his class environment. There is still a need, even so, to take notice of geography; but how much more was this the case when Cobbett was a boy. Then the physical environment – that is to say the influence of such things as soils, climate, elevation, aspect and local natural resources – had considerable bearing on the social and economic life of different regions, districts and even parishes. That this could have been particularly so in Cobbett's case can be tested by trying to imagine what sort of a man he would have grown into if his father, instead of being a small farmer in West Surrey, had been a London grocer, a Nottingham weaver or a Deptford shipwright. The difference would certainly have been most evident in the things for which he eventually became most famous. He would undoubtedly, if he had become a writer, have become a different sort of writer, and there would have been no *Cottage Economy*, no *Woodlands*, no *English Gardener*, and, above all, no *Rural Rides*. Equally, if he had become a politician, he might well have ended up as a Radical, but it is most improbable that he would have become the unusual sort of Radical that Farnham Cobbett actually and ultimately became.

Some of the influences exerted on Cobbett by an eighteenth-century country childhood can be guessed at more confidently than others. They seem to have been adequately documented by Cobbett himself. Others we can only wonder about. It was surely the influence of his early environment, for example, that made him and kept him a countryman, even though he was to spend so much of his life divorced from the countryside. It was not merely that he never lost his taste for farming and gardening or his interest in the life and sports of the countryside, but also that he never lost his distaste for urban life. He spent, on and off, a third of his life in London without ever once recording any liking for the place. So far as he was concerned, it was, in physical terms, a noisy, dirty, unhealthy place in which he constantly caught colds. In political terms, it was the Great Wen, the symbol of almost everything that had gone wrong in England in the course of his lifetime; a place that produced none of the country's food and little enough of its real wealth, but consumed far more than its proper share of both.

It was as part of making him a countryman that Surrey gave him that deep and enduring love of nature which so enlivened his writing in later life. He was able to read a countryside, as he rode across it, as spontaneously as a scholar reads a known text, and was never unaware of the underlying rocks that formed the skeleton of the land or of the nature and quality of the soils that fleshed it. He was, however, a child of the heaths and wastes of Surrey, as well as of the fertile, intensively-cultivated land of the Wey Valley, and this led, in his case, to a certain internal conflict that was never resolved, for the farmer in him tended to differ from the naturalist. If the Wey Valley made him the one, the untouched heaths – with their wide, uncluttered landscapes and their undisturbed wild life – probably made him the other.

He never rode through a countryside without noticing the presence or absence of birds, or without commenting on their flight and song habits and how they responded to the snows of winter. He would remark on its wild flowers, its native trees, the shapes of hills, cloud formations, and speculate on the origins of the mists that swirled over the Downs. These were all things he wrote about, almost unconsciously, while he was conducting his series of ostensibly political investigations into the state of agriculture and of country life that became, eventually, *Cobbett's Rural Rides*. He wrote about them, moreover, with something of the freshness and wonder of a child realising for the first time the difference between scrub oak and forest oak, lark and linnet, downland and fen. The interest and delight he took in these things was of such an enduring quality that they must have been with him ever since he was an urchin engaged in bird scaring or running truant after the hare-hounds.

On the other hand, born as he was in the Wey Valley, where every activity was directed towards crops and cropping, he grew up with a profound conviction that land was for using, and that those lands which could be used to the best advantage would always provide the more beautiful landscape. He was too much of a professional farmer to succumb to the comparatively new cult of the Picturesque. The wild mountains and desolate crags that had become so attractive to the romantic writers of the day did little more for him than remind him of how little they would produce in the way of food.

So it was that, although none of his contemporaries left behind them better descriptions of the English countryside and the American wilderness, he defied his readers to think of him as anything but a farming writer when it came to country subjects. Only a year before he died, he wrote, 'I have, for my part, no idea of *picturesque beauty* separate from *fertility of soil*. If you can have *both*, as on the banks of CLYDE, and on the skirts of the *bays* and *inlets* in Long Island, then it is delightful: but, if I must have *one* or *the other*, any body may have the *picturesque beauty* for me.'[37]

Cobbett was never, in fact, the unfanciful man he claimed to be. It is true that he saw in a fine stand of timber, a well-cultivated root field or a full rickyard a beauty that more romantic writers might have failed to see. But it is equally true that fertility, for him, represented food, and what he wanted most of all, for Englishmen in general and the rural poor in particular, was an abundance of food. But his claim that he never saw beauty in anything except a fertile landscape was a contradiction of all that he wrote about so much else in the countryside that had little or no connection with fertility. It was as if Constable had claimed that the only thing he could admire and paint was a haywain.

One of Cobbett's characteristics as a soldier, a farmer and the head of a household was the great emphasis he always put on neatness, order and timeliness. These are, of course, farming virtues, and nowhere are they more necessary than in a hop-garden. For there the plants have to be spaced out across the field with a mathematical exactitude imposed on them by the requirements of stringing, and the ground has to be kept as clean as a garden bed or cleaner. The Wey Valley at that time grew 'the finest hops in England' and Cobbett's father had a hop-garden in which Cobbett had laboured:

The first work that I ever did in my life, was to tie the hop shoots round the bottom of the poles with rushes; and . . . even as soon as I could stand on my feet, those feet used to help trample the rushes, spread upon the floor for that purpose, in order to make them pliant to tie with.[38]

It is that mention of rushes, however, which reminds us of another, and more important lesson that Cobbett must have first learnt in the Surrey of his childhood. It was the lesson of Economy, something that would concern him throughout his adult life, and would have a profound effect on his political thinking.

Economy [he wrote] means management and nothing more; and it is generally applied to the affairs of a house and family, which affairs are an object of the greatest importance, whether as related to individuals or to a nation.[39]

He was not an altogether successful manager of his own domestic economy, but this never prevented him from writing, with singular fervour, about the economic affairs of the nation or, indeed, about the cottage economy.

The cottage economy – the sound management of the cottage household – had to be based, he maintained, on a policy of maximum self-sufficiency. This, in its turn, depended on having access to land on which food could be grown or reared, and to commons, wastes and woods where the products of nature could be harvested. The rushes used for tying the hops offer one small example of this policy at work. They cost nothing but the labour involved in cutting them and treading them into pliability, and they saved the hop-grower the price of string. But at least some bread, meat, milk, beer, fuel and clothing could all, when he was a boy, be got in the same way, so long as the cottager had, as he had then in Surrey, a garden to dig, a strip on the open field and access to the common and wastes. These things would keep him at least partially outside the money economy while still allowing him to live and feed better than his descendants would for generations to come.

This was the way of life that the young Cobbett saw practised by all but the most indigent or the most idle. But when he returned to the South Country after an absence of more than twenty years, that way of life was disappearing. The cottager, having lost most of his access to the land, had become wholly and solely a wage-earner. Since wages were low and prices high, his wife, as often as not, joined him in the field and, because she no longer had the time or the means for them, gave up her breadmaking, brewing and bacon curing and failed to pass those traditional skills to her children. One consequence of entering wholly into the money economy is an increasing reliance on the brewer, the baker and the candlestick maker and on earning the wages with which to pay them.

Cobbett could not reconcile himself to this passing of a way of life he remembered so fondly from his childhood, especially as it resulted, in an inflationary period, in a rapid lowering of the labourer's standard of living and the appearance, for almost the first time in generations, of endemic food hunger. He refused to believe that the old ways could never return, and he wrote his *Cottage Economy* in order to keep alive the domestic skills that were in danger of being abandoned and forgotten. He attacked the enclosers and the engrossers, even though, as a progressive farmer, he knew the benefits of enclosures and had himself added farm to farm at Botley. He could not accept the 'philosophical' argument of the day which was that the nation benefited doubly from enclosures, since they not only increased the productivity of the land, but also that of the farm labourer, who would no longer waste his time growing his own food but would be driven to greater industry working full-time for a wage.

He had an almost pathetic belief that the old ways would return. In the course of one of his Rural Rides he came across a farmer who let out one of his fields in quarter-acre strips to his labourers for allotments and remarked:

This fashion is certainly a *growing* one; it is a little step towards a *coming back* to the ancient small *life* and *lease* holds and *common-fields*! This field of *strips* was, in fact, a sort of *common-field*; and the 'agriculturalists' as the conceited asses of landlords call themselves . . . might . . . begin to suspect, that the '*dark age*' people were not so very foolish, when they had so many *common-fields*, and when almost every man that had a family had also a bit of land, either large or small.[40]

The reference to the 'dark ages', which he always placed in inverted commas because he considered them to have been, so far as country people were concerned, rather more enlightened than the age he lived in, reminds us of how much importance Cobbett, in his maturity, attached to the past. Whether the historical perspectives that increasingly dominated his thinking had their origins in the countryside of his boyhood is conjectural. However, it was probably his sense of the imminence and importance of the past that helped, in the end, to provide him with almost all that he

33

had of a political philosophy and with most of his political criteria.

He wrote, for the most part, as a polemicist, but he always aspired to be an historian and for many years planned to write, or rather rewrite, the history of England. He would be responsible, eventually, for starting, though not for writing, a *Parliamentary History of England* and the *Complete Collection of State Trials* that was later to be known to generations of lawyers and historians as *Howell's*. The two histories he did write – *The English Reformation* and *Regency and Reign of George IV* – demonstrated that he was too prejudiced for even the most partisan of his supporters to be able to accept him as a sound historian. Nevertheless, his particular interpretation of the immediate and distant past of the English so coloured his thinking, his politics and his writings that it is difficult to understand how such a profound sense of history developed.

It could be argued that it came, as all of his education came, solely from reading. Most of us, however, can read history books without suffering from his particular compulsion, which was to summon up the past so that it might always sit in judgment on the present. One need not rely on such an imponderable as the folk memory to suspect that some few intimations of antiquity seeped into him, through his pores as it were, during his Farnham childhood.

Farnham had, after all, been a place of settlement since prehistoric times. There were flint deposits in the nearby chalks, and worked flints of the Paleolithic Age can still be found in comparative abundance in the vicinity of what must have always been an important river crossing and crossways at Farnham. There is an ancient tumulus on top of the Crooksbury Hill Cobbett so frequently mentioned. The Pilgrim's Way, one of the oldest of all the pre-Roman routes, runs close to the town. Briton, Roman, Saxon and Norman have all left tangible evidence of settlement. Farnham formed, at various periods, part of the Kingdom of Wessex, of the See of Winchester, of the earldom of Leofwine, Harold Godwinson's brother, and of the manor, sixty hides, or some five thousand acres of Wey Valley land, which William the Conqueror gave to the new Bishop of Winchester, who was his half-brother. Another bishop, Henry de Blois, who was the Conqueror's grandson and King Stephen's brother, built the castle at Farnham that was later modified into a palace for the bishops of Winchester. It was in the grounds of that palace that the young Cobbett worked for a short period as garden boy. On the outskirts of the town the Cistercians built, in 1178, Waverley Abbey, the first of their abbeys in England. The ruins of that foundation were, in Cobbett's day, contained inside the estate of Sir Robert Rich, from whose gardens Cobbett, as a boy, stole the best of the strawberries.

It would be idle to assume that, when he was climbing Crooksbury Hill or working in the grounds of the castle Henry de Blois had built, the youthful Cobbett was consciously absorbing the lessons of history. Yet the past, then, must have seemed closer and more relevant to the present than it ever would again. For this was still a self-contained and self-continuing civilisation that had produced, so far as the common people were concerned, few sudden discontinuities. The last relevant change in their way of life to be remembered by the people of Farnham could well have been the Reformation.

Certainly Cobbett, in later life, would always maintain that the Reformation constituted the most important watershed in the whole of English history – not so much because it had brought about a change of religion as because it had brought about a change of landowners. The monks, he argued, had been far less demanding as landlords, and more deeply committed to caring for the poor than any of the *novi homines* who replaced them. The Reformation, therefore, had brought little but loss to the common people.

Henry VIII, who had engineered the English Reformation, and Elizabeth I who had re-established it, were, so far as he was concerned, two of the greatest villains in English history. In the still staunchly Protestant England of the eighteenth century, his could hardly have been the official version of the Reformation, nor was it one he could have constructed from the history books of the time. It could, however, have been a version handed down in garbled fashion from father to son by his peasant ancestors, who may well have thought a good landlord and the relief of poverty more important than any amount of doctrinal argument over Transubstantiation.

It is sometimes said that men inherit their political beliefs more frequently than they come to them by reasoning. If and when they do so, they are, however unconsciously, acknowledging the influence of history. Cobbett had a highly developed sense of history; which may have been why his particular form of radicalism, when he came to it, was far closer to the traditional radicalism of the South Country peasants than it was to that of the Jacobin intellectuals and the new urban proletariat. For there was, among the peasants of the south-eastern and eastern counties, a long tradition of radicalism which, every now and again in history, manifested itself in violence. Since Cobbett, in some ways, became the heir and last representative of that tradition, it is worth emphasising that this was an essentially peasant radicalism that was seldom or ever concerned with philosophical or political theories, but was wholly concerned with the ancient rights and the bellies of the poor.

The Surrey peasants had joined the men of Kent when they marched, under Wat Tyler, on London in 1381, largely because their pockets had been threatened by the new poll tax. The men from Farnham, it is recorded, turned aside at Southwark in order to burn the brothels. They did so, not for high moral reasons, but for typically peasant ones. The houses were the property of their feudal overlord the Bishop of Winchester, who represented most of what there was of central government in Farnham. The Bishop, it should be said, had leased the houses to William Walworth, Lord Mayor of London, who had, in his turn, sub-let them to the 'frows of Flanders'.

Surrey men joined Kentish men, once more, when they marched on London under Cade in 1450 and under Wyatt in 1554. They fought, for the most part, on the Parliamentary side in the Civil War, which was, in many respects, a war that had its origins in a dispute about taxation. Finally, in this respect, they took an active part in that last of all peasant movements in England, the 'Captain Swing' riots of 1830 when, according to the Surrey county historian, 'The south-eastern counties began to wear the look of a country where revolution was in the air.' He added also, 'William Cobbett was a native of West Surrey, and it is not impossible that his frequent presence in the neighbourhood of his old home had something to do with the spread of radicalism . . .'[41]

It had largely been the need for radical reform of conditions among the rural poor that had led Cobbett to abandon the Tory party and to become, in his own way, a Radical. Was he, by doing so, returning to his roots, or had his been no more than another case of political conversion?

It is easy, perhaps, for the biographer to discover or exaggerate childhood influences that might have made Cobbett what he was. But always, in the end, he has to find some explanation for Cobbett's Arcadianism, and for his hatred of the new industrialised and urbanised civilisation that was settling over England, blotting out its past. Why was it that, while most other Radicals were worrying over how to establish popular control over this new civilisation, only Cobbett was worrying over how to destroy it?

Most of his last twenty years in politics were devoted to pleading with his countrymen to turn back from change. 'Stop', he seemed, in effect, to be saying. 'The England we are destroying was a far better place for the common man to live in than the England we are now building. I can prove it to you by Alfred the Great and Edward

III, by St. Augustine, Fortescue and the monks of Beaulieu, for I know as much about them as I know about Pitt and Wellington and Castlereagh. I can prove it to you in terms of beer, bread and bacon, of strip-fields and common rights and comfortable cottage homes, of self-sufficiency for the industrious and relief for the indigent, for I remember how things were half a century ago, when I was a plough-boy in Surrey.'

He was, in short, enquiring, with a growing anger, 'What is the cause that the former days were better than these?' Was he 'enquiring wisely'? What was the difference between the myth and reality of Arcadia? He was, in his own overstated way, right about the horrors of the present and the future. But he was factually wrong to attribute so many felicities to the past. He was guilty, if one may invent such an ugly word, of the Arcadianisation of history, and for this, if for nothing else, the influences and memories of a Surrey childhood were at least partly responsible.

CHAPTER TWO

Exit into the World

Les vrais paradis sont les paradis qu'on a perdus.
Marcel Proust: *Le Temps Retrouvé*

Apart from that rocky Peloponnesian plateau whose inhabitants, in classical times, were principally goatherds noted for their stupidity, Arcadias can have no more than a metaphysical existence. They are countries to be looked back on or forward to but never to be lived in. So it was with Cobbett. He had to leave Farnham before he could, many years later, begin to remember Arcadia.

It was not easy, however, to leave Farnham, and he only succeeded in doing so at his third attempt. When he was about fourteen, he had worked in the gardens of the Bishop of Winchester's Palace, where his 'employment was the clipping of box-edgings and weeding beds of flowers'.[1] Splendid though the grounds of what has now become a Centre for International Briefing still are, they failed to provide him with all that he wanted:

I had always been fond of beautiful gardens; and a gardener who had just come from the King's gardens at Kew, gave such a description of them as made me instantly resolve to work in these gardens. The next morning, without saying a word to anyone, off I set with no clothes except those upon my back, and thirteen half-pence in my pocket. I found that I must go to Richmond, and I accordingly went from place to place, inquiring my way thither.[2]

Then, as always, he preferred to obey impulse rather than reason. Richmond lay a long, hot, summer's day away, and the bread, cheese and small beer he bought for his refreshment left him, when he finally arrived, with no more than threepence in his pocket. As he walked through Richmond 'in my blue smock-frock and my red garters tied under my knees', he saw, in a bookseller's shop window, a copy of Swift's *Tale of a Tub*. The oddity of the title induced him to spend his last coppers on it. Then:

38

I was so impatient to read that I got over into a field, at the upper corner of Kew Gardens, where there stood a hay-stack. On the shady side of this I sat down to read. The book was so different from any thing that I had ever read before; it was something so *new* to my mind, that, though I could not at all understand some of it, it delighted me beyond description; and it produced in me what I have always considered a sort of birth of intellect.[3]

Whether it was a birth of intellect or not, it was almost certainly the first book he had ever bought for himself. As such, it was his first introduction to that world of books which he would, within a few years, enter and inhabit for the rest of his life. It was almost as though, having kissed a girl for the first time, he had promised himself to acquire the habit just as soon as he could afford it.

After a night spent in the haystack, the boy began to walk through Kew Gardens reading his book. It was then that 'The singularity of my dress, the simplicity of my manner, my confident and lively air, and doubtless, his own compassion besides, induced the gardener, who was a Scotsman, I remember, to give me victuals, find me lodging, and set me to work.'[4]

Simplicity, confidence and liveliness would always be three of Cobbett's most important qualities. They appear to have been, in the domestic man, entirely admirable qualities, for they, more than anything else, attracted people to him. His simplicity gave him a frank and open approach, his confidence made him diffident in no man's company, and his liveliness gave him a most engaging turn of humour. In his public life, however, simplicity all too often became a licence to be brutally rude, confidence grew into an almost intolerable cockiness, and liveliness demonstrated itself in savage sarcasm and ridicule. The private man was always able to turn strangers into instant friends, and to attract to himself, at almost every stage of his career, patronage and willing support. The Scots gardener was to be no more than the first of a succession of men who would be eager to help Cobbett for no sounder reason than that they had taken an immediate liking to him.

The only other thing known about the Kew interlude is that Cobbett was laughed at by a boy of about his own age whom he was, some forty years later, to attack constantly for his politics and his immorality, oppose in the matter of his divorce, and denigrate to posterity in his *Regency and Reign of George IV*:

It was during this period that I was at Kew, that the Present King and two of his brothers laughed at the oddness of my dress, while I was sweeping the grass Plat at the foot of the Pagoda.[5]

Cobbett was eventually reclaimed from Kew by his father, who set him to work on his farm for the following five years. His next attempt to escape into the outside world came in 1782, when he was nineteen. He was sent to pass some time with an uncle at Portsmouth, but he had got no nearer than Portsdown when he had his first glimpse of the sea:

> No sooner did I behold it than I wished to be a sailor. I could never account for this sudden impulse, nor can I now. Almost all English boys feel the same inclination: it would seem that, like ducks, instincts lead them to dash on the bosom of the water.[6]

Hardly had he felt the impulse than he succumbed to it. He immediately had himself rowed out to a man-of-war, the *Pegasus*, in order to enlist. The ship's captain, the Hon. George Berkeley, however, would have none of him:

> The Captain had more compassion than is generally met with in a man of his profession: he represented to me the toils I must undergo, and the punishment that the least disobedience or neglect would subject me to. He persuaded me to return home, and I remember he concluded his advice with telling me that it was better to be led to the church in a halter to be tied to a girl that I did not like, than to be tied to the gangway or, as the sailors called it, married to Miss Roper. From the conclusion of this wholesome counsel, I perceived that the Captain thought I had eloped on account of a bastard. I blushed, and that confirmed him in his opinion . . . I returned to the plough, but I was spoiled for a farmer.[7]

His first impulse to run away had done no more than lead him from the gardens at Farnham Castle to the gardens at Kew. This second attempt would have changed him from a farmer into a sailor, and it reflects a tendency that would, in future years, puzzle his friends and enrage his enemies: namely a willingness to change the course of his thoughts and actions almost in a minute. It earned him a reputation for being, at the best, inconstant and, at the worst, a turncoat.

Since the Navy had refused him, he had, for once, time in which to consider his next change of course, for change, he had determined, there now had to be:

> I had, before my Portsmouth adventure, never known any other ambition than that of surpassing my brothers in the different

40

labours of the field; but it was quite otherwise now; I sighed for a sight of the world; the little island of Britain seemed too small a compass for me. The things in which I had taken the most delight were neglected; the singing of the birds grew insipid, and the heart-cheering cry of the hounds, after which I formerly used to fly from my work, was heard with the most torpid indifference.[8]

None the less, it was once again a sudden impulse that led to his next and last attempt to escape from Farnham:

It was on the sixth of May, 1783, that I, like Don Quixote, sallied forth to seek adventures. I was dressed in my holiday clothes, in order to accompany two or three lasses to Guildford Fair. They were to assemble at a house about three miles from my home, where I was to attend them; but, unfortunately for me, I had to cross the London turnpike road. The stage coach had just turned the summit of the hill, and was rattling down towards me at a merry rate. The notion of going to London never entered my mind till this very moment, yet the step was completely determined on, before the coach came to the spot where I stood.[9]

He arrived in London with no more than half a crown of his holiday money left. Nevertheless:

By a commencement of that good luck, which has attended me in all the situations in which fortune has placed me, I was preserved from ruin. A gentleman who was one of the passengers in the stage, fell into conversation with me, and he soon learnt that I was going I knew not whither or for what. This gentleman was a hop-merchant . . . and . . . it appeared he had often dealt with my father . . . His house became my home, he wrote to my father and endeavoured to prevail on me to obey his orders, which were to return immediately home. I am ashamed to say that I was disobedient. Willingly would I have returned, but pride would not suffer me to do it.[10]

Since Cobbett remained obdurate, his benefactor, the hop-merchant, set about finding him employment in London. According to Huish,* though Cobbett himself never mentioned it, he was recommended, in the first instance to a draper who wanted a counter assistant. 'But the first qualification for such a position is gentility, and the draper advised the young rustic, who came to him

* Robert Huish, *Memoirs of the Late William Cobbett* (London, 1836).

41

attired in short and light yellow breeches, a fustian coat, a red plush waistcoat and a pair of hob-nailed high-lows, to return without delay to the plough.'[11]

It is difficult to imagine a genteel Cobbett spending his life measuring out yards of lace and matching up ribbons. Since that opportunity was denied him, however, the hop-merchant looked for something else:

He was preparing an advertisement for the newspaper, when an acquaintance of his, an attorney, called in to see him. He related my adventures to this gentleman, whose name was Holland, and who, happening to want an understrapping quill-driver, did me the honour to take me into his service, and the next day saw me perched upon a great high stool, in an obscure chamber in Gray's Inn, endeavouring to decipher the crabbed draughts of my employer . . .[12]

He was, at first, of little use to Holland:

I could write a good plain hand, but I could not read the pot-hooks and hangers of Mr. Holland. He was a month in learning me to copy without almost continual assistance, and even then I was of but little use to him; for, besides that I wrote a snail's pace, my want of knowledge in orthography gave him infinite trouble . . .[13]

Few men, however, were ever quicker than Cobbett at picking up new skills and fresh knowledge. The time soon came when 'Mr. Holland was pleased to tell me, that he was very well satisfied with me, just at the very moment when I began to grow extremely dissatisfied with him.'[14]

Following the plough and running after the hare-hounds had been bad preparations for the gloomy office in Gray's Inn, where candles had to be burned in daytime, work began at five in the morning and lasted till eight or nine at night, and almost the only person who spoke to him was 'The *laundress*, as Mr. Holland called her. Those gentlemen of the law, who have resided in the Inns of Court in London, know very well what a *laundress* means. Ours was, I believe, the oldest and ugliest of the sisterhood . . . It would be wronging the Witch of Endor to compare her to this hag, who was the only creature that deigned to enter into conversation with me.'[15]

The work itself seemed to him infinitely boring:

When I think of the *saids* and *soforths*, and the counts of tautology that I scribbled over; when I think of those sheets of seventy-two words, and those lines two inches apart, my brain turns.[16]

His only respite from the Gray's Inn dungeon was on Sundays, when he usually took a walk in St. James's Park in order to look once more at trees, grass and water, as if to reassure himself that these things still existed. It was small wonder that when he came, some dozen years later, to write about this, his introduction to London life, he described it as the only part of his life that had been totally unattended with pleasure. He rounded off the description – he was still testing his powers as a writer – with this bravura passage:

Gracious heaven! if I am doomed to be wretched, bury me beneath Iceland snows, and let me feed on blubber; stretch me under the burning line, and deny me thy propitious dews; nay, if it be thy will, suffocate me with the infected and pestilential air of a democratic club-room; but save me from the desk of an attorney.[17]

Little though he liked his attorney's desk, the nine months he spent at it had certain not unimportant consequences. It set him, for the rest of his life, on clerkish courses. The improvement in his 'orthography' allowed him, when he joined the Army, to avoid most of the hardships of life as a recruit, for it led, very rapidly, to an appointment as regimental clerk. He would, thereafter, pass more of his life at a desk than anywhere else.

It is arguable, moreover, that it was Gray's Inn that gave him a sufficient smattering of the law to turn him into the barrack-room lawyer he undoubtedly became, not only when he inhabited a barrack-room, but throughout his career. Almost every climactic moment in that career was to be marked by a law suit, for he was both litigious and frequently litigated against. He had a lawyerly fondness for precedents and documents, and spoilt some of his best political writing by quoting, in full, anything from a treaty to a letter that might be thought to support his argument of the moment. He hated, and had some reason to hate lawyers, but he loved the Common Law, and could quote Bracton, Fortescue, Coke and Blackstone with any Inn of Court man. As an essentially didactic writer, it was, perhaps, permissible for him to urge his readers to follow what he wrote rather than imitate what he did.

Nevertheless there was a certain element of humbug in the advice
this incurably litigious man included in his *Advice to Young Men*:

> In all situations of life avoid the *trammels of the law* . . . One
> good rule is to have as little as possible to do with any man who is
> fond of lawsuits . . . Such persons, from their frequent litiga-
> tions, contract a habit of using the technical terms of the courts,
> in which they take a pride, and are, therefore, companions
> particularly disgusting to men of sense.[18]

Further evidence of Cobbett's love-hate attitude to the law is
provided by the fact that he turned all four of his sons into lawyers.
The three oldest, William, John Morgan and James Paul, became
barristers, while the youngest, Richard, joined a firm of solicitors
in Manchester still known as Cobbetts, although the last partner of
that name, Sir Walter Cobbett, died in 1955. William and James
Paul proved themselves true sons of their father in that, besides
practising law, they wrote books about it.

Cobbett never actually planned his departure from Gray's Inn. It
was, once again, obedience to a sudden impulse that freed him
from his attorney's desk. During one of his Sunday walks in St.
James's Park:

> I happened to cast my eye on an advertisement, inviting all loyal
> young men, who had a mind to gain riches and glory, to repair to
> a certain rendezvous, where they might enter into His Majesty's
> Service, and have the peculiar happiness and honour of being
> enrolled in the Chatham division. I was not ignorant enough to
> be the dupe of this morsel of military bombast; but a change was
> what I wanted; besides, I knew that marines went to sea, and my
> desire to be on that element had rather increased than dimin-
> ished by my being penned up in London.[19]

He resolved, there and then, to become a Marine and went
immediately to Chatham, taking care to let no one learn of his
intentions. The next morning:

> I found myself before a Captain of a marching regiment. There
> was no retreating. I had taken a shilling to drink His Majesty's
> health, and his further bounty was ready for my reception. When
> I told the Captain that I thought myself engaged in the Marines:
> 'By Jasus, my lad', said he, 'and you have had a narrow escape.'[20]

Since regiments in those days did their own recruiting, this was the first contact Cobbett had with anyone from the 54th of Foot. The recruiting officer in question was Captain Lane, one of the few officers in his regiment for whom Cobbett would retain any degree of respect or affection. He was to be of some help to Cobbett later, but at this stage he did no more than attempt to reassure the new recruit by informing him that he had joined a fine regiment which was, at that moment, enjoying the delights of that best of all foreign stations, Canada. There, after preliminary training at the Depot, Cobbett would be sent to discover for himself the richness and beauty of the Nova Scotian countryside and the friendliness of the natives.

Cobbett enlisted on 4 February 1784, that is, less than a year after peace had been signed with the United States. He was then slightly more than a month under twenty-one, although, because he always believed he was three years younger than he actually was, he claimed to be rising eighteen. Since there was no immediate prospect of another war, he was, perhaps, an unusual recruit. The Army had fallen away considerably in both efficiency and repute since the great days of Marlborough, and peacetime service in its ranks had, for a number of reasons, become unattractive. In times of war men could enlist 'for the duration only'. But in peacetime, no limit had, as yet, been set to the length of the engagement, and a man might be kept in the Army until he was too old to be of any further use, in which case he would be turned off with little more by way of a pension than a licence to beg.

Almost all the conditions of service were bad: discipline was both capricious and cruel and pay, for all practical purposes, was negligible. It was not surprising, therefore, that young men from respectable families who were not actually in desperate need or desperate trouble, seldom enlisted in peacetime. Even in wartime, when patriotic fervour could combine with the prospects for plunder, promotion and adventure to outweigh the brutality and squalor of life in the ranks, recourse still had to be made, as often as not, to impressment.

The Army, in short, was commonly thought to contain the scum of the nation in its ranks and the pick of the boobies in its officer corps. It was, as reputations go, an exaggeration, but one that survived well into this century. Moreover, as is so often the case, it came dangerously close to being self-fulfilling. While there were some men who, like Cobbett, enlisted out of no more than boredom, such evidence as we have suggests that they were few.

The Army, as a consequence, had to pay high bounties and set low standards if it was ever to get its recruits. Even a crack cavalry regiment like the 1st Dragoon Guards could not afford to be overselective. General Robert Long, writing of his days as a subaltern in that regiment, described how, in 1792, he was sent out in charge of a recruiting party. He was instructed to enlist 'only Protestant natives of Great Britain . . . no apprentices, seamen, marines, militiamen, colliers, stragglers, vagrants or possible de- serters . . . not any man not perfectly straight, well-featured, in every way well-made, and not heavy-limbed . . . not older than thirty nor younger than seventeen . . . men over twenty to be at least five feet seven inches tall.' He was authorised to offer a bounty of fourteen guineas per head, an extravagant bribe con- sidering that no serving trooper could expect to receive even fourteen pennies in his hand out of his week's pay. To spur their recruiting ardour, there was also a bounty of five guineas to share between the members of the party for every man recruited. By 1792 war with France must have seemed imminent, and young men must have been considering enlistment. Yet after Long and his party had scoured the countryside for eight weeks, they returned to the regiment with no more than eight recruits.[21]

For ordinary regiments of the line standards were set even lower. There was no medical inspection, and any man who was not obviously crippled or incapable would be accepted. Nothing was required by way of literacy, intelligence or good character. Liter- acy, indeed, could be a disadvantage. George Farquhar, the playwright, drew on his own army experience when he wrote *The Recruiting Officer* (1706). He had his Captain Kite turn down a 'scoundrelly attorney' whom his sergeant wanted him to enlist, because 'I will have nobody in my company that can write: a fellow that can write can draw petitions – discharge him this instant.'

Cobbett's father plainly thought that the peacetime army was no place for any son of his. As soon as he found out what William had done he wrote to him, offering to buy him out. William, however, refused to be bought out and, by refusing, made any return to Farnham and farming in the foreseeable future impossible. Until then, none of his sudden decisions had been irreversible. Now that he had sold himself, for an indefinite period, to the King, he had finally achieved his exit from Arcadia.

He spent no less than thirteen months at the Chatham Depot, an unusually long stay in an age when the common complaint of regiments in the field was that they were sent as replacements recruits who had spent so little time in training that they arrived not knowing even the rudiments of their drill. But as he explained:

I enlisted early in 1784, and, as peace had then taken place, no great haste was made to send recruits off to their regiments. I remained upwards of a year at Chatham, during which time I was employed in learning my exercise, and taking my tour in the duty of the garrison.[22]

The length of his stay at the Depot helped to start him on the path to a series of extraordinarily rapid promotions. He was, from the day he appeared, an obviously unusual peacetime recruit – strong, tall, active, intelligent, sober, industrious and literate. As such, he stood out, as he always would, from the generality of men, and more specifically, in this case, because of the calibre of the men enlisted with him. The consequence was that he was very quickly promoted and arrived, eventually, at his regiment, not as a half-trained recruit, but as a man who had already proved his value to the Army and with a recommendation for his further advancement.

Though he certainly had to learn his 'exercise' while he was at the Depot, this was, perhaps, the least important of the many lessons he learnt at Chatham. Quite apart from learning, for the first time, about hierarchies of power and how large bodies of men may be organised, which are of value to any politician, Chatham taught him a great deal about grammar, wakened him to ambition, and exposed him, for the first time in his life, to hunger. Each of these experiences was to have a marked influence on his subsequent career.

In later life, Cobbett would often refer to the seven-odd years he spent in the Army as his 'cap-and-feather days'. If that suggests that they were entirely gay, swaggering and carefree ones it misleads us. Few men, in fact, have been less inclined to indulge in what T. E. Lawrence, a century and a half later, would describe as 'the cat-calling carnality of barrack-room life'. The average private soldier, then as now, looked to beer and women, when he could afford them, to provide the relief he needed from the burdens of army routine. If they could not be afforded, then talking about them, skylarking and brawling would help to pass the off-duty hours.

Cobbett, however, devoted his leisure hours, and some of his duty ones as well, to the suddenly-revealed delights of self-education: 'My leisure time, which was a very considerable portion of the twenty four hours, was spent, not in the dissipations common to such a way of life, but in reading and study. In the course of this year I learnt more than I had ever done before.'[23]

He subscribed to a circulating library at Brompton, though it is

47

difficult to see how he afforded to do so on a private's pay. It was not a very considerable library, but he managed to read most of the books in it more than once. In later life he deplored this somewhat indiscriminate attack on the world of books:

> Novels, plays, history, poetry, all were read and nearly with equal avidity . . . Such a course of reading could be attended with but little profit; it was skimming over the surface of everything. One branch of learning, however, I went to the bottom with, and that the most essential branch too, the grammar of my mother tongue.[24]

Cobbett's father, who had been all that he had had, as a boy, by way of a teacher, was, as Cobbett himself remembered, ignorant of the principles of grammar, and his son had found, while still working in Gray's Inn, that he was handicapped by his lack of understanding of that essential discipline. Now, however, Fate, taking, as so often in Cobbett's career, the form of a patron, forced him to become a student of grammar:

> It is very probable that I should never have thought of encountering the study [of grammar], had not accident placed me under a man whose friendship extended beyond his interest. Writing a fair hand procured me the honour of being copyist to Colonel Debeig, the commandant of the garrison . . . Being totally ignorant of the rules of grammar, I necessarily made many mistakes in copying, because no one can copy letter by letter, nor even word by word. The Colonel saw my deficiency, and strongly recommended study. He enforced his advice with a sort of injunction, and with a promise of reward in the case of success.[25]

The injunction, one assumes, was a threat to return Cobbett to normal duties if his grammar did not improve. Since, for most men, the calm of the commandant's office would seem preferable to the hurly-burly of the parade ground, this would have been inducement enough. There was also other advice to the same purpose which reveals something of the impression the young Cobbett must have made on people who were then his social and intellectual superiors. He had, while at Gray's Inn, formed a friendship with Benjamin Garlike, a young man of similar age who was then embarking on a career in the Diplomatic Service that would lead him, before his death at an early age, to the position of British

48

Envoy at Constantinople. He wrote to Cobbett, either just before or just after he had enlisted:

> Now then, my dear Bill, it is for you to determine whether you shall all your life yield an abject submission to others, or whether you yourself shall be a guide and leader of men. Nature has done her part towards you most generously; but her favour will be of no avail without a knowledge of grammar. Without that knowledge you will be laughed at by blockheads: with it, you may laugh at thousands who think themselves learned men.[26]

For Garlike to have seen in the unsophisticated and rustic youth such clear indications of all he would ultimately achieve as 'a guide and a leader of men' demonstrates prescience on his part and reveals something of the sheer force of Cobbett's personality.

Colonel Debeig recommended Bishop Lowth's *Short Introduction to English Grammar* as a suitable textbook, and it was this that Cobbett now proceeded to master:

> The pains I took cannot be described: I wrote the whole grammar out two or three times; I got it by heart; I repeated it every morning and every evening, and when on guard I imposed on myself the task of saying it all over once every time I was posted sentinel.[27]

The Army did not expect their private soldiers to devote their spare time to study, and barrack-room life never made that study easy:

> The edge of my berth, or that of the guard-bed, was my seat to study in; my knapsack was my bookcase; a bit of board lying on my lap was my writing table . . . I had no money to purchase candle or oil; in winter time it was rarely that I could get any evening light but *that of the fire*. and only *my turn* even of that . . . I had to read and to write amidst the talking, laughing, singing, whistling and brawling of at least half a score of the most thoughtless of men, and that, too, in the hours of their freedom from all control. Think not lightly of the *farthing* that I had to give, now and then, for ink, pen or paper. That farthing was, alas! a *great sum* to me![28]

So it was that the future grammarian was trained, and by that training became one of the masters of English prose. What was more immediately important, however, was the fact that mastering

Lowth's *Grammar* entitled him to the reward Colonel Debeig had promised. He was confirmed in the post of garrison clerk and was: 'soon raised to the rank of a corporal;* a rank which, however contemptible it may appear in some people's eyes, brought me a clear twopence *per diem*, and put a very clever worsted knot on my shoulder too'.[29]

There are various reasons that might explain why it was that the older Cobbett, a leading Tory publicist, became, in a comparatively short space of time, a Radical leader of considerably greater importance. Yet, if one single reason has to be found, it was probably his almost obsessive hatred of food hunger that led to his radicalisation.

When he returned to farming and the countryside, after an absence of more than twenty years, he was genuinely and deeply horrified to discover that the farm labourers, the people who produced the food, were being denied their necessary share of what they produced. They and their families had been reduced, for the most part, to a condition of semi-starvation. He devoted so much of his energy, thereafter, to fighting this particular evil that Lord Cockburn, a fellow-Reformer but a Whig, was probably justified when he referred to him, with Whiggish superciliousness, as a 'Radical of the belly'. Cobbett, in short, fought, not for any abstract Radical theories about equality – he was never an egalitarian – but to prevent the English labourer being permanently reduced to living on soup, like the French, on burgoo, like the Scots, or on potatoes, like the Irish. If he came to harbour one enduring principle through his frequently contradictory political career, it was 'That the law of nature, as well as the law of the land, gives every soul in the community a *right* to a sufficiency of food.'[30]

Given Cobbett's farming background, it was natural that he should always be concerned, as both farmer and politician, with the production and distribution of the nation's food. His observing, enquiring, analytical mind drove him further. He took an active interest, wherever he went, in the nature and quality of the food that people ate. Not the least interesting part of his writings is concerned with the different food tastes of the Americans, the Scots and the English. He was well before his time, in an age when those who could afford to do so ate grossly, in adopting a frugal diet

---

* Cobbett gave different versions, at different times, of how, where and when he won his rapid promotions. It is possible that he did not acquire his 'very clever worsted knot' until he had spent some months with his regiment in Nova Scotia. See also the footnote on page 61 concerning his promotion to Regimental Sergeant-Major.

for himself and advocating a wholesome and balanced one for everyone else. Yet there is little in all of this that explains his particular hatred of hunger. Nor was it a matter of compassion. His compassion, though it ran deep, was confined to narrow channels, and it would be wrong to describe him as a generally compassionate man. Nevertheless, wherever he saw hunger, whether it was among the Scots, whom he disliked, or the Irish, whom he pitied, or among the 'chopsticks' whom he loved, he was most deeply angered.

He could have had little or no experience of hunger in his youth. Even the bread-and-cheese, apple-pudding diet he lived on when he stayed with his grandmother would have been filling enough to stay a growing boy's appetite. At The Jolly Farmer there would have been all he could eat of at least the basic elements of an eighteenth-century diet – bread, beef, bacon and beer. Nor would he have seen much food hunger around him in Surrey, for he had been born into a community whose food supplies had been at least adequate for several generations.

We know, however, because it was always referred to when he wrote about his army days, that he was quite suddenly exposed to months of semi-starvation when he was a recruit at the Depot. If one may theorise on the basis of experience, it is probably true to say that those who have known nothing in their lives but food hunger are less scarred by it, mentally, than those who are suddenly and unexpectedly forced to experience it. That is, as many former prisoners of war will agree, a deeply degrading experience, and one almost impossible to forget. Those who have gone through it will never again be able to take food for granted, nor will they be able to accept, without anger, the proposition that it is part of the human condition that some part of mankind must always starve.

If we are to understand why it was that Cobbett went so hungry at Chatham, some reference has to be made to army pay and allowances at that time. For a private soldier in a line regiment these totalled tenpence (10d.) a day, though a trooper in a cavalry regiment would get slightly more since he had a horse to care for. Fourpence of the day's pay represented the official messing allowance, which was supposed to cover the cost of the rations issued and the fuel needed for cooking. The spending of this money was not left to the soldier, but was done on his behalf by the Quartermaster. It was a long-established tradition that some of it would stick to the Quartermaster's hands, either in the form of money not spent or rations not issued and subsequently resold. That tradition would have been even easier to uphold in all the comings and goings of a Depot than in the closer community of the regiment.

The remaining sixpence a day was, theoretically, the private's cash wage, which, once again theoretically, had to be paid to him every seven days. Here again, however, it was thought better not to leave the spending of it entirely to the soldier. The system of 'stoppages' ensured, in fact, that he never saw all and seldom saw very much of it at the end of the week:

> Of my sixpence, nothing like fivepence was left to purchase food for the day, indeed, not fourpence. For there was washing, mending, soap, flour for hair-powder, shoes, stockings, shirts, stocks and gaiters, pipe-clay and several other things to come out of the miserable sixpence.[31]

The reference to purchasing food reflects the fact that the messing allowance had become quite insufficient in a period of rising food prices, with the consequence that soldiers had to supplement their rations out of their own pockets. Since it was 1792 before Parliament agreed to increase the messing allowance by a penny-halfpenny (1½d.) a day in order to allow the all-important bread ration to be maintained, part of that ration, in Cobbett's time, had to consist of brown rather than white bread. 'When I was a recruit at Chatham barracks, in the year 1783, we had brown bread served out to us twice in the week. And, for what reason God knows, we used to call it *tommy*.'[32]

If this should seem a minimal hardship, it needs to be explained that, when bread provides an important part of the total diet, it is difficult to eat enough of it unless it is either made of wheat or else is accompanied by a sufficient quantity of relish in the shape of meat, butter or cheese. Fighting troops, even in the last war, frequently had to survive for quite long periods on a diet of bully beef and biscuits. If the bully had been removed, no quantity of biscuits could have maintained them at fighting pitch for long. The German army, for its part, relied heavily on the dark and highly nutritious *Komissbrot*, but this was accompanied, even at the worst of times, with a piece of sausage or a small tin of meat.

Cobbett's position, then, was that the Army, while he was at Chatham, could not and did not provide him with enough food to keep him adequately fed, and failed to leave him with enough money to buy extra food every day. In fact 'The whole of the money not expended for us at market, was twopence a-week for each man.'[33] Yet 'I was as tall as I am now; I had great health and great exercise.'[34]

It is not surprising that what he principally remembered and wrote down of those days was the effect hunger had on himself and on others. Whatever else he was writing about, the theme of hunger recurs:

> To buy a pen or a sheet of paper I was compelled to forego some portion of food, though in a state of half-starvation.[35]

> I remember well . . . the pangs of hunger felt by me during the thirteen months when I was a private soldier, previous to my embarkation for Nova Scotia.[36]

> We had several recruits from Norfolk (our regiment was the West Norfolk) and many of them deserted from sheer hunger. They were lads from the plough-tail . . . I remember two that went into a decline and died during the year, though when they joined us, they were fine hearty young men. I have seen them lay in their berths, many and many a time, actually crying on account of hunger. The whole week's food was not a bit too much for one day.[37]

> I remember, and well I may! that, upon one occasion, I, after all absolutely necessary expenses, had, on a Friday, made shift to have a halfpenny in reserve, which I had destined for the purchase of a *red-herring* in the morning; but, when I pulled my clothes off at night, so hungry then as to be hardly able to endure life, I found that I had *lost my halfpenny*! I buried my head under the miserable sheet and rug and cried like a child.[38]

These are not the comments of a man who had forgotten what it was like to be 'so hungry as to be hardly able to endure life'. All of them were written, in well-fed tranquillity, long after the event, but the anger shows through, an anger that would always come to the surface whenever and wherever he came across starvation. A great deal of what powered his politics is revealed in a passage he wrote, forty years later, when he was riding round the countryside studying the state of the nation:

> The labourers here *look* as if they were half-starved . . . Talk of '*liberty*' indeed; '*civil and religious liberty*'; The *Inquisition with a belly full*, is far preferable to a state of things like this. For my own part, I really am ashamed to ride a fat horse, to have a full belly, and to have a clean shirt upon my back, while I look at these wretched countrymen of mine; while I actually see them reeling with weakness; when I see their poor faces present me nothing but skin and bone, while they are toiling to get the wheat

and the meat ready to be carried away and devoured by the tax-eaters.[39]

If Cobbett entertained any ambition as a boy, it probably amounted to no more than a desire to become as good a farmer as his father and a better one than his brothers. His urge to discover a way of life more adventurous than Farnham could provide failed to resolve itself, however, into a single, irresistible ambition until he joined the Army. What was important now about his stay in Chatham was that it revealed to him, not only that he was ambitious, but also that he possessed the will-power and the intelligence to pursue his ambitions. He discovered, in short, that he was considerably more capable than his fellows, and that this was apparent to his superiors. This would always be true of him in a very material sense, for, whatever people thought of him in later life, few would ever find it possible to ignore him. But he had to be placed in the company of the type of man then recruited into the Army for his qualities to become immediately apparent. There he stood out like a good, heavyweight hunter in a group of pit-ponies.

It is difficult to decide when it was, at Chatham, that he first began to realise that the world, or at least the military part of it, could be his oyster. Certainly, his appointment as garrison clerk, and his rapid promotion to Corporal must have suggested to him that the way upwards might not be too difficult for a man of his ability. 'There is no situation where merit is so sure to meet with reward as in a well-disciplined army. Those who command are obliged to reward it for their own ease and credit.'[40]

His own merit was something that he began, almost too readily, to take for granted. Benjamin Garlike had already assured him that Nature had done her part towards him most generously, and Colonel Debeig, without putting it into such fulsome terms, had appeared to concur. There was no superfluity, among the Chatham recruits, of men as intelligent, sober, industrious and literate as himself.

What there remained for him to do was build on his innate advantage over others through a rigid process of self-education. It was not merely a question of adding a mastery of grammar to his already valuable ability to read, figure and write legibly and at speed. It was also important that he should excel at drill, learn how the Army organised itself, and master such subjects as officers were presumed to have mastered in their study of tactics and strategy. For he had made up his mind to win further, and unlimited promotions. Commissioned rank, in the Army of those days, was normally obtained by purchase. There were some officers, however, who won promotion from the ranks, and Cobbett had already begun to believe that it might not be impossible for him to do the same. He was not, in this respect, being over-optimistic, for he was eventually offered a commission in an effort to induce him to stay in the Army. He sometimes said in later life that, had he accepted the offer, he would certainly have ended his career as a General. He never, of course, lacked self-confidence, and the self-approbation that grows from it.

For the moment, however, all of his energies had to be devoted to the task of learning his trade as a soldier and acquiring the further education that would support his still seedling ambitions. The private soldier's 'exercise' was not very complicated. There was a large amount of ceremonial drill, in addition to which he had to learn to march long distances, handle musket and bayonet, and perform such elementary manoeuvres as turning from column into line and advancing in skirmishing order. There is no reason to believe that Cobbett found any of this difficult. He was always a quick learner, and he started with the initial advantages of knowing his left from his right and of being able to read and understand a drill manual. He was strong and active enough to think nothing of carrying a fourteen-pound musket and a deal of heavy accoutrement on the long marches and parades required of him. Indeed, he must have been more than ordinarily proficient at his 'exercise', for he would, in two or three years' time, be made responsible for the drilling of an entire regiment, officers included.

Given his lifelong passion for neatness, cleanliness and order, he could never have been anything other than smartly turned out. He was too abstemious to go boozing, too chaste to go whoring and too industrious to be idle. In short, there was nothing in his conduct, on or off duty, that could do anything but win him the approbation of his officers.

Looking forward to what might be required of him if he gained a commission, he now added to his study of grammar attempts to learn French, geometry and fortification. He read Watt's *Logic* and the Duke of York's *Military Exercises and Evolutions*. Indeed, there was probably no period in his eight years of service when his private hours were not devoted to improving his education and preparing himself for more important duties in the Army. His duties in the garrison office must have taught him, in a more practical way, how the Army was run. He must have begun to learn something of the difference between theory and practice when it came to such matters as pay, messing allowances, muster rolls and courts martial. Finally, the Army taught him, as Gray's Inn had not, how to adapt himself to the desk work that would, from then on, occupy most of his working life.

It was at Chatham, then, that his ambitions first manifested themselves in any definable form. He would win promotion. He would hope for a commission. He would aspire to becoming a General. Meanwhile, he would devote every hour that could be spared to the task of training and educating himself for these things. But:

> As promotion began to dawn, I grew impatient to get to my regiment, where I expected soon to bask under the rays of royal favour. The happy day of departure at last came: we set sail from Gravesend, and, after a short and pleasant voyage, arrived at Halifax in Nova Scotia.[41]

A great deal of what Cobbett wrote about his army days displayed him, quite unintentionally, at his worst. He presents himself, to all but the most partisan reader, as a self-centred prig and careerist at Chatham and as something worse in his regimental career. Much of this lies in the writing, for Cobbett could never, under any circumstance, see faults in himself. Yet he did not, in fact, spend all his waking hours at Chatham improving and advancing himself and isolating himself from his fellows and the lighter occupations of garrison life. For one thing, he either fell, or came close to falling in love with the Brompton librarian's daughter. The passion for self-education that drove him to read his way through every book in the library twice may, therefore, have had its origins in a different and more painful passion. For, though we do not know whether it ever amounted to anything more than making eyes at her, we do know that the affair, such as it was, was quickly over. The librarian's daughter married a London stationer, and departed.

Even this, however, leaves us with a picture of a Cobbett too serious for his years and our taste. However, when Cobbett revisited Chatham, some forty years later, what he remembered were not the hours he had spent with his books, but rather those that had been passed in the company of girls who may have been prettier than their daughters:

> Here I was got into the scenes of my cap-and-feather days . . . Upon looking upwards towards the fortifications and the barracks, how many recollections crowded into my mind! The girls . . . do not seem to be *so pretty* as they were thirty eight years ago; or am I not so quick in discovering beauties as I was then?

Have thirty eight years corrected my taste, or made me a hypercritic in these matters? . . . One thing I will say for the young women of these towns, and that is, that I always found those of them that I had the great happiness to be acquainted with, evince a great desire to do their best to smooth the inequalities of life, and to give us 'brave fellows', as often as they could, strong beer, when their churlish masters or fathers or husbands would have drenched us to death with small.[42]

CHAPTER THREE

Canada, Love and the 54th

Travel, in the younger sort, is a part of education; in the elder, a part of experience.

> Francis Bacon: *Of Travel*

When the transport carrying replacements for the 54th of Foot entered Halifax harbour, Cobbett was disappointed by what he saw:

> When I first beheld the barren, not to say hideous, rocks at the entrance of the harbour, I began to fear that the master of the vessel had mistaken his way; for I could perceive nothing of that fertility that my good recruiting Captain had dwelt on with so much delight.[1]

That first impression of Nova Scotia never altered. When, in later life, he had a barren and forbidding landscape to describe, he would often refer to it as Nova Scotian. He was almost fifty years older, for example, when he described a particularly hilly part of Surrey, which is, incidentally, thought of as something of a beauty spot today, as:

> Verily the most villainously ugly spot I ever saw in England. This lasts you for five miles, getting, if possible, uglier and uglier all the way, till, at last, as if barren soil, nasty spewy gravel, heath, and even that stunted, were not enough, you see some rising spots which, instead of trees, present you with black, ragged, hideous rocks. There may be Englishmen who wish to see *Nova Scotia*. They need not go to sea, for here it is to the life.[2]

It was not only the Nova Scotian scenery that displeased him. He, being a traditionalist, found something ridiculous in the Nova Scotians themselves:

> Nova Scotia had no other charm for me than that of novelty. Everything I saw was new; bogs, rocks and stumps, musquitoes

58

and bull-frogs. Thousands of captains and colonels without soldiers, and of squires without stockings or shoes. In England, I had never thought of approaching a squire without a most respectful bow; but, in this new world, though I was but a corporal, I often ordered a squire to bring me a glass of grog, and even to take care of my knapsack.[3]

This may seem a somewhat snobbish observation, but, if one is to understand Cobbett, it is necessary to appreciate that when he attacked the officers, the squirearchy and the aristocracy, he attacked them not for their class, but because he thought them unworthy members of that class. The man who was brought up in Farnham and moulded by the Army never doubted that the structure of society had to be hierarchical. He no more questioned the existence of hereditary landowners and legislators than he questioned the existence of a Commander-in-Chief. What he wanted was that they should fulfil what he considered to be the duties of their heritage and position. What he deplored and attacked was that a degenerate age had produced degenerate men who refused to live up to his expectations. Few of them, he would insist, were worthy of their ancestors, and too many of them, being upstarts, had no ancestors to be worthy of.

It may well be that the American custom of bestowing and accepting meaningless titles, a custom which, apparently, the Loyalists had brought with them to Canada, was what first taught Cobbett to realise that the titles he respected did not necessarily guarantee men he could respect. Certainly, when he later came to live in the United States, the American fondness for honorifics gave him some amusement and a considerable amount of ammunition. It seemed to him that it was part of the republican hypocrisy he derided, that every township should be full of squires without land, judges who had never seen a law school and colonels who had never fired a shot in anger or led their men farther than the nearest grog-shop.

Cobbett soon discovered, however, that there were parts of Canada that did not resemble Nova Scotia.

We staid but a few weeks in Nova Scotia, being ordered to St. John's, in the province of New Brunswick. Here, and at other places in the same province, we remained till the month of September, 1791, when the regiment was relieved and sent home.[4]

Here, around St. John's and Fredericton, he found a less rugged and more fertile countryside, with great forests to explore, game to

59

shoot and an abundance of the rivers, creeks and waterfalls he always considered a necessary part of any pleasing landscape. Here, also, he found a farming people who, in the course of time, came to welcome him as one of their own. He is remembered principally today for his descriptions of an English countryside that has largely changed or disappeared. Yet some of his finest descriptive writing was reserved, not for the English counties as he rode across them, but for his memories of the forests, rivers, lakes and farmlands of the countryside that stretches northwards from St. John's to Fredericton.

Almost as soon as Cobbett had arrived in Halifax his experience in the orderly room at Chatham ensured a similar post for him as regimental clerk. 'In a very short time, the whole of the business, in that way, fell into my hands; and at the end of about a year, neither adjutant, pay-master or quarter-master could move an inch without my assistance.'[5]

But it was not only in clerical matters that he made himself indispensable, for 'The *military* part of the regiment affairs fell under my care in like manner.'[6] Since there is no other account of how this happened than Cobbett's, we have to accept it, even though the cartoonist Gillray had great fun with it in later years. Cobbett wrote:

About this time the new *discipline*, as it was called; that is to say, the mode of handling the musket and of marching &c, called *Dundas's System* was sent out to us in little books,* which were to be studied by the officers of each regiment, and the rules of which were to be immediately conformed to . . . it ordered and commanded a *complete change*, and this change was to be completed before the next annual review took place. To make this change was left to me, who was not then twenty [i.e. twenty-three] years of age, while not a single officer in the regiment paid the least attention to the matter; so that when the time came for the annual review, I, then a *Corporal*, had to give lectures of instruction to the officers themselves, the Colonel not excepted, and for several of them, if not for all of them, I had to make out, upon large cards which I bought for the purpose, little plans of the position of the regiment, together with lists of the words of command, which they had to give in the field . . .[7]

---

* The 'little book' was almost certainly the *Principles of Military Movement Chiefly Applied to Infantry*, written by General Sir David Dundas (1788). An abridgement of this was made the first official drill manual of the British Army.

It was probably at this stage that Cobbett ceased to feel that he owed deference to anyone, least of all to his officers. The Great Disrespecter, in short, was emerging, and that, ironically enough, was also a part of his army education:

> There was I at the review, upon the flank of the Grenadier Company, with my worsted shoulder-knot, and my great, high, coarse, hairy cap; confounded in the ranks amongst other men, while those who were commanding me to move my hands or my feet, thus or thus, were, in fact, uttering words which I had taught them; and were, in everything except mere authority, my inferiors, and ought to have been commanded by me. It was impossible for reflections of this sort not to intrude themselves; and, as I advanced in experience, I felt less and less respect for those whom I was compelled to obey.[8]

All who have had any experience of regimental life would agree that there is only one man in the regiment who can be allowed to know more about its conduct and drill than the sergeants, on the one hand, and the officers on the other. He has to be, and can only be, the Regimental Sergeant-Major. Everything else apart, therefore, it was impossible to leave the only man who understood Dundas's System 'confounded in the ranks'. Consequently, in what was probably one of the most rapid promotions ever to take place in the British Army in peacetime 'I became Sergeant-Major to the regiment . . . being raised from Corporal to Sergeant-Major at once over the heads of thirty Sergeants . . .'*[9]

Cobbett, oddly enough, never included his mastery of the new drill among the reasons for his promotion. If he found any single reason, apart from his overall and obvious superiority to others, it lay in his adoption of the motto, *Toujours prêt*:

> I can truthfully say, that I owe more of my great labours to my strict adherence to [toujours prêt] . . . than to all the natural abilities with which I have been endowed; for these, whatever

---

* Cobbett, in later life, offered two different versions of how and when he was promoted. In 1809 he wrote that he had been raised to Sergeant as soon as he arrived in Canada, but was not promoted to Sergeant-Major until a year later. This does not tally with the account given above, which he recorded in 1830, at an age when old men may be forgiven for having forgotten the details. The discrepancy is, however, unimportant. What indubitably happened is that, within three years at the most, he rose from raw recruit to Regimental Sergeant-Major, without once having seen combat, or having been obliged, by battle casualties, to step into dead mens' shoes.

may have been their amount, would have been of comparatively little use, even aided by great sobriety and abstinence, if I had not, in early life, contracted the blessed habit of husbanding well my time. To this, more than to any other thing, I owed my very extraordinary promotion in the army. I was *always ready*: if I had to mount guard at *ten*, I was ready at *nine*; never did any man or anything wait one moment for me.[10]

Since Cobbett wrote about his army career with an air of wonder at himself and even more than his usual degree of self-approbation, one has to assume that his 'very extraordinary promotion' surprised even himself. The other non-commissioned officers, with perhaps twenty years of service behind them, may have felt something more than surprise at being passed over in this manner. At the time, however, they showed little or no resentment. Cobbett, in all modesty, explained why:

Being, at an age *under twenty years* [i.e. twenty-three] raised . . . over the heads of thirty Sergeants, I naturally should have been the object of envy and hatred; but this habit of early rising . . . really subdued these passions; because every one felt, that what I did he had never done, and never could do.[11]

In order to emphasise that point, he gave a description of a typical day in the life of Sergeant-Major Cobbett:

Long before any other man was dressed for parade, my work for the morning was all done, and I myself was on the parade, walking, in fine weather, for an hour perhaps. My custom was this; to get up, in summer, at day-light, and in winter at four o'clock; shave, dress, even to the putting of my sword-belt over my shoulder, and having my sword lying on the table before me, ready to hang by my side. Then I ate a bit of cheese, or pork and bread. Then I prepared my report, which was filled up as fast as the companies brought me in the materials. After this I had an hour or two to read, before the time came for any duty out of doors.[12]

He was already, in the matter of food, exercising that abstemiousness he was to practise and preach for the rest of his life. One habit, however, which he acquired in his army days, he subsequently abjured and denounced; it was an addiction to tea and coffee:

Experience has taught me that those slops are *injurious to health*; until I left them off (having taken to them at the age of 26) even my habits of sobriety, moderate eating, early rising; even these were not, until I left off the slops, sufficient to give me that complete health which I have since had. I pretend not to be a 'doctor'; but I assert, that to pour regularly, every day, a pint or two of *warm liquid matter* down the throat, whether under the name of tea, coffee, soup, grog, or whatever else, is greatly injurious to health.[13]

As to his hour or two of reading every morning, these were devoted to his continuing process of self-improvement. Some of that time was passed in further studies into French and English grammar, and the rest in 'learning geometry and fortifications'. Yet the more he gained in erudition, the more he learnt to despise those less erudite than himself. His new position brought him, for example, into 'Close contact, at every hour, with the whole of the epaulet gentry, whose profound and surprising ignorance I discovered in a twinkling . . .'[14]

Intellectual snobs may flourish in civilian society, but it is imprudent, even now, to parade as one in army circles. In Cobbett's day, and in Cobbett's position, it might have been fatal:

I had a very delicate part to act with those gentry; for, while I despised them for their gross ignorance and their vanity, and hated them for their drunkenness and rapacity, I was fully sensible of their power. My path was full of rocks and pitfalls; and, as I never disguised my dislikes, or restrained my tongue, I should have been broken and flogged for fifty different offences, had they not been kept in awe by my inflexible sobriety, impartiality and integrity, by their consciousness of their inferiority to me, and by the real and almost indispensable necessity of the use of my talents. They, in fact, resigned all the discipline of the regiment to me, and I very freely left them to swagger about and get roaring drunk.[15]

It is difficult to believe that Cobbett was so candidly objectionable in his army days as this particular passage suggests, but since it was written more than twenty-five years after he left the Army, he was probably attributing to Cobbett of the 54th attitudes that only Cobbett of the *Political Register* could afford to sustain.

None the less it is obviously true that Cobbett, by now, disliked and despised almost every officer in the regiment, though no doubt he did so covertly rather than overtly. He particularly despised the

Adjutant, Lieutenant Hall, which, since Hall had risen from the ranks just as Cobbett hoped to do, seems particularly unjust of him. But then 'class solidarity' was never among Cobbett's loyalties. He took particular pleasure, in fact, in deriding Hall's attempts to conceal his want of education:

It is the custom in regiments to give out orders every day from the officer commanding. These are written by the Adjutant, to whom the Sergeant-Major is a sort of deputy. The man I had to do with was a keen fellow, but wholly illiterate. The orders which he wrote most cruelly murdered our mother-tongue. But, in his absence, or during a severe drunken fit, it fell to my lot to write orders. As we both wrote in the same book, he used to look at these. He saw commas, semi-colons, colons, full points and paragraphs. The questions he used to put to me, in an obscure sort of way, in order to know why I made these divisions, and yet, at the same time, his attempts to disguise his object, have made me laugh a thousand times . . .[16]

The upshot was that Hall eventually left the editing and writing of orders entirely to Cobbett, who doubtless felt even more superior to his superiors as a consequence. But what Cobbett most frequently brought up in later life in connection with the Adjutant was the affair of the New Brunswick Commissioners. They had been sent out to examine and report upon the state of the provinces of New Brunswick and Nova Scotia. The final stage of that enquiry brought them to Fredericton, where the 54th was then stationed:

As the arrival of every stranger was an excuse for a roaring drunk with our heroes, so this ceremony took place. But the Commissioners had their report to make. And what did my ass of an Adjutant do, but offer to make it for them![17]

The Adjutant, once he had sobered up, realised that he had promised more than he could perform. Cobbett, for his part, had for some time been importuning for a week's leave so that he and a friendly sergeant could go pigeon-shooting on a distant farm. Some rather delicate fencing followed:

He talked to me at first in a sort of ambiguous manner. He said the Commissioners wanted him to do it, but d . . . n them, he would not do it for them . . . I affected not to understand him, turned the matter as soon as I could, and so we parted . . . The Adjutant knew that I had the [pigeon-shooting] at heart. What does he now do, but come to me after talking about the report again, affect to lament that he should be so much engaged with it, that there was no hope of my being permitted to go on my frolic, till he had finished the report . . . Tacked on to the pigeon-shooting, the report became an object of importance, and I said, 'perhaps I could do something, Sir, in putting the papers in order for you'. That was enough. Away he went, brought me the whole mass, and tossing them down on the table: 'There', said he, 'do what you like with them; for d . . . n the rubbish, I have no patience with it.[18]

Cobbett, of course, produced a splendid report:

As was the case with everything that I meddled with, [it] was done in so clear, correct, and, in point of penmanship, so beautiful a manner that, I have been told, the Duke of Kent, when he afterwards became Commander-in-Chief of those provinces, had it copied, and took away the original as a curiosity.[19]

The original, however, was in Cobbett's handwriting, and so was the very thing that could not be shown by Hall to the Commissioners:

The Adjutant got over this difficulty by copying the report; and, having shown it, and had it highly applauded, 'Well, then' said he, 'here, Sergeant-Major, go and make a fair copy.' That was the most shameless thing I ever witnessed.[20]

Cobbett's work on the Commissioners' Report can be regarded as his first introduction to public affairs. At that time, however, such matters did not seem to interest him greatly, since he states that he 'd . . . d' the papers as heartily as the Adjutant had done, and persevered with them only as the price of his pigeon-shooting. In truth, however, there was little he liked better in later life than quarrying statistics, reports and Parliamentary papers for evidence that would support his arguments.

While he was in the 54th, he produced a small pamphlet or primer on arithmetic for the instruction of the other ranks, and also an article that circulated in the regiment giving a humorous and largely apocryphal account of life in the orderly room and the duties of a sergeant-major. This reveals that, even though politics did not, as yet, interest him greatly, his urge to instruct and his lively and enlivening sense of humour were already dominant characteristics. Indeed, though he quite unconsciously presents himself, in his accounts of his army life, as a conceited, overweening and frequently unpleasant individual, it is noticeable how, in those same accounts, sufficient humour creeps in to make the reader decide not to abandon him in disgust.

Not all of Cobbett's time with the 54th, however, was spent in taking over as much of the running of the regiment as was feasible, or in promoting his own intellectual and professional advancement. He was country-bred and eager to engage, once more, in country pursuits, and was still youthful enough for ginger to be at least warm in his mouth. Moreover he had, then as always, many engaging qualities which his rapid promotion could have done little to diminish in country eyes. He was, therefore, a man to be welcomed in the farming community, and his ability to come quickly on to friendly terms with almost anyone not associated with him in a professional capacity allowed him to take advantage of that welcome.

As a consequence, he derived more pleasure and better entertainment from his time in New Brunswick than probably most other members of the St. John's and Fredericton garrisons. He was, for the first time since he had left Farnham, placed in a countryside whose beauty was not marred for him by any all-pervading infertility of the soil. What there was of wilderness he could explore and hunt in; what there was of farmland he could visit and judge and discuss with those who farmed it. He was not even dismayed by 'the horrible climate; the land covered with snow seven months of the year; the danger of death if any man be lost in the snow for only ten minutes . . .'[21]; for he mentioned how much he enjoyed those winter days 'with a bright sun over our heads, and with snow, dry as hair powder, screeching under our feet'.[22] Besides:

> Winter is the great season for jaunting and dancing (called frolicking) in America. In this province, the rivers and the creeks were the only roads from settlement to settlement. In summer we travelled in canoes; in winter in sleighs on the ice and snow.[23]

He always loved rivers, lakes and streams in his landscapes, and one of his happiest pieces of descriptive writing concerned the river of St. John as it changed with the changing seasons:

> That river, as well as all the creeks running into it on both sides, were so completely frozen every year by the seventh of November, or thereabouts, that we could skate across it and up and

down it, the next morning after the frost began, while we could see the fish swimming under the ice on which we were skating. In about ten days the snow came; until storm after storm . . . made the mass, upon an average, ten feet deep . . . [In the month of April] the melting of the snow turned the river into ice again. Soon after this, the symptoms of breaking-up began to appear . . . the creeks, where the masses were not so large, and the lakes where the freezing had not been so severe, began to give way, and you every now and then heard a crack at many miles distance, like the falling of fifty, or a hundred, or a thousand very lofty timber trees coming down all together. These cracks indicated that the ice was bursting asunder . . . Towards the end of May, the whole surface of the river moved downwards with accelerating rapidity towards the sea . . . until the sun and the tide had carried the whole away, and made the river clear [until November] during which time, the sun gave us melons in the natural ground, and fine crops of corn and grass . . . [and] began . . . to make us cast off our furs, and to resume our dresses as men, instead of those of bears.[24]

Yet, even in the wilderness, it was the fertility of the soil, that could express itself in fine trees, sweet pastures and an abundance of wild life, that most attracted him:

On the sides of these creeks the land is, in places, clear of rocks; it is, in these places, generally good and productive; the trees that grow here are the birch, the maple, and others of the deciduous class; natural meadows here and there present themselves; and some of these spots far surpass in rural beauty any other that my eyes ever beheld; the creeks abounding towards their sources in waterfalls of endless variety . . . and always teeming with fish, while water-fowl enliven their surface, and while wild pigeons, of the gayest plumage, flutter in thousands upon thousands, amongst the branches of the beautiful trees, which sometimes for miles together, form an arch over the creeks.[25]

He went on shooting expeditions during which he may well have encountered bear as well as the wild pigeons and other small game he hunted, for he writes of carrying his sword and a brace of pistols with which to defend himself against them. On one such expedition, at least, he was accompanied by his closest friend in the regiment, Sergeant Smaller, who was:

A Yorkshire man, who began learning his ABC (under my direction), and who, at the end of the year, was as correct a writer as I ever saw in my life. He was about my own age; he was promoted as soon as he could read and write; and he well deserved it, for he was more fit to command a regiment than any Colonel or Major I ever saw.[26]

On this particular excursion into the woods, 'amongst the melting snows', Cobbett fell down exhausted, at night-fall, just when it had begun to rain heavily. Smaller, having torn his shirt into rags in an unsuccessful effort to light a fire with a spark from his pistol, then carried Cobbett for five miles to the nearest house. Since Cobbett could never, at any time of his life, have been anything but a heavy burden, it was no wonder that Smaller arrived coatless, shoeless and with his feet and legs 'cut to pieces and covered with blood'. The eighteenth century was one in which strong men were permitted, even encouraged, to weep:

> The moment he put me down and saw that I was still alive, he burst into a flood of tears that probably saved his own life; which, however, was there saved only to be lost in Holland under the Duke of York.[27]

Cobbett never explained why a flood of tears should have saved Smaller from dying of exhaustion; but, writing twenty years later, he could not avoid using his now-dead rescuer as a text for one of his homilies on the need for Army Reform and promotion by merit:

> How often has my blood boiled with indignation at seeing this fine, this honest, true-hearted and intelligent young man standing with his hand to his hat before some worthless and stupid sot of an officer whom nature seemed to have designed to black his shoes. And does not the English Army contain many a Smaller now?[28]

Not everyone in the ranks of the 54th was as noble as Smaller, nor was every one of Sergeant-Major Cobbett's trips into the wilderness undertaken solely for pleasure:

> I went through a track of the woods, of about a hundred miles, where no man had ever ventured before to go alone; and this I did for the purpose of putting a stop to desertion, by showing the regiment that I *myself* was able to follow the fugitives, and,

68

accordingly, after that we had no more desertion to the United States.[29]

In the Army of those days, desertion and mutiny were constant threats to which, in an uneasy quadrilateral of force, the lash and the gallows were the answer. With a newly independent and still half-hostile country to the south, desertion was a greater danger in Canada than in almost any other station. The attempted mutiny, two or three years later, of the Quebec garrison demonstrated this clearly. The Duke of Kent, who had recently been made Commander-in-Chief in Canada, was a zealous disciplinarian. In an attempt to prevent the drunkenness then almost endemic among the troops he put the grog-shops out of bounds. This angered the men and shortly afterwards a plot was discovered which involved the subversion of all the troops in the garrison. Once this had been achieved, the officers would be murdered and the mutineers would march south as an organised body to take service in the American army. The fact that the conspiracy was discovered before it got beyond a handful of men in the Duke's own regiment, the 7th Royal Fusiliers, did not mean that it could never have succeeded. The severity of the sentences imposed at the subsequent court martial revealed how seriously the whole affair was taken.

Cobbett, however, when he was not pigeon-shooting or deterring potential deserters, was sufficiently impressed by the strangeness and the beauty of the Canadian countryside to come away from it with memories that eventually had to be put into words. Long before he embarked on his *Rural Rides*, he made himself famous as a descriptive writer with his accounts of the Canadian and American countrysides. No one could have written about them as he did if he had not already possessed the gift of looking at nature with something more than the tourist's or farmer's eye. Hazlitt, one of his most perceptive if not one of his most friendly critics, said of those American pieces, 'If he had sat down to look at himself in the glass, instead of looking about him like Adam in Paradise, he would not have got up these articles in so capital a style.'[30]

Nothing could more neatly have pointed to the difference between Cobbett the polemicist and Cobbett the descriptive writer. The polemicist, though he wrote with considerable skill, force of argument and humour was, as often as not, self-regarding. He wrote through his own beliefs and prejudices, with no attempt to consider that there might be an alternative view. He used the world, in short, as a mirror that must reflect nothing but Cobbett. It was only when he was forced, by the strangeness of his Canadian surroundings, to consider the natural world that he lost all consciousness of himself and his arguments. It was then that he discovered that he could observe and describe a scene as though he were, indeed, the First Man, walking through that strange Garden in the dew-cool dawn of that First Day. It is probable that he never valued this gift of his as highly as we do. He increasingly thought of himself as a dialectician and allowed argument to obtrude on his descriptions of the English countryside, often to their detriment. It was only in his earlier descriptions of the North American scene that he was content to remain, most memorably, a descriptive writer.

These Canadian days were also, since he was young and active and country-bred, days for physical enjoyment: 'I found time for skating, fishing, shooting and all the other sports of the country of which, when I left it, I had seen and knew more than any other man.'[31]

That last claim exposes what would always be one of his most irritating weaknesses as a writer: his tendency to exaggerate; his seeming inability to deal in anything but superlatives. If he had claimed to have known more about Canada than any other man in his regiment, he might still have been claiming too much. His then commanding officer, Major Lord Edward Fitzgerald, had travelled farther in the Canadian wilderness and probably learnt more about it than he had. The difference between them lay in the fact that Cobbett lived to write about it, whereas Fitzgerald did not. But his claim goes further. It is so absolute that it can be taken to mean that Cobbett knew more about the Canadian wilderness than any native *coureur-de-bois*.

Although that was nonsense, there was one special factor that did add to Cobbett's very real knowledge of the region and its inhabitants. He managed, whilst he was in Canada, to fall in love, not merely once, but twice. The first passion led him, eventually, into marriage. The second, wasted though it was, gave him what amounted to an invitation to enter the Canada of the Canadians. Cobbett's love-life – if that is the right word for it – was one of basic simplicity. Indeed, if we ignore the Brompton librarian's daughter, there seem to have been only two women in his life. The first was the Ann, Anne or Nancy (he used all versions) whom he married. The second was an American, a certain Miss Smith, with whom he dallied – there is no other word for it – during his last two years in Canada.

Cobbett was close on twenty-four, already a sergeant-major, and still stationed at St. John's in New Brunswick when he first saw

Ann Reid. This was in the winter of 1786–7 when Ann was no more than thirteen years old. Her father was Sergeant Thomas Reid of the Royal Artillery whose unit was then close to finishing its tour of duty in Canada. Impulse and calculation combined to convince Cobbett that here was a girl who would grow into the woman he must marry:

> I sat in the same room with her for about an hour, in company with others, and I made up my mind that she was the very girl for me. That I thought her beautiful was certain, for that I had always said should be an indispensable qualification; but I saw in her what I deemed marks of that sobriety of conduct which has been by far the greatest blessing of my life.[32]

If he needed any further confirmation of the soundness of this first judgment, it came very soon, when he was able to add evidence of Ann's industry to the favourable opinions he had already formed of her beauty and sobriety:

> It was now the dead of winter, and, of course, the snow several feet deep on the ground, and the weather piercing cold. It was my habit, when I had done my morning's writing, to go out at break of day to take a walk on a hill at the foot of which our barracks lay. In about three mornings after I had first seen her, I had, by an invitation to breakfast with me, got up two young men to join me in my walk; and our road lay by the house of her father and mother. It was hardly light, but she was out on the snow, scrubbing out a washing-tub. 'That's the girl for me', said I, when we had got out of her hearing.[33]

If Cobbett exhibited a certain market caution even whilst he was falling in love at first sight, this was certainly no more than his peasant ancestors would have expected of him. Indeed, a pretty face, a sober mien and a scrubbed washing-tub probably amounted to rather less proof than many of those ancestors would have required of a future bride's work-worthiness and bed-worthiness. Her cooking, brewing, bacon-curing and butter-making might all have had to be tested before she was duly certified as being both industrious and pregnant and so led to the altar. Cobbett probably knew, however, that Ann came of a hard-working family for, when it had first arrived in Canada, her mother had added to the family income by taking in washing and she herself 'was employed in assisting her poor mother to wash soldiers' shirts.'[34] As for the rest, Ann was probably too young and Cobbett too chaste and too

71

impetuous for all the preliminaries to a Farnham courtship to be necessary. He courted in haste and never, perhaps, repented of it:

> From the day that I first spoke to her, I never had a thought of her being the wife of any other man, more than I had thought of her being transformed into a chest of drawers; and I formed my resolution at once, to marry her as soon as I could get permission, and to get out of the army as soon as I could.[35]

His decision to get out of the Army, according to this passage, preceded his other and later decision to bring certain officers of his regiment to a court martial, and this last was not, therefore, a course that was forced on him by his passion for justice, as is so often suggested. Permission to get married was necessary only because Ann was under age. At that time, females could be legally married at the age of twelve, though males had to be at least fourteen. Sergeant Reid might well have agreed to Sergeant-Major Cobbett marrying his daughter there and then had the requirements of the Horse Guards not taken precedence. The 54th was suddenly ordered to Fredericton, a hundred miles up-river, and at the same time other units of the St. John's garrison, including the Royal Artillery, Sergeant Reid and family, were relieved and embarked for England.

It was at that moment that Cobbett realised that he had to become 'a real and sensible lover. I was aware that when she got to that gay place WOOLWICH, the house of her mother and father, necessarily visited by numerous persons not the most select, might become unpleasant to her, and I did not like, besides, that she should continue to *work hard*. I had saved *a hundred and fifty guineas*, the earnings of my early hours in writing for the paymaster, the quartermaster and others, in addition to the savings of my own pay. *I sent her all my money* before she sailed; and wrote to her, to beg of her, if she found her home uncomfortable, to hire a lodging with respectable people; and, at any rate, not to spare the money, by any means, but to buy herself good clothes, and to live without hard work, until I arrived in England.'[36]

It was expected that the 54th would be ordered home by 1789 at the latest, but the then famous 'Nootka Affair' blew up. This, in 1788, made the war between Britain and Spain over sovereignty in Vancouver Island a possibility and, as a consequence, the regiment did not get back to England until the final days of 1791:

> As the malignity of the devil would have it, we were kept abroad *two years longer than our time*. Mr. PITT, (England not being so

tame then as she is now) having knocked up a dust with Spain about Nootka Sound. Oh how I cursed Nootka Sound, and poor bawling Pitt too, I am afraid.[37]

Meanwhile there was Cobbett, young, lusty and, after his own fashion, wildly romantic, left for four years in Fredericton, many thousand miles away from Woolwich and his Ann. He may not have realised it, but he was more than half ready to fall in love again, and more than half ready to repent of it, before he finally married his Nancy.

Miss Smith's Christian name is unknown: nor can it even be firmly established that her surname was Smith since Cobbett, who was the only man ever to record the affair, never gave her a name. He did, however, give details of her background, her home and her family which matched those he gave, in an entirely different context, for a New Brunswick family called Smith, in whose company he had spent most of his spare time in his Fredericton days. 'Miss Smith', therefore, only exists, and that anonymously, in the account of the whole affair that Cobbett wrote some forty years later. Even then, he only brought her back into existence to serve as a text for a sermon on how such affairs ought to be conducted in general – 'Nor has a man any right to *sport* with the affections of a young woman, though he stop short of positive promises.'[38]

It was very usual for him, when he was wearing his homiletic hat, to point to himself as an example whenever righteous behaviour came under discussion. This, however, was the only occasion when he publicly held himself up as an example of a man who had once misbehaved, though that misbehaviour, he emphasised, had stopped this side of actual 'betrayal':

There are cases . . . in which you are deluded into something very nearly resembling sincere love for a second object, the first, still, however, maintaining her ground in your heart; . . . cases in which you are not guilty of injustice or cruelty; but cases in which, nevertheless, you *do wrong*; and as I once did a wrong of this sort myself, I will here give you a history of it . . . the only atonement that I can make, or ever could have made, for this only *serious sin* that I ever committed against the female sex.[39]

In the long account that followed, it was typical of Cobbett that more attention should be paid at the beginning to the landscape and the farmscape than to the love affair. It all started with one of his excursions in the New Brunswick woods, armed with pistol and sword against the bears. Night fell, and he tried to make a nest for himself between two fallen trees. Sleep however, was impossible. It was cold; he felt sick from all the water he had drunk during the heat of the day; the noise made by bears prowling around alarmed him:

> Lest one of them should find me in a defenceless state, I had roused myself up, and had crept along as well as I could . . . I arrived at a large and well-built log dwelling-house . . . in the middle of a moonlight night, the hoar frost covering the trees and the grass. A stout and clamorous dog, kept off by the gleaming of my sword, waked the master of the house, who got up, received me with great hospitality, got me something to eat, and put me into a feather-bed, a thing that I had been a stranger to for some years . . .[40]

In the morning he discovered that:

> I had got into the house of one of those YANKEE LOYALISTS who, at the close of the revolutionary war (which until it had succeeded was called a rebellion), had accepted of grants of land in the King's Province of New Brunswick; and who, to the great honour of England, had been furnished with all the means of making new and comfortable settlements. I was suffered to sleep till breakfast time, when I found a table, the like of which I have seen so many times in the United States, loaded with good things.[41]

He found, in fact, something more than a hospitable family and a good breakfast, for everything around him delighted him:

> If Nature, in her very best humour, had made a spot for the express purpose of captivating me, she could not have exceeded the efforts which she had here made . . . Here was everything to delight the eye, and especially of one like me, who seem to have been born to love rural life, and trees and plants of all sorts . . .[42]

The spot, surrounded by hills, had large expanses of natural meadows, fine trees and the flowing waters he always loved which 'came down in cascades, for any one of which many a nobleman in England would, if he could, give a good slice of his fertile estate; and, in the creek at the foot of the cascades, there were, in season, salmon, the finest in the world, and so abundant, and so easily taken, as to be used for manuring the land . . .'[43]

The salmon had been put to good use, since there stood, next to the log cabin:

A very good field of Indian Corn, by the side of which there was a piece of buckwheat just then mowed. I found a homestead and some very pretty cows. I found all the things by which an easy and happy farmer is surrounded . . .[44] . . . The master and the mistress of the house, aged about fifty, were like what an English farmer and his wife were half-a-century ago. There were two sons, tall and stout, who appeared to have come in from work, and the youngest of whom was about my age . . .[45]

But, what was eventually far more important, there was also:

Another member of the family, aged nineteen, who, (dressed according to the neat and simple fashion of New England whence she had come with her parents five or six years before) had her long light-brown hair twisted nicely up, and fastened on top of her head, in which head were a pair of lively blue eyes, associated with features of which that softness and that sweetness, so characteristic of American girls, were the predominant expressions, the whole being set off by a complexion indicative of glowing health, and forming, figure, movements, and all taken together, an assemblage of beauties, far surpassing any that I had ever seen but *once* in my life . . .[46]

Here, then, was his Miss Smith; but here, also, were all the other Smiths, and their company, their farm and the scenery to enjoy. The attractions of the first, in those early days, failed to outweigh the attractions of these others:

What, then, did I fall in love at once with this bouquet of lilies and roses? Oh! by no means. I was, however, so enchanted with *the place*; I so much enjoyed its tranquillity, the shade of the maple trees, the business of the farm, the sports of the water and the woods, that I stayed at it to the last possible minute, promising, at my departure, to come again as often as I possibly could; a promise which I most punctually fulfilled.[47]

Fulfilling it led, shortly, to his falling in love, and life became complicated for a man of high moral principles. He was no Macheath, prepared to be happy once t'other dear charmer was away. Nor did the fact that his attachment to Nancy was well-known in the district protect him:

75

My *prior engagement*, though carefully left unalluded to by both parties, was, in that thin population, and owing to the singular circumstances of it, and to the great talk that there always was about me, *perfectly well known* to her and all her family . . . So that here was no *deception* on my part; but still I ought not to have suffered even the most distant hope to be entertained by a person so innocent . . .[48]

Cobbett was not altogether the conceited coxcomb this passage suggests, for Miss Smith had soon begun to behave 'in a way to which a chap much less sanguine than I was would have given the tenderest interpretation . . .'[49] He took no advantage of this, but yet could not bring himself to endure the disadvantage of giving her up. He suffered equally, in short, from the pangs of love and the pangs of remorse:

My affection for her was very great; I spent no really pleasant hours but with her; I was uneasy if she showed the slightest regard for any other young man; I was unhappy if the smallest matter affected her health or her spirits; I quitted her in dejection, and returned to her with equal delight; many a time when I could get leave but for a day, I paddled in a canoe two whole succeeding nights, in order to pass that day with her. If this was not love, it was first cousin to it . . . Many times I put to myself the questions: 'What am I at? Is not this wrong? *Why do I go*?' But still I went.[50]

Although, like another Viola, he never told his love, it had no need of telling:

It is when you meet in company with others of your own age that you are, in love matters, put most frequently to the test, and exposed to detection. The next-door neighbour might, in that country, be ten miles off. We used to have a frolic, sometimes at one house and sometimes at another. Here, where female eyes are very much on the alert, no secret can long be kept; and very soon father, mother, brothers, and the whole neighbourhood looked upon the thing as certain, not excepting herself, to whom, however, I had never once even talked of marriage, and had never even told her that I *loved* her. But I had a thousand times done these by *implication*, taking into view the interpretation she would very naturally put upon my looks, appellations and acts; and it was of this that I had to accuse myself. Yet I was not a *deceiver* . . .[51]

If he could have found a single excuse for abandoning his Nancy, he would have taken it:

> If I had received a *cool* letter from my intended wife; if I had only heard a rumour of anything from which fickleness in her might have been inferred; if I had found in her any, even the smallest, abatement of affection; if she had but let go any one of the hundred strings by which she held my heart . . .[52]

If any of these mean loopholes had been available to him, then he would not only have married his Miss Smith, but he would also have left the Army and settled in Canada, for:

> Young as I was; able as I was as a soldier; proud as I was of the admiration and commendations of which I was an object; fond as I was, too, of the command which, at so early an age, my rare conduct and great natural talents had given me; sanguine as was my mind and brilliant as were my prospects; yet I had seen so much of the meannesses, the unjust partialities, the insolent pomposity, the disgusting dissipations of that way of life, that I was weary of it; I longed, exchanging my fine laced coat for the Yankee's farmer's home-spun, to be where I should never behold the supple crouch of servility, and never hear the hectoring voice of authority again; and, on the lonely banks of this branch-covered creek, which contained (she out of the question) everything congenial to my taste and dear to my heart, I, unapplauded, unfeared, unenvied and uncalumniated, should have lived and died.[53]

This account of the Miss Smith affair seems to reveal Cobbett at his best and his worst as both writer and man. The glib reference in the last passage to 'the supple crouch of servility' is the almost automatic language of the aged hack who has already turned out too many thousand newspaper articles, while the sneers at 'insolent pomposity' and 'disgusting dissipations' reveal the attitudes that were, by then, almost obligatory ones for the 'Great Disrespecter' to strike. Yet there are also passages of real and, for Cobbett, rare heart-searchings. Few poets and fewer prose writers would have remembered and, remembering, would have recorded so truthfully and so simply, what it was like to be young, and to fall in love against the grain of one's will and one's conscience. This is one of the few occasions when Cobbett dealt as faithfully with his own nature as he generally did with the world of nature.

Nevertheless it is worth remembering that he could approach the same theme with considerably less feeling when he found it could serve him in one of his interminable literary arguments. Nine years earlier he had been engaged in a prolonged argument with a certain Morris Birkbeck on the subject of emigration to the United States. Birkbeck had himself settled in what was then the frontier country of Illinois, and had written urging Englishmen to follow him there. Cobbett, an 'authority', by then, on the North American wilderness, advised them not to. If they had to emigrate, and he deplored the necessity, then Englishmen would do better in the already settled country of the Eastern United States. For, he said, he had seen how the American Loyalists, who already had some experience of pioneering, had settled in the New Brunswick wilderness. Here, in spite of all the aid that the English government had given them, and in spite of the material success of their settlements, they 'still *sighed for Connecticut*, and especially the women, young as well as old, though we gay fellows with worsted or silver lace upon our bright red coats did our best to make them happy . . . while we drank their coffee and grog by gallons, and eat their fowls, pigs and sausages and sweet-meats, by wheel-barrow loads . . .'[54]

There are few of the pangs of ill-fated love in that account. If we are to recapture the 'dying fall' of his New Brunswick idyll, we have to return to that other account, and to the end, for end there had to be, of his affair with Miss Smith:

The last parting came; and now came my just punishment. The time was known to everybody, and was irrevocably fixed; for I had to move with a regiment, and the embarkation of a regiment is an *epoch* in a thinly-settled province. To describe this parting would be too painful even at this distant day, and with the frost of age upon my head. The kind and virtuous father came forty miles to see me, just as I was going on board in the river. *His* looks and words I have never forgotten. As the vessel descended, she passed the mouth of *that creek*, which I had so often entered with delight; and though England, and all that England contained, were before me, I lost sight of this creek with an aching heart.[55]

If to kiss and to tell be a fault, then not to kiss and to tell must be even more blameworthy. Yet with a man as conscious of his own probity as Cobbett to deal with, even a solitary confession of weakness comes like dew in the desert. The affair of Miss Smith had given him 'a great deal of pleasure and also a great deal of pain, both in their extreme degree; and both of which, in spite of the lapse of forty years, now make an attempt to rush back into my heart'.[56]

CHAPTER FOUR

A Passion for Justice

> My deeds upon my head! I crave the law.
>> Shakespeare: *The Merchant of Venice, Act IV*

Cobbett's ability, his comparative youthfulness, his enterprise, and, perhaps, the romance surrounding his courtship of Ann had all, according to him, made his name known in army circles outside the regiment, and in civilian ones throughout New Brunswick. The courtship, for example, was:

> A matter of so much notoriety and conversation in the Province, that GENERAL CARLETON . . . who was the Governor when I was there, when he, about fifteen years afterwards, did me the honour, on his return to England, to come and see me at my house in Duke Street, Westminster, asked, before he went away, to see my *wife*, of whom *he had heard so much* before her marriage.[1]

His local reputation, he claimed, was such that:

> The fame of my services and talents ran through the whole country. Every good man respected me. I was invited to visit people in all parts of the provinces. While we lay at Fredericton in New Brunswick, I had the settling, or rather the preventing, of eight or nine law-suits.[2]

And yet he had, for some years, been eager to quit the Army. He had grown to resent the discipline he was subject to, disliked and despised most of his superiors, and had developed a very lively appreciation of his own merit, all of which could have added up to one reason. He wanted to marry, and that could have provided another, even though, as a sergeant-major, he would have been entitled to marry on the strength. He may have concluded that the Army had already taught him all that it usefully could. It had served him as school, university and Grand Tour combined, and had helped him discover and develop his talents. Now, there was little more that it could do for him in the way of education and, if he wanted to take those talents to a more profitable market, the time had come to leave.

All of these things he almost certainly considered. What finally decided him, however, was another factor. He was already developing what some of his biographers have described as his passion for justice. That is probably too large a name to give to the powerful instinct that undoubtedly dictated much that he did in the course of his life. His passion was never for justice in any general or abstract sense. Indeed, it would be more accurate to say that he hated injustice rather than that he loved justice, and that he was only capable of discovering injustice in certain specific cases. Nothing would deter him from fighting what he conceived to be an injustice that affected him, or any of the causes and people he was interested in; but equally, nothing would induce him to attack obvious injustices done to those for whom he felt indifference or hostility. He would always be proud of the fact that there was not a scrap of impartiality in him.

Such as it was, his passion for justice first revealed itself when he began to consider the condition of his fellow soldiers. He decided that they were not being dealt with fairly by certain officers of the 54th. He did not come to this conclusion, as he could well have done, because of the harshness of the discipline they were subjected to, the lack of any care for their welfare, and the emptiness of an existence in which the grog shop provided the only relief from a routine of drills, ceremonial parades and a constant preoccupation with turnout. These he accepted as an unavoidable condition of military service, even though he had a personal horror of the cat which was the almost universal instrument of enforcement. What he discovered to be an injustice, and decided to fight against, was that the officers of the 54th, like most of the officers in most of the regiments, were indulging in peculation.

That established, he took it upon himself to be the instrument of their punishment. He decided that, as soon as he had collected sufficient evidence, and the regiment had returned to England where he could gain access to those in authority, he would obtain his discharge and proceed to bring the peculators to a court martial. It was an extraordinary decision to take, and one which, if his plans were discovered, would place him in great danger. Nevertheless, once he had decided on his purpose, he began to work single-mindedly towards it.

It would always be both his strength and his weakness that he could concentrate on the particular to the exclusion of almost everything else. When he fought what he conceived to be an injustice he gained strength from the force of his different passions, for he had as great a depth of hatred for the oppressor as he had of compassion for the victim. His weakness arose from the fact that the force of these equal passions so possessed him that he tended to ignore everything else. He considered neither reason nor prudence. He abandoned any duty he might owe to loyalty or decency, but charged into the fight like an enraged bull, eager to gore and trample whatever might get in his way. Except that there was little that was ox-like about him, when this mood possessed him he closely resembled Kipling's prototypal Saxon:

> The Saxon is not like us Normans. His manners
>   are not so polite.
> But he never means anything serious till he
>   talks about justice and right.
> When he stands like an ox in the furrow with
>   his sullen eyes set on your own,
> And grumbles, 'This isn't fair dealing,' my son,
>   leave the Saxon alone.[3]

Cobbett's conspiracy – for that, in its initial secrecy, was what it was – had taken a long time to mature:

> This project was conceived so early as the year 1787, when an affair happened, that first gave me a full insight into regimental justice. It was shortly this: that the Quarter-Master, who had the issuing of the men's provisions to them, kept about a fourth part of it to himself. This, the old sergeants told me, had been the case for many years; and they were quite astonished and terrified at the idea of my complaining of it. This I did, however; but the reception I met with convinced me that I must never make another complaint, till I got safe to England . . .[4]

The Quartermaster was not, in the end, involved in the matter of the court martial. He had, perhaps, by then retired from the Army or died, as had one other man originally involved. By 1790 the Army List gave Major-General Frederick as Colonel-in-Chief of the 54th and Lieutenant-Colonel A. Bruce as its commanding officer. He, however, was already absent from the regiment on sick leave, and would shortly be entered as deceased. In his absence, Major Lord Edward Fitzgerald, who had transferred into the regiment from the 19th of Foot some two years earlier, was in command. Of the officers under him, Captain Powell was listed as the second senior Captain and Lieutenants Seton and Hall were listed as Paymaster and Adjutant respectively.

All of these are more or less relevant names, though only Fitzgerald's is still remembered for reasons quite unconnected with Cobbett. It is interesting, though not necessarily significant that, Cobbett apart, the only members of the 54th of that period who have some mention in history are Major John André, who, in 1780, was hanged by the Americans as a spy, and Major Lord Edward Fitzgerald, who died of his wounds after being shot by the British after the abortive Dublin rising of 1798. It is true that a recently gazetted British Brigadier-General called Benedict Arnold, whose desertion to the British Army had been the cause of André's capture and execution, had led a brigade which included the 54th in the attack on New London, where the regiment had gained its nickname of 'The Flamers' by burning a great deal of enemy shipping, but this was hardly sufficient to make him a member of that regiment.

Fitzgerald would, eventually, be instrumental in getting Cobbett his discharge. He had already made a name for himself as an efficient and gallant officer during the American War whilst serving in the 19th of Foot. When he transferred to the 54th he was, according to the regimental historian, an unusually enlightened and painstaking officer who made the welfare of his troops his main consideration. He insisted, for example, on having his men properly housed while they were at St. John's, and set them to work building their own barracks, in spite of the objections raised to such officious and unofficial action by the local Barrack Master, who was nominally in charge of such matters.

Cobbett, however, made no mention of Fitzgerald when he claimed, in later years, that 'I built a barrack for four hundred men, without the aid of either draughtsman, carpenter or bricklayer; the soldiers under me cut down the timber and dug the stones, and I was the architect . . .'[5] His repeated claim that all the officers of the 54th were drunken rogues who paid no attention whatsoever to the welfare of the troops is made to appear too sweeping in some of the letters that Fitzgerald wrote, at that time, to his mother. In one he tells her that 'I have got a garden for the men which employs me a great deal. I flatter myself that next year it will furnish the men with quantities of vegetable . . .' In another, which describes his daily routine, he appears to contradict Cobbett's account of how the regiment was exercised. He wrote:

I get up at 5 o'clock, go out and exercise the men from 6 to 8, come home and breakfast; from that time I read, write and settle

the different business of the Reg^t; at 4 we dine, and at half after
six we go out to parade and drill till sun-down.[6]

Cobbett describing how he exercised the regiment when the
matter was left to him, wrote:

I always had it on the ground in such time that the bayonets
glistened in the *rising sun*, a sight which gave me delight . . . If
the officers were to go out, eight or ten o'clock was the hour,
sweating the men in the heat of the day, breaking in upon the
time for cooking their dinner, putting all things out of order and
all men out of humour . . .[7]

Cobbett, it will be seen, admired Fitzgerald to the point of
claiming, as entirely his own, an attention to the troop's welfare
that he had at least to share with his commanding officer. But the
two men had more than solicitude for their men in common.
Fitzgerald, like Cobbett, but unlike most others in the regiment,
loved the Canadian wilderness. He travelled in it extensively, and
once made a remarkable journey on foot through the unmapped
forests that lay between St. John's and Quebec. At the end of that
journey he was arrested, since the Army thought that no one but a
deserter would have been desperate enough to have made it. The
Indians, however, showed more appreciation of his skill as a
woodsman: the leader of the Six Nations made him an honorary
chief of the Great Bear Tribe. Even when he took home leave,
Fitzgerald refused to travel in any orthodox manner. Instead of
taking passage, decorously, from St. John's, he made a long and
difficult journey down the length of the Mississippi and on into
Mexico before embarking for England.

It is something fanciful to imagine that each may have recognised in the other that underlying spirit of rebelliousness that
would, in due course, drive each of them out of the Army, and turn
each in his different way towards subverting the established order.
It was, perhaps, paradoxical that it should have been the Duke's
son who became an ardent republican and revolutionary and led an
armed rebellion against the Crown, while it was the son of a
peasant with republican sympathies who turned High Tory and
monarchist, and who so offended republican sentiment in the
United States that he was finally obliged to leave that country in
haste.

There is nothing paradoxical, however, in the fact that Cobbett,
never a notably deferential man, displayed considerable respect
for Fitzgerald while he was alive and risked unpopularity by

praising him after he was dead. They were, after all, and in many ways, two of a kind. So it was that, in 1800, when Cobbett had just returned to England to be fêted by the Tories as their champion in America, he went out of his way to point out, to Pitt of all men, the many virtues of the Irish Jacobin whom British troops had so recently shot:

> I remember that, in dining with Mr. Pitt at Mr. Windham's . . . the former asked me about *Lord Edward Fitzgerald*. We talked about him a good deal. I gave the company present . . . an account of his conduct, while at the regiment; I spoke in very high terms of his zeal for the service, and I told Mr. Pitt that Lord Edward was the only sober and the only honest officer I had ever known in the army.[8]

If Cobbett felt it necessary to denigrate every other army officer in order to be able to praise Fitzgerald, it was because he undoubtedly held the whole of the officer corps in contempt. Much of it arose from his own intolerance and feelings of superiority. Some of it, however, was more objectively based, for even by eighteenth-century standards, there was much that was wrong with the 54th, and with conditions in the Canadian garrisons.

Many of the troops garrisoned in Canada had formed part of the defeated army that moved north from the former thirteen colonies at the end of the American War. They had, therefore, left a comparatively civilised and settled country for a much wilder one whose European population was less than a tenth of that in the United States. Much of that population was French-speaking and there was an influx of Loyalist refugees who were strangers in this setting almost as much as were the British soldiers. The climate was harsh, the garrisons were isolated, for the most part, in small towns and settlements, and there was little or none of the social life that Boston or New York could have provided.

The Army had the disheartening task of guarding a vast, unexplored and ill-defined territory against a potential enemy who had already driven it out of what was now the United States, had already attempted one invasion of British Canada, and was already talking of a 'manifest destiny' that would extend the Republic from the Atlantic to the Pacific, and from the Gulf of Mexico to Hudson's Bay. No man who thought of such things would have considered the military situation an encouraging one. The depth of republican, anti-British and pro-French feeling in the United States made another war seem probable. The fact that neither side was prepared to honour the peace treaty in full appeared to provide continuing reason why one should start.

Morale in the 54th cannot have been heightened by the fact that it had been too long abroad for the comfort of the troops, many of whom could have served for most of their active careers without once seeing home. The regiment had left England in 1755, less than a year after it had been raised, and it was not to return until 1791. The last sixteen years had been spent on the distant North American station, eight of them in an unsuccessful war against the Americans.

Defeat in war is always demoralising. For the 54th, there was the additional factor that they must have found it difficult to understand *why* the war had been lost. They had remained in New York when much of the Army was marching through the Carolinas under Cornwallis, to a briefly enjoyed victory at Camden and the dreadful day when the world turned upside-down at Yorktown. Defeat and surrender on the battlefield force men to accept a reality that those not present may find it difficult to recognise. There must have been many in the 54th who would have talked about being betrayed by the generals and the politicians, and who would have agreed with Cobbett's later argument that the war should never have been lost:

It is, indeed, very true, that it was out of the power of America and her allies to renew the contest; and it is not less true that it was out of their power to have continued the contest . . . At the very moment when His Majesty was thus compelled to act upon the *defensive* against his rebel subjects; at that moment, the army which lay at New York, placed under proper commanders, and two millions of money, placed in honest hands, would have re-established his authority from New Hampshire to Georgia.[9]

Even if Cobbett had been right in his estimate of the military situation in the closing years of that war, he ignored the political realities. It had already been decided that further attempts to re-establish and sustain British rule in the thirteen colonies would be futile. Nevertheless, what he wrote was probably what he had been taught in the regiment, which, when he joined it in 1784, must still have been discussing the defeat Britain had suffered in America.

The reference to 'proper commanders' suggests one objective reason for his attitude towards his superiors, while that to 'two millions of money placed in honest hands' reveals another. Generations of grudging taxpayers and parsimonious Parliaments had so starved the Army of funds that large numbers of German troops had to be used in America, largely to the detriment of the British cause, because the Army could not afford to pay a wage that would attract sufficient English recruits. There were not even funds enough to equip, arm and pay the thousands of American Loyalists who had volunteered to take arms against their fellow Americans. What was worse was that not all of the funds that were available were spent on pursuing the war to a speedy conclusion.

The combination of indolence and corruption at Staff level did much to prolong the American War, and prevented it being brought to a speedy conclusion in Britain's favour, as was entirely possible in the earlier stages. Even as late as 1780, when the war was well on the way to being lost, Admiral Rodney commented bitterly on the subject to Lord Edward Germain, then Secretary for the Colonies. In a letter dated 22 December 1780 he wrote:

Nothing but the affection an Englishman bears . . . to his King and Country irritates my mind when I behold her treasures squandered, her arms inactive, and her honour lost, and by the very men entrusted with the most important and honourable confidence of their sovereign and his ministers, paying not the least regard to the sufferings of the country, but retarding the completion and extinction of the rebellion to make the fortunes of a long train of leeches, who suck the blood of the state, and whose interests prompts them to promote the continuance of the war, such as quarter-masters and their deputies *ad infinitum*, barrack-masters and their deputies *ad infinitum*, commissaries and their deputies *ad infinitum*, all of which make princely fortunes and laugh in their sleeves at the generals who permit it, and by every means in their power continue to discountenance every active measure, and, instead of having an idea of speedily concluding this unhappy war, their common discourse turns on what may happen in two or three ensuing campaigns.[10]

If the Admiral knew about these things in 1780, one can be sure that canteen and latrine gossip had brought them to the attention of every private soldier well before 'this unhappy war' had ended. The troops would have grumbled about these higher forms of peculation in a way they might not have grumbled about the lesser peculations their regimental officers engaged in, for these were a part of army tradition, and there is no greater traditionalist than the serving soldier.

Peculation in the regiment had a history that went back to the days before there had been any standing army, and when the regiment was, in Fortescue's words, 'a commercial company raised by men with the necessary capital . . . and agreeing among themselves as to the sharing of profits'.[11] Although the Crown had become solely responsible for the maintenance of the regiments, some remnants of their commercial origins survived in the purchase and sale of commissions and the distribution, in wartime, of prize money. Both of these ensured that the profit motive should remain a part of soldiering.

The purchase of a commission was a comparatively large investment, even though the market price varied from regiment to regiment and fluctuated with market conditions. However cheaply it was purchased, however, a junior officer's pay never provided a reasonable return on the capital invested. By the end of the eighteenth century a subaltern's pay would not even cover his mess bills. Poorer officers, therefore, had to look elsewhere if they were to enjoy incomes they could live on, and it was here that the tradition of the regiment as a commercial enterprise came to their aid. Just as Falstaff had 'misused the King's press damnably' and taken a profit out of the three hundred pounds entrusted to him, so the tradition survived that it was no great crime to make a profit out of the running of a regiment. There were several ways in which this could be done. Muster rolls could be padded, so that pay and allowances could be drawn for non-existent soldiers. Messing and clothing allowances could be handled by those who had the spending of them so as to leave a profit. Stoppages and residual pay could be manipulated to the officer's advantage. The Army never sanctioned such peculations, but accepted them rather as a custom which, if modestly followed, would seldom be objected to officially. The sergeants of the 54th, indeed, were astonished when Cobbett objected to the Quartermaster keeping back a fourth of the rations.

But Cobbett, that uncomfortable man with a passion for justice, would always have a particular hatred for anything that even suggested corruption, whether it took the form of patronage, pensions, profit-taking or peculation. He refused to acknowledge that it could be hallowed by tradition or in any way justified by the British habit of maintaining its armed forces on the cheap. It is against this background, then, of a recently defeated and partially demoralised regiment, serving in an isolated garrison on a potentially hostile and dangerous frontier, where there was little for underoccupied and underpaid officers and men to do but drink, gamble and brawl, that Cobbett's proudly asserted incorruptibility must be measured.

The conditions described were not peculiar to that period, that station and that regiment. Some twenty years later, just before war did in fact break out again between Britain and America, General Sir Isaac Brock was required to report on the preparedness and morale of the Canadian garrisons. The following comments are typical of many that were contained in that report. Of his own regiment, the 41st, he said, 'It is an uncommonly fine regiment but wretchedly officered'; of another regiment he said, 'The 48th has been ten years in this country, drinking rum without bounds . . .'[12] (In spite of this, those same British regiments succeeded in defeating the American attempt to invade by land, but General Brock himself was killed in the engagement at Queenston Heights.)

Once Cobbett had discovered the Quartermaster with his hands, as it were, in the ration waggon, and had it forcibly impressed upon him that he was never to question such practices, he decided that he had to operate as what might nowadays be called a 'mole'. He made it his private duty to discover what other forms of peculation might exist in the regiment. He was in a good position to do so, for all the business of the regiment passed through his hands. He began to study the books that had been left to his sole control with a different and more suspicious eye, and there is something pleasantly naïve in his confession that 'the circumstance which first disgusted me . . . was, the abuses, the shocking abuses as to money matters, the peculation, in short, which I witnessed . . .'[13]

Having found what any less ingenuous sergeant-major would have expected to find, he had to ask himself what he should do with his discoveries. He was not, and never would be a man for those simpler loyalties that bind men together collegiately. Nevertheless, such loyalties as even he felt he owed his regiment did something to weaken his passion for justice until he was again reminded of the depth of his dislike for those who were superior to him only in authority:

If my officers had been men of manifest superiority of mind, I should, perhaps, not have so soon conceived the project of bringing them, or some of them, at least, to shame and punishment.[14]

There is nothing, of course, like a little personal animosity to sharpen the pace at which one feels obliged to engage in an impersonal pursuit of justice. So it was that 'from this time forward, I began to collect materials for an exposure, upon my return to England. I had ample opportunities for this, being the keeper of all the books, of every sort, in the regiment, and knowing the whole of its affairs better than any other man.'[15]

He continued this secret assembling of evidence for four full years, but 'the winter previous to our return to England, I thought it necessary to make extracts from the books, lest the books themselves should be destroyed. In order to be able to prove that these extracts were correct, it was necessary that I should have a witness as to their being true copies.'[16] This was a ticklish situation for any 'mole' to find himself in. Enlisting a second 'mole' meant revealing the conspiracy and so more than doubling the risks of detection.

I hesitated many months. At one time I had given the thing up. I dreamt twenty times, I dare say, of my papers being discovered, and of my being tried and flogged to death. At last, however, some fresh act of injustice towards us made me set all danger at defiance.[17]

What the fresh act of injustice was, nobody knows, but it stimulated him to recruit a secondary 'mole': 'I opened my project to a corporal whose name was William Bestland, who wrote in the office under me, and who was very bound to me, for my goodness to him.'[18]

This Bestland was 'a very little fellow: not more than about five feet high', and an oddly assorted pair they must have looked as:

To work we went, and during a long winter, while the rest were boozing and snoring, we gutted no small part of the regimental books, rolls and other documents. Our way was this; to take a copy, sign it with our names, and clap the regimental seal to it, so that we might be able to swear to it, when produced in court.[19]

Cobbett would be at one end or the other of litigation on several future occasions, but he would never again prepare his case so carefully or take so many precautions on his way to court. In the future he would, all too often, charge at the law like a bull, depending, perhaps over-optimistically, on the power of his name and his pen outside the court, and on the power of his tongue inside it.

The time eventually came for the regiment to return to England and it disembarked at Portsmouth on 3 November 1791, though not before Cobbett and Bestland had been thrown into a moment of confusion:

There was talk of searching all the boxes &c., which gave us great alarm and induced us to take all the papers, put them in a bag, and trust them to a custom-house officer, who conveyed them on shore to his own home, whence I removed them in a few days after.[20]

By 19 December 1791, Cobbett had obtained his discharge from the Army, after what was, for those days, a remarkably short enlistment. Orders for the Plymouth garrison on that day contained the following announcement:

Sergeant Major Cobbett having most pressingly applied for his discharge, at Major Lord Edward Fitzgerald's request, General Frederick has granted it. General Frederick has ordered Major Lord Edward Fitzgerald to return the Sergeant Major thanks for his behaviour and conduct during the time of his being in the regiment, and Major Lord Edward Fitzgerald adds his most hearty thanks to those of the General.

Nothing could have been more handsomely done, though, if the General had known what was contained in the bag so recently recovered from the custom-house officer, there would have been neither thanks nor discharge for Cobbett, but an immediate court martial. One wonders, however, what Fitzgerald, that fellow rebel, whose name would be removed from the Army List in little more than another year, would have made of it, if he had known. As it was he handed Cobbett the following document on the day of his discharge:

By the Right Honourable Major Lord Edward Fitzgerald, commanding His Majesty's 54th Regiment of Foot, whereof Lieutenant General Frederick is Colonel.

These are to certify that the bearer hereof, William Cobbett, Sergeant Major in the aforesaid regiment, has served honestly and faithfully for the space of eight years, nearly seven of which he has been a non-commissioned officer, and of that time he has been five years Sergeant Major to the regiment; but having very earnestly applied for his discharge, he, in consideration of his good behaviour and the services he has rendered the regiment, is hereby discharged.

Given under my hand and the seal of the regiment, at Portsmouth, this 19th day of December, 1791.[21]

Fitzgerald, it would seem, had as high a regard for Cobbett as Cobbett had for him. It is possible, however, that suspicion was beginning to gather around Cobbett. The search of the baggage may be put down to routine, but Bestland failed in his attempt to obtain his discharge at the same time as Cobbett. This was a very necessary part of the conspiracy, for it was essential to have the evidence confirmed by Bestland:

> I had solemnly engaged with him not to have recourse to [it], unless he was first out of the army; that is to say, out of the reach of the vindictive and bloody lash . . . But there was a suspicion of his connection with me, and therefore they resolved to keep him.[22]

Meanwhile, however, Cobbett had more personal matters to attend to. He went in search of his Nancy, and 'found my little girl *a servant of all work* (and hard work it was), *at five pounds a-year*, in the house of a Captain Brissac; and without hardly saying a word about the matter, she put into my hands *the whole of my hundred and fifty guineas unbroken!*[23]

Cobbett, as he should have been, was greatly impressed by having the soundness of his original choice confirmed in this useful manner. Indeed, some thirty-five years later, he used the incident to point out to young lovers the heights of virtue and prudence women could and should aspire to:

> Need I attempt to describe what effect this example ought to have on every young woman . . . ? Admiration of her conduct, and self-gratulation on this indubitable proof of the soundness of my own judgement, were now added to my love of her beautiful person. Now, I do not say that there are not many young women in this country who would, under similar circumstances, have acted as my wife did in this case . . . But when *her age* is considered; when we reflect that she was living in a place crowded, literally *crowded*, with gaily-dressed and handsome young men, many of whom really far richer and in higher rank than I was, and scores of them ready to offer her their hand; when we reflect that she was living amongst young women who put upon their backs every shilling they could come at; when we see her keeping the bag of gold untouched, and working hard to provide herself with but mere necessary apparel, and doing this while she was passing from *fourteen to eighteen years of age*; when we view the whole of the circumstances, we must say that here is an example, which, while it reflects honour on her sex, ought to have weight with every young woman whose eyes or ears this relation shall reach.[24]

Cobbett married his Ann at Woolwich on 5 February 1792. There are times when he was almost unbearably self-satisfied, but he was never more so than when he was discussing his choice of a wife. Ann does, indeed, seem to have been a remarkably loving, loyal, industrious and, perhaps, long-suffering mate. He, for his part, was for most of the time, an admiring, faithful, attentive, and almost excessively uxorious husband. Ann bore him, often in difficult circumstances, no fewer than thirteen children, though only seven of them survived childbirth or infancy – a reasonable score for those days. She was never her husband's equal in intelligence or learning; her daughters even had to write her letters for her. But Mary Russell Mitford, when she visited the Cobbetts in the days of their prosperity at Botley, wrote:

> Everything was excellent, everything abundant – all served with the greatest nicety by trim waiting-damsels: and everything went on with such quiet regularity, that of the large circle of guests not one would find himself in the way. I need not say a word more in praise of the goodwife . . . to whom this admirable order was mainly due. She was a sweet, motherly woman, realising our notion of one of Scott's most charming characters, *Ailie Dinmont*, in her simplicity, her kindness, and her devotion to her husband and her children.[25]

Henry Hunt, Cobbett's fellow Radical commented, in later days, that Mrs. Cobbett seemed unable to keep or train her servants, not having been brought up in a household where servants were kept. (There is no one like a good Radical for noticing such matters.) Cobbett never mentioned his wife in his published writings except to praise her, which he did whenever the opportunity occurred. One such occasion is relevant at this point, for it deals with what might have happened to him if he had not got married:

> A fourth part of the labours I have performed never would have been performed *if I had not been a married man* . . . I should, all the early part of my life, have been rambling and roving about as most bachelors are . . . I might have done *something*; but perhaps not a thousandth part of what I have done . . . for the chances are, that I, being fond of a military life, should have ended my days ten or twenty years ago in consequence of wounds, or fatigue, or, more likely, in consequence of the persecutions of some haughty and insolent fool, whom nature had formed to black my shoes, and whom a system of corruption had made my commander. *Love* came and rescued me from this

state of horrible slavery; placed the whole of my time at my own disposal; made me as free as air; removed every restraint upon the operations of my mind, naturally disposed to communicate its thoughts to others; and gave me for my leisure hours a companion, who, though deprived of all opportunity of acquiring what is *called learning*, had so much good sense, so much useful knowledge, was so innocent, so just in all her ways, so pure in thought word and deed, so disinterested, so generous, so devoted to me and her children, so free from all disguise, and, withal, so beautiful and so talkative, and in a voice so sweet, so cheering, that I must . . . have been a criminal, if I had done much less than that which I have done; and I have always said, that if my country feels any gratitude for my labours, that gratitude is due to her full as much as to me.[26]

Was Ann Cobbett ever as beautiful as her husband believed her to be? We have only his word for how she looked when she was in the bloom of her youth. A portrait of her in her middle age hangs in the Farnham Museum. It is true that the journeyman portraitists of that age are not always the most reliable witnesses, but the ageing brunette who looks out of that portrait seems, in contrast to the vigorous, small-eyed, masterful man whose leg of mutton face looks out of the companion portrait, a somewhat plain and homely person who could never have had anything but youth and a fond eye to elevate her to beauty.

All of this, however, is to anticipate the effects of living happily, in theory, for up to forty years. At this time Cobbett had only just ceased being a 'rambling roving bachelor', and had only just got married. Much as he would always revel in the private joys of matrimony, he would never, at any time in his life, allow it to interfere with public affairs. At this moment he still had a court martial to pursue, and he had taken no more than a first step towards pursuing it in public.

On 14 January 1792, less than a month after his discharge and just over a fortnight before his marriage, Cobbett wrote to Sir George Yonge, the Secretary of War. The letter contained a petition to the King and an explanation of what it was he asked for. This was to have Lieutenant-Colonel Bruce, Captain Powell and Lieutenants Seton and Hall brought to a court martial on the following charges:

a) Embezzlement of monies rightfully belonging to the NCOs and men of the regiment, or to the regiment itself.
b) Depriving troops of rations and clothing due to them.

c) Falsifying accounts.

d) Over-complementing the muster rolls in order to draw pay and rations for non-existent soldiers.

Bruce had died, and so was dropped from the proceedings. Cobbett's general charges were whittled down, as the affair proceeded, to the more specific but less damaging charges of:

a) Making a false muster of seven men.

b) Mustering as soldiers men who had acted as servants.

c) Making five false returns.

d) Misapplying work money earned by privates and NCOs.

e) Taking firewood from fuel issued for troops.

f) Selling two years' clothing whilst men wore rags, and obliging them to accept an inadequate sum in lieu.

g) Signing false certificates about clothing.

h) Taking over the baking of the men's bread, cheating them of the right amount of flour and selling the rest.

Cobbett was to complain that these were only some of the charges he had preferred and that the most material parts had been omitted from the charges that were left. Indeed, though the consequences must have been serious for the accused if they were convicted, the charges had been sufficiently reduced to make what had been started as a crusade against peculation as a system seem little more than a haggle over the regiment's housekeeping. But Cobbett had a long way to go before even these lesser charges were considered. For a number of reasons both the Government and the Army resented and resisted his call for justice.

Courts martial sometimes had to sit in judgment on civilians, but there were few cases of a civilian forcing a court martial to be held on serving officers against whom the Army had not, and would not itself, prefer charges. It was, in effect, having its hand most inconveniently forced by Cobbett. Politicians and generals were, of course, aware that peculation was a traditional, widespread, and almost necessary part of Army practice. It was highly improbable, however, that any of them would welcome a case that could bring that fact to the attention of the general public.

Although Pitt had built his reputation on his skilful handling of financial problems, he was notorious for his refusal to find adequate funds for the Army. If his enemies could show that this encouraged and perpetuated peculation and might lead to a recurrence of the disasters experienced during the American War, his administration might have been exposed to damaging attacks.

There must have been some members of that administration who wondered, as Cobbett's enemies did in later years, whether his motives were as laudable as he claimed at the time and later:

> The object . . . was to bring certain officers to justice for having, in various ways, wronged both the public and the soldier. I was so situated as to save England thousands and thousands of pounds during the time that my regiment was stationed in New Brunswick. My vigilance was incessant; and I pursued the interest of the government at home, with as much zeal as if my life depended on the result. I would take my oath that I never saw any man that did the same, whilst I was in that country, with the exception of General Carleton, the Governor, and the unfortunate Lord Edward Fitzgerald, who was a really honest, conscientious and humane man . . .[27]

Was he, in short, what he claimed to be, a simple, straightforward and embarrassingly honest man demanding no more than justice for the taxpayer and the soldier? Or was he carrying out a political purpose and acting, whether innocently or otherwise, on behalf of the Government's enemies? When political motives were imputed to him in later years, Cobbett claimed that he was, at that time, a political innocent:

> The reader will recollect that this was in 1792, a time when the principles of demolishing governments were little known and little dreaded. Let it be considered that I had just arrived in England; that I was a perfect novice in politics, never having, to my recollection, read even a newspaper while abroad . . .[28]

He was a Tory, though already an unorthodox one, when he wrote that passage, and very much involved in politics. He must, therefore, have known that his disavowal was somewhat disingenuous: claiming to be a novice in politics is not the same as claiming to be apolitical. Indeed, he spoilt the whole argument by adding the following apologia:

> Previous to my leaving England for France,* previously to my seeing what republicanism was, I had not only imbibed its principles, I had not only been a republican, but an admirer of the writings of Paine. I will not be blamed by those who duly reflect. Instead of blame, I am not without hope, that the reader

---

* i.e. immediately after the affair of the court martial.

will find something to commend, in a person who, having imbibed erroneous opinions, was so soon taught, by experience, to correct them.

This suggests that he was at least radically inclined, if not politically motivated, at the time of the court martial, and not disinclined, therefore, to embarrass the government. It is right for us, who can follow the whole of his career, to believe that a passion for justice would always dictate his actions. But it was not unreasonable for his enemies to claim that, at the time of the court martial, that passion had been seasoned with radicalism and sharpened by his hatred of the officer class. Such arguments, however, belong to the future, when he would frequently be taunted with his behaviour over the court martial. At this stage, there were difficulties to overcome before that court martial could become even a possibility.

Cobbett's letter to Sir George Yonge was answered, ten days later, by a request for him to attend at the War Office.

I was shown into an ante-chamber amongst numerous anxious-looking men, who, every time the door which led to the great man was opened, turned their heads that way with a motion as regular and as uniform as if they had been drilled to it. These people eyed me from head to foot, and, I shall never forget their look, when they saw that I was admitted to Paradise without being detained for a single moment in Purgatory. Sir George Yonge heard my story, and that was apparently all he wanted of me. I was to hear from him again in a day or two . . .[29]

When Cobbett had heard nothing for fifteen days he began to suspect that an attempt was being made to starve him out. He wrote again to remind Yonge that, since he had little money, to keep him waiting in London much longer would be to ruin him. The reply came that a court martial had been agreed to, that the matter had now been passed to Sir Charles Gould, the Judge-Advocate General, and that it was proposed to hold the trial, not in London, as Cobbett had requested, but in Portsmouth, where the 54th was still stationed. Cobbett immediately wrote back protesting at 'the very unexpected and alarming circumstances of its being proposed to hold the Court-Martial at Portsmouth.'

I have placed myself in London . . . for no other purpose than the prosecution of this affair, never imagining it possible that charges of such importance and such general concern, would be investigated anywhere else . . . All I wish is a fair and impartial trial. But this I freely declare I cannot expect at Portsmouth . . . There the regiment is quartered, there the accused have formed connections, and there all the witnesses I may call upon will be totally in their power . . . In London I should think myself perfectly safe, and should give my evidence without fear. At Portsmouth I shall be a friendless, unsupported individual, surrounded with a host of enemies, and I should look upon my life as being in danger.[30]

He had been known, while he was serving, as 'Lawyer Cobbett', which suggests that he was not entirely popular. A regiment always looks after its own, and it now formed a protective circle around the accused officers, and there was no one in the 54th on whom Cobbett could count. Indeed, as the passage suggests, he expected a counter-attack and, as he took that possibility seriously, he may already have had some ideas of the form it would take. Captain Powell, who now acted as spokesman for the accused, had also written to the Judge Advocate-General insisting that the court martial should be held at Portsmouth, since the expense of travelling to London to be tried would be a heavy drain on their pockets. He added, rather neatly 'We are soldiers of fortune, not men of fortune.'[31]

The courage and audacity with which Cobbett now faced his opponents were admirable in themselves and surprising in a man who had, for eight years, been subject to the commands of his superiors. He went over everyone's head and wrote to Pitt himself. After explaining his position he ended with the following dignified, and possibly menacing protest:

I have now, Sir, done all a man can do in such a case. I have proceeded regularly, and, I may add, respectfully, from first to last; if I am allowed to serve my country by prosecuting men who have injured it, I shall do it; if I am thwarted and pressed down by those whose office is to assist and support me, I cannot do it; in either case, I shall be satisfied with having done my duty, and shall leave the world to make a comparison between me and the men I have accused.[32]

The scandal that would attend a court martial held in London would be bad enough, but to have Cobbett appeal to public opinion, with some reference to those who had 'thwarted and pressed him down' would be worse. Pitt accordingly yielded, and gave Cobbett his court martial in London. This, however, no longer sufficed. Cobbett had asked for the regimental records to be secured, and this had not been done. If they had been destroyed, changed or hidden, the primary evidence he relied on would be missing, while the signed and sealed copies, which might have served as secondary evidence, could not now be used since Bestland had not been discharged and Cobbett had sworn not to call him as a witness if he was still subject to military discipline.

Cobbett's case, carefully prepared over four years, was falling apart. And now another, and greater danger threatened. He intended to go to Portsmouth in order to discover, if he could, what had in fact happened to the regimental records, but 'As I was going down to Portsmouth, I met several of the sergeants coming up, together with the music-master . . . I was told by a Captain Lane who had been in the regiment,* that they had been brought up to swear, that, at an entertainment given by me before my departure from the regiment, I had drunk "the destruction of the House of Brunswick".'[33]

If this were proved, the tables would have been effectively turned. The toast, if given, amounted to sedition, and as he was a serving soldier at that moment, would have come under the Mutiny Act so that, far from court-martialling his officers, they would have court-martialled him. Cobbett, of course, denied ever having uttered the words:

> I had talked pretty freely on the occasion alluded to; but I had neither said, nor thought, anything against the King, and, as to the House of Brunswick, I hardly knew what it meant . . . I was told they would send me to Botany Bay; and, I now verily believe, that, if I had remained, I should have furnished a pretty good example to those who wished to cure military abuses . . .[34]

This, then, was the regiment's counter-attack. Whether the sergeants and the music-master were marching to London merely to perjure themselves, or whether Cobbett, 'talking pretty freely', had really given the toast will never be known. The farewell party, probably in the Sergeant's Mess, would certainly have been a beery occasion, and even Cobbett may have got drunk enough to voice some of the republican sentiments he then, on his own admission, entertained. This was certainly the first time in his life anyone had

---

* Lane was the friendly officer who had recruited him.

accused him of holding political views of any description, a fact that does something to strengthen the theory that, in the matter of the court martial, politics had infiltrated his passion for justice.

The court martial was set for 24 March. Cobbett had left for Portsmouth on 20 March, but, having met the sergeants, apparently went no farther than the village of Fratton. From there, according to him, he wrote once more to Gould:

> Stating over again all the obstacles that had been thrown in my way, and concluding by demanding the discharge of a man whom I should name, as the only condition upon which I would attend the court-martial. I requested him to send me an answer by the next day, and told him, that, unless such an answer was received, he and those to whom my repeated applications had been made, might do what they pleased with their court-martial; for, that I confidently trusted, that a few days would place me beyond the scope of their power. No answer came, and, as I had learned in the meanwhile, that there was a design to prosecute me for sedition, that was an additional motive to be quick in my movements.[35]

In all the controversy concerning the case that continued for years Gould resolutely denied that he had ever received this letter, and asserted that all he had from Cobbett had been a letter saying that he had to be in the country until the day before the hearing, but would return in time to attend. The court martial duly opened on 24 March, but to an anti-climax. Cobbett, the key figure in the case, was not there.

Powell, Seton and Hall were formally charged and Cobbett was then called as a witness. When, by ten o'clock he had failed to appear, a messenger was sent to his lodgings to summon him. He was not there either, but his landlady said she believed that he had been called to his father's sickbed, but had left no address. The court accordingly adjourned for three days. When it reconvened, and Cobbett still failed to appear, there was nothing left for it to do but declare that 'The said charges against these officers are, and every part thereof is, totally unfounded.'

A great deal of indignation was expressed at Cobbett's conduct, and the Judge Advocate-General enquired of the Law Officers whether, on the facts as revealed, Cobbett could be criminally prosecuted. The Officers gave it as their opinion:

> We think that Cobbett, unless he can be proved to have conspired with others, wilfully and maliciously to prefer these

charges, could not be criminally prosecuted. The parties injured by his conduct, which is certainly most highly blameable, might maintain actions in the case against him.

Those 'parties' immediately announced that they would, indeed, sue Cobbett just as soon as they could find him, but this, of course, they failed to do. There is a story, which may or may not be true, that they were told that he was hiding in his father's house at Farnham, and that they sent a private of the 54th called Johnston, disguised as a beggar, to verify the report. Cobbett was sitting at dinner when Johnston knocked on the door. He recognised him, in spite of his disguise, asked him to come in, and offered him food. While he was eating, Cobbett sent his brother to fetch the parish constable, and when he arrived, said:

I charge this man with being a deserter from the 54th Regiment of Foot. His name is John Johnston, and as a proof that my accusation is true, he shall be immediately stripped and the marks will be found on his back of the hundred lashes which he received when I was Sergeant Major of the Regiment.

While the constable was questioning and stripping Johnston who, so far as spying went, had surely to be classified as an unskilled labourer, Cobbett was able to pack his bag, steal out of the house, collect his wife in London and slip across the Channel to France. It is a suitably picaresque story which, *se non è vero, è molto ben trovato*. All that is established, however, about the end to the affair of the abortive court martial is that while Powell and the others were still looking for Cobbett in order to sue him, he and his wife had landed at St. Omer in France on one of the last days in March 1792.

Although the four-year-long affair actually ended at the moment when Cobbett failed, for the second time, to answer to his name in court, the scandal it gave rise to never really died away in the course of his lifetime. His enemies would, in later years, frequently taunt him with having blustered about justice and then run away. He had been rash enough, in one of his letters to Gould, all of which were subsequently published, to write: 'If my accusation *is* without foundation, the authors of cruelty have not yet devised the tortures I ought to endure. Hell itself, as painted by the most fiery bigot, would be too mild a punishment for me.'

When Gillray published his lampoon in 1809, one of the plates showed Cobbett being claimed from the court room by the Devil himself. That was a good year for anti-Cobbett literature, for J.

Hatchard of Piccadilly also published an anonymous pamphlet which did much to revive memories of the scandal of 1792. It dealt, in some detail, with the court martial, as seen from the viewpoint of men who claimed to have been falsely accused, and it reproduced many of the letters that had passed between Cobbett and Gould.

The author was, very probably, Powell. It caused a sufficient stir for Cobbett to feel obliged to answer it in a long article in his *Political Register* (from which many of the quotations used here have been taken). Why Powell waited so long before publishing his version of the affair is something of a mystery. It may be because the regiment had been sent abroad again on active service not very long after the court martial. It may have been because, later, when it had returned to England, Cobbett was for a time high in the Government's favour, and it could have been impolitic for a serving officer to attack him. By 1809, however, he had fallen out of favour, and the Government's only wish was to silence him, which it managed to do shortly afterwards by having him imprisoned in Newgate for seditious libel.

Years before Powell's pamphlet, however, and almost immediately after the court martial, Ridgway, a London printer, had published a fifteen-page pamphlet that would do much, over the years, to perpetuate the theory that the court martial had really been an attack on the Government, and that Cobbett had been, and would always be a potential rebel and traitor. The title page ran:

The
SOLDIER'S FRIEND
Or
CONSIDERATIONS
On The
LATE PRETENDED AUGMENTATION
Of The
SUBSISTENCE
Of The
PRIVATE SOLDIERS
Written by a Subaltern
(Price Two-Pence, or One hundred Copies 10s.6d.)

The pamphlet attacked the officer corps for having, by its peculations, reduced the funds voted by Parliament for the soldiers' subsistence allowance. It also attacked Parliament because, instead of punishing the peculators, it had voted an extra £23,000 a year to make up the deficit, thus making the taxpayers pay for the officers' dishonesty. The subject, it can be seen, was closely related to the charges Cobbett had brought against the officers of the 54th. Since the pamphlet was first published in June 1792, less than three months after Cobbett had fled to France, it was always believed that he was either its author or part-author.

This he steadily denied, most specifically in an article he wrote in 1805, though he did there admit that information he had given at the time of the court martial to 'a person with whom I was acquainted' may have provided some of the information on which the pamphlet was based. It was, at that time, important for Cobbett not to be thought responsible for a work which, if it did not actually amount to an incitement to mutiny, still went out of its way to promote disaffection in the ranks. It was not until 1833, two years before his death, that he finally acknowledged authorship.

He did not need to do so for, crudely though the pamphlet was written, it bore the stamp of Cobbett's mind and Cobbett's later style. It ran into at least two editions, and was widely read in the armed services. It was believed to have had considerable influence on some of the ringleaders of the dangerous, almost revolutionary mutinies that took place at Spithead and the Nore in 1797.

A few quotations, taken almost at random, must convince any student of Cobbett that in this, his first essay at polemics, the true Cobbett style was already taking shape.

On Parliament:
If anything done in that wise and equal Representation of the People called the House of Commons, were worth a thought from a man of sense . . .

On Officers:
The world is often deceived in those jovial, honest looking fellows, the Officers of the Army . . . I could mention characters in this *honourable* profession that would shine amongst the *Seed of Abraham*, or do honour to the society of Stock Jobbers.

To the Soldiers:
If you should have the fortune to become a non-commissioned Officer, and were to deduct but a penny from a man unlawfully, you know, the consequence would be a breaking and a flogging, and refunding the money so deducted; but here you see your Officers have been guilty of the practice for years, and now it is found out, not a hair of one of their heads is touched . . . How comes it, then, that the Law is so softened towards your officers? Because the ruling Powers look upon your Officers as Gentlemen, and upon you as Beasts . . .

102

On the Crown

Soldiers are taught to believe everything they receive, a *gift from the Crown*; cast this notion from you immediately . . . I would have you know that you are not the servant of *one man* only; A British soldier can never be that. You are the servant of the whole nation . . . I would have you look upon nothing you receive as a *Favour* or *Bounty* from Kings, Queens or Princes; you receive the wages of your servitude; it is your property . . . which property your rapacious Officers ought never to seize on, without meeting punishment due to their infamy.

It was, as can be seen, good, inflamatory, democratical stuff. If Cobbett did not write it, as he would later write the American pamphlets attacking democracy, and later still the Manchester Lectures demanding universal suffrage and annual Parliaments, then there is no value anywhere in textual comparisons, and no one should ever attempt to attribute a piece to an author on the strength of its style.

Cobbett had, in the space of three short months, become a civilian, a married man, a litigant, a public figure, an author, a rebel and an exile. Encouraged by all this, he now set out to make his fortune in a new and different world.

CHAPTER FIVE

A Desire to Instruct

Young man, there is America – which at this day serves for little more than to amuse you with stories of savage men and uncouth manners; yet shall, before you taste of death, show itself equal to the whole of that commerce which now attracts the envy of the world.

Edmund Burke: *Of Americans and their Fishing Industry*

When the 54th landed in Portsmouth at the end of 1791, Cobbett was determined to do three things: to obtain his discharge; to get married; to bring the matter of the court martial to a successful conclusion. These, however, were all matters for immediate action, and we can only guess at what he proposed to do in the longer term.

His later writings, fortunately, provide some faint clues as to what was in his mind at that time. There was nothing for him in Farnham, where the small family farm and public house already had to support his parents and at least one married brother. He could not, hating the legal life as he did, return to Gray's Inn. There was little, indeed, that a man with such a sound conceit of himself and determined, henceforth, to be his own master, could hope to do anywhere in England. He now, quite justifiably, counted himself a knowledgeable and educated man, but he possessed neither fortune, qualifications nor patrons, and men educated beyond their prospects – curates, schoolteachers, Grub Street scribblers – were two a penny.

If he drew on what he had already acquired by way of self-knowledge, which, in one way or another, is what we all do, he would have realised that he still had a strong desire to see more of the world, that it was difficult, if not impossible, for him to serve under others, and that he had both the desire and the ability to instruct. He had, after all, had the training and instructing of an entire regiment, including its officers, and had discovered in himself a mind 'naturally disposed to communicate its thoughts to others.'

There are, perhaps, only three ways by which a man so disposed can gratify his desires. He can teach; he can turn to didactic

writing; he can engage in politics. Cobbett would, eventually, turn
to the last two. At that time, however, he could not be certain that
he had a talent for either. *The Soldier's Friend* could no more have
convinced him that he was a writer than his reading of Paine and his
half-fledged ideas about republicanism could have convinced him
that he was a politician. He did, however, know from past experience that he could train and instruct others, and this, one imagines,
must have made him consider teaching. Though it would have been
difficult for him, in his comparatively poverty-stricken and un-
qualified state, to open a school in England, there was no reason
why he should not plan to do so in that other English-speaking
country, the United States.

He differed from Burke in that he had already had some
personal experience of North America. Although he would have
agreed with him about the vast potential wealth of the United
States, he would have differed from him in expecting to find
nothing there but 'savage men and uncouth manners', though he
did, eventually, find enough of those to keep his pen busy for a
decade. The American Loyalists in Canada, and in particular the
Smith family, had taught him that uncouthness and savagery are no
more than comparative conditions. Had not the Smiths, after all,
sat down by the waters of the St. John River and wept for
Connecticut? And had not men no better qualified than himself
founded universities, become judges, ambassadors and State Gov-
ernors in the United States? And was that not now a country where
republican sentiments served as a commendation rather than, as
they increasingly did in England, a reason for a rapid passage to
Newgate or Botany Bay?

Although Cobbett, as a consequence of the court martial, now
had to leave England precipitately, it is still reasonable to assume
that he had intended to leave in any case, and that the manner of
his leaving did not mean that he fled without either a plan or a
purpose. His purpose was to settle in the United States where he
would open a school. His plan was to spend a preliminary year in
France in order to complete his education. A man might succeed in
passing for educated in those days if he had neither Greek nor
Latin. He would find it difficult to do so, however, if he had no
fluency in French, which was then the second language of every
civilised man, as English is today. He already had a theoretical
knowledge of the language for he had studied it in Canada when he
was still convinced that it was his destiny to become a general.
Now, however, needing more than a theoretical knowledge of the
language, 'To France I went for the purpose of learning to speak
the French language, having, because it was the language of the

military art, studied it by book in America. To see fortified towns was another object . . .'[1]

The reference to 'fortified towns' reveals how strongly the army years continued to influence him. Indeed, the Army would never entirely cease to exert an influence on him, even when he was, in his Radical days, arguing for its abolition. It had turned him, for ever, into a man of strict routines and regular habits. It had given him reason to believe that he was an expert on all matters of defence, strategy and military organisation. It had also given him an almost obsessive interest in all forms of military engineering.

In later years, when he was riding the length and breadth of Britain and writing the *Register* articles that would eventually be brought together as *Rural Rides*, he never passed a fortification, an encampment, a military academy or a barracks without pausing to comment. The remains of an Iron Age hilltop camp with ditch and earthwork defences would interest him as much as an overgrown Elizabethan gun emplacement that could still be made use of in the defence of Southampton if the French should invade. The sight of the new barracks at Colchester, or the new Military Academy at Camberley enraged him as much as the sight of the Martello Towers positioned round the South Coast, or the Grand Military Canal and the casemates that honeycombed the cliffs around Dover. All of these represented to him Pitt's squandering of the nation's wealth, when any competent soldier would have told him that they offered no defence against a *Grande Armée* that had fought its way across Europe from Toulon to Moscow.

Given an enduring interest in such matters, it was not strange that a newly-discharged sergeant-major should want to spend some time in the country where Vauban had shown the world what military engineering could achieve. But, if the Army had convinced him that French fortifications were as much worth studying as the French language, it had also taught him that North America was something more than a wild and savage continent, and that the United States might well be the country for an ambitious and independently-minded man to settle in. It seems odd that a man now so generally considered to have been an epitome of John Bull should, at that time, have thought of himself as one of nature's Americans; but such, nevertheless, was the case:

My determination to settle in the United States was formed before I went to France, and even before I quitted the army. A desire of seeing a country so long the theatre of a war of which I had heard and read so much; the flattering picture of it given by

106

Raynal;* and, above all, an inclination for seeing the world led me to this determination. It would look a little like coaxing for me to say that I had imbibed principles of republicanism, and that I was anxious to become a citizen of a free state, but this was really the case.† I thought that men enjoyed here a greater degree of liberty than in England; and this, if not the principal reason, was at least one, for my coming to this country.[2]

One should never question the honesty with which, at any one time, Cobbett held to an opinion. He was never, or very seldom, dishonest either with himself or his public. He was, however, inconstant, and could be discovered on Monday supporting the opposite of what he had firmly believed in the Friday before last. It was typical of him, therefore, that he should have fallen in love with the United States before he had ever set foot in it; that he should fall out of love with it almost as soon as he began to live there; and that he should fall at least partially in love with it once more once he had settled, again, in England. America, however, still lay over the horizon when Cobbett and his wife slipped over the Channel and landed in France.

Once the Cobbetts had reached St. Omer they went no farther into France than the nearby village of Tilques. Here they spent the next six months, after which they proposed to winter in Paris before embarking for the United States. Cobbett, who had the gift of absorbing knowledge as easily as a sponge absorbs water, made himself fluent in French in a comparatively short time and passed what he afterwards referred to as the 'happiest six months of my life'. It was, indeed, a protracted honeymoon, and before it ended Ann was pregnant.

Cobbett would, for the rest of his life, remain a keen student and shrewd interpreter of French affairs, and seemed almost as much at home with the French language as his own. He would, for many years, take a violently anti-Gallican stance, but his hatred was for French politics rather than the French people, of whom he wrote,

* The reference is to the Abbé Raynal's *Tableau et Révolutions des colonies anglaises de l'Amérique Septentrionale* (Amsterdam, 1781).

† *The Life and Adventures of Peter Porcupine*, from which this passage is taken, was written to deny some of the accusations brought against him by his enemies in the United States. One of these was that he had had to flee both England and France because of his activities as a sneak-thief, and that he had come to the United States only out of necessity. 'Not so', in effect, the passage replies; 'I came to the United States because I wanted to, and because I was once as foolish as yourselves, and held democratic and Jacobinical principles.'

when he was already the staunchest anti-Jacobin in the United States:

> I should be the most ungrateful monster that ever existed, were I to speak ill of the French people in general. I went to that country full of all those prejudices, that Englishmen suck in with their mother's milk, against the French and against their religion: a few weeks convinced me that I had been deceived with respect to both. I met everywhere with civility, and even hospitality, in a degree that I had never been accustomed to. I found the people, among whom I lived, excepting those who were already blasted with the principles of the accursed revolution, honest, pious, and kind to excess.[3]

It is commonly accepted that Cobbett remained uninvolved in politics until he had settled in the United States and had produced his first pamphlet in 1794. It is all the easier to believe this because whenever, in later life, he changed his political stance, he generally gave the impression of doing so in a single leap, rather than by a series of cautious shuffles. That, after all, is the way in which the radically-minded republican who fled from England emerged, two or three years later, as the most outspoken Tory, monarchist and anti-Jacobin in all of Philadelphia. This is, however, too simple a reading of Cobbett's political progress. There were always conditions, experiences, impressions antecedent to his political attitudes, and it can very reasonably be argued that what he saw and experienced in France in 1792 had an effect on what he decided were his politics in 1794.

March to September 1792 were decisive months in the development of (what was later to be known as) the French Revolution. It was the period in which legitimacy in that country was finally destroyed. The Austrians declared war and crossed the French frontiers, and this, more than anything else, destroyed whatever chances were left for constitutional reform and a British-type monarchy. It also led to the death, imprisonment or flight of such constitutionalists as still endeavoured to make themselves heard above the clamour of the revolutionaries in the new National Assembly where, in true comradely fashion, the Girondists and the Jacobins were engaged in condemning each other to death for counter-revolutionary activities. When the Jacobins emerged from this, for the time triumphant, they had no better solution to offer a country terrified by the combined threats arising from invasion on the frontiers and counter-revolution in the provinces than to organise themselves for further executions and the mob for further massacres. The Tuileries were stormed and, largely as a result of Lafayette's equivocal posturings, the Swiss Guard and a few aged courtiers still faithful to their loyalties were put to the sword. The King was deposed and imprisoned, soon to be subjected to revolutionary justice and executed. The sporadic class war that had expressed itself in the countryside through the burning of various chateaux and the slaughter of their owners was now extended to include, among its victims, large sections of the clergy and the bourgeoisie. Before Cobbett succeeded in leaving France, the September Massacre in which some 13,000 prisoners were murdered by the mob, would signal the official opening, as it were, of the Reign of Terror.

We have, with the passage of time, been educated into accepting the French Revolution as a possibly rough, but still necessary and desirable harrowing of the political soils of Europe: a cultivation that would prepare the seed-bed for all our democracies. This was not, however, how it seemed to the vast majority of contemporary Europeans who watched in horror while the French carried out, in the sacred name of democracy, larger atrocities and bloodier wars than any reactionary government of the *ancien régime* would have dared even contemplate. So far as the French themselves were concerned, their Revolution was immediately expensive and ultimately self-defeating, for it brought them nothing more beneficial, in the next half-century, than Napoleon.* So far as the rest of Western Europe was concerned, it constituted such a warning of the horrors that could be committed in the sacred name of the people that it set the cause of Parliamentary democracy back for at least another generation.† So far as Cobbett was concerned, it at least started the process whereby that radically-minded son of the people developed into the anti-Jacobin who wrote as Peter Porcupine, and the constitutionalist who was William Cobbett, the Father of Reform.

It is, of course, true that his conversion to Toryism owed more to the American than to the French experience. But when, many years later, he was reconverted to radicalism, he was not, at the same time, reconverted to republicanism. Even when he was

* One inquisitive writer has demonstrated that not the least of the benefits Napoleon conferred on the French was to reduce the average height of Frenchmen, for most of the nineteenth century, by no less than an inch and a half. The country, having had so many of its fittest and youngest men slaughtered in his wars, was left to breed future generations from unfit or ageing stock.

† The British example is a relevant one. The youthful Pitt, introducing a measure for Parliamentary Reform in 1782, lost it by the narrow margin of fourteen votes. At that date, such a measure seemed more likely to succeed than it did even when Grey came to power in 1830.

calling for 'great change' in England, he would have nothing to do with either revolution or republic though at least some of his fellow Radicals were not entirely averse from threatening Britain with both. This must be directly attributed to what he had seen of the French Revolution personally, as well as to what he came to know about it in his days as an anti-Jacobin. The man who, to his last days, supported the monarchy though he hated the monarch, who supported the supremacy of Parliament though he hated the oligarchs, and who supported the rule of law though he hated the judges, was also the man who had himself seen what happened once legitimacy had been destroyed in France.

The time that he spent at Tilques was not, of course, long enough to fix all of this in Cobbett's mind; but if we ignore his French experience, we fail to understand one of the few lasting influences on his changing habits of political thought. The dilemma of the Radical who wishes to bring about change but fears to destroy legitimacy is a familiar one, even today, when universal suffrage is supposed to offer entirely peaceful and legitimate means for bringing about a revolution in society without also bringing about a revolution in the streets. In the days when it seemed that change could only be brought about by violence from below, the problem was more acute and especially so for Cobbett. For agitators can never limit the effects of their agitating. They can move the people to action, but they cannot control the actions the people then take. So it was with Cobbett. He could successfully incite the people to demand change, but he could not prevent some of them demanding that which he wanted least: change brought about by violence and the destruction of most or all of the nation's existing institutions. It took other, less eloquent Radicals to steer the British away from revolution and from the violence associated with the Luddites, Captain Swing and the early Chartists.

G. D. H. Cole claimed that the French Revolution provided the aristocracy and plutocracy of Britain with an enduring excuse for reaction. He wrote more as a socialist than as an historian. As the first, he subscribed to the notion that every revolution must, in the end, flower into socialism. As the last, he should have known that the opposite is more often the case. Many things can come out of the barrel of a gun, but democracy* is seldom one of them. Cobbett

---

* One has to be cautious, these days, in the use of such label-words as democracy. Except where I qualify it by placing it in inverted commas, I use it here in the still often-accepted sense of meaning a Parliamentary democracy, though even then this has to be further defined by insisting that this means a system under which a multi-party, limited-term legislature is elected, by universal suffrage, for the purpose of either providing or controlling the Government.

was neither an aristocrat nor a plutocrat, and he was only one of millions of Englishmen who came to believe that a democracy so dearly-bought and so temporarily sustained as the French had attained was not worth the having.

Apart from commencing the process that would turn Cobbett into an immediate Tory and a life-long anti-revolutionary, Cobbett's short stay in France turned him into a Francophone and something of an expert in French affairs. He would, over the next ten years, make the most that he could, as a propagandist, out of the atrocities of the Terror, and the excesses committed by the French in the course of their wars and the ostensible cause of revolution. Atrocity propaganda never makes the best of reading, but the pamphlets he wrote on these subjects deserve study even today, if only to remind us of what the French Revolution cost the rest of Europe in bloodshed and destruction. But, even when he had ceased to be primarily an anti-Jacobin, his chief interest lay, until at least 1816, in foreign affairs, and his chief claim to fame resided in the knowledge he had of French and American politics. The journal which made him famous, *Cobbett's Political Register*, which he published in London weekly from 1802, would, in fact, devote more columns every week to the former than to the latter, though he wrote as an expert on both. He had, indeed, condemned himself, as it were, to the task of interpreting the French, first to his American readers and subsequently to his English ones. A heavy price, perhaps, to pay for the six months he spent in Tilques.

At this stage, however, he still had to get away from Tilques and from France, and that was not altogether easy. He did not, himself, write about the difficulties, beyond saying: .

I did intend to stay in France till the spring of 1793, as well to perfect myself in the language as to pass the winter at Paris; but I perceived the storm gathering; I saw that a war with England was inevitable, and it was not difficult to foresee what would be the fate of Englishmen in that country where the rulers had laid aside even the appearance of justice and mercy. I wished, however, to see Paris, and had actually hired a coach to go thither. I was even on the way when I heard, at Abbeville, that the king was dethroned and his guards murdered. This intelligence made me turn towards Hâvre-de-Grace, whence I embarked for America.[4]

His youngest daughter, Susan, was rather more informative when she wrote to her brother, John Morgan, then in the United States, in 1835. In that long letter she recorded, not her father's, but her mother's recollections of their flight, some forty years earlier, from revolutionary France:

> At one place, which they arrived at on a Sunday, they were very closely examined and made to unpack everything and show all papers, and, as the man could not understand English, he made Papa read the contents of them to him in French . . . the reason the man was so particular in his examinations, was because Mama had no passport . . . this man chose to suspect that she was a Frenchwoman, and she would not give him an opportunity of being undeceived by speaking, for she was so insulted at his behaviour that she would not answer him when he spoke to her, and this confirmed him in his suspicions.[5]

It is heartening to find that Ann, who was generally described as gentle and self-effacing, could be quite as obstinate as her husband, and quite as capable of being indignant at being taken for French. There can have been few recently-married women of eighteen who, in the midst of a developing revolution, would not have chosen to babble away indefinitely in English in order to allay such sans-culotte suspicions. Nor was this the only difficulty the Cobbetts met with:

> There was, of course, a great deal of parleying wherever they stopped. When they got to Hâvre-de-Grace . . . the people in the street came running to the carriage and climbed up to look in at the windows, the coachman being much frightened thereat; he begged them to put the windows down, and drove very slowly through the streets till they came to the 'Municipality', where Papa was closely questioned . . . but they were polite here. They stayed, Mama thinks, a fortnight at Hâvre-de-Grace waiting for a vessel.[6]

Although Cobbett never actually reached Paris, he had, nevertheless, been in correspondence with Mr. Short, the American Ambassador there, and had obtained from him a letter of introduction to Thomas Jefferson, who was then Secretary of State. At that time, the United States was an infant among the nations. Nevertheless, the American Ambassador in Paris was a person of some consequence, and Thomas Jefferson was even more important. How did Cobbett, an unknown would-be emigrant, enlist the aid of the first to win an introduction and recommendation to the second?

There are other questions which suggest themselves. In the first place, there is the matter of passports. How did Cobbett, slipping secretly away from a possible prosecution for sedition, obtain one for himself, and how did Ann, who had none, succeed in leaving England and entering France? That is, perhaps, more easily answered than the problem of Cobbett's finances at that time. He had earned nothing, when he left France, since leaving the Army eighteen months earlier, yet here he was, after six months of idle living in that country, hiring a coach for his journey to Hâvre-de-Grace and buying passage for two from there to America.

It is true that he had, halfway through his Army service, amassed the one hundred and fifty guineas, which were entrusted to Ann and returned to him intact four years later. How he had managed to save as much on a soldier's pay, even though he was, for part of that time, a sergeant-major, remains a mystery that cannot be entirely explained by his abstemious habits and by his industrious moonlighting. (It could perhaps be said that he was doing as much to damage the efficiency of the regiment by doing the work of his superiors for them as the latter were achieving by fiddling the accounts.) His earnings and savings in the next four years must have been exhausted by his expenses over the court martial, expenses which he had described to Gould as ruinous. None the less, on leaving England 'I had, in the whole world, but about 200 guineas, which was a very great deal for a person in my situation.'[7]

It was a great deal, though Ann's contribution must have accounted for most of it. But two hundred guineas were not a great deal when they had to support the two of them while they lived and travelled abroad. It was characteristic of Cobbett that he never allowed himself to worry about money, though he frequently had need to. He no more doubted that it would come to him whenever he needed it than Elijah doubted the ravens. One of his early letters to England after he had settled in Wilmington in the United States, suggested that the ravens had not failed him:

It is generally said, and often with much justice, that a rolling stone never gathers moss; this, however, was not the case with me; for though my rambles in France cost me above a hundred and ninety guineas, and though I was reduced to about eighteen at my arrival in Wilmington, I am now better off than ever, notwithstanding my expenses in my family have been enormous.[8]

Cobbett, who had already been across the Atlantic each way, had nothing to say about the voyage that took Ann and himself to Philadelphia. Susan, however, in the same letter to her brother, wrote that her mother remembered that it had been very dangerous, that it had taken eight weeks, and that 'The name of the captain was Grenouille, the passage was very dangerous and the captain very diligent and skillful. The name of the vessel she does not remember, but it was on board her that Papa looked at a map and fixed upon Wilmington as a place where he would go and settle and keep school.'

In 1829 Cobbett wrote *The Emigrant's Guide*, a fascinating work designed as a sort of *vade mecum* for the many British emigrants then leaving for America. Memories of that long-ago voyage across the Atlantic in the company of a young and heavily-pregnant Ann undoubtedly coloured much of what he wrote. It is not one of his better-known works, though it is typically Cobbettian in its combination of dogma, politics and sensible, down-to-earth instruction. It also offers a picture of what it was like to cross the Atlantic when such a journey was, in itself, an adventure:

Of Ships to Choose:
I have crossed the Atlantic three times in American ships, once in an English merchant ship, once in a king's ship, and once in a king's packet; and I declare, that the superiority of the Americans is decided, and so decided, that if I were going to cross again, nothing should prevail on me to go on board of any ship but an American one.[9]

Of Provisions for Steerage Passengers:
You have, in fact, every thing in the steerage which you have in the cabin, if you take proper pains to lay in the stores. Neat's tongues recently salted are excellent things . . . now and then an egg . . . a bottle of brandy . . . to be judiciously administered in *bribes* to the *black cook*. He would bid you toss your money into the sea; but he will suck down your brandy; and you will get many a nice thing prepared by him, which you would never get, if it were not for that brandy . . . The cooking place, called the cabboose, is for the whole ship, and you, if in the steerage, must seize your opportunity . . . A large bag of biscuits of the *best* quality and fresh made . . . I regard as a store against short allowances and famine. Flour, in its various modes of use . . . Apples, excellent, refreshing; and apple puddings are easily made. Your wife will sit up in her berth, in very rough weather, and make the puddings . . . The cook will boil them for you . . .[10]

Of Sleeping Arrangements:
The berths are placed along the side of the ship; these berths are

separated by boards, and are so constructed as to prevent your rolling out when the ship leans to one side. Every man's senses will guide him in choosing the best berth he can for his wife, and every decent single man will give way in such a case. At the best, however, it is a state of great inconvenience: without any description from me, a married man will easily conceive the many awkward, ludicrous, and painful circumstances that must here occur . . . As to the work of undressing and dressing, however, this is managed in a very decent manner. If there were men so brutal as not to go upon the deck, and leave the women to themselves, the Captain would instantly interfere . . .[11]

Of Modesty and Necessity:

The greatest and most injurious inconvenience is, that the modesty of English women too frequently restrains them from relieving themselves by going to the usual place for that purpose, which place is, and must be, upon the deck, and within sight of all those who are upon the deck. This reluctance, however amiable in itself (and very amiable it is), has often produced very disagreeable, not to say fatal consequences. That mode of relief has been pointed out by nature; it is indispensable to animal existence; retention to a certain extent is destructive; and the sufferings experienced on this account are very great. *French* women must be excellent sailors; but English or American women, must change their natures, before this can cease to be a subject of really serious importance. Use every argument in your power to get over this difficulty with regard to your wife; lose no opportunity of over-coming her scruples; be very attentive to her in every circumstance and point attending this matter; and, if she be in a state, from her sea-sickness, (which is frequently the case) not to admit of removal from her bed, you must be prepared, not only with the utensile suitable to her case, but you yourself must perform the office of chamber-maid . . .[12]

When he wrote in this mood, Cobbett was, to use his own phrase, 'very amiable'. Every voyage, however, must have its end, and the Cobbetts landed safely in Philadelphia at the end of October 1792.

By the 2 November 1792, Cobbett had sent Short's letter of introduction to Thomas Jefferson. In the covering letter he asked whether a place could be found for him in some government office. He described himself as being:

Ambitious to become a citizen of a free state. I have left my native country, England, for America. I bring with me youth, a small family, a few useful literary talents, and that is all.[13]

Within two or three years he would be maintaining that nothing could persuade him to abandon his allegiance to George III and become an American. By then, of course, he had become something less of a republican and a democrat than he might still have been when he approached that most republican of all democrats and most democratic of all republicans, Thomas Jefferson. This apart, there was still a certain disingenuity in the letter. He was certainly still youthful, if that be measured in terms of energy and vigour, but he was only a few months short of thirty, and that was, in terms of average life expectancy at that time, already well into middle age. There was a certain hope value, moreover, that attached to his reference to 'a small family'. Ann had not, as yet, been delivered of her first child, and a family of two is a small one indeed.

The most intriguing part of this letter, however, is the reference to his 'few useful literary talents'. If, by this, he meant anything more than that he was an excellent copyist, then it contradicts the generally accepted idea that he had no notion, at that time, of becoming a writer. Nevertheless, his letters which have survived from that period demonstrate that he already possessed a gift for exposition, and a fluency of language that might well have encouraged many a better educated man to believe that he was destined for a life of authorship. There were, moreover, the small book he had written for the instruction of his fellow soldiers, the Report he had put together for the New Brunswick Commissioners, the long and difficult correspondence that had arisen out of the court martial, and *The Soldier's Friend*, all of which could serve to persuade him that he was not claiming too much.

The reply he received, three days later, can hardly have been the one he had hoped for:

Philadelphia. Nov 5th. 1792

Sir,

In acknowledging the receipt of your favour of the 2nd. instant, I wish it were in my power to announce to you any way in which I could be useful to you. Mr. Short's assurance of your merit would be a sufficient inducement to me. Public Offices in our government are so few, and of so little value, as to offer no resource to talents. When you shall have been here some small time, you will be able to

judge in what way you can set out with the best prospect of success,
and if I can serve you in it, I shall be very ready to do it.

> I am,
>> Sir,
>>> Your very humble servant,
>>> Th. Jefferson.[14]

In later years Cobbett would frequently praise the United States
for spending far less on the whole of its administration than the
British Government spent annually on sinecurists. In 1792, however, Cobbett could probably have wished that the American
Government were prepared to spend the little more that would
have provided him with employment. He strongly resented Jefferson's refusal, though it was politely, even handsomely expressed.
He would, of course, become one of Jefferson's severest critics,
principally because, as soon as he took to American politics, he
took to them on the opposite side. Would he have taken to politics,
or have taken to the politics he did, or ever have come to be so
critical of Jefferson if the latter had been able to find him a post in
government? All that is known is that, even four years later, the
memory of that rejection rankled:

> I will just observe on this letter, that it was thankfully received,
> and that, had I stood in need of Mr. Jefferson's services, I should
> have applied to him; but as that did not appear likely to be the
> case, I wrote him a letter some few months afterwards, request-
> ing him to assist a poor man, the bearer of it, and telling him that
> I should look upon the assistance as given to myself. I dare say he
> complied with my request, for the person recommended was in
> deep distress, and a *Frenchman*.[15]

The sting here lies in the tail. Jefferson was the leader of what
might fairly be called the Gallican party in the United States,
Cobbett often accused him of being more of a Frenchman than an
American, and of neglecting the true interests of his own country in
order to support anything that would further the cause of France
and the Revolution.

As there was to be no post for him in a government office,
Cobbett now moved to Wilmington, the small town on the Delaware whose existence, according to Susan, he had first discovered
from a map. He was not to stay there for long, nor was he to open a
school there. He would, in later years, develop and publish his own
rather unusual ideas on how children should be educated or, to be
more accurate, on how they should not be educated. He had, of

course, been left to educate himself, and had done so with conspicuous success. What had been beneficial to him must, in his view, be beneficial to everyone else. Children, therefore, should not be sent to school and college, but should be left to educate themselves, with no more outside assistance than could be acquired from books, practical experience, and a sympathetic and patient parent. All formal systems of education, he maintained, were stultifying, and all pedagogues, professors, schools and universities, as a consequence, harmful.

He could never have held to these views in later life as stoutly as he did had his critics been able to reveal that he had himself once worked as a pedagogue, and had kept school, even though it had only been in Wilmington. He was spared that embarrassment. He arrived in Wilmington with a pregnant wife, eighteen guineas in his pocket, a great deal of self-confidence, and a willingness to undertake almost anything. It never entered his mind that he might fail to make his way, in some manner or other, in this new world he had come to.

CHAPTER SIX

The Birth of Peter Porcupine

Writers, like teeth, are divided into incisors and grinders.
Walter Bagehot: *Shakespeare – The Individual*

The American Republic had hardly been born before it began to
serve its intermittent purpose as a country of refuge. People
flocked to it to escape, not only the poverty and land hunger, but
also the politics of Europe. There were United Irishmen escaping
the consequences of 'the troubles', English and Scottish Radicals
hoping to find in the new Republic the Utopia denied them in
Britain, and Frenchmen fleeing from the Utopia that had been
created for them in France, or from much the same sort of situation
that the negro uprisings had created in the French West Indies.

Of these, only the French refugees suffered from the disadvantage of speaking little or no English. There were many such
Frenchmen in and around Philadelphia, which at that time served
as the capital of the Republic. Some of them were men of substance, well able to afford the services of anyone who, speaking
their language, could also teach them the language of the country
they had arrived in. It was Cobbett's good fortune that he was
particularly suited to that task and, as he soon discovered a whole
clutch of Frenchmen living in a boarding-house in Wilmington, he
abandoned the idea of opening a school, and turned himself
instead to teaching them English.

Forty years later, in the letter already quoted, Susan Cobbett
described what her mother remembered of that period. Her father
'found a great many Frenchmen there . . . who wanted to be taught
English. Papa then went regularly to the boarding-house where
they lived, and taught them, and they gave him a great deal of
money . . . Mr Matthews was one of those French gentlemen, but
he was so pleased with Papa's company that he would insist on
living in his house.'[1]

There must have been other Frenchmen who, like Mr.
Matthews, enjoyed Cobbett's company, for Susan added:

They continued to receive boarders for some months, but Mama
found them disagreeable and got to dislike Wilmington, and Mr

Matthews thought Papa might do much better . . . in Philadelphia . . . and so to Philadelphia they went in the Spring.

There was advantage in the move, since Philadelphia was bound
to contain more Frenchmen than Wilmington. But there was also
the problem of Wilmington itself to consider, for Cobbett had
come to dislike it as much as his wife. In his case it was entirely
because of the Wilmingtonians who, being democrats almost to a
man, were pro-French in their sympathies and anti-British in their
politics. Cobbett, who had already begun to find such attitudes
intolerable, would write, three or four years later:

This Wilmington (and it is a pity, too, for it is a delightful little
place), this Wilmington, in Delaware, was the most abominable
sans-culotte of any town in the whole continent . . . They
caballed and harangued and demonstrated with more industry
and virulence than even the virtuous town meetings of Boston
and Philadelphia . . . People wonder at this factious disposition
in the Wilmingtonians, seeing that they are mostly Quakers,
which usually signified men mild, peaceable and obedient to the
laws. But the Quakers of Wilmington differ from all other
Quakers in America; they frown and look fierce, and, if contradicted in conversation, not honey but wormwood drops from
their lips; they are a sort of Puritans in a Quaker dress.[2]

There was another and sadder reason why both of the Cobbetts
wished to leave Wilmington, and it was described in the letter that
Cobbett wrote, a year later, to his London friend, Rachel
Smithers:

I told you that we had a little boy; my wife was brought to bed of
a second boy about the middle of last March, but it was still-born
. . . But now prepare your tender heart to pity us. On the 3rd of
June our other dear little fellow was snatched from us . . . the
dearest, sweetest, beautifulest little fellow that ever was seen.
We adored him . . . I am sure I shall never recover his loss. I feel
my spirits altered. A settled sadness seems to have taken possession of my mind; nor do I wish to be diverted from it. For my
poor Nancy, I cannot paint you her distress; for several days she
would take no nourishment. We were even afraid for her . . . I
am happy, however, that my Nancy is re-established – thank
God, our means enabled me to change houses directly.[3]

The change took him to Philadelphia, and to a house at No. 81 Callowhill. In spite of his determination not to be diverted from his sadness, that also eventually came to an end, and Cobbett returned to his more normal condition, which could be described as one of pugnacious ebullience. But the sadness had been genuine and, while it lasted, there had been nothing that could please him in America. His strongest private emotion would always be love for his family. Until he grew old and increasingly eccentric there would always be between him and his children a mutuality of affection that was as genuine as it was unusual. He was able to reveal to them all the gentleness, sympathy, playfulness and understanding that were seldom allowed to surface in his public life.

As for Ann, her sorrows were soon to be allayed by the birth of her first daughter, also called Anne and also, confusingly, nick-named Nancy, who was followed, two years later, by a son called William. Although she bore no more children in America, she gave birth to no fewer than ten more after her return to England, though only five of them survived infancy. In twenty-odd years of child-bearing, therefore – from 1793 to 1814 – she was pregnant no less than fourteen times and had, so far as rearing her children was concerned, a success rate of precisely fifty per cent. Such fecundity left her little time for continuing to mourn those who had been lost.

Family life must have passed happily for the young Cobbetts in Philadelphia, in spite of the bad beginning. Cobbett was seldom, until the end, unhappy in his domestic life, but, when he was an old man and writing his *Advice to Young Men*, he kept looking back on those days:

I began my young marriage days in and near Philadelphia . . . I had business to occupy the whole of my time . . . but I used to make time to assist (my wife) in the taking care of her baby, and in all sorts of things; get up, light the fire, boil the tea-kettle, carry her up warm water in cold weather, take the child while she dressed herself and got breakfast ready, then breakfast, get her in water and wood for the day, then dress myself neatly and sally forth to business.[4]

When Ann was recovering from the death of her son, the weather being very hot, she found it impossible to sleep. Things were made worse by the howling of the Philadelphian dogs, also unsettled by the heat:

They made a noise so terrible and unremitted that it was next to impossible that even a person in full health and free from pain

121

should obtain a moment's sleep. I was, about nine in the evening, sitting by the bed. 'I do think,' said she, 'that I could go to sleep *now*, if it were not *for the dogs*.' Down stairs I went, and out I sallied, in my shirt and trousers, and without shoes or stockings; and, going to a heap of stones lying beside the road, set to work upon the dogs, going backward and forward, and keeping them at two or three hundred yards' distance from the house. I walked thus the whole night . . . and I remember that the bricks of the causeway were, even in the night, so hot as to be disagreeable to my feet. My exertions produced the required effect: a sleep of several hours was the consequence; and, at eight o'clock in the morning, off I went to a day's business . . .*[5]

Cobbett's solicitude for his wife came to its height in thunder storms. Thunder and lightning terrified her, and both were common in Philadelphia:

I knew well, of course, that my presence would not diminish the danger; but, be I at what I might . . . I used to quit my business and hasten to her the moment I perceived a thunder-storm approaching. Scores of miles have I, first and last, *run* on this errand in the streets of Philadelphia! The Frenchmen who were my scholars used to laugh at me exceedingly on this account; and sometimes, when I was making an appointment with them, they would say, with a smile and a bow, '*Sauve la tonnerre toujours, Monsieur Cobbett*.'[6]

Those same Frenchmen were now affording him a good living. He charged each of them six dollars a month, and found, as a consequence, that 'I earned about 140 dollars per month, and which I continued to do for about two years and a half. I taught English to the most respectable Frenchmen in the city . . .'[7]

Yet, whether it was because his sadness had not, as yet, departed, or whether it was because of his own spirit of contrariety, he now found everything American distasteful:

This country is good for getting money, that is to say, if a person is industrious and enterprising. In every other respect the country is miserable. Exactly the contrary of what I expected it. The land is bad; rocky; houses wretched; roads impassable after the least rain. Fruit in quantity but good for nothing. One apple or peach in England or France is worth a bushel of them here. All is burning or freezing. There is no spring or autumn . . . The

---

* Cobbett was always, nevertheless, a great dog lover and fancier.

people are worthy of the country – cheating, sly, roguish gang. Strangers make fortunes here in spite of all this, particularly the English. The natives are by nature idle, and seek to live by cheating, while foreigners, being industrious, seek no other means than those dictated by integrity, and are sure to meet with encouragement even from the idle and roguish themselves; for however roguish a man may be, he always loves to deal with an honest man . . .[8]

One has only to compare this early description of America and the Americans with the one he gave, twenty years later, in his *A Year's Residence in the United States* to see that the first was born out of spleen. Even his picture of the honest and industrious Englishman making good amongst the idle Americans failed to correspond with popular opinion in England, where the 'smart' Yankee had already acquired the reputation of being more than a match for any half-dozen slower-witted Englishmen.

One can understand, however, why Cobbett, in that frame of mind, found few friends among the natives, and why, as he explained to Rachel Smithers, 'The greatest part of my acquaintance in this country are French merchants from St. Domingo and Martinico'.

While his view of America continued so jaundiced it was natural for him to start thinking of leaving the country. His French friends must have filled him with stories of the beauty and riches of the West Indian islands, for he wrote, in the final passage of the letter to Rachel Smithers:

To one of those islands I shall probably go in about eight or nine months; and in that case, if I live so long, I shall be in England in about three years. For I do not intend to stay much above a couple of years in the Islands. Take care of my trunk and box, if you please, till you see or hear from me . . . Doctor Priestley is just arrived here from England. He has attacked our English laws and Constitution in print and declared his sentiments in favour of those butchers in France. He has, however, been attacked in his turn by an Englishman here. I will send you one of those pieces in another ship. Accept my love and God bless you.
Wm. Cobbett.[9]

Cobbett never got to the Islands, and did not get back to England for another six years. Even then, far from leaving the United States of his own free will, he had to be forced out of the country by the attacks made on him by his American enemies. The reason for this change of mind is hinted at in the reference to Doctor Priestley. For, although Cobbett coyly concealed it, the Englishman who had attacked the doctor for his unpatriotic writings was Cobbett himself. It was that attack which first set him off pamphleteering, and which tied him, for the next six years, into the complicated pattern of American journalism and politics.

In his own version of how he came to write and publish his *Observations on the Emigration of Doctor Priestley*, Cobbett maintained that it had been the product of chance. In so far as that particular pamphlet was concerned, he was telling the truth, even though the implication that, had it not been for chance, he would never have turned politician and pamphleteer is less certainly true. When one considers various incidents in his past career – the challenge to the 'Establishment' posed by his activities over the court martial, *The Soldier's Friend,* the republicanism he had subscribed to before fleeing to France, and had abjured once he had discovered that the French republicans were 'butchers' and the Wilmingtonian ones 'Puritans' – it is difficult to accept that he was, before Priestly landed in the United States, entirely without political opinions and literary ambition.

Cobbett's explanation, in short, reveals *how* he came to write the first of his American pamphlets, but fails to say *why*. Patriotism alone is seldom sufficient to push most people into print. Yet, as he set them out, the circumstances, if not the motives that gave rise to the pamphlet are clear. Joseph Priestley, the celebrated savant and dissenter, had just landed in the United States. He had been the victim of the Birmingham mob, which had recently attacked, ransacked and burnt his house and laboratory. That mob, he maintained, had been incited to violence by the British Government, which resented his support for Radical causes at home and the French Revolution abroad.

Priestley's arrival as a political refugee in New York attracted much the same sort of publicity as Solzhenitsyn's arrival in the West did in our day, though the two were, of course, refugees for opposite reasons. In Priestley's case, almost every Democratic Club and 'liberal' Society in New York presented him with an Address. Each greeted him as one of Freedom's heroes, and as the virtuous victim of a monarchical, reactionary and tyrannical system that was Freedom's sole enemy. In his replies to those Addresses, which were published in most of the journals, Priestley confessed to the heroism and confirmed the victimisation.

Cobbett knew nothing about Priestley or his politics until one of these journals was brought to his attention:

THE BIRTH OF PETER PORCUPINE

Newspapers were a luxury for which I had little relish, and which, if I had been ever so fond of, I had not time to enjoy. The manifestoes, therefore, of the Doctor . . . and the malicious attacks upon the monarchy and the monarch of England which certain societies thereupon issued through the press, would, had it not been for a circumstance purely accidental, have escaped, probably for ever, not only my animadversions, but my knowledge of their existence.[10]

The 'circumstance purely accidental' arose from the fact that one of his French students, 'A person that we in England would call a Coffee-house politician', chose to improve his English by reading aloud from a New York newspaper, and the paper he read from contained both the Addresses to Priestley and his replies to them:

My scholar, who was a sort of republican, or, at best, but half a monarchist, appeared delighted with the invectives against England, to which he was very much disposed to add. Those Englishmen who have been abroad, particularly if they have had time to make a comparison between the country they are in and that which they have left, well know how difficult it is, upon occasions such as I have been describing, to refrain from expressing their indignation and resentment; and there is not, I trust, much reason to suppose that I should, in this respect, experience less difficulty than another. The dispute was warm as might reasonably be expected between a Frenchman, uncommonly violent even for a Frenchman, and an Englishman not unremarkable for *sang-froid*; and the result was a declared resolution on my part to write and publish a pamphlet in defence of my country, which pamphlet he pledged himself to answer; his pledge was forfeited; it is known that mine was not. Thus, Sir, it was that I became a writer on politics.[11]

If it was a pledge or wager, it was certainly a somewhat loaded one. If the Frenchman already had enough English in him to write a reply to Cobbett's pamphlet, he would have stood in no need of Cobbett's lessons. One cannot help feeling that Cobbett was already ripe to produce a pamphlet, if not about Priestley, then about something else equally irksome on the American scene. The Frenchman, in short, was no more than the trigger which, once pulled, released the first of Cobbett's political buckshot. A great deal of such shot would be released in the next few years, and he could boast, at the end of his first American exile:

My labours were without intermission . . . There were published from my pen about twenty different pamphlets, the whole number of which amounted to more than half a million copies. During the last three years, a daily newspaper, surpassing in extent of numbers, any ever known in America, was the vehicle of my efforts. I might safely have asserted, that there was not in the whole country, one single family in which some part or other of my writings had not been read . . .[12]

That prodigous volume of writing, however, still lay before him when, in accordance with his pledge to the Frenchman, he set about getting his *Observations* published. It was an age when it was not as difficult as it is now for a man to get himself into print. Printing and paper were cheap, and almost every bookseller of any consequence was also a publisher.* Philadelphia itself was, at that time, a centre of the publishing trade, but it was also a stronghold of those Americans who held what Cobbett would have described as 'democratical and Jacobinical' views. The mob was a politicised one, and was inclined to express its belief in democracy by dealing roughly with anyone it considered to be lacking in respect for such republican virtue as had been manifested in the great American and French Revolutions. The least that could be expected of its displeasure was a breaking of windows though, where the offence was blatant, the offender could expect to have his house attacked and burnt, or to be tarred and feathered and run out of the city on a fence-rail.

Cobbett, consequently, found it difficult to find a bookseller willing to publish what was, in effect, a root-and-branch attack on the latest of all the democratical heroes, Doctor Priestley, and his host of fulsome admirers in New York. The leading booksellers and publishers in Philadelphia were, at that time, Matthew Carey and Thomas Bradford. Cobbett chose, in the first instance, to offer the pamphlet to Carey, because 'I knew Mr. Bradford retained a rooted hatred against Great Britain, and concluded, that his principles would prevent him from being instrumental in the publication of anything that tended to unveil one of its most bitter enemies.'[13]

He did not, perhaps, realise that Carey, an Irishman who had been imprisoned in his native country for his nationalist views, was himself a democrat, a Gallican and a pamphleteer in those causes:

* In those happy days, any bookseller who wanted to expand turned himself into a publisher, and so produced much of what he sold in his shop. Publishing had not, as yet, turned itself into a separate profession that gentlemen could engage in without actually having to sell books, stationery and pens across a counter.

Mr. Carey received me as booksellers generally receive authors (I mean authors from whom they hope to get little by): he looked at the title from top to bottom, and then at me, from head to foot. – 'No, my lad,' says he, 'I don't think it will suit.' – *My lad!* – God in heaven forgive me! I believe that, at that moment, I wished for another yellow fever to strike the city . . .[14]

Cobbett now left the pamphlet with Thomas Bradford:

The next day, I went to him, to know his determination. He hesitated, wanted to know if I could not make it a little *more popular*, adding that, unless I could, he feared that the publishing of it would endanger *his windows*. *More popular*, I could not make it. I never was of an accomodating disposition in my life. The only alteration I would consent to, was in the title. I had given the pamphlet the double title of *The Tartuffe Detected*; or *Observations &c*. The former was suppressed, though, had I not been pretty certain that every press in the city was as little free, as that to which I was sending it, the *Tartuffe Detected*, should have remained; for the person on whom it was bestowed, merited it much better than the character so named by Molière.[15]

The pamphlet was eventually published, but with more than merely *Tartuffe Detected* omitted. It bore the names of neither the publisher nor the author. This was the only work Cobbett had published in 1794, but in the following year he published no fewer than four. The first of these, *A Bone to Gnaw for the Democrats*, was also anonymous, the only clue to its origin being the information on the title page that it had been 'Published for the Purchasers'. By 1796, however, Bradford had published a fourth edition of *Observations*. This contained some additional material, but, for the first time, it was described on the title page as 'By Peter Porcupine'. On the bottom of that page the reader was informed that the work was 'Published by Thomas Bradford, Printer, Book-Seller and Stationer, No 8, South Front-Street, Philadelphia'.

Cobbett, later that year, would write of these first pamphlets of his, with understandable bitterness:

It was not till long after the public had fixed the seal of approbation on these pamphlets that they were honoured with the bookseller's name. It was something curious, that the second, and third, and fourth editions should be entitled to a mark of respect, that the first was not worthy of. Poor little innocents! They were thrown on the parish like foundlings; no soul would own them, till it was found that they possessed the gift of bringing in the pence. Another singularity is, that they got into better paper as they advanced. So the prudent matron changes her little dirty ragged wench into a fine mademoiselle, as soon as she perceives that the beaux begin to cast eyes on her.[16]

As for Carey:

Mr. Carey has sold hundreds of *Observations* since that time, and, therefore, I dare say, he highly approved of them, when he came to a perusal. At any rate, I must not forget to say, that he behaved honourably in the business; for he promised not to make me known the author, and he certainly kept his word . . . This circumstance, considering Mr. Carey's politics, is greatly to his honour, and has almost wiped from my memory, that contumelious '*my lad*'.[17]

Once *Observations* had been published, Cobbett continued to tutor Frenchmen for a time because this assured him of a living. But his first two pamphlets, though they had not brought him much in the way of money, had yet been far more successful than he could have dared hope. They had attracted a great deal of public attention, and had deserved to do so for, although they suffered from some of a novice's literary weaknesses, they were, on the whole, as witty, as well-written and argued, and as hard-hitting as most of what he would produce later. They were also, in the American context, entirely novel and daringly different:

I knew not one British subject in America besides myself who was not afraid to own his country and his King . . . Such truth as I had published, no man had dared to utter in the United States since the rebellion. I knew that these truths had mortally offended the leading men amongst the Democrats, who could, at any time, muster a mob quite sufficient to destroy my house, and to murder me.[18]

He could not, therefore, object to the immunity that anonymity conferred on him, even though he could grumble that the first two pamphlets had been parentless. Yet a name of some sort had become essential to him if he was to become a professional writer, even though it could only be a pseudonym, for his pamphlets had aroused a great deal of public and hostile criticism. One of his critics, writing anonymously in the *Aurora* newspaper, had said of this new and mysterious author, that he 'pricked his enemies with his quills like a porcupine'. Cobbett immediately decided to turn an insult into a boast. If they thought him a Porcupine, he would make it a matter of pride to remain one.

It was an age for pseudonyms in politics. They allowed a man to say in print what it may not have been politic to say in person. Classical names abounded, for they suggested classical virtues. There was scarcely a newspaper of the period that did not contain something from the pen of a *Brutus*, a *Cato* or a *Cicero*. Some of the most powerful political writing had been published in America under the name of *Publius*, and in England under that of *Junius*. Cobbett wanted something plainer, for he already saw himself acting as the plain man's guide to politics. He had a talent for nicknames. He also had the true journalist's ear for alliteration. Nothing was simpler for him, therefore, than to add Peter to Porcupine and acquire a parent for his writings.

It did not take his enemies too long to discover and publish the true identity of Peter Porcupine. It was as William Cobbett that he was sued for libel and threatened with deportation, and it was as William Cobbett that he eventually fled from the United States to escape financial ruin. But it was as Peter Porcupine that he had brought these disasters on himself by pricking too many Americans with too many quills in too many of their tender places. Long before then, however, the Americans first heard of Peter Porcupine when, in February 1794, that name appeared as the author of a new and scurrilous pamphlet called *A Kick For A Bite*.

Peter Porcupine occupied a position that could, with hindsight, be described as one of considerable historical importance. He was the only English writer of any note – Thomas Paine was in a French prison – to live in the United States during the last decade of the eighteenth century. Since he was a remarkably observant man, he took notice of much that was occurring in those eventful years: being a writer, he recorded, not only what he himself saw and experienced, but also what people thought and argued about. He was, if one likes, another Xenophon recounting his own adventures and another Herodotus reporting the strange manners and politics of a distant and largely unknown tribe. Yet Porcupine's writings are now little more than another curiosity of literature.

The late G. D. H. Cole maintained that this was because Cobbett never began to write at the summit of his powers until he became a Radical. This seems to be a political rather than a literary judgment, and one that is not entirely supported by the evidence contained in the yellowing pages that can now be read only in the statutory libraries. Cobbett certainly became a more practised and skilful writer than Porcupine, but it cannot be said that he was more vigorous or more vivid. Indeed, Porcupine possessed a certain gusto, an almost naïve enjoyment of his new-found powers as a polemicist, that would, in the older Cobbett, grow stale. A desire to experiment with both form and content would give way to the confining influences of an accustomed style and settled habits of thought. If one balances the one set of advantages against the other, nothing but the reader's political preferences can lead him to believe that Tory Porcupine was any less effective as a writer than Radical Cobbett.

Nevertheless G. D. H. Cole was stating no more than the obvious when he wrote, 'Of all his American pamphleteering, all that is now alive is his *Life and Adventures of Peter Porcupine.*'[19] And indeed, if one ignores the problems of access (nothing of Porcupine's, apart from *Life and Adventures,* has been re-published since his *Collected Works* were brought out in a limited edition in 1801) one has to seek an explanation for this in the different audiences Porcupine and Cobbett dealt with.

Cobbett occupies a central, if minor, place in British politics and in the history of Parliamentary democracy in any country. Porcupine was never an actor in American politics, and cannot easily be accepted by Americans as a reliable and trustworthy chronicler of a formative period in their history. He wrote as a propagandist, and as a propagandist he cheerfully abused almost every hero in the American pantheon and derisively trampled on what was to become known as the American dream. He showed no more respect for the infant republic than he did for its Founding Fathers. Washington, he reminded his readers, had been a traitor to the King whose uniform he had once worn, had probably been responsible for firing on Frenchmen attempting to parley under a flag of truce, had been ultimately responsible for the judicial murder of Major André, and had almost certainly, as President, overdrawn his salary in order to lend money at interest. Jefferson, on the other hand had always been more of a Frenchman than an American. His opposition to a treaty with Britain arose from his reluctance to pay the debts he owed his British creditors. His Pantisocratic ideas about a nation made up of American yeoman farmers and his ridiculous theories about slavery, negroes and the science of anthropology all proved that he was a hypocritical, intriguing, dangerous, and all too learned fool. Congress was largely recruited from jumped-up ostlers, tavern keepers, contractors and land speculators, all of them engaged in feathering their own nests while indulging in rodomontades on republican virtue.

These represented the true Americans no more than did the

town mobs who shouted against the British King, strutted around as imitation Jacobins, smashed Tory windows and taught their children to parade the streets singing:

> Englishman no bon for me,
> Frenchman fight for Liberty.[20]

The true Americans – as opposed to those who had done well out of the rebellion, had been bribed with French gold, corrupted with French ideas, or were malcontents and refugees from British justice – were, he maintained, still Loyalists at heart. They deplored the rebellion that had separated them from their mother country, had interfered with their trade and had exposed them to the revolutionary theories of the American Jacobins and the violence of the mob:

> During my residence in the United States . . . I never met with a man . . . who did not regret the separation . . . from the mother country . . . I never knew one American who, in his calm and candid moments, did not acknowledge that the country was much happier before the rebellion than it ever had been since.[21]

A man who could persuade himself of the truth of such a sweeping statement could, of course, persuade himself of anything. Nevertheless he persisted in his belief that, if one ignored the Democrats and the American Press which they largely controlled, the 'real' Americans continued to see the French, rather than the British, as their natural enemies.

Porcupine's success with his American readers was, therefore, very largely, *un succès de scandale*. Those he thought of as the 'real' Americans undoubtedly enjoyed him and may, in some instances, have agreed with him. The majority, however, read him in order to be shocked. What he wrote seemed to them to be a sort of political pornography: they read him in order to be titillated by his perversity. Later generations of Americans, not surprisingly, have found little to interest them in such a scurrilous version of one of the heroic periods in their history.

Porcupine's later works did, for a time, find favour in Britain, but there, also, they have ceased to be read. One may wonder why. There have, after all, been other, no less prejudiced and no more amusing English writers whose unflattering descriptions of later generations of Americans have lived to become classics.

The answer may lie in the insularity of the British, who are seldom interested in the history of other nations except in so far as it has affected British history. Porcupine was read in England for as long as there was a danger that the United States might change the course of the war by entering it on the side of the French, for the main thrust of his writing was directed towards preventing that. Once Washington had assured America's neutrality, that particular danger receded and, when it revived in 1812, the French war was on its way to being won and Cobbett was back in England and a Radical taking the opposite side of the argument. He could not have wanted Porcupine's opinions revived, and the American war, in terms of the global struggle, had become a side-show. Porcupine's works, as a consequence, were no longer of any great political importance. His version of America was no longer relevant, even to those in England who took an interest in American affairs.

Porcupine's America, consequently, remains buried in Porcupine's works. In what follows, no attempt has been made to describe the American scene in the 1790s as historians would recognise it. What is presented, instead, is a sketch of the American situation as Porcupine saw it, for without his blinkered and highly selective eyes, a great many of his American pamphlets and much of his American journalism have neither context nor significance.

The American nation seemed to Porcupine to be an uncomplicated one. He made no distinction between New Englanders and Georgians, between backwoodsmen and New Yorkers, between those who were descended from Anglo-Saxon, Celtic, Dutch, French or Negro stock, between those who were recent immigrants and those original Americans so misguidedly called Red Indians. The only distinction that concerned him was that which separated those Americans who were pro-French and anti-British from those who were of an opposite inclination. He was prepared, perhaps, to accept that most of them were, to some extent or other, republicans, just as he might have admitted that there was a large central section that was content to be merely American and cared not a damn for either the French or the British. Being himself a man of extremes, he was concerned with the extremes of American opinion, with those who desperately wanted either the French or the British to prevail in the global struggle that was then in its early stages.

In all of this he started from the simple position that he was an Englishman and a patriot. That patriotism was none the less ardent for having been only recently revealed. The man who had left England in order to become an American and a republican found no difficulty in now rebuking the Americans for not being Englishmen and monarchists. His was, indeed, a patriotism of a particular and personal kind. He once described his wife, admiringly, as 'a patriot of the soil'. He could well have described himself as the opposite. He needed to be removed from his native soil before patriotism, in its commonly recognised forms, could take over. He could be patriotic about England so long as he was in America, and almost as patriotic about America whilst he was in England. His tended, as Hazlitt said, to be a patriotism of contrariety:

> He cannot agree to anything established . . . When he is in England, he does nothing but abuse the Boroughmongers and laugh at the whole system; when he is in America, he grows impatient of freedom and a republic. If he had staid there a little longer he would have become a loyal and loving subject of His Majesty King George IV.* He lampooned the French Revolution when it was hailed as the dawn of liberty by millions: by the time it was brought into almost universal ill-odour . . . he had turned with one, two or three others, Bonapartist.[22]

It was this uncomplicated patriotism, blossoming in exile, that made Cobbett a High Tory for the next fifteen years. It also determined Porcupine's politics whilst he was in the United States. It would always be difficult to credit Cobbett with anything that resembled a coherent political philosophy, for he was a politician of the belly rather than of the head. Hazlitt, once again, said of him that he had 'no fixed or leading principles, (and did not appear) ever to have thought on a question till he sits down to write about it'. Since Hazlitt was, himself, something of a political theorist, one can understand his impatience. Porcupine did, in fact, have one 'fixed and leading principle'. It is best expressed in the saying attributed to the Arabs: 'The friends of my enemy are my enemies: the enemies of my enemy are my friends.'

Who his American friends would be was easily determined. The two largest political groupings at that time – they were more than factions but rather less than parties – called themselves the Federalists and the Republicans, though, since they were also referred to by other names, it would be almost less puzzling to call them Hamiltonians and Jeffersonians after Alexander Hamilton and Thomas Jefferson who provided them with a large part of their different philosophies. Porcupine was scarcely interested in their

---

* Hazlitt refers, here, to Cobbett's second American exile in 1817–19, and the point of the comment is that, when Cobbett was in England, George IV, whether as Regent or King, had no more constant and vociferous an opponent than Cobbett. It is true, however, that his father had no more loyal and admiring a subject than Porcupine so long as Porcupine was in America.

philosophies, for American domestic politics barely concerned him. As a consequence, the great debates about the powers of a Federal Government, about State Rights, about the North-Western Territories, about monetary and fiscal policies, State and Federal franchises, land tenure and land settlement – these, and many other equally important matters, failed to attract his attention unless they could provide him with ammunition to use against his opponents, or unless they had an ultimate bearing on foreign policy.

His allegiances were, of course, quickly decided. Although the Hamiltonians were far less ardently in favour of the British than the Jeffersonians were of the French, they were, from 1794 onwards, determined to treat with Britain, and not be dragged into the war on the French side. Before then, the great body of American opinion had supported the French cause, partly because of the alliance that had helped the Americans to arrive at their republic, partly because it was difficult for them to change from the belief that monarchies in general and the British one in particular must always be hostile and pose a threat to their independence.

Because of this, most Americans initially viewed the development of a republic in France as entirely favourable to their own security. Every revolution in history has felt the need to be buttressed by sister revolutions and has worked to help them emerge. The Americans, moreover, being the first of the modern republicans, received the news of the arrival of a French Republic with all the complacency that follows when a people feels it has been flattered by being imitated. As Porcupine put it, 'The vanity of the Americans was highly gratified at the thought of having set the *example* to the most populous and powerful nation in the old world.'[23]

As the French Revolution developed into the Terror, however, and as that, in its turn, produced what seemed likely to be an endless war between the Revolution and all established forms of government, American public opinion began to divide. That division, more than any of the arguments over domestic policy, helped to establish the identities of, and the differences between, the two emerging political parties in the United States. Porcupine was fortunate in this respect, for such clear-cut differences in foreign policy allowed him to discover his future opponents immediately.

The Jeffersonians clung, with a truly conservative fervour, to the conviction, not as yet put into words, that there could be no enemies to the Left. They saw the Jacobins completing the task that had, to their great regret, been left unfinished in the United States. They were bringing about a social as well as a political revolution, and this the Jeffersonians had been unable to achieve in America. It was natural, therefore, for them to want Jacobinism to prevail in Europe. More pertinently, they wanted it to establish itself in the United States, where they feared an aristocratical or even a monarchical form of government might be in the making.

The Federalists or Hamiltonians, on the other hand, wanted to stabilise the situation. They preferred strong and centralised government to any form of continuing revolution, such as the French might export. They did not feel that they owed the French so much of a debt of gratitude for such support as they had given them during the struggle for their independence that they had now had to imitate those who had begun by imitating them. The French had, after all, been their traditional enemies until they had lost Canada, and only then had the British replaced them in that role. The French King had only and tardily come to the support of the American revolutionaries in order to avenge the humiliations inflicted on his nation in the French and Indian war. Had not Vergennes, that King's Minister, talked at its end of the feelings of 'Indignation and of vengeance that the very name of English must inspire in every patriotic Frenchman'?

There was every indication that revolutionary fervour had strengthened, rather than replaced, the natural chauvinism of the French people, who might still wish to re-establish their lost North American Empire, even if they had now to call it a republic. France, therefore, could, in Porcupine's opinion, easily revert to posing a double threat, ideological as well as territorial, to the American Republic. It could be argued, therefore, that if a French monarch had found it possible to support American republicans against a British monarch, there was no logical reason why those same republicans should not now support a British monarch against the French Republic.

In this equal struggle of opposing sympathies, neutrality seemed to many Americans to be the best compromise. Neutrality, however, was more easily defined than achieved. The course and nature of the war, and the mere facts of geography, subjected the United States to pressures it could not possibly ignore. Those different pressures came from three of the greatest of the European powers, France, Britain and Spain, and though they might, to America's great advantage, cancel one another out, Americans could not be confident that this would happen, nor, indeed, could they do very much to help it happen. For although the United States was, in European terms, a very minor power, with only the beginnings of a navy or national army, it was still, in the eyes of the belligerent powers, capable of influencing the course of what was rapidly developing into a global war. If the American Government honoured the terms of the Franco-American Treaty of 1778, even if only to the extent of helping to defend French possessions in the West Indies and opening its ports to French naval vessels, privateers and prizes, the balance of naval power in the Atlantic would be affected. This Britain could not afford, and her counter-measures would, almost inevitably, force America into the war as a belligerent and ally of the French. This was the development that British diplomacy sought to avert as strenuously as French diplomacy sought to bring it about.

Porcupine was, almost from the beginning, seized of this danger. He maintained that there would have been no war if Britain and America had stayed united. Hence:

It is not true (as Priestley stated) that the granting of the independence of America was an 'advantage to England'. It was, on the contrary, the greatest evil that ever befell her. It was the primary cause of the present war, and of all the calamities it has brought upon England and Europe. If England and the American States had continued united, they would have prevented France from disturbing the peace of the world. That fatal measure . . . has created a power who will be capable of assisting France in any of her future projects against us, and whose neutrality . . . must be purchased by us at the expense, first of commercial concessions, and finally, by much more important sacrifices.[24]

He went on to add, with some prophetic insight:

In short, it laid the foundation of the ruin of the British empire, which can be prevented by nothing but a wisdom and energy, which have never yet been marked by the councils of our Government, in its transactions with the American States.[25]

The stakes, consequently, were high, and America had, once again, become a vitally important battlefield on which the French and British would fight each other, not, this time, with armies, but through politicians, diplomats, overt and covert agents, conspiracies, bribes, blockades and propagandists. It was a battle concerned primarily with moving American public opinion decisively one way or the other.

The manner in which each of the three European Powers attempted to exert pressure on the Americans varied. Spain was once again in possession of Louisiana and the Floridas, and it was for some time Spanish policy to believe that the new federation of American states would not endure. When it split up, some at least of those states might revert to Spanish rule. The Bourbon monarch in Spain, moreover, had no liking for republics, even though formerly, in alliance with France, he had had some small part in helping to establish the American one. So, until the collapse of the first coalition against Republican France, and the first intimations that an Anglo-American détente might be in the making, Spain saw little need to conciliate the Americans, to whom they denied freedom of navigation down the Mississippi, and from whom they still claimed large areas of territory in Georgia and Kentucky. The Pinckney Treaty of 1795–6, which defined the boundary of Louisiana and Florida and guaranteed free navigation of the Mississippi was a consequence of European, rather than American politics.

Everything changed when Spain was forced, in 1796, to become an ally of France, and a Spanish Bourbon was obliged to support the Jacobins who had so recently executed every French Bourbon they could lay their hands on. Spain then became, in every sense of the word, a French satellite. Her Minister in Philadelphia, the Chevalier Charles Martinez d'Yrujo, began to duplicate French propaganda against the British almost as soon as he arrived in that city, and drew Porcupine's fire as a consequence. He made all that he could of the Blount Conspiracy* and publicly accused Secretary of State Pickering of being pro-British, and of working too closely with the British Minister in Philadelphia, Robert Liston.

From then on, Spain was important in America only because of her subservience to France. Porcupine, and Cobbett after him whilst he was in his Tory phase, thought that Spain would be forced to cede the Floridas and Louisiana to her French masters. If the French were then to land an army in New Orleans, they would be in a position to dictate policy to the Americans, who would either have to fight them or join them. Those territories were, in fact, ceded by secret treaty in 1800. In 1803 a French expeditionary force did set out to occupy New Orleans, but never got there because of the unsuccessful attempt it made to occupy Santo Domingo en route. Napoleon then agreed, in an uncharacteristic fit of political myopia, to the Louisiana Purchase, whereby he sold

---

* This was an attempt – actual or imaginary – to use British forces and Indian auxiliaries to conquer the Floridas, passing through United States territory in order to do so. The plan was hatched by mercenaries, headed by Blount, and it is doubtful whether the British Government was ever involved, although it cannot have been entirely unaware of what was proposed.

the largely uncharted land west of the Mississippi to the Americans for fifteen million dollars. It has to be said that, in this respect, Cobbett displayed a sounder understanding of geo-politics than Napoleon. We find him writing on this subject to William Windham, when he was back in England, and just before hostilities with France were resumed after the Peace of Amiens:

> If war were to break out between us and France just at the time that the latter are about to set foot in Louisiana, we should have the Americans on our side, because with our help they could prevent the sweep of the French settlement; but, if the French army be once safely landed and has solid possession of the mouth of the Mississippi, I should not wonder if America were to join in the war against us, and, when that takes place, Adieu to British Independence.

And in a subsequent letter:

> If I am not the most mistaken of mortals, the fate of Louisiana will decide the fate of Great Britain. The colonizing of it and the Floridas must produce one or two things; an open rupture between America and France, or a sort of family compact between these two dreadful nations; if the former, Great Britain may retrieve all by joining America; if the latter, it is by no means inconceivable that France should evacuate her new dominions in America, and give up the whole Northern Continent to the United States, upon condition that they will first join her in ruining and subjugating Great Britain. The idea of dividing the world between two great powers is worthy the mind of Buonaparte.[26]

Years earlier, Porcupine had already urged the British Government to forestall the French by attacking New Orleans and seizing it from the Spaniards. That Government, however, had recently had its fingers burnt over the Blount Conspiracy: consequently there was no British attack made on New Orleans until 1814. By then it was American territory; the attack was repulsed and Cobbett had turned Radical and was as much opposed to taking the city from the Americans as he had been in favour of taking it from the Spaniards or the French.

The French position in the United States when Porcupine first started pamphleteering was very different from that of the Spaniards. They could offer no physical threat to the United States because they occupied no territory in the Americas. Their strength there lay in immaterial things. They could draw on the gratitude Americans owed the French for the assistance given them in the War of Independence. They could point to the common bonds that must always exist between sister republics, and that must unite them in opposing the tyranny of monarchs. They could claim what was owed to them from the loans extended to the colonists during that war, as well as what was due to them under the 1778 Treaty. Their greatest strength, however, lay in the fact that both the French and their Revolution were popular in the United States, whereas the British and their monarchy were not.

Very many years later, Cobbett described the climate of opinion in the United States at the outbreak of the French war in the following words:

> The people of America, still sore from the wounds of their war against England for liberty, were so loud and enthusiastic in the cause of the French, that the far greater part of the young men, hoisted the famous tricolour cockade; and everything seemed to indicate that the Government would be forced into a war with the English in aid of the French. I took the English side; the force of my writings gave them effect; that effect was prodigious; it prevented that which both Governments greatly dreaded; peace between America and England was preserved . . .[27]

He was undoubtedly making the most of his past achievements, as old men are wont to do. He could not, and did not prevent an Anglo-American war single-handed, though he probably did more in that cause than any other Englishman in the United States. Where he certainly succeeded was in making the French far less popular in America than they otherwise might have been, though it has to be added that the people who did most to discredit the French were the French themselves. Their diplomacy was surprisingly clumsy; their conspiracies and duplicity obvious, and their arrogance insufferable to all but the most ardent of their American partisans. They soon managed to dissipate much of the goodwill they had accumulated over the years, and more of it was blown away by the great gusts of anger and laughter with which Peter Porcupine assailed them.

What he achieved was to destroy with ridicule the three successive French representatives in the United States, Messieurs Genet, Fauchet and Adet. He revealed, in detail, all that had been most atrocious in the French treatment of Frenchmen, Germans, Dutchmen and Swiss and made the most any man could of the way the French Government had behaved in the matter of the

American Commissioners and what came to be known as the XYZ Affair. He attacked almost every American Jacobin with a ribald ferocity it must have been difficult for his victims to bear, and those victims ranged from Jefferson, Randolph and Madison down to the Philadelphian bully boys who fuddled themselves drinking toasts to the Revolution and swaggered about wearing French cockades in their hats and singing 'Ça Ira' with a Yankee twang to their French. That this was efficient is evidenced by the fact that, quite early in his crusade, Talleyrand, then ostensibly an emigré but in fact a French agent, attempted, not very skilfully, to bribe Porcupine to change his tune.

There was little that the British could do at that time to win the hearts and minds of the American public, even though Hammond and Liston, successive British Ministers in Philadelphia, worked skilfully at government level to keep America neutral. Almost everything that was done to advance the British cause at the popular level was done by Porcupine, with a few American Tories, such as the Fennos, supporting him. Nevertheless, it was an infinitely more difficult task to make the British popular in America than it was to make the French unpopular.

The British had more than memories of the American War to overcome. The two countries were still in dispute over a number of matters which were also the cause of considerable anger to ordinary people in both countries. Although the Treaty of Paris was more than ten years old, neither side had, as yet, honoured all its undertakings. The boundary problems had not been settled and Britain had not, as yet, withdrawn her posts on the Mississippi. The Americans had not paid their pre-war debts to their English creditors and had failed to keep their undertaking to compensate the Loyalists for their confiscated properties. The British were accused of inciting the Indians to raid along the frontier settlements and the Americans were suspected of planning, once more, to invade Canada. What was most damaging to Anglo-American relations, however, was the British blockade, in the course of which some three hundred American vessels were declared prizes, the West Indian ports were closed to American shipping, and hundreds of American sailors were taken off American ships and press-ganged because they were of British birth.

Many of these problems were eventually solved or made less contentious. Both Washington and John Adams, the two Federalist Presidents, were cautious men, who preferred talk to threats and negotiation to war, and the British were at least as eager to negotiate. John Jay's Treaty with England of 1794 did much to ease the tensions, even though the Democrats burnt Jay and most of the

Senate in effigy for having negotiated and agreed to it. All of these were matters about which Porcupine wrote in his pamphlets and his newspaper until his readers must have tired of his long and sometimes tedious expositions of the British case. He seldom read as well when he was presenting a case as he did when he was attacking one. The first made him solemn and legalistic, the other released all his humour and ribaldry.

He believed, and with some justification, that he had done his country a considerable service, and was supported in that belief by the praise and rewards offered him by the British Embassy in Philadelphia and the Government and Tory press in England. Liston offered him, on behalf of the Government, a 'great pecuniary award' for his 'gallant and effectual stand against the French influence'. This he refused, though the refusal gained him nothing at the time since most Americans already believed that he was, indeed, a paid British agent. Liston, who had come close to being compromised by the Blount Conspiracy, was particularly grateful to Porcupine for defending him in that matter. Edward Thornton, who became Chargé d'Affaires when Liston left, was a friend and constant correspondent, and Lord Henry Stuart, who was attached to the Embassy, used Cobbett as his criterion whenever he had to assess how much any American he spoke to sympathised with Britain. He would ask him:

'How do you like Mr Cobbett's writings?' If they applauded, he set them down as sincere friends of England: if not, if he found them even cold in their commendations, he set them down as enemies.[28]

At the end of his stay in the United States, when he had come close to being ruined by lawsuits, five thousand dollars were raised for Cobbett by public subscription in New Brunswick, and when he called at Halifax on his way back to England, the Duke of Kent, who was then Commander-in-Chief in Canada, went out of his way to do honour to 'this great British patriot'. Meanwhile at Westminster, William Windham, before he had ever met Cobbett, declared that he deserved his statue in gold for the service he had done his country in the United States.

These things need to be remembered if only because Porcupine was soon to be subsumed by Cobbett. It is seldom that one man wins fame twice in his life – once as a Tory and again as a Radical. We may today remember the Father of Reform but we have largely forgotten the man who deserved a golden statue for his services in

America. No impartial contemporary of Cobbett's would have made that mistake.

An enormous gulf should have separated the man who taught English to Frenchmen and the one who had made it his duty to the world to confound and condemn French policies and support British ones. It was a gulf that Cobbett jumped so easily that nothing seemed more natural. He did not, of course, confine himself to matters of high politics. Much of his writing was concerned with his personal and literary vendettas and the ordinary scandal and gossip of the day. When he was concerned with these, he was, indeed, a Porcupine, darting his quills in all directions. When it came to politics, however, he was something contrary to Bagehot's dictum. He both bit into the subject and chewed on it. Very many years later, Heinrich Heine was to write, 'Alter Cobbett, Hund von England! Ich liebe dich nicht . . .' There was, in short, something of the bulldog as well as of the Porcupine in the man who would always inimitably remain William Cobbett.

CHAPTER SEVEN

Porcupine's Progress

> For he might have been a Roosian,
> A French, or Turk or Proosian,
> Or perhaps Ital-ian!
> But in spite of all temptations
> To belong to other nations,
> He remains an Englishman!
>   W. S. Gilbert: *H.M.S. Pinafore*

Although Porcupine published only one pamphlet in 1794, in the following year he published no less than four. All of these were more specifically political than *Observations* had been, all were printed by Bradford, and the last two carried the name of Peter Porcupine as author. In 1795 he also published his first book, an English Grammar for Frenchmen called *Le Tuteur Anglais* in its first edition but *Le Maître Anglais* in its second and subsequent editions. Much later in his life he described why he had written it:

> When I . . . came to teach the English language to French people in Philadelphia, I found that none of the Grammars then to be had, were of much use to me. I found them so defective, that I wrote down instructions and gave them to my scholars in manuscript. At the end of a few months this became too troublesome; and these manuscript-instructions assumed the shape of a *Grammar* in print, the copy-right of which I sold to Thomas Bradford, a bookseller of Philadelphia, for a hundred dollars, or twenty two pounds, eleven shillings and sixpence; which Grammar, under the title of *Maître d'Anglois*, is, as I have just observed, now in general use all over Europe.[1]

Cobbett was not, in this instance, claiming too much. Generations of French schoolchildren and adults were to use this Grammar to acquire such knowledge of the English language as the French allow to be necessary. Similarly, generations of English schoolchildren would still, well into this century, be issued with *Cobbett's English Grammar*, so that they might learn, with less pain than otherwise, some of the intricacies of their own language.

Porcupine, like Cobbett after him, attracted hostile critics as swiftly and as surely as a cast ewe attracts maggots in midsummer. As a consequence, three of the pamphlets he published in 1796, *The Scare-Crow*, the well-known *Life and Adventures of Peter Porcupine*, and *Remarks on the Pamphlets Late Published Against Peter Porcupine*, had to be devoted to personal, rather than political, matters. The repercussions from his political pamphlets had made it necessary for him to explain and defend himself, and to answer his critics with at least three blows for every one they had dealt him. Apart from these, he published three more political pamphlets of which one, *The Bloody Buoy*, was the first of the several works he devoted to a detailed study of the atrocities committed during the French Revolution. As if these were not enough to keep a man fully employed for a twelvemonth, he also began work on *A Prospect from the Congress-Gallery*, the first instalment of what he intended to be a regular series of reports on proceedings in Congress. He was clearly obeying the same urge as was to lead him, some eight years later, to originate in England the reports on proceedings in Parliament that are now known as *Hansard*, but were originally called *Cobbett's Parliamentary Debates*.

Porcupine's readers, accustomed to his pamphlets, seemed likely to find *A Prospect* too factual, there being little of Porcupine in it and a great deal of Congressional oratory which is usually even more difficult to read than it is to listen to. That, at least, was his publisher's opinion. Bradford objected, moreover, to the form Porcupine proposed for the work:

> I proposed making a mere collection of the debates with here and there a note by way of remarks. It was not my intention to publish it in Numbers, but at the end of the session, in one volume. But Mr Bradford, fearing a want of success in this form, determined on publishing in Numbers. This was without my approbation . . . When about half a Number was finished, I was informed that many gentlemen had expressed a desire that the work might contain a good deal of original matter, and few debates. In consequence of this, I was requested to alter my plan: I said I would, but that I would by no means undertake to continue the work.[2]

The first Number was a success, and Bradford now pressed for a continuation of the series, offering to raise the payment for each instalment from eighteen to one hundred dollars. Porcupine would have accepted, had not Bradford's son let it slip that, if it were not continued, 'Their customers would be much disappointed; for that his *father had promised* a continuation, *and that it should be very interesting.*'[3]

This produced such an outburst from Porcupine as no modern author would dare indulge in:

> What! a bookseller undertake to promise that I should write, and that I should write to please his customers too! No; if all his *customers*, if all the Congress, with the President at their head, had come and solicited me; nay, had my life depended on a compliance, I would not have written another line.[4]

A Prospect was consequently dropped, though the notion of reporting and commenting on Congress was immediately embodied in another and different periodical which Porcupine started. This was a monthly political review called *The Political Censor*. The first Numbers were printed by Benjamin Davies who had, for a time, replaced Bradford. But Porcupine had not merely changed publishers: he was already moving towards becoming his own publisher. Once this happened, Porcupine, and Cobbett after him, would never depart very far from the business of publishing what they wrote and selling the works that resulted over their own counters.

Eight Numbers of *The Political Censor* appeared in 1796–7 before Porcupine abandoned that periodical in order to launch a daily newspaper. Over that period the *Censor* continued to report proceedings in Congress, but, perversely enough, in the manner that Bradford had wanted and Porcupine had been unwilling to adopt. That is, it developed as a journal of opinion rather than as one of record. The debates became less important than Porcupine's commentaries on them, and the reporting gained considerably in liveliness and vigour as a consequence.

The *Censor*, short-lived though it was, represents an important stage in Porcupine's career. He had gone at least half-way to discovering the type of journalism that Cobbett would later exploit so successfully. The political weekly has suffered a serious decline in England in recent years, but for well over a century it represented all that was best in British political journalism and exercised an almost undue influence on the course of politics. Much of this is owed to what Cobbett built up, over thirty-odd years, through his *Political Register* which, in its turn, owed something to Porcupine's *Political Censor*. It is interesting that Porcupine should later have abandoned his political monthly in order to launch a daily newspaper which lost him money, for Cobbett was to make similar attempts in the future only to lose even more money than

Porcupine had. The genius of both lay in commentary rather than in *reportage,* and the political weekly, in the end, proved itself to be the only vehicle that could carry the particular *mélange* of argument, political news, gossip, scandal, opinion and propaganda that would always represent Cobbett's immediate reactions to current events.

Yet even this was not all that Porcupine produced in 1796. He undertook, at Bradford's request, the translation of two works from the French. The first was Moreau de Saint-Mery's *Topical and Political Description of the Spanish Part of Saint-Domingo*, and the other Marten's *Law of Nations*, then one of the standard works on international law. This last, which ran into four editions and was republished in London, added considerably to Porcupine's nodding acquaintance with the law but, undertaken in addition to all his other work, it forced him to earn his fee in a manner that only a man of his prodigious energy could contemplate:

I translated it for a quarter of a dollar a page; and I made it a rule to earn a dollar while my wife was getting breakfast in the morning, and another dollar after I came home at night, be the hour what it might: and I earned many a dollar in this way, sitting writing in the same room where my wife and child were in bed and asleep.[5]

It must have been gratifying to be able to add:

The President, the Vice-President, and every member of Congress had a copy of the work, which is now to be found in most of the law-libraries in the United States.

Finally, it is probable, though not proven, that Porcupine was the author of two satirical poems published by Bradford in that year. Their titles, *The Democratiad* and *The Guillotina* certainly point in his direction. Porcupine was experimenting at this time with different forms of writing; but neither he nor Cobbett had any gift for verse. They could never do more than put together collections of jingling rhyming couplets that had not one tenth of the power and humour of their prose.

A fourth edition of *Observations* also appeared in 1796 with several additions made to it, including a rather boring political fable, after the style of Aesop, called *A Farmer's Bull.* By the end of the year, when Porcupine had already turned publisher, he brought out American editions of Mackenzie's *An Answer to Paine's Rights of Man* and Playfair's *The History of Jacobinism*, adding a 'Letter from Peter Porcupine' to the first and an Appendix containing 'A History of the American Jacobins, commonly denominated Democrats' to the second.

Cobbett was an extraordinarily prolific writer, so much so that, in later life, he was frequently accused of using his sons as ghost writers; but he needed only to remind his critics of all that Porcupine had produced in that single year of 1796, when his only son was an infant and he himself had no money to spare for ghost writers, to prove that, even when he was a novice, he was still capable of turning out as much work as any three other writers taken together.

By March 1797 he was fully occupied with launching his daily newspaper, *Porcupine's Gazette*, and the fine flow of pamphlets began to abate. He was now a journalist far more than a pamphleteer, and though he would publish other pamphlets before he left the United States in 1800, most of them were enlargements and reworkings of his newspaper articles. He was moving towards that professionalism in writing which would be so much a characteristic of Cobbett. With him a speech or lecture would, as often as not, turn into a newspaper article, the article would expand into a pamphlet and the pamphlet, eventually, into a book.

The pamphlets of this later period that are still worth attention include *The Cannibal's Progress*, another examination of French atrocities, though this time inflicted on the Swabians by the invading French troops; and two attacks on Tom Paine, the first being *A Letter to the Infamous Tom Paine in Answer to his Letter to General Washington*, and the second a muck-raking *Life of Thomas Paine*, based on a pamphlet by Oldys, an English pamphleteer. This was one of the few works he would come to regret when he turned Radical and took Paine as his guide in his study of monetarism.

In those early years from 1795 to 1797, when Porcupine was solely and magnificently a pamphleteer, he wrote with a freshness, a gaiety, an enjoyment of his own new-found powers that necessarily disappeared as writing became his constant and almost only occupation. Those early pamphlets, moreover, did more than set Porcupine on his way as a writer. They were primarily responsible for almost everything that happened to him thereafter in America.

What needs to be remembered about the background to this time is that the United States was still in the making and that this was the Age of Enlightenment. It was a good time, therefore, for political theorists; for the political parties were beginning to take shape and their members were beginning to cast around for the policies that would best defend their special interests and for theories that would do something to justify their different predilections and prejudices.

It almost seemed as though every man at all active in politics or letters had turned system monger at that time. Even within the broad divisions that separated the Federalists from the Republicans there existed a multiplicity of schools and no shortage of prophets. There were Jacobins and counter-revolutionaries, Pantisocrats and Technocrats, Free Traders and Protectionists, Free Thinkers and Fundamentalists, Slave Owners and Abolitionists, Levellers and Capitalists. There were even simpler souls like Doctor Thornton and Noah Webster who believed that the native virtues of Americans would be lost unless they could be saved from using the English language. They must, therefore, invent a new, and entirely American language, even if this meant printing the alphabet upside down, spelling words phonetically, and compiling a dictionary that could perpetuate these necessary and wholesome innovations.

Any outsider with an eye for the absurd who could remain uninfected by these imported and home-bred philosophies, must have found much to laugh at in the activities of at least some of the ideologues, so differently engaged in making the United States a fit place for planters, backwoodsmen, Boston bankers, New England manufacturers, traders, isolationists, atheists, episcopalians or land speculators to live in. The gulf between high political theory and low political gerrymandering was delightfully obvious. There was something inherently comical in watching the Philadelphian mob pretending to be French sans-culottes, or in hearing Virginian plantation owners prattle about Liberty, Equality and Fraternity before proceeding to argue in Congress that every three of their slaves ought to count for one white man when it came to calculating the number of representatives they might send to sit there.

Porcupine was precisely that sort of outsider, and the ideologues presented him with ideal targets. This was at once his strength and his weakness. It was his strength because it gave him a wealth of absurdities to expose. It was his weakness because he refused to look beyond those absurdities towards the values that would ultimately emerge: values that have been of some benefit to free men in every country and every age. From the American point of view, the only valuable thing he contributed to those debates was laughter. But the only consequence that was of serious concern to him was that nothing should emerge from them that might damage British interests. In that climate of intense political and philosophical speculation, the whole of his own political philosophy consisted of being an Englishman. If this made him a Tory, then it was because that corresponded with his native instinct, his national interest and his particular position as the sort of writer he was.

He defined that position, almost unthinkingly, in the first of all his American pamphlets:

> System mongers are an unreasonable species of mortals: time, place, climate, nature itself must give way. They must have the same Government in every quarter of the globe, when perhaps there are not two countries which can possibly admit the same form of Government at the same time. It is always done by little and little. When completed it presents nothing like a *system*; nothing like a thing composed and written in a book.[6]

He would never, either as Porcupine or Cobbett, write a passage that more clearly revealed his instinctive conservatism. A healthy mistrust of 'systems'; a feeling that, if things have got to be changed, it is always best to change them 'by little and little', and an unspoken belief that every country's politics ought to reflect the uniqueness and traditions of its people rather than whatever is currently fashionable among political philosophers – these gut-reactions add up to almost all the internal guidance any reasonable Tory should need. Which is not to say, however, that Tories have never turned unreasonable and gone whoring after theories, systems and elegant, self-sufficient philosphies.

Porcupine was not, all in all, the sort of polemicist contemporary Americans had grown used to. He was, in the first place, an Englishman writing as an Englishman in a country where it had become unusual for anyone to attempt to define, let alone defend, British interests. Those of his pamphlets that were primarily concerned with foreign affairs – that is to say with Anglo-American, Franco-American and Anglo-French relationships – were argued with great seriousness, but from a viewpoint that seemed perversely contrary to everything most Americans had subscribed to since the Revolution. But even in these pamphlets, and above all in those that were concerned with the domestic American scene, he dared to laugh at most of what Americans had come to hold most sacred.

And yet, in spite of all this, or perhaps because of it, he achieved considerable success: his pamphlets were widely read and brought him a considerable return once he had shaken himself loose from Bradford's tutelage. That success can only partly be accounted for in terms of the outrage he caused and the number of hostile critics he accumulated. What best explains that success is that he succeeded in making Americans laugh, even though there must have been many who suspected that they were being invited to laugh at themselves. In short, almost everything that happened to Porcupine in America is more convincingly explained in terms of his humour than of his politics.

Had he not been so ribald at America's expense, he would have been able, had he desired it, to spend the rest of his life in that country, even though he had spent all of it as a Tory and a serious defender of the British cause. It was, in the end, his ability to make Americans laugh at themselves that won him his readership and led to his downfall. He succeeded in making the mob suspect that it might not, after all, represent all that was best in Republicanism and that Republicanism might not represent the best form of government. At the same time he succeeded in making many in high places suspect that they might be going around with some of their moral and intellectual fly-buttons undone.

Porcupine undoubtedly enjoyed himself at his work. Every new hostile critic – and at one time it seemed as though every Phila-delphian, New Yorker or Bostonian capable of putting two thoughts and four sentences together and on paper had rushed into print against him – added to his readership and his renown. Moreover, since he was an irredeemably pugnacious man, he greatly enjoyed the literary brawling he so gleefully provoked. But more than any literary or debating success, what he valued was that he had made Americans laugh.

An anti-Porcupine cartoon published by a Philadelphian print-seller called Moreau provided him with an opportunity to point this out. It was one of those elaborately allegorical works the age delighted in. It portrayed Porcupine trampling on his critics and all their works while in the background George III in the shape of a lion, and accompanied by Satan, held a bag of gold out to him. Meanwhile, in the foreground, America, depicted as an eagle, drooped her wings and wept over the bust of Benjamin Franklin. Of this last, Porcupine wrote:

> This is almost the only part of the print to which I find fault; for, if by America, the people of America be to be understood, I believe most of those who have read my essays will do me the justice to say, that I have endeavoured to make America laugh instead of weep.[7]

As for all the other anti-Porcupine publications, he hurled defiance at the critics and welcomed the publicity they gave him:

'Dear Father, when you used to set me off to work in the morning, dressed in my blue smock-frock and woollen spatter-dashes . . . little did you imagine that I should one day become so great a man as to have my picture stuck in windows, and have four whole books published about me in the course of a week.' Thus begins a letter which I wrote to my father yesterday morning, and which, if it reaches him, will make the old man drink an extraordinary pot of ale to my health. Heaven bless him! I think I see him now, by his old-fashioned fire-side, reading the letter to his neighbours. 'Ay, Ay,' says he, 'Will will stand his ground wherever he goes.' – And so I will, father, in spite of all the hell of democracy . . . When I had the honour to serve King George, I was elated enough at the putting on of my worsted shoulder-knot, and afterwards, my silver-laced coat; what must my feelings be then, upon seeing half a dozen authors, all *Doctors* or the devils knows what, writing about me at one time, and ten times that number of printers, bookbinders and booksellers, bustling, running and flying about in all directions to announce my fame to the impatient public . . .[8]

It was a robust age, and the 'Doctors or the devil knows what' could scarcely have been accused of being squeamish when it came to attacking Porcupine. He was called 'the celebrated manufactur-er of lies and of filth'. He was told that he had left England to avoid being hanged, and France to escape being imprisoned as a sneak-thief. His 'talent at lies and Billingsgate rhetoric' had attracted the attention of the British Government, with the result he had been enlisted as a British agent in America. He had not possessed a shirt to his back when he first arrived in the country, but had now 'taken a house for the sale of his poison, at the enormous rent of twelve hundred dollars a year, and had paid a year's rent in advance'. The public could, consequently, begin to understand 'the overflowings of his gall against the Republic of France and all the Republicans of this country, as well as his devotion to the cause of tyranny and of Kings'.

The Life and Adventures of Peter Porcupine was written in reply to such accusations. It set out, to the great benefit of his future biographers, the story of Porcupine's life up to that point, and it served to rebut, dispassionately and with a great deal of docu-mentation and well-reasoned argument, every one of the several allegations made against him. Porcupine chose as an epigraph or motto for that work, a quotation from Shakespeare – 'Now, you lying varlets, you shall see how a plain tale will put you down' – and he concluded the Preface with a splendid cry of defiance to all his critics:

> Let them write on, till their old pens are worn to the stump; let the devils sweat; let them fire their balls at my reputation till the very press cries out murder. If ever they hear me whine or complain, I will give them leave to fritter my carcass, and trail my guts along the street, as the French sans-culottes did those of Thomas Mauduit.[9]

This, however, was dealing with his critics in general terms. There is little point now in discussing the specific literary quarrels he engaged in with various American publicists and publishers, although one or two examples of his method will give some flavour of his style. Samuel Bradford and his son Thomas had become his bitter enemies after he had left them and had, in *Life and Adventures*, described how they had cheated him while he wrote for them and had threatened legal action against him as soon as he had left them. They were unwary enough, eventually, to bring out, under the pseudonym of Tickletoby, an anti-Porcupine pamphlet which they called *The Impostor Detected*. It repeated most of the slanderous gossip about him then current, and went on: 'You can declaim and scandalize with the greatest hero of Billingsgate, yet in sober argument and chastity of manner, you are a mere nincompoop.' Porcupine's reply included the following passage:

> Chastity! Chastity from the pen of a Bradford! Chastity, I say, from No. 8 South-Front Street! *Chastity* from *the bawdy book-shop*! – I have no pretensions to an over-stock of modesty or squeamishness. I have served an apprenticeship in the army; yet I have often been shocked to see what the Bradfords sell. Not, perhaps, so much at the obscenity of the books, as at the conduct of the venders. I do not know a traffic so completely infamous as his. In London it is confined to the very scum of the Jews. It is ten times worse than the trade of a bawd: it is pimping for the eyes: it creates what the punk does but satisfy when created. These *literary panders* are the purveyors for the bawdy house.[10]

There was no man he quarrelled with more frequently and more publicly than Benjamin Franklin Bache, old Franklin's grandson, and the owner and editor of *The Aurora*, the Philadelphian newspaper that gave most support to the Democratic and Gallican causes. Shortly after *Porcupine's Gazette* had been launched, *The*

Aurora published a dangerous attack on Porcupine by an anonymous correspondent. Porcupine answered it at length:

> Now, pray, is this of your [i.e. Bache's] manufacture, or is it really from a correspondent? If you own it is yours, I assert that you are a liar and an infamous scoundrel: if you do not, your correspondent has my free leave to take those appellations to himself . . . Having thus settled the point of courtesy, give me leave, my sweet sleepy-eyed sir, to ask you what you could propose to yourself in publishing not only what you knew to be a falsehood, but what you must, if you are not quite an idiot, perceive everyone else would look upon as such? Do you dread the effect of my paper; and do you imagine that a poor miserably constructed falsehood of your publishing will tend to obstruct its success? If you do, you are egregiously mistaken. Not all that you and your correspondent can say, not all the reports of your spies, nor all the assignats of your Gallic friends disposed of in bribes,* will ever rob me of a single subscriber . . . I cannot for my life see, why you should wrangle with me. 'Two of a trade can never agree.' Very true: but I hope in God my trade is very different from yours. We are, to be sure, both of us newsmongers by profession; but then the articles you have for sale are very different from mine . . . I am getting up in the world, and you are going down; for this reason it is that you hate me, and that I despise you.[11]

One wonders how many authors and journalists would wish, in these effete and mealy-mouthed days, that it were still possible to deal with publishers and editors in such a direct and knock-them-down manner.

All of this, however, can still be considered as no more than the normal give-and-take of literary intercourse in those post-colonial times. Where Porcupine ran into greater danger was when he began to attack those who were already beginning to be thought of as the Founding Fathers, when he set about the Jeffersonians in their entirety, and when he even dared to question the superiority of republicanism over all other forms of government.

Having parted from Bradford, Porcupine stayed with Benjamin Davies as his publisher for only so long as it took to bring out three

---

* It was always part of Porcupine's argument that Genet, Fauchet and Adet, successively French Ministers in Philadelphia, bought support for French revolutionary causes with bribes and, in particular, subsidised Bache and *The Aurora*.

copies of *The Political Censor* and one pamphlet. By July 1796, he had set up for himself as bookseller, printer and publisher of his own and other mens' works. In that month he moved into new premises on Second Street which he rented from John Oldden, a wealthy Philadelphian Quaker, for the considerable sum of £300 a year, or some $1200. The premises included a double-fronted shop with living quarters above it, and here he set up his two printing presses and opened his bookshop.

The financial risk involved seemed to him justifiable. He had failed to buy back the copyrights of his early works from Bradford, but all that he had written since then was selling well, not only in America, but also in England, where John Wright, his future and sometime partner, was beginning to act as his agent, reprinting some of his pieces in *The Anti-Jacobin* of which he was then the publisher, and arranging for British editions of the longer works. He also undertook to keep Porcupine supplied with all the English books and journals he needed for sale in his bookshop. *The Political Censor* was selling so well in the local market that Porcupine was able to put an advertisement in the front of the sixth Number announcing:

> Persuaded of the utility this Censor may be of, if extensively read, the editor has printed a double edition of it, and by that mean has been enabled to reduce the price to *One Quarter of a Dollar*.

Yet, if his prospects seemed favourable, he was not allowed to embark on his new career as a bookseller and publisher without being made to realise, for the first time perhaps, the risks he was running:

> Till I took this house, I had remained almost unknown as a writer. A few persons did, indeed, know that I was the person, who had assumed the name of PETER PORCUPINE; but the fact was by no means a matter of notoriety. The moment, however, that I had taken a lease of a large house, the transaction became a topic of public conversation, and the eyes of the Democrats and the French, who still lorded it over the city, and who owed me a mutual grudge, were fixed upon me . . . I knew . . . the Democrats . . . could, at any time, muster a mob quite sufficient to destroy my house and murder me . . . My friends grew . . . anxious for my safety. It was recommended to me, to be cautious how I exposed at my window, anything that might provoke the people; and, above all, not to put up any *aristo-*

cratical portraits . . . I saw the danger; but I also saw, that I must, at once, set all danger at defiance, or live in everlasting subjection to the prejudices and caprices of the democratical mob. I resolved on the former . . .[12]

Consequently, he filled his shop windows with portraits and prints of members of the British Royal Family, British Ministers, Bishops and Judges, and successful British Admirals: 'Such a sight had not been seen in Philadelphia for twenty years. Never since the beginning of the rebellion, had any one dared to hoist at his window the portrait of George the Third.'

Within a few days his landlord, Mr. Oldden, received an ill-spelt, anonymous letter which declared, *inter alia*:

A certain William Cobbett alias Peter Porcupine, I am informed is your tenant. This daring *scoundrell*, not satisfied with having repeatedly traduced the people of this country, vilified the most eminent and patriotic characters amongst us, and *grosly* abused our allies the French . . . has now the astonishing effrontery to expose those very publications at his window for sale, as well as certain prints indicative of the prowess of our enemies the British and the disgrace of the French . . . When the time for retribution arrives, it may not be convenient to discriminate between the innocent and the guilty. Your property therefore may suffer. For depend upon it brick walls will not skreen the rascal from punishment . . . I advise you to save your property by either compelling Mr Porcupine to leave your house, or at all events oblige him to cease exposing his abominable productions or any of his courtley prints at his window . . . In this way only you may avoid danger to your house and perhaps save the rotten *carcase* of your tenant for the present.

A HINT

In the event, no attack was made on Porcupine and Mr. Oldden, far from being intimidated, offered to give the property to Porcupine as a gift. This was refused, but the occasion produced a pamphlet that ended, rather splendidly, in this manner:

Of all the stupid inventions that ever entered the brains of this bungling clan, the cut-throat letter to Mr. Oldden is the most ridiculous. Had they studied for years, they could not have found out anything that would have pleased me so well. It will for ever silence their clamours about the liberty of the press; it will prove to the people . . . the truth of what I have always told them; that is, that these 'pretended patriots', these advocates for liberty and equality, would, if they had become masters, have been a divan of cruel and savage tyrants. That they knew nothing of liberty but the name, and that they make use of that name merely to have the power of abolishing the thing . . . I will continue to publish and expose for sale what I please . . . I will never cease to expose . . . the enemies of the country in which I live, so long as one of them shall have the impudence to show his head. Hitherto I have given acids only, I will now drench them with vinegar mixed with gall.[13]

The pamphlet concluded with the announcement that it came 'FROM THE FREE PRESS OF WILLIAM COBBETT, JULY 22 1796'. The dubious freedom of the American press would, from now on, be used by Porcupine as a text to illustrate the difference between the theory and practice of republicanism. Any Democrat scribbler was free to libel and insult the British monarch, British politicians and all loyal Britons, wherever they lived, with impunity. But, if one of those same loyal Britons, who happened to be living in the United States, dared to defend his country or to attack its traducers, he was immediately at risk from the mob and ultimately, as he soon discovered, from the law. His passion for justice quickly persuaded him that this was intolerable, and from that moment, his criticisms of the Democrats and the Jacobins began to expand into a sweeping criticism of what he saw as the hypocrisies of republicanism. He had discovered a new and hydra-headed Tartuffe, which persuaded him to embark on the policy he outlined in a later pamphlet, 'I concluded that I might . . . go as great lengths in attacking the enemies of my country as others went in attacking its friends.'[14]

In other words, if some were given a licence to libel, all must be given it. He claimed as much in the Introduction he wrote for the first number of *The Censor*. After pointing out that the American Government had provided postal facilities for newspapers only in order to give the public access to information, he described how this facility had been used by newspaper editors to misinform the public:

The French revolution burst forth like a volcano . . . The editors, perceiving the partiality of the most *numerous* class of their subscribers for this revolution, and all the novel and wild principles it has given rise to, have been seduced by their love of gain, to flatter that partiality, by extolling those principles at the expense of every thing, their own private interest excepted . . .

156

To countervail the malignant efforts of these retailers has ever been my wish . . . But, alas! what can a straggling pamphlet, necessarily confined to a single subject, do against a hundred thousand volumes of miscellaneous falsehood in folio? . . . In opposing a literary monster like this, I am aware that a Porcupine, with all his quills, can never hope for complete success: but . . . this I shall attempt in a monthly work . . . In this work I shall take a review of the political transactions of the past month; give an account of every democratic trick, whether of native growth or imported from abroad; unravel the windings of the pretended patriots . . . and, I trust, I shall be enabled to give monthly a sketch of political affairs more satisfactory, because more correct, than has ever yet appeared in this country . . . The newspapers are supported by subscription, and for that reason the *Censor* shall not. As long as people read, so long shall I write; and, when the bookseller advertises me that the work lies on his shelf, it will be a very good hint for me to draw in my quills . . . Here, then, begins a *bellum eternum* between the fabricating *Quidnuncs* and me. – There is my glove, gentlemen; take it up as soon as you will.[15]

His purpose could not have been more clearly revealed. The attacks against him had been extended from single critics to those who influenced public opinion and the behaviour of the mob. He, in his turn, would reply by widening the scope of his own attacks and counter-attacks until they encompassed, not only his personal enemies, but the American system itself. *The Censor*, however, soon proved to be too occasional a vehicle to support the full load of his ambitions. On Saturday, 4 March 1797, the first copy of his daily newspaper, *Porcupine's Gazette*, came out with an 'ADDRESS TO THE PUBLIC' on its front page. What was contained in that Address should still be of interest to any journalist. On the technical side, it set out what sort of news would be published and how it would be obtained both locally and from abroad. Would-be correspondents and advertisers were welcomed, methods of distribution were explained, and a claim was made that more subscribers had already been obtained than any two other Philadelphian papers could boast of.

More interesting, however, was Porcupine's statement of purpose:

My politics, such as they are, are known to everyone; and few, I believe, doubt of their continuing the same. Protestations of impartiality I shall make none. They are always useless and are besides perfect nonsense, when used by a news-monger; for, he that does not relate the news as he finds it, is something worse than partial; and as to the other articles that help to compose a paper, he that does not exercise his own judgement, either in admitting or rejecting what is sent to him, is a poor passive tool and not an editor . . . I wish my paper to be a rallying point for the friends of the Government.* Here they may speak their minds without reserve . . . without fearing that their productions will be rejected, or gutted, or frittered away, for fear of offending this or that person, society or nation. I have not descended from the *Censorial* chair merely to become a newsmonger. I have not made this sacrifice for the sake of augmenting the number of retailers of small-beer politics. In short, I have not taken up that cut-and-thrust weapon, a daily newspaper, without a resolution, not only to make use of it myself, but to lend it to whomsoever is disposed to assist me . . . I should not conclude, perhaps, without thanking my subscribers; but I trust they will give my silence on this subject the proper interpretation. I never was master of the God-bless-your-honour style.

One wonders how many newspaper proprietors would launch a new paper today as honestly or as well, just as one wonders how many newspaper unions would allow them to do so. It is the right, indeed the duty, of all men, including news-mongers, to have opinions. G. K. Chesterton once wrote, 'Bigotry may be roughly defined as the anger of men who have no opinions' and a publicist who boasts, as is often done these days, of his impartiality, is probably lying. If he is not, then he is, by Chesterton's definition, confessing himself a bigot, and would probably be better employed publishing railway timetables.

Between his pamphlets, *The Censor* and his new cut-and-thrust weapon, *The Gazette,* Porcupine had worked towards a position from which he could publicise almost every opinion he held on almost every subject on which he thought it worth having an opinion. He was able, moreover, to demonstrate, more convincingly than ever before, how little he thought of impartiality. This did not prevent him, as a news-monger, from treating the news seriously, even though he may have been somewhat selective in what he reported. In his liberal use and analysis of documentary evidence he may well be thought of as a pioneer of what is now called investigative journalism.

As an investigative journalist, then, Porcupine covered a great many of the contemporary situations of national and international

---

* Which was then Federalist and consequently neutralist and not markedly pro-French.

importance. He was, for those days, fair in his factual reporting but less than impartial in his conclusions. He dealt with the Whisky Rising which he reported with great accuracy, even though those reports led him to conclude that it was all the fault of the Democrats and their French paymasters. Nor could he refrain from pointing out, with considerable pleasure, that it was something odd that a nation that had risen in rebellion because the British had placed an excise duty on tea should now have to send an army against those Western settlers who had objected to a similar duty being placed on whisky which was, given the state of communications, almost the only way in which they could dispose of their surplus grain.

He considered, in great detail, the facts involved in Edmond Randolph's resignation as Secretary of State (1795) and that unfortunate man's attempts to explain and vindicate his conduct. After publishing, in full, the French minister Adet's despatches, which had been so miraculously captured and published by the British, and all the letters exchanged between Randolph and Washington, he concluded, almost inevitably, that Randolph had, indeed, attempted to elicit bribes from the French and had rightly been dismissed as a consequence. Since Randolph is now generally given the benefit of the doubt, this was an excellent example of how investigative journalism can be made to result in whatever conclusion the investigative journalist desires.

And so it went on. Washington's retirement, the British treaty, the behaviour of the French Ministers in Philadelphia, the seizure of American shipping by both the British and French navies and numerous other matters of immediate concern in American politics were carefully investigated and made to yield the conclusions Porcupine wished to arrive at. These, generally speaking, were that the French were bloodthirsty and arrogant bullies, that they were attempting, alternatively, to bribe and bully the Americans into an alliance, that the Democrats were their more-than-willing accomplices in this, and that the British were, at the worst, defending their interests in a life-and-death struggle with the French, had no interest in American affairs apart from this, and were, indeed, that country's natural allies and trading partners.

The Gazette, however, had to be a newspaper as well as a vehicle for Porcupine's opinions. As such it reported international affairs, war news, local gossip, Congressional debates, shipping news and prices, and anything that Porcupine considered relevant or interesting in what went on around a hundred different parish pumps and town meetings in the United States. What he reported was not what we have come to think of as history: it was too selective and too much directed towards a single purpose for later historians to be able to accept it as a reliable account of what was then happening. But it does contain much of the raw material from which history can eventually be assembled, and, as such, it has been, to my mind, unduly neglected by historians looking, perhaps too single-mindedly, for impartial and therefore reliable evidence.

A layman, however, who has any interest in the past, would find it interesting to look at events that were to become part of accepted history from Porcupine's critical and far from impartial viewpoint. This is especially the case when he was reporting and discussing those aspects of foreign affairs that form part of all our pasts. One can, if one wishes, ignore the picture he painted of the French revolution and its immediate aftermath. It is different from the one we are now accustomed to, for few, since his time, have been willing to accept his argument that it was an unmitigated disaster for mankind. One can, therefore, ignore the atrocity pamphlets and articles. Such things, nowadays, are referred to as 'hate propaganda', even though atrocities are atrocities whether it is French aristocrats, Russian kulaks or Chinese peasants that are massacred.

But, when he mentions that the old Empress of Russia has just died, and wonders how this will affect the pattern of shifting alliances in Europe; when he argues that the battle of Cape St. Vincent was indeed a victory for the British which would influence the course of the war for years to come; when he wonders how long the Directorate can survive in Paris, and what will happen to the new satellite republics the French had set up in Batavia, Switzerland and Italy – then we might indeed feel that we are being brushed by the skirts, at least, of history.

He thought of himself, and would continue to do so for all of his life, as something of an expert on foreign affairs. And it is true that this former ploughboy displayed, on occasion, what has to be described as prophetic insight, even in his ribaldry.

The pages of *The Gazette* reflect, for example, his growing interest in the career of a man he described as one of the French bandit-generals then operating in Italy. When Bonaparte, for it was he, returned in triumph to Paris, Porcupine, who always enjoyed translating and publishing in full those official entries in *Le Moniteur* that were particularly rich in bombast and references to the great Romans, described with glee how the members of the Directorate, worried by his growing popularity, urged him to depart for the conquest of England in the following terms:

Go, and by the punishment you inflict on the Cabinet of London, strike terror into all Governments which shall dare to doubt the power of a nation of freemen. Pompey did not disdain to crush a nest of pirates. Greater than the Roman General, go and chain down the gigantic pirate who lords it over the seas . . .

Porcupine's comment on this started in ribaldry and proceeded into something approaching prophecy:

After this there was a *patriotic drunk*, just such ones as we have seen in Philadelphia . . . They have determined on the fate of this poor fellow [Napoleon]. If he ever gets out of sight of land, he is gone . . . Mind what I say *Master Bonaparte* . . . get into their berth while the mob is in good humour; and then, like old *Oliver*, case yourself with iron, and rule the monsieurs with a rod of the same metal.[16]

Within two years, Napoleon had become First Consul, and five years later, no longer content to be a French Cromwell, he made himself Emperor.

Porcupine's constant sniping at the French was welcomed in England, but proved increasingly embarrassing to the American Government which was seeking to maintain good relations with both Britain and France. Above all, it infuriated the Democrats, the American Jacobins, and such emigré Scots Radicals and United Irishmen as had landed in America. That, of course, was part of its purpose. And so long as he did no more than that, he was safe from all but the editors and pamphleteers who took the opposite side, and the possible attentions of the mob.

It was when he began to criticise the men of power – even, on occasion, those whom he nominally supported – that he began to attract more powerful enemies. He did not even respect that most recent and sacred of dead cows, Benjamin Franklin. He generally referred to him as 'the almanack-maker' or 'the lightning-rod man' and allowed no one to forget that he had been, in his time, a prodigious producer of bastards:

As a *moralist* the Doctor's example is certainly a useful one; especially in a country like this that is thinly inhabited. 'Increase and multiply' is an injunction that this great man had continually in mind; such was his zeal in the fulfillment of it, that he paid very little attention to time, or place, or person.[17]

Porcupine had, of necessity, to show some respect for Washington, but he could never like him. Nothing annoyed him more than the fact that he had become, to a certain extent, a cult figure in England:

The Reverend Arthur Homer D.D. . . . has thought proper to represent GENERAL WASHINGTON, the man who, while he bore a commission under his and Dr. Homer's Sovereign, was the very first in the Colony of Virginia to subscribe to a fund for raising troops to fight against that Sovereign; the man who afterwards commanded the rebel army, who in cold blood, and contrary to the laws of war, executed the gallant ANDRE; the man, in short, whose fame rests on his having been the principal instrument in cutting off an empire from the crown of Britain; this is the man whom the Reverend Arthur Homer has thought proper to represent as *THE GREATEST AND MOST VIR-TUOUS character that the New World has ever produced.*[18]

Commenting on the fact that Washington had appeared at the opening of the first Federal Congress in a suit of clothes entirely of American manufacture:

Every farmer of sense knew that the suit cost as much as a middling farm would sell for. In fact this suit of the General's, like many other of his tricks, was well enough calculated to amuse the ignorant part of the people, and to persuade them that America could exist totally independent of England . . .*[19]

When Washington retired, attacks were made on him in the press by various correspondents using such pseudonyms as 'Valerius', 'Pittachus' and 'A Calm Observer'. These accused him of what amounted to peculation in the matter of drawing his salary and allowances during his Presidency. They were answered by Hamilton and Wolcott, and Treasury accounts were reproduced. Porcupine published the whole of this exchange without comment, but added, in a footnote at the end:

This establishes one unpleasant and embarrassing fact; to wit, that General Washington, *instead of refusing to accept any salary* (which his admirers have said was the case), actually *overdrew*

* Until he discovered, in the course of the 1812 War, that the United States had started its own wool industry based on imported Merino sheep, Cobbett firmly believed that Americans could not long survive without British textiles and consequently could not maintain an embargo on British imports.

his salary, and had, from June 1790 to June 1795, constantly several thousand dollars of the *public money* in his hands. Whether he did let this money out at usurious interest, as it was asserted, will, perhaps, never be known.[20]

If he could treat in this manner a man who was dead, and another who was for a long time at the head of a government he had to support if only because it was less Anglophobic than the Democrats, it is easy to imagine how he dealt with the Democrats themselves. He was less inclined to make fun of Jefferson than of the others, though he tended to laugh at his philosophical pretensions and to remind him of the inglorious part he had played in the War of Independence. Moreover, Jefferson had a vested interest in severing all connections with Britain:

> Jefferson, a man who was deeply indebted to the English merchants, and who hated England because he had injured her, was . . . appointed Minister Plenipotentiary to France, where he resided till the new Federal Government was formed . . . This man was totally devoted to . . . France, and the whole time of his embassy was taken up in contriving . . . the means of turning the channel of the American trade from England to France.[21]

Commenting on the Presidential election, in which John Adams narrowly defeated Jefferson, he wrote:

> It is a notorious fact, that in this election, the partisans of France . . . were ranged in opposition to the friends of the Federal Government. I do not insinuate that Mr Jefferson would now wish to see this government subverted; but it is well known . . . that he has ever been opposed to the principles on which it is established . . . His partiality for the destructive system of the upstart rulers of France is also well known. His *philosophy* and politics perfectly harmonize with theirs.[22]

Porcupine reported in full the inaugural speech lauding Adams which Jefferson, as Vice-President, made in the Senate, adding, in a footnote:

> A declaration more false and hypocritical than this, never disgraced a public assembly. Not only had Jefferson been the rival candidate of Adams, not only had he seen every base and wicked art made use of to degrade and disappoint his opponent, but it was notorious, that he himself had written several most

artful and infamous libels against the man whom he here pretends to love and respect, and for whose life, health, and continuance in office, he affects to pray![23]

It is difficult, in Porcupine's version, to recognise the sage of Monticello and the man who gave his name to a version of democracy which, however unattainable, formed part of the American dream. He was less restrained when it came to Jefferson's followers. Madison, 'who was a mere tool of Jefferson', he described in a manner that may well, in later years, have influenced Dickens who, as a young man, once worked on a newspaper with which Cobbett was connected:

> Madison is a little bow-legged man, at once stiff and slender. His countenance has that sour aspect, that conceited screw which pride would willingly mould into an expression of disdain, if he did not find the features too skinny and too scanty for its purpose. His thin sleek hair, and the niceness of his garments are indicative of that economical cleanliness, which expostulates with the shoe-boy and the washerwoman, which flees from the dangers of a gutter, and which boasts of wearing a shirt for three days without rumpling the ruffles.[24]

Equal and even more scurrilous attacks were constantly made on a host of other Democratic worthies. Included among these were M'Kean, the Chief Justice of Pennsylvania and Democratic candidate for the Governorship of the State, and Benjamin Rush, an eminent Philadelphian physician and savant, who had once been Surgeon-General to the Armies of the Middle Department and was a Democrat, an enemy of Washington and a close friend of Paine and Jefferson. Porcupine also disliked 'the vile Dallas' sufficiently to offer a reward of ten dollars to anyone who could prove that the future Secretary to the Treasury had not a scrap of English blood in him. That reward was won by a man who claimed he had proof that Dallas had been born in Jamaica of Scottish parents. Thereupon a Scots reader wrote to protest at this slur on his race. Dallas, he swore, was an entirely Irish name.

And if these personal attacks were not sufficient, Porcupine's writings had a tendency to invite Americans to laugh also at their most prized institutions. In his reporting of Congress, for example, he dwelt on such parts of their proceedings as revealed Members in their most pretentious and ridiculous aspects; for the motley band of ambitious, inexperienced statesmen in Congress at that time seemed to excel in absurdity.

He reported in full that precursor of all Watergates, the affair of
Randall and Whitney. These two entrepreneurs, having an opportunity to acquire twenty million acres of Indian Territory, had
thought to gain permission from Congress by offering shares in the
land company they had set up to all Congressmen willing to vote
the motion through. When this was exposed by one who had been
approached and had refused, with what solemnity did Member
after Member stand up and swear, with his hand on his heart, that
he knew nothing of Randall, or if he did, had never been
approached by him, or if he had been so approached, had spurned
his offers! Taken together with the Randolph affair, and the fracas
that resulted when Congressman Lyon spat in Congressman
Griswold's face, whereupon the two started a duel with a pair of
tongs on one side and a cudgel on the other, anyone seeking to
demonstrate that there was a certain lack of probity and decorum
in Congress never needed to look far for proof.

There was the more solemnly absurd case of the debate on the
Naturalization Bill in 1795. William Branch Giles, maintaining
that a revolution was about to sweep Britain, suggested that the
British aristocracy might, as a consequence, flee to the United
States for refuge. He therefore proposed that no foreigner should
be allowed to become an American citizen unless he first re-
nounced all his titles. Madison supported the amendment, which
was duly passed. A New England representative maintained,
however, that this was not enough. Foreign aristocrats seeking
citizenship should also be required to renounce the right to own
slaves. Thereupon Madison, who came, like Giles, from Virginia,
declared that this was a different matter altogether. Property was
sacred, and it was the right of every freeman and citizen to own
slaves, even though he might not be allowed to own a title.

Porcupine's comment on all this was simple:

'Tis a pity the poor devils [of British aristocrats] are not apprized
of all this. It would certainly be an act of humanity . . . to let
them know what blessings are in *store* for them; they seem
attached to their Coronets and Coach-and-sixes at present; but
were they informed that they can have as much homony and fat
pork as they can gobble down (once every day of their lives),
liberty to chew tobacco, and smoke all the week, and to ride out
on the meeting-going mare on Sundays, it might tempt them to
quit their baubles and their poor bit of an Island without a
struggle, and fly to the free state of Virginia.[25]

It was not merely the representatives of the Republic who came under attack. By now, Porcupine was beginning to see in republicanism itself the cause of almost all that he disapproved of in the life of the American nation. He never had any liking for negroes and was not, himself, an Abolitionist. But he began to collect examples of how the existence and treatment of slaves revealed the hypocrisy that underlay the statement that 'all men are born equal'. The freedom of the press equally was based on humbug, as was the administration of justice in the courts. Republicanism led to immorality and a loosening of family ties, and to prove this he published lists of advertisements culled from other newspapers, of which the following is merely one example:

> Whereas my wife, Betty, has eloped from my bed and board, and has behaved in an unbecoming and indecent manner, by propagating the human species in a way other than the one prescribed by law: this is to caution all kinds of people, both *black*, *white* or *piebald*, against trusting her on my account (*harbour her they may if they can*); as I will not pay one *mille* of her contracting after this date. JOHN BOLTON.[26]

It is only when one considers where Porcupine's writings were taking him that one begins to realise that they seemed to conform to an overall pattern. There was more to them than the exaggerated patriotism of an Englishman exiled in a foreign country and surrounded by frequently hostile natives. There was more, even, than an innate pugnacity and a gift for scurrilous criticism. Over the years he had, perhaps without realising it, developed a sense of mission. He had also, he thought, detected a wide-spread conspiracy to frustrate it.

When he started writing, his purpose had been to persuade Americans to abate their hostility towards Britain. To achieve that, he had embarked on a root-and-branch attack on the Jacobins and their supporters in the United States. This had won him English, as well as American readers, and had brought him into contact with English as well as American critics. The former were, for the most part, Whigs or Radicals who continued the strain of republicanism that had never entirely disappeared from British politics. It became his duty, as he saw it, to demonstrate to the British what republicanism was really like, and what it had produced in America and France. He sought to prove that the United States, far from possessing the most perfect system of government, possessed a most imperfect one; that far from being administered by wise and virtuous men, it was administered by corrupt rogues

166

and vainglorious fools; that far from producing the greatest possible degree of prosperity and happiness for all the people, it produced poverty, contention, and discontent amongst most of them.

It could be that there lay, in his subconscious mind, an even greater ambition. If he could convince the British that a republic was so much worse than the constitutional monarchy they lived under, why should he not attempt to do the same to the Americans? Why should he not be able to persuade them that their Republic had failed them, that independence would eventually ruin them and place them under the domination of France, and that their best course, by far, would be to return to their former allegiance to the British Crown? He was in a unique position to make that attempt. He reached more readers, he claimed, than any other man then writing in America, and though he aroused a great deal of opposition, he also attracted many supporters. When anything happened, people had got into the habit, so one of his supporters assured him, of asking what Porcupine had to say about it. His name was frequently mentioned in Congress where he was considered sufficiently dangerous for pressure to have been put on John Adams to order his deportation as a British agent under the new Alien and Sedition Acts. If all of this seems far-fetched today, one has to remember that the first French Republic endured for barely a decade, and that those who knew most about the United States at that time were also those who most frequently prophesied the imminent collapse of the Federation.

Cobbett always subscribed to the conspiratorial theory of politics. This would, eventually, lead him to discover THE THING, that elaborate conspiracy in which politicians, landowners, bankers, jobbers, economists, Scotsmen, Jews and Quakers came together in order to ruin the country and destroy all that he, Cobbett, fought for. Porcupine's theory was a simpler one, and one that many people still believe in. It was, roughly speaking, a conspiracy of those on the left in politics to mould public opinion through their monopoly of the Press:

While the press, which is now become the ruler of the opinions of men, was, in America, thus enlisted under the banner of the republicans; in Europe circumstances rendered it not less devoted to their service. France, which on the Continent gave the fashion in sentiment as well as in dress, was compelled to espouse their cause, in justification of her own conduct; and though it was excessively ridiculous to hear her monkeys chatter about giving liberty and happiness to the British colonies, the envious nature of Europe, who all, either openly or secretly, rejoiced at the humiliation of England, listened to them not only with patience, but with pleasure and applause.[27]

As for the situation in Britain itself:

There is, in ninety nine hundredths of mankind, a propensity to approve of whatever is crowned with success: hence many of those, who, while the issue of the contest was doubtful, expressed a becoming detestation of the conduct of America, have, since the close of the war, appeared among the forwardest to congratulate her on the event, and to eulogise those who were, and who still are, branded with the name of rebels . . . The British press, than which nothing ever was, or ever can be, more servile, kept an exact pace with the delusion of the nation, till, at last, it became a matter of course for us to read of the American rebellion (which has been softened into a *revolution*), not only as a justifiable but a meritorious act, which has led to the formation of a Government the most perfect in the world.[28]

All one can add to this is that, if one is going to indulge in conspiracy theories, it is generally best to make the conspiracy world-wide.

When Spain, after the collapse of the first European Alliance, became, in effect, a French satellite, Porcupine was doubly outraged. As a monarchist, he thought it indecent for a Bourbon king to come to terms with the sans-culottes. As an Englishman, he deplored the fact that his country had lost an ally and gained an enemy. He lost no time, therefore, in blackguarding Charles IV, the Spanish nation, and the Chevalier Carlos Martinez d'Yrujo* who had recently taken up the post of Spanish Minister in Philadelphia. The Chevalier was, according to Porcupine, half a Frenchman and more than half a Jacobin, which is why he immediately dubbed him 'Don Sans-Culotte de Carmagnola Minor'.

There was policy as well as outrage behind this blackguarding. Porcupine had for some time been urging the British Government to come to an alliance with the United States for the purpose, if nothing else, of taking over all the Spanish possessions in North America before these were ceded to the French and occupied by them. As soon as d'Yrujo arrived *en poste*, he somewhat imprudently embarked on a public dispute with Secretary of State

---

* The name was sometimes spelled De Yrujo in the French fashion.

Pickering over the fulfilment of the terms of the recent Spanish–American treaty concerning the military posts on the Mississippi. Even more imprudently, his secretary, Don Fatio, had sent a copy of the letter setting out the Spanish grievances to the offices of *The Gazette,* together with a note that ran:

> Sir,
>   From the known impartiality of your Gazette, I am directed by the Chevalier d'Yrujo to hand you for publication the annexed translation of his last note to Colonel Pickering.

Nothing in Spanish diplomacy could have been more misguided, or have suited Porcupine better. He proceeded, in a series of abusive articles, to inflame public opinion against the Spaniards in an attempt to make it difficult for the American Government to negotiate these problems peacefully. That government, however, had little as yet by way of a navy or standing army, and could not afford to fall out with Spain, however much it might aspire, one day, to plant the American flag in Louisiana and the Floridas. The more Porcupine attempted to whip up anti-Spanish sentiment, the more he embarrassed the American Government. Consequently, when d'Yrujo, infuriated by the scandalous material Porcupine was publishing about himself and his monarch, asked the Federal Government to institute proceedings against Porcupine for criminal libel, that government consented.

To institute an action for criminal rather than civil libel was to attempt to exact a harsher revenge, for the first could result in imprisonment and fines whereas the second could produce only damages. The criminality of the libel could only be proved if it could be established that it was one likely to bring about a breach of the peace. Since d'Yrujo and Cobbett were unlikely to engage in fisticuffs – the former was a very small man – the prosecution sought to prove that the newspaper articles were likely to excite Spaniards 'to hatred, hostilities and war against the United States'.

Porcupine, or rather Cobbett, for Porcupine had to disappear when the law was involved, appeared quite unconcerned. The first his readers learnt about it was from a less than conciliatory passage in *The Gazette*:

> It is said that Genet is in town incog., and it is generally supposed that he has been invited hither as a chamber councillor for the Spanish Minister in his prosecution of *P. Porcupine*, which we have pleasure to inform our readers is in a fair way of coming to a head. The little Don, we are informed, has for some time past,

been extremely assiduous in his addresses to Miss M'Kean, the amiable daughter of poor Pennsylvania's Chief Justice. – What were his motives in commencing this suit we shall leave our readers to divine . . . A question for lawyers. – Is it possible for *a man* to write a libel on *a monkey*, though the monkey be the tool of *a baboon*?[29]

The 'little Don' did, in fact, marry 'the amiable Miss M'Kean'. Since her father was one of Cobbett's most bitter enemies, this produced what seemed a dangerous alliance of father-in-law and son-in-law equally determined, though for different reasons, to bring about Cobbett's downfall.

Cobbett's insouciance, and determination to continue saying what he thought of d'Yrujo, Charles IV and M'Kean, revealed an admirable spirit, but he had, at this time, a second chicken coming home to roost, also carrying a writ for libel in its beak. There had been another Yellow Fever epidemic in Philadelphia that year, and Doctor Benjamin Rush had been advertising his 'Depletion' cure for that disease in all the newspapers. That cure rested on a simple theory he had arrived at in the previous epidemic of 1793. Yellow Fever produces persistent haemorrhages and vomiting. These, Rush concluded, were evidence of excessive pressures being generated inside the patient's system. The remedy, therefore, was simple. The patient had to be severely and repeatedly bled and purged, and kept on a starvation diet, until those pressures subsided. The disease would then become no more dangerous than the common cold.

When Rush now began to insist that his was the only cure for Yellow Fever, Cobbett, with his awkward habit of consulting the statistics, discovered that more of Rush's Yellow Fever patients died than those of any other doctor. He ran a series of articles examining Rush's results and making fun of his theories. He nicknamed Rush 'Doctor Sangrado', after the physician in his favourite novel, Lesage's *Gil Blas*, who used to call in the barber-surgeon to take 'six good porringers of blood' from Gil's sick master every three hours, saying that it was 'a gross error to suppose that blood is necessary to the conservation of life'. Cobbett's gloss on this entirely fictional theory was:

> Every farmer's son is, in some degree, a *practical phlebotomist*. I have cut the throats of scores of geese and little pigs, and I have always perceived that *the moment the blood was out of the body the poor creature died*.[30]

He continued the anti-Rush campaign, in which he was supported by other physicians and by John Fenno of *The Gazette of the United States*, until Rush started proceedings against him for libel. That case, for various reasons, did not come to court for another two years, during which time d'Yrujo's action came to a conclusion.

An action for criminal, as opposed to civil, libel was normally tried in a Federal court. Cobbett, accordingly, had been bound over to appear before Judge Peters at the next sitting of the Federal District Court. This suited neither d'Yrujo nor his future father-in-law, since it was by no means certain that a Federal judge would deal as firmly with Cobbett as M'Kean proposed to do. D'Yrujo, therefore, appealed to have the case removed to the Supreme Court of Philadelphia, alleging that Cobbett, by continuing his libels, had made the matter an urgent one. Permission for the removal was granted, and M'Kean immediately bound Cobbett over to keep the peace. If this meant ceasing to say what he thought of d'Yrujo, Charles IV and M'Kean, Cobbett found it impossible to comply, even though he had given recognisances of two thousand dollars.

On 18 November 1797, Cobbett was arrested on a Sheriff's warrant and brought before M'Kean in chambers. There, to M'Kean's disgust, he refused to answer questions and was only saved from immediate imprisonment by friends who stood bail for him. When he eventually appeared before a Grand Jury, M'Kean, who presided over the case, was clearly intent not only on seeking personal revenge, but also on making such an example of him as would deter all other scandalising newspaper editors. His summing up was extremely hostile, and how the Grand Jury dared to disagree with him is a puzzle. It could have been that M'Kean's reputation for dealing out extremely rough justice, his close connections with d'Yrujo, and his unconcealed dislike for Cobbett affected the outcome, for the Grand Jury divided ten against nine in Cobbett's favour, and a Bill of Ignoramus was returned.

Cobbett had now escaped, by only one vote, from the Scylla of d'Yrujo, but the Charybidis of Rush still loomed over him. This should have made him cautious, but it merely succeeded in making him more venomous. He very soon rattled off a pamphlet, *The Democratic Judge*, which consisted of nothing more than an attack on American justice and an exposure of his persecution by M'Kean, whom he abused immoderately. He had, however, learnt one lesson, which was that he must not risk having to appear before M'Kean when the Rush case came up. Since he was a British subject, he had the right to appeal to the State court to have that case heard by a Federal court. The difficulty was that the appeal had to be heard by the Philadelphian Bench under the presidency of M'Kean himself. The outcome was inevitable. After reserving his decision for three months, M'Kean dismissed the appeal out of hand. Cobbett's account of those preliminary hearings, though full of bitterness, must still rank with Bardell v. Pickwick as one of the most amusing descriptions of the law at work.

Before the actual case was tried, M'Kean had been elected Governor of Pennsylvania, and the post of Chief Justice of that State had become vacant. Judge Shippam was the next in line, but M'Kean delayed making the appointment until the case of Rush v. Cobbett had been heard. This, according to Cobbett, was only done to ensure that Shippam, who was something of an Anglophile, dealt as harshly with Cobbett as M'Kean would have done.

Cobbett now began to appreciate the danger of his situation. He managed to delay the hearing for almost eighteen months by objecting to the jury lists, but his right to object was limited, and it became clear that a packed jury must eventually be nominated. He therefore decided to remove himself, his family, and as much of his property as he could, out of the jurisdiction. He acquired a shop and premises in New York, and, on 18 November 1799, he wrote to Edward Thornton:

> Yesterday all my goods sailed for New York, so that they are no longer, I hope, within the grasp of the sovereign people of Pennsylvania. I have some few things left at my house in 2nd. Street, which will there be sold by auction.[31]

Among those 'few things', however, were the page proofs of his latest and most ambitious publishing venture, *The Collected Works of Peter Porcupine*, which could not easily be removed in their unbound state. He was, moreover, owed considerable sums in uncollected accounts, for the irony of his situation was that, *The Gazette* apart, all his writing and publishing ventures were profitable. His latest pamphlet, *The Cannibal's Progress*, had sold 20,000 copies in its first edition, and would, eventually, sell over 100,000 copies, including a German translation made for the benefit of the Pennsylvanian 'Dutch' who obviously took an interest in the atrocities committed by the French in Swabia. He was also about to bring out an American edition of Anthing's *History of the Campaigns of Count Suvarov*, to which he had added a long account of the recent Italian campaign. All in all, there could not have been a worse time for him to move.

Nevertheless, move he did, and he had great hopes of

establishing himself in New York as the leading bookseller and publisher in that city. He returned to Philadelphia early in December because he had been told his case was about to come up. He was then informed that it would be delayed, returned to New York, only to learn that, on 12 December, his case had been heard *in absentia*. Shippam's summing up was quite as hostile as M'Kean's had been, and he ended with this injunction to the jury:

> Every one must know that offences of this kind have for some time past too much abounded in our city; it seems high time to restrain them – that task is with you, Gentlemen. To suppress so great an evil, it will not only be proper to give compensatory, but exemplary damages; thus stopping the process of this daring crime.

Crime, this time, it was not, since the action was in tort. Nevertheless, the jury, finding for the plaintiff, assessed his damages at $5,000, a larger sum than had ever before been awarded for libel in an American court. Costs, which were assessed at $2,000, also went against Cobbett. Added to this he was now in great danger of forfeiting the $2,000 recognisances he had entered into when M'Kean had bound him over. As his capital was entirely tied up in his business, Cobbett now faced ruin.

His lawyers immediately appealed against both the verdict and the damages awarded, but the appeal failed. Rush was so certain of the outcome that, even before the appeal had been heard, he had all the property Cobbett had left in Philadelphia seized, and it was later sold for pitifully little in a sheriff's auction. The unbound pages of his twelve-volume *Collected Works* went for waste paper.

Cobbett refused, for almost six months, to admit defeat. The British Minister, acting probably through Thornton, seems to have advanced him the five thousand dollars he needed for the payment of damages. This was, it would appear, merely a bridging loan, for the Loyalists of New Brunswick were raising a similar sum by subscription in order to ease the hardships inflicted on one of England's champions by the Yankees.

The Gazette, however, had to be discontinued, though not, Cobbett maintained, because of Rush. In the last Number, published in New York in January 1800, he took farewell of his readers, to whom he explained:

> My Gazette, Gentlemen, instead of being a mine of gold to me, as it has generally been supposed, has never yielded me a farthing of clear profit . . . The other branches of my business

enabled me to support the loss incurred by the publication of my paper . . .

It would have been most unlike him, however, to end with a whimper, and so he went on:

There are some few things, on which I humbly presume, I may be permitted to congratulate myself. Yes, I must congratulate myself on having established a paper, carried it to a circulation unparalleled in extent, and preserved this circulation to the last number, without the aid of any of those base and parasitical arts, by which patronage to American papers is generally obtained and preserved . . . I congratulate myself on never having, in a single instance, been the sycophant of the Sovereign People, and on having persisted . . . in spite of the *savage howlings* of the SANS-CULOTTES and the *soothing serenades* of the FEDER-ALISTS (for I have heard both under my window) – I congratulate myself on having, in spite of all these things, persisted in openly and unequivocally avowing my attachment to my native country and my allegiance to my king . . . Finally, I congratulate myself on having the entire approbation of every man of sense, candour and integrity, the disapprobation of every fool, the hatred of every *malignant* whig, and the curse of every villain.

Chastened, he quite certainly was not, nor was he inclined to spare those who had brought him low. He had already, in *The Democratic Judge*, had such revenge as he could hope for on M'Kean. He now started a monthly journal called *The American Rush-Light*, its punning title revealing all that it was intended to do, which was to continue to attack Rush and all his theories, with digressions that allowed him to vent his feelings about American justice, the freedom of the press in that country, the history, character and behaviour of M'Kean, and every detail of what he considered to have been his persecution. Cobbett's polemical writings can never be unreadable for anyone with a taste for the *genre*. These, however, were unworthy of him, not so much for the style, which was quite adequately vigorous and vituperative, but because he was doing little more than indulge, almost interminably, the belief that he had been persecuted and his almost childish thirst for revenge.

Publishing *The Rush-Light* did him even more damage. His Philadelphia lawyers were reduced to begging him to leave the country as soon as possible, not only because of the matter of the recognisances, but also because his new publications had given cause for new libel actions against him. Rumours reached him that the Government was now seriously considering having him deported. Cobbett had been less than kind to John Adams when, during the campaign for the Presidency, the old scandal about Pinckney's appointment to succeed him as Ambassador to St. James had been revived. He wrote to Thornton: 'But what will they do? – I know not. Yet, what they *can* do I know they *will* . . . To send me *home* would not be *wise*, but, as they do not always fall upon the wisest course, it is not impossible that they may do it.'[32]

He consulted Alexander Hamilton about the new libel actions threatened against him. Hamilton offered, if and when they came up, to defend him in court and take no fee for doing so. He did, however, beg Cobbett to keep that fact secret. He did not, until he had to, want to publicise the fact that he supported a man the President disapproved of and might soon deport.

For some time Cobbett wavered between a prudent desire to retreat to England and an equally strong desire not to let his enemies see that they had put him to flight. 'To flee from a *writ* . . . is what I will never do; for though, generally speaking, to *leave the United States*, at this time, would be little more disgraceful than it was for Lot to run from Sodom . . . yet, with a writ at my heels I will never go . . . to an Englishman, a subject of George the Third, it would be an unsupportable disgrace.'[33]

Prudence, however, prevailed in the end, and he made plans to leave the United States at the beginning of June, for the matter of the recognisances was due to come up in July. His London Bookshop, for that was what he had named it, was, in spite of everything, doing good business, and he now arranged for a friend and business associate, John Morgan, to take it over, lock, stock and barrel. Morgan later announced that he would rather follow Cobbett to London and go into partnership with him there, so the sale was transferred to John Ward Fenno, who paid Cobbett $7,000 down and promised the rest by instalments.

By 25 April, Cobbett was able to write to Thornton:

I shall be able to carry home about 10,000 dollars: which . . . will leave me wherewith to open a shop some where in the West End of the town . . . That I shall have friends and customers I will not doubt; but I do, as I have always done, place my principal dependence upon my exertions, which, thank God, have never yet failed me . . .[34]

He sailed from New York, on board the packet boat *Lady Arabella*, bound for Halifax and Falmouth, on 11 June 1800. So ended his first stay in the United States. He had, however, ensured that some small after-taste of Porcupine should be left behind him. He had written a *Farewell Address to America*, to be published in the newspapers after his departure. It reflected, very fairly, his state of mind at that moment, for it echoes his love and his hatred of America, his defiance of his enemies there and his regret at leaving the friends he had made:

> When people care not two straws for each other, ceremony at parting is mere grimace; and as I have long felt the most perfect indifference with regard to the vast majority of those whom I now address, I shall spare myself the trouble of a ceremonious farewell. Let me not, however, part from you in indiscriminating contempt. If no man ever had so many and such malignant foes, no one ever had more friends, and those more kind, more sincere, more faithful. If I have been unjustly villified by some, others have extolled me beyond my merits; if the savages of the city have scared my children in their cradle, those children have, for their father's sake, been soothed and caressed by the affectionate, the gentle, the generous inhabitants of the country, under whose hospitable roofs I have spent some of the happiest hours of my life. *Thus* and *thus*, Americans, will I ever speak of you. In a very little time I shall be beyond the reach of your friendship and your malice . . . but being out of your power will alter neither my sentiments nor my words. As I have never spoken anything but truth *to* you, so I will never speak anything but truth *of* you . . . Although you have as a nation treated me most ingratefully and unjustly, I scorn to repay you with ingratitude and injustice. To my friends, who are also the real friends of America, I wish that peace and happiness which virtue ought to ensure, but which I greatly fear they will not find; and as to my enemies, I can wish them no severer scourge than that which they are preparing for themselves and their country. With this I depart for my native land, where neither the moth of democracy, nor the rust of federalism doth corrupt, and where thieves do not with impunity break through and steal five thousand dollars at a time.

Yet the last word of all should be left, perhaps, to the man who was the first of Porcupine's victims in America. In a letter to his friend, Rev. T. Lindsay, Dr. Priestley wrote, just a month before Cobbett sailed:

At this time he [Cobbett] is by far the most popular writer in this country, and, indeed, one of the best in many respects. He now publishes a paper called the *Rushlight*, which in sarcastic humour is equal, if not superior, to anything I have ever seen. Till he began to censure the conduct of Mr. Adams, he was cried up by all his friends; though they now pretend to be ashamed of him.[35]

PART TWO

GREAT COBBETT

Man is only truly great when he acts from the passions.
Benjamin Disraeli: *Coningsby*

CHAPTER EIGHT

The Homecoming: 1800–1802

> God! I will pack and take a train
> And get me to England once again!
> Brooke: *The Old Vicarage, Grantchester*

If Cobbett had fought, almost to the water's edge, against being forced to leave the United States, this was not so much because he still wanted to cling to America but rather because he could not bring himself to admit that Rush and M'Kean had defeated him. This apart, he had for some time accepted and even welcomed the fact that his American venture was drawing to its close. His chief concern had been to salvage all that he could in the way of capital and future business connections so that he might make a good start in England.

His patriotism, inflamed by years of struggle with American Anglophobes, had helped him to construct an exile's England that bore little or no resemblance to the country he had so gladly left in 1792. Then he had wanted nothing more than to become an American and a republican. Now, when he sailed from New York on 2 June 1800 on board the packet-boat *Lady Arabella*, bound for Halifax and Falmouth, he had a positively Panglossian conviction that he was returning to the one country where all was for the best in what was otherwise, perhaps, not the best of all possible worlds, being full of French Jacobins and American Democrats.

At Halifax Cobbett was given something close to a hero's welcome. He was fêted by its leading citizens, who were still engaged in raising the $5,000 needed for the Rush case. The need to put their hands in their pockets increased the indignation they felt about his sufferings at the hands of the Yankees. The Governor, Sir John Wentworth, had him to dinner. The Commander-in-Chief, HRH The Duke of Kent, sent for him two or three times in order to consult him, in the most flattering manner, on various military and political matters. He even sent the ducal carriage to convey the Cobbetts to the annual Military Review, at the end of which the Royal Commander-in-Chief rode over to invite the former Sergeant-Major to give his opinion in public on the conduct

181

of the exercise and the turn-out of the troops. Cobbett wrote to Thornton:

> How peculiarly gratifying this is to me I leave you to imagine. When I was last in Halifax I helped, as a soldier on fatigue, to drag the baggage from the wharf to the Barracks.[1]

They had a fair voyage to Falmouth, even though Cobbett, as one would expect, found people to quarrel with and matters to quarrel over. What most concerned him was the behaviour of two Lieutenants of the 26th who had joined the ship at Halifax:

> Mrs Robertson had a maid (I mean a female servant), with whom these fellows made free, almost in the presence of our wives; they smoked Mrs Cobbett almost to death; they talked in the most vulgar strain, and even sung morsels of bawdry in her presence.[2]

The *Lady Arabella* was chased by a French privateer in the approaches to the Channel. The French would certainly have thought that notorious Francophobe, Peter Porcupine, a prize worth having and holding but as things turned out they escaped capture and reached Falmouth at the beginning of July, whereupon 'all the *gentry*, as they stiled themselves, went on shore and left us to get out of the ship as we could. At the custom-house they were exulting in the embarrassment they had thrown in my way . . . when, to their utter astonishment, the Collector asked if it was that Mr Cobbett who had gone under the name of Porcupine, and upon receiving an answer in the affirmative, ordered the Cap[t]. to send on board to tell me, that he would be happy to oblige me in any way he could.'[3]

Mr. Pellew, the Collector, did all that he could to make the Cobbetts' stay in Falmouth a pleasant one, and it was from there that Cobbett wrote to John Wright in London:

> I have taken the liberty to give a draft on you for £20. I brought off only £50 in cash, and as I have remained here and at Halifax much longer than I thought there would be an occasion for, I was apprehensive I should fall short. Mr Pellew of this place, who, by the by, is a brother of the gallant Sir Edward Pellew, offered me whatever I might want, and I gave him the above-mentioned draft. Do not fail to accept it, and I will be careful to lodge the cash with you before the time of payment arrives.[4]

It was the sort of request John Wright would become all too familiar with over the next dozen years, during which period he would act as Cobbett's manager, editor, partner and confidant. Wright, who was then about thirty years old, had left his native Norwich in his youth in order to enter the bookselling business in London. He had done sufficiently well at this to have established himself as a bookseller at No. 169 Piccadilly, premises which were subsequently taken over by Hatchards when Wright was made bankrupt in 1802. It was here that in 1797 Canning, Hammond, Frere and Gifford had founded the *Anti-Jacobin* for which Wright acted as publisher, as he did for its successor, the *Anti-Jacobin Review*. Cobbett and Wright had established a business relationship long before either had met the other: on the basis of their common interests in bookselling and anti-Jacobinism Wright had undertaken to act as Cobbett's London agent.

So it was that Cobbett hired a post-chaise and drove with his family through the summer countryside to London. There he took lodgings, for a short time, in St. James's Street, though he soon moved from there to Wright's premises in Piccadilly, where he stayed until he acquired a house and shop of his own in Pall Mall and publishing premises in the Strand. As soon as Cobbett had arrived in London he was made aware of how important it was in various political and literary circles to have been Peter Porcupine:

> Very soon after my arrival, I was invited to dine at MR WINDHAM'S, who was then Secretary at War, and did dine in the company of Pitt, who was very polite to me . . . I was well aware, that Mr Pitt never admitted newspaper writers to such an honour . . .[5]

In addition to Windham and Pitt, Cobbett met Canning, Frere, Hammond and Hawkesbury (later Lord Liverpool) at that dinner, and it is probably true that Pitt, who had little regard for scribblers, whether they supported him or not, went out of his way to be amiable. Cobbett brought up, courageously one might think, the subjects of Lord Edward Fitzgerald and of his own involvement in the abortive court martial of 1792. No one wished to pursue this last subject, although 'in fact, they all well knew that what I had complained of was true, and that I had been baffled in my attempts to obtain justice, only because I had neither money nor friends.'[6]

From Cobbett's point of view, however, the most immediately important person at that dinner was George Hammond, whom he had met in his Philadelphia days when Hammond was still the first Minister Plenipotentiary to the United States. He was now Under-

Secretary for Foreign Affairs, and the Government expert on American politics. As an old America hand, he already knew a great deal about Cobbett, and as a co-founder, with Canning, of the *Anti-Jacobin*, he knew enough about journalism to realise how valuable Cobbett might be to the Government, if he could be provided with a suitable vehicle and be harnessed to it.

'My first visit,' Cobbett wrote to Thornton, 'was to Mr Hammond, from whom I met such a reception as might be expected from his own goodness joined to Mr Liston's and your recommendation.' In the course of that visit Cobbett unfolded his plans for opening a bookshop and publishing house and for conducting, in conjunction with the London Bookshop in New York, a brisk export trade in books and journals to the United States. 'He approved, but urged, in addition, the undertaking of a daily paper; and we parted with a promise, on my side, that I would neither rent a house nor take any other step, till he saw me again.'[7]

It seems probable that the former publisher and editor of *Porcupine's Gazette* had already formed plans of his own for a London newspaper, for he remembered, thirty years later, that he had 'felt more than ever disposed to use my talents in support of the system as it was then going on; which stood in real need of support, for Bonaparte was making fearful progress; and I resolved in my mind to set up a daily paper'.[8]

He had done no more than look around for premises for this newspaper before he again dined with Hammond, Frere, and various other Tory politicians and publicists. After dinner, 'Mr George Hammond made me an offer of a Government paper. The Government had two, the TRUE BRITON and the SUN, the former a morning and the latter an evening paper. They were *their property*, office, types, lease of houses and all; and the former was offered me *as a gift* . . . This was no trifling offer. The very types, presses &c. were worth a considerable sum . . . My refusal of SIR ROBERT LISTON'S offer* had convinced them, that to offer money was of no use.'

Cobbett refused Hammond's offer of the *True Briton* as firmly as he had earlier refused Liston's offer of money. It was not only that

---

* The Pitt government had wanted to reward Cobbett for his work as Peter Porcupine. Liston, when he was Minister in Philadelphia, had been empowered to offer him 'a great pecuniary award'. When Cobbett refused this, an offer was made to reward or advance any of his relations in England he might care to nominate. Cobbett, that true-blue incorruptible, turned that down also, for the somewhat priggish reason that his relations 'having rendered no public service, had no right to live on the taxes paid, in part, by other labouring people.' Cobbett had every right to object to the 'tax-eaters', but it is less certain that he had any moral right to prevent other Cobbetts joining them.

he valued his independence and guarded it jealously, but also that
there were sound tactical and Tory reasons for not accepting it. As
he put it, shortly afterwards, in a letter to Thornton:

> Most assuredly the offer was great; but there were also great
> objections to my accepting it. You know what the villains of
> America, and their partizans in England would have said; and,
> indeed, you will clearly perceive, as did Mr Hammond and Mr
> Frere . . . that for me to be able to do the government any
> service, I must be able to say that I am totally independent of it,
> in my capacity of proprietor of a newspaper . . . Mr HAM-
> MOND did not appear at all surprised at my answer . . . and
> said . . : 'Well, I must say, that I think you take the *honourable*
> course and I sincerely wish it may also be the profitable one.'[9]

By 1830, however, perhaps because he thought it essential to put
a Radical gloss on his Tory past, Cobbett had persuaded himself
that he had refused Hammond's offer for a somewhat different
reason and in an entirely different manner. The issue was no longer
whether or not he could serve the Government better if he were
seen to be independent of it. It was rather that unless he *were*
independent he would be fatally false to himself. All of this, he
declared, he had explained to Hammond by the simple process of
quoting to him the 'Fable of the Mastiff and the Wolf':

A fat sleek mastiff came across a starved-looking wolf in the
wood. Touched by his condition, he suggested that he should leave
the wood and return with him to the kennels. There he could share
with him all the benefits of domesticated life, and pass the rest of
his days between eating and sleeping. The wolf gladly agreed, but,
as they trotted homewards together, happened to ask the mastiff
why he had a mark around his neck. 'Oh', said the other, 'it is only
the mark of *my collar* that my master ties me up with.' '*Ties you
up!*' exclaimed the wolf. 'Give me my ragged hair, my gaunt belly,
and *my freedom!*' and so saying, he trotted back to the wood.'

'From that moment,' Cobbett added, 'all belonging to the
Government looked on me with great suspicion.'[10] Little of this,
however, rings true. It would be some years after 1800 before the
Government began to suspect Cobbett of being anything more
dangerous than too High a Tory or too zealous a supporter of the
war against the French. Nor can one easily believe that he would
have answered Hammond's businesslike offer of the *True Briton*
with anything as fanciful and literary as a fable, least of all one in
which Cobbett, who was always fair of flesh and ended up, before
he died, as one of the heaviest men in the House of Commons, put

185

himself forward as a gaunt-bellied wolf. None the less it was as true in 1800 as it was in 1830 that Cobbett valued his freedom above almost everything else. It was natural for him, therefore, to resist and resent anything that even suggested that he could be bought, bullied or rewarded into supporting a cause. Hammond's offer of the *True Briton* must have seemed to him to embody some such suggestion, even though, to almost anyone else, it would have seemed no more than a well-earned and entirely proper offer of government patronage. Certainly the leading Tory pamphleteers and journalists he now began to meet – Reeves, Bowles, Ellis, the two Giffords (John and William), Canning and Vansittart among them – would have seen it in that light since they, after the established custom of the time, were all Pitt's placemen, sinecurists or pensioners.

They were also men who knew enough about Peter Porcupine to realise what a valuable addition to their ranks William Cobbett could be. For all of them, as he wrote later, 'looking upon me as a *fellow-labourer*, had . . . *sent their pamphlets to me* at Philadelphia; and . . . had written me laudatory letters.'[11] Though he would, over the next decade, work closely with many of them and form friendships with some of them, he came, in the end, to despise all of them because they had been willing, as he had not, to build their careers on patronage.

Initially, it would seem, he entertained no feelings against patronage as a system even though his spirit of independence made him reject it for himself. Even seventeen years later, when he had for long been a bitter enemy of the 'Pitt system', he recalled how, after turning down Hammond's offer of government patronage because 'I shall be able to give the Government much more efficient support, than if any species of dependence could be traced to me', he remembered that he had added, with most uncharacteristic humility, 'At the same time, I do not wish to cast blame on those who are thus dependent.'[12]

By 1830, however, he was very willing to cast precisely such blame, for he was by now convinced that it was on the basis of patronage that Pitt had built his hated system with, as Cobbett saw it, all its corruption and nepotism, its bought seats and sold votes, its retinue of profiteers and parasites, and its fifth column of scribblers who, however much they may have lacked conviction, were always prepared to be as persuasively Tory as they were paid to be. He now cheerfully described those Tory writers who had received him as a colleague in 1800 as 'a low, talentless, place and pension-hunting crew'.[13] To prove his point he listed all the posts, pensions and sinecures their writings had earned them, ending up

'And NICHOLAS VANSITTART, ESQUIRE, who had written a pamphlet to prove that *war enriched the nation*, I found, O God! a *Commissioner of Scotch Herrings*! Hey dear! as the Lancashire men say: I thought it would have broken my heart'.

There were two of that band, however, who, having been his friends and benefactors in the past, he now felt had been slightly less contemptible:

REEVES and WILLIAM GIFFORD were the only ones of talent. The former . . . politics aside, as good a man as ever lived . . . William Gifford despised Pitt and Canning and the whole crew; but he loved ease and was timid . . . and all his life had to endure a conflict between his pecuniary interest and his conscience . . . Both lived and died bachelors; both left large sums of money; both spent their lives in upholding measures, which, in their hearts, they abhorred, and in eulogising men, whom, in their hearts, they despised; and in spite of their literary labours, the only chance they have of being remembered for even ten years to come, is this notice from a pen that both most anxiously wished to silence many years ago . . . Amongst the first things that REEVES ever said to me, was: 'I tell you what, Cobbett, we have only two ways *here*; we must either *kiss* their . . . . . or *kick* them; and you must take your choice at once.'*[14]

'I', Cobbett proudly remembered thirty years later, 'I resolved to kick.' And so, in due course, he did, although that was far from being the choice he made in 1800. If, in the next few years, he had to kick any Tory arses, as opposed to Whig or Evangelical or Jacobinical ones, it was because he had persuaded himself that there was something fundamentally un-Tory in whatever he was kicking.

If one looks for such staging posts in a man's life, then refusing the offer of the *True Briton* can be thought of as the starting point of Cobbett's political career in Britain. Although it seemed obvious to everyone, including Cobbett, that such a career lay in front of him, he certainly never envisaged having to oppose the Government when he now set about founding his own independent newspaper, which he called *The Porcupine*.†

* There is no other evidence than Cobbett's to prove that these two were Tories only for pay. Their contributions to the *Anti-Jacobin*, and Gifford's editing of the *Quarterly Review* suggest that they were High Tories of the old school, untainted by liberalism, and with just as much conviction to their politics as any ranting, rip-roaring radical.

† Towards the end of its life the paper was renamed *The Porcupine and Anti-Gallican Monitor*.

How Cobbett hoped to finance a newspaper is a mystery. He had written to Thornton, while still in New York, of his hopes of being able to return to England with $10,000 capital. If he did ever command as much, there was little enough of it left over after he had provided for his travel and living expenses and for the cost of setting up a bookshop and publishing house in Pall Mall. Whatever he actually invested in *The Porcupine* was quite insufficient, even though it was probably added to by Gifford, who joined him in the investment and lost some £300 as a consequence. Thirty years later, Cobbett recalled how 'I set up my daily paper; but I knew nothing of such a business, which demanded thousands in place of a few hundreds.'[15]

In those early days, however, he had no reason to believe that a shortage of capital might limit or frustrate any of the ventures he was now putting in hand. He had made handsome profits in the United States out of his bookshop and publishing house, and it was reasonable for him to expect to do even better out of a similar enterprise based in London and serving the American and West Indian markets as well as the British one. His friend John Morgan, who had been something of a sleeping partner in his Philadelphian venture, had come over to London to become an active partner. In the United States John Ward Fenno, who had bought Cobbett's New York bookshop, and Ezra Sergeant, who had been Cobbett's clerk in Philadelphia, were prepared to act as their American agents. Cobbett, in addition to selling and exporting other men's books and newspapers, had plans for publishing or republishing several works of his own. He was convinced that these activities would be so profitable that he could undertake the additional business of publishing a newspaper almost as a sideline.

He wrote to Thornton, early in October, that 'my News-paper Office will be at No. 3 Southampton Street, Strand, and my house and shop at 18 Pall Mall; the former costs £106 a year, and the latter £308 a year. These are vast undertakings; but, says the old proverb; 'a faint heart never won a fair lady'. And lady *fortune* is, of all others, the least apt to yield to a timid lover.'[16] Cobbett, then the staunchest of King and Church Tories, nailed his politics, as it were, to the mast by calling his bookshop The Crown and Mitre, and by hanging up a sign displaying those loyal symbols.

He was still, of course, something of a hero in government circles, and he may have been made even more willing to invest by being introduced to Thomas Raikes, a Governor of the Bank of England and a close friend of Pitt's, who had 'concluded his visit by offering me any service in his power, "and," said he, "when I say *service* I mean money".'

Much of Cobbett's time was spent in preparing the *Works of Peter Porcupine* for publication. His first attempt at publishing this had been frustrated by the sale of the page proofs at sheriff's auction in Philadelphia. He now added a long *Preface* and an even longer *Summary View of the Politics of the United States from the Close of the War to 1794* to Volume One and brought all twelve volumes out in May 1801 in a 1,000-set edition. It was an ambitious undertaking for his first publishing venture in England, but the financial risk was lessened because more than 750 sets had already been subscribed for. No fewer than 350 of these went to the United States. In Britain, subscribers included each of the Royal Princes, the Archbishop of Canterbury, the Bishops of London and Durham, the Foreign Office, Oriel College Oxford, and a cross-section of peers, clerics and academics, together with such leading politicians as Addington, Castlereagh, Cowper, Canning, Grenville, Hawkesbury and Malmesbury. There were also subscribers from Lower Canada, Jamaica and New Brunswick, including, in each of those colonies, the Governor, Chief Justice and leading members of the provincial Assemblies.

The publication, so well subscribed for, must undoubtedly have brought Cobbett in some money, though probably not the $20,000 clear profit he had told Thornton he expected to make. But, even before he had put the *Works* before the public, he had launched his daily newspaper. In September 1800 he had written to Thornton 'No prospectus has yet been published, but the paper is much talked of through this end of the town, and I have no doubt of its success. Much depends upon one's having a tolerable confidence in one's *self*.'

When the first Number of *The Porcupine* came out on 30 October 1800, the first claim it made was to independence. 'The *Porcupine* never was, in America, nor shall it be in England, the *blind instrument* of party.' It would express no other views than those of its publisher, who would 'feel no restraint but that of decency and candour'. No one, however, could have doubted what those views were and, indeed, he summarised them very neatly, two or three years later, in his *Political Register*, the weekly journal that succeeded *The Porcupine*:

I had no intention to range myself in a systematic opposition to His Majesty's Ministers, or to their measures. The first object was to contribute my mite toward the support of the authority of that Sovereign, whom God had commanded me to honour and obey. The uniform intention of my writings was, and is, to counteract the effects of the enemies of monarchy . . . to check

189

the spirit and oppose the progress of levelling innovation, whether proceeding from clubs of Jacobins, companies of traders, synagogues of saints, or boards of government; to cherish an adherence to long-tried principles, an affection for ancient families and ancient establishments.[17]

Memories of the hated Doctor Rush had not, apparently, faded, for he announced that *The Porcupine* would not accept any 'quack advertisements', even though this would mean a loss to him of £500 a year. He had, in later years, to adopt a rather more commercial attitude to newspaper publishing, and advertisements for patent medicines and cures were certainly accepted by the *Political Register*. At that stage in his career, however, he was still sufficiently uncommercial (and priggish) to boast of the fact that, although copies of *The Porcupine* were not to be seen in any of London's innumerable pot-houses, it had 'the superior advantage of being generally read by persons of property, rank and respectability'.[18]

Unfortunately, there did not seem to be enough readers of this sort. Most daily newspapers of that period would have expected to survive on sales of between 2,000 and 3,000 copies but, although sales of *The Porcupine* increased from 700 to 1,500 within five weeks of its launching, they seem to have increased little, or not at all, thereafter. There were various reasons for this failure, but the most important was probably that Cobbett, that inveterate enemy of all petty peculators, had refused to pay Francis Freeling, the Secretary of the Post Office, his customary rake-off.

Once Cobbett had refused to pay Freeling's fee of five guineas a year for the despatch of a newspaper to America or the West Indies, he found that his export trade was hindered, that the charge for delivering American and Continental newspapers to him had been raised, that Post Office advertisements which had been promised him had been withheld, and that it had become difficult to satisfy out-of-town orders for *The Porcupine* because the Clerks of the Roads, the Post Office officials in charge of such mail, held up deliveries. By June 1801 Cobbett had written to the Postmaster General, Lord Auckland, complaining of this treatment, claiming 'I can have little doubt as to the source of this cowardly hostility', and ending 'while these things are, my Lord, we may talk about the *liberty of the press*, we may say we possess it, we may boast of it as the birthright of Englishmen; but it will exist nowhere, except in the imaginations of those who are unacquainted with the facts, which I have here had the honour of submitting to your Lordship'.[19]

In later years Cobbett was more inclined to attribute the failure of *The Porcupine* to his own probity rather than to Freeling. 'I could not *sell paragraphs*. I could not throw out hints against a man's or woman's reputation in order to bring the party forward to pay me for my silence.'[20] However, by the end of November 1801, barely a twelvemonth after he had so hopefully launched it, Cobbett had to acknowledge that he could no longer afford to keep *The Porcupine*. He sold it, therefore, to John Gifford, one of the founders of the *Anti-Jacobin Review*, and wrote, in later years, that he had lost in all some £450 he could ill afford over the venture. Gifford must also have found it difficult to make *The Porcupine* profitable for, only two months later, he allowed it to disappear through merger with Heriot's *True Briton* which, being a government newspaper, did not have to attract a large readership in order to survive.

Cobbett may well have regretted his boast that *The Porcupine* would never be found in the London pot-houses. If it had been taken by only a proportion of them, it might have survived, although the then state of public opinion admittedly made it improbable that pot-house readers would approve of *The Porcupine*. It was not, in this case, a question of its being a 'quality' as opposed to a 'popular' newspaper: the reading public was still too small for that distinction to have been reached. It was rather that its opinions were bound, at that particular period, to be unpopular with almost everyone. By 1801 any newspaper that argued for the continuation of the war with France would be bought and read only by the most obstinate of anti-Jacobin Crusaders.

Certainly, urging a continuation of the war could not have made Cobbett popular with the new administration under Addington which had been formed for the specific purpose of putting an end to the fighting. For Pitt had resigned in the January of that year, partly because of the King's refusal to allow Catholic Emancipation to go forward, but partly also, one suspects, because he was unwilling to be associated with the only sort of peace the French were likely to agree to after their victories at Marengo and Hohenlinden had made them the masters of Europe and had left the largest part of Pitt's war policy in ruins.

Agreeing to the terms Napoleon would now exact was a task better left to an Addington than a Pitt. Addington was, after all, a man distinguished only by his lack of distinction, and one who owed his position in politics almost entirely to the fact that his father had been the Pitt family's doctor, a circumstance that may have encouraged another British Prime Minister to write of him, a century later, that he carried into politics 'the indefinable air of a village apothecary inspecting the tongue of the State'.[21] In 1801, however, when Addington started on the negotiations that would end, in March of the following year, in the Peace of Amiens he was supported by almost everyone in politics, Whig or Tory and by the majority of a public that had, after eight years of military failures, grown war-weary enough to be eager for peace at almost any price.

Nevertheless, *The Porcupine* was not the only paper to oppose the Government's negotiations for a peace. When, at the beginning of October 1801, a preliminary agreement for one was reached and the London mob, hearing of it, danced in the streets, Cobbett wrote to Windham:

The newspapers (which must never be forgotten when we are speaking of public opinion) are ranged thus: the *True Briton* and the *Sun*, the *Herald* and the *Times* justify the Peace through thick and thin; and the latter (the *Times*) which has been enlisted by the Foreign Office, extols my Lord Hawkesbury at the expense of Mr Pitt! This, all things considered, is humorous enough. These four papers, which are not the best possible supports that a cause can have, are opposed by the *Morning Chronicle*, the *Morning Post*, the *Courier*, the *Star*, the *St James's Chronicle* and *The Porcupine*.[22]

Cobbett had not yet realised that Pitt, although he stayed away from the House, fully supported Addington's efforts to obtain a peace. Robert Banks Jenkinson, Lord Hawkesbury, the future Earl of Liverpool and Prime Minister, was then Addington's Foreign Secretary, and the man Cobbett would refer to in future years with loathing as 'the stern path of duty man'.

Nothing written in opposition to the Peace attracted more attention than the series of articles Cobbett himself published from day to day in *The Porcupine* in the form of *Letters to Lord Hawkesbury*. These caused a sufficient stir to lead Cobbett and Morgan to engage in their second book publishing venture for, in November 1801, they were republished in book form under the title of *Facts and Observations Relative to the Peace with Bonaparte*. Cobbett found it impossible to leave the argument there, but, after the sale of *The Porcupine*, he no longer had a newspaper in which to publish his next series of 'Letters' on the subject, which were addressed, this time, to Addington. They were published, therefore, in January 1802, in a book called *Letters to the Right Honourable Henry Addington on the Fatal Effects of the Peace with Bonaparte*. The two books sold sufficiently well for another to be brought out the same month in which the two series of 'Letters' appeared in a single volume containing 259 pages of text and 96 pages of Appendices. Cobbett's views on the Peace, therefore, unpopular though they were, could not be entirely ignored in either London or Paris.

The 'Letter' form was particularly suited to Cobbett's style. He had already used it effectively in America. The 'Letters' to Hawkesbury and Addington, however, were much more carefully and reasonably argued, and were less enlivened by his scurrilous wit. This was, quite clearly, an occasion for reasoning rather than fighting with men he agreed with politically, even though they had now been led astray by their desire for peace and their less than complete, and less than Cobbettian understanding of foreign affairs and the French character.

Nevertheless those not used to the robust methods of arguing he had developed in America could be forgiven for believing that he had suddenly engaged in a sustained and damaging attack on a government which had every reason to expect his support, and on a foreign policy almost everyone in the country supported whether they otherwise approved of the Government or not. It was suggested by some that he was actuated by spite, that he had expected to be rewarded for his services in America and had, instead, been slighted by Pitt and ignored by Addington. It was an unworthy suggestion, especially as he had very clearly outlined his position in the first paragraph of his first 'Letter' to Addington. 'The treaty,' he wrote, 'appears to me to have laid the foundations of the ruin of the *colonies*, the *commerce*, the *manufactures*, and the *constitution*, of the kingdom. This being sincerely my opinion, it is my duty to endeavour to convince others of its justness, and thereby to produce such a change of measures, as may yet save us from the destruction with which we are threatened.'[23]

Yet, in spite of this clear statement of his position, he still felt it necessary, in one of his 'Letters' to Hawkesbury, to refer to the allegations that he was motivated by chagrin and writing out of spite:

It has been said that I acted from pique against Mr ADDINGTON, Mr PITT, or your Lordship, from one or all of whom I had received *some slight*. But, my Lord, you know that, as far as relates to yourself, this imputation is totally groundless; and I declare to you that it is equally so with respect to Mr ADDINGTON and Mr PITT, the former of whom stands first, after the Princes, on the list of the subscribers to my works*, and the latter has shown me marks of commendation, of which many a better

* The reference is to his recently published *Collected Works of Peter Porcupine*.

and greater man than myself would have been proud . . . In short, my Lord, till this unfortunate peace was made public, I entertained no other sentiment towards your Lordship, Mr ADDINGTON, or Mr PITT, than that of respect.*[24]

Cobbett, of course, always found that disrespect came more easily to him than its opposite: it is part of the polemicist's prerogative. It is probable, therefore, that many of those who had previously lionised him now began to think of him as an inconveniently awkward critic, though his loyalty to King, Country and the Tory Cause was not, as yet, in dispute. Lord Auckland, a member of the Government, and himself a pamphleteer, had already noted in his Journal, 'The Porcupine will, having charged his quills with a sufficient quantity of venom, discharge them in a series of letters to Lord Hawkesbury.'[25] Nor, at this stage, were there lacking people who warned him that, in this matter, he would stand alone. Yet there were others ready to admire the style of his attack upon the Government, and even some who supported it.

The style of that attack attracted the attention of Johannes von Müller, the Swiss historian, who was then in London. He wrote to his brother that Cobbett's 'Letters' to Hawkesbury and Addington had to be compared, for their eloquence and impact, with the Philippics of Demosthenes. But Cobbett was no more a Demosthenes than Addington was Philip of Macedon. There were others, however, more important than Müller, who supported Cobbett for the substance rather than the style of his attacks on the Government's foreign policy. Prominent among them was William Windham who, along with Grenville, now led the New Opposition and saw in Cobbett the man who could best maintain in public and in print the opposition he himself was leading in Parliament to Addington's peace policy in general and the terms attaching to it in particular.

Cobbett, indeed, had plunged into politics far more quickly and at a much higher level in England than Peter Porcupine had in Philadelphia. There is always some danger of allowing those politics, which are now no more than memories of complicated and once-important cabals and conspiracies and struggles for power, to

* Cobbett had been told by Heriot of the *True Briton* (whom he shortly afterwards had reason to thrash) that Pitt had said that 'Cobbett, given enough rope, would certainly hang himself'. Cobbett wrote of this 'I was deeply wounded, but after inquiry, I have every reason to believe it to have been a base and wicked misrepresentation, fabricated by a servile wretch, who had the impudence to regard me as his competitor for the favour of the Ministry.' In view of Cobbett's subsequent campaigns against Pitt and the 'Pitt system', this trivial example of tale-bearing and back-biting is not without significance.

obliterate the man. Cobbett's private life would never again be divorced from British politics, but a private life he certainly had, although little is known about it in those early years when he was not, as yet, a national figure.

We do know that he revisited Farnham soon after his return to England and immediately after the dinner party at which he had met Pitt. There is a long and justly famous passage in his *A Year's Residence in the United States* (published in 1818), in which he describes that visit and the emotions he felt at the time and, doubtless, embellished in later years:

> When I returned to England in 1800, after an absence from the country parts of it of sixteen years, the trees, the hedges, even the parks and the woods, seemed so *small*! . . . When, in about a month after my arrival in London, I went to *Farnham*, the place of my birth, what was my surprise! . . . My heart fluttered with impatience, mixed with a sort of fear, to see all the scenes of my childhood; for I had learnt before the death of my father and mother. There is a hill, not far from the town, called *Crooksbury Hill* . . . [which] was a famous object in the neighbourhood. It served as the superlative degree of height. 'As high as Crooksbury Hill' meant, with us, the utmost degree of height. Therefore, the first object that my eyes sought was this hill. *I could not believe my eyes!* . . . I, for a moment, thought the famous hill removed, and a little heap put in its stead; for I had seen in New Brunswick a single rock . . . ten times as big, and four or five times as high! The post-boy, going down hill, and not a bad road, whisked me, in a few minutes, to the Bush Inn, from the garden of which I could see the prodigious *sand-hill* where I had begun my gardening works. What a *nothing*! But now came rushing into my mind, all at once, my pretty little garden, my little blue smock-frock, my little nailed shoes, my pretty pigeons that I used to feed out of my hands, the last kind words and tears of my gentle and tender-hearted and affectionate mother! I hastened back into the room. If I had looked a moment longer I should have dropped . . .[26]

Being Cobbett, however, and a Cobbett, moreover, with eighteen more years of political embroilments behind him than he could have expected to accumulate when he revisited Crooksbury Hill, he had a political moral to draw from this re-editing of his emotions and memories:

> When I came to reflect, *what a change*! What scenes I had gone through! How altered my state! I had dined the day before at the

Secretary of State's, in company with *Mr Pitt*, and had been waited upon by men in gaudy liveries! I had had nobody to assist me in the world. No teachers of any sort. Nobody to shelter me from the consequences of bad, and no one to counsel me to good, behaviour. I felt proud. The distinctions of rank, birth and wealth, all became nothing in my eyes; and from that moment (less than a month after my arrival in England) I resolved never to bend before them.[27]

By the time he wrote those lines his politics had put him into the law courts on more than one occasion, had confined him in Newgate for two years and driven him out of England for a similar period and would, very shortly, drive him into bankruptcy. But even in 1801, when he had been back in England for little more than a year, his politics were already beginning to have some effect on his domestic and business life quite apart from contributing to the early failure of *The Porcupine*.

News that an agreement had been reached on the Preliminaries to the Peace began to reach London early in October, and the city and its citizens prepared to go *en fête*. Cobbett, of course, saw no reason for rejoicing. On 7 October he wrote to Windham about the 'delirium of the multitude' which was waiting for ratification of the Preliminaries to be confirmed. 'A grand illumination is preparing at all the Public Offices. Two thousand lamps, I am told, are prepared for the War Office and the Horse Guards. The swinish multitude, having nothing better to do, have, all this day long, been assembled, to the amount of three or four thousands, in St. James's Park, waiting for the arrival of the ratification and for the consequent firing of guns.'[28]

News of the ratification came on 10 October, and Otto, the French Envoy, later the Comte de Mosloy, and Lauriston, later a Marquis and a Marshal of France but then Napoleon's ADC, were cheered to the echo by the London mob who, taking the horses out of their carriage, pulled them in triumph through the streets to Whitehall. The man-drawn procession passed in front of Cobbett's house, and that same day he wrote, once more, to Windham:

I look forward to a revolution with as great certainty as I do to Christmas or New Year's Day. This is the first time an English mob ever became the cattle of a *Frenchman*; and they are willing to be such now, not because they love the Frenchman as such, but because he is one of those who have killed kings and queens and noblemen and have destroyed rank and property. This indication of the temper and sentiments of the lower orders is a most awful consideration.[29]

That night all the houses and shops, as well as the Government offices in that part of London were illuminated in honour of the Peace. The Government had requested that this should be done. Cobbett, of course, ignored the request. He placed no candles in his Pall Mall windows, even though, as he wrote in his letter of protest to Lord Pelham, the Home Secretary, the following morning, 'I had reason to expect that . . . my dwelling house here as well as my printing office in Southampton Street would be attacked.'[30] Although Cobbett had already asked at Bow Street for protection, none was afforded him. 'About eight o'clock in the evening my dwelling house was attacked by an innumerable mob, all my windows were broken, and when this was done . . . the villains were preparing to break into my shop . . . and had actually made one of the shutters give way. Fearing that the cannibals might murder myself and my children, I now ordered my windows to be lighted; but even this . . . did not satisfy this unlawful and ferocious rabble, who ever and anon howled out that I was the publisher of *The Porcupine*, and the attack continued at intervals till past one o'clock this morning. During the whole of this time not a constable nor peace officer of any description made his appearance, nor was the smallest interruption given to the proceedings of this ignorant and brutal mob.'[31]

A similar attack was made on Cobbett's printing house in Southampton Street, where his clerk was put in fear of his life and sufficient damage was done to stop the newspaper printing for the next two days. It is at least probable that, in addition to his financial problems, these intimations of his unpopularity as a newspaper publisher, more violently expressed than anything that had happened to him at the hands of the Philadelphian mob, finally forced him to the conclusion that *The Porcupine* had to be sold.

Selling *The Porcupine*, however did not save Cobbett from an even worse display of mob violence when, on 27 March 1802, the Peace of Amiens was finally signed and London rejoiced even more wholeheartedly. He was still determined not to illuminate his Pall Mall premises. 'In the same degree that I perceived the illumination . . . was to be compulsory, I became resolved not to submit to the degradation.'[32] His position this time, however, was a more difficult one:

On the evening before the Proclamation, I saw my wife actually confined in that situation, which, above all others, requires comfort and tranquillity . . . I began to grow apprehensive of the consequences of resistance. To hazard the life of her, who had been my companion and support through all the storms I had

197

endured; to make this sacrifice was no longer to be thought of, and I had made up my mind to yield, when she bravely determined to be removed to the house of a friend, rather than her husband should submit to the mandates of a base and hireling mob.*[33]

Pelham, on this occasion, had listened to Cobbett's request for protection. The Bow Street Runners and, eventually, a detachment of Horse Guards were sent to protect him from the mob. His house, none the less, was under siege for an hour and a half, and was more seriously damaged than it had been the previous October. This time Windham, a man of considerable daring and courage despite what appeared to be a weak constitution, came to Cobbett's aid and, setting about the mob with his cane, assisted in the arrest of six of the ringleaders. Three of these were subsequently committed for trial. Cobbett, always suspecting conspiracy, pointed out, subsequently, that each of them was connected, in some way or another, with the General Post Office, and so, by implication, with Freeling.

The jury found the three guilty on lesser charges, for Cobbett had agreed that the most serious charge which, on conviction, would have led to their death sentences should be dropped. In passing their verdict, the jury recommended the accused, all of them young men, to the mercy of the court. When Cobbett was asked if he would join in the jury's recommendation he replied, 'Certainly not. I came here to ask for *justice*, and not for *mercy*.' It was a revealing remark. His passion for what he conceived to be justice could never be doubted. He was capable, in certain, strictly-defined instances, of great depths of compassion. He would always, whether he could afford it or not, dispense alms to those he thought of as the deserving poor. But charity in the Christian, or even the philanthropic sense he would always reject. Only those who deserved it would ever be worthy of his support, and no one who had injured him would ever receive his forgiveness. The court was more charitable than he was. It fined the three youths and bound them over for two years. But even then Cobbett had the last word. 'My rescinding the capital charge,' he wrote, 'was an act of clemency, and as such it was felt, and *publicly acknowledged*, by Mr Mackintosh, the counsel for the prisoners.'[34]

The failure of *The Porcupine* Cobbett attributed to the Government's abandonment of the policies the newspaper had been founded to support, most notably the continuation and more

---

* The child, produced four days later, was still-born.

vigorous prosecution of the war against the French. He felt bewildered by what he thought of as a betrayal, not only of the country but, perhaps more importantly, of himself. As many do, under such circumstances, he attributed to those he thought of as traitors to the cause a greater hostility to himself than was reasonable. They, through Freeling and the Post Office, had made it impossible for *The Porcupine* to continue. They had encouraged such hacks as Heriot to attack him in the government-owned press. They had been behind that mob violence and the attacks on his premises. No one in politics, apart from Windham and a few others in the 'New Opposition' now agreed with the policies he had risked so much to support in America and had so lately been praised for in England. As early as the end of November, 1801, he had revealed how he felt about this in a letter to Windham who had, by now, assumed the combined roles of father figure, patron and political guide:

> The *light* is now extinguished completely. One half of the papers are devoted to France, and the other half to the Ministry . . . The French prints will extol the virtues of Bonaparte, and the Ministerial prints will nod assent. Well, I wash my hands of the consequences. I have done all I could do without reducing my family to beggary. The great base men of this country have drenched me with ingratitude, and I see no law, either moral or divine, that forbids me 'to mock when their fear cometh', as it certainly will come at no very distant period.[35]

One cannot help feeling that Cobbett, for all his feelings of betrayal, felt some relief at being able to revert to that position in politics he had occupied for so long in America and would, for the most part, occupy for the rest of his life in England. He was, by instinct, a man of the Opposition, even if it were an Opposition of no more than one. From there he could always maintain and proclaim his prized independence and integrity, and from there it was always easier to exercise his talent for 'mockery'.

At this particular moment his hurt feelings combined with his financial necessities to convince him that a gesture was necessary. His bookselling, publishing and exporting business had not, as he had thought it would, made him financially independent. John Morgan, who had become his partner at the Crown and Mitre, must already have decided to return to America, which he did in the following year. It was no longer sensible, and had perhaps become impossible for Cobbett to continue, single-handed, with a venture that had been founded with such high Tory fervour that

now seemed misplaced. He could not, as he explained to Windham, continue with his grand and patriotic design:

> My resolution is taken, I will take the Crown and Mitre from the
> house, and will efface the names of the princes; because the
> princes and the bishops approve of the infamous Peace. To do
> this without insulting the Church and the Throne, I must leave
> my house . . . My partner and I agreed to keep this house merely
> as a rallying-point for the loyalty and religion of the press; but as
> such it is now useless, and we have nothing to consult but our
> interests. I would scorn to lend my hand to support a govern-
> ment administered by the Hawkesburys, the Addingtons and the
> Bragges. The very circumstance of such men ruling with uninter-
> rupted sway is quite sufficient to dissuade every subject from all
> those duties that flow from a love of his king and country. You,
> Sir, are the only person in the nation to whom I owe an account
> of my public conduct, and, therefore, I shall tell to nobody else
> what I have now taken the liberty to trouble you with.[36]

No more than eighteen months had passed since his homecom-
ing yet already almost all of his plans and ventures had foundered.
Cobbett's bitterness must have increased as the passing months
confirmed all that he had said about the humiliating, dangerous
and spurious nature of the Peace that the Government had signed
and the nation had applauded. It would not, in fact, be long before
most Englishmen had come round to his way of thinking, though
by then, of course, he was already beginning to think contrariwise.

Meanwhile, however, he still had his way to make in the world
and by the beginning of 1802 he had brought out the first Number
of his *Political Register*.

CHAPTER NINE

Cobbett of the Register

> You cannot hope
> To bribe or twist
> Thank God!
> The British journalist.
> But seeing what
> That man will do
> Unbribed, there's no occasion to.
> Humbert Wolfe: *Punch*

We mostly think of Cobbett, these days, as the philosophical and, on the whole, kindly author of *Rural Rides* or *Cottage Economy*. His contemporaries, however, thought of him, for better or worse, as Cobbett of the *Register*. It was that most famous and infamous of all political weeklies which eventually led Hazlitt to describe him, in his essay on 'Mr Cobbett',[1] as 'a kind of *fourth estate* in the politics of this country'.*

If the *Register* transformed Cobbett into an apparently per- manent and increasingly prominent feature of the British political scene, it also changed him in a more personal manner. It quickened the gradual process of his politicisation and changed him from a free-ranging polemicist into a man almost totally immersed in domestic and Party politics.

Cobbett had a habit of starting his articles, his books and his chapters with what he called a 'motto' and we would call an epigraph, meaning no more in both cases than 'the text to the sermon'. Cobbett never actually used it, but if one had to select a 'motto' suitable for thirty-five years of the *Register*, 'Solvitur Scribendo' ('we solve it by writing about it') might be appropriate. For Cobbett was, pre-eminently, a political journalist who, week by week and month by month, wrote himself into his various and varying political beliefs. It was the *Register* that provided him with the space he needed for that continuing exercise.

---

* The Press, until it lost its monopoly in the moulding of public opinion, was frequently referred to as 'the fourth estate'. Nevertheless that phrase was first coined by Hazlitt in an attempt to describe the particular phenomenon that was Cobbett of the *Register*.

The *Political Register* was launched in January 1802. Before discussing what Cobbett made of that journal and what that journal made of him, it is worth reconsidering what his political attitudes were at that time and how he had arrived at them. For if we are all, as Aristotle said, 'political animals', most of us are only moderately so, whereas it would be difficult to name another English writer of distinction who developed into such an immoderately political animal as Cobbett had become within a few years of launching his *Register*. From then on he would find it increasingly difficult to discuss even a potato in non-political terms.

Cobbett had come to his politics slowly, as, indeed, most of us do. He was thirty-two before he created Peter Porcupine and thirty-nine before he published the first number of the *Register*. When he first settled in Philadelphia he was, on his own admission, as uninterested in the theory and the business of politics as any intelligent and opinionated man could be.

His politics came to him in America by way of his patriotism, the propaganda and intrigues of French agents, and the Anglophobia of the Jeffersonians. However, since that patriotism made it impossible for him to become an American subject or think like an American, his politics remained the politics of a foreigner and an exile. That is to say he was concerned with the domestic and Party politics of the Republic only to the extent that they had, or might have, any significant effect on Britain's foreign policy and her conduct of the war. In those matters he made himself an expert, and was probably more conscious of the growing importance in global politics of Anglo-American relations than anyone in London. A year after he had returned to England, he included in his *Letters to Addington*, the following passage protesting against the insularity, ignorance and arrogance of the British in their dealings with the United States:

> The sage who owns the *True Briton*, speaks of it as a country 'at *so great a distance* as to be little interesting to Englishmen' . . . our financiers and politicians affect to regard that nation as being independent from us in *form* only, as a mere colony, where the foolish people hew the woods and till the land to no other end than that of earning money to pay for British manufactures . . . Men of all parties imitate the servants of the King, who have long seem ashamed or afraid to turn their eyes to America; but be you well assured, Sir, that if fortune does not speedily favour us in France, America, which we obstinately persist in treating with contempt, will, with the co-operation of a power that knows how

to manage her better, give us the most mortal of those blows under which you have doomed us to sink.[2]

Cobbett was what might be described as an early Atlanticist. That is, he was one of the few Englishmen of his time to insist on the importance to both countries of good Anglo-American relations. Whether he was arguing with the Americans, who were, on the whole, hostile to the idea, or with the British, who were uninterested in it, this was one argument he never abandoned. It was the argument that, more than any other, involved him first in American and subsequently in British politics.

To be an Englishman in the United States so shortly after the War of Independence, and to write in such a partisan manner about Anglo-American relations necessarily involved Cobbett in as many Party battles and as much political controversy as any other journalist, congressman or cracker-barrel politician of the time. Yet he could not, whilst he was in America, be properly described as a Party man. If he gave some support to the Federalists, it was not because he was particularly attracted to their politics. They were, after all, republicans, and his French experience had inoculated him against any further attacks of republicanism. They were, however, republicans with a difference. That is to say they were not as firmly committed as the Jeffersonians and the American Jacobins were to anti-monarchical and anti-British policies. They could more easily be converted to Atlanticism than the others, and he supported them in much the same way as a zealous missionary supports those most likely to be proselytized. But it would be true to say that his only Party at that time was England, and his only politics the defence and advancement of her interests abroad. He started, in short, from the premise that patriotism *was* enough.

Since he was never given to understatement or self-doubt, his patriotism at that time was unquestioning, absolute, and so enthusiastically expressed that we, in these more moderately patriotic days, read him on that particular subject with some embarrassment. He wrote for England in much the same way as Chauvin, some years later, would speak for France. As for the Americans, who were by no means prissy about their patriotism, Cobbett would still have thought that that Yankee demi-Nelson, Stephen Decatur, had been somewhat half-hearted in his approach to the matter. 'Our country! In her intercourse with foreign nations may she be always right; but our country right or wrong' has become a useful tag for later generations to use or laugh at. Cobbett, so long as he was in the patriot mood, found it impossible to consider that England could ever be in the wrong.

That being so, his patriotism led him into more than a partial immersion in American politics, an early Atlanticism and a joyful crusade against the Jacobins. It also led him into British party politics and turned him into what may best be described as an Unpremeditated Tory. He started to write in the dawn of that period in which we still live; one in which rival lay ideologies have produced far more doctrinal and actual warfare than the clash of religions. He soon found, however, that it was not all a question of attack. It was not enough to demonstrate, as he did so dashingly, that the New Orders in Europe and America were alternatively or conjointly corrupt, hypocritical, inefficient, tyrannical, blood-thirsty and aggressive. Those he attacked were conducting similar attacks on the established order of things in Britain. They, for their part, argued that there could be neither justice nor freedom nor fraternity in that country until it, also, became part of the New Order with a Republic, a National Assembly and guillotines set up in St. James's Park. Since their own truths were, by definition, self-evident, it was by no means difficult to find faults in the traditional truths of the British.

It was almost impossible for a man of Cobbett's temperament to leave even one such attack unanswered. Consequently, in addition to scourging the Jacobins and Republicans wherever he could discover them, he soon found himself defending what in the end amounted to every least jot and smallest tittle of the existing British Establishment. The British monarchy, Church, aristocracy, legal system and style of politics had to be proven superior, not only to what had replaced them in the new Republics, but also to anything else that had been devised by the wit of man. There would never again be a time in his long political career when he would find so little to criticise in England and so much to criticise everywhere else.

All of this, as soon as it was heard of in Britain, had the effect of dragging him, backwards as it were, into the cockpit of British party politics. There he was immediately recognised, and acclaimed by those who agreed with him, as one of the best of the High Tory fighting cocks. He was in much the same case as M. Jourdain, in Molière's *Le Bourgeois Gentilhomme*, who had spent forty years of his life speaking prose without knowing it. He had spent eight years in the United States as a patriot without realising that this proved him a Tory.

Toryism, however, suited his temperament, his instincts and his prejudices better than any of the other political creeds he later indulged in. Indeed, he was more than half a Tory and less than half a Radical for the whole of his life. He had, perhaps, too much passion and too little scepticism ever to be wholly a Tory, just as he had too much reverence for the past and too little faith in the future ever to be wholly a Radical. But, whether he was nominally Tory or Radical, he would always have the countryman's and farmer's instinct for doing things in the traditional way, and more than their customary suspicion of everything that was new-fangled, foreign or threatening of change. If these qualities did not, by themselves, qualify him as a dyed-in-the-wool reactionary, they were dominant enough to ensure that he could never properly be classified as a Progressive.

Although Cobbett's emergence as a Tory may have been unpre-meditated, there was nothing in his behaviour in 1802 when he started the *Register* to suggest that he objected to such a label. Indeed, had he been more of a politician and less of a Tory, *The Porcupine* might not have failed. The attacks on his Pall Mall premises, combined with his growing unpopularity in government circles, would have persuaded a less opinionated and more supple man that his particular form of Toryism had become dangerously unpopular with almost everyone in England, including the major-ity of those who thought of themselves as Tories.

Addington's coalition was predominantly a Tory one in spite of including so many of the Whigs who had deserted Fox and the Old Opposition in order to pursue the anti-Jacobin crusade. Now, however, there had been a change of heart, and the Government was wholly committed to a policy of negotiating a peace with the French, and in this it was supported by most of the politicians outside government as well as by public opinion. Cobbett, how-ever, still held to the views that had first established him as a Tory whilst he was in America. As a staunch monarchist he was as dogmatically anti-Republican as he was anti-Jacobin. As a hyper-patriot he saw no reason for ending the war until the French had been conquered. As a self-declared expert on foreign affairs he was obsessed by the need to return the French to their traditional frontiers and to destroy their threat to the British position over-seas, especially in the Americas.

Cobbett, in so far as his politics were concerned, had one quality most politicians would pray to be spared. He was generally too far in front of events or too far behind them to be able to preach to the converted. At this stage he had, in a comparatively short space of time, fallen too far behind. War fever and anti-Jacobinism had both gone out of fashion, and that for at least two reasons. The people were increasingly weary of a war that had brought them unprecedented levels of taxation, growing inflation and a debased currency, an enormous increase in the National Debt, a diminution of their liberties marked by the suspension of Habeas Corpus and the passage of the Treasonable Practices and the Seditious Meetings Acts, the growing threat of invasion, insurrection in Ireland, political unrest in Scotland and in many of the factory towns in England, mutinies in the Navy and, except for a precariously maintained mastery of the seas, an almost complete lack of victories. It even seemed to many of them that Nature herself had turned Frenchwoman, for there had not been one good harvest in England since 1793, and food hunger was growing.

As for the once popular anti-Jacobin pack, it had, as all but a few of its members now acknowledged, run out of scent. Napoleon had, as it were, shot their fox. Within weeks of becoming First Consul he had, like so many dictators, set about reducing the power of those who had put him into power. These things being so, it seemed to most British politicians that there was no longer any ideological necessity for continuing the war and every practical reason for bringing it to a conclusion. But if peace were to be negotiated, its proponents argued, it had to be negotiated now, before it became a peace imposed by an ultimate victor on the ultimately vanquished.

Pitt, who had been reluctant to go to war in 1793, now tacitly supported Addington's attempts to end it. All those of his supporters who had remained in government, and most of those who had resigned with him, followed him in this. Only a few refused either to serve with Addington or to acquiesce with Pitt, but these included Grenville, Spencer, Windham, and, for a time, Canning, and they now came together to form the New Opposition. They constituted, at that time, a mere handful of Abdullamites, bitterly opposed to Addington, unwilling, any longer, to support Pitt, and extremely critical of the Government's policy of seeking a peace with the French at that particular stage of the war and according to the terms then under discussion. This New Opposition found in Cobbett a most useful ally. By helping him start his *Political Register* they established, for so long as they remained in Opposition, an organ that was increasingly successful in expressing their views and an editor who outstripped many of them in the fervour with which he advanced them. Cobbett, for his part, found himself once more in the position he had occupied in Philadelphia. He had made himself the spokesman outside Parliament for a small, and initially unpopular minority, for those who belonged to what Napoleon and many in Britain contemptuously referred to as the 'war party'.

The few months that elapsed between the sale of *The Porcupine* and the launching of the *Register* are puzzling ones for any biographer. This is almost entirely because Cobbett, in later years, provided explanations of his financial and business position at that time which differed from what he told Windham when he was actually engaged in raising the money with which to start the *Register*.

There is some suggestion that Windham had found the *Letters to Lord Hawkesbury*, published in *The Porcupine*, so strongly in accordance with his own views on the peace negotiations then in progress that he had asked Cobbett not to sell the paper and had offered him financial assistance in continuing it. That offer came too late. Describing his situation in 1801 many years later, Cobbett wrote, 'My daily paper was soon gone, and with it *more* than all that I possessed in the money way.'*[3]

Cobbett's was too valuable a voice, in Windham's view, to be silenced for lack of capital. Windham, aided by Dr. Laurence or Lawrence, as Cobbett frequently spelt it, the Regius Professor of Civil Law at Oxford and Member of Parliament for Peterborough, proposed to Cobbett the starting of a weekly political journal. This would be a less expensive undertaking than a daily newspaper and Windham offered to raise the necessary capital – some £600 – by private subscription. As Cobbett phrased it some thirty years later, 'If I had not been aided by a private subscription, set on foot by MR WYNDHAM and the good DR LAWRENCE, this famous Register never could have been begun.'[4]

All of this suggests that Cobbett was, at that point, suffering from something more than a mere lack of liquid capital. Nevertheless, discussing the project in a letter to Windham, he was at some pains to prove otherwise:

> I sunk about £750 in the *Porcupine* . . . The remainder of my capital was joined to that of my partner, Mr Morgan, who, soon after our partnership was formed, returned to the United States of America, with many of the towns of which we carry on a sort of mercantile trade of considerable magnitude, and not

---

* Professor Stephen Koss, in the first volume of his *Rise and Fall of the Political Press in England*, wrote that Cobbett had been 'the recipient of Treasury support to the tune of £3,000 for the *Porcupine*, a daily that began in 1800 and quickly folded'. I have failed to uncover the evidence on which this statement is based. It certainly contradicts Cobbett's behaviour and all that he said to Hammond when he refused the *True Briton*. There is, however, a suggestion that £3,000 was the sum Windham offered to invest in *The Porcupine* if Cobbett would agree to keep it going.

contemptible in point of profit. But from that trade I cannot withdraw any considerable sum. My duty towards both my partner and my family would forbid such a step . . . I disclaim all desire to derive pecuniary advantage from the proposed under-taking . . . I have business quite sufficient to satisfy all my wants and all my wishes.* Its success is so certain, and so perfectly independent of every one in England that I might, without the least injury thereto, shut up my shop and retire to the country . . . Such, too, is the nature of my concerns, and the situation of my property, that I might, were *self-interest and security* my ruling object, fold up my hands and let the storm take its course.[5]

He quoted from this letter extensively in an article he published in the *Register* in 1805. Unfortunately, however, he had, earlier in that article, referred to how he had turned down Hammond's offer of the *True Briton* and had, instead, 'embarked on my own bottom; and, it is well known, that my enterprise was unsuccessful. The difficulties which this gave rise to are not to be described. I was saved from utter ruin by a friend, and it is right, that all those who are good enough to set any value on my labours, should be informed that that friend was MR PENN,† who . . . took me by the hand the very week that I came to England, and, when I stood in need of his aid, most liberally gave it to me. I have wanted, and have found other friends too; but MR PENN I shall always regard as my preserver.'[6]

The deception, if deception it was, is understandable. Cobbett may just have been saved from ruin by Penn, but it was still important for him to convince Windham that his was no hired or hireable pen. A man as independent as Cobbett had always to insist that his independence be recognised. It was a point he made in his letter to Windham:

I am . . . willing; I am even anxiously desirous, to conduct the publication now proposed; but that desire, great as it is, will not suffer me to do, or to accept of any thing, that shall, in the smallest degree, work a forfeiture of that independence, to preserve which, I have, all my life-time, practised, and I still do practise, industry and economy to their utmost extent.[7]

* When quoting this passage in the 1805 article he inserted at this point, in parentheses, 'In this I most grievously deceived myself, by the bye.'
† One of William Penn's descendants. The Penn family owed Cobbett some small debt of gratitude. As Peter Porcupine he had written strongly in favour of the (unsuccessful) claim they made for the return of their vast Pennsylvania estates, confiscated in the War of Independence.

There were eight subscribers in addition to Windham, all of them, one assumes, members or supporters of the New Opposition. They accepted Cobbett's demand for complete autonomy in the running of the *Register*, and must have lived up to their agreement, for Cobbett paid them a handsome tribute some five years later:

> Thus the foundation of the *Register* was laid; being, I trust it will be thought, a foundation as fair and honourable as any of which the mind of man can possibly form an idea. It was building upon a rock; and the house has stood, accordingly, in spite of the wind and the floods. In asserting my own character, I am not, however, to forget the support thus received from the truly patriotic spirit of the New Opposition. I have strictly observed my part of the engagement, and so have they; for, never upon any occasion, has one of them attempted, by means either direct or indirect, to thwart the course of my mind. They have sometimes agreed, and sometimes disagreed with me; but they have never attempted to exercise anything resembling a power of dictation; they have never offered advice in a manner other than that in which they would naturally offer it to one another; and, if there have been a few instances, in which MR WINDHAM has discovered more than ordinary solicitude with regard to my writings, his influence has been exerted in favour of his bitterest enemies, those by whom he had been most despitefully used, and most basely misrepresented.[8]

Of all these sponsors, by far the most important so far as Cobbett was concerned was certainly Windham. Indeed, the next five years of Cobbett's life could be described as his 'Windham Period', for Windham influenced him as no man had before or ever would again. Theirs was a relationship in which, given the differences in their respective positions, age and experience, patronage necessarily played a part. But there was also, between them, an affinity that over-leapt patronage and extended well beyond politics. It was an affinity that resulted in what was probably one of the closest and most genuine friendships Cobbett ever enjoyed.

Cobbett was at that time as self-taught in politics as he was in everything else. Windham completed his political education. He brought him into the political argument at a higher, more intimate and more sophisticated level than any he had been accustomed to as Peter Porcupine. He made him a member, for the first time in his life, of an active, distinctive and influential political grouping. That it was a splinter group rather than a recognisable political party did nothing to reduce the effect membership of it had on Cobbett. He had to learn to work with others and to a policy, something he had never needed to endure in his free-ranging American days. He had to accept, to some small extent, the responsibilities as well as the freedoms of the political writer for, although the New Opposition formed an inconsiderable fourth grouping in politics, its voice could not be entirely ignored. Such men as Windham, Canning and Grenville had to be listened to in Parliament and the *Register* carried their argument, with growing effect, to the public.

That argument became increasingly convincing, as Napoleon proved by his actions in Europe that the Peace of Amiens was, indeed, what the New Opposition and the *Register* had always prophesied it would be – 'a disgraceful and hollow truce'. The renewal of hostilities in May 1803 provided the group with its final justification but removed its *raison d'être*. It held together for another three years, even though it no longer had the Peace to argue against, but by 1806 its various members were back in the parties and coalitions they had defected from in 1801. Only Cobbett failed to find, and had no desire to find a political party to cling to. He had, by then, acquired such a dislike of governments and such a taste for opposition that he was already well on his way to becoming that sort of 'fourth estate' Hazlitt had described.

Cobbett and the *Register* were probably as useful to Windham as Windham was to Cobbett. What made their relationship so close, however, was the fact that they were, in some respects, men of similar character and taste. They were both countrymen, and both were interested in preserving what they thought of as the native vigour, courage and ferocity of the race. Consequently, they worked together to preserve the old sports of the countryside that were now beginning to be considered brutal, and to resist those who, either out of puritanism or misplaced benevolence, sought to abolish them as part of the continuing process of educating and civilising the English. Both men were deeply concerned with schemes for Army Reform. Both were ardently patriotic and violently anti-Jacobin, these being the qualities that had led them, however temporarily, to keep company with the High Tories. But what they had most in common was that dangerous form of intellectual honesty or arrogance that made it difficult for them to be good party men.

William Windham was a man whose adventurous spirit and love of sport would have placed him firmly amongst the Corinthians had he not devoted so much of his adult life to politics and the arts. He had, in his youth, volunteered for an expedition to the North Pole in which another young Norfolk man, Horatio Nelson, was engaged. A prolonged attack of sea-sickness, however, had led to his being put ashore in Norway, from where he had returned to England in a Greenland whaler. When the craze for ballooning swept England in 1785, he was one of the few amateurs who actually went aloft. He was a close friend of Samuel Johnson, an amorist of some note, and popularly considered to be the finest orator in the House of Commons after Burke had died.

The Windhams of Felbrigg Hall had been part of the Norfolk Whig establishment ever since the days of Walpole. William Windham, consequently, had entered politics as a friend and supporter of Fox. Burke and the French Revolution had caused him to break with Fox and join Pitt as his Secretary at War. When Pitt resigned Windham worked to form the New Opposition to Addington before eventually taking office, along with both Fox and Addington, in the Ministry of All Talents. Such seeming inconstancy had earned him the nickname of 'Weathercock Windham' but, like Cobbett, he knew how to make the best use of what had been intended as an insult. During the Norfolk election of 1806 he had some hedge-poet follower compose the following verses, which his supporters sang lustily in the streets of Norwich:

> Let fools who without sense or reason will bawl,
> With their jeers try our feelings to shock;
> O come to the Poll, Norfolk Freeholders all!
> We'll vote for the old WEATHERCOCK.
>
> Let Peer-courting sycophants promise or rail,
> For their flumm'ry we care not a feather;
> When their turn is once served, all their promises fail –
> Our WINDHAM's a COCK for all WEATHER.[9]

Cobbett, of course, had already gained a reputation as an ingrate and a turncoat for having refused Pitt's patronage and for having turned against Addington. No one, however, could justifiably impugn either man's honesty. Cobbett was known to be incorruptible, and Windham was frequently referred to as 'high-souled Windham'. Indeed, he was so given to examining his conscience that he doubted, at the start of his career, whether he would ever make a politician. Samuel Johnson, however, reassured him, saying: 'Don't be afraid, Sir, you will soon make a very pretty rascal.'[1] Windham never succeeded, however, in becoming a rascal and for lack of that political attribute, failed to become Prime Minister, although he was, in other respects, better fitted for such a post than an Addington or a Perceval.

Since Windham was, in some ways, the parent of the *Register* and the man most completely in Cobbett's confidence, it was to him that Cobbett exposed his reasons for wanting to publish such a paper:

> I have so long exerted myself for my king and country. I have endeavoured to do, and I have really suffered so much for them, in almost every way that a man can act or suffer, that to desire to promote their interest and their honour is become the leading propensity of my mind.*[10]

He then proceeded to discuss the class of reader he wanted to reach. They were oddly defined for a writer whose political fame and influence would eventually be based on the fact that he wrote to and for the common people; but at this stage in his career he put it down that 'the opinions of the multitude would be of very little consequence'. However, Cobbett was, at that time, a fiercer opponent of what we would now call democracy than almost anyone else then in politics.

Nevertheless, it still comes as something of a shock to find the future Populist and Radical, the man who, more than anyone else, can be said to have invented the popular Press, writing the following passage:

> A publication, addressed to the passions and prejudices of the multitude, may raise a mob, and may, in some cases, quiet a mob; it is a desperate remedy that is sometimes made use of to destroy, and sometimes to preserve, lawful authority. But it will never produce any lasting effect; it will never work a change in the temper and feeling of a whole nation; it will never raise that gentle steady flame of patriotism, which alone can lead to great national actions, and which is so much wanted at the present awful crisis. To raise this flame and to fan it when raised, the publication I propose appears to me to be the most efficacious that can be devised.[11]

How could he know, writing that, that in no more than eight years time he would be raging inside Newgate precisely because the Government had believed that he had been over-successful in addressing himself 'to the passions and prejudices of the multitude'? At this stage, however, he was doing no more than plan the *Register*:

* The 'sufferings', presumably, referred to the court actions against him in America.

It will contain an abundance of useful information, its principles will be unexceptionable, its expense will be trifling, it will circulate freely through the post-office, it will be something between a newspaper and a magazine, uniting the activity of the former with the durability of the latter. Such a publication, conducted with great diligence and care, some talent, unwearied perseverance, and an inviolable attachment to truth, will, if anything can, awaken the dormant spirit of the nation, and form a rallying point for the now scattered friends of the king and the country – To set this publication on foot, and to support the chances of the losses on it *for one whole year*, would require a fund of 600l. How that fund is to be raised is not for me to say . . .'[12]

In the middle of January 1802 Cobbett wrote again to Windham informing him that 'Mr. Elliot and Mr. T. Grenville called on me yesterday and informed me that the whole of the sum was raised, exclusive of the five thirties that I have obtained. If so, so much the better. The greater the fund, the greater will be my ability to render the work useful and of extensive circulation.'[13]

He then announced, triumphantly, 'The first Number of the new work will be ready for delivery tomorrow, but the great number of copies will prevent its distribution taking place till Wednesday.' If there were some who had doubts about the success of such a venture, Cobbett did not share them. 'My literary friends persist in treating my plan with coldness. They are full of doubts. I have had none; and, since I have seen a proof of the 1st Number complete, my confidence is stronger than ever.'

The paper, which was, at different times, variously styled *Cobbett's Weekly Political Register*, *Cobbett's Weekly Political Pamphlet* and finally *Cobbett's Weekly Register* was, from the first, successful. It sold for tenpence, and most of the people Cobbett considered 'capable of forming an opinion', from the King downwards,* made a point of reading it and of wondering how they had managed in former times without a *Register* to applaud or attack every week.

Cobbett was triumphant about the bargain he had struck with the Commissioners of Stamps, who 'regard me as a new species of

---

* Cobbett, referring to the old King's fondness for the *Register*, wrote, in 1809: 'I have been told, that the King, when he visited Cufnells in 1804 . . . said, the moment he entered the house, "*Where is* MY FRIEND *Cobbett's* paper?"' (Hampshire Letter No. 3)

lunatic; but, as they are in general, not conjurors, they by no means disheartened me. They did, tho', what was much better; they granted me a discount on the stamps to the amount of 8½ per centum, which was 4½ more than I at first expected.'

The paper was printed in the first year by T. C. Hansard of Peterborough Court, Fleet Street, who also printed the first *Annual Register*, which consisted of two volumes, each containing twenty-six of the weekly Numbers bound into a single volume, the annual cost being £2.15s. Describing his printing arrangements to Windham, Cobbett wrote: 'My printing will be somewhat dear; but my printer is the very best in London. A man of letters perfectly conversant in French, of great attention, and great means of dispatch, from the number of hands he can at all times command. Ten per cent for such advantages is no object.' Hansard's extra ten per cent must, in the end, have proved a luxury, for the following year the printing was taken over by Cox and Baylis of Great Queen Street. By 1805 the paper was on sale not only from three different centres in London, but also in Dublin and Philadelphia.

Since the only by-line allowed was that announcing 'Mr Cobbett's Letter to . . .' whatever politician or philosopher he thought it necessary to devote a leading article to, it is difficult to name the other contributors, though it is almost certain that Canning and William Gifford were amongst them. The paper depended so considerably on letters from pseudonymous correspondents that one suspects that some of them, at least, had been either solicited or commissioned by Cobbett. The only mention of regular contributors is made in a letter Cobbett wrote to Windham when the *Register* was first launched: 'The French Government and the Politics of the Continent I shall leave to Tierney and Robson.* The (Official) Gazette articles to a compiler.† The Parliament, Notices of Books and some other matters I shall take upon myself.'[14]

In fact, Cobbett probably wrote half, and more than half of each week's copy himself. In October 1802 he wrote to Windham: 'The *Register* of tomorrow is closed. I have written it *half* with my own hand. I have sometimes done worse, and sometimes a great deal better . . . I wish there was more time for handling such copious subjects.' Cobbett considered the book reviews, all of which he wrote himself, to be particularly important. 'These *Notices of New Books*,' he wrote to Windham, 'is perhaps the most valuable head

---

* Tierney and Robson were both Members of Parliament. Tierney was, perhaps, a part owner of the *Morning Post*, and is best remembered for having fought a bloodless duel with Pitt.
† This compiler was, in all probability, John Wright.

of the work. They must generally be short; but it requires not much room to say something pointed and efficacious on any of the topics, of which the works I shall notice will treat.' As he had done in America, Cobbett took care to notice only works that would give him an excuse for drawing a political moral, and that moral, in spite of what he had written to Windham, was frequently a lengthy one.

If the *Register* was, in the first place, a journal of opinion, and of Cobbett's opinions at that, he was also anxious to make it the best of all current journals of record. He pointed this out in the Preface to Volume 8 of his *Annual Register*, published at the end of 1805:

> In closing this volume, I think it proper to point out the utility of this work, as a Register of the transactions between nation and nation. One of the principal objects of the undertaking, was to insure to my readers the possession of *all* the authentic documents . . . In every other work professing to be a Register of the times, the compilers have, for some reason or other, contented themselves with a *selection* of documents . . . Every selection must depend upon the taste, or the opinion of the person selecting, and must produce a representation which, in greater or lesser degree, is deficient in point of impartiality . . . In the opinions and statements of my own, I am not inclined to deny that prejudice and passion have frequently had their influences . . . [but] I fear not to repeat, that, under the three heads; first of PUBLIC PAPERS; Second, of FOREIGN OFFICIAL PAPERS; and Third, of DOMESTIC OFFICIAL PAPERS, the *Political Register* contains a collection such as is to be found in no other work.[15]

This was perhaps the only occasion when Cobbett admitted that his opinions might be born out of his passion and his prejudices. Yet, such is the vanity of human wishes, if the *Register* is ever looked at today, it is precisely in order to discover the passages in which those passionate and prejudiced opinions have been recorded. Few ever go to that work in order to read in full the letters exchanged between the French and Austrian Ambassadors, the American Note protesting against the conduct of the British blockade or the Petition against Lord Melville from the county of Kent, complete with a list of its signatories.

This passion for publishing all important records soon produced what would now be called 'spin-offs' from the *Register*. The first such, however, owed more to Cobbett's political passions than to his regard for posterity. It took the form, for reasons to be explained, of a French language journal for sale on the Continent.

The Peace of Amiens might have ended the fighting war, but it had not put an end to the ideological one. There were continuing arguments over the terms of the treaty and not altogether unjustified accusations of bad faith were launched on both sides; a recent attempt to assassinate Napoleon was attributed to the British and cries of *Perfide Albion* were, of course, heard. More importantly for Cobbett, Napoleon, who had already applied censorship and a primitive form of mind control to his own people, now began to exhibit the irritation common to dictators when they are criticised from abroad. There were still British newspapers, the *Register* prominent amongst them, which, in spite of the Peace, continued to take an anti-Gallican and anti-Bonapartist stand.

Napoleon objected to this as though it were a form of *lèse-majesté* and a legitimate reason for action. The French Ambassador in London complained to the Government and demanded action against the offending editors, amongst whom Cobbett was particularly mentioned. There was an article to the same effect in *Le Moniteur* of which Cobbett wrote to Windham:

The Ministers are upon their knees. Curious cloak for their cowardice to affect not to believe that Buonaparte is the author or authorizer of the article in the *Moniteur*! Sir, be assured that we approach the end of those liberties, which have so long been the possession of Englishmen. Buonaparte has nothing to do but to request a prosecution of some one printer; the Ministers will order it, and, if the Attorney-General represents punishment as necessary to the *preservation of peace with France*, the jury will find guilty . . . One decision of this sort silences the press for ever.[16]

What Cobbett was referring to was the fact that the Government had responded to Napoleon's pressure, and had prosecuted for seditious libel, not Cobbett, but a French emigré called Peltier, the publisher of an anti-republican paper called *L'Ambigu*. He had been found guilty precisely because both the presiding judge and the prosecuting counsel had told the jury that there would be war again with France if he were acquitted. Judgment against Peltier, however, was never executed, but this did not prevent Cobbett from attacking the whole of the British press for its cowardice in the face of such attacks on its freedom.

To demonstrate how little he himself was cowed, Cobbett now started a monthly journal in French which he called *Le Mercure Anglois*, or *Cobbett's English Mercury*. This consisted of French translations of his most outspoken anti-Gallican and anti-Bonapartist *Register* articles, and, since French was the diplomatic and political language of Europe, it must have been read in many of the politest circles on the continent. *Le Mercure* did not have a long life; the renewal of the war perhaps assured that. Nevertheless, while it survived, Cobbett was in the unusual position of being able to air his political views to the British, the Americans and the Continentals all at the same time.

By 1804 the reporting of Parliamentary affairs, which Cobbett had reserved to himself, began to take up less space in the *Register* than before. This was because in that year Cobbett launched, as a completely separate venture, a series of periodical reports of the debates and business of Parliament. Those reports, then called *Cobbett's Parliamentary Debates*, have survived to this day although, now known as *Hansards*, they are no longer produced by a private publisher but have become, as it were, Parliament's own parish magazine.

In the same year Cobbett was persuaded that there was still an important area that was being left unrecorded. That was the state of informed public opinion as it was expressed in the newspapers of Britain, France and America. He therefore started another weekly publication which he called *Cobbett's Spirit of the Public Journals*. This consisted, in his words, of 'Letters, Essays &c. &c. taken from the English, America and French journals . . . the subjects being all of that nature which renders them interesting to politicians'.[17] British politicians, however, appeared to be too insular to be interested in the opinions of any paper, domestic or foreign, apart from those contained in the newspaper they habitually bought. The *Spirit of the Journals* survived for no more than a twelvemonth. Nevertheless, with the *Register*, the *Mercury*, the *Debates* and the *Spirit of the Journals*, Cobbett had proven his desire to become the recorder of his age.

Cobbett may have been as impartial as any Recording Angel when it came to publishing a set of statistics *in toto*, but he was inclined to be partisan when it came to selecting what statistics he should publish. For example, in pursuit of his theories about Republican morality he reproduced in full the figures published in *Le Moniteur* covering births, marriages, divorces and deaths in Paris for the year 1801–2, and found them extremely gratifying. They showed that a quarter of all babies had been born out of wedlock and that the proportion of divorces to marriages was not much less than one to three. This, of course, allowed him to use 'French Morals' as the heading for his article. Even more encouraging was the fact that Paris was shrinking, for the statistics showed that, in spite of five thousand bastards having been born in that year, there had been more deaths than births:

> The divorces and bastards exhibit a horrid total; and when we perceive that more than one-third of the whole of the persons who die, expire in poor-houses and hospitals, we may form some judgement of the prosperity and happiness of the people. This is the scene of gayety, and the emporium of the fine arts, to which English fools are flocking for pleasure and refinement.

Combining anti-Gallicanism, morality and tongue-in-the-cheek statistics in this manner reminds us that the *Register* was not solely a political journal or a journal of record. There were, especially during Cobbett's 'Windham period', certain fringe subjects to which he often returned. A favourite one was the need to preserve the ancient sports of the people and, through them, the vigour of the race. He not only kept publishing articles in defence of such popular delights as bull-baiting, single-stick fencing, quarterstaff play and boxing but also kept Windham supplied with a somewhat bizarre collection of material that might support the latter's speeches in the Commons. Thus he wrote to remind him that 'Marat was a *chemist*, Le Bon a *lawyer*, Collet d'Herbois a *player*, and not one of them a *bull-baiter*, I dare be sworn'. In a memorandum sent to Windham on the same subject he produced an argument containing something that dangerously resembled an undistributed middle: 'Of all the bull-baiting in England one half is carried on in Staffordshire and Lincolnshire. The best soldiers in the kingdom . . . come out of those counties, particularly Staffordshire . . . Wherever the Staffordshire regiment goes, it is followed by a score of bull-dogs . . .'[18]

As it was with bull-baiting, so it was with boxing. In a long *Register* article Cobbett pointed out that ever since the *bien pensants* had made boxing matches illegal, even to the extent of stopping Englishmen settling a dispute with their fists, there had been a great increase in stabbings, violent assaults and other un-British methods of deciding an argument. Nor was this the only thing to consider, for 'it is the political view of this subject which appears to me to be most worthy of attention . . . Commerce, Opulence, Luxury, Effeminacy, Cowardice, Slavery; these are the stages of national degradation. We are in the fourth . . . Of the symptoms of *effeminacy* none is so certain as a change from athletic and hardy sports to those requiring less bodily strength, and exposing the persons engaged in them to less bodily suffering; and when this change takes place, be assured that national cowardice is at no great distance.'

Since he was Cobbett, however, it was difficult for him to conclude an argument before he had in some way personalised it: 'Belcher [the prizefighter] has, by the sons of cant . . . been held up to us as a monster, a perfect ruffian; yet there are few persons who would not wish to *see* Belcher . . . and scarcely a female Saint, perhaps, who would not, in her way to the conventicle, or even during the snufflings there to be heard, take a peep at him from beneath her hood.'[19]

The 'sons of cant' and the 'female Saints' were, of course, all those Evangelicals, Quakers, Methodists and Abolitionists who wanted to put an end to sport in England and slavery in the West Indies. They wanted, as Cobbett saw it, to give freedom to the negroes while depriving Englishmen of the freedoms they had once enjoyed. In place of the bull-baitings, boxing matches, wrestling, racing and singlestick fighting that had exercised and amused their ancestors they were being offered education, Sunday Schools, tracts, psalm-singing and politics:

> They proposed schools and badges for the poor. They were hostile to rural and athletic sports, to those sports which string the nerves and strengthen the frame, which excite an emulation in deeds of hardihood and valour, and which imperceptibly instil honour, generosity, and a love of glory. Men thus formed are unfit for the puritanical school; therefore it was, that the sect were incessantly labouring to eradicate, fibre by fibre, the last poor remains of English manners . . . Too many of the rulers of this land were hunting the common people from every scene of diversion, and driving them to a Club or a Conventicle, at the former of which they sucked in the delicious rudiments of earthly equality, at the latter, the no less delicious doctrine, that there was no lawful king but King Jesus.[20]

In Cobbett's eyes the leaders and very personification of these latter-day saints were William Wilberforce and Hannah More, and he never, from now on, had a good word for either. Wilberforce had 'talents, which in spite of twenty years' cultivation, still remained far beneath mediocrity; [and] an abundant stock of that presumption of which a conceit of extraordinary purity was at once the cause and the effect'. As for Hannah More, 'Gifford now possesses undeniable proof, *juridical* proof, that Mrs Hannah More has several times received the sacrament from the hands of a layman. This decides the controversy. The British Critics have had the same evidence conveyed to them, and have been called upon to give up their heroine, as they promised they would, the moment she was *proved* to be a Methodist. It is a fearful thing to think of, that this woman had under her tuition the children of a large portion of England.'[21]

The *Register* gave frequent evidence of Cobbett's interest in Army Reform and of his support for Windham's proposals in this direction. There were numerous articles in which Windham's speeches on the subject were fully reported, and in which the mechanics, as well as the politics of Army Reform were examined. Pitt's reluctance to enlarge and professionalise the regular army, and his reliance on the militia and the Fencibles for home defence stood in the way of such reforms and was, perhaps, the first cause of Cobbett's growing opposition to Pitt's system of government. When Windham finally came back into government as Minister of War and the Colonies in 1806, his reluctance to carry out the changes in the Army which Cobbett and he had planned and agitated for provided one reason for the breach between them.

Cobbett, as one would expect, wrote a great deal about the actual conduct of the war, once it was resumed, and shrewdly analysed the conduct of the different armies and the different generals in the various theatres of war. He generally, and sometimes unreasonably, found it easier to praise French troops and French Generals than British ones and, whatever his varying judgments of Napoleon may have been, he never doubted the military genius of a man whose career he had followed ever since the early Italian campaigns. He had, when he was still writing as Peter Porcupine, recognised him, not as just another dashing Republican army commander, but as a future French Cromwell at a time when Bonaparte was still thought of as another ambitious military adventurer liable to suffer, sooner or later, the same fate as Pichegru.

But Cobbett did not aways confine himself, in military matters, to events of national and international importance. He devoted a great deal of time, for example, to the case of Private Lutz and the Invincible Standard. It was a case which allowed Cobbett to engage in a controversy in which his passion for justice and his delight in provoking others could be equally satisfied. It also revealed those qualities in him that entitle him to be described as a pioneer of investigative journalism.

Put briefly, the Lutz affair grew out of an argument that unexpectedly developed over who, at the battle of Alexandria fought on 21 March 1801, had actually captured the Standard of the French 21st demi-brigade, known – unfortunately in view of their defeat –

as 'The Invincibles'. When that Standard was brought back to England, it was a tangible symbol of the first considerable victory over the French that the British Army had won in some eight years of war. It was eventually, by the King's order, hung over the tomb of Abercromby, the hero who had fallen, fatally wounded, at the moment of triumph.

News of the victory had, quite naturally, been received with great enthusiasm throughout Britain, and nowhere with more enthusiasm than in Scotland. For here was a famous victory in which the Army had been commanded by a Scot and which, according to reports, had been made possible by the dash and courage of a Scottish regiment, the 42nd Royal Highland Regiment, popularly known as the Black Watch. In addition, it had been a soldier of that regiment, a certain Sergeant Sinclair, who had been credited with the capture of the Invincibles' Standard. It was accepted, however, that Sinclair had later been wounded in a French counter-attack and left senseless on the ground, so that it had been a certain Private Lutz who had actually carried the Standard back to the British lines.

There was reason enough in all of this for the Scots to rejoice. The Highland Society met under the chairmanship of the Duke of Atholl in order to record their pleasure at the fact that the 42nd had 'nobly maintained the hereditary glory of the Caledonian name'. It was agreed that a subscription should be started so that the Society could present every member of the regiment with a medal, and the Officer's Mess with 'an elegant and characteristic cup (of the value of 100 guineas)' so that 'even in their convivial hours that achievement of the 21st of March may never be forgotten'.

The resolution to this effect ended on a somewhat self-congratulatory note: 'The love of glory is the most striking passion of the human heart. All that the hero asks, in return for his efforts and his toils, is that his fame be celebrated . . . How appropriate, then, is the measure now proposed.' The 'elegant cup', when the silversmith had finished it, carried an engraving depicting Sergeant Sinclair cutting down the French Ensign and seizing the Standard.

So the matter stood until, more than a year later, Cobbett came across a report of a murder trial then being heard at Winchester Assizes. The accused was that same Private Lutz who had brought the Standard back to the British lines. After his regiment, the Queen's Germans, also known as the Minorca Regiment, had returned to England, Lutz had been attacked, in the barrack-room, by a drunken fellow-soldier. In the scuffle that followed, Lutz's assailant had impaled himself on a naked bayonet that had been left sticking out from a bunk, and had died as a consequence.

If Lutz had been able to speak better English the case would probably never have come to a trial, for at the worst he had acted in self-defence and more probably it was a case of death by misadventure. This eventually emerged at the trial and Lutz was acquitted.

In the course of the trial, however, the defending officer, who was Lutz's Adjutant, had referred to the accused's exemplary conduct as a soldier. He then went on to explain to the court that it had, in fact, been Lutz who had shot the French ensign and captured the Standard which he had then brought back to headquarters together with a French dragoon he had made prisoner. Cobbett was so interested in this different account of how the Standard had been taken that he had Lutz brought up to London. There he spent several days questioning him after which he referred his evidence to officers of the Queen's Germans and the General Staff who had been present during the battle for corroboration. When this was given he arranged, through Windham, for Lutz to be brought before the Cabinet so that they could hear his story which was, even for those days, an unusual one.

Lutz had been born in Alsace and, like most Alsatians of his class, spoke German rather than French as his native tongue. Although' he was then only twenty-five, he had already been a soldier for more than ten years and had served in no less than five different armies and taken part in innumerable battles. He had been conscripted, as a boy, into the French revolutionary army, from which he had deserted in order to join the French Royalist forces led by Condé. When these had been disbanded he had enlisted in the Russian Army, and when that withdrew from Italy, he had taken service with the Austrians. He had been taken prisoner by the French at Castel Nuovo, and had been recognised by a former comrade as a deserter. He then escaped from prison to avoid execution, rejoined the Austrians, and was taken prisoner, once more, this time by the Spaniards at Milan. He was then sent, with other prisoners of war, to Barcelona, but the transport carrying them was captured by a British man-o'-war and taken to Minorca. He, and many of the other prisoners, enlisted in the regiment then being raised there which was known as the Queen's German Regiment, and this eventually formed part of General Stuart's Foreign Brigade which was recruited almost entirely from foreigners such as himself.

The Foreign Brigade, along with the 42nd, had formed part of the reserve at the Battle of Alexandria. When The Invincibles, supported by French cavalry, attacked the British rear, the 42nd were sent to repulse them. Far from driving them from the field, as popular opinion had it, the 42nd was over-run and in danger of being annihilated when General Stuart sent his Foreign Brigade in to recover the situation. It was the Queen's Germans who eventually put The Invincibles to flight and repulsed the French cavalry counter-attack, and it had been Lutz who had killed the French ensign and captured the Standard. He had then killed one French dragoon and taken another prisoner before he returned with his trophies to his regimental headquarters. There his commanding officer had been so impressed with his achievements that he ordered him to report with the captured Standard to the Adjutant General. That officer had given Lutz what few guineas he had in his pocket, together with a certificate recording his exploits, and the Standard had been sent to Abercromby, to console him, in his dying hours, with a symbol of his victory.

The Cabinet, convinced, eventually, of the truth of Lutz's story, had him promoted to Sergeant and sent back to his regiment, but not before Cobbett had had his portrait painted and had arranged for prints made from that portrait to go on sale in London and abroad, the proceeds of the sales to go to Lutz. He also began, in the *Register,* a series of articles which covered, in fullest detail, the whole of Lutz's career, the events connected with the capture of the Invincibles' Standard, and the false claims that had been made by Sergeant Sinclair, so ably, if innocently, supported by the officers of the 42nd and almost every man in Scotland, including the members of the Highland Society.

This, needless to say, exposed him, immediately, to the wrath of the Scots, while many of the London newspapers also seized the opportunity to turn on their new, slightly bizarre, colleague who already had the reputation of being more of a Yankee than an Englishman and was considered to have brought a low, scurrilous and thoroughly American style of writing to London.

So the *Morning Chronicle* remarked:

The [*Register*'s] narrative certainly will give great offence to the 42nd regiment, who are represented to have been in a very shameful situation when rescued by the German regiment . . . If the narrative be true, Sergeant Sinclair has been guilty of lies and misrepresentations . . . [but] it certainly will afford us great pleasure to find that the merit of an exploit so highly extolled belongs to a British regiment and a British soldier, and not to a *French* deserter, which Antoine Lutz was . . . We feel, however, what we are sure every *British heart* must feel . . . It does not show much of the *English spirit* to insinuate that the *foreign* corps had a greater share in the victory of the 21st than any of our *native* troops.

Cobbett refused to horsewhip the editor of the *Morning Chronicle* for this attack on his patriotism because 'I will not disgrace the lash by bestowing it on sentiments so mean, so grovelling, so detestably vile and base'. He scourged him, instead, in print. He warned him against attempting to prejudice the public against Lutz by referring to him, whenever possible, as 'the French deserter'. Far from being a deserter, Lutz had rallied to the cause of the rightful rulers of France and had fought in some fourteen battles as a result. But then the *Morning Chronicle* had supported the French Revolution, and so this was 'a step which the writer must naturally abhor'. As for Cobbett, all he had wished to do was to ensure justice for 'this gallant, though friendless foreigner'.

The editor of *The Pilot* had been even more insulting. The *Register* articles on Lutz, he declared, had been written 'for the purpose of exalting, by a tortuous and most insidious construction, the valour of a French emigrant over that of a brave Highlander, [and had] exhibited these details with all the sneering malevolence of an *anti-British* mind'. Cobbett gave this editor a milder answer, perhaps because he had not referred to Lutz as a deserter, or perhaps because he thought, quite wrongly, that the editor was a Scot, and therefore had some cause for grievance. He had, Cobbett wrote, somewhat disingenuously, no feelings of animosity towards either Sergeant Sinclair or the Scots. Nevertheless, 'there is but *one* wreath of invincible laurel; before I can restore it to LUTZ, I must take it from the brow of the Highlander'.

This by no means mollified *The Pilot*. 'Our French trumpeter must not blow his coarse notes against *us* as Scotchmen, for we had not the honour to be born in that portion of the country; we are Englishmen, but we recognise no distinction between ourselves and our fellow subjects in the North. The mean and dastardly illiberality with which [Cobbett] has calumniated the Scotch, the cowardly insinuations against one of our bravest regiments, and the attempt to raise the French character by a depreciation of the British, are all functions that belong exclusively to a man, who announces every week that "we are a lost and degraded nation"*
. . . We know *his* principal object is money.'

There was, perhaps, a modicum of substance in the reference to money. Cobbett never was a commercial newspaper proprietor in the sense of writing in order to increase his sales or to attract more

---

* The editor of *The Pilot*, who may well have served Dickens as a model for Mr. Pott, the editor of the *Eatanswill Gazette*, was referring here to Cobbett's constant attacks on his fellow countrymen for having lost their taste for the ruder sports and acquired, instead, a longing to make peace with the French.

advertisers. He wrote, very largely, in order to ease his own feelings and, if it so happened, to arouse the feelings of others, and he never cared what the public thought of him. Nevertheless, the Lutz articles did so much to increase his sales that his print order rose to five thousand copies a week. They were closely followed in America and Europe as well as in England, and a request came to him from Berlin to have them translated into French. The editor of *The Pilot*, therefore, may well have been suffering from professional jealousy, for this, indubitably, had been a scoop.

However, it was Cobbett's passion for justice that started it all. He seemed, moreover, to have grown very fond of Lutz, who was not, as he had expected, 'a huge German *grenadier* with monstrous whiskers on his face, [but] a little, young, smooth-faced Frenchman; well-set, indeed, and of a manly countenance and deportment, but only five feet six inches high'. Lutz was, moreover, an undoubtedly brave man, a thoroughly professional soldier and a staunch anti-Jacobin. Any one of those qualities was bound to be attractive to Cobbett: in combination they were irresistible.

Nevertheless, as the Scots continued their clamour against him – one retired Scots officer publicly called on the Attorney-General to prosecute Cobbett for libelling the Highlanders – something more than a desire to see justice done began to motivate Cobbett. He had grown up with perhaps more than his proper share of the antipathy so many Englishmen felt at that time towards the Scots. Now that antipathy began to develop into something approaching Scotophobia, and this quality marked much of his thinking and writing until, in the last years of his life, he actually visited Scotland. There, contrary to all expectations, he was warmly received by the people he had jeered at and derided for so long and, as a consequence, the Introduction to his *Scottish Tour* contains something as close to an apology and a recantation as he ever achieved.

Towards the end of the Lutz controversy, a pamphlet was published in Edinburgh and London whose purpose was fully explained in its title and sub-title. These ran: '*Invincible Standard. Falsehood and Magnanimity Detected and Exposed in a Vindication of the Forty Second Highland Regiment Against the Pretensions of Mr William Cobbett and the Claims of Anthony Lutz*.' This less ephemeral type of attack did not greatly concern Cobbett. He had had pamphlets enough written against him in America. However, it did mark the start of what was to become a seemingly endless flow of anti-Cobbett pamphlets in Britain.

If the Lutz Affair had revealed that the *Register* had made enemies among the Scots and the London newspaper editors, its politics had succeeded equally well in arousing the anger and hostility of the Government and the government-paid scribblers. None of this perturbed Cobbett who celebrated the second year of his journal's existence by publishing an article on *Effects of the Register*:

> In casting my eye upon the date of the present sheet; in reflecting that this day closes the second year of my labours, it is impossible not to look back to the time when those labours commenced; and if, in surveying the changes . . . I feel a considerable degree of self-satisfaction, I shall not, I trust, merit the charge of inordinate vanity . . . The circulation of the Register . . . may be regarded as a criterion of the political opinions of the well informed part of the community . . . The work began with a sale of less than *three hundred* . . . there are now sold upwards of *four thousand* . . . [yet] the Ministers are affecting the utmost contempt for the effects of my work, [but] lose no opportunity of expressing their hope, that the numbers of its sale are fast upon the decline . . . They have attempted to establish no less than *six* periodical papers of one sort or another, for the express and *openly-avowed* purpose of destroying the *Register*, all of which have, in due succession perished, not for want of funds, it will readily be believed, but for want of readers . . . In estimating the effects of the *Register*, it should be remembered, that it is not like a common newspaper, looked over and then thrown away; and that in consequence of its being preserved, and being so convenient for reference, each number is read, first or last, by several persons . . . I do not think it is being over-sanguine to suppose that every number is read by ten persons, making an aggregate of forty thousand readers. These readers, too, are, for the most part, persons whose opinions have weight with those who hear them, for . . . I always reflect with peculiar satisfaction that the *Register* . . . disdains the success, which is to be derived from the approbation of the thoughtless, the ignorant, or the low . . . I trust that, of all the political writers . . . no one has ever shown less inclination than myself to take unfair advantages of his opponents. Those opponents are circulating their writings through sixpenny publications; on mine I put a price nearly double, rejecting, at the same time, the aid of those baits by which the needy, the grovelling, the idle, the foolish and the profligate are usually attracted; and appealing to the better qualities, the better feelings, to the sense, the reason, the public spirit, the honour and the loyalty of the nation.[22]

Cobbett in an unpleasantly self-congratulatory mood, certainly, and feeling vindictive enough to hit out at the Ministers and his fellow-editors. Yet he had some reason to feel pleased with himself. The *Register* had not, like the *Porcupine*, folded, but was establishing itself, in spite of government hostility, as a new form of journal with a new style of journalism. If Cobbett was crowing like the most self-satisfied of bantam cocks, he had at least established a good dunghill from which to crow.

CHAPTER TEN

The Enemy Discovered

A man cannot be too careful in the choice of his enemies.
                    Oscar Wilde: *The Picture of Dorian Gray*

By 1802 Cobbett had almost persuaded himself that Pitt, whom he had revered as a war-leader and anti-Jacobin, had, in fact, been responsible for most of the failures in the war and almost all the ills that afflicted Britain. It was then that, perhaps unwittingly, he took the first steps in a political pilgrimage that would lead him away from Tory politics and deposit him on those fringes of Radicalism where Reformers, Populists, Levellers and Jacobins kept uneasy company with one another.

Every stage of that long and frequently divergent pilgrimage would be reflected in his political writings. If *Important Considerations for the People of This Kingdom* (1803) was the last great piece he wrote from a purely Tory point of view, almost all the rest of his journalism, for the next ten years at least, can be thought of as a series of increasingly savage attacks on Pitt, on memories of Pitt, and on the system Pitt had created. Looked at as a whole, they constitute a political polemic of truly epic proportions, one that might even be described as his *Pittiad*.

From that Pittiad almost everything in Cobbett's subsequent politics flowed – Reform, his economic theories, his hatred of the new 'capitalism', the birth of that conspiracy theory of politics that swelled into *The Thing*, his populism and so, eventually, his own particular and personal style of Radicalism. But it had all started, not because he was initially in favour of Reform – he rejected it – nor because he was then a populist – he disregarded the working class – but because he had taught himself to hate Pitt and all his works. Cobbett, in short, was a man whose politics had to start from opposing and hating, though this sometimes led him to find reasons for proposing and supporting alternative and more positive solutions.

Cobbett had started, as a Tory, with an assortment of generic rather than specific enemies. These included the Foxite Whigs, because they had supported the French Revolution and opposed

228

the French war; the Parliamentary Reformers, because they were 'democratical'; the Catholic Emancipationists, because they threatened to weaken the Established Church; and the Evangelicals and other 'liberal' reformers, because they would soften the English by substituting Sunday Schools and psalm singing for fairs and bull-baitings.

These were all, however, peripheral enemies since they had no control and little influence over the course of the war. The signing of the Peace of Amiens in March 1802 had provided Cobbett with more definite enemies in the form of Addington and his ministers. It cannot be said, however, that he hated Addington or Hawkesbury in exactly the same way as he would come to hate Pitt. He attacked them in the *Register* with ribaldry and contempt rather than hatred. Addington, for obvious reasons, was generally referred to as 'the Doctor', and Canning's rather weak squibs on that theme appeared in the *Register*, the following being a typical specimen (the King had given Addington a large house in Richmond):

> In Richmond's shades the Premier sat,
> Discoursing o'er his wine;
> "What name, dear Hiley, shall we give
> To this sweet place of mine?'
>
> A wicked wag the question heard
> Behind a neighb'ring tree;
> "Call it, *dear Doctor!*" straight he cried,
> "The VILLA MEDICI."*

Not all the attacks on Addington, however, seemed as innocuous and as tolerable. In the end it was decided to strike back at Cobbett personally, rather than as the spokesman for the New Opposition. The Ministerial press and various Government pamphleteers launched a series of attacks on Cobbett, all of which purported to prove that he was no more than a Grub Street hack not worth the listening to. The public was told from a dozen

---

* Oddly enough, it had been in a Whig newspaper, *The Oracle*, and not in Cobbett's *Register* that Canning had published the best known of these squibs, which ran:

> Pitt is to Addington
> As London is to Paddington.

Hiley Addington was the Prime Minister's brother.

different sources that he was a hireling, a turncoat and a scribbler who now slandered the Government only because he had expected a greater reward for his services in America than Mr. Pitt had been prepared to offer him. The *True Briton* called him 'an American scribbler', and it was everywhere suggested that he had been out of England for so long that he had become something of a foreigner, which was why he criticised his fellow countrymen so frequently.

In this last respect, Cobbett had given these enemies a certain amount of ammunition. He had never been 'a patriot of the soil', which meant, generally speaking, that he had to be abroad before he could stop criticising those at home. He was, of course, convinced that he never criticised Englishmen except for England's good, and so was doing no more than patriotism demanded of him. It was, however, a form of patriotism many of his compatriots failed to understand. Even something as tangential as the Lutz Affair had suggested to many Britons, not all of them Scotsmen, that there was something un-English about this most English of Englishmen.

These attacks and counter-attacks proceeded briskly in 1803 until, on 18 May, a resumption of the war with France was proclaimed. If this was something that Napoleon and, by implication, the French were eager for, that was far from the case in Britain, where both Government and people had adjusted themselves to peace and found the process of re-adjustment difficult. Addington, like all post-war Prime Ministers, had begun to economise on the armed forces, reducing both the Navy and the Army to a condition closer to their old, peacetime establishments. The taxpayers had begun to look forward to an easing of the financial burdens Pitt had inflicted on them. Peacetime trading had been restored and the Stock Exchange was booming. Now, after several false alarms, war had returned and a nation that was materially and psychologically unprepared for it fell into a state of near-panic, for Napoleon had already assembled a large army at Boulogne. As the First Consul rode through Amiens on his way to review his invasion forces he could have read, written in large letters on the gate of that town which faced towards Calais, the words THE ROAD TO ENGLAND.

But if all was purposeful and warlike bustle in France, almost everything was in a state of confusion in England. Naval vessels that had been paid off now had to be hastily recommissioned and manned. The Militia and the voluntary forces that had to swell the Home Army received swarms of men who could not, for the moment, be either armed, trained or officered. There was panic on the Stock Exchange, Consols fell as low as forty, and the Prince of

Wales withdrew to his hunting lodge at Weedon which, being in the centre of England, was arguably as far removed from Napoleon's Grenadiers as was feasible.

Windham, who had been inspecting defences in Norfolk and Suffolk, wrote to Cobbett that there had been no delivery of muskets, powder or artillery for the Militia and an invasion force could expect to land unopposed. Cobbett, who expected the invasion to come any day, replied:

> When this time comes, my intention is to go instantly *into the Army*, taking wife and children to some tolerably secure place first; for, in such a crisis, that man will be best off who has a sword in his hand, and certainly he will be more likely to serve his king as a soldier than as a writer, of which latter tribe there will be but very few wanted when force, physical force, is become all in all things.[1]

To this Windham had replied, 'What sort of situation have you thought of for yourself in the Army? It is a matter of some consideration, and in fact, whether you cannot be otherwise better employed. I should wish', he added, rather plaintively, 'that we could be somewhere together.'[2]

Since the invasion never materialised, the forty-year-old ex-Sergeant-Major and the former Secretary at War thirteen years his senior never found it necessary to face Napoleon's Grenadiers on an English beach. Cobbett, indeed, must have been one of the few regular soldiers of that period who never had occasion to flesh his sword or fire a shot in anger. He had already found, however, that he could still be patriotically employed, if only as a member of the 'writing tribe'.

The *Morning Post* of 5 June had published a proposal that every newspaper should, henceforth, devote some of its space 'to the purpose of arousing the people to the defence of the country'. Cobbett responded to this appeal far more effectively than any other newspaper editor in England. He immediately sat down and wrote a long article which he called *Important Considerations for the People of This Kingdom*. But he did not publish this under his name in the *Register*. He gave it, instead, to Yorke, the former Home Secretary, with a request that it should be handed to Addington for him to deal with as he saw fit. The only proviso made was that if it were to be published, it had to be published anonymously.

So it was that this allegedly unpatriotic and hostile Grub Street hack provided Addington with just the powerful piece of

231

propaganda he needed. Addington, who saw no need to look such a gift horse in the mouth, 'accepted it, in which he showed his sense of duty to be above party pique'.[3] Cobbett was offered payment, which he refused, whereupon the Government spent several thousand pounds on having the piece printed and distributed to the nation. Within little more than a week a sufficient number of copies had been sent to the minister of each parish in England and Wales for him to be able to place one copy in every pew and distribute several more in the aisles, where the poor worshipped. He also received two extra copies, printed as posters, with instructions to fix one to his church door and to display the other 'in some such public part of the parish as you may deem best fitted for making it known among the parishioners'.

The accompanying circular explained that this was to be done so that 'at this moment of crisis, His Majesty's subjects should be fully apprised of the danger in which their property and their lives, their liberties and their religion are threatened, in order that their energies may be called forth, and that, under God's providence, the safety of the realm may thereby be provided for, and its ancient honour maintained'.

Important Considerations is seldom discussed, these days, by students of Cobbett's work. This may be because such a traditional and, indeed, Tory specimen of patriotic propaganda fits incongruously into the later work of a Radical who would, in a very few years, be advancing almost diametrically opposite doctrines. Yet any two or three passages are enough to reveal that Cobbett could write as a Tory quite as powerfully as he wrote when he became a Radical.

Important Considerations started with a factual, sober and well-researched account of the sufferings the French had already inflicted on the countries they had occupied and the peoples they had conquered. Cobbett had described such things before in his American days, and he described them well. He then went on to explain why, having plundered and mastered Europe, Napoleon now wanted to resume the war against a country so patently eager for peace as Britain:

Having, under the name of *Equality*, established in his own person and family a government the most pompous and expensive, while the people are pining with hunger and in rags; having, with the word *Liberty* continually on his lips, erected a despotism the most oppressive, the most capricious, and the most cruel that the Almighty, in his wrath, ever suffered to exist, Napoleon feared that while there remained upon the earth, and especially

232

within a few leagues of France, a people enjoying all the
blessings of freedom, their sentiments and their example would,
by degrees, penetrate through his forest of bayonets, his myriad
of spies, and would, first or last, shake the foundations of his
ill-gotten power.

When Cobbett came to that part of the work in which he warned
his readers of what to expect if England also were occupied, there
is something that would seem dismayingly familiar about the
prophecy to those in France who experienced the Nazi occupation:

Such of our manufactories as are moveable they would transport
to France, together with the most ingenious of the manufacturers, whose wives and children would be left to starve. Our
ships would follow the same course, with all the commerce and
commercial means of the kingdom. Having stripped us of everything, even to the stoutest of our sons and the most beautiful of
our daughters, over all that remained they would establish and
exercise a tyranny such as the world never before witnessed. All
the estates, all the farms, all the mines, all the remaining
manufactories, all these they would bring Frenchmen over to
possess, making us their servants and their labourers. To prevent us from rising and uniting against them, they would crowd
every town and village with their brutal soldiers, who would
devour all the best part of the produce of the earth, leaving us
not half a sufficiency of bread. They would divide us into
separate classes; hem us up in our districts; cut off all communications between friends and relatives, parents and children, which latter they would breed up in their own blasphe-
mous principles; they would affix badges upon us . . . or clothe
us in the habits of slaves.

Cobbett ended the piece with a passage which, although it may
seem somewhat florid today, is still quoted when his 'finer' writing
comes under discussion. What is more relevant, however, is that it
was very much to the taste of his contemporaries:

The sun, in his whole course round the globe, shines not on a
spot so blessed as this great, and now united Kingdom. Gay and
productive fields and gardens, lofty and extensive woods, innumerable flocks and herds, rich and inexhaustible mines, a mild
and wholesome climate, giving health, activity and vigour to

fourteen millions of people; shall we. who are thus favoured and endowed; shall we who are abundantly supplied with iron and steel, powder and lead; shall we who have a fleet superior to the maritime force of all the world, and who are able to bring two million of fighting men into the field; shall we yield up this dear and happy land? No; we are not so miserably fallen; we cannot, in so short a space of time, have become so detestably degenerate . . . Mighty, indeed, must be our efforts, but mighty also is the meed. Singly engaged against the tyrants of the earth, Britain now attracts the eyes and the hearts of mankind . . .

If one judges it by its immediate effect on the public, this must rank as the most powerful piece of writing Cobbett ever produced. He himself never doubted its effect. 'There are about eleven thousand Clergymen in England and Wales,' he wrote some six years later, 'and my real belief is, that all of them together, in the whole of the preceding eleven years, had not, whether by writing or preaching, moved the people so much as I moved them in one single week.'

Nevertheless, until 1809, Cobbett was content to leave the authorship of *Important Considerations* a secret to be shared only with Addington and a few others. The newspapers thought that it had been written by Lord Hawkesbury and others claimed that John Reeves, the anti-Jacobin, was its author. The latter, indeed, was publicly thanked by Queen Charlotte at one of her Drawing Rooms for having written such a patriotic and rousing piece. 'The King,' Cobbett wrote, 'expressed the highest approbation of the work . . . He was not, I dare say, told who was the author, nor was it necessary that he should be; for I wanted nothing of him by way of reward, no, not even a "*thank you*".'[4]

By 1809, however, Cobbett was a Reformer and a Radical, which meant that he was, after the fashion of the time, constantly accused of being a revolutionary, a Jacobin and a Leveller. He was not, and never could be, any one of those, but he was worried that the attacks made on him might, by association, become attached to the cause of Reform. He knew from his Tory days how easy it was to spread the suggestion that all Reformers were Jacobins and all Jacobins traitors. Since his enemies had, by this time, dug back into his past to the extent of reviving the scandals associated with the seventeen-year-old affair of the abortive court martial and his alleged perjury and subsequent flight, he also thought it necessary to go back over his life, from his first soldiering days onwards, in order to show that, in or out of the Army, in America or England, he had never behaved otherwise than as an honest man and a patriot.

This brought him, eventually, to 1803 and the fact, which he now published, that he, and he alone, had been the author of *Important Considerations*. At this stage he turned on those Hampshire worthies who were vilifying him because he had requisitioned a meeting at Southampton at which almost 2,000 freeholders had signed a Declaration in favour of Reform:

> They would fain represent me as a *low* and *insignificant* person; a person of no consequence; a person by whom the county ought to be ashamed to be led . . . As to being a *low* person, I never, in point of birth, pretend to be a *high* one. I never put on any airs . . . I have not the presumption to wish to *lead* the county [but] I *always* had weight and power. Wherever I was, I was a *leader* . . . But let them efface, if they can, the fact that a production of mine, when its author was unknown, was sent to every parish throughout the kingdom under *government authority* and at the *public expense*. When those who attempt to lower me in the estimation of the people of this county shall have produced any thing to be so honoured as this production of mine, and shall have refused, as I did, to take any compensation for it; when they have given such irrefragable proofs of ability, public spirit and disinterestedness, then let them pretend to place themselves upon an equal footing with me; but not before; till then, let them keep their due, that is to say, an inferior place. In every way in which we can be compared, except as to mere money, I am their superior.[5]

Important Considerations revealed that Cobbett could influence public opinion more powerfully than almost any other journalist in the kingdom. It was a fact which explained why it was that, out of all the publicists in England, he always attracted the most attention and gave rise to the most controversy. He was himself, of course, a contentious man, but in those days a journalist could be more contentious than he and still not have his name recognised beyond the other end of Fleet Street. It was this ability to communicate, quite as much as what he communicated, that turned him into a man governments attempted, in vain, to enlist or silence. *Important Considerations*, therefore, did more than mark the high point of Cobbett's career as a Tory. It also marked the point at which he finally convinced politicians and public alike that he was, in the words that G. K. Chesterton used to describe him, 'the noblest

English example of the noble calling of the agitator'.[6] Even his enemies never again considered anything he did to be unimportant, any more than they expected that anything he wrote would be uncontentious.

Why, however, did Cobbett insist that *Important Considerations* be published anonymously? That he took no money for it may be credited to his patriotism, but that he took no credit for it when it would have silenced all those who questioned his patriotism seems strange. It may have been that he feared that its impact would be less if it became known that it had been written by a 'warmonger'. More probably, however, as a member of the New Opposition, which had continued to refuse Addington its support even though the Peace of Amiens had collapsed, he had no wish to be seen offering the Government even such indirect aid as *Important Considerations* provided. He trusted Addington no. more as a war-leader than he had trusted him as a peacemaker, and he attacked him as fiercely after May 1803 as he had ever since he had come to power in 1801.

What was significant was that he had early discovered that attacks on Addington had also, by implication, to be attacks on Pitt. Not only had such men as Hawkesbury and Addington originally been Pitt's creatures 'whom he had cherished, only because they were little and low, only because they suited him as instruments', but they had enjoyed Pitt's support in coming to peace with the French. He had written to Windham, as early as 7 October 1801: 'Mr Pitt's city friends deny that he has had any hand in the Peace, while his enemies contend that he has, and while we (I mean Gifford and myself) have proof positive of the fact, a fact which we shall boldly state at all times when we think it necessary.'

If supporting the Peace was, in Cobbett's view, one political vice that Pitt shared with Addington, the creation of an 'upstart system' was another. In 1802 Cobbett launched an attack on Addington which was, tangentially at least, meant to include Pitt. He gave the article the ominous heading of THE PITT SYSTEM:

We believe Mr Addington to be a very *honest* man, but what is that? Honesty alone is not a recommendation for a footman, and shall it be for a first minister? There are several persons in the ministry possessed of very good talents, but they want weight, they want consequence, they want birth. At no period of our history were the powers of Government ever shared by so few men of family. A race of merchants and manufacturers, and bankers and loan-jobbers and contractors, have usurped their place, and the Government is very fast becoming what it must be expected to become in such hands.[7]

Cobbett's hatred of the *novi homines* who had acquired wealth as industrialists, merchants or financiers, and had then acquired land and political power through wealth was one of his most enduring aversions. He hated their growing influence as much when he was a Radical as when he was a High Tory. As a Tory, however, he hated them because they were replacing the 'men of family' on the land and in politics, while as a Radical he hated them for having imposed the factory and 'commercial' system on what had once been an agrarian country.

But even as a Radical, Cobbett continued to find some values, albeit increasingly theoretical ones, in 'men of family'. When he attacked them as 'Normans', which he did frequently, it was precisely because he thought they had abandoned what he considered to have been Norman ideas about *noblesse oblige*. He quoted, approvingly, the old Norman proverb 'Il vaut mieux qu'une cité périsse qu'un parvenu la gouverne'. If this seems a somewhat snobbish, not to say elitist attitude for a Radical leader of peasant origins to adopt, it is the peasant origins that are most relevant. When the land was farmed almost solely by tenants the character and attitudes of the landlord were matters of the utmost importance and it was commonly, and not unjustifiably believed that, just as the land was best farmed by the son of the last man who farmed it, who would understand it better than any newcomer, so it was with landowning. So, also, would it be with serving the State. Families which had, from generation to generation, provided the country with its officials and politicians were more likely to produce capable officials and politicians than any others.

All politicians of that age were, by modern standards, corrupt: the patronage system ensured as much. But it was possible that men of family would be less blatantly corrupt than parvenus, either because they were already well endowed by the corruptions of their ancestors and needed no more in the way of honours and pensions, or else because they could accept additional honours and pensions as part of a rightful progression to further greatness rather than as a sudden and obvious bribe. The descendant of a King's bastard could be a Duke and agree to enter the Cabinet with considerably more propriety than would attend the purchase of a baronetcy and a seat in Parliament by a West Indian Nabob or the son of a Cotton King.

Cobbett supported the New Opposition because of its attitude towards the war rather than because it was, on the whole, made up of members of the old Whig aristocracy; but he resented even more than they did the large number of 'upstarts' Pitt had included in his Government and who now served Addington:

> This upstart system naturally grew out of the peculiar circum-stances under which Mr Pitt came into power. It was adhered to, with some exceptions, from the first moment of his administra-tion to the last; he appears never to have voluntarily and cordially given the hand to anything great, whether of birth, character, or talent.*

Cobbett's attacks on Pitt became more sustained and more complicated in the early months of 1804 when Addington's incom-petence as a war leader was forcing him out of office and Pitt was negotiating the terms under which he would form a new adminis-tration. Central to the political situation now was the fact that Fox, after his visit to Napoleon had convinced him that an equitable and enduring peace was impossible, no longer opposed a second war against Bonapartist France as he had opposed the first against Revolutionary France.

This allowed the New and Old Oppositions to come together in what they saw as their common duty, which was so to defeat the French as to come to a better peace than had been obtainable at Amiens. Their first task, as they saw it, was to remove Addington, whose only support came from the King, and to instal in his place a government so broadly based that it would enjoy the support of the nation.

Cobbett, an enthusiastic supporter of both the *rapprochement* and the policy, campaigned vigorously for 'A ministry of men of *talents* and of *great public influence* collected from ALL THE PARTIES *that have hitherto existed*, taking as a bond of their union, an inflexible determination to resist the aggrandizement of France'.* This represented, in at least two respects, a shift in his political attitudes that he was at some pains to explain. He had previously attacked Fox mercilessly for his support of the Ameri-can and French Revolutions and his opposition to both wars. Now he not only approved of him as a future Minister but had also, in some ways, moved towards Fox's attitude to war with the French.

---

* It can be argued – and was, indeed, by Lord Rosebery – that Pitt, who thought of himself as a 'liberal' and a Whig of sorts until the day of his death, brought a new governing class into existence in order to curb the powers of the old Whig oligarchy. Pitt had been, it should be remembered, a Reformer until the necessities of war had driven such considerations out of his politics.

This was that war was a matter, not of ideologies, for both Jacobinism and anti-Jacobinism were no longer relevant, but of Britain's true interests. It was clearly not in her interests to have the French dominate Europe and control the European coastline from Venice to Hamburg. Nor was there the slightest substance now in the old French argument that war had been forced on them and that they could only defend their Revolution by carrying it into all the countries of Western Europe. Napoleon had shown himself more intoxicated by *La Gloire* and more avaricious of territory than any of the Bourbons, and his campaign of conquests obviously had to be reversed. Once that was achieved, however, peace became both possible and desirable, no matter what régime the French chose to be governed by.

Within a few years, Cobbett had absorbed these ideas so completely that he would argue that the restoration of the Bourbons and of the *ancien régime* must form no part of Britain's war aims. From there it did not take him long to arrive at a final and complete reversal of his old anti-Jacobin and anti-Gallican attitudes and to argue that the war had never been fought to defend British freedoms, but had been fought by the British oligarchs and the tyrannical monarchies of Europe to crush freedom in France. It was in this manner that the author of *Important Considerations* eventually found himself defending Napoleon at a time when the vast majority of his fellow countrymen, whatever their former beliefs, had concluded that there could be no peace in Europe until he was destroyed.

That time, however, was still to come. In 1804 Fox and Windham had agreed, because the war had lost its ideological content in the one case, and in spite of that fact in the other, that it still had to be fought until a better peace than Amiens was achieved. Addington could lend no strength to this new, predominantly Whig coalition of forces. It seemed increasingly possible, however, that Pitt might be prepared to join a government of All the Talents, although he would only do so as its leader.

Cobbett's attitude to this was confused, if not equivocal. He poured scorn on those Addingtonians who, alarmed by such possibilities, argued that any alliance between such old enemies as Fox and Pitt must be an unnatural one. They 'stigmatized that co-operation subsisting between Mr Pitt, Mr Fox, Lord Grenville and Mr Windham, who are now not to agree because they once disagreed'. This did not, however, prevent him, a few months later, when all plans for such a coalition had collapsed, from writing in the second of his *Letters to Pitt*:

Not only have I never spoken of your return to the *prime* ministry as an event to be wished, but, whenever the subject has been agitated, I have positively declared my dissent from such a wish. The truth is, Sir, that having considered the nature and tendency of the whole of your system; having arrived at a thorough conviction, that the system points directly, and is proceeding with hasty strides, to the subversion of the Church, the ancient Aristocracy the Throne, and, of course, the Liberties and Independence of England; and, not less firmly convinced that your system is, and must remain, inseparable from your possession of the first place amongst the servants of the King, I thought it my duty to endeavour to prevent your return to that place.[9]

Cobbett may, at that time, have entertained the idea that Pitt would agree to serve under his quarrelsome and somewhat capricious cousin, Grenville. If he did, he must have been one of the few men in England who thought that possible. In the event, when the King was finally obliged to ask Pitt to form a government because Addington, his favourite, no longer commanded sufficient support in Parliament, no broad-based government of any sort emerged. The King resolutely refused to have the hateful and Jacobinical Mr. Fox, whose name he had personally ordered to be removed from the list of Privy Councillors, as one of his Ministers. Pitt, after no one knows how much argument, had to agree to exclude him, and Windham and Grenville, as a consequence, felt in honour bound to refuse office.

Pitt, therefore, had to form a government from his personal followers and from many of those who had served under Addington, even though he had recently described these latter as 'incapable and imbecile'. This was promptly seized on by Cobbett, whose 'Pittiad' had resumed its fullest flow. He published, in two parallel columns, the names of Addington's 'incapable and imbecile' Cabinet and those of Pitt's 'capable and efficient' one. Lo and behold, with only three exceptions, the names were the same. At which he commented, 'It appears, that as to the *number* of "Noses", the present cabinet possesses a superiority of one tenth over the last.'[10]

It was from the moment that Pitt formed a government from which Fox, Grenville and Windham had been excluded, that Cobbett began to publish, either in serial form or as specific articles, what amounted in the end to a sustained and all-embracing criticism of every aspect of Pitt's foreign, military, economic and social policies. These were interspersed, as was so often his custom, with purely personal attacks, few of which were justified and many of which were immoderate even by contemporary standards.

Those articles that continued from week to week included the series entitled *The State of the Parties* and the six *Letters to the Right Honourable William Pitt*. Their theme was resumed in subsequent years in, for example, the series published under the title of *Perish Commerce* and in the *Letters to William Roscoe*. The theme was never, in fact, abandoned. Long after Pitt was dead his supposed iniquities were revived in almost every comment Cobbett made on current political and social policies. What had been specific to the 'Pittiad', and to such individual articles as *Paper Aristocracy*, *A Stock-Jobbing Nation* or *A Multitude of Laws* formed a springboard from which he launched his attacks on half a dozen of Pitt's successors. Tedious though these ancient polemics may seem today, there still resides in many of them a small core of relevance that could give modern politicians reason to believe that Cobbett still has something to contribute.

Although Cobbett was a more or less regular churchgoer and generally spoke well of religion, he was not, as his contemporaries saw him, a conventionally religious man. If he eventually came to any religion, it was one of the modern, 'sociological' kind that preaches salvation through 'social justice'. However, since social justice is more of a political than a religious concept, it is fair to say that he came closer to making politics his religion than he ever came to making his religion his politics. But, since he had not been born a cradle-politician, he had, in effect, to construct his own Catechism as he struggled towards it. The beginnings and the body of that Catechism are to be discovered in his 'Pittiad'. There, perhaps unwittingly, he attempted to define those articles of Faith which, once followed, would allow him to be reborn as a Radical.

Although Cobbett's 'Pittiad' had grown out of his almost total preoccupation with the problems of the French war, it became the vehicle which led him away from the concept of the war as a struggle against the French towards the concept of the war as the source of all Britain's domestic ills. In short, the 'Pittiad' developed from an attack on Pitt as a war leader for what he had failed to do to the French, into an attack on him as a politician for what he had succeeded in doing to the British.

The 'Pittiad' proper, or rather that portion of it that was represented by the *Letters to Pitt*, had started, as was usual with Cobbett, as an answer to attacks that had been made on him as a consequence of his support for the new Fox–Windham Opposition:

The Treasury writers have accused me of 'deserting Mr Pitt. whom I had so highly extolled, and of going over to Mr Fox, whom I had so severely censured'. And thus I am, by way of allusion, charged with a crime almost as heinous as any that man can commit. But, to desert, a man must first be enlisted, and if I might be said to be enlisted, it was in the cause of which I regarded you as the champion; and not in your personal service.

It was true, he went on, that he had formerly extolled Pitt as 'the great asserter of the cause of my country and of monarchy . . [and as] the person who was at the head, who was the rallying point of all those who were opposed to the principles and natural conse- quences of the French revolution'. He had, along with so many others, trusted Pitt's sincerity when he assured the country that he would never be satisfied with a peace that brought a false security, but would continue the war until 'an adequate, full and rational security had been assured', and until Europe had been restored to 'her settled and balanced constitution of general polity'. All of this, moreover, Pitt had promised to achieve 'without the creation of new debt'.

Each of these promises, Cobbett told Pitt, had been broken, 'Because you, either from choice or from necessity; impelled either by your interest, your ambition, or the consequence of your errors, changed your course in politics'. If it was now said that Britain could no longer afford to continue the war, then Fox and the rest of the Opposition had been right to call Amiens a 'peace of necessity' and Pitt had deceived the country when he had sworn such a necessity could never arise. If he had been mistaken in his judg- ment, then he should apologise for his errors, and if he had deceived the country then he should apologise for his deceit. 'Forgiveness, from me, would have been readily granted; but, I never would have put it in your power again to mislead, again to disappoint, again to disgrace either myself or my country.'

These were bold words considering that Pitt had already come to power again and was leading the country in yet another French war. They were followed by even bolder and more wide-ranging criticisms which held no traces of the forgiveness Cobbett had promised. But then, of course, Pitt had failed to apologise either to the country or to Cobbett whom, in all probability, he continued to ignore up to the day of his death.

Those criticisms amounted to a detailed denunciation of Pitt's strategy during the war and his behaviour during the peace. The war strategy had not been a difficult one to criticise since its obvious lack of success had already provided as much criticism as any ordinary man might require. Cobbett, however, insisted on something more detailed by way of a criticism, and set about providing it.

Pitt's war strategy had rested, broadly speaking, on three assumptions:

a) That Britain's naval supremacy allowed her to adopt a largely defensive policy so far as the land war was concerned.

b) That, with the aid of British subsidies, the European Powers could be persuaded to put into the field armies large enough to defeat the French with no more than an occasional stiffening of British troops.

c) That France, which had embarked on the war in a state of national bankruptcy, did not possess the financial or material resources for a prolonged struggle whereas Britain's wealth, credit and foreign trade would allow her to fight a war along such lines for as long as was necessary without weakening her finances or imposing an undue burden of taxation on her people.

The naval strategy was the only one that had, by 1805, achieved any success. It had prevented invasion; it had maintained an at least partially successful blockade of Europe; it had produced successes that could be measured, not only in terms of defeats inflicted on the combined French, Spanish and Dutch fleets, but also in terms of colonies and stations in India, Africa and the West Indies the British had been able to seize. (It was one of the symbols of the overall weakness of the British position by 1801 that most of these had to be returned either to the French or their original owners under the terms of the Treaty of Amiens.)

The cost of a naval strategy, however, was enormous, not only in terms of the ship-building programme but also in terms of all the crimping and pressing needed to keep the ships manned and the hardships and the cruel disciplines that were an essential part of maintaining the fleets at sea year in and year out. That these were popular neither with the people at home, who went in constant fear of the press gang, nor with the sailors on distant foreign stations or manning the blockade was demonstrated by the caution with which the Government handled the highly dangerous mutinies of 1797. Moreover, as Trafalgar had revealed, a false positioning of the Home Fleet, or one important naval battle lost would have destroyed every advantage naval supremacy had given to Britain. The French could then have invaded and occupied Britain and so put an end, for the foreseeable future, to the war in Europe.

Such disasters had been averted, but, as Cobbett kept pointing out, neither naval supremacy nor the blockade had produced the advantages that had been claimed for them. The blockade had proved a double-edged weapon. It had turned neutral and even friendly countries into potential enemies. It had given rise to the Berlin Decrees of 1806 and the counter-blockade of Britain commonly known as the Continental System. It had forced the French into even more military adventures because of their need to find, inside Europe, resources that had been denied them by the blockade. As a consequence, they gained control of the European coastline from the Baltic to the Mediterranean, and there was little the British fleets could do to halt the coastal trade that kept France and the French armies supplied from the granaries, factories and forests of half a continent.

Cobbett's main criticism, however, was that not all the fleets and all the Nelsons that Britain could produce would have any effect on Napoleon's domination of Europe. Armies could only be defeated by armies, and in this case, apparently, only by British ones. But a victorious Napoleon would surely turn his attention to a naval strategy so that he might deal with the only power still in the field against him. With all the resources of Europe at his disposal he must, eventually, succeed in building two warships for every one that Britain could build.

Pitt's policy of Continental coalitions and subsidies was easier to criticise. Its failures were almost too evidently proof of the absurdity of attempting to buy the defeat of the French with money. The £9 million in gold that had, by 1801,* been poured out in subsidies to the Austrians, Prussians, Russians, Sardinians and a motley collection of impecunious German Princes had led to nothing except the defeat of their armies and a further extension of French power. Cobbett, whose heroes had long been Edward III and Henry V, never stopped pointing out that it was not thus that the French had been defeated at Crécy and Agincourt.

Such a policy was one more symptom of the weakening in the fabric of the nation for which he held Pitt responsible. It was something he remembered after the war had been won and Pitt's policy of alliances and subsidies had, ironically enough, had some part in the winning of it. Long after Waterloo had been won, and even longer after Pitt had been buried, Cobbett wrote:

The Pitt crew boast of their achievements in the war. Why! what fools could not get the same, or the like, if they had *as much money* to get it with? Shooting with a *silver gun* is a saying among game-eaters. That is to say, *purchasing the game*. A waddling fat

---

* The total spent on such subsidies had grown much larger before the war ended.

fellow, that does not know how to prime and load, will in this way, *beat* the best shot in the country. And this is the way that our crew *beat* the people of France.[11]

Such British troops as Pitt had sent on his various expeditions to the Continent had achieved nothing, and had achieved it with the loss, by 1801, of 60,000 other ranks and 1,300 officers. This, according to Cobbett, proved how wickedly perverse Pitt had been to reject the plans for Army Reform which Windham and he had drawn up and advocated. The failure of British troops, he maintained, was entirely due to the failure of the officer corps he had learnt to despise when he was with the 54th. From the Duke of York downwards, he wrote, the Army was now commanded and led by incompetent amateurs who owed their positions to birth, money or influence.

Not all of these criticisms were justified, even though events had appeared to make them so. This was a different sort of war from any that had previously been fought. There were few in Britain or on the Continent who knew how to oppose their conventionally trained armies to the People's Army the Revolution had produced and Napoleon used with such genius.

But it was when Cobbett came to attack the third leg of Pitt's war policy, which was that Britain's most potent weapon and her surest guarantees of ultimate victory were her wealth and France's poverty, that Cobbett's writings really bit. That part of his 'Pittiad' amounted to something approaching heresy, for Pitt's reputation rested, very largely, on his supposed success in the management of the nation's finances. All Cobbett's instincts and prejudices had already convinced him that the consequences of Pitt's financial policies were, in purely social terms, disastrous. What he now attempted to do was to prove that they were equally disastrous in economic terms. To do so, he had to acquire a better understanding of economic theory than his process of self-education had, as yet, provided.

He consulted his mentors, Windham and Doctor Laurence. The latter, being an academic as well as a politician, advised him to read Adam Smith and George Chalmers. Cobbett did so, and emerged with an undying contempt for those particular Scottish 'feelosofers' and for all their followers and successors from Bentham to Ricardo. He then turned to statute law and read his way through every statute that had been passed since the days of William III that had anything to do with finance, banking or taxation. Still unsatisfied, he turned to the work of the man he had attacked so violently when he was Peter Porcupine, one he was still inclined to think of as an enemy of all established order. Although he did not study him intensively until he was imprisoned in Newgate, Cobbett discovered in Tom Paine's *Decline and Fall of the English System of Finance* economic arguments he could immediately understand and agree with. It was Paine, then, who finally opened his eyes to what he conceived to be the evils of Pitt's taxing and funding system.

Cobbett had always, until this time, written in the Aristotelian belief that man is, by nature, a political animal. Henceforth, the main thrust of his writing would suggest that he had come to believe that his readers were economic animals before they were political ones. If these writings began to acquire a *gravitas* that left ever less room for irony and humour, they still demonstrated his great talents as a simplifier and *grand vulgarisateur* in the field of economics, even though he had entered it so recently.

Cobbett may have been anticipating the journalism of the future when he began to concentrate on economic argument, but, as he came more or less untutored to the subject, he had to argue almost everything from first principles. Events appeared to have proved Pitt entirely mistaken in his belief that Britain's wealth, trade and credit must win her the war. But how had he arrived at such a belief, if belief it was? He had, Cobbett wrote, fallen into the error of equating what was true of individuals with what was true of nations:

> Amongst individuals wealth gives power and power gives security, but this is only because there is another and greater power which secures the wealth; and, as there is no such power to superintend the wealth of nations, the rich nation is no more secure than the poor one; nay, it is much less secure, being placed in a position similar to that in which a rich man would be without the protection of the magistrate, presenting to the plunderer the strongest of temptations with the weakest of obstacles.[12]

Napoleon and the outcome of the late war provided Cobbett with all the text he needed for his sermon. Britain had embarked on that war with a sound currency, great national wealth and credit, low taxes and comparatively little poverty. Although her ability to borrow seemed almost limitless, the National Debt was not disproportionately large and seemed likely to be reduced by the Sinking Fund Pitt had already instituted. France had started the war in a state of apparent bankruptcy, with almost no backing for the *assignats* – the paper money introduced during the Revolution – beyond the value of the lands that had been confiscated. Now, after eight years of war, the positions had been reversed. France had a currency backed by gold and Britain had paper money and the inflation that went with it.

Cobbett found no difficulty in attributing all this to the Pitt System, and most specifically to the policies Pitt had followed with regard to the land, the war and the National Debt. While the French had solved their land problem by confirming the peasants' title to it and relieving them of the feudal dues and tithes that had once burdened them, the British had followed a policy of dispossessing the peasants and imposing an ever heavier burden of rents, rates and taxes on the farmers. While Pitt had paid foreign princes to fight Britain's battles in Europe, the French had set about winning their campaigns and occupying large parts of that Continent. As a consequence, much of the wealth and most of the resources of Europe were now under French control. Napoleon, it might be said, had conquered and plundered whilst Pitt had subsidised, taxed, borrowed and lost.

Pitt had relied on his funding policy to provide more security for his borrowings than taxation alone could provide. The Sinking Fund had originally been instituted by Walpole, but that great English statesman had subsequently abandoned it. Pitt had revived it as a means of containing and ultimately reducing the size of the National Debt, but the scale of his borrowings made this impossible, and the Fund now served the purpose of supporting government credit and of allowing it to borrow more largely and even more expensively. It still operated so as to redeem an annual proportion of the National Debt, but that proportion was not cancelled, and continued to bear interest at the taxpayer's expense. The Government's monthly purchases of stock prevented a fall in the value of past issues and acted as a guarantee for the payment of interest on future issues. The result was that an increasing proportion of revenue had to be devoted to the payment of interest. In an inflationary period, when the nation as a whole was suffering from a fall in real values, the only section of the public protected against that fall was that which invested in government stock, and the only people to profit from the policy were those who dealt in the loans. The bankers, jobbers and brokers were kept both busy and prosperous.

This policy, as Cobbett saw it, of protecting the investors and speculators at the expense of those who owned and worked the land was the direct result of Pitt's borrowing and funding policy, and that had had its origin in Pitt's vision of Britain as a commercial and trading nation rather than one that relied on the land and a policy of self-sufficiency. This was, Cobbett declared, to give predominance to wealth, and, raised to the status of highest national policy, it was a sure sign of a decline in all that had once made Britain great:

> It is not the mere possession of the wealth that we are to regard as a mark of national decline; but the estimating of that wealth too highly, and particularly the confiding in it as a means of preserving ourselves against the assaults of a warlike enemy, a sort of confidence that was never yet entertained by any nation not in the last stages of its degradation.

According to Cobbett, the 'Predominance of Wealth' had led to a noticeable decrease in the Englishman's willingness to fight, a decrease that was demonstrated by the Regular Army's inability to recruit, the fact that the Militia could only be manned by means of compulsory balloting and the Navy could only continue to operate by liberal use of the press gang. 'Of all the marks of national decline, none is so unequivocal as that disposition which leads a people systematically to stand on the defensive . . . They first endeavour to purchase tranquillity at the expense of their honour; and, failing that, forced at last into war, their best hope is to avoid being conquered and yoked – the resentment of such a people, their bitter reproaches against their enemy, are not occasioned by his insults, but by the compulsion they are under to meet him in arms.'

Cobbett's desire that his countrymen should 'pluck bright honour', if not from the pale-faced moon, then at least from the French, was evidence, perhaps, of his romanticism. His resentment of one particular of the Government's failure to do so was frankly childish. In the preliminary negotiations for the Peace, Napoleon had demanded, and the Government, supported by Pitt had agreed to, the abandonment by the Crown of its ancient title of King of France, together with the elimination of the fleur-de-lys from the royal arms. Cobbett devoted the whole of one of his *Letters to Pitt* to this 'degrading surrender of the Lilies'. Pitt had referred to this as being something that was 'harmless as a feather', something that could very easily be conceded when more important matters concerned with the acquisition and restitution of territories and the payment of compensation were being negotiated. This seemed to Cobbett to be treating something that affected the national honour and the prestige of the Crown with outrageous levity. Only a man so preoccupied with, and corrupted by, considerations of money and trade as Pitt was could ever have agreed to treat the 'surrender of the lilies' so lightly, or would have allowed that surrender to be 'huddled in amongst objects merely pecuniary, and, consequently, vile; objects which would not be worth contending for in arms; items which would not have been disgraced by being found in the day-book of a loan-jobber or a Jew.'

The 'Pittiad', however, was on the whole concerned with other, and more serious matters. Pitt's inflationary and paper-money policies were changing the traditional patterns of agriculture and, for the first time since he had left Farnham, Cobbett's farming instincts came to the surface as he contemplated what was happening in the countryside. Landowners could no longer afford to grant long leases at fixed rents. Although it was commonly conceded that there was nothing more conducive to bad farming than annual tenancies, these were all that the majority of landlords would now grant. Ever-increasing rents, when added to the existing burdens of war taxes and a soaring Poor Rate, would have made farming completely unprofitable if prices, which had been rising steadily, should begin to drop.

One of the basic measures of farming profitability has always been the market price of wheat. This had varied considerably during the war years, more as a consequence of poor harvests than of anything else. Addington had prepared a Bill, which Pitt subsequently passed through Parliament, to encourage wheat growing by providing an export bounty whenever wheat came into surplus. This, of course, kept bread prices high, and so angered Cobbett that he devoted the whole of his *Fifth Letter to Pitt* to the subject of the Corn Bill, and the effect it, together with the policy of general enclosures, would have on the rural poor.

The arguments he deployed were ones he sustained for the rest of his career, and he sustained them, on this occasion, with savage sarcasm. If export bounties were a certain guarantee of increased production, then why not, he asked, encourage the export of all those other things that might be thought to be currently in short supply, such as soldiers and sailors? Bounties might add to the number of acres put to wheat growing, but they would not add a single bushel to the production per acre. On the contrary, a policy of 'up corn, down horn' would actually decrease the yield since there would be far less manure to return to the land, and the stored fertility of the ploughed-up downlands and ancient pastures would soon be exhausted.

Nor were high wheat prices of any benefit to the farmer himself, for if his profits were raised, his rent would be raised accordingly, just as the opposite must promptly occur if his profits were decreased. For rent, in an annual tenancy system, was the means by which the landowner ensured that the profits of farming should not exceed the level of profit of other enterprises.

So far the argument was one popularly pursued by most economists of the day. But Cobbett now turned to the subject which was just beginning to concern him. That was the relationship between food prices and wages in so far as these affected the farm labourer and the rural poor. The price of the quartern loaf, as he demonstrated in one of his carefully compiled charts, had risen from an average of fivepence three farthings over the decade ending in 1760 to one of a shilling over the thirteen years ending in July 1804; but there had been no equivalent rise in farm wages. This meant that, irrespective of the state of the harvest, the labourer could purchase more bread in 1760 than he could in 1803. Neither increased production nor export bounties were capable of doing anything but increase his hardships for he would be deprived of any opportunity of enjoying cheaper food in times of surplus, the rate of Enclosures would quicken and, since wheat-growing was one of the least labour intensive of all farm crops, the demand for labour would fall. These things alone were responsible for the fact that, under the Pitt Policy, poverty had increased until one-eighth of the population was drawing parish relief:

> Any law to encourage or permit the exportation of corn, is a law to abridge the domestic consumption; a law to check population by creating want and misery; a law to depopulate the hamlet and to people the work house, to add to the more than a million of miserable paupers already in existence.

The reader might think to recognise in this the more familiar figure of the author of *Rural Rides* and *The Poor Man's Friend*. It would be premature to do so, since Cobbett, at this stage, was using the state of agriculture and the condition of the rural poor as no more than examples of the folly of Pitt's economic policies. Even the argument against the export of wheat was no more than a part of the more serious argument he had launched against what he saw as Pitt's policy of turning England into a predominantly commercial and trading country. He was opposed in principle to any large increase in the country's foreign trade, and it is in this, perhaps, that we can find the bedrock on which he built all his future political and economic theories.

He first dealt with this subject extensively in a series of *Register* articles under the title of *Perish Commerce*. Though these appeared in the November and December numbers of 1807, that is a year after Pitt's death, they constitute both part of the 'Pittiad' and the start of Cobbett's Sisyphean task of attempting to turn the nation back towards self-sufficiency. None of the other subjects he tackled would so clearly reveal him for what he was – a man of the old, agrarian civilisation attempting to analyse and cure the ills of the new industrial civilisation that had emerged during his absence from England.

In prolonged and furious debates with politicians and economists, in article after article in the *Register*, in works as diverse as *Rural Rides*, *Cottage Economy*, *A Year's Residence* and anywhere else that permitted it he continued to preach the doctrine that the nation could only remain sound and the cottager could only remain contented if both accepted the virtues of self-sufficiency.

Britain, he insisted, produced and could continue to produce everything, or almost everything that Britons should want so long as they remained what they had always been – husbandmen, craftsmen and small, cottage-scale industrialists. To remove them from this ancient 'small way of life', to place them in factories and towns, to engage them on an ever-increasing scale in industry and commerce degraded them from their former freedoms and brought the nation no benefit. There was little enough of what they produced that they could afford to consume, and the growing proportion of it that was exported enriched only the industrialists, the merchants, the financiers and all other members of the new 'upstart class' he so bitterly resented. As he wrote himself into these theories, his former pride in Britain's position in the world, in her colonies, her trade and her influence was exchanged for what would come to be called a Little Englander philosophy. Colonies were expensive luxuries maintained for aristocratic boobies to administer and merchants to plunder. A policy that insisted that Britain should dominate world trade could only have a short existence. It would invite competition and be the cause of endless future wars. Whatever was exported Englishmen would not be able to consume, and whatever was imported they should not want to consume. The barley that was sent abroad could have been turned into malt at home and used to produce the home-brew that had once been such an important part of the working man's diet. In its place he had to acquire a taste for the unhealthy, unnutritious, expensive and foreign habit of tea-drinking.

He was never less than convinced that his arguments would eventually be accepted. 'Pitt is gone; commerce, as the foundation of a system of politics, will soon follow him, and, let us hope that

Englishmen will once more see their country something like it formerly was.' Meanwhile he raged because commerce had made those same Englishmen 'dependents of the upstarts of trade'. And so he returned to the argument with which he had started the 'Pittiad', and which he never relinquished. For the growing supremacy of commerce meant, for him:

> The almost entire extinction of the ancient country gentry, whose estates are swallowed up by loan-jobbers, contractors and nabobs, who for the far greater part not Englishmen themselves, exercise in England that sort of insolent sway, which by the means of taxes raised from English labour, they have been enabled to exercise over the slaves of India or elsewhere; the bestowing of honours upon the mere possessors of wealth, without any regard to birth, character or talents, or to the manner in which that wealth has been acquired; the familiar intercourse of but too many of the ancient nobility with persons of low birth and servile occupations, with exchange and insurance-brokers, loan and lottery contractors, agents and usurers, in short, with all the Jew-like race of money-changers.[13]

This constant repetition of what nowadays would be seen as his racial and class prejudices may worry the modern reader more than they ever worried his contemporaries. What is important, however, is that they seem to obscure the very germ of his arguments. However, although his abuse was generic, it usually had some specific reference to his current contentions.

In, for example, the passage just quoted, one can, with a little understanding of the man and his period, particularise his targets, and so come closer to understanding their connections with the 'Pittiad'. When he wrote about the upstarts who were 'for the greater part not Englishmen', then – Jews apart – he was almost certainly thinking of the Barings. In 1770 Sir Francis Baring, the grandson of an immigrant German cloth merchant, had founded Baring Brothers, the banking house that would have far greater influence in world money markets than any other in Europe. As a Member of Parliament, his unwavering support of Pitt had brought him a baronetcy, though it was left to future members of the family to collect the earldom and three other peerages that supported their position in British political life. The Barings had, from their first emergence into affluence, made a practice of acquiring and enlarging country estates, either by purchase or marriage, and Cobbett disliked them if only for that. In later years his *Rural Rides* would be full of references to the Baring habit of 'adding field to field', and of unflattering description of the manner in which the various members of the family managed their estates, their tenants and their labour.

At this time, however, Cobbett was more concerned with the influence the Barings had on Pitt's financial policies and with their Bank's function as an issuing house for foreign loans. He took particular exception to the fact that Baring Brothers had floated the loan which allowed Napoleon to convert the credits he had obtained from selling Louisiana to the Americans into cash. Sir Francis, moreover, had become chairman of the East India Company, which explains the reference to Nabobs as well as to loan-jobbers.

The 'bestowing of honours upon the mere possessors of wealth' must certainly refer to the peerage given to Robert Smith in 1797. When he was made Lord Carrington, it was said that he was the only tradesman George III had ever agreed to ennoble, and that he had only done so at Pitt's insistence. Robert Smith was the son of a Nottingham industrialist and banker, and he had, from 1786 onwards, taken on the never easy task of managing Pitt's private finances. Since Pitt was always in debt – Parliament voted £40,000 to pay off his creditors after his death – Carrington cannot have been altogether successful in that task. However, he controlled no less than five seats in the House of Commons, and these were invariably at Pitt's disposal. One way or another, therefore, the peerage had been well earned.

Cobbett's savage attacks on the Government had already, in Addington's day, brought him into trouble that augured ill for the future. There had appeared in various numbers of the *Register* of 1803 a series of articles under the pseudonym of *Juverna* which questioned the competence of the Irish Government and attacked leading Irish Ministers, from the Lord Lieutenant of Ireland downwards, for their harsh and stupid repression of the native Irish. Memories of the attempted French invasion under General Hoche in 1796, of the Orange rising of the following year, and of the United Irishmen's rebellion of 1798 were fresh enough to ensure that Whitehall should be particularly sensitive to anything that suggested a revival of sedition in Ireland.

Spencer Perceval, later Prime Minister but then Addington's Attorney-General, demanded disclosure of *Juverna*'s identity so that action might be taken against him. Since Cobbett initially refused to disclose his sources, action was started against him as the publisher of articles 'maliciously intending to move and incite the liege subjects of His Majesty to hatred and contempt of his royal authority'; and he wrote to Windham saying 'Now, Sir, I really stand in need of help.'[14]

The case was heard before Lord Chief Justice Ellenborough and a special jury on 24 May 1804. Cobbett's defence, which he would use again on similar occasions, was that he was too loyal a subject and too demonstrably a patriot ever to associate himself with sedition. Although he called Windham, Yorke, John Reeves, Lord Henry Stuart and Lord Minto as character witnesses, his responsibilities as publisher of the *Juverna* articles could not be avoided. He was found guilty and fined £500. The same verdict and the same fine resulted from a subsequent action brought against him by William Plunket, the then Solicitor-General for Ireland.

Cobbett may well have thought that this was a re-run of the Dr. Rush case, though, with Perceval and Ellenborough arrayed against him, it was more like a preliminary run of the 1810 trial that would put him in Newgate. His fines, in the Rush case, had been paid for him by subscribers and friends, and he now expected something similar to happen. He wrote again on 20 July to Windham, telling him that an unknown subscriber in Oxford had sent him £50 'towards the expenses of my law persecution', and added:

There remains £471 to pay, and, without selling stock or goods at auction, raise this I cannot. They insist, too, as far as Plunket is concerned, to be paid in very short time. It is a shame for me to ask for anything; and I only want to be furnished with the money upon my bond or note at 8 or 9 months, when I shall be well able to pay, if please God I live and have my health; and, if not, why then I am sure my wife and children would find merciful creditors.

It is not clear whether Cobbett succeeded in raising the £1,000, but it is clear that he thought it possible to bring about some mitigation, for he now handed to the Attorney-General the original manuscript of *Juverna*'s articles. This revealed that *Juverna* was, in fact, the Hon. Robert Johnson, a Judge in the Irish Court of Common Pleas. Perceval insisted that this could not affect the outcome of Cobbett's case, and immediately entered an action against Johnson. The Government then fell, that case never came to trial, and in 1806 a *nolle prosequi* was entered and Johnson was allowed to retire on pension. The journalist's unwritten law concerning non-disclosure of sources was, perhaps, less clearly defined and less frequently observed in those days than it is now, but there were many at that time who found much to blame in Cobbett's conduct.

In this wartime period, when the Jacobins were attempting to promote unrest and revolution in Ireland and in mainland Britain, governments had, almost of necessity, to pay such close attention to the press that journalists expressed their views at some peril. Nevertheless Cobbett's 'Pittiad' was, for all its scurrilities, non-actionable. Cobbett's *Register* unquestionably came under close scrutiny, but the law officers could discover nothing to act against and Pitt, who had little time for journalists even though he followed the custom of those days of retaining a government press and a host of pamphleteers, seems never to have considered Cobbett worth proceeding against.

This was so even when the Melville impeachment case allowed Cobbett to launch his most damaging attacks on Pitt and the Pitt System; attacks that brought him, for the first time, into the company of such well-known Radicals as Major Cartwright, Sir Francis Burdett and Colonel Wardle, the Member for Oke-hampton. Henry Dundas, Viscount Melville, had been one of Pitt's earliest political supporters and adjutants, and was, moreover, along with Canning and Wilberforce, a member of the remarkably small group of men who enjoyed Pitt's friendship. When, after the Tenth Report of the Commission of Enquiry – concerning misuse of public funds – a Motion of Censure on Melville was moved in the House, which was passed by the Speaker's casting vote, and which even Wilberforce supported, Pitt, according to Lord Rosebery, 'pressed his hat on his head, and it was seen that this was to conceal the tears trickling down his cheeks . . . Some have ascribed [Pitt's] death to Ulm, and some to Austerlitz; but, if the mortal wound was triple, the first stab was the fall of Dundas.'[15]

It can be seen, therefore, that although he could have ignored the rest of the 'Pittiad', Pitt had reason to resent the relish with which, in number after number, Cobbett followed the course of the Melville affair. Other Prime Ministers might eventually have turned to the courts for protection, and it was, perhaps, only his death that prevented Pitt from doing so.

Quite apart from the opportunity it gave him to attack Pitt through his friends, the Melville case provided Cobbett with two further lines of attack. The first arose from the fact that Dundas was a Scot and had, for a decade or more, been recognised as the uncrowned King of Scotland, dispensing posts and patronage with a liberal hand to his compatriots. Cobbett, like many other Englishmen, saw the Scots as a band of out-of-pocket adventurers who had flocked south ever since the days of James I and VI in order to advance themselves at the expense of the English. Certainly Melville, whether as Lord-Advocate, Home Secretary, Treasurer to the Navy, or in any other of his numerous positions of influence, had never allowed a Scottish name to constitute a bar to advancement in politics, promotion in the Navy or to a place of influence and potential enrichment in India.

What was more important about the Melville case was that it set Cobbett off, once more, on his self-appointed task as the smeller-out and scourge of corruption. As Cobbett of the *Register*, he was no longer confined, as Sergeant-Major Cobbett had been, to petty peculation inside the 54th of Foot. Every placeman, pensioner, sinecurist and peculator in the kingdom could now come under his jurisdiction. An important part of his journalism, from now on, would be what those who agreed with him might call investigative, and what those who suffered from it, muck-raking. It was from now that he began to acquire, in terms of his unwelcome honesty and incorruptibility, the reputation of being the Robespierre of British journalism. His frequent revelations of how Lord Tomnoddy had been made a Colonel of the Horse Guards at the age of ten while his father, who commanded some following in Parliament, had been appointed Keeper of the Tapers for life, with a salary of ten thousand a year and a pension for half that amount to his heirs for the next three generations, shocked his contemporaries rather less than similar revelations would shock us today. Yet it is still a fact of political life, that a man who cannot, or will not exercise patronage, will find it difficult to attain power and impossible to retain it for long. All that has changed is that clients, these days, are publicly paid and privately advanced, whereas it was more customary to exercise patronage in the opposite way in Cobbett's day.

The 'Pittiad' did not cease, or even falter, after January 1806, when Pitt died. There were some conventions Cobbett would always observe, but *de mortuis* was not one of them. He danced, in effect, on Pitt's tomb with quite as much joy as he would dance, in later years, on Perceval's, on Castlereagh's and on George IV's. In February he devoted an article in the *Register* to the motion recently passed in Parliament to give Pitt a public funeral and burial in Westminster Abbey. It was there agreed that a suitable monument should be placed 'to the memory of that excellent statesman, with an inscription expressive of the public sense of so great and irreparable a loss'.

Windham and Fox opposed the motion upon general principles, but they also expressed the view that Pitt had not been an excellent statesman and that his loss was by no means irreparable. Cobbett thought they had not gone far enough, since they 'admitted much which I am not disposed to admit, and which I am certain the people of England will deny. To describe the particular measures of this minister, is a task not to be performed in a short space, either of time or of paper; but it is one which I look upon it as my duty to perform, and which duty I assuredly will not neglect, nor delay, nor listlessly discharge.'[16]

Nor, of course, was he either negligent or listless in that task. Did people say Pitt had been a man of great talents? He 'never gave *proof* of any talents, except as a debater. He was a great debater. But that was *all*; and that, from the use which he made of it, was pernicious to his country . . His eloquence was frothy. In all matters of state, he was conspicuous for nothing but the imbecility of his plans. In all his schemes, whether of war or of peace or of interior economy, you can trace the shallow mind.'

Was it claimed for him, quite falsely, that he had doubled the country's trade? Then why was it not also said that he had 'tripled the number of tax-gatherers; that he had tripled ten-fold the bank-notes; that he had banished specie out of the kingdom; that he had more than doubled the number of parish paupers; that he had effaced the Lilies and yielded the honour of the Flag; and that, under his administration, the power of France had broken through all bounds, and had finally extended itself over every part of Europe? Had it been forgotten, also, that Pitt had more than tripled the pension and place list in number of names as well as in amounts of sums? Did no one remember that he had defended Melville and actively participated in the illegal application of Naval Money?'

Was it said that his death was greatly regretted by the people? 'This is an impudent and insulting falsehood. That he may be regretted by those who were looking up to his power for emoluments, or for shelter I am far from meaning to deny; but, that he is regretted by *the people of England* is a falsehood which never shall pass uncontradicted by me. They do not regret his loss; they regard it as no loss at all; they look upon his death as the first dawn of their deliverance from an accumulation of danger and disgrace. Let him be wept by the Cannings and the Jenkinsons and the Huskissons; *they* have, indeed, *lost* by his death. Let the City of London erect a monument to his memory, it will become both them and him. To be praised, wept and honoured by the swarm of contractors and jobbers is due to his memory. He loved them; they were the part of the community that he selected for his own.'

It was a piece few men would have written about a man so recently dead, but it revealed three things about Cobbett of some importance. He had become an increasingly angry man, and would, for the most part, remain one for the rest of his life. He had discovered his enemies and his reasons for hating them. And he had revealed how dangerous it was, whether in life or in death, to have William Cobbett as an enemy.

CHAPTER ELEVEN

Cobbett's Farming Ventures

Those who labour in the earth are the chosen people of God . . .
generally speaking the proportion which the aggregate of other classes
of citizens bear in any state to that of its husbandmen, is the proportion
of its unsound to its healthy parts . . .

Thomas Jefferson: *Notes on Virginia*

Peter Porcupine had once laughed at what he then held to be the
higher lunacy of Jefferson's notions about farmers, notions that
George Orwell might have reduced to the simple proposition:
'Farmers good; others bad'. By 1805, however, Cobbett of the
Register would have come close to supporting such a proposition –
which Jefferson, incidentally, had long since abandoned in the
interests of gaining and retaining the Presidency.

If the Pittiad had done nothing else for Cobbett, it had, as *Perish
Commerce* demonstrated, reminded him of urban and industrial
iniquities and country virtues. It was one more reason why, after
more than a dozen years of city life, and twice as many spent away
from the land, he now turned farmer. He would, henceforth, live
as a man who was never wholly a farmer and never wholly not one,
and this profoundly affected his fortunes, his domestic life, his
politics and his writings. The original peasant – who hitherto had
lain, more or less dormant under the soldier, the polemicist and the
politician – finally emerged to make Cobbett the last agrarian
politician and writer of any standing in British politics and literature.

When Cobbett left his premises over the bookshop in Pall Mall
in 1803, he bought the lease of a house at No. 15 Duke Street,
Westminster. Here the *Register* and the other publications associated with it were born, some to flourish, some to die soon after
birth. The *Register* certainly flourished. It had, by 1805, a steady
sale of some 4,000 copies a week, with additional runs of another
1,000 or more when his articles were of particular interest to the
public. What this meant in terms of profit cannot be estimated, but
there is no reason to doubt his later claim that his income at that
time was in excess of £5,000 a year. He had amply justified his boast

259

that, given pen, ink and paper, and access to the reading public, he could always, in a remarkably short space of time, earn whatever he needed in the way of money.

Soon after the *Register* was launched he was obliged to find someone who could assist him in its running. Having almost certainly been the creditor who had put John Wright into a debtor's prison, he was now the one who procured his release and, from early in 1803, Wright began to work for him as a sort of general factotum. He was soon left to deal with the publishers, the printers and the paper makers. He did all, or most of the sub-editing. He compiled the Reports and Official Papers and dealt with layout. Even Cobbett's own articles, which were often written in such haste that he had no time for rereading and correction, were increasingly left to Wright for polishing.

Wright had taken rooms over a tailor's shop at No. 5 Panton Square, but he spent an increasing part of his time in the Cobbett household. The children, now four in number,* accepted him as part of the family while Cobbett, starting as an employer, developed in many ways into a surrogate father to a man not many years his junior. Wright, for his part, added to the role of sedulous apprentice that of dutiful son. The arrangements worked so well that Cobbett found, by 1804, that he could leave most of the day-to-day management of his affairs, both business and private, to Wright. This set him free to satisfy what had, by now, become a consuming ambition. This was to acquire a farming property not more than a day's coach-ride from London to which he could remove himself and his family, and from which he could still, through daily letters and periodic visits, control his publications and keep in touch with politics.

Although he was beginning to take as much interest in agrarian problems as in international ones, he never contemplated abandoning either national politics or journalism. Indeed in December 1807, with two years of farming and country living already behind him, he wrote in one of his *Perish Commerce* articles, 'One of my correspondents remonstrated with me as with a *farmer*; it may, therefore, be of use to observe here that I am not one; that, in all likelihood, I never shall be one, and that, of course, I am perfectly disinterested upon that score'. It might have been more candid to add that he was already in possession of four farms, was looking for more, and was confidently expecting to build up a prosperous estate in land to leave to his children.

* These were Anne, b. Philadelphia, 1795; William, b. Philadelphia, 1798; John Morgan, b. London, 1800; and James Paul, b. London, 1803. Eleanor, Susan and Richard were all born at Botley between 1805 and 1814.

In 1804, however, his plans were less defined. A country place would allow him to escape from a city life he had come to hate and to bring his children up as country bred rather than as Cockneys. His health would benefit – he suffered from what were probably bronchial complaints whilst he was in London. He would have more time for writing and for the country sports he loved. Above all, he would be able to farm and garden and plant trees, occupations he had delighted in as a boy.

A final consideration, perhaps, was that farming might allow him to do what he had never before succeeded in doing, which was to accumulate capital. His current income, and his position as proprietor of the *Register*, would allow him to borrow whatever capital he would need to start him in farming, and he never doubted his ability to redeem his mortgages in a comparatively short time out of the profits of his farming.

In 1804 he began to pay frequent visits to Surrey and Hampshire, the counties he knew best. He was staying at Grange Park, Alresford, home of the close friend and shooting-companion of his Philadelphia days, Lord Henry Stuart, when he first came across the Hampshire village of Botley and the small farming estate of Fairthorn which lay on the outskirts of the village in the valley of the Bursledon River, some five miles from Southampton and seventy from London. The estate consisted of two medium-sized farms, two smaller ones, a large farmhouse built on a hill with grounds running down to the river, and several cottages. It was later described as covering 500 acres, but this probably included some of the parcels of land Cobbett had added to it.

By July 1805 Cobbett had arranged the necessary mortgages, completed his purchase and moved himself and his family into their new home. The following month he wrote joyously to Wright:

Botley is the most delightful village on the world. It has everything, in a village, that I love and none of the things I hate. It lies in a valley; the soil is rich, and thick-set with woods; the farms are small, the cottages neat; it has neither workhouse nor barber nor attorney nor justice of the peace, and though last not least, no Volunteers.* There is not justice within six miles of us, and the barber comes three miles once a week to shave and cut hair! 'Would I were poetical', I would write a poem in praise of Botley.[1]

---

* This is a reference to his opposition to Pitt's ideas for a large Volunteer force and to his own preference for an all-Regular army.

There can be nothing more pleasant for an active and vigorous man with an independent income, a love of farming and a liking for country sports than to acquire a handsome farming estate and to set about improving it. Cobbett was such a man, which is not to say that he treated his farming as a hobby, part-time farmer though he always was. He applied himself to his farming just as seriously as he had once applied himself to his education and later to his politics. He had many of the qualities that make for a successful farmer. He absorbed knowledge rapidly, so that what he had not already learnt about farming during his childhood he soon learnt from his new neighbours and from books. This was not enough, however, for a man of his speculative and analytical turn of mind, so he began to question existing methods and to experiment with new ones. In this he was aided by his passion for figures. He had used statistics lavishly in his journalism, and in his farming he was an early exponent of what is now called the statistical method. He was always weighing, measuring and estimating things, whether it was the number of bastards born in Paris in 1798 or the weight of a given number of swedes grown under different conditions in the same field.

Laymen may not, perhaps, realise how important statistics are in farming. Yet the more accurately a farmer can cost each of his undertakings, the better he is, generally, at pricing, measuring and estimating, the more likely he is to succeed. But, amateur economist and statistician though he was, Cobbett was never a good manager of money and, like so many other enthusiastic 'improvers', he over-invested.

If he had started as a poorer man he might well have ended up as a wealthier farmer. But, with a large income and the *Register* behind him, he could borrow almost at will. He persisted in sinking more and more borrowed capital into his various ventures, never believing that anything could happen to himself, or to his publishing business that could ruin his credit.

He over-invested in a number of ways, not all of them common among farmers. The Army had given him a passion for neatness and order, and so he planted new hedges, put up new fences and gates, tidied and re-planted woods until every corner of his holding was in parade order. He also had a passion for forestry which led him into buying up existing woodlands and planting new ones. Timber can be a profitable crop, but it is a very long-term one. Cobbett 'borrowed short in order to invest long' as his enemies, the bankers and jobbers, would have put it.

But his greatest farming weakness was that he suffered from that greed for more land which is as obsessive with farmers as a desire for more gold is with misers. Yet even from the start, he was never aware of what his capital position was, for that depended, very largely, on his credit, which depended, in its turn, on the success of the *Register*. This involved him in a somewhat speculative form of accounting, and as both he and Wright were extremely muddled accountants, his affairs were generally in some state of confusion. This was the case from the very beginning of Botley for, when he was completing the purchase, he wrote to Wright:

> I am this day going to take possession of the place at Droxford, in virtue of the notes you sent me the other day. But there will be wanted a good deal of money for the purchase of stock there and for the payment of my bills here. You will, therefore, by return of post, send me an account of your receipts and disbursements on my account. I shall then see what I am able to rely upon. But I want *immediately* 20 pounds to pay here, so you must send it by return of post.[2]

The accounts must have satisfied him, for shortly afterwards he wrote to thank Wright for presenting them 'made out with your usual clearness and celerity'. But hardly a week passed from then on without Cobbett demanding money 'by return of post' for he was drawing on Wright for his day-to-day expenses as well as for his investment capital, and this did little to help his accounting. Money was needed for a pair of 'Normandy cows' or a brace of grey-hounds, or a pointer dog, or nursery stock for his garden and his plantations, or for 'a suit of clothes for John and another for me, lest people should take me for a heathen philosopher, upon the maxim that the arses of such gentlemen are always to be seen through their pocket-holes'. So it was that, irrespective of Cobbett's purchases of land, there was an outflow of cash and credit that took little account of the profits that might be expected from farming or publishing.

And still Cobbett insisted on adding acre to acre. In 1807 he bought another 87 acres, most of it woodland, largely because it bounded his land and so would 'drive trespassers and poachers another half mile from me'. The asking price had been £3,200 and he wrote to Wright, 'I made a lumping offer of £3,000 and we met at 3,000 Guineas to be paid in notes at 2, 4 and 6 months. I wrote to Mr. Higham for his help, and he has promised it to me.'[3]

In the previous year inflation had brought about an all-too familiar publishing problem, a steep rise in the cost of paper, and Wright must have written advising caution in matters of expenditure, for Cobbett replied:

The rise in the price of paper is a very serious thing; but I have no other way of facing it, except by economy, if I *can* increase that. We have not drunk six glasses of wine since you left us. Almost all the money I draw is expended in preparations for planting . . . In short, I am drawing 5 pounds at a time to add 50 trees at a time to my real property; and, unless I do it now, I lose years of my life, which it is now too late to do. The pecuniary pinches give me great uneasiness at times; but they will cease before it be too long . . . much about the time that my grand planting scheme will be actually completed.[4]

Having started the letter swearing to economise, Cobbett ended it by telling Wright that 'there is a little coppice, which I think will have to be sold, which I intend you shall have . . . I am very desirous that you should have an inch of land that you might set your foot upon and say "This is mine"'. Whereupon he gave the owner of the coppice an accommodation bill at two months to secure its purchase.

If Cobbett was, in some respects, a spendthrift, it was seldom if ever for purposes of self-indulgence. He himself was always prepared to eat frugally, drink sparingly and live simply. What he spent on his farms may have been, in part, for his own gratification, but the main purpose was to build up, in the years that were left to him, a substantial estate he could leave to his sons, each of whom he proposed to bring up as a countryman, a sportsman and a farmer. There is something heart-warming in the fact that a large part of his domestic expenditure was devoted to entertaining his friends, for whom he kept open house, and in promoting and engaging in the sports of the countryside. He was, as Wright's 'little coppice' demonstrated, extremely generous: gifts of game, fruit and early vegetables used to flow from Botley to his friends and acquaintances in London.

And so Cobbett continued on what many might have considered to be his improvident way. In 1810 he already knew that he was to be brought to trial for seditious libel, and that he would, if convicted, be sent to prison and come close to being ruined. He spent the early months of that year putting his affairs in order and paying off such of his creditors as he could. He also arranged for his brother-in-law, Lieutenant Reid, to take over the management of the Botley farms whilst he was in prison. Yet only a month before his trial he wrote to that same Lieutenant Reid that he was proposing to buy 'an estate as large as all that I now possess . . . Three fine farms, two small ones, and some detached parcels of property, some in houses and some in land, including a fine chalk-pit, and having as much timber on it as I already have'.[5]

Since the purchase could only be completed with more borrowed money, and since he well knew the Government was willing to ruin him and his creditors were waiting to pick up the spoils, this was yet another example of land-hunger over-riding common prudence. In this respect there was always a gap with Cobbett between precept and practice. The man who attacked Pitt so bitterly for his spend-thrift ways with the taxpayer's money, who advised 'Young Men' to financial prudence and 'Cottagers' to the strictest domestic economy was himself incapable of controlling his domestic expenditure or of managing his capital investments cautiously.

Yet he had made the move to Botley full of plans for the money he would make and the money he would save from such a move. At the end of 1805 he discussed his domestic plans with Wright:

Mrs Cobbett and I have now fixed upon our plan and scale of living. [he wrote in an early letter from Botley.] We intend to live here from the first of May to the Queen's birthday in every year; to take a lodging in town for the three winter months and, of course, to get rid of the house and furniture in Duke Street as soon as I can get to town and put up the curtains so as to make the House look neat and handsome. Suppose a winter lodging for 13 weeks to cost us 3 guineas a week. Suppose my coach-hire to cost 20 pounds a year (ten trips between London and Alton). Suppose £20 a year for a store-room; that makes £80 a year. Very well; the house rent, the taxes, the water-duty, and the interest of money upon goods and wear and tear of goods in Duke Street (besides the interest upon what I paid for the lease) amounts to more than £240 a year. The garden stuff is worth £25 a year. The milk will not cost us above a third part of what it costs in town; bread is one-ninth cheaper (an immense sum in a year), the meat about an 8th cheaper. In short, I am fully convinced that, exclusive of the considerations of *health*, and taking into account postage &c. &c. attendant upon this distant situation, that the saving would be at least 300 pounds a year.[6]

It was a calculation Mr. Micawber might have approved of and, like most of Micawber's financial projections, it failed to reflect the reality of things. Cobbett continued, for the best of reasons, to over-invest and over-spend until, when he fled to America for the second time in 1817, his enemies announced that he had done so to avoid his creditors and published a list showing that he owed, at that moment, no less than £32,650, of which £16,000 represented mortgages on the Botley farms. They also accused him of absconding with creditors' money, and to this Cobbett, by then in America, replied:

> The sons and daughters of Corruption harp a good deal upon the circumstances of my having taken away a few hundred pounds in ready money . . . What! did they imagine I counted it *anything* to carry with me money enough to pay my passage and to furnish me with food and lodging for a few months? . . . I left behind me a farm covered with stock of all sorts, a house full of furniture; an estate which, with its improvements, had cost me forty thousand pounds, and which was mortgaged for less than seventeen thousand; copyrights which were worth an immense sum, and a current income from my writings of more than ten thousand pounds.[7]

Cobbett's investments were often a source of anxiety to his family. With the purchase of Botley he entered on a financial spiral from which he could never escape. His reaction, whenever he needed money, was to set up another writing and publishing project, the hypothetical profits from which would be invested in his farms long before they materialised. His family, therefore, while worrying about his publishing ventures, worried even more about the encouragement these gave to his farming investments. His wife must have been specially apprehensive for, shortly after the move to Botley, Cobbett wrote to Wright:

> I have one caution to give you, which I beg you will observe; and that is never to speak or hint, in the presence of Mrs Cobbett, anything relative to my pecuniary concerns or concerns in trade of any sort or kind. She has her own ideas about such matters, which cannot be altered. I have never mentioned *The Spirit of the Journals* to her; and there is no occasion for it. She knows I have lost so much by printing &c. that she is fearful of every thing of this kind. I cannot blame her anxiety, but, as I cannot remove it, it is better not to awaken it – Always reserve these matters for tête-à-tête opportunities . . .

By that time Ann had seen her husband prosperous and ruined in America, she had lived through the demise of *Porcupine's Gazette*, *The Rush-Light* and *The Porcupine*. What Cobbett's children felt about his expensive passion for farming was best demonstrated when they had grown up and Cobbett, with his customary resilience, was bouncing back from bankruptcy and penury. He had returned from his second American exile leaving his son, John Morgan, to manage his publishing business in the United States and to conduct the American side of an export–import business he had started as a seedsman and nurseryman. This was designed to introduce useful American crops such as Indian Corn and the Locust tree to England and English farm and garden seeds to America.

In 1820, however, Cobbett had to declare himself bankrupt, and Botley was finally lost to the family. In 1821 'My family, after having for years been scattered about like a covey of partridges that had been sprung and shot at, got *once more together*, in a hired lodging at Brompton . . .'[8] At that stage Major Codd, an old friend of Cobbett's, offered him the lease of a house in the then countrified suburb of Kensington. Its chief attraction was a four-acre walled garden, most of which was laid down to grass. The kindly Major thought that such an unusual example of *rus in urbe* might console Cobbett for the loss of his Botley broad acres and allow him to play at farming by keeping a couple of cows and by growing fruit and vegetables for the household.

That hope was echoed in a letter that his oldest daughter, Anne, sent to John Morgan Cobbett in New York:

The house we are in at present, at Brompton, we find too small, and we have got one in our eye at Kensington, which has four acres of land, quite enough for Papa's amusement, though not sufficient to drag him into any great expenses.[9]

Anne, it has to be said, under-estimated her father, who now set about turning the 'rough and sour meadow' into a nursery in which there were no less than 450 beds containing a million 'seedling forest trees and shrubs and about three thousand young apple trees'. The youngest Cobbett daughter, Susan, wrote of this in later years:

All went pleasantly for a good bit. The large piece of grass induced the keeping of cows for our use, a little dairy was built and we made butter. [But] Major Codd was mistaken in thinking that but little could be spent in the walled-up 4 acres . . . The grass was taken up and there was a vast deal done in digging and trenching for sowing the seeds and planting out the young trees . . . the men at times stood so close together that they could not well work. There were as many as 100 at a time at work in that four acres. All this, and the importation of American seeds, fruits and timber was very fine, but it ran away with a great deal

267

of money which the *Register* so plentifully brought in during the years at Kensington.[10]

Whether Cobbett's additional role as a seedsman and nursery-man was a profitable one must be doubted. What is clear is that, once again, his pen and his *Register* had to provide the means with which he could indulge his passion for growing things. Kensington alone provided insufficient scope. In 1827 Cobbett leased an 87-acre farm from the Barn Elm estate. This was in run-down condition, though he described it as 'the richest land I believe in this whole world, except those marshes which bring disease along with their riches'.* He put his only surviving brother in charge of the farm, but the latter's increasing infirmity led him to publish in the *Register* a celebrated advertisement for a farming apprentice:

I want neither science nor advice. I want *legs* that will move nimbly and willingly, and a young head capable of *learning*. The lad ought to be *stout* and not stunted, he ought to be able to read and write a little; but two things are indispensable; namely that his father be a *farmer*, and that the son has lived on a farm in *England* all his life . . . He is to sit at table with my brother and my niece (who is the housekeeper), and, when I am at the farm, with me also; and is to be treated in every respect as the *young farmer of the house*. He is never to quit the farm; except on my business and to go to the parish church on the Sunday . . . He will here learn all about the cultivation of Indian Corn, Mangle Wurzle, and of several other things not very common. He will learn to sow and rear trees, and to plant and prune them. He will learn how to raise seeds of various sorts . . . how to grind and dress wheat and Indian Corn . . . how to make beer; to see butter and cheese made before breakfast time; and he will have constantly before his eyes examples of early rising, activity, punctual attention to business, *content with plain living*, and Perfect *sobriety*. Now, if any farmer, who is of *my political principles, full up to the mark*, have such a son, nephew or grandson, to dispose of in this way, I shall be glad to hear from him . . . It is, I hope, unnecessary to add, that this is a farm-house without a *tea-kettle* or a *coffee-pot*, and without any of the *sweets* that come from the *sweats* of African slaves. Please to

---

* The Essex marshes and the fenlands of East Anglia were then, as now, some of the most productive areas in Britain. Malaria, or the ague as it was then called, was, however, endemic in them and crops were more liable to blight and mildews than were those grown on drier soils.

observe, that I do not want a *young gentleman*; but a good, sturdy lad, whose hands do not instinctively recoil from a frozen chain, or from the dirty heels of a horse or an ox. I hope that the lad . . . will never have been at an *establishment* vulgarly called a *boarding-school*; if he unfortunately have, and should suit in other respects, I must sweat the boarding-school nonsense out of him . . . If he have a mind to improve himself in study, here are books, and all the other means of well employing his leisure hours . . .

P.S. The *great qualities* are, a fitness to *give orders*, and *spirit to enforce obedience*; and, above all things, never to *connive* at the misconduct of the men . . . It will be quite useless to engage a soft, milky thing, that has not the courage to make a lazy fellow stir, or to reprove a perverse one . . .

N.B. I will have no one, who has a near relation that is a *tax-eater* of any sort.[11]

Cobbett's increasing dogmatism in farming and political matters is demonstrated in this advertisement, and it was at Barn Elm that his farming idiosyncracies were most publicly revealed. He had, by now, departed from the more conventional manner of life he had practised at Botley and, perhaps under the influence of the ideas he had assembled for his *Cottage Economy*, was insisting, more than he ever had before, on a regime of the strictest self-sufficiency.

It was at this time that he claimed that nothing proceeding from wheat* or which was not 'the produce of the soil of England' had been consumed at Barn Elm, and wagered £100 that no one could find 'under any roof, nay under six roofs, any twelve persons that have so many inches of red upon their cheeks'. Because he had excluded spirits, sugar, tea, coffee and all groceries from the household there had been no illness in it. 'The accursed tea has not been here to shake our nerves, and the brandied wine and the vitrioled spirits, and the abominable brewer's poison have been kept away from under this roof, and we have been well though close upon the border of a marshy meadow which, I was told, would give us all agues and typhus fevers.'

To demonstrate how well they lived under such a régime he described how two young men out with their dogs and their guns had been breakfasted when they called at the Barn Elm farm-

---

* Cobbett was, at that time, endeavouring to move agricultural policy away from that emphasis on wheat production that had been one consequence of the war and one of the reasons for General Enclosures. He thought that this might be achieved by persuading farmers to grow Indian Corn *as a grain crop*.

house. He had given them 'about four pounds of solid fat bacon, without a morsel of lean in it, but exquisitely good, rosy as a cherry, and transparent as glass'. Accompanying this home-produced delicacy were a pudding made of home-grown maize meal and mutton suet and swedes off the farm, the whole boiled in one pot with the bacon. The meal was rounded off with a pot of home-brewed ale (thirty gallons to the bushel of malt) and bread made from home-grown and home-ground rye flour and maize meal. Our less robust modern stomachs might persuade us that there was a vomit in every mouthful of such a breakfast, but Cobbett remarked that his guests 'praised the victuals exceedingly', and that the whole meal had cost him less than threepence a head.[12]

It was, perhaps, more of a 'political' breakfast than an example of the old-fashioned country hospitality Cobbett had generally practised. It was not, however, the only occasion when political and economic theories dominated events at Barn Elm. Cobbett had long believed that factories were not needed and that the land could always give employment to all who wanted it, even if this meant returning to the spade and the flail in place of the plough and the threshing machine. Barn Elm land was in such a dirty condition when he entered the farm that this gave him an opportunity to put his theory into practice, with, perhaps, some farming benefit to himself. Digging was still a better method of ridding the land of couch grass and other perennial weeds than any system of ploughing then available, and Cobbett advertised offering work to any men prepared to dig Barn Elm.

Scores of out-of-work labourers replied and were set to work digging most of the farm's 87 acres. This would have been an inordinately expensive form of tillage had Cobbett not announced that they would be paid only in kind. Each man accordingly received two pounds of bread, half a pound of cheese and two pounds of meat a day. Many of the Radical leaders accused him of bringing the hated 'truck' system into agriculture, which did nothing to worry him since he had no objections to the truck system, which he saw as a variant of the old 'living-in' system under which single farm labourers had been hired for centuries. As he pointed out, his diggers were actually receiving more food than they could have purchased had he paid them the current money wage.

Business man and capitalist though he had to be, Cobbett never really accepted the money economy. He had no objection to earning a large income for himself, but he was instinctively opposed to any system that measured a man's work and worth in cash terms. A labourer, he argued, would be better off with a full belly, a warm back and a rain-tight roof than he would be without them but with money in his pocket, for in the process of turning that money back into food and warmth he was placing himself in the hands of those unnecessary middlemen, the shopkeepers and tradesmen. He had, at the turn of the century, seen something close to a moneyless economy in the United States, where the old Continental currency had lost most of its value and, in the Western Settlements at least, men had grown accustomed to living by self-sufficiency and barter.

Barn Elm was held on a short lease which was not renewed when it expired in 1830. Mr. Colebrook, his landlord, apparently complained about the state of the land and the crops at Cobbett's outgoing, which suggests that, whatever the politico-economic benefits of spade-culture may have been, it was not entirely successful when it came to couch grass. Cobbett, of course, denied that the farm had suffered at his hands, but his enemies rejoiced at the suggestion. *The Times* and the *Farmer's Journal*, generally referred to by Cobbett as *The Bullfrog's Blunderer** gleefully described how 'Farmer' Cobbett had left the land at Barn Elm 'a bed of weeds' and reported on 'the hue of misery' that hung over the entire farm, from the empty granary and rickyard to the dilapidated and empty styes and the meagre root crop.

Cobbett answered them in a *Register* article which listed the yields of the excellent crops he had grown on the farm and gave the names and addresses of the many expert judges who had admired them. He described the improvements he had made to the holding and all that he had contributed to agricultural science through his experiments there, not least the establishment of Indian Corn as a crop suitable for British farming conditions. He warned Mr. Colebrook against issuing statements about dilapidation that could be proved libellous and the article ended with the proud boast that 'Cobbett's Corn will succeed in *any summer* in England. I have the crop to *show* to any one that may choose to see it, and this is the best answer to all gainsayers'.

Cobbett was nearly seventy when he had to quit Barn Elm. Age, however, had done nothing to blunt his appetite for further farming ventures. In 1831 he advertised for the tenancy of a farm and was offered and accepted a long lease of Normandy Farm at Ash in West Surrey. And so, in some respects, he finally came home, for Ash was no more than four miles from Farnham and he

---

* 'Bullfrog's' because it supported the large farmers who had, by adding farm to farm, swollen themselves up like bullfrogs; 'Blunderer' because the paper did not support all Cobbett's farming theories.

had come back to farm land that he had known and run over as a boy. He was able, therefore, to spend the last four years of his life as a part-time farmer and, having been born on a farm, to die on one.

Nevertheless he continued to divide his time between his farm and London, and to devote some of it to the last of his *Rural Rides* into Scotland, Wales and Ireland. When he at last won a seat in Parliament in 1832, he gave up his house with the four-acre garden in suburban Kensington and took one closer to the Houses of Parliament at 21 Crown Street, Westminster. This, family troubles apart, must soon have proved too expensive for him, since his last London residence was over his business premises in Bolt Court off Fleet Street. There was perhaps something symbolic in this move away from Westminster. The House of Commons he always disliked; journalism he excelled in; the land he loved. He died more closely connected by residence and inclination with the last two than with the first.

Looking back, in his latter years, he counted his blessings, as old men sometimes do. They included his farm at Barn Elm, his house in Kensington and his office in Bolt Court. 'What more than this,' he wrote, 'can I want? I have horses at my will; always not less than half a dozen men to start at my call. God has blessed me with health and strength very rare at my age. Has ambitions its calls upon me? What can it suggest beyond the farm that I have? Beyond the real power which I possess of upholding my friends and beating down my enemies?'[13]

Ambition may well have made one more call on him which he, ever optimistic in such matters, never realised must be left unfulfilled. For the past thirty years he had worked – no one more assiduously – in order to provide a prosperous farming estate for his sons to inherit. When he died, Cobbett was so close to insolvency that even the *Register*, the first and main source of the family's prosperity, could not be continued for more than a few months. It was even less feasible to renew the lease of Normandy Farm and to continue, however modestly, in agriculture. So it was that, for the next generation of Cobbetts at least, those connections with the land that their father had held so dear were lost.

Cobbett was never merely a writer who took up farming. Far less was he a farmer who took up politics and writing. He was, by any standards, a man whose achievement it was to make an important and lasting contribution to an understanding of rural England. His upbringing at the tail of a plough would not, by itself, have given him the authority that was eventually his. That authority came to him slowly as Cobbett of the *Register* developed, successively, into Cobbett of Botley, Cobbett of Barn Elm and Cobbett of Normandy Farm.

CHAPTER TWELVE

Domestic Life and Domestic Theories

> Let me be no assistant for a state
> But keep a farm and carters.
> Shakespeare: *Hamlet*

Such assistance as Cobbett had given the state had, for the most part, consisted of savagely criticising the manner in which it had been governed. He had no intention of withdrawing such assistance because he had progressed to keeping a farm and carters. But his criticisms were now concerned with country and farming matters quite as often as with matters of foreign and economic policy. Since most Britons still lived in the country and the principal business of the nation was still farming, Cobbett's political writings did not, therefore, necessarily become parochial. He could attack the Pitt System through Enclosures, Poor Rates, depopulation, corn laws, food prices and farm wages quite as satisfactorily as he had attacked it for bungling the war, creating a paper aristocracy, ruining Ireland and grossly extending the power and sphere of central government.

As a writer, he concerned himself solely, now, with the *Register*, and would continue to do so for the next dozen years. The *Register* however, began to reflect his new life at Botley, not only in the space given to country and farming politics, but in that also given to private and domestic matters. Cobbett had more time to devote to these, and the digressions he had always indulged in were now used to advance his developing views on such topics as marriage, diet, exercise, sport, gardening and the education of children. Later in life, when he turned to authorship, he wrote a series of books around these subjects, but they had already begun to be mentioned, if only by way of digressions, in his journalism. He never doubted that his own experiences as husband, father, farmer and countryman entitled him to pronounce on such matters *ex pede Herculem*. We can, as a consequence, gain a clear picture of life at Botley from even his widest generalisations on these subjects. Education is a case in point.

As soon as Cobbett had settled his family at Botley he wrote to John Wright that he was sending his oldest daughter to a school at Winchester and his two older sons to another at Twyford. This last was the establishment in which Alexander Pope, one of Cobbett's few literary heroes, had started his education. Another item in its favour was that the master, although a 'noisy hawbuck' was sufficiently radical in his politics to be a Burdettite, and Cobbett was beginning to believe that his own political future lay in supporting that famous parlour Radical, Sir Francis Burdett, rather than Windham who, as the prospect of a return to office increased, was proving to be more and more conventionally a Whig and a member of a self-protecting Establishment.

His friendship with Windham was to survive, however, until the latter actually took office in 1806. Consequently Cobbett felt able to write to him also about the education of his children. 'My three children I shall now put to school . . . My intention is to make the boys fit to *fight* their way through life; for who can be so weak as to imagine that we shall, or they will ever see many days of tranquillity!' The school would, he pointed out, teach them 'to write English, to speak French; to read a little Latin' if it did nothing else. For the rest, it was his intention to 'teach them by precept and example, to ride, to play at single-stick, and, above all things, to *work at husbandry*'.[1]

Windham, a scholarly man who had been educated at Eton and the Universities of Glasgow and Oxford, may have thought this a somewhat Spartan form of education, but there was nothing startingly unorthodox in the division Cobbett had made between what the ushers would be allowed to cram into his sons at school and the other, more important matters he hoped to train them to at home. The ushers, however, must have failed in their task, for he soon wrote to Wright that 'the school project has failed. William tells me that *something* is continually making him cry. When he saw me he was ready to burst . . . You have helped to make him so in love with home, and you must have the teaching of him *another year* or two. His mother cannot live without him, and they must be humoured.'

At least one more school was tried, but it also proved unsatisfactory and Cobbett decided, as best suited his affectionate disposition and his experimental mind, to educate them – or, rather, allow them to educate themselves – at home. They never had, he wrote almost thirty years later, '*teacher* of any description; and I never, and nobody else ever taught any one of them to read, write or anything else, except in conversation, and yet no man was ever more anxious to be the father of a family of clever and learned persons'.*[2]

Cobbett was now well past his anti-Jacobin fervours and so could allow himself to be influenced by the educational theories put forward by Rousseau in *Emile*. He agreed entirely with the latter's theory that children should be taught through pleasure and kindness rather than through pain and compulsion. Since the body had to be nurtured before the mind, the first thing to attend to was their health. At Botley, therefore, each child had his or her 'flower-bed, little garden, plantation of trees; rabbits, dogs, asses, horses, pheasants and hares; hoes, spades, whips, guns; always some object of lively interest, and as much *earnestness* and *bustle* about the various objects as if our living had solely depended on them. I made everything give way to the great object of making their lives happy and innocent'.[3]

The education of their minds, Cobbett insisted, should always consist of a leading out rather than a stuffing in. The child would educate himself once he was given access to knowledge and provided with examples of how pleasurable and serviceable knowledge could be. How this was done at Botley is described in *Advice to Young Men*:

A large strong table in the middle of the room, their mother sitting at her work, the baby, if big enough, set up in a high chair. Here were inkstands, pens, pencils, India-rubber, and paper, all in abundance, and every one scrabbled about as he or she pleased. There were prints of animals of all sorts; books treating of them; others treating of gardening, of flowers, of husbandry, of hunting, coursing, shooting, fishing, planting, and, in short, of everything with regard to which we had something to do . . . The book-learning *crept in* of its own accord, by imperceptible degrees. Children naturally want to be *like* their parents, and to do *what they do*; the boys following their father, and the girls their mother; and as I was always *writing* or *reading*, mine naturally wanted to do something in the same way . . . What need had we of schools? What need of teachers? What need of *scolding* and *force* to induce children to read, write and love books?[4]

* Cobbett was, perhaps, claiming too much. His letters from Newgate reveal that the sons who had come to London in order to keep him company were being taught, not only by himself, but also by a variety of schoolmasters, including, to his great amusement, a dancing master.

Cobbett was prepared to admit, albeit grudgingly, that not all fathers, however loving, could do as he had done at Botley, where 'my occupation, to be sure, was chiefly carried on at *home*'. But if, in the last resort, a child had to be sent to a school, then 'let it be as little populous as possible . . . *Jails*, *barracks*, *factories*, do not corrupt by their *walls*, but by their condensed numbers. Populous cities corrupt from the same cause; and it must be the same with regard to schools, out of which children come not what they were when they went in'.

Schools, and universities, were, he argued, factories for cramming their pupils full of too much learning and too little knowledge, since they considered that 'learning consisted *solely* in the acquirement of a knowledge of the meaning of words in various languages, which knowledge is to be derived from books'. They encouraged intellectual arrogance, and feelings of superiority in those who were sent to them because their parents were wealthy, and of subservience in those who got to them although their parents were not. Worst of all, they kept children isolated for far too long from the world of adult experience. 'If boys live only with boys, their ideas will continue boyish . . .'

Cobbett was addressing himself here to the problems of the middle classes, of those who were free to decide *how* and not *whether* their children should be educated. When it came to the problems of educating the masses, he produced theories which have dismayed educationalists and 'social engineers' up to this day, and which seemed to justify Karl Marx's dismissal of him as a man who 'looked for popular liberty rather in the past than in the future'.

This was an age when every *bien pensant*, whether of the Evangelical or Utilitarian persuasion, was promoting schemes for bringing literacy to the illiterate. Cobbett was by no means opposed to a working man bettering himself by educating himself, but he was permanently suspicious of organised attempts to force education on him. He argued, in the first place, that the *bien pensants* invariably confused education with book learning:

If the farmer understands well how to conduct the business of his farm, and if, from observation of the seasons and the soil, he knows how to draw from the latter as much profit as therefrom can be drawn; if the labourer be expert at ploughing, sowing, reaping, mowing, making of ricks and fences . . . if this be the case, though neither of them can read or write, I call neither an *ignorant* man. The education of these men is a finished one, though neither may ever have looked into a book.[5]

As one of the most successful of all auto-didacts, and an advocate of the virtues of self-help and self-sufficiency, he further believed that when a man wished to educate either himself or his children he should do as Cobbett had done. That is, he should attend to that task himself and not leave it either to the State or to any charitable organisation, none of whom could be trusted not to have ulterior motives. Yet Cobbett's principal arguments were always political ones. As long as he was a Tory with no very high regard for the 'democratical mob' he had argued that education would destroy the hardiness, vigour and independence of the common people, and would reduce the English to a tract-reading, psalm-singing, Methodistical race of toadies. As a Radical, he feared much the same thing, though for different reasons. He had come to believe, by then, that his chief duty was so to expose and foster and focus the discontents of the poor that the Pitt System would collapse for want of popular support. Thereupon Merry England would be reinstated.

Education could prevent this, for it would be used by the Establishment to soften, rather than strengthen, the legitimate discontents of the oppressed. They would be taught to read the corrupt, time-serving newspapers, the pietistic tracts and edifying books that all sought to convince those who read them that everything was for the best in this world below, and that once this had been accepted, all would be even better for them in the world above.

Popular education, in short, was no more than another eleemosynary device serving the abhorred and abhorrent 'comforting system'. It would encourage the poor to forget their discontents, accept their poverty and be grateful to their betters, so ignoring those political imperatives which required them to nurse their discontents, hate their poverty, and work to bring down those who had been responsible for it. Whether discontent is, or is not divine remains a matter for political, philosophical and theological argument. What seems indisputable is that universal education – which was not introduced until 1880 – has not had the effect that Cobbett anticipated and feared. Far from softening and silencing what he had come to regard as the necessary discontents of the poor, education has so nurtured them that they now flourish as they never did in his days of deep poverty and spontaneous violence.

If Cobbett's writings on education were partly based on his own political prejudices and partly on what he had learnt from educating his children at Botley, then most of what he wrote about

278

marriage was either theoretical and moralistic, or else was based on his own experiences as Ann's husband. He had no other experience to draw on, for he was strictly monogamous and puritanically chaste, qualities which had the effect of making him all the more uxorious.

Few prose writers have ever written so poetically – and on occasion so fulsomely – on the subject of the happy marriage. Even fewer have insisted that the woman must bring quite so many moral and domestic virtues to the wedding bed in order to achieve it. The qualities he insisted on in a wife, and had, so far as his public was concerned, found in Ann, included sobriety, frugality, cheerfulness, constancy, modesty, industry, cleanliness, neatness, good temper and skill in every one of the domestic arts. Beauty was also important when it came to choosing a wife, but for a somewhat topsy-turvy reason: an ugly girl was, he believed, more likely to have been seduced before marriage than a pretty one. 'Which is the most likely to resist; she who has a choice of lovers, or she who, if she let the occasion slip, may never have it again?'⁶

His own experience of women had convinced him that no man could be happy with a wife who moped or giggled immoderately; who was idle, sluttish, fond of finery, flighty, extravagant, or given to chewing her food too slowly. Masterful, pertinacious, argumentative and intellectual women all made bad wives, and no sensible man would ever consider his wife ignorant if she was a good cook, housekeeper and mother but was unable to play the piano or discuss the latest plays and novels.

But once a wise choice had been made, and once the paragon had been courted, wedded and bedded, certain duties devolved upon the husband if he wanted the union to be a happy one. The most important of these were concerned with the need to sustain and nourish the young wife's self-esteem and self-confidence. This was best accomplished by always preferring her company to anyone else's, and by being unremittingly attentive, unwaveringly faithful, and, it would seem, tirelessly amorous. The last was a duty that might become onerous, if only because 'Nature has so ordered it, that men shall become less ardent in their passion after the wedding-day, and that women shall not. Their ardour increases rather than the contrary; and they are surprisingly quick-sighted and inquisitive on that score.'⁷

A husband who continued in his bachelor ways and spent his time with his boon companions should expect to be cuckolded. Adultery was, of course, a more serious offence for a woman than for a man, not because the sin was greater, but because it could have different consequences. The male adulterer 'only brings *shame* upon his wife and family; whereas the wife, by her breach of her vow, may bring the husband a spurious offspring to maintain.' Yet the husband who passed his evenings in coffee-houses and taverns was actually inviting his wife to engage in this most serious of all matrimonial crimes. At the least he was encouraging her to retaliate by gadding about to tea-parties, and everyone knew that the gossip and frivolous behaviour of women around the tea table was a training for the brothel. At the worst, his neglect of the marriage bed, or his drink-impaired performance in it, would sooner or later oblige his wife to look elsewhere for the satisfaction of the 'ardours' that marriage had aroused.

That situation, however, would ease once child-bearing had begun, for, 'when the *child* comes, it divides this ardour with the father; but, until then, you have it all; and if you have a mind to be happy, repay it with all your soul . . . let your words and looks and manners be just what they were before you called her your wife'.

Child-bearing, which was, of course, the principal purpose of marriage, must continue unremittingly until the passing of the years brought it to its inevitable close. Thereafter the husband should, if it lay in him, continue to be kind and attentive to his wife. By then, however, 'time and others things have, in most cases, blunted her feelings, and rendered a harsh or stern demeanour in the husband a matter not of heart-breaking consequence'.

The proper attitude of a wife to her husband at all stages of their marriage was one of unquestioning obedience. 'Reason has said, and God has said, that it is the duty of wives to be obedient to their husbands; and the very nature of things prescribes that there must be a *head* of every household, and an undivided authority . . . Am I recommending tyranny? Am I recommending *disregard* of the wife's opinions and wishes? By no means: on the contrary, though I would keep anything disagreeable from her, I should not enjoy the prospect of good without making her a participator . . . A woman when patiently reasoned with on this subject, must be a virago in her very nature not to submit with docility to the terms of her marriage vow.'

So much for Cobbett's views on marriage, which would not be complete, however, without one further reference to the subject of children. Cobbett had an almost pagan respect for fertility in all of its forms. This being so, he valued the mother even more than he valued the wife. She could never be more beautiful in his eyes than when she held a babe to her breast, had an infant in the cradle, a toddler clutching at her knee, and all the older products of her womb clustered around her.

The value he placed on all forms of self-sufficiency forced him to believe that it was an offence against nature and common sense to put any child out to a wet-nurse. Although he was too modest to say as much, fecundity and good milking qualities were included among his other *desiderata*. That same modesty led him to attribute to women rather more pudor than they themselves might have considered sensible, for, much as he valued procreation, he was most violently opposed to the growing habit of employing male midwives.*

It would be easy for modern experts to decide from all this that Cobbett's attitude towards women, marriage and procreation was a compound of the humbug and male chauvinism considered typical of the Victorians. He was, in certain respects, a premature Victorian. When he wrote, as he so often did, about the virtues of self-help, diligence and thrift he seemed to be anticipating Samuel Smiles rather than reflecting the world of Henry Fielding. Yet when he wrote about women he was looking backwards, beyond even Fielding, to a long line of peasant ancestors. It had always been for them a matter of great and equal importance so far as their livelihoods were concerned that their fields, their livestock and their women should all be both fertile and serviceable.

There are now fewer peasants in England than in any other country in Europe, and we have grown out of the habit of believing that fertility can still be an important criterion. But for Cobbett, as for most of his contemporaries, it was still the most important of all qualities. It is far from fanciful to believe that his regard for fertility lay at the very root of his politics. His 'Pittiad' was based on it. A man who, however misguidedly, took it as an article of faith that English fields and English herds would always be productive enough to supply all the food that Englishmen might ever need to eat, was bound, in the end, to believe that a system that condemned so many of them to starvation must be perversely conceived, malignly administered and contrary to every tradition and instinct of the race.†

A worship of fertility lay beneath his moral and political

---

* Cobbett was once given a bedroom at an inn which he could only leave in the morning by passing through an outer bedroom in which a lady was sleeping. Mr. Pickwick confronting the middle-aged lady in yellow curl-papers was no more embarrassed than Cobbett was when, as an early riser, he sought to leave his room and get to his breakfast. (*Rural Rides*, 10 October 1826.)

† Cobbett relied on ancient authorities from Bede to Fortescue to prove that the English had always been a hearty, meat-eating, beer-swilling, well-nourished race of eupeptics, and that it had taken a Pitt to destroy these blessings. More modern authorities have demonstrated that, from time immemorial, periodic famine kept the population of England to below three million until food production began to increase in the seventeenth century, and the *Rosbifs* emerged.

objections to 'the monster MALTHUS, who has furnished the un-
feeling oligarchs and their toad-eaters with the pretence that *man
has a natural propensity to breed faster than food can be raised
for the increase*'.[8] One could argue that Cobbett, who himself
supported the Malthusian theory in his Tory days, only turned
against it because he had turned Radical, there being little room
in any Radical philosophy for the proposition that the human
condition is only marginally and precariously capable of improvement. This would, however, be to ignore Cobbett the moralist.
Although Parson Malthus had advocated nothing more drastic, by
way of birth control, than continence and late marriage, Cobbett
maintained that his theory could have no other outcome than
to persuade men to accept as natural all manner of unnatural
practices, such as contraception, onanism and sodomy.

A large part of Cobbett's radicalism grew out of his ferocious
opposition to the influence of the Malthusian theory as it was
actually interpreted and acted upon by contemporary politicians.
Since the population of England was increasing at that time at a
rate we now associate with a country like Bangladesh, Malthus
seemed justified, and politicians would have been failing in their
duties if they had not considered the future problems of a country
that was rapidly becoming incapable of feeding itself from its own
resources.

Such consideration produced various possible solutions, each of
them equally odious to Cobbett. The strictest Utilitarians suggested that paupers who insisted on breeding should be ineligible
for relief, and that they and their children should be left to starve or
not as Fate and common sense ordained. This was never accepted,
but there was considerable support for the idea that the diet of the
poorest and most numerous section of the population should be
debased. It took less land to keep a labourer alive on potatoes,
soup and tea than to maintain him in bread, meat and beer. The
poor, however, could not easily be persuaded to live on potatoes,
and even when they did, they continued to procreate, paying no
regard to the nation's problems.

Emigration, some argued, could provide a useful, if partial
alternative, but not all the poor were criminals who could be
transported to Botany Bay, and not all of them could be persuaded
by the Emigration Societies to try their luck in the Americas.
Meanwhile the Speenhamland System, under which the poor
received relief from the rates according to the size of their families,
actually encouraged the resident poor to breed. The burden this
placed on the parish rate finally persuaded the politicians that Poor
Law reform had become a necessity. Cobbett's longest and most

bitter struggle was against the new Union system that emerged, which abolished the ancient system of outdoor relief and shut paupers away from the community in workhouses. There, 'those who have command over the poor, keep the married women separated from their husbands; do not suffer them to see each other but once in so long a time; and then, for only so many minutes, and never out of the presence of the overseer; and all this for the odious, the shameless, the beastly purpose of preventing that increase in family which the parson at the marriage has joined with the parties in praying God may take place, and which God himself has said shall be considered a blessing'.[9]

Cobbett did not become seized of these problems as soon as he had moved to Botley. But, although he devoted much of his time there to farming and domestic matters, politics continued to obtrude, and his personal involvement increased as he saw, all around him in the countryside, concrete examples of the damage created, as he maintained, by the Pitt system. An opposition to that system that had started with almost theoretical objections to its economic and social consequences, was now strengthened by contact with the miseries of the rural poor and by every change for the worse in the old country way of life.

Cobbett was not the man to take such things lightly, and his daughter Anne remembered how deeply his political passions affected him, even in the privacy of his home. 'He felt as he wrote. Would look pale with earnestness in the subject, folding his hands which would seem to get thinner and thinner, and his voice would falter. This was the case when he wrote some of his best *Registers* – upon the subject of the poor; the church; the honour and glory of his country.'[10]

Anne had, indeed, been brought up to recognise the depths of her father's political emotions. According to her, when Cobbett returned to England in 1800 and had refused to be rewarded for his services in America, he asked Pitt to give his daughter, then aged five, a small present that would, in future years, remind her of her father's connections with that great man. Pitt had accordingly presented the infant Anne with a locket which had, 'in the centre W.P. in pretty filigree letters of gold', and which contained a lock of his hair. When Cobbett turned against Pitt, three years later, his anger over the Peace of Amiens was so great that he burnt the hair and erased the initials, 'greatly to my grief'.[11]

Political animal though he was, Cobbett avoided discussing politics with his guests all the time he kept open house at Botley. That open house was important to him, not merely because it increasingly served as a meeting place for his London and country friends, but also because he placed great value on the old English tradition of simple but unstinted hospitality. In later life he would complain that formal invitations and elaborate soirées had replaced the old country habit of keeping open house for one's friends, and he was delighted to rediscover in the United States habits of simple hospitality that had disappeared from England.

Mary Russell Mitford visited Botley when the Cobbett's days there were drawing to their close. They no longer lived at Fairthorn but, for reasons of economy, had rented 'Sherecroft', a house in the village which, she remembered, reminded her of her host since, like him, it was 'large, high, massive, red and square'.

'There was,' she wrote, 'a constant flow of visitors for the hour or for the day, and the visitors were of all ranks, from the Earl and his Countess to the farmer and his dame. The house had room for all, and the hearts of the owners would have had room for three times the number. I never saw hospitality more genuine, more simple, or more thoroughly successful in the great end of hospitality, the putting of everybody completely at ease. There was not the slightest attempt at finery, or display, or gentility. They called it a farmhouse, and everything was in accordance with the largest ideas of a great English yeoman of the old time'

However one anonymous guest thought it necessary to point out, as so many others did, that there was always, with Cobbett, some distinction to be made between precept and practice:

From the manner in which Cobbett wrote his *Register* one would have supposed that he lived as an English yeoman, eating a leg of mutton, a dish of bacon and beans, and drinking a glass of home-brewed ale. I do not know how this may be on ordinary days; but this I can state, that when Cobbett entertained, he did so in good style, sensibly and solidly. There was on the table, and well-served, everything that any man of wholesome appetite in the station of a gentleman or a gentleman-farmer could require – a good soup, a good fish, a good roast and wholesome vegetables. I never saw a finer baron of beef at any nobleman's county ball at Christmas time than I have seen at Cobbett's table, and he seemed to have a peculiar pleasure and pride in standing up before it, a large carving knife and fork in hand, ready to give a prime cut. He drank pretty freely of ale out of a large tankard.[12]

Apart from keeping open house for his friends, Cobbett was able to enter into village and county life more fully when he was at Botley than he ever would again. He organised single-stick matches and village sports. He hunted, coursed and shot, occupations he delighted in and wrote about with great charm. No sportsman could fail to enjoy his analysis of the place sport occupied in country life, or of the differences between hunting men and shooting men. He could interrupt a serious passage of political argument to comment on the habits of pheasants in the snow, to describe a gundog he had once owned or a day he had spent shooting in Philadelphia with a lawyer who insisted on fudging the bag. Purists might quarrel with his insistence that what the Americans of his day called quail were really partridge, and what they called partridge were pheasant, but they will forgive him that for his descriptions of woodcock shooting on Long Island. Opposition to field sports was, apparently, as strong in his day as now, and all shooting men will recognise and applaud the arguments he put up in defence of his sport which are contained in *A Year's Residence in the United States*.

Although he shot over dogs, in the old-fashioned way, he by no means approved of Botley being poached. One of the purposes of acquiring more land had been to remove potential poachers to a greater distance. His farm account book records a scale of rewards to his staff: '40s for each poacher or shooter, that shall be prosecuted to conviction, if I pardon him; and the whole of the penalty if I take the penalty'. Yet he was a staunch opponent of the series of new and harsher Game Laws passed in the time of George IV to protect the new sport of battues which made night poaching a transportation offence, and an affray with gamekeepers a hanging one.

The only indication that he took any interest in fishing, and then hardly a sporting one, was when he discovered shortly after he came to Botley that the salmon peel ran up the river at the bottom of his garden. He wrote off to Wright immediately for a trammel net, with which he caught so many fish that he boasted in his next letter that the catch would more than pay for the cost of the net. One must doubt whether any fish were sold for this purpose, but shortly after there was a letter to Windham concerning a parcel of fine salmon being sent to Mrs. Windham.

How popular Cobbett was with his neighbours in the county, it is difficult to know. The villagers of Botley liked him well enough to give him a rousing welcome on his return from two years' imprisonment in Newgate, but the Botley parson, Mr. Baker, refused to allow the church bells to be rung in his honour. Cobbett enjoyed a protracted feud with Baker. Although he had started life at Botley as a regular church-goer willing to be on good terms with both Church and parson, he found in Baker a man quite as quarrelsome and as opinionated as himself. They were friends at first but were bound to fall out, even without Cobbett's increasingly Radical views on tithes, pluralities and the correct status and function of parish priests. Cobbett was, perhaps, the last man to object to anyone being political but Baker was a typical High Tory churchman of that period, and his sermons seemed so full of his politics that Cobbett once declared he deserved to be horse-whipped for them in his own pulpit.

The Botley doctor did something very close to that. After a violent quarrel with Baker in the vestry he took his riding crop to him to settle the argument. Even the parish clerk took exception when Baker ordered him to thrash his wife for failing to come to church, and retorted that Baker would do better to take a stick to Mrs. Baker. The villagers probably enjoyed all the ridicule Cobbett heaped on the parson in print, especially as Baker had a reputation for being particularly greedy in the matter of his tithes. 'He had his nose in your sheep-fold, your calf-pen, your milk pails, your sow's bed, if not in the sow herself.'[13]

Cobbett, of course, waged a continuing war against tithes. When he published his very popular *Twelve Monthly Sermons* in 1821, being determined not to allow the Evangelicals all the best tunes, he devoted one of those sermons to *The Duties of Parsons and the Institution and Object of Tithes*. In it he quoted innumerable authorities from Holy Scripture to Elfric's Canons to prove that tithes, as they then existed in England, were no part of God's ordinances, and that even the ancient Israelites, who had invented them, took no more than a tenth of any *increase* in the crop and not a tenth of the entire crop. There may, he argued, have been some justification for them in pre-Reformation England, for then the parish priest had appropriated only one-third to the tithe to himself, and was bound to dedicate the rest to the upkeep of the parish church and the succour of the parish poor. His Protestant successor, being a married man, kept the whole for himself and left the upkeep of the church and the relief of the poor to be met by the parish rates. Cobbett also objected to what he considered to be the gentrification of the clergy, many of whom were squarsons rather than humble priests. As such they employed curates to attend to the spiritual needs of their parishioners whilst they, as Justices of the Peace, sat on the Bench and dealt out temporal, and frequently harsh justice to them.

Cobbett himself had the reputation at Botley of being a good, if exacting master. Idle hands were immediately dismissed, but others stayed with him for years and were, as the farm accounts show, paid better than average wages. Those wages, moreover, were adjusted to the size of the man's family, for Cobbett would allow none of his men to claim parish relief even though he claimed that he had paid over £2,000 in Poor Rates during his tenure of Botley.

The case of Jesse Burgess, however, allowed his enemies to attack his reputation as an employer. Burgess was a youth Cobbett had engaged for the year. He ran away, having been paid his wages, because he disliked Cobbett's insistence on early rising. Cobbett sent the village constable to apprehend him and, eventually, Burgess's mother and brother were taken up for helping the boy to escape arrest. The brother brought an action against Cobbett for unlawful arrest, claiming £1,000 damages, but was awarded only £10, which Cobbett claimed as a victory. He had to devote a long *Register* article to this comparatively trivial incident because London was placarded with notices proclaiming 'Cobbett the Oppressor of the Poor'. These were almost certainly Government-inspired, for this was an unexpected opportunity to turn the tables on a writer who had, for years, attacked the Government for its neglect of the poor. Cobbett, however, may have had the last word:

> When Mr Canning looks back to the time, when I dined at his house in Putney, and when he paid me so many just compliments for my exertions in my country's cause, I can hardly think, that he did not view with some degree of shame such attempts on the part of persons who were publicly said to have written under his particular patronage.[14]

There was, however, a lighter side to Cobbett, most frequently expressed in his letters to Wright, which came nearer to being completely spontaneous and artless than anything else he ever wrote. When, in his early days at Botley, his cook fell in love with the local blacksmith, Cobbett wrote to Wright, 'She wants sadly to get into the embraces of her Vulcan. What a devil of a hissing there will be with the *fire* of the blacksmith and the *grease* of the cook. Having a taste for poetry, you may make a good smutty epigram out of this.'

Whether or not a smutty epigram did emerge, it is something of a relief to discover that strait-laced Cobbett was prepared to enjoy it if it did. His letters to Windham were friendly but considerably more formal, though a certain amount of domestic detail, such as the progress of Mrs. Cobbett's pregnancies, might be included. Nevertheless, Cobbett could start a seriously political letter to his patron with a joke about Pitt that was at least slightly bawdy. 'What more I had to tell you was relating to the person who once said that Mr Pitt was like a fine lady that had become a whore; that is his *reputation* was gone, but that he was still a good *piece* in debate.'[15]

Various writers have left us pen-portraits of Cobbett. Mary Russell Mitford described him in his Botley days, before his own imprudent pen and his numerous enemies had driven him from there. 'There was,' she wrote, 'something of Dandie Dinmont about him, with his unfailing good humour and good spirits – his heartiness, his love of field sports, and his liking for a foray. He was a tall, stout man, fair and sunburnt, with a bright smile, and an air compounded of the soldier and the farmer, to which his habit of wearing an eternal red waistcoat contributed not a little. He was, I think, the most athletic and vigorous person that I have ever known.'

Cobbett would not have appreciated being compared to Dandie Dinmont, the hearty farmer out of Walter Scott's *Guy Mannering*. Scott's novels were then the rage, but Cobbett hated the novels and despised their author to such an extent that, when he was in Scotland, he wanted to visit Robert Burns's widow in order to assure her that one single page written by her late husband was worth more than a whole cart-load of Scott's works.

Miss Mitford's description of Cobbett, however, tallies to a large extent with a later one given by Hazlitt:

The only time I ever saw Mr Cobbett he seemed to me a very pleasant man – easy of access, affable, clear-headed, simple and mild in his manner, deliberate and unruffled in his speech . . . His figure is tall and portly; he has a good sensible face – rather full, with little grey eyes, a hard square forehead, a ruddy complexion, with hair grey or powdered; and he had on a scarlet broadcloth waistcoat with the flaps of the pockets hanging down, as was the custom for farmers in the last century . . . I certainly did not think less favourably of him for seeing him.[16]

The last description of him in his old age comes from a more hostile source, for *The Scotsman* had not a single good word for Cobbett when he lectured in Edinburgh in 1832:

We witnessed the performance of the London lion yesternight. Cobbett is a stout man about five feet ten inches high, with a hoary head, a florid complexion, and a remarkably hale appearance. His form is rather clumsy and his gait somewhat slouching. His forehead is phrenologically fine; it is both high and prominent and well developed in all the leading organs. Under it is a

pair of small eyes set very near one another, giving his countenance an expression of craft and abating a good deal from his
otherwise good looks. His mouth is small, and with the aid of
well-filled cheeks, gives his face, when he laughs, an exceedingly
comic expression . . . His speech is plain and distinct, though his
'*Hofficers*' and '*Harmy*' betray the Cockney. His voice is clear
and agreeable, his manners as a speaker free, animated and
varied, but never impressive or eloquent . . . He has considerable powers of mimickry and excels chiefly in lively graphic
sketches and touches of humour.

The writer may have known a good deal about phrenology but,
as a Scot, he could hardly be expected to distinguish a soft
Hampshire accent from a sharp Cockney one.

CHAPTER THIRTEEN

The Agrarian

But a bold peasantry, their country's pride,
When once destroy'd, can never be supplied.
A time there was, ere England's griefs began,
When every rood of ground maintain'd its man.
Oliver Goldsmith: *The Deserted Village*

The combined effects on the English chopsticks of war, the aftermath of war, the Industrial Revolution and of a series of bad harvests were to force large numbers of them off the land to suffer new forms of hardship in the crowded factories and *bidonvilles* of the Lancashire cotton towns. Those still left on the land, however, were condemned to unprecedentedly low standards of living which the Poor Law could do little to make endurable. The consequence was widespread and continuing food hunger.

For Cobbett, the man who had once gone hungry at the Chatham Depot; the man who had lived in America where no one ever needed to go hungry; the man who believed, as an article of faith, that England had, until then, always been the best-fed country in Europe; for Cobbett of Botley, then, every evidence of the food hunger that was spreading through the countryside was proof of complete political failure on the part of successive governments. The primary purpose of politics, he argued, was to ensure that everyone in the country enjoyed, and could afford to enjoy, an adequate and sustaining diet. In short, he came very close to advancing the not altogether unreasonable proposition that food was the purpose of politics and that politics should, if necessary, be about little else than food.

By such standards, the politics of his day had gone notably astray, a situation he regarded as evidence of original sin. What he failed, perhaps, to appreciate was the role played by the Industrial Revolution. He was not to know that the first stages of industrialisation in any country can only be completed on the back of agriculture and at the expense of the peasants – hunger being, perhaps, the least price the latter are asked to pay.

Since Britain was the first country to industrialise, Cobbett could not even consider the possibility that it was not the war, the Pitt System and paper money that produced hunger in the countryside, but the underlying and unavoidable influences of a new economic law working its way through the social system. Even if he had been told that this was the case he would, very reasonably, have refused to believe it. It seemed far more sensible to create a more practical demonology in which Pitt, the vile 'feelosofers', the paper money men and the Jews were in their various ways solely responsible for food hunger, enclosures, rural depopulation and all the other current ills of the countryside.

Food now began to be mentioned in Cobbett's writings more frequently than almost any other subject. He wrote about it, with varying degrees of understanding and anger, as a consumer, a dietician, a farmer and a politician. As a consumer and dietician he belonged to what might be described as the minimalist school: as a farmer and politician he was a maximalist.

He was, himself, an apparently frugal consumer. In an age when almost everyone who could afford to do so ate and drank immoderately, and many of those who could not afford to do so merely drank, Cobbett preached and practised abstemiousness with regard to food, and something approaching abstinence with regard to drink. Not infrequently he congratulated himself for doing so. 'How little eating and drinking is sufficient for me,' he wrote, triumphantly, in *Advice to Young Men*. 'Who, what man, ever performed a greater quantity of labour than I have performed? What man ever did so much? Now, in great measure, I owe my capability to perform this labour to my disregard for dainties . . . I am certain that, upon average, I have not, during my life, spent more than *thirty-five minutes a-day at table*, including all the meals of the day.'

This was probably true. He may have kept 'a gentleman's' table when he entertained at Botley, but he seems to have been almost indifferent to what he ate when he was alone. All that he insisted on was that it should be plain, wholesome, less than filling and should consist principally of meat. He ordered a mutton chop for his dinner every day for a year whilst he was in Newgate prison. When he was on his own in London he lived happily, for weeks on end, on legs of lamb. In the not unarduous course of his Rides he frequently fasted from breakfast to supper. His favourite drink was milk-and-water and, in spite of all the dinners he had to attend and all the toasts he had to drink in his political career, he drank little wine and no spirits. Drunkenness he abhorred. At the end of what was to be one of the last of his Rides he boasted that 'I verily believe that I shall be the first human being that ever came into Scotland

and went out of it again without tasting, wine, spirits, beer or cider. Everybody drinks too much; and it is not just to reproach the working people with drunkenness, if you, whose bodily exertions do not tend to provoke thirst, set them the mischievous example, by indulging in drink, until the habit renders it a sort of necessity of life.' Of course he considered beer a necessary of life both for himself and for the farm labourers, for whom it served the double purpose of supplementing their diet and replacing what they had lost through sweat.

The farmer and the politician in him, however, could lead him to write about food, whether in its raw state or on the table, with the same sort of gloating relish that Charles Dickens later brought to the subject. He made a point, in the course of his Rides, of visiting the market in each fresh town he entered. In Nottingham, for example, 'Being a great connoisseur with regard to the article of meat, I saw here a greater number of fine sirloins of beef than I had ever seen in any one market before, After I got back to the inn, I hankered after one of these sirloins of beef, went back, had it sewed up in cloths, and brought it to London. It was not of the largest size; but with the third part of the suet left in, it weighed 61 lbs, and was whiter and fatter than any one of the same size that I ever saw before.'[1]

More to a political than an agricultural purpose was the description of American food he sent back in the very first *Register* article he wrote in his second exile to the United States in 1817. He was staying at an inn on Long Island:

We eat by ourselves; and it really *is eating*. We have smoked fish, chops and eggs for breakfast, with bread (the very finest I ever saw), crackers, sweet cakes; and when I say we have such things, I do not mean that we have them for *show*, or just enough to smell to; but in *loads*. Not *an egg*, but a dish full of eggs. Not a snip of meat or fish; but a plate full. Lump sugar for our tea or coffee;* not broke into little bits the size of a hazel nut, but in good thumping pieces. For dinner we have the finest of fish, bass, mackerel, lobsters; of meat, lamb, veal, ham &c. The supper is like the breakfast, with preserved peaches and other things.[2]

* Cobbett seemed to accept drinks abroad he would have roundly condemned at home. So it was that he drank in American those 'slops from the tea-kettle' which he had described in England as 'a destroyer of health, an enfeebler of the frame, an engenderer of effeminacy and laziness, a debaucher of youth, and a maker of misery for old age'.

Here, the modern reader might say, was a man who was both *gourmet* and *gourmand*. His readers, at that time, in England knew otherwise. For this was a passage in an entirely political article, and it ended: 'And for all this and excellent cider to drink, with the kindest and most obliging treatment, we pay no more than *twenty-two shillings and sixpence a week each*. . . . Here, then, we are able to live at an Inn, one of the most respectable in the whole country, at the rate of 59 pounds a year, while the pay of the common farming man is not much short of that sum.'

The political purpose of the passage becomes clear once it is realised that Radical William Cobbett had a very different opinion of the United States from that once held by Tory Peter Porcupine. It could now be held up to the people of England as an example of what was possible in a country where there were no tax-eaters. There, even farm labourers came close to being able to live off lobsters and excellent cider, whereas in England only the tax-eaters could afford such a diet, whilst those who actually produced the food saw little more than bread and potatoes on their tables from one year to another. Cobbett generally managed to associate food with the condition of the chopsticks and politics with both.

Although food, and concern for the labourer's diet constituted an important part of Cobbett's agrarian philosophy, they were by no means the whole of it. One cannot discuss that philosophy, if such it was, without reference to *Rural Rides*; but the nature and purpose of that collection of *Register* articles, written over a period of ten years (1822–1832), is now commonly misunderstood or ignored. The Rides were not undertaken in order to provide a description of a countryside that has largely changed and a rural way of life which has completely disappeared. They were undertaken, at a time of increasing unrest in the agricultural counties which culminated in what Cobbett called 'the rural war', for entirely political purposes. He wanted to measure the devastation caused in country areas, as he maintained, by the Pitt System.

Each article, therefore, was primarily a political polemic. If the collection is now read for its literary rather than its political message, this is no more than what has happened to such depoliticised works as *Gulliver's Travels* and *Animal Farm*. Cobbett was a fine, perhaps a great descriptive writer who could never resist the temptation to digress from his theme in order to set a scene or a character, or to discuss any one of his own innumerable quirks and quiddities. *Rural Rides* continues to be read because the skill and humour of the descriptive writing and the odd attractiveness of the personality that obtrudes itself have ensured that it is Cobbett's politics that are now treated as digressions while the digressions that were, in a serious political writer, an occupational hazard, are treated as the very core and purpose of the work.

As Cobbett grew older, the political purpose of the *Rides* became clearer, and the tone of the writing grew more polemical and shrill. As a consequence, the penultimate *Ride*, through the south of Scotland, is now seldom, if ever read. Indeed, every edition of *Rural Rides*, save one, that has been published since Cobbett's death, stops the Northern Tour, which included Scotland, abruptly at Alnwick. The exception is the three-volume edition of *Rural Rides*, which was edited and brilliantly annotated by G. D. H. Cole. But even Cole, who was interested in Cobbett solely because of his politics, thought the tour through Scotland too political to be interesting. Yet it is precisely because of its concentration on politics that the Scottish Tour affords us a summary of most of the opinions Cobbett had finally arrived at as a farmer, a politician, and as the last of the notable agrarians.

Cobbett had never before been north of the Tweed. Since he had earned a reputation as a Scotophobe, he feared a more hostile reception than he had grown accustomed to by 1832, when the Reform Bill had been passed and the 'Great Reformer' was greeted by enthusiastic crowds wherever he travelled in England. Indeed the London and Edinburgh newspapers, never friendly to him, cheerfully prophesied that he would be thrown back into the Tweed as soon as he had crossed it, by the rightfully indignant Scots he had so continually traduced. He entered Scotland, therefore, apprehensively, but still hugging his prejudices. Like so many Southerners of that time, he had been brought up to believe that Scotland was a barren country where there would be little of any agricultural interest to see; but once he had got as far as Cockburnspath in Berwickshire, the richness and productivity of the red soils between the hills and the sea astonished him. The size of the farms and the depopulated state of the countryside, however, so confirmed everything he had expected of the Scots that he wrote, triumphantly, 'Here we are amongst the mischief'. A large part of the book he subsequently published on his Northern Tour was devoted to various descriptions and definitions of that 'mischief'. When he got to Edinburgh, he wrote two long 'Letters' for the *Register* under the heading of *Cobbett's Advice to the Chopsticks in the South of England*. However tedious the rest of the Northern Tour may be to read, these embody so much of his agrarian philosophy that they deserve to be read in full. Indeed, Cobbett himself thought so much of them that he instructed his printers to strike off ten thousand copies of each of them for distribution and sale to the same chopsticks at the price of one penny a copy.

'You know,' he began, 'that many gentlemen in England have *Scotch bailiffs*. You know that these bailiffs are always telling you how good and obedient the labourers are in Scotland, and how WELL OFF they are. The Government and the parsons tell you the same thing; and they tell you, that if you were as well-behaved as the Scotch, and as quiet, you would be as well off as they are. Now, then, I will tell you how well off the Scotch labourers are.'

Few today would accept that the Scottish working man is more submissive, more long-suffering, and less inclined to robust protest than his English counterpart. But the arson and rioting associated with the 'Captain Swing' rebellion (1830–1) had been confined to the south-eastern counties of England, and had had no counterpart in Scotland. Yet, as Cobbett now set out to prove, the Scottish farm labourer had even more to rebel against than the chopsticks.

First, however, he had to set the scene and assure the chopsticks that Scotland was not all barren hills and moors. He described the great farms that stretched for hundreds of acres; the fine farmhouses fit for gentlemen rather than mere tenant-farmers; the large rick-yards holding, frequently, more than a hundred corn stacks, each yard with its threshing machine driven by steam or, if coals were too far for carting, by a water-wheel or windmill, and with never a barn or a flail to be seen.* There were cattle courts and sheep pens to hold the livestock fed, in winter, off the magnificent crops of turnips grown in hundred acre blocks in fields kept as free of weeds as a garden border. As for the quality of the soil: 'The land is the finest that I ever saw in my life, though I have seen every fine vale in every county in England; and in the United States of American I never saw any land a tenth part so good.'

Such a Land of Goschen must sound attractive to the chopsticks, who would expect to live well where the farming was so prosperous. 'Oh! how you will wish to be here! "Lord", you will say to yourselves, "what pretty villages there must be there; what nice

---

* The threshing machine had become at once the cause and the symbol of many of the farm labourer's discontents in the corn-growing counties of England. It did away with the continuing winter task of threshing the sheaves on the barn floor with a flail, so adding considerably to seasonal unemployment and reducing what a labourer could earn in a year. The almost certainly apocryphal 'Captain Swing' took his name from the hinged, upper part of the flail with which the sheaves were struck which was called 'the swing'.

churches and church-yards; oh! and what precious nice ale-houses! Come, Jack, let us set off for Scotland! What nice gardens we shall have to our cottages there! What beautiful flowers! And what prancing and barking pigs we shall have running out on the common, and what a flock of geese grazing upon the green".'

The rich lands of East Lothian would, until British farming collapsed with the ploughing of the American prairies, constitute a showcase in which all that was new and fashionable in farming could be exhibited. Here the patterns were set for English farmers to follow, and they were patterns Cobbett hated. Here, and in the Tweed Valley, lay the Dukeries where estates covering large parts of a county were owned by one, often absentee, landlord whose sole interest it was to draw all that he could from his estates to support the splendours of his existence in London or Paris or Rome.

The land, consequently, was divided into farms considerably larger than those in England, and these being let at rack rents which often amounted to five or even six pounds an acre, could only attract money-conscious, hard-driving tenants who knew that they had to practise large-scale, mechanised farming and sweat their labour before they could expect to make any profit. The result, as Cobbett saw it, was 'one farmer drawing to one spot the produce of the whole country all around, a sort of manufactory of corn and meat'.

That sort of 'factory farming' was not yet common in England, though it was Cobbett's greatest fear that the enclosers and engrossers there would produce something on the Scottish pattern, and with similar results – a countryside with no small proprietors, few inhabited villages, and emptied of people. It was his duty to warn the chopsticks of this, and so, having set up his conversation with his fictional interlocutors, he set about doing so:

Stop! stop! I have not come to listen to you, but to make you listen to me; let me tell you, then, that there is neither village, nor church, nor ale-house, nor garden, nor cottage, nor flowers, nor pig, nor goose, nor common, nor green.

To English eyes this would still seem true of East Lothian, where farms are large and the villages, where they exist, possess few of the traditional amenities of the English village which Cobbett valued so highly. The absence of villages and the prevalence of the threshing machine, driven by steam, wind or water, convinced Cobbett that 'in this country of the finest land that ever was seen, all the elements seem to have been pressed into the amiable service of sweeping the people from the face of the earth'.

But, he had his two chopsticks arguing, no farm can be run without labourers, and 'out of such a quantity of corn and of beef and mutton, there must be some come to the share of the chopsticks to be sure!' 'Don't be too sure, yet;' Cobbett replied, 'but hold your tongue and hear my story.'

· It was the story of his chief grievance. The new, entirely commercial forms of farming meant that the countryside no longer sold only its surpluses to the towns, but all that it produced. This had to be so because the Pitt system had made it essential for the farmers to have the money with which to satisfy the enormous demands made on them by way of taxes, rents and rates. The consequence was that those who produced all the food were left with the least of it, and this, Cobbett found, was even more the case in Scotland than in England:

> The cattle and the sheep walk into England upon their legs; the wheat is put into ships, to be sent to London and elsewhere; and as to the money that these are sold for, the farmer is allowed to have a little of it, but almost the whole of it is sent away to the landlord to be gambled or otherwise squandered away. Almost the whole of the produce of these fine lands goes into the pockets of the lords; the labourers are their slaves, and the farmers their slave-drivers.

The condition of the East Lothian farmworkers under the 'bothie' system did, indeed, do something to justify Cobbett's claim that they were worse treated than the negro slaves in America. Each slave, at least, had a capital value which would be lost if he was not maintained in good working order whilst, in Scotland, 'the hiring is for a year, beginning on the 26th of May, and not at Michaelmas; the farmer taking the man just at the season to get the sweat out of him; and if he die, he dies when the main work is done'.

Under the bothie system, the Scottish farmworker neither lived in, when single, nor could he expect a cottage of his own when he married. 'The single labourers', Cobbett told his chopsticks, 'are kept in this manner; about four of them are put into a shed, quite away from the farm-house. Here these men live and sleep, having a certain allowance of oat, barley and pea-meal, upon which they live, mixing it with water or with milk when they have the use of a cow. They are allowed some little matter of money besides to buy clothes with; but they never dream of being allowed to set their foot within the walls of the farm-house. Pretty well, that, for a knife-and-fork chopstick of Sussex, who has been used to sit around the fire with the master and the mistress, and to pull about and tickle the laughing maids! Pretty well, *that*!'

The state of the married farm labourer on these 'steam-engine farms' was even worse, as Cobbett now demonstrated:

> There is a sort of *barrack* erected for these to live in. It is a long shed, stone walls and pantile roof, and divided into a number of *boothies*, each having a door and one little window, all the doors being on one side of the shed, and there being no *back-doors*; and as to a privy, no such thing for them, appears ever to have been thought of. Each distinct *boothie* is about seventeen feet one way and fifteen feet the other. There is no ceiling, and no floor but the earth. In this place a man and his wife and family have to live.

At Botley, Cobbett had gone to great expense building new cottages for his labourers, in which they lived rent-free. Each had a garden, though in later years he forbade anyone to grow potatoes in them. Their fuel they could have for the cutting, and no man was ever thrown out of his home because of sickness or old age. The housing of the Scottish farm labourers in these bothies infuriated him and, since they could be and were evicted for the slightest misconduct, led him to produce what was, perhaps, the first denunciation of the tied cottage in English literature. 'The labourer is wholly at the mercy of the master, who, if he will not keep him beyond the year, can totally ruin him by refusing him a character. This family has no HOME; and no home can any man be said to have who can thus be dislodged every year at the will of his master.'

The family's diet was another cause for anger. Food constituted the largest part of the husband's wage, he receiving no more than four pounds a year in cash, and being unable, therefore, to improve his diet with bought food:

> The married man receives for the whole year sixty bushels of oats, thirty bushels of barley, twelve bushels of peas, and three bushels of potatoes, with ground allowed him to plant the potatoes. The master gives him the keep of a cow for the year round; but he must find the cow himself; he pays for his own fuel; he must find a woman to reap for twenty whole days in harvest, as payment for the rent of his *boothie*; he has no wheat; the meal altogether amounts to about six pounds for every day in the year; the oatmeal is eaten in porridge; the barley meal and the

pea-meal are mixed together and baked into sorts of cakes upon
an iron plate put over the fire; they sometimes get a pig and feed
it upon potatoes. Thus they never have one bit of wheaten bread
or of wheaten flour, nor of beef nor of mutton, though the land is
covered with wheat and cattle.

Worst of all, in Cobbett's opinion, was the fact that the Scottish
labourer, if he was dismissed or left of his own accord, could not,
without recommendations from the farmer and the minister, find
further employment. In such a case, there was not even a system of
parish relief for him to fall back on. The statute of Elizabeth I that
had established a Poor Law in England did not apply to Ireland and
only partially applied to Scotland, which was why vagrants and
beggars from both countries travelled, if they could, to England.

Cobbett discovered that, in the case of Scottish vagrants, special
contractors were employed on the English side of the Border to
round them up and cart them back to their home parishes in
Scotland, and that some of them had been apprehended and
returned in this fashion no less than twenty times. Yet it was a
half-Scottish Whig, Brougham, who now led the movement so to
emasculate the Poor Law as to reduce the English paupers to
something resembling the state of the Scottish ones. 'Is not this,'
Cobbett wrote, 'the greatest shame that ever was witnessed under
the sun?!'

Cobbett's compassion flowed, perhaps, all the more deeply for
being restricted to no more than a few channels. It is also possible
that it could only flow in the same direction as his politics. A parson
once said to him that his religion seemed to be altogether political,
to which he replied: 'Very much so, indeed; and well it may – since
I have been furnished with a creed that makes part of an Act of
Parliament.' If the parson had said that his compassion was equally
political, Cobbett might not have had such a ready answer, for it
was always difficult to decide whether his politics sprang out of the
compassion or his compassion out of the politics. This was why, in
the end, his *Advice to the Chopsticks* turned out to be purely
political advice. 'There, chopsticks of Sussex,' Cobbett wrote
when he came to his peroration, 'you can now see what English
scoundrels, calling themselves "gentlemen" get Scotch bailiffs for.
These bailiffs are generally recommended to the grinding ruffians
of England by the grinding ruffians of Scotland. The Scotch
landowners have told the English landowners how they manage
the matter here. The English fellows find that they can get nobody
in England to treat men in such a way, and, therefore, they bring
them up from Scotland, and they pick the hardest and cruellest

fellows they can find in Scotland; so that we have not, by any means, a fair specimen, even of Scotch bailiffs. I advise you to have your eye upon every man who has a Scotch bailiff; for, you may be sure, that his intention is to bring you down to the shed and the brose; to prevent you from ever seeing knife or fork or bread again . . . I do most strongly urge you to attend at all elections, *whether you have votes or not* . . . Though, according to the Reform Bill, you are *not to vote*, yet you have *the right* of petitioning, and if you make use of that right, and in a proper manner, we shall never again see those days of degradation of which we have seen so many.'

Demagoguery, certainly, and like most demagogues Cobbett overstated his case, as he discovered when he got to the West of Scotland and found far less of the 'mischief' he had come across in the Lothians. Yet it had, on this occasion at least, been demagoguery in a proper and worthy cause.

It was because those changes in the countryside that Cobbett most hated – depopulation, rack-renting landlords, 'steam-engine farms', hungry and degraded farm workers and the destruction of the 'ancient small way of life' – were more advanced in the Lothians than they were, as yet, in England that the Scottish Tour embodies so much of his agrarian philosophy. His anger ensured that what was implicit and diffused in his other works, and in the earlier parts of *Rural Rides*, should here be concentrated and made explicit. His abiding belief was in the richness and adequacy of the land of Britain. It, alone, could produce all the wealth the nation needed. Those who laboured to produce that wealth had an historic and inalienable right to their proper share of it, a share that had primarily to be expressed in terms of a sufficiency of bread, meat and beer. The very fertility of the Lothian lands seemed to him to have made such a whittling down of that right all the more reprehensible and all the more disgusting.

But not even the Scottish Tour could be devoted solely to agrarian politics. A farmer, a social observer and a ribald journalist lived inside the same skin as Cobbett the politician. The farmer, for example, being of an experimental frame of mind and a good judge of livestock, was interested in the new breeds he came across in Scotland; and it was not long before he had decided to acquire some Angus cattle, a small flock of Blackface sheep and a few of the wonderfully pretty Ayrshire cows he had learnt to admire. He was by then stocking Normandy Farm, and he proposed to test the ability of these breeds to prosper on the heaths and sandhills of West Surrey where only the local 'heath-croppers' could currently survive.

He tested the Angus cattle and the Blackfaces in a thoroughly practical way – with his teeth. He found that Angus meat was 'exceedingly fine in the grain'. Even more to the point, it produced '*tender* beef-steaks, a thing I have not met with before in more than one out of ten beef-steak jobs'. The same could be said for the Blackfaces, so long as they were not less than five years old when slaughtered. At that age they produced 'exceedingly fine mutton', even though it was something deficient in fat since 'the same pains are not bestowed here on making the mutton fat as are bestowed in England'. This was an observation that reminded him of the only occasion he would admit to when he had been less than fair to a Scot. 'The reader recollects that the Scotch youth who came to see me at Kensington, would not eat his breakfast that my daughter had prepared for him because the beef was "*vary fot*", and really my rage upon that occasion would have been less violent had I known that the general taste of his countrymen was against the very fat meat.'

It was as a social observer rather than a politician that he visited a bothie on a farm near Dunfermline in which six farm labourers lived in conditions of primitive squalor. These men were each allowed 'two pecks of coarse oatmeal a week and three "chopins"* of milk a day. They have to use this meal, either by mixing it with cold water or with hot; they put some into a bowl, pour some boiling water upon it, then stir it about and eat it; and they call this BROSE. I saw some of the brose mixed up ready to eat; and this is by no means bad stuff, only there ought to be half-a-pound of good meat to eat along with it. The Americans make "brose" of the corn-meal; but then they make their brose with milk instead of water, and they send it down their throats in company with buttered beef-steaks. And if here was some bacon along with the brose, I should think the brose very proper; because in this country, oats are more easily grown in some parts than wheat is.'

The practical farmer, it will be noticed, had accepted the fact that oats were more easily grown in Scotland than wheat, and the social observer was far less prepared than the politician had been to declare that the Scots were being forced to live on that which in England 'is only given to horses and pigs'. Indeed, the private Mr. Cobbett, who was a fine judge of eating, developed a taste for porridge which is, after all, only a step along from brose. 'Every morning but one, while I was at Edinburgh, it formed the principal part of my breakfast; and I greatly preferred it, and should always

* A Scottish liquid measure – containing about an English quart.

prefer it, to toasted bread and butter, to muffins, to crumpets, to bread and butter, or to hot rolls.'

Nor did he conceal the fact, as he travelled through the squalid Scotch villages, that the villagers seemed not to suffer from such a diet. 'The people look very hearty, and by no means badly dressed, especially the little boys and girls, whose looks I have admired ever since I entered Scotland; and about whom the parents seem to care much more than they do about their houses or themselves. They do not put the boys to work hard when they are young, as they do in England; and, therefore, they are straighter and nimbler on foot.'

There was a certain innate honesty in Cobbett the reporter that all too often dissolved into rhretoric when the political commentator got to work. It was probably the reporter rather than the commentator who went on to observe: 'But here is a total carelessness about the dwelling-place. You see no such things as a little garden before the door; and none of those numerous ornaments and conveniences about the labourers' dwellings, which are the pride of England, and by which it is distinguished from all other countries in the world.'

The honest observer in him obliged him, in the end, to abjure some, at least, of his Scotophobia. Far from being thrown back into the Tweed by the Scots, they gave him a lion's welcome. Bells were rung in honour of the 'Great Reformer', and the crowds took the horses out of his carriage in order to pull it themselves. Cobbett, of course, had no objection to being lionised. In his subsequent book, therefore, he pointedly referred to the hard-working, friendly and estimable people of Scotland, who were so misrepresented in England and so grievously oppressed at home. It was not in Cobbett, however, to abandon a long-held prejudice in its entirety. He stuck firmly to his belief that the Scots had always exerted a malign influence on the English, but added that he attributed this, now, not to the Scots people as a whole, but to their scoundrelly 'feelosofers' and those 'grinding ruffians' the Scottish landowners. These had, he explained, perverted the gullible English: the first with their pernicious economic theories; the others by their example.

He claimed, at the start of his book, that he had written it in order to dispel some of the vulgar prejudices Englishmen had inherited in a thousand years of dealings with the Scots. Although he, himself, was eminently fair in such matters and was immune from prejudice, yet even he had had 'Strong feelings excited in my mind against Scotland generally by the scoundrelly feelosofers who preached up a doctrine tending to cause the people of England to be treated like cattle.' Because of this, 'even I could not make it out how it was that Scotland should spew forth so many monsters.'

The Scottish landowners aroused him to more than merely political hostility. Old though he was by then, he set about them in that lively, scurrilous style that had first established him as a writer worth reading in America, forty years earlier. They were, he argued, more corrupt and greedy than even the worst of their English counterparts though he did not spare even these as he rode North.

In Northumberland, for example, the sight of 'the endless turrets and lions of Alnwick Castle, and the 'flag flying on the battlements to indicate to the vassals around that the descendant of Hotspur was present in the castle' immediately led him to remind those vassals that the person in residence was actually 'Duke Smithson, commonly called Percy'. The fact was that the present Duke was the grandson of a most respectable person called Smithson who, having married the Percy heiress, had changed his name for hers. His heirs, after a protracted lawsuit, had inherited the name, estates and titles of the Percies, but the incumbent Duke of Northumberland was a Tory, a boroughmonger and a staunch opponent of Reform. He had, therefore, to be reminded that he was no true 'Norman' but, with Smithson blood in his veins, something of an imposter.

Almost every great estate he passed after crossing the Border revived memories of past scandals. The sight of Ayton Castle recalled the late John Fordyce, who had owned it until his death. He had, amongst other things, been Receiver-General of the Land Tax in Scotland and had suffered the misfortune of being £100,000 out in his accounts when he quit that post. Creevey had attacked him in the House of Commons, but the scandal had died down. Cobbett was fighting Creevey for one of the Manchester seats in the 1832 election, and he now wondered whether Creevey, if elected, would still endeavour to recover the money, or whether the fact that Fordyce had been the Duke of Gordon's brother-in-law would silence him.

A similar political animosity stirred in him when he passed the gates to Roxburgh (now Broxmouth) Park, on the outskirts of Dunbar. The sight of the Park immediately led Cobbett to revive the story of the comical misfortunes of 'Duke Gawler'. John Gawler had acted as second to Sir Francis Burdett when he fought a duel with another celebrated Radical, James Paull, over the Westminster Election of 1807. Cobbett had at one time collaborated and later quarrelled with both and some of his animosity towards Burdett must have rubbed off on the luckless Gawler, whose subsequent misfortunes would not otherwise have been revived with quite so much relish.

The fourth Duke of Roxburgh had made Gawler, who was his second cousin, his heir, and the latter confidently expected to inherit both the title and the estates. In anticipation of that event, he obtained the King's permission to change his name to Ker. The octogenarian Sir William Innes, however, contested the will, and the House of Lords eventually confirmed him as the rightful heir and fifth Duke of Roxburgh. This might have represented no more than a postponement of Gawler's expectations had not the fifth Duke, within eight days of his first Duchess's death, married a twenty-year-old girl who promptly produced a male heir, and so put an end to all Gawler's hopes.

'To this dukedom of ROXBURGH,' Cobbett now wrote, 'appertains an immense estate. Lord! how "DUKE GAWLER" would have revelled in the possession of this estate. His heir apparent would have had DICK GURNEY for a huntsman, instead of creeping under the gabardine of this brewer-banker in order to be shuffled into a seat for the city of NORWICH, in consequence of the recommendation of that famous patriot BURDETT.'

Ancient scandals unfortunately nearly always need lengthy explanations; and this has made Cobbett's journalism, and such works as *Rural Rides*, partially unintelligible to a modern reader. The short passage just quoted contains a whole broadside of insults whose force and economy of expression are not immediately apparent.

Gawler's 'heir-apparent' was Charles Henry Bellenden-Ker, who was then fighting one of the Norwich seats as the Reform candidate. As such, he deserved Cobbett's support, but those on the Radical side of politics seem seldom to have found it difficult to hate one another for personal as well as doctrinal reasons. Bellenden-Ker had been recommended by Burdett, which was reason enough for Cobbett to think poorly of him. He was also a leading member of the Society for the Diffusion of Useful Knowledge and was in receipt of a comfortable income in his capacity as Secretary to the Master of the Rolls. The first, so far as Cobbett was concerned, made him part of the 'comforting system'. The second condemned him as a sinecurist. Even in a fellow-Reformer, such iniquities were not to be ignored.

As for 'Dick' Gurney, who was also a Reformer, he was even more precisely the sort of man Cobbett loved to hate. He was a member of the well-known Quaker family, and the Quakers as a whole had so markedly succeeded in finance, the corn trade,

304

brewing and other branches of commerce that Cobbett generally referred to them as 'the Jew-like fraternity'. The otherwise inexplicable reference to Gurney's 'gabardine' was therefore an extra, not over-subtle insult. The Gurneys had, in the course of little more than a century, prospered exceedingly, and had become great landowners in Norfolk and men of power in political and banking circles in London. 'Dick' Gurney, therefore, could not escape being an upstart so far as Cobbett was concerned. Nor, as a banker, could he avoid being a paper-money man. He was a brewer, which meant that he was one of those who lured the poor away from their home-brewed beer to drink the unwholesome and doctored concoctions all brewers dispensed. Finally, he was Burdett's friend, and so no better than a pseudo-Reformer and a Whig.

Cobbett never got past the south of Scotland on his tour. He had to rush south for the General Election of 1832 in which he finally won a seat in the first Reformed Parliament. He departed swearing that he would return and tour the Highlands, if only to investigate what the Duchess of Sutherland had been up to by way of her Clearances. But, if he was consistently abusive and scurrilous about the Scottish 'lords', he was even more brutally abusive about the Scottish 'feelosofers'. Almost every one of them, from 'that nasty palaverer, Brougham' down to Jeffery of the *Edinburgh Review* – a journal always referred to as 'Old Mother Mange' for no obvious reason other than its support for Malthus – came under his lash. If they had remained in Scotland they were attacked for misleading their fellow countrymen. If they had migrated to London they were attacked for having perverted the English.

John Ramsay McCulloch, the economist, Ricardo's disciple and sometime editor of *The Scotsman*, for example, was advised to quit Edinburgh and join his fellow 'renegados' in London: 'Now, "Peter" McCulloch, empty Peter, impudent Peter, brazen Peter, Ricardo-lecture Peter, *Scotch* Peter . . . write no more paragraphs but go and join your associates Mr Brougham and Doctor Birkbeck to enlighten us, the benighted "loons o' th' Sooth".' (Cobbett's use of what can only be described as music-hall Scots was one of his more distressing habits.)

John Black, on the other hand, was a Scot who had migrated to London, where he had become editor of the *Morning Chronicle*, which was then a Radical paper. He was a scholarly man who had accumulated a large library, which led Cobbett to refer to him, sarcastically, as 'Doctor'. The fact that he was a fellow-Radical and a fellow-editor did nothing to save him from Cobbett, for Black not only supported the Utilitarians, but was also one of those who had advised the rick-burning, rioting Sussex chopsticks to imitate the wise and prudent behaviour of the Scottish farm labourers. Cobbett, having been in Scotland for no more than a few days, was convinced that Black knew nothing about either the English or the Scottish chopsticks. 'You are a Scotchman, Doctor; but you know nothing about Scotland. You live in England; but you know nothing about England. *Books* have been your teacher, and you ought not to trust the stuff put forth by the scribbling coxcombs, fools and knaves that are dead. It is not yet a week since I set my foot in Scotland, yet I have seen enough to make me clearly understand the ground-work of your errors.'

It is probably true that the Scottish Tour had some influence on Cobbett's Scotophobia, changing it from a general prejudice to a particularised one. That country, he explained in his book, 'has always been injured by the selfishness and treachery of those whose birth ought to have taught them to be their protectors; and the renegado villainous feelosofers who have come to London from Scotland, have been, and are the corrupt tools of the Scottish oligarchy for selling their own country, and of the English oligarchy for pillaging and enslaving the people of England.'

No biographer can discuss Cobbett's agrarianism without referring to *Rural Rides*. Although the Northern Tour, which properly constitutes the last part of that work, may be tedious to read, it does, by its very concentration, convey the strange mixture of politics, farming, economic theory, careful social observation, personal prejudice and much-relished scurrility that was so characteristic of agrarian Cobbett and of *Rural Rides*. But the Northern Tour was almost the last piece that Cobbett wrote, and he had, by then, abandoned his former attempts to fight on a wider agrarian front. When he first undertook his Rides, eleven years earlier, he still entertained hopes of being able to form a comprehensive agrarian movement in which landowners, farmers and farm workers would all combine to destroy the Pitt System and return the nation to its ancient and country way of life.

The landowners had, for the most part, preferred to join the Pitt System rather than fight it. Cobbett had reasoned with them over this for several years. He had never questioned the necessity for landowners, property being, in his opinion, the basis of civilisation, though he had argued that land could not be owned absolutely, but was held subject to such rights as the poor had always had in some part of its produce. However, being innately conservative, he naturally preferred the owners and supposed trustees to be men whose long descent had made them an integral part of the rural community. In the end he was forced to conclude that, if such men could not see that paper money, high taxes, rack rents, short leases and falling farm prices would, in the end, leave them with untenanted or unprofitable farms and a growing burden of debt, he could do nothing further to save them. He left them, as he said, to the bankers, the jobbers and the Jews, from whom they would borrow until the day finally came when the loans were called in and the moneylenders became the landowners.

It was after he had come to that conclusion that a character he called 'Squire Jolterhead' began to figure prominently in the political articles Cobbett sometimes wrote in the form of dramatic dialogues. 'Jolterhead' was the personification of all the long-established, slow-witted landowners who could never understand why it was that the ancient order of things had changed, nor why the moneylender, the tax collector, the sly London attorney and the bum bailiff were so frequently to be found in his parlour. Each of these was constantly claiming money he no longer had, even though he had, by then, put down his hounds, sold his horses, sacked his gamekeeper, felled his timber and ploughed up his park to grow turnips.

There was a time, in the post-war period of agricultural depression, when Cobbett had more success among the farmers. Indeed, in the early 1820s, when there was a drastic fall in farm prices, it seemed possible that he would become spokesman and leader of a Farmers' Party, something that had never before, and has not yet disturbed political life in Britain. He came closest to success in 1823 when, with the aid of Sir Thomas Beevor of Hargham Hall, he organised his famous Norfolk Petition.

He had, by then, come close to converting the farmers to his belief that their ills did not arise from falling farm prices but from the Pitt System. If the National Debt and the interest paid on it could be reduced, if government expenditure could be curtailed, and if patronage and corruption could be eliminated from politics, then the level of farm prices would be immaterial. Rents and taxes would fall even quicker than farm prices, and cheaper food would allow the burden of the parish rate to be so reduced that it no longer amounted to a second rent.

Cobbett's arguments prevailed to the extent that the four principal proposals made in the Petition came close to approximating to the policies around which the Radical politicians were beginning to form something resembling a Radical Party. Essentially, these were:

a) The sale of all Crown and Church lands into private ownership; the proceeds to be devoted to a substantial reduction of the National Debt.

b) A further lessening of the burden of taxation imposed by servicing the Debt. This would result from 'an equitable adjustment' which would reduce, perhaps even abolish, the interest paid to stockholders and the purchasers of government annuities. It had always been Cobbett's argument that the Government had been floating its loans at a heavy discount* and for paper money. If interest continued to be paid on these at face value and in gold, present and future taxpayers would be most unjustly penalised and the tax-eaters most unjustly rewarded.

c) A reduction of the standing army 'to a scale of expense as low as that of the army before the war'.†

d) The immediate abolition of all sinecures, pensions, grants and emoluments not merited by public service.

The farmers possibly failed to realise how improbable it was that any administration, whatever its politics, would agree to their demands. The Radicals, for their part, were in the happy position of being able to advance policies they would not, for at least a century, be elected to operate. When they were finally elected to power they were as unwilling as all previous administrations even to consider policies that would have the effect of drastically reducing the power and scope of government and of destroying its credit, and so its ability to borrow. Sound money, less government and low taxes are always popular with politicians who have no immediate prospects of power.

The Norfolk Petition, however, for all its improbabilities, was enthusiastically supported by the majority of those who attended a duly summoned meeting of the Norfolk electors and in the following months similar meetings were held and similar resolutions were passed in other primarily agricultural counties. Slowly, however, the farmers' desperate position eased, and with that their support for Cobbett waned. Farm prices improved slightly; the post-war recession 'bottomed-out'; the resumption of cash payments did something to halt inflation. The Government moreover offered the farmers an alternative to Cobbett's radical remedies, and one that,

---

* Pitt, in the course of his first administration borrowed £334 million for which he received only some £200 million in cash. The lenders, in short, forced him to issue low interest coupons at a heavy discount. When Peel resumed cash payments in 1819, the stockholders were in the fortunate position of being paid their interest in sound money and at face values, having invested originally at a discount and in paper money.

† The one-time 'war-monger' and advocate of an entirely professional army had, before the end of the war, turned peace-monger and would, eventually, propose the total abolition of any standing army, though this was not actually insisted on until he gave his Manchester Lectures in 1832.

traditionally, farmers have never been able to reject. They were offered protection and another Corn Bill and so were, to a large extent, cured of their petitioning, their radicalism and their willingness to listen to Cobbett.

He, in spite of all his zeal for the agricultural interest, was as violently opposed to all Corn Bills as any Cobdenite of the subsequent generation. Corn Bills meant two things, so far as Cobbett was concerned: higher food prices for the poor, who had no votes, and appeasement of the farmers, who had. The first created even more need to destroy the Pitt system, but the second silenced the protests of those who might otherwise have helped to bring that about.

Consequently, whilst the farmers, for the most part, deserted Cobbett, he, for his part, began to desert them. He started to criticise and ridicule at least the 'bullfrogs' among them and those who sought to solve their problems by starving their labourers. They were so greedy for land that there was one farmer at Uphusband who now 'held as one farm, the lands, that men now living, can remember to have formed *fourteen farms*, bringing up, in a respectable way, fourteen families.'[3] There were farmers in Sussex who actually put bells around the necks of their labourers, as though they were cattle. But above all, Cobbett ridiculed those farmers whose temporary wartime prosperity had given them ideas above their station, so that they began to assume the manners and airs of 'gentlefolk'. Their ruin, he joyfully told them, was close at hand:

When the old farm-houses are down (and down they must come in time) what a miserable thing the country will be! Those that are erected now are mere painted shells, with a Mistress within, who is stuck up in a place she calls a *parlour*, with, if she have children, the 'young ladies and gentlemen' about her: some showy chairs and a sofa (a *sofa* by all means): half a dozen prints in gilt frames hanging up: some swinging book-shelves with novels and tracts upon them: a dinner brought in by a girl perhaps better 'educated' than she: two or three nick-nacks to eat instead of a piece of bacon and a pudding: the house too neat for a dirty-shoed carter to be allowed to come into: and everything proclaiming to every sensible beholder, that there is here a constant anxiety to make a *show* not warranted by the reality. The children (which is the worst part of it) are all too clever to *work*: they are all to be '*gentlefolks*'. Go to the plough! Good God! What, 'young gentlemen' go to plough! They become clerks or some skimmy-dish thing or other. What misery is all this! What a mass of materials for producing that general and *dreadful convulsion* that must, first or last, come and blow this funding and jobbing and enslaving and starving system to atoms.[4]

So, in the end, out of all those who, between them, represented the agricultural interest, Cobbett was left with only the chopsticks to lead. But, while this was happening, he had, for a number of reasons, begun to expand his natural constituency to include industrial workers. The Luddite troubles, the Nottingham riots, the Peterloo massacre of 1819, the march of the Blanketeers had all served to bring the condition of this new industrial proletariat to his notice. He had no interest whatsoever in industry, but his Rides had brought him, for the first time, to the Lancashire cotton towns and into contact with the mill hands. Moreover, the last three seats he contested before Oldham – Coventry, Preston, and Manchester – were all industrial seats where the majority of his votes had to be won from among the factory workers.

As his concern for them increased, so his anger against their employers swelled, and he now included the 'Cotton Lords', whom he addressed with mock reverence as 'Seigneurs of the Twist, Sovereigns of the Spinning Jenny, Great Yeomen of the Yarn', among his political and class enemies. It was now that he acquired the title of 'The Poor Man's Friend'; though no one can say whether it was bestowed on him or whether he took it as a consequence of having used that title for a series of six Letters he addressed to 'the working classes of Preston' immediately after failing to win a most unruly election in that town. Thus it was that the man who had originally thought to put himself at the head of an agrarian party embracing all the rural classes finally emerged as the more or less acknowledged leader of what was, in effect, the first English working-class movement, consisting of an uneasy and unnatural alliance between the chopsticks and the mill hands.*

Although Cobbett achieved so much in many different spheres he took most pride in the fact that 'My efforts have, all my life long, since I became a man, been to cause some addition to be made to the food, the drink and the raiment of the industrious classes.'[5]

His was the age of the 'Improvers' and it seems strange that

---

* Cobbett always believed, however, that the chopsticks would, in the end, constitute the most active and forceful wing of that alliance. The 'great change' he looked for would not, he said, take place until the chopsticks actually forced the Government to pay attention to the poor man's grievances. He thought that such a moment had arrived when the 'rural war' of 1830 broke out.

Cobbett, who hated enclosures, 'factory farms', and most forms of mechanisation, who derided the new Board of Agriculture that had been set up to advance agricultural science, has himself to be thought of as one of the most ambitious of all the Improvers. This was not, perhaps, the case when he farmed on a largish scale at Botley. There he followed traditional farming practices, though with a greater emphasis on forestry than was, perhaps, customary.

It was when he farmed in a smaller way on Long Island and at Barn Elms, and when he turned seedsman and nurseryman at Kensington, that he conducted most of his experiments in cropping and cultivations. Here, again, one must distinguish between what he achieved as a practical farmer and grower, and what he wrote as an educationalist and populariser.

His real interest in the science of agriculture probably started when he was in prison in Newgate. There, where he could manage his Botley farms only through correspondence, he had much time for reading, and devoted some of it to studying the standard works on agriculture. He found little that was new to him in any of them until he came across Jethro Tull's *Horshoeing Husbandry*. Its theories about the advantages of using 'a sort of Vineyard Culture' for ordinary farm crops seemed at once so sensible and so practical that he wrote, in later years, that this one book had 'done more to promote good agriculture than all the other works of all the countries put together'.[6] This may, however, have been a publisher's puff, for in 1822 Cobbett brought out a new edition of Tull's book with an Introduction and an account of his own farming experiments added to it.

Tull, however, set Cobbett thinking about the science, as well as the politics, of farming, and turned him into an earnest advocate of the drill, the horsehoe and all forms of rowcrop cultivation. These led him, eventually, to the *Ruta Baga* or Swedish Turnip, a crop for which he developed an almost excessive enthusiasm. In his Long Island exile, when he was producing his first (largely) non-political book *A Year's Residence in the United States*, he devoted most of the first part of it to a *Treatise on Ruta Baga*.* This described the various experiments he had carried out with the growing, harvest-

---

* The section of *A Year's Residence* dealing with the growing of the *Ruta Baga* was, somewhat unexpectedly, translated in to French in 1834 under the title *De La Culture des Betteraves*. Beetroot, or rather what was to become sugar beet, was a crop that had been encouraged in France ever since the British blockade had forced the French to look for an alternative to West Indian cane sugar. The swede is not, of course, a sugar beet, but advice for growing the one is equally serviceable for the other.

ing and utilisation of that root and revealed that he had in him the qualities that would, in a later age, have been required of an agricultural scientist. He used what would now be called replicated plots to test various methods for preparing the soil and planting and growing the crop, and kept careful measurements and records for every one of them.

Anything Cobbett was interested in he turned propagandist for, even if it was in a treatise on root vegetables. There was a strong element of the ridiculous in the way he invested quite ordinary farm crops with political virtues or vices. Just as the potato – 'the lazy root' – was the curse of Ireland and would, if the borough-mongers had their way, become the curse of England, so the swede became the 'radical root' – presumably because it was useful, added to the overall food supply, but could not be used as a substitute for bread. Cobbett even went so far as to suggest that no English farmer could be considered a good Radical unless the 'radical root' figured prominently in his cropping.

Cobbett had returned from America in 1819 full of another such enthusiasm for what he called the Locust Tree, which is more properly known as the False Acacia *(Robinia Pseudacacia)*. This grew well in the United States, where its timber was used as an alternative to oak, especially in ship-building. Under favourable conditions the tree grows into timber more rapidly than oak, and the wood is at least as durable and as strong.

Cobbett brought a quantity of 'Locust' seed back to England and grew it on in his Kensington nursery. Henceforward his *Register* articles and other works were full of references to the advantages of this 'new' tree. As a consequence he claimed to have sold over a million saplings in the course of a few years, to the great economic advantage of all forestry owners and to the ultimate benefit of a nation which could no longer grow oaks quickly enough to meet the demands of the shipyards.

Some people, however, thought Cobbett was perpetrating a hoax on the public. One of these was Samuel Copland, a well-known farming journalist of that period. In his massive encyclopedia *Agriculture Ancient and Modern* he started from the indisputable fact that the 'Locust' was no new introduction. John Tradescant, the gardener and plant collector, had brought the False Acacia to England in 1640, and it had been grown ever since then as an ornamental tree in parks and gardens. It could be bought, Copland pointed out, from any one of dozens of nurserymen at a very much lower price than Cobbett was charging for it as a 'Locust'. But because of all the 'puffing-off' of the tree that Cobbett had done 'Cobbett's admirers swallowed his egotistical humbug, and actually believed that he had introduced an entirely new species.'[7]

Cobbett's reputation as an expert arboriculturalist stood high after he published *The Woodlands* in 1825, this being his 'Treatise on the planting, cultivating, pruning and cutting down of Forest Trees and Underwoods'. He was often consulted by landowners on the planting up of their estates, a subject frequently mentioned in *Rural Rides*. Indeed, there may still be locust trees growing that owe their existence to William Cobbett.* In spite of this, his dream of filling the forests of England with locust trees never materialised. Copland, who strongly disapproved of 'this locust mania' wrote 'His object was to make money by the sale of the plants; and as the purchasers would have had to wait thirty or forty years before the truth or falsehood of his representations could be tested, he trusted to the chapter of accidents to be beyond the reach of censure before that period expired'. The Forestry Commission recently gave a less subjective reason for the failure of the false acacia as a forest tree in England. 'It requires a very high light intensity, and probably the only place that trees of the required light intensity to make the planting in sufficient numbers to be viable commercially is to be found is in the Allegheny.'[8]

Cobbett devoted no more than two pages of *A Year's Residence* to his experiments with Indian Corn (maize, corn, *Zea Mays*) which he thought cropped best if transplanted as seedlings. It was, however, a crop that attracted his attention, being much the heaviest yielding of all the cereals and capable of being made into bread and other foods for human consumption besides being a feed grain on which all farm animals thrive. It suffers, however, from being frost sensitive and from requiring long periods of sunshine before the grain will ripen. It could not, therefore, be safely grown in Europe anywhere north of the Loire.

Cobbett made it a practice to send his sons, in turn, to tour in France – two of them, on his advice, wrote books on their travels. His eldest son, William, however, did not bring back material for a book but some seed taken from a dwarf strain of Indian Corn he had found growing in a Frenchman's garden. His father grew this on in his Kensington nursery and found, to his delight, that the grain ripened in an English autumn. This reawakened his interest

---

* There are still locust trees at Hargham Hall in South Norfolk – the home of that Sir Thomas Beevor, Bt., who was Cobbett's patron and partner in the Norfolk Petition – which were originally planted on Cobbett's advice. The present Sir Thomas Beevor told me that they have been cut down and allowed to stool three times, so contributing to the payment of three lots of Death Duties.

in a crop which, if it could be brought to harvest in England, could be used to drive out the hated potato as a bread substitute, and could also, because of its high yields, be used in the cottager's garden plot to increase his self-sufficiency.

There is no need here to enter into explanations of why dwarf characteristics allow maize to be grown in more northerly areas, though it is on that basis that dwarf strains are now specifically bred. Once again Cobbett had, as he thought, something new and useful to introduce into British farming and, being Cobbett, he promptly wrote *A Treatise on Cobbett's Corn*, and even had the work printed on paper made from the spaths or husks of the corn cobs.

The *Treatise* is, perhaps, one of Cobbett's most digressive and randomised works and is, for that reason, worth reading by those who have not the slightest interest in Indian Corn. After starting it with an attack on 'our schools and universities where everything is taught, but that which is the most useful and honourable of all; namely the means of raising food' several noble and learned men, including Sir Walter Scott, were attacked by name for confessing, or even boasting of their total ignorance of everything connected with agriculture. He then came to his own achievements:

The introduction of the Locust Tree was a matter of such vast importance that I never dreamed of anything to exceed it in point of value to the country; but, it certainly will be exceeded by the introduction of the plant of which I am about to treat . . . I shall show what a blessing this plant will be to the English labourer, and how it will and must drive the accursed soul-degrading potatoe out of the land into which it never ought to have come.* . . . Much of the ease and happiness of the people of the United States is ascribable to the absence of grinding taxation; but that alone, without the cultivation of Indian Corn, would not, in the space of only about a hundred and fifty years, have created a powerful nation. . . . I have very frequently observed that I believed England to be the richest agricultural country in the world, bating the want of Indian Corn; and that, if it had that, it would exceed every other country beyond all comparison. I regarded our sun as wholly insufficient for the

* Cobbett's hatred of the potato was expressed in a variety of ways. The following is perhaps the most absurd: 'It was one of the greatest villains upon earth (Sir WALTER RALEIGH), who (they say) first brought this root into England. He was hanged at last! What a pity, since he was to be hanged, the hanging did not take place before he became such a mischievous devil.'

purpose of ripening this valuable crop, until the accident of which I shall speak induced me to make the trial, which, upon a scale sufficiently large to obviate every doubt, has now convinced me of the contrary.

The accident was, of course that 'Two ears of this corn were brought to England, early in the year 1826, by Mr William Cobbett, who obtained them from a gentleman in the province of Artois, who had cultivated the plant in his garden a good many years, but who seemed not to have a very distinct recollection of the manner in which he came to the seed. My son was convinced that it would ripen in England and that the crop would be greater than that of any other Indian Corn.'

It did ripen, for several seasons, in Cobbett's walled Kensington garden. As a consequence, the seed of 'Cobbett's Corn' was put on sale at his seedsman's shop and was widely advertised in the *Register* which, on appropriate dates, contained articles advising farmers that the time had come to prepare the soil, to plant or to harvest the rich crop flowing from Cobbett's discovery. Parcels of seed were despatched to selected farmers in every county of England for distributing to their farmhands so that they, also, might benefit. And so it was that maize came to be referred to in farming circles as 'Cobbett's Corn' for generations to come.

In the end, however, it might as well have been referred to as 'Cobbett's Folly'. His Indian Corn, alas, failed to ripen when grown on a farm scale, and it ceased to be grown as anything but a green crop until very recently. Even now, when dwarf hybrids specially bred for more northerly climates are available, maize cannot safely be grown as a grain crop in any but the most southern counties of England. Cobbett's dwarf corn was almost certainly one such hybrid, but it would, of course, fail to breed true, so that its valuable characteristics would disappear in the course of a few plant generations.

As was customary with him, the whole of the *Treatise* was interspersed with anecdotes, the most amusing of which concerned the success he had had on Long Island when he fed his horses on Indian Corn. Every farmer there kept a light waggon and a good pair of horses for taking produce into New York or 'for taking the wife out a-visiting'. His horses were much on a par with those of his neighbours, but they, 'amidst all their long-faced gravity and absence of ambition and rivalry, have, nevertheless, one species of folly; that, in going upon the roads, it is looked upon as a sort of slur on one, if another pass him going in the same direction . . . You will see an old Quaker, whom to look at as perched in his waggon, you would think had been cut out of stone a couple of hundred years ago, lay his whip upon the "creatures" if he hear a rattle behind him . . . and on they go, as fast as they can scamper. It would have been a shame to pass two years and a half amongst these happy people without contracting their habits, and therefore my horses had their trials upon the road; sometimes we were victorious and sometimes we were defeated, but never the latter without pretending that we did not want to go so fast. Until the year 1819, I used to feed as others did, with oats, barley, rye and cut chaff; but in that year I had a great stack of corn which I had purchased in the ear. My horses therefore, had nothing but corn for the whole of the year, and they beat every pair of horses on the road, till at last nobody that knew them ever attempted a rivalship. It was the corn', he added triumphantly, 'that forced the horses along.'

One other experiment gave Cobbett great cause for pride. This concerned the straw-plat affair. Most women at that time wore straw hats in summer, and the material for making them had to be imported from Italy, as the straw from harvested English cereals was not of a sufficiently fine quality. Cobbett came across a Leghorn bonnet, as they were called, which had been made in the United States from bleached and dried grasses that he identified as a mixture of burnet and smooth-stalked meadow grass. This gave him the idea for launching an entirely new cottage industry which would allow the labourer's wife to earn money by gathering and bleaching these grasses and plaiting them into straws suitable for the milliners to make hats out of. He set about this business very seriously, drew up lists of suitable grasses and dates for their gathering, and experimented with various methods of bleaching and plaiting before he was sufficiently satisfied with the result to communicate it to the Secretary of the Society of Arts. That Society awarded Cobbett its Silver Medal for this discovery and he wrote about it in his *Cottage Economy*, ending with the comment: 'I am strongly disposed to believe that the manufacture, the establishment of which I am endeavouring to promote, will be beneficial to my country in many respects, and particularly, that it will tend to better the lot of the labouring classes.' Then, remembering how he had been persecuted and imprisoned by the Pittites, he also remembered what he had said when he emerged from prison in Newgate: 'the only way in which I should seek to be revenged of my enemies, was by rendering services to that Country of which they were the insolent oppressors'. Quite apart from the fact that Cobbett never ceased blackguarding his enemies until the day he died, there is still something remarkable in a man who can turn a home-made Leghorn bonnet into an instrument of political revenge.

There was a strong element of the White Knight about Cobbett who, although he hated machinery, was always acquiring or inventing gadgets which he then proceeded to press on his fellows as being the means by which a better and more economical life could be lived. Among these were the hand-mill he had made so that wheat no longer had to be sent to the miller, who invariably cheated; the machine for separating maize kernels from the cob; the American stove he imported which would save all the expensive fuel then used in open fireplaces, and the Dutch oven he constructed which, placed in front of such a stove, allowed all the work done on the kitchen range to be carried out, more economically, in the parlour.

Cobbett was always fertile of ideas. Not all of them were sensible, nor many of them practical. The most worthy of them were concerned with the land and how it could best be made to serve all mankind, and it was that which, in the end, stamped him as an agrarian above everything else. For him, truly, ripeness was all. Much of his writing and most of his politics may be forgotten; but his basic philosophy deserves to be remembered. Some of it, at least, is contained in another passage in his *Treatise on Cobbett's Corn*:

An old farmer in Hampshire, who was very rich, and whose silly neighbours were persuading him to have his daughter taught music, said: 'Na! talk of muzik indeed; gi' me two flails and a cuckoo'. I dare say that this saying was as old as the English language. The two flails make a very pretty sound at all times. The voice of the harbinger of summer is also delightful; but here was the *idea of wealth* most aptly associated with that of pleasant sounds. The cuckoo never comes till *old May-Day*; and two flails going in the same barn at that time of the year, indicates that there is a good store of grain in the barn at that distance from the preceding harvest, and that, therefore, the farmer is rich. I like two flails and a cuckoo very well, and they have charmed my heart many and many a time, even when I was a little boy.

CHAPTER FOURTEEN

The Road to Reform: 1805–10

The English are free, only forty days, once in seven years; and the use
they make of their freedom, shows that they deserve to be enslaved all
the rest of their lives.

Jean-Jacques Rousseau: *Social Contract*
(Quoted by Cobbett to the Electors of Westminster.)

To pretend that Cobbett can usefully be discussed in isolation from
the world of politics would be as idle as pretending that Nelson
could be discussed without reference to the sea. So far political
discussion has been confined to indicating how far Cobbett's
character influenced and determined his politics. Henceforth his
politics determined his career. Almost everything of any importance that happened to him from around 1805 onwards happened
to him for essentially political reasons.

Cobbett had a passion for justice, and a great fund of compassion for those he conceived to be the victims of injustice. He was
intellectually and physically fearless, although there were occasions when he realised that prudence might become a necessity. He
was, in a corrupt age, totally incorruptible, which led him to hate or
despise those who were not. This, even more than his opinionated,
quarrelsome nature, distinguished him and isolated him in society.
The oligarchs who exercised patronage, and the politicians, office
holders, military men, churchmen, journalists and writers who
were their clients were, for the most part, so conditioned by what
were then thought to be the reasonable necessities of government
that they failed to realise the extent to which they had themselves
been corrupted and had become responsible for the corruption of
others. They were almost incapable, therefore, of understanding
Cobbett's attitude to such matters, and refused to believe that it
was based on moral conviction. They preferred to attribute it to
personal and political malice.

Yet he was, in spite of all that his enemies alleged, a true patriot,
though his ultimate loyalty was to the England of his childhood
rather than the England he still lived in. Although he was as
properly xenophobic as any other Englishman of his day and

318

background, he still contrived to be, in some respects, a citizen of the world. Consequently he tried harder perhaps than any other publicist, to interpret and explain the Americans, French, Spaniards and other foreigners to his stubbornly insular countrymen. This was generally done, admittedly, for political reasons. He saw advantages in demonstrating how, in one respect or another, things were better managed abroad than they were in England. Nevertheless he did attempt to educate his readers to a better understanding of foreigners and foreign affairs.

Although he was, by all accounts, calm and amiable in his private life, it is truly surprising how often, in writing about him, one has to say that he hated, and that he did so with a permanence, a vindictiveness and a lack of proportion that no public cause could justify.

Anger, indeed, was his principal weapon but, although it gave great force to his writing and his preaching, it all too often removed him by at least one step from reality and made him see the world of politics with what amounted to a political form of tunnel vision. It was strange that a man who could look at the countryside with so much perception and describe its subtlest variations with so much sympathy and truth should, when it came to politics, become almost incapable of seeing things otherwise than in terms of absolute black or absolute white. Politics appeared to coarsen his emotions and blunt his sensibility. Indeed, he held coarseness and bluntness to be virtues. If the liberal mind is one that makes a man conscious of the many-sided nature of political truth, Cobbett was proud of the fact that there was not one drop of stultifying, milk-and-water liberalism in his veins.

The older Cobbett grew, the more Radical he became. The fact that he developed politically in what many would consider to be a widdershins direction leads one to wonder whether, for all his country-bred conservatism, his qualities had not always been Radical ones. That heady mixture of compassion, anger and hatred is certainly more commonly found on the 'left' of politics than it is on the 'right'. But when one considers how limited his compassion was and how vast his hatreds were such an explanation becomes too simple.

He instinctively believed, like most Radicals, that injustice must breed anger, and anger hatred. Ergo, the depth of his compassion for the chopsticks and the intensity of his anger at the apparently wilful destruction of the 'small, ancient way of life' of the English countryside more than justified all his hatreds. It was both right and necessary, therefore, to hate variously the Jacobins and the anti-Jacobins, the Pittites and the Whigs, the corrupters and the corrupted, the decadent aristocracy and the upstarts, the money men and the placemen, the Jews, Scots, Methodists, Quakers and Evangelicals, the industrialists and the 'feelosofers', not to mention almost every contemporary historian, novelist, newspaper editor and journalist.

As a Radical, he hated, or at least quarrelled bitterly with large numbers of his fellow-Radicals – because they were Malthusians, or Utilitarians, or republicans, or Owenites, or revolutionaries, or atheists or disagreed with his monetarist theories, or merely because they were living in sin with another man's wife. It was much the same with his fellow-Reformers once he had been converted to Reform. He hated a moderate Reformer almost as much as he hated a borough-monger, for in that matter he rapidly developed into a Maximalist and ignored the art of the possible. He wanted more than the abolition of the rotten boroughs, equal representation, universal suffrage and secrecy of the ballot. He demanded, among other things, annual Parliaments sitting alternately in Westminster, York, Bristol and other regional centres; the exclusion from Parliament of all members of the Executive and all servants of the Crown; and members who were delegates rather than representatives and who were debarred from receiving payment or patronage of any kind.

It is possible, of course, to argue that political hatreds ought not to be taken at much more than face-value; that they are an essential element of the party-political game; that they are often more useful as instruments for change than whole sessions of reasoned and reasonable argument. But even if one accepts that, Cobbett's hatreds, which invariably spilled over into his politics, did not always and solely correspond to the required hatreds of party politics. They were as much intra-party hatreds as they were inter-party ones. Many were personal prejudices blown up into political principles. Some of his prejudices and preferences, moreover, seemed to belong to the party he currently opposed rather than the one he supported.

It may, for example, have been entirely suitable for a born-again Radical to hate all factory owners, landowners, financiers and tax-eaters collectively, but there were few or no Radical principles that justified hating all, or nearly all Abolitionists, Evangelicals, Malthusians, educationalists, economists or Scotsmen. There were, in fact, contradictions in Cobbett's politics; and they not only prevented him from achieving such success as a politician as his skills as an agitator entitled him to; they also made it almost impossible for him to be a good party man and even made it difficult, on occasions, to decide whether he was on the right or the left in politics. If one said that he was a man whose conservative instincts quarrelled with his radical emotions and that his native prejudices quarrelled with both, this would still fail to account for all of his inconsistencies.

He was, for example, a monarchist, even in his most Radical moods. On the other hand, he disliked the House of Guelph, hated George IV and abused most of the British monarchs from Henry VIII onwards more mercilessly than any Jacobin. He was a staunch Church of England man who came in the end to advocate complete freedom of religion even though he continued to hate all Dissenters, Deists and Atheists quite as much as he came to hate tithes, bishops and pluralistic parsons.

Whereas most Reformers believed they were fighting for a future in which political power would lie in the hands of the people, Cobbett fought for Reform because he thought it would destroy the Pitt System, reverse the Industrial Revolution and restore the agrarian civilisation the people themselves had abandoned. He first opposed and later supported Catholic Emancipation until it was accomplished, and then declared that it was not religious but economic relief that was needed if the Irish problem were to be solved. On the other hand he only reluctantly abandoned his opposition to the abolition of slavery, thought negroes were better off as slaves, and wrote, 'Some means should be taken to put a stop to the increase of Blacks in this country . . . It is truly shocking to see the number of English women, who are married to Negroes: our streets and public walks are continually disgraced by the disgusting spectacle: and whom are we to blame but ourselves?'[1]

It has frequently been said that English Radicalism has always owed more to Wesley than to Marx. Cobbett, nevertheless, hated Dissenters as much when he was a Radical as he had when he was Peter Porcupine and a High Tory. Such primitive prejudices must have seemed almost as shocking to most of his fellow-Radicals as they do to us today. Certainly 'Old Mother Mange' (that determinedly liberal journal The Edinburgh Review) attacked him for his attacks on Dissenters quite as often as it attacked him for his Scotophobia. Cobbett gloried in such attacks, for these were not only the prejudices he had been born to, but they added weight and substance to his writings. In voicing them he was also voicing the prejudices of the people.

His most violent hatred, which was reserved for the Jews, probably gave less affront to his fellow-Radicals and the bienpensants. To some, however, it may have seemed a somewhat old-fashioned prejudice that was rapidly becoming irrelevant. Cobbett recognised that his was a departure from current trends of liberal and even Radical thought when he wrote: 'My dislike of the Jews is that which our forefathers had of them.'² Consequently, he usually produced historical reasons for his hatred. He rejoiced that his great hero, Edward I, had chased the Jews out of England, and regretted that those villains, Cromwell and William III, had brought them back. 'In France the Jews were the rapacious farmers of taxes, in Poland, in Germany, in Hungary; every where, where they have been allowed to practise their arts of plunder, they have produced ruin to the people, and very frequently to the state . . . Bonaparte, when he had become a tyrant, insolently put these wretches upon a level with the French people . . . Some of you have said that they have been put upon a footing with Christians in the United States of America. I have never heard of but one Jew being admitted to any public trust at all, and he was no more than a sherriff of a county. So far from encouraging and favouring the Jews, the Americans detest them.'³

In 1821 Cobbett published his celebrated 'Sermons' in twelve monthly numbers. In 1830, when a Petition to remove the civil disabilities of the Jews was presented to Parliament, his anger was so intense that he published a thirteenth 'Sermon' which he called *Good Friday or The Murder of Jesus Christ by the Jews*. In this he clearly and vigorously stated his reasons – religious, historical, social and economic – for hating that race:

> The strongest of all the proofs of our religion is to be found in the clear and repeated prophecies that they should be dispersed amongst the nations and should have no *inheritance*, except the possession of *their own bodies*, or, as the prophet Ezekiel describes it, the monopoly of their own *filthiness*; that is to say, that they should, in no country on earth, have any immunities, any privileges or possessions in house, land or water, any civil or political rights; that they should everywhere, be deemed *aliens*; and always at the *absolute disposal of the sovereign power of the state*, as completely as any inanimate substance thrown on the land by the winds or the waves.

Cobbett saw no inconsistency in quoting an Old Testament prophet to justify his attacks on the Jews. This particular prejudice of his, however, involved other and more relevant inconsistencies. He had long been a supporter of Catholic Emancipation and had, on and off, been a friend and admirer of Daniel O'Connell, the great 'Liberator'. In 1830, however, after O'Connell had forced Catholic emancipation on the Government, and after he and certain other Catholics had at last taken their seats in Parliament,

322

Cobbett, instead of rejoicing, launched a virulent attack against O'Connell and the Duke of Norfolk for having supported the petition to remove civil disabilities from the Jews. He addressed a *Register* article to O'Connell whose tone can be judged from the following quotation. 'So much for you and the Jews; but I should like to see you down upon your knees before your big crucifix, thumping your breast with one hand, putting your other hand behind your back to be shaken by a Jew, who is pointing with his finger and mocking at the crucifix.'[4]

As for that leader of the English Catholics, the Duke of Norfolk, he had spoken in favour of the petition in the House of Lords, saying, 'As an English Catholic, but lately admitted to a seat in this House, I should be most ungrateful if I did not support the prayer in this petition'. Cobbett's comment on this in the *Register* was entirely characteristic of a man who would always allow innate prejudice to override even closely-held political beliefs. The author of the recent *History of the Protestant Reformation in England* and the man who had fought so long to procure full political rights for Catholics, wrote:

> If it really was gratitude that prompted His Grace to support the petition of the anti-Christians; if he was conscious that he owed his seat in the House to any Jew-like influence; then the more the pity for us that he should have obtained that seat, and we Protestants ought to be the last to join him in his expressions of gratitude. If he considered himself vested with the sanction of the people of England, then, indeed, this is being grateful to us with a vengeance, and God help all those (Jews only excepted) who anticipate a bettering of our state as the consequence of Catholic emancipation.[5]

The most significant passage here was the one in which he asked the unfortunate Duke whether he considered himself 'vested with the sanction of the people of England'. For Cobbett believed that the Duke of Norfolk had no authority to speak for 'the people': he also believed, and with some justification, that he, William Cobbett, possessed that authority to a greater degree than any other man in England. On occasions such as these he did not even pause to consider whether he was speaking as a Radical and a Reformer, for he knew he was speaking as the voice of the people.

What he was voicing was an ancient, deep-rooted, popular prejudice that had been recently reinforced by the growing hatred the working classes felt for the new capitalism. Whether or not some of his fellow-Radicals might have felt embarrassed at having such an essential element of Radical philosophy expressed in such an illiberal manner was irrelevant. What was relevant was the fact that the charge of being either Jews or Jew-like could be added to all the other crimes of the new capitalist class.

We nowadays may appreciate better the dangers to which that particular prejudice may lead. Nevertheless, it is still difficult to believe we also appreciate that it is no more logical to hate a man because he is a capitalist, or a kulak, or a reactionary, than because he is a Jew, or a negro, or a priest. We are scarcely entitled to judge Cobbett according to present standards of accepted wisdom, seeing that our wisdom is still, in so many respects, no greater than that of our forebears.*

One can argue at great length over the type of label to attach to Cobbett's politics. Was he, as his concern for social justice, for Reform, for freedom of the Press and of religion suggests, an authentic man of the left, or was he rather, as his respect for traditional institutions, his mediaevalism, his dislike of everything but minimal government suggest, really a man of the right? If, as seems obvious, he was both, then what combination of titles – Tory-Radical, Radical-Tory, Christian-Democrat, Agrarian-Conservative, Radical-Nationalist – would best describe him? It would, perhaps, be simplest to settle for 'Populist', a political label that avoids all problems of ideology but does say something about Cobbett's undoubted ability to form, voice, and lead popular opinion.

Yet that would describe only one aspect of him. The problem that all who write about politics have to struggle with is that, whatever lengths we may go to in attempting to classify our politicians, there is still no taxonomy of politics which even a half-trained taxonomist would recognise as valid. That Cobbett was, in certain moods, and at certain stages of his career, a Populist seems as certain as that he was, in other moods and stages, both a Radical and a Tory. Yet he was as capable of defying popular opinion as he was of leading it. None of his biographers, therefore, has the right to claim him for any particular political party. Were he ordered to put a label on Cobbett, our half-trained taxonomist would be more than justified in classifying him as *sui generis*. Even if that is a minimal type of classification it is one which is amply

---

* However little political theorists may like it, history still demonstrates that no popular movement can succeed unless it appeals to the prejudices as well as the aspirations of the people. Every great populist leader has had to bring as much conviction to his hatreds, mindlessly destructive though they might be, as he brings to any of his more reasonable and constructive proposals. This is, sadly, as true of the prophets of democracy as it is of the prophets of other creeds.

supported by Cobbett's own preference for forming, from time to time, an autonomous Opposition Party of one.

Pitt died on 23 January 1806. Little more than a week later Lord Grenville took office at the head of what came to be called the Ministry of All Talents. It was, substantially, a Whig administration formed from a coalition of the Old and New Oppositions, including Fox, with a leavening of former Pittites. Windham returned to the War Office, but this time in the more important role of Secretary of State for War and the Colonies. Within a matter of days the *Register* had begun to attack this new administration quite as vigorously as it had ever attacked Pitt's. By the end of the month Cobbett's close connections with Windham had been severed.

Cobbett had made the mistake of believing, under the influence of such recent critics of Pitt as Fox, Grenville and Windham, that the new Government would immediately undertake the task of destroying the Pitt System. He was, of course, immediately disillusioned, largely because he had been naïve enough to ignore several important facts of current political life. One of these was that Pitt, largely speaking, had not actually invented the Pitt System. If one overlooks the economic policies forced on him by the necessities of war, Pitt's style of government had conformed to the manner in which Britain had been governed for the best part of a century, and would continue to be governed even after the first Reform Bill. Moreover, there was hardly one important member of Grenville's Cabinet, except for Fox, who had not, at one time or another, served under Pitt and had not, questions of war and peace apart, supported Pitt's policies.

Few of the new Ministers, therefore, were as eager as Cobbett to initiate 'great change'. Indeed, even modest change would have been difficult to achieve at that particular time. There would have been a great weight of military, bureaucratic and political inertia to overcome if traditional methods of governing the country were to be abandoned, just as there would have been powerful new forces to neutralise before any of the changes Cobbett advocated could be accomplished.

The rapid industrialisation of the country, for example, could not easily be halted, however much the agrarian Cobbett resented it. Nor would it have been possible to deny the new 'upstart' industrial and financial magnates some growing share of political influence. So long as the war, which Cobbett had so enthusiastically supported, continued, any government would have been bound to raise new taxes and new loans and been forced to pass measures that limited personal freedoms.

Patronage will probably always be a source of corruption, but no autocracy, oligarchy or democracy has ever been able to dispense with it entirely. In that age, when no more open or moral method for paying politicians and government servants a living wage had been arrived at, patronage had proved to be far more serviceable than patriotism, and its attendant corruption was accepted as an almost 'necessary evil' of good government.

These political realities Cobbett obstinately refused to recognise. He should not have entertained the slightest hopes, however, that the Grenvilles would agree with him. No other family, in the whole of the Whig oligarchy, was so notoriously arrogant, rapacious and self-serving. The various Grenvilles and Temples were already in receipt of some £60,000 a year of public money in the form of pensions and sinecures, and Grenville himself drew £6,000 a year by virtue of his appointment for life to the sinecure post of Auditor of the Exchequer. Now that he was Prime Minister he was also, ex-officio, First Lord of the Treasury, but he still refused to surrender his sinecure even though it theoretically placed him in the position of having to check, as Auditor, every expenditure of public funds he had sanctioned as First Lord. One of his first acts as Prime Minister, indeed, was to require Parliament to approve this anomaly.

The *Register* immediately condemned such a flagrant abuse of public funds in an article which developed into a vigorous attack on the Grenvilles singly and severally. That article rapidly brought into the open political disagreements that had been developing, for some time, between Cobbett and Windham. The latter, for example, had never been able to agree with Cobbett's economic theories. He had, after all, served under Pitt and had never objected to his economic policies, merely to his war policies. But Windham did object to Cobbett's increasing support for Sir Francis Burdett, who was not only a Radical, but also a Reformer, and Cobbett and he had at one time agreed that Reform was both dangerous and unnecessary. If Cobbett had begun to depart from that belief, Windham, for his part, now had to abandon the cause of Catholic Emancipation, which Cobbett and he had supported in their opposition days. The King's obstinate refusal to allow emancipation to go forward had provided the Ministry with sufficient reason for leaving it out of its programme.

Such disagreements rapidly developed into an open clash of personalities. The correspondence and messages that passed between them during that fateful month of February 1806 reflect the course of their quarrel. On 4 February, as soon as he had heard of Windham's appointment, Cobbett had written to him: 'This day 22 years ago I 'listed as a soldier – tomorrow 14 years ago I was married. This month of February has always been a lucky month for me; for I can truly say, that the news of this morning (I allude to the List of new Ministers) has given me as great pleasure as I ever before felt in my whole life.'⁶

Great pleasure would soon give way to great chagrin. Once again, as when he had returned from America in 1800, Cobbett announced that he expected no personal rewards for his services, even though it was generally expected in Whig circles that he would be given either a seat in Parliament or an office of profit for what he had done through the *Register* in bringing the Whigs back into office.

This did not mean, however, that Cobbett did not expect to be listened to and have his advice respected, above all by Windham. He promptly began, therefore, to shower Windham with ideas about what now ought to be done and recommendations as to who ought to be in and who ought to be out of the Government. If he asked nothing for himself, he was still insistent that such friends of his as Dr. Laurence and Mr. Penn must be found posts, and by the same token, that his old enemies of *The Porcupine* days, Lord Auckland and Mr. Freeling, be turned out of office.

Windham, naturally enough, ignored such advice. What concerned Cobbett even more was that he also ignored the plans for reforming the regular army that the two of them had discussed so frequently in former days. Windham had no intention of forcing these on a Cabinet that was perfectly willing to continue with Pitt's ideas for leaving the regular army unreformed and for enlarging the Militia and Volunteer forces instead.

Cobbett formally submitted his plans for the regular army to Windham, but he must have sensed that the new Minister was a somewhat different man from the one who had consulted him and corresponded with him on an almost daily basis for the past four or five years. In a noticeably stiff covering letter, therefore, he declared: 'It may as well be laid down as a rule, that while you are a Minister, *I* shall never intrude upon your time by personal application to you upon any occasion whatever. Your time is now too precious to be spent in *parler pour parler*.'⁷

It would have been better, perhaps, if some time could have been devoted to *parler pour parler*. Instead, John Wright had to act as a messenger between them, and it was from Wright that Cobbett soon learnt how angry Windham was, and how wide the breach between them had become. Windham had probably been irritated

by all the unsolicited advice his former adviser plagued him with,
but his anger arose more directly from the rough treatment the
Grenvilles had received in the *Register*. That journal had always
acted, when necessary, as Windham's mouthpiece; now he had to
explain to his leader and his Cabinet colleagues that he was in no
way responsible for its hostile treatment of them.

Windham must have sent a message through Wright ordering
Cobbett to cease all such attacks for, on 23 February, Cobbett
wrote to him:

> The other parts of your communication give me great pain;
> because, though Wright merely repeats what was said to him,
> there is, running through the whole of his language and his
> manner, such an evident appearance of sorrow that . . . I cannot
> help concluding that the impression upon his mind was, that on
> account of the article relative to Lord Grenville, I had incurred
> your serious displeasure. This would have seriously affected me,
> whose chief pride it had been to endeavour to further your
> views, and whose almost sole consolation has been the posses-
> sion of your countenance and friendship [were it not that] I
> cannot think myself justified to retract one word of what I have
> said. The question relating to the Auditorship is open to the
> judgement of the world . . . I will not disguise either to you or to
> the world that I clearly perceive, from the manner in which he
> [Grenville] has begun, and from the retention of so many of the
> Pitt sect about him, an intention to preserve the accursed
> system, which I hope to see annihilated.

Windham, it would seem, had done more than order an obstinate man to swallow his opinions. He had also, as the same letter
reveals, slighted him as a writer. 'Wright states that you appear
extremely vexed at the prevalence, or supposed prevalence, of an
opinion that "all the most violent parts" of the *Register* were either
written or suggested by you . . . I must confess myself proud
enough to hope that, from having my writings imputed to him, no
man's character has ever suffered an injury.'

When two proud and opinionated men clash in this manner,
friendship is generally the first casualty. On 28 February Windham
recorded in his diary: 'Came away in carriage with Fox, got out at
end of Downing Street, and went to office, thence to Cobbett.
Probably the last interview we shall have.' In his last letter to
Windham, written in March, Cobbett revealed, by the stiffness of
his manner, that he realised that their correspondence and their
former intimacy had come to an end. It began: 'Loath as I am,

particularly after the remark of your last letter but one, to trespass upon your valuable time'; it ended, after a certain amount of pettifogging argument, 'When you have described *your* plan [for army reform] to Parliament, *mine* I will thank you to return to me at No 5 Panton Square'.

Cobbett would, in future years, quarrel with and part from other political friends and allies. Judging by the relish with which he then proceeded to blackguard them in the *Register*, he enjoyed the quarrels and never regretted the partings. With Windham it was different. Cobbett was genuinely saddened and hurt by the breach, and never lost his affection and regard for the man who had once been his patron, guide and friend. Although he later published a series of critical articles in the form of *Letters to Mr Windham* in the *Register*, he, almost uniquely, avoided speaking or writing ill of a man whose politics had become no less repugnant to him than those of any other Whig borough-monger.

The Grenville article can be seen as one of those sudden climaxes that would, time and again, change the whole design of Cobbett's politics. If there had been no breach with Windham, would Cobbett have been absorbed into the Whig establishment and have pursued a respectable though unexciting career in establishment politics? All that we know of his character suggests that, in the long term, this could never have happened. On the other hand he might well have taken longer to arrive at his Radicalism had he stayed with Windham until the latter's death in 1810.

That there had been, for Cobbett, a design, and that it revolved around Windham had, up to that moment, been abundantly clear. Cobbett had always seen in Windham a future Prime Minister. Part at least of his friendship for him had been invested in an attempt to convince him that he was the one man in England who possessed the qualities that were needed if Napoleon was to be beaten, the Pitt System destroyed and the nation returned to its ancient virtues. That investment, never perhaps an entirely sound one, had now been lost. And with it Cobbett lost such influence as he might have hoped to exercise in Government circles. Henceforth he would have to turn to the people, rather than to the established politicians for his authority and his mandate.

Since he had, by now, ditched the Whigs as unceremoniously as he had once ditched the Tories, the majority of politicians were convinced that his double apostasy had effectively deprived him of political credibility. This did not, however, greatly affect the sales and influence of the *Register*. People in and out of politics continued to read it because of the vigour of Cobbett's writing, and because his views, however outrageous, were never less than interesting. But few of his readers now found themselves agreeing with his views, for they were no longer the views of either the Government or the Opposition. Those most likely to agree with them were to be found among the Radical Reformers; and for this reason Cobbett found himself attracted into that circle in which such men as Major John Cartwright, Sir Francis Burdett, Henry Hunt and James Paull laboured to prepare the country for Reform and 'democracy'. Burdett was no longer in Parliament, but his attacks, in and out of the Commons, on the Pittites had so attracted Cobbett as to allow him to forget that he had once hated the man for his Jacobinical sympathies. The *Register*, accordingly, supported Burdett, and Burdett, one supposes, agreed with the *Register*.

Major Cartwright, one of the founders of the pre-war Reform movement, had already made friendly overtures to Cobbett, at a time when the latter was still a staunch supporter of a New Opposition that was neither Reformist nor Radical. The venerable and venerated major had written to him during Pitt's lifetime to congratulate him on his articles analysing the Melville scandal, saying 'it was only lately that I became a reader of your *Weekly Register*, your energy, your indignant warmth against peculation, your abhorrence of political treachery, and your independent spirit command my esteem'.[8] The Major, an eminently honest man, was undoubtedly sincere, but the fact that he enclosed some of his own pamphlets on the need for Reform, mentioned 'that public spirit and courage which were once the characteristics of England', and ended the letter with the injunction 'We must not despair', suggests that he was aware of the advantages that could accrue if Cobbett of the *Register* were converted to the cause of Radical Reform.

The two men exchanged theories and visits and soon discovered that they had more than 'an indignant warmth against peculation' in common. Both were deeply interested in agriculture. Both were ex-servicemen (Cartwright had been a sailor before he became a soldier) and, as such, had plans for reorganising the defences of the country, though Cobbett wanted an enlarged and more professional regular army while Cartwright, with memories of the ancient Saxon *fyrd* in his mind, wanted to put every able-bodied man under arms. Where, for the time being, they differed was over the need for a reformed Parliament.

The reforms that Cobbett wanted were to existing economic and fiscal policies, and these, he argued, could be achieved through Parliament as it was at present constituted. All that was necessary was to persuade the Commons to refuse the Executive supply, as they had done in the days of Hampden, and the Pitt System would collapse, the tax-eaters would disappear, and the ancient freedoms of Englishmen would be restored to them.

Cartwright turned to history and to theories about the Anglo-Saxon Witenagemot rather than to Pitt's economic policies to find support for his argument that things would not go better in England until every free Englishman had a voice in the election of his government. These appeals to the somewhat apocryphal history of the English people were far more important to the pre-war Reformers, most of whom were drawn from the middle and upper classes, than they were, later, to those members of the working class who supported the Radical and Reformist cause after 1815. They, in varying degrees, would be influenced by the egalitarian theories released by the French Revolution and were far more interested in equality and the notion of democracy than in any attempt to resuscitate the Witan.

Characteristically enough, when Cobbett was converted to Reform, it was for Arcadian and antiquarian reasons rather than for Jacobinical ones, even though he never lost sight of the economic argument. Hazlitt wrote of Burdett, for example: 'There is only one error he seems to labour under (which we believe he also borrowed from Mr Horne Tooke or Major Cartwright), the wanting to go back to the early times of our Constitution and history in search of the principles of law and liberty . . . Liberty, in our opinion, is but a modern invention . . . A man may be a patriot, without being an antiquary.'[9]

Cobbett, far more of a Populist than Burdett, also borrowed from Cartwright. Like him, he went back, in the end, to the early times to find more justification there for Reform than was provided by his 'Pittiad', his hatred of upstarts and his concern for the poor. It is difficult to understand the philosophy that underlay Cobbett's particular brand of Radicalism; or his arguments for Reform, unless one appreciates how much these were influenced by the historicity of such men as Cartwright and Burdett. It was they who turned his mind towards those dubious historical arguments that underlay his eventual and abiding belief that all the economic and political ills of the English had begun with the Dissolution of the Monasteries. It was a belief that allowed Cobbett to become a Radical Reformer without ever becoming a 'progressive' and without ever wholly subscribing to those theories about democracy and equality on which true Radicalism was based.

With Cobbett it always came back to the land. He accepted Cartwright's theory that in pre-Conquest days every freeman had

had a voice in the election of the Witan. Feudalism, he argued, had substituted tenure for status, and the concept of freeman was submerged by the concepts of vassalage and villeinage. When feudalism decayed, and all men, in theory, became free and equal under the law, the new landowners who had plundered the Church, and the lawyers who served them, had ensured that the commons of England should be represented in Parliament, not on the basis of being *freemen*, but on the basis of being *freeholders*, and not less than forty shilling ones at that. Most of the land of England, however, was occupied and farmed by tenants and copyholders, and, although these were now, in legal terms, 'free' tenures, they carried no rights of suffrage. Thus it was that the new landowning aristocracy gained control of the county vote and ownership of the seats left to the ancient and now decayed boroughs, and through these had arrogated to themselves the right to decide who should speak for the commons of England in Parliament. Cobbett's ultimate arguments for Reform, powerful and popular though they were, appealed essentially to the folk memory. The true Radicals, on the other hand, appealed to the novel and intoxicating ideas of the American and French Revolutions.

In June 1806, however, Cobbett, although he had parted from Windham and the Whigs, had not as yet been converted either to Reform or to mediaevalism. All his political efforts were devoted to his 'Pittiad'. He was publicly raging at Parliament's recent decision to spend £40,000 on settling Pitt's private debts, when one of the first by-elections of the new Parliament was announced. This was at the near-rotten borough of Honiton in Devon.* Mr. Cavendish Bradshaw, one of the two sitting Members, had just accepted the office of Teller of the Irish Exchequer and had, as a consequence, to offer himself for re-election.

This example of 'Pittite corruption' led Cobbett to publish in the *Register* two *Letters to the Electors of Honiton*. He castigated Bradshaw who had, since being 'constituted one of the guardians of the public purse, taken care to obtain a place by the means of which he will draw into his own pocket, some thousands a year out of that purse'. He then proceeded to call upon some 'independent, honest and zealous man' to stand against Bradshaw, and upon the Honiton electors to vote for him if he materialised. No one, in fact, did materialise, whereupon Cobbett wrote his second Letter to the

---

* Honiton, with some 400 electors eligible to vote, was hardly an entirely 'rotten' borough, as Old Sarum so notoriously was, despite the fact that almost every voter was publicly up for sale to the highest bidder.

electors telling them: 'I did, upon hearing of the approaching vacancy, use my efforts to prevail upon other men to afford you an opportunity of evincing your good sense and uprightness, and, having failed in these efforts, I have thought it my duty to afford you this opportunity myself.'[10]

There is evidence which suggests that Cobbett did not, at that time, feel that he had a mission to enter Parliament, a place for which he always expressed a mixture of contempt and dislike. The sense of mission came later, for at that moment he could have entertained no hopes of defeating Bradshaw. He was saved from persevering with his gesture by the unexpected intervention of that remarkable man, Thomas, Lord Cochrane (1775–1860), later tenth Earl of Dundonald.

Although Cochrane at this time was only thirty-one, he was already a national hero for his dashing exploits, first as commander of the *Speedy* sloop-of-war, and later as captain of the *Fortuna* frigate. He had just returned to Plymouth after a cruise in which prizes to the value of £150,000 had been captured, and was proceeding on leave when, on reading the London newspapers, he came across mention of Cobbett's appeal for someone to stand against Bradshaw at Honiton.

Cobbett was just about to pay his first visit to Honiton in a coach put at his disposal by Colonel Bosville, a prominent Reformer. By a strange coincidence a certain Mr. Cochrane Johnstone, one of Cobbett's friends and Lord Cochrane's uncle, told him he was about to travel to Plymouth to greet his nephew. Cobbett offered him a seat in the coach as far as Honiton, and was surprised to find, when they arrived in that town, a letter awaiting him from Cochrane 'informing me, that his Lordship, having read my address to the people of Honiton, and having perceived that I had resolved to stand myself, *merely because I could find no other independent man to oppose Mr Bradshaw*, he had determined to accept my general invitation, and that he was actually on his way to put his purpose into execution. In an hour afterwards, having stopped at Exeter to provide lawyers &c., his Lordship arrived.'*[11]

If the object really was to defeat Bradshaw, then Cobbett had found a more likely candidate than himself, and he willingly stood down, though he remained in Honiton to assist in the election. He also found, in Cochrane, a lifelong friend and political ally, and one who was almost the only Radical politician of any importance with whom he would fail to quarrel.

* Cobbett's enemies alleged, and he stoutly denied, that Mr. Cochrane Johnstone's presence at Honiton was evidence that this was a put-up affair, to produce a *coup de théâtre* by suddenly injecting a national hero into the election.

There are certain similarities in the three men whose friendship Cobbett valued most. Fitzgerald, Windham and Cochrane were all aristocrats; they were all, in their different ways, politicians, rebels and eccentrics, and they were all adventurers. One must also suppose that each of them saw in the son of the Farnham peasant some reflection of their own idiosyncracies. They were, perhaps, the only men to whom Cobbett remained obstinately loyal.

Just as he had spoken up, in 1800, for Fitzgerald, the Irish rebel, so in 1814 would he speak up for Cochrane, the convicted fraudster who was dismissed the Navy, fined, imprisoned and threatened with the stocks. In 1832, when he passed Cochrane's birthplace in Culross, the memory of the wrongs done to his friend still rankled:

> To reflect upon his treatment always fills me with indignation inexpressible, knowing as I did, and I do, that even if the thing imputed to him had been a crime, he was innocent of that crime; and remembering, as I do, all the base means that were used to render him despicable in the eyes of the people, whom he had served in Parliament with more zeal and fidelity than any man I had ever known.*[12]

Cochrane, however, was not yet in Parliament, and the Honiton by-election failed to put him there. The fact was that the Honiton electors always voted, as they put it, for 'Mr Most'. Many of them actually obtained credit from the Honiton shopkeepers against what they would earn at the next election. Bradshaw, they knew, always paid five guineas a vote. When they asked Cochrane what he would pay he replied not a penny, and was accused as a consequence of attempting to rob poor men of their rights. After Bradshaw had won the election Cochrane had it announced that he would now pay ten guineas to every man who could prove that he had refused Bradshaw's five guineas and had voted for him instead. It was a neat manoeuvre, for at the General Election of the following year Cochrane was elected for Honiton in the mistaken belief that he was willing to pay twice the going rate for each vote.

* Cochrane had been convicted for a fraud that had involved rigging Stock prices by spreading a rumour that Napoleon had abdicated. An uncle of his was probably one of the men responsible, but Cochrane himself was even more probably innocent. The many enemies he had made in the Navy and in politics had almost certainly conspired to ruin him. Cobbett lived long enough to see his friend, by that time the hero of the Wars of Independence in Chile and Greece, given a 'free pardon' and have his rank in the British Navy restored to him. He did not survive, however, to see him made Vice-Admiral of the White and, eventually, Rear-Admiral of the United Kingdom.

The Honiton by-election contributed significantly to Cobbett's political education. It had allowed him to see for himself the extent to which corrupt electoral practices emasculated political argument and reduced all theories about electoral choice to a farce. Three months earlier he had still been able to write: 'Of what has been denominated Parliamentary Reform I have always disapproved. Of universal suffrage I have witnessed the defects too attentively, and with too much disgust ever to think of it with approbation.'[13]

After Honiton, he may not yet have been converted to universal suffrage, but he had become a Reformer to the extent of believing that corruption had to be eliminated from the electoral process. When he first presented himself as a candidate at Honiton, he had given a pledge to the electors that 'Whether you elect me or not, I never, as long as I live, either for myself or any one of my family, will receive under any name, whether of salary, pension or other, one single farthing of public money, [and I will never] give one farthing of my own money to any man, in order to induce him to vote, or cause others to vote for me.'*

After the Honiton election he wrote: 'For my *own sake* I have no desire to be in the House of Commons; for, though it would be contemptible affectation to pretend to doubt of my own ability to discharge the duties of a Member, yet my habits do not lead me that way, nor any way that takes me from my home. But, if I think that I can serve the country more effectually by becoming a member of parliament, a member of parliament I will, if I can, certainly become; and the present impression upon my mind is, that if neither of the candidates for the *City of Westminster*, do, at the next election, make a declaration against accepting of the public money, I ought to afford the electors of that city an opportunity of choosing a man that will make that declaration.'[14] In short, if he could shame no one else into doing so, Cobbett was prepared to present himself as the 'anti-Corruption' candidate on any and every suitable occasion. It took no more than a shuffle to move on from there to open support for Reform.

It was at Honiton that Cobbett first discovered that the rough-

* Cobbett was reminded of that pledge by his enemies in future years. Whether accepting money raised by public subscription is the same as accepting public money is a matter of fine distinction. Cobbett certainly accepted at various times large sums raised to allow him to fight an election. Sir Thomas Beevor instituted a public fund to allow him to fight the Preston election of 1826. Cobbett himself suggested in 1830 that the readers of the Register should subscribe 10,000 guineas to get him into Parliament.

and-tumble of elections, however corruptly conducted, was greatly
to his liking. Any man with his fondness for the more robust
country sports was bound to enjoy an occasion that, more than
anything else, resembled a cross between a single-stick meeting
and a rowdy country fair. There were voters to be brought in from
the outlying districts and 'treated' until the drink ran out of their
ears. Candidates were not as cautiously segregated as they are
today; in those days they had to appear on the same platform, and
each had to attempt to make himself heard over the cheers of his
supporters and the jeers of his opponents. The election itself might
be spread over several increasingly turbulent days, since the
returning officer could, if he chose, delay the pace of the voting by
requiring any elector liable to vote for the wrong side to establish
his identity and to swear that, not being a Papist, he was eligible to
vote. Ditches might be dug and fences erected to make access to
the voting booth more difficult, and rival gangs of bludgeon men
might fight with each other and with would-be voters to prevent
known supporters of the opposition ever getting to the poll.
However much Cobbett may have disapproved of such practices,
he was sufficiently combative to enjoy them; and the reference to
the 'candidates for the City of Westminster' revealed how his mind
was already working.

The Westminster constituency was, by its nature, one of the very
few in the country where the Radical Reformers could hope to do
well. It had a 'scot and lot' franchise, that is, one in which payment
of a local rate gave an entitlement to vote. It had a large electorate,
many of whom were journeymen and small traders, sufficiently
educated to take an interest in politics and sufficiently independent
to vote as they pleased. Although there was a growing Radical
tradition in the constituency, its two seats had for some years been
held, by tacit agreement, by one Tory and one Whig. Charles
James Fox, who had been the Whig incumbent, died on 13
September 1806, and Cobbett promptly started the long series of
political essays and electoral addresses that are collectively known
as *Letters to the Electors of the City of Westminster*.

They were, he told them, independent electors, unlike the
electors of boroughs, 'where their numbers are small, or where
they are, in some way or other, dependent upon one or two rich
men'. All the greater was their duty, therefore, since 'the possessor
of the elective franchise is the holder of a trust; he acts not only for
himself, but for his country in general'. He told them that if only a
handful of honest and independent Members could be returned to
Parliament they could, by their exposure of the evils of the present
system, bring about its reform. He admitted that some 300 seats in

the Commons were controlled by the Government and the borough-mongers, but that still left some 120 county and city seats where, if only the electors did their duty as patriots and honest men, Members could be returned who would be prepared to put an end, at last, to the Pitt System. It was to those constituencies, he urged, that the 20,000 honest and independent electors of Westminster must now set an example.

There were three elections in Westminster in the space of a year. In the by-election following Fox's death the Government caught the Radicals unprepared. Richard Brinsley Sheridan, the dramatist and Whig politician, who had remained close to Fox in spite of having deserted the then opposition to serve under Addington, was immediately put up. By agreement between the Whigs and the Tories, he then stood down in favour of Lord Percy, a not very distinguished son of the Duke of Northumberland, who was elected unopposed.

Cobbett had already attacked Sheridan for his political opportunism in 1804, when he published a book with the title *The Political Proteus; a View of the Public Character and Conduct of R. B. Sheridan Esq*. Sheridan was the sort of man he enjoyed hating, and he hated him even more now that he himself had joined the Radicals than when he had been a Windhamite. Sheridan, it must be said, provided him with a great deal of ammunition. He was notoriously venal, and both he and his son were sinecurists. He was a close friend of the Prince Regent and so a member of the hated Carlton House set. His parentage and his connections with the theatre made him, according to Cobbett, little better than a vagabond. Moreover Cobbett, who had once loved the theatre, was now, in his Radical days, inclined to disapprove of most of the pieces played in it, and thought Sheridan's were precisely the frivolous, unprincipled sort of plays that were corrupting the morals of the public.

These defects in Sheridan's character were discussed at length in the *Register* and on the hustings when, in November of that year, Grenville called a General Election and both the Westminster seats had to be fought for. Lord Percy vacated the seat he had won only two months earlier, and Sheridan stood in his place, with Admiral Sir Samuel Hood contesting the other seat for the Tories. The Radicals, this time, were well prepared for the fight. James Paull, the quarrelsome former East India merchant, who had already lost one arm in a duel, was their candidate. Francis Place, the Radical tailor of Charing Cross, was put in charge of organising the working-class vote. Burdett, an extremely wealthy man – he had married the daughter of Coutts the banker – financed Paull, and Cobbett more or less ran the election from the hustings and in the columns of the *Register*, which offers an extremely funny account of the eventual contest.

Sheridan abused Cobbett and Cobbett Sheridan. The crowd shouted Sheridan down and he appealed to Cobbett to quieten his mob, whereupon Cobbett pointed out that it was impolite to refer to the Westminster electors as 'a mob'. Sheridan, referring to Cobbett's plan for reducing the interest paid on the National Debt, said that he 'detested his recommendation for breaking faith with the public creditors'. His audience, many of whom might well have been tradesmen to whom he owed money, thereupon chanted 'Hear! hear! Richard Brinsley Sheridan DETESTS BREAKING FAITH WITH CREDITORS'.

When Paull was accompanied to the hustings by a marrow bones and cleavers band, Sheridan promptly acquired a larger and grander band. When Sheridan hired 200 bludgeon men to guard him and then stiffened them with a contingent of sailors from Admiral Hood's ship, Paull was escorted to and from the hustings by a vast crowd of young apprentices and tradesmen, and Cobbett boasted that there was 'not one play-actor not one vagabond' among them.

Although Sheridan and Hood were duly elected, they had never expected to have to fight this new, enthusiastic, and comparatively well-organised opposition, for the Radical Reformers had almost ceased to exist as a political force since the outbreak of war, and would not, indeed, begin to amount to anything significant until after the war. Paull, however, had collected sufficient support at the poll to persuade the Radicals that the Westminster seats, at least, were winnable, and when the Government fell in March 1807, they paired Paull with Burdett as their candidates. The two quarrelled, however, and fought their duel. Both were wounded, Paull more seriously than his opponent, and the Radicals, thoroughly wearied of Paull's quarrelsome habits, adopted Lord Cochrane instead. Paull refused to be dropped, stood as an Independent, and came bottom of a poll which was headed by Burdett and Cochrane. The Whig-Tory alliance in Westminster had been defeated, and two famous men had been returned to the Commons as Radical Reformers. Paull, who was financially embarrassed, committed suicide shortly afterwards.

If Cobbett revelled in the Honiton and Westminster elections, it was, perhaps, because elections in those days presented politics to the people as a form of street theatre, and there was, in Cobbett, a strong streak of theatricality. But if there was an actor lost somewhere inside the politician, there was also a dramatist lost somewhere inside the writer.* Some of Cobbett's best political writing was written in dramatic dialogue, and his descriptive writing often amounted to what would, in a play, have been stage directions.

More important was that, in these elections, Cobbett had begun to discover his true audience. The *Register* might continue to be written for and read by the upper and middle classes, but an increasing proportion of his other work would, like his election speeches, be directed towards explaining his version of politics to the masses. If he succeeded in this, it was largely due to his ability as an orator and his gift for straightforward exposition as a writer. It could be said of him that, by bringing politics, in this way, to the people, he prepared the way for bringing the people into politics. However Cobbett's dramatic instinct all too often led him to present politics to the people in the form of melodrama, and it may be that democratic politics have suffered from a certain theatricality, from a tendency to prefer illusion to reality, ever since.

Cobbett spent the years between and after the Honiton and Westminster elections very largely at Botley, which now became something of a meeting place for many of the leading Radicals. But neither farming nor hospitality could be allowed to interfere with Cobbett's journalism. Articles on subjects too various to detail travelled every week from Botley to London, where the assiduous Wright prepared them for the printer and for next week's *Register*. They were written in the unmistakeable Cobbett style, but they were now coloured by his newly acquired convictions as a Radical and a Reformer.

Many of his articles were still concerned with foreign affairs and the conduct of the war. Cobbett was as critical of the various Royal Dukes who enjoyed possibly unmerited commands as he was of Wellington and Moore for their apparent failures in Spain. He even began, for the first time, to criticise the continuation of the war. Since the French 'are by nature disqualified for the enjoyment of what we call freedom', they might as well have Napoleon to rule them as any other despot. To continue the war merely in order to restore the Bourbons was folly. Neither the French nor the Spaniards wanted the Bourbons back, while as for the Dutch, Swiss, Rhinelanders and Italians, they actually preferred the tyranny that might come with French rule to the tyranny they had known under

* Cobbett wrote three plays in the last ten years of his life. They were all political squibs, but he was very proud of them as satirical comedies and hoped to have them staged. There is no record of their having been produced in the professional theatre, although one, *Surplus Population*, is as good as most standard Victorian melodramas and considerably more funny, even though it was primarily written as an attack on Malthus.

their former rulers. Britain, therefore, should leave the Continent to the French so long as the French agreed to leave the oceans, the colonies and the British Isles to the British.

On domestic policies he was, naturally, even more critical, whether he wrote as a Radical, an agrarian or an anti-Pittite. But, whether he recognised it or not, there was a growing need for him to be moderate in his criticisms. Under wartime legislation the freedom of the press had become something close to an illusion. Those papers that could not be bought by the Government could be put out of business by withdrawing advertisements and creating difficulties over Stamp Duty and postage. If this did not succeed, the laws of sedition and libel were sufficiently elastic to place an over-critical journalist or editor in constant danger of prosecution and imprisonment.

Cobbett never flinched from making enemies, but he had never before succeeded in equally antagonising two political parties by his successive desertions. And although there were many powerful men who would be very willing to see him silenced, the days when Grenville and Windham could be counted on to protect the *Register* were past.

Cobbett did, indeed, attempt to put some restraints upon his pen, and he constantly warned Wright to modify or soften anything in his articles that might put him in danger of the law. Some such danger must have arisen early in 1807, for he wrote to Wright, 'What you have told me has given me some uneasiness, on account of the *trouble* that *prosecutions* would give me . . . I am deeply impressed with the necessity of *caution*; but, if they are resolved to plague me, plague they may. Should anything of this sort happen, I am determined to plead *my own cause*, be the consequence what it may.'[15]

Cobbett entered 1809 determined to be equally critical and cautious; but it was the year in which a scandal concerning the Duke of York, his mistress Mrs. Anne Clarke, and the sale of army commissions was at its height; in which two Radical newspaper editors, Perry of the *Morning Chronicle* and Leigh Hunt of the *Examiner*, were about to be prosecuted for sedition; and in which a detachment of local militia mutinied in Ely.

CHAPTER FIFTEEN

Newgate: 1810–1812

Nothing can render them popular but some degree of persecution.
Jonathan Swift: Thoughts on Religion

Shortly after the Westminster Election of 1807 Walker, the Corn-
hill print seller, published a cartoon with the punning title 'The
Head of the Poll'. It showed a burly Cobbett holding up a pole on
the top of which a diminutive Burdett was perched. Burdett was
shouting 'Huzza – Liberty and Independence', while underneath
him Cobbett is commenting: 'The finest puppet in the world,
Gentlemen – entirely of my own formation. I have only to say the
word and he'll do anything.' This cartoon reflected the growing
belief that the Radical Reformers, of whom there were fewer than
half a dozen in Parliament, were making themselves heard only
because of Cobbett. Cartwright's pamphlets, Burdett's oratory
and Hunt's demagoguery would, it was widely believed, have all
gone for nothing had it not been for the *Register*.

This was, however, to attribute too much to William Cobbett.
By the same token it attributed too little to that small band of men
who had struggled to keep the cause of Reform alive even though,
in the patriotic and xenophobic climate of a bitter war, they had
acquired the reputation of being a bunch of 'democratical' theorists and Jacobinical revolutionaries no more worth listening to than
so many Jack-o'-Bedlams. But Cobbett, now he had joined them,
might easily turn out to be a different, more popular, and more
dangerous sort of animal.

However much the *Register* was now disliked in Whig and Tory
circles, it was still required reading for those who took an informed
or professional interest in politics. Moreover *Letters to the Westminster Electors* had revealed that it was on the way to becoming
required reading for those members of the working class who were
both literate and politically active. Many had begun to pool their
pennies in order to subscribe to the *Register*, which was read aloud,
passed around and discussed in scores of London ale-houses and
other meeting places. Both Addington and Grenville could test-
ify – as Pitt might have done – that it was a journal capable of
inflicting too much political damage to be ignored.

Spencer Perceval, who was now Chancellor of the Exchequer and would, by October 1809, become Prime Minster, had been saying ever since 1804 that Cobbett would have to be dealt with. He had then, as Attorney-General, prosecuted Cobbett for seditious libel in the '*Juverna*' case, and had not bothered to conceal his Tory and patrician dislike for such a renegade scribbler. 'Who,' he had then asked the presiding judge, Lord Chief Justice Ellenborough, 'who is Mr Cobbett? Is he a man of family in this country? Is he a man writing purely from motives of patriotism? *Quis homo hic est? Quo patre natus?* He seems to imagine himself a species of censor, who, elevated to the solemn seat of judgement, is to deal about his decisions for the instruction of mankind.'[1] Ellenborough, disliking Cobbett no less, had nodded and had fined the accused £500.

Cobbett's enemies in positions of power had multiplied since then, especially among the military. He had laughed at the Royal Dukes for playing at soldiers and had particularly mentioned HRH the Duke of York who, as Commander-in-Chief, had seemed to contribute little to winning the war. As for the long list of British generals, Cobbett had written that England needed 'something more than the wisdom and courage of our generals, great as they may be, and aided as they are by Prussian discipline and by Hanoverian troops.' They grumbled at this in the Service Clubs, and grumbled even more when he criticised the conduct of Wellington and Sir John Moore in the Peninsula.*

In 1809, however, Cobbett's attacks became dangerous enough to concentrate the Government's attention. This was the year of the affair of Mrs. Anne Clarke, the demirep who had been the Duke of York's mistress. So long as the Duke kept her she had supplemented what he allowed her in cash by conducting, with or without her lover's connivance, a brisk and almost public sale of army commissions, promotions and exchanges. The public first heard of this when Colonel Wardle raised the matter in the House of Commons. The Government supporters' first reaction was to attempt to shrug it off as a disgraceful Jacobinical conspiracy got up to smear the Royal Family, the Duke and the Army. The Colonel, however, produced so much prima-facie evidence that a Parliamentary Committee of Enquiry had to be agreed to, whereupon

---

* In his autobiography Sir James McGregor, then Director General of the Army Medical Department in the Peninsula, recorded how once, when he attended on Wellington, 'I found him in a miserable small room, leaning over the fire. He was attentively reading some printed paper. I could see that it was Cobbett's *Register*, just received with the letters from England. After perusing it for a few minutes, he threw it on the fire . . . He was in a very bad humour.'

Cobbett wrote to Wright: 'I wonder you had not written to give me your opinion about Mr Wardle.* This is an admirable fellow. I will perform a pilgrimage to see him. Oh! the damned thieves! "A Jacobinical conspiracy." Damned hell-fire thieves. The Duke must go.'[2]

The enquiry, which dragged on for months, was, so far as the journalists were concerned, the news event of the year. A series of reluctant witnesses – army officers, lawyers, go-betweens, servants and even a parson who had wanted to preach a sermon before the Royal Family and so obtain a deanery – provided ample evidence of Mrs. Clarke's business activities and did little to remove the suspicion that the Duke had, in some way, been party to them.

Mrs. Clarke herself was by far the most colourful witness. She gave her evidence with a cheerful, even willing candour it would have been difficult for a more respectable woman to sustain. She felt no desire to spare the Duke, who had by now turned her off,† and she stated that she had been forced into the business of selling patronage only because her lover had been too mean to support her properly, although he was by no means unwilling to allow her to supplement her income in this manner. In an effort to discredit her evidence witnesses were brought to show that she had forged the Duke's signature, attempted to blackmail him, passed herself off as a widow when she was not, and had conspired with Colonel Wardle to disgrace the Duke, all of which was probably true but did little to disguise the fact that the Government was attempting to blacken her character in order to whitewash the Duke's. The impression left was that she was a cheerfully dishonest whore who saw no reason why her own dishonesty should be taken as in any way proving the honesty of others.

At the end of these lengthy proceedings Parliament voted, though not overwhelmingly and, it would seem, against the burden of the evidence, to exonerate the Duke. He, however, resigned as Commander-in-Chief, though still swearing his absolute innocence. The generals of the 'Military Club' agreed with him. They met to pass a resolution expressing their appreciation of all that he had done for the Army and their belief in his integrity, a step that

* Cobbett refused to use Wardle's military rank in order to distinguish him from the 'Military Club' which, he alleged, was attempting to dictate how Britain should be governed.

† Wardle had alleged in the Commons that Mrs. Clarke's successor to the Duke's favours, a certain Mrs. Carey, had actually set up an office in the City for the sale of commissions, with a list of the prices asked prominently displayed. This charge does not seem to have been pursued.

further convinced Cobbett that Britain was in greater danger than ever of being put under some form of military rule.

All of this would have been meat and drink to any journalist, however loyal to the Establishment. To one who was hostile to the Government and who had dedicated himself to the exposure of corruption and the destruction of the system, the case seemed heaven-sent. For months on end the largest part of the *Register* was devoted to full-length reports of the evidence presented and to the debates on the matter in Parliament and the newspapers. Each report was accompanied by Cobbett's analysis of the proceedings. This, naturally, supported Mrs. Clarke and derided all who attempted to discredit her. Perceval, in particular, came under attack, both for having attempted to forestall Colonel Wardle by using *agents provocateurs* to uncover a quite different case of corruption not involving the Duke, and for himself being a sinecurist with his hand plunged deep into the public purse. The *Register* reminded its readers that, although Perceval's salary as Chancellor of the Exchequer was officially £2,600 a year, he was actually drawing a total of £8,851 a year by virtue of the other, largely sinecure posts that he held. In addition to this, his brother, Lord Arden, received £12,562 a year for life from various sinecures which would revert to Perceval if Arden predeceased him.

Cobbett was now plunging into deep and dangerous waters. There were increasing complaints in Parliament and the Government press about the libellous, seditious and ruffianly articles appearing in certain Whig and Radical journals, and calls for even more restraints to be placed on them. The Law Officers, ignoring Cobbett for the moment, moved at the end of the year against Leigh Hunt of *The Examiner* and Perry of the *Morning Chronicle*, the latter having republished in his paper an article of Hunt's which was alleged to be an attack on the monarch. Early in 1810 the two men were charged with uttering seditious libels; Perry came to trial first and the jury refused to convict, whereupon the case against Hunt was dropped.

In such a climate dangers attached to any reports or comments that could be construed as seditious. Because of that Cobbett had argued throughout his articles on the Mrs. Clarke case that, if the boasted freedom of the English press meant anything, it meant that full and honest reports on matters of public interest could be neither libellous nor seditious whether they concerned a royal personage or not. Such arguments may have persuaded the Law Officers that to prosecute Cobbett would be as fruitless as prosecuting Perry had been. Nevertheless Cobbett had sworn to Wright that he would give his enemies no cause for action. On the other hand he was triumphant over the part that the *Register* had played in the Mrs. Clarke affair, and argued that Canning, Castlereagh and Perceval had all been forced to admit that corruption did exist in high places and had to be investigated.

Cobbett, therefore, was equally poised between caution and a desire to continue his attacks, when the Ely Mutiny case was first brought to his attention. This concerned men of the Ely Militia who had refused orders, either because they had not been paid their statutory 'marching guineas' or because of a dispute over stoppages made for their goatskin knapsacks (both reasons were given by Cobbett at different times). It could not be described as a very serious mutiny; but a squadron of cavalry from the German Legion was summoned from Bury St. Edmunds, the amateur soldiers were surrounded, a summary court martial was called and five ringleaders were sentenced to five hundred lashes apiece, part of this sentence being later remitted. Cobbett wrote, many years later, 'I, in my *Register*, expressed my indignation at this, and to express it too strongly was not in the power of man.'³

In order to understand why Cobbett was sufficiently indignant to throw necessary caution to the winds, it has to be remembered that he had long grumbled about the Germanisation of the British Army which, under the influence of the German-trained Royal Dukes, had had to adopt German-style uniforms, disciplines and drills. What he resented most, however, was the presence of large bodies of Hanoverian troops in England. They were there, he argued, to act as a Praetorian Guard for the 'Military Club' in case it should ever become necessary to subdue the English. One reason for his indignation, therefore, was that it had been 'a body of Hanoverian horse that was brought from Bury St. Edmunds to *compel these young Englishmen to submit to be flogged*'.

The flogging itself was another reason. Everything Cobbett had written about his soldiering days revealed his personal fear of the lash and his determination to do nothing that would earn him a flogging. This placed him in some difficulty when he was discussing his schemes for Army Reform with Windham, for the lash had become the almost only means, apart from the gibbet, for maintaining discipline in the armed services. In 1804 General Sir Robert Wilson had published his *Inquiry into the Military Force of the British Empire* and in it had recommended abolition of the lash. Cobbett thought this impossible in an army that was recruited from what was commonly believed to be the scum of the nation. As he wrote at that time to Windham:

The fact is, that military discipline is to be enforced only by *fear* of the consequences of disobedience. There are different ways of keeping alive this fear, and I do not recommend the lash; but the punishment must be *severe*. The Germans run the gauntlet; how would that be relished in England? . . . The French shoot offenders at once. Would that be liked better? It is the mode of recruiting that renders the lash necessary, absolutely necessary . . .

But the intensity of his hatred of the lash, and, perhaps, the first cause of it were not fully revealed until 1811, in an article written for the *Register* from Newgate. At that time the Judge Advocate General had just issued instructions limiting the maximum sentence at a drumhead court martial to three hundred lashes and restricting the use of the cat for minor offences so as to encourage alternatives to what he called 'corporal infliction'. Why, Cobbett asked, did he talk about 'corporal infliction' when he meant flogging? '*Flog is flog* . . . and it means to whip the naked back (and sometimes, *other parts*) of a soldier with a thing called a *cat*; that is to say with nine strong whip-cords, about a foot and a half long, with nine knots in each, and which cords are fastened, like the thong of a whip, to the end of a stick about two feet long . . . As to flogging upon parts *lower down* the back, I do not know that it is now practised; but I saw it done myself, in a meadow of the Bush Inn at Farnham by the Surrey Militia; and, though I was then but a little boy, I remember that an officer who was an enormously fat man, beat the Drummer with his stick, because he did not flog the soldier hard enough.'[4]

A week after the Ely incident, Cobbett wrote the *Register* article his enemies had been waiting for. The opening passage, although the most rhetorical, was possibly the least incriminating: 'Well done, Lord Castlereagh! This is just what it was thought your plan would produce . . . Five hundred lashes each! Aye, that is right! Flog them; flog them; flog them! They deserve it and a great deal more. They deserve a flogging at every meal time. "Lash them daily, lash them duly." What, shall the rascals dare to *mutiny*, and that, too, when the German Legion is so near at hand! Base dogs! . . . What, mutiny for the sake of the price of a knapsack! . . . and then, upon the appearance of the German soldiers, they take a flogging as quietly as so many trunks of trees.'

This might have passed as rhetoric rather than incitement had he not then added two passages:

I do not know what sort of a place ELY is; but I really should like to know how the inhabitants looked one another in the face, while this scene was exhibiting in their town . . .

And then:

This will, one would hope, teach the *loyal* a little caution in speaking of the means, which Napoleon employs (or rather which they say he employs), in order to get together and to discipline his conscripts. There is scarcely any one of these loyal persons, who has not, at various times, cited the *hand-cuffings*, and other means of *force* as a proof, a complete proof, that the people of France *hate Napoleon and his government*, assist *with reluctance in his wars*, and would fain see another revolution . . . I hope that the loyal will, hereafter, be more cautious in drawing such conclusions, now that they see, that our 'gallant defenders' not only require physical restraint, in certain cases, but even a little blood drawn from their backs, and that, too, with the aid and assistance of *German* troops.[5]

The Attorney-General, Sir Vicary Gibbs, immediately filed an information against Cobbett for sedition, but no attempt was made to bring him to trial for several months. Cobbett departed to Botley by no means certain that a trial was inevitable. The Government, he thought, might be holding the threat of one over him to bully him into a more accommodating mood.

Wright now began to play some part in the proceedings. He was not only the correspondent to whom Cobbett poured out his alternate fits of defiance and apprehension: he acted also as the go-between who endeavoured to discover how serious the Government was in its intention to proceed against Cobbett. John Reeves, the King's Printer and Cobbett's old friend, was used as an intermediary with the Government. It was his task to discover whether or not the case would be pursued.

Cobbett's letters to Wright during this period clearly reveal his differing states of mind. On 22 July 1809 he wrote:

It is quite useless to *fret* and *stew* about this. I must meet it. They may, probably, confine me for two years; but that does not kill a man, and may, besides, produce even good effects in more ways than one. But the main thing is to be *prepared* for the thing. There is a *possibility* of *acquittal*, though they push their malice to its full extent. Let us, therefore, be prepared; let us take all proper precautions, and then wait the chapter of accidents . . .

What I would do, in case of imprisonment, is this. I would make F. Reid come and take charge of my lands &c. I will, *even now*, cut off all expenses of table, dogs &c., so as to make up for the loss; and I would have such a plan of economy as should enable me to have my family near me, if possible, without additional expense.

In November 1809 he was writing:

Be sure to tell Hansard, or any of them, from me, that I hold the thing in contempt, that I am no more afraid of the rascals than I could be of so many mice. And, really, if we have an *honest* jury, it will be a famous thing altogether.

On other occasions Cobbett wanted Wright to send him details of how Horne Tooke had successfully defended himself in the celebrated treason trial of 1794, and instances, if any existed, of it having been held tyrannical to use foreign mercenaries against Englishmen. For if it came to a trial, Cobbett was determined to defend himself, as Horne Tooke had done, forgetting perhaps that Tooke had been trained both as a parson and a barrister, and so could be considered capable of making his points to the judge on the Bench and to the congregation in the jury box.

Meanwhile, in April 1810, Burdett had published in the *Register* a letter (which Cobbett later claimed to have written for him) accusing the House of Commons of having acted illegally in imprisoning John Gale Jones, a Radical surgeon, for an alleged breach of Parliamentary privilege. Speaker Abbott immediately held Burdett in breach of privilege and issued a Speaker's warrant for his arrest and imprisonment in the Tower. Something resembling an insurrection followed. Burdett barricaded himself in his house, declaring the warrant to be illegal and calling on the City authorities to protect him. Lord Cochrane and other supporters rushed to his defence – Cochrane with a barrel of gunpowder which he proposed to use in order to mine the front of the house. Crowds of Londoners gathered outside and the Government had to call in all available troops and Volunteers before Burdett would consent to be marched off to the Tower, where he stayed until Parliament was prorogued.

There was a move to summon Cobbett to the Bar of the House of Commons, since, although it was not established that he had actually written the offending letter, he had certainly published it. This was not, however, agreed; Members contented themselves with having the offending letter in the *Register* read out to them by the Speaker.

If the Government had ever hesitated over bringing Cobbett to trial, it hesitated no longer. On 15 June 1810, Cobbett, together with his printer, publisher and bookseller were tried at the Court of the King's Bench by Lord Chief Justice Ellenborough sitting with a special jury.* The Attorney-General, Sir Vicary Gibbs, led for the prosecution, lawyers for the three other defendants entered pleas of guilty and Cobbett, against the advice of his friends, entered a plea of not guilty and defended himself.

He did so extremely badly, partly because he had at last realised what the Government he had goaded intended, and partly because he was not, as yet, the confident orator he later became. He denied that what he had written was libellous, and then qualified this by adding that it was no more libellous than much that passed unpunished in other newspapers. He attempted to quote anti-flogging speeches that had been made recently in Parliament and was promptly stopped by the judge. Worst of all, he admitted on several occasions that his article had been written hastily and in anger, and may have been mistaken in certain particulars – an admission that was tantamount to confessing, at the very least, to libel by negligence.

The Radicals had hoped that Cobbett, if convicted, would achieve the sort of martyrdom on which the Party could be built. Instead, he made such a poor showing that Francis Place, his former brother-in-Radicalism, was disgusted and never spoke to him but once again. During the trial, as Place later described it:

> Cobbett made a long defence, a bad defence, and his delivery of it and his demeanour were even worse than his matter. He was not at all master of himself, and in some parts where he meant to produce great effect, he produced laughter. So ludicrous was he in one part, the jury, the judge and the audience all laughed at him.[6]

Sir Vicary Gibbs, in his final address, made a sharp distinction between Cobbett and the other accused, if only because, in this case, the printer and the publishers had been employed by the author, and not vice-versa. Consequently, when it came to judgment, Hansard, Cobbet's printer, was sentenced to three, and

---

* Cobbett always maintained that special juries were, by their very method of selection, rigged juries and therefore bound to bring in the verdicts the Executive desired.

Budd and Bagshaw his publishers to two months' imprisonment respectively. For Cobbett, however, he demanded greater punishment, for 'whatever of malignity resulted from the publication, to him it was attributable, and whatever arose from it of base lucre and gain accrued to him alone'.

Gibbs then enumerated the different ways in which Cobbett's article had injured, and had been intended to injure the most vital interests of a nation struggling in a bitter war:

a) It had been designed 'to encourage the soldiers to impatience, insubordination and disgust', and by abusing them for submitting meekly to their punishment, it had served to encourage others to acts of mutiny.

b) It had held the German Legion up to contempt, and represented them 'as persons who could be of no use in the general service of the country, who could only be useful in quelling disturbances among our native troops'.

c) By upbraiding the civilian inhabitants of Ely for not interfering while the mutineers were receiving their just punishment he was fomenting civil disorder.

d) By deriding 'the loyal' who maintained that the French only fought for Napoleon under duress, and by insinuating that English soldiers were being worse treated than French conscripts, he was making a mockery of patriotism besides turning the truth upside down.

Each of these, he told the jury, was a libel designed to promote the subversion of society itself. As for Cobbett's defence that other newspaper libels had been allowed to pass unpunished, that was an additional reason for exemplary punishment for, since he had been encouraged by *their* example, it was so much the more important that others should not, in the future, be encouraged by *his*. He finished by reminding the jury that 'the army, against whom this libel was in a peculiar manner directed, called on the Court for justice against its traducer'.

Ellenborough, in an extremely hostile summing-up, described the article as 'a most infamous and seditious libel', whereupon the jury felt no need to leave the jury box before bringing in a verdict of guilty. Judgment was reserved and Cobbett was ordered to give bail for his future appearance in court for sentencing.

Cobbett returned to Botley fearing that he was a ruined man and suspecting that he was facing something half-equivalent to a death sentence. Jail fever – the typhus that was almost endemic in the prisons in those days – meant that, however short the sentence, by no means all who went into prison could expect to come out.

In the twenty days between trial and sentence, Cobbett engaged in a series of negotiations that were subsequently much argued over by Cobbett and his enemies alike, and were often used by the latter to discredit him. Cobbett remembered how, in 1804, he had bargained with the Government over the *Juverna* case. Then, by surrendering Judge Johnson, he had gone some way towards mitigating the penalties imposed on him. Why should he not now offer to surrender the *Register* and journalism in return for a guarantee that the penalties in this case would be remitted? With Cobbett silenced, the Reform movement would lose its most powerful voice and the Government its most irritating critic. Cobbett, for his part, would be able to retire to Botley and lead a farmer's life, something that his despairing family was now begging him to do.

The negotiations were, once again, arranged through Reeves, Wright acting as intermediary. At first it seemed that the Government was willing to indulge him, and Cobbett prepared a farewell article for what he intended to be the last number of the *Register*: 'I have never,' he wrote, 'written merely for the sake of gain . . . I cannot, of course, after what has taken place, think it proper, let the pecuniary loss be what it may, to continue any longer this publication . . . It must be manifest that, if the Work was continued, *it could not be what it has been* . . . It is manifest that, if continued, it must be nearly, if not quite, the exact opposite of what it has hitherto been, and, therefore, those who have most highly valued its existence must, of course, be the most desirous that it should cease to exist . . . I know that there will, nevertheless, be enough persons to say *that I have deserted the Cause*; but I shall ask, *whose cause*? Well, if putting a stop to this work be an injury to the country, let it be recollected that it is *the country* itself who have condemned me . . . I will not attempt to disguise my extreme disappointment and mortification at this decision against my writings . . .'

That mortification was expressed by carefully listing the names of all those who as judge, prosecuting counsel and jury had forced him to 'lay down at the height, at the very pinnacle of its circulation, a Work which has long found its way into every part of the civilised world'.* To these he added the newspapers, who had, with few exceptions, always been hostile to him and would glory at his fall. 'I, by anticipation, heartily wish them joy of their triumph, and leave them, without the smallest particle of envy, in full

* The circulation of the *Register* at that time was around 6,000 copies a week, which was as high as that of most daily newspapers, and higher than any other weekly journal.

possession of all the honours and all the happiness attached to their profession. To that profession I, this day, *cease to belong* . . . I NEVER WILL AGAIN, UPON ANY ACCOUNT, INDITE, PUBLISH, WRITE OR CONTRIBUTE TOWARDS, ANY NEWSPAPER, OR OTHER PUBLICATION OF THAT NATURE, SO LONG AS I LIVE.' It is probable that no other English journalist has ever taken such a bitter (and premature) leave of his trade as Cobbett proposed to take at that moment.

Cobbett's angry valediction was never published. He had already sent it off when he learnt, from both Wright and Reeves, that it was by no means certain that, having closed the *Register*, he would not still be brought to judgment. The Government, Reeves suggested, was unlikely to hold its hand, and the most that he could hope for from the Court was that the sacrifice Cobbett had made would be taken into consideration when he was sentenced. In later years Cobbett insisted that 'no proposition of any sort was ever made by me, or by my authority, to the government'. All that he had done, seeing how distressed his wife was when he returned to Botley, had been to write to his attorney suggesting that such a proposition *might* be made. 'The letter was hardly got to the post-office at Southampton before the courage of my wife and eldest daughter returned. Indignation and resentment took place of grief and alarm, and they cheerfully consented to my stopping the Letter.'[8] He accordingly sent a friend off in a post-chaise to London to prevent his attorney taking any action.

It is a more attractive version of what happened, but the letters to and from Wright and Reeves, and the valedictory article itself, prove that it is specious. The more accurate version was published in *The Times* in 1812 and again in 1816 as part of a continuing attempt to discredit Cobbett, since Wright, who was by then a bitter enemy, had provided that paper with the full story. The manuscript of the article was actually produced in court in 1819 in the libel action that Wright himself then brought against Cobbett. On this occasion, as on one or two others, Cobbett ignored the facts in order to bluster his way out of an unpleasant episode from his past.

In the light of the role the *Register* was to play in the next quarter of a century, the Government appears to have been at least unwise not to have accepted Cobbett's offer to withdraw from politics and journalism for ever. The politicians, however, enjoyed having Cobbett, as they thought, at their mercy. Spencer Perceval's brother-in-law, Lord Redesdale, for example, shook him by the hand and wished him joy on the day that Cobbett was found guilty.

An unnamed Member of Parliament speaking to a member of the Government said: 'Why, here's Cobbett squeaking; he'll give up the *Register*, if you won't send him to Newgate'. He then went on to suggest that, if the pressure on Cobbett were kept up, 'he might submit even more and begin to write for the government', to which the reply was 'Damn him, he has changed too often already – he would not be worth a louse to us.'⁹

On 5 July 1810 Cobbett was brought back to London and lodged in the King's Bench prison. Three days later he was brought before Ellenborough and a full bench of judges for sentencing. He was condemned to two years in prison and a fine of £1,000, and was required in addition to give bail for £3,000 and find two sureties for £1,000 each for his keeping the peace for seven years following his release.

The question of where he would be imprisoned was important to him. If it was in a London prison he might, under certain circumstances, be able to write for the *Register*, which he was now determined to continue, and, through frequent visitors, to maintain his contacts with politics and his farms. Four of his friends, led by Major Cartwright, had already announced that, if he was put into a provincial jail, they would take up lodgings nearby in order to visit him and act as his contacts with the outside world. This became unnecessary, however, since he was lodged in Newgate, and in Newgate in those days influence and money could procure almost everything except freedom.

The Sheriff of London, Alderman Wood, was both influential and a Cobbettite, as was Francis Maseres, Cursitor Baron of the Exchequer, who made a point of visiting Cobbett in prison in his full regalia of wig and gown. These and other frequent visitors such as Cochrane, Burdett and Cartwright showed that Cobbett was no ordinary prisoner. That fact, and the payment of twelve guineas a week, ensured him accommodation in a set of apartments formerly inhabited by the governor of the prison, and all that he required in the way of food, service, visitors and the constant presence of various members of his family. Henry Hunt described Cobbett's period of imprisonment as 'not much more than living two years in London in lodgings'.

A fuller description of how Cobbett lived in Newgate, was recorded in his *Journal* by Louis Simond, a Frenchman resident in the United States who was then touring England. Part of that tour included a visit to Newgate, where he marvelled at the way the different groups of prisoners were treated, with the 'state prisoners' moving freely about, playing fives and generally entertaining themselves. Since he was a regular reader of the *Register*, which he described as containing 'a good deal of information and entertainment, together with some treason', he enquired whether Cobbett was one of them. The turnkey who was his guide replied 'Oh! no, he is too great for that' and led him to a grated door, 'Through which I could see a carpeted room – Mr. Cobbett's room. He has a key of the grated door, and therefore free access to this leaded roof, which is extensive, high and airy, with a most beautiful view of St. Paul's and over a great part of the city.'

What particularly struck Simond, however, was that 'his family is with him, and he continues to pour out his torrent of abuse as freely as ever, on everybody and everything in turn. Mr. Cobbett seems to me to furnish, without intending it, the same sort of evidence in favour of the existence of the liberty of the press in his own country, as a philosopher of antiquity gave of the existence of motion.'[10]

The comfort of Cobbett's existence in Newgate, however, did nothing to lessen his anger at his imprisonment which increased and intensified his personal problems, domestic and financial. At the moment of his imprisonment his wife was in her almost customary state of advanced pregnancy. Cobbett accordingly raged that 'I must now have a child *born in a felon's jail* or be absent from the scene at the time of the birth'. Ann, more stoical than her husband, took lodgings in Smithfield that were as close to Newgate as she could find. This caused Cobbett to grumble again that she was 'amidst the incessant rattle of coaches and butcher's carts and the noise of cattle, instead of being in a quiet comfortable country-house with neighbours and servants and everything necessary about her'. While he grumbled, Ann endured Smithfield, a dangerous confinement and the loss of the child with, as Cobbett was forced to admit, 'the greatest composure'.

Thereafter she divided her time between Newgate and Botley, where Cobbett bombarded her with letters of advice on how to economise over the housekeeping, keep away from Rev. Baker, and stop wearing flannel underwear: 'I must repeat to you my advice about wearing less flannel. Pray do leave off some of it. It rubs you and it scrubs you, all to pieces. I am sure it does you harm; and I hope you will tell William to tell me that you have left off the *Breeches*, at any rate. I do not like to see you with *waistcoats* and *breastplates*; but the *Breeches* is the worst of all. Now, pray mind what I say about these nasty Breeches.'[11]

He refused to allow his imprisonment to hinder the task of educating his children. Relays of them came to London to stay with him in Newgate, and from there went to a nearby school to supplement their father's instruction, for he could not spare the time to teach them, among other things, dancing, about which he wrote to his wife:

> But the *dancing*! They have had 4 lessons, and they are as eager to get to it as they ever were to get to play . . . They did not go out all day yesterday. They put on their pumps and danced the best part of the day; and laughed till their jaws ached, and so did I. John has got all the capers, and he skips and twists himself about like a grasshopper, I would have the girls of the Village get themselves in order for dancing, for these fellows will soon be ready to hand them about.[12]

It was not all laughter, however, for, whether the children were at Botley or in Newgate, Cobbett followed his somewhat Squeersian method of educating them. Those who were in Hampshire had to write him frequent letters, the youngest of them actually learning their ABC in the process. The older ones had to keep him informed about work on the farms or, if they were with him in Newgate, improve their arithmetic by doing the farm accounts. William, the oldest, was taught something about journalism by having his father dictate his *Register* articles to him.

Cobbett's financial and business problems were not so easily solved. His court case had cost him, what with fines and fees, £5,000, and his living expenses in Newgate, where he entertained almost daily, came to well over £1,000 a year. As soon as he was sentenced most of his numerous creditors pressed him for payment, and he might well have had to sell Botley had not Burdett come to his aid with a loan of £3,000, and had Swann, his papermaker, not offered to wait for payment of the large sums owed to him. It was ironic, perhaps, that Cobbett had, for once, attended to his business affairs in the months whilst he was waiting for the trial. He had, except for the mortgage, paid every one of his debts as a farmer. What he was now faced with were debts he did not even know that he owed as a publisher.

The *Register* had probably always been profitable. His other publications – *Parliamentary Debates*, *History of Parliament* and the collection of *State Trials* which he had started in 1809 – had lost money, although Cobbett had always thought of them as valuable and profitable ventures. John Wright's muddled accounting and Cobbett's willingness to leave all financial matters to him were responsible for this state of affairs. Wright's salary had never been fixed; he drew what he wanted as he wanted it. He had, moreover, been promised a large share of the profits from the part-publications once their sales had passed a certain figure which had never been attained, and he drew considerable sums against those hypothetical profits. He had covered these drawings in his rudimentary accounts by allowing debts due to the printers and papermakers and other tradesmen to remain unpaid, and it was for these that Cobbett was now being dunned.

Wright had probably never gone any closer to dishonesty than allowing the muddle to continue, and Cobbett, as his employer, had the ultimate responsibility for permitting him to do so. Indeed, when Wright had engaged a young barrister called Howell to edit the *State Trials* series, Cobbett had warned him against allowing Howell to expect that he would have any share in the profits or any access to the accounts of the business. 'Only think,' Cobbett had written to Wright, 'of having another person invested with a right, a *legal* right, to make us account, *us* whose accounts the devil himself would never unravel. No, no; you and I were never made to have our accounts unravelled by any one but ourselves.'[13]

Given such encouragement, Wright naturally assumed that all was well between himself and his employer so far as accounting went. He was wrong to do so. As soon as Cobbett, because he was in Newgate, had the true facts of his publishing finances forced on him by his creditors, he changed from being a paternalistic and benevolent employer into an extremely hostile one. He ordered Wright to discharge the various writers and compilers he had engaged to assist him, and to take on their work himself. He also insisted that Wright should immediately present him with a full account of all the monies that had passed through his hands during the years of their collaboration.

When Wright managed to produce a statement recording something of those years of muddled accounting, Cobbett swore that he had been systematically robbing him, and claimed that Wright owed him at least £12,000. This Wright stoutly denied. All that he would admit to was that he had drawn some £500 against future profits. Cobbett, as one would expect, called him rogue and scoundrel, and they finally agreed to allow the matter to be settled by arbitration. William Cooke, a lawyer of Lincoln's Inn who specialised in bankruptcies, was chosen as arbitrator, and he finally decided that Wright owed Cobbett no less than £6,500.

Wright was unable and unwilling to pay any such sum. Cobbett dismissed him, and they parted on terms of enduring hostility. Cobbett was now forced to sell the *Debates*, *History* and *State Trials* to Hansard, who removed Cobbett's name from those publications and substituted his own. Hansard retained Wright to act as editor for the first two, and Howell to do the same for the *Trials*, which does not wholly account for the fact that, whilst the

Debates have, ever since, been referred to as Hansard's, generations of lawyers have always referred to the *Trials* as Howell's.

Cobbett was now left with the task of running his farms by
correspondence and of managing the *Register* single-handedly and
from prison. This last he proceeded to do with the utmost vigour.
The 'torrents of abuse' which Louis Simond referred to poured out
of Newgate and were not only more abusive than ever before, but
were also, for a time, doubled in quantity. Cobbett, reacting to a
need for money in his usual manner, decided that, if one *Register* a
week was profitable, two a week would be doubly so. He must have
been too optimistic in his calculations, for after a year he reverted
to a single number published weekly.

What was very clear to his readers was that Cobbett, who had
always been most strongly motivated by anything that could be
construed as what he saw as an injustice done to those of his
countrymen he supported, was now even more strongly motivated
by what he considered to have been a gross injustice done to
himself. Every article in the *Register* that he signed carried, under
his signature, the address: 'State Prison, Newgate', to which he
sometimes added the comment, 'where I have just paid a thousand
pounds fine to THE KING; and much good may it do to His
Majesty'. He never, for the rest of his life, forgot the two years in
Newgate, nor did he ever forgive the Establishment for having put
him there. However altruistic a Radical Cobbett may have been,
he was also a basically vindictive man. Until then, he may have
hated the policies more than he hated the policy-makers: after
Newgate he unquestionably allowed personal and class hatreds to
dominate his politics.

Nonetheless the facts of the Ely Mutiny case suggest that his
prosecution and sentence were not entirely unjustified. Just as he
had once done in America, Cobbett had pushed comment beyond
the limits of legal tolerance and, as it had in America, the law
exacted its penalties. A similar article written 130 years later,
during Britain's second war against Germany, would have invited a
similar prosecution, even though the Government then was one in
which the leading Radicals of the day were prominently represented.

Although he had made a poor showing at his trial, Cobbett's
imprisonment turned him into a national figure. What Swift had
said of the Christian Church applied equally to him: 'Nothing could
render him popular but some degree of persecution'. He was never
solitary in his imprisonment. Radical and Whig politicians visited
him constantly and, if Cobbett's letter to Thomas Creevey is a
guide, were solidly, if somewhat monotonously entertained. 'I

seldom do anything after two o'clock, when I dine. The best way is to favour me with your company at *dinner* at *two*, and then the day may be of *your appointing*, I always being at home, you know, and every day being of equal favour . . . I give beef-stakes and porter. I may vary my food to mutton chops, but never vary the drink.'[14]

He was also, in the course of his imprisonment, 'visited by persons whom I had never seen before, from *one hundred and ninety-seven cities and towns of England, Scotland and Ireland*, the greatest part of whom came to me as the deputies of some society, club or circle of people in their respective places of residence.'[15] The fact was that the misery and growing discontents of the period were beginning to make the Reformers more popular, and a wide range of people now saw in Cobbett the very voice and symbol of Reform;' not least because, during his two years in Newgate, Cobbett wrote no fewer than 364 political, and by no means restrained articles for the *Register*.

The most numerous, and in his eyes the most important of these dealt with economic matters. He had, from the first, decided to use his enforced withdrawal from the world as a period during which he would attempt to fit his various arguments about the National Debt, paper money, taxation, poverty and prices into a series of linked articles that would explain to his fellow countrymen the reasons for their economic ills. He had attempted as much before, when his readers were too preoccupied with the war and the need to pay for it to believe such controversial stuff. Once the war, however, the continuation of which he now described as folly, came to its end, he was convinced that the truth of his economic theories would become self-evident. He told an American friend who visited him in prison: 'This nation is drunk, it is mad as the March hare, and mad it will be till this beastly frolic is over . . . My plan is to write that now which I can hold up to the teeth of my insolent enemies and taunt them with in the hour of their distress.'[16]

It began to seem, indeed, that he might not have to wait for the end of the war to be justified. Ricardo, with whom Cobbett seldom if ever agreed, had recently argued that, whatever the Government and the Bank of England said, the suspension of cash payments under the Bank Restriction Act of 1797, and the flood of paper money that had resulted, had produced a steady and continuing decline in the value of the currency. His arguments, which in this respect were the same as Cobbett's, had forced the Government to appoint a Bullion Committee, and it had reported that even Bank of England paper, let alone that issued by the country banks, had failed to retain its value in spite of being legal tender. It recommended a return to a gold-backed currency within two years.

Meanwhile the effects of printing money were being made obvious in other ways than in rising rents, prices and poverty. Country banks had begun to fail, most notably in Salisbury. De Yonge, a Dutch Jew, had recently been prosecuted for selling guineas at a premium to seamen who then smuggled them abroad. Goldsmid, the banker, had been unable to meet his commitments and had committed suicide instead. And yet Nicholas Vansittart, who was later Chancellor of the Exchequer, had persuaded Parliament to reject the Bullion Committee's report, and had declared that Bank of England notes still retained the full confidence of the public.

Cobbett, before his imprisonment, had written a series of articles about the De Yonge case under the title 'Jacobin Guineas'. He now produced another series of articles in the form of *Letters to the Inhabitants of Salisbury* which, after rehearsing his former arguments against paper money, the funding system and the predominance of commerce, flatly stated that a return to the gold standard would immediately produce a disastrous deflation unless it was accompanied by that 'equitable adjustment' of the National Debt for which he had argued for so long. Such an adjustment, however, could only be brought about by a reformed Parliament, for the present one was controlled by the supporters and beneficiaries of the borrowing, paper-money system, and nothing would induce them to abandon that system for so long as they controlled the Legislature.

Cobbett's arguments, which were complex and wide-ranging, were, perhaps, no more and no less valid than those advanced by better qualified economists. He was right to see in the printing-press inflation one of the root causes of the growing poverty in England. He may have been wrong, however, not to foresee that, after a disastrous post-war decade, the industry and commerce he so despised would once again provide Britain with a stable currency and stable prices. Nevertheless, he thought so highly of these articles – 'the best of my life' – that he published them in book form in 1815 under the title *Paper Against Gold and Glory Against Prosperity*. Since he could never be entirely gloomy, even when he was wearing his economist's hat, the fly-leaf carried the notice 'Retail Price 20s in Paper Money'.

Cobbett never departed from his basic economic arguments, which were to him the most fundamental and most important of all the political arguments. Unlike most of his fellow-Reformers, he saw Parliamentary Reform, not as a political end in itself, but as a necessary preliminary to economic reform. Nevertheless the economy was not all that he wrote about in Newgate.

He wrote also a series of articles on *The King's Illness and the Regency*. In 1810 the King's illness had finally and permanently deranged him and the Regency had to be re-established. There were, once again, disputes along Party lines concerning the powers that should be granted the Regent. He was popularly supposed to support the Whigs, and it was confidently expected that he would dismiss Perceval and his father's other Ministers and call on Grenville and Grey to form a Ministry. The Whigs, therefore, wanted to maximise and the Tories to minimise the Regent's powers until, quite suddenly, the position was reversed. Perceval became willing to grant the Prince all, or almost all that he wanted and was accordingly retained as Prime Minister, whilst the Whigs let it be known that they had been unable to take office because of the problem of Catholic Emancipation. This was not enough for Cobbett, who at that time hated the Tories even more than the Whigs and hated Perceval, his 'persecutor', most of all. He decided, therefore, that the Prince had been alternately bribed and blackmailed into retaining the Tories. Cobbett always subscribed to the conspiratorial theory of politics, and he would return to this particular 'conspiracy' when he first became involved, in 1813, in defending Caroline of Brunswick's reputation and her rights as a wife, mother and future Queen. His articles then in the *Register*, which took the form of *Letters* to his American friend *James Paul*, hinted darkly at the existence of THE BOOK, a work which, if it had been published, would so have discredited the Prince Regent that he had agreed to retain Perceval as Prime Minister in return for having THE BOOK suppressed.

There was as little substance in this argument as in Cobbett's other conspiratorial theories. The Prince Regent, in the first place, had never seemed to worry about the publicity that attached to all his many love affairs, in or out of marriage. In the second place THE BOOK was published, and even advertised in *The Times*. *The History of the Regency and Reign of George IV*, when it came out in 1830, proved to consist of little more than a rehash of Cobbett's conspiracy theory. It was, in short, an account of how the then Prince Regent, having grossly maltreated his 'innocent', 'virtuous', and eventually 'martyred' wife, had been blackmailed by Perceval with THE BOOK, and had, as a consequence, been forced to keep the Tories in power throughout the whole of his regency and reign.

Of greater interest is the series of *Letters to the Prince Regent on the Dispute with America* which came out of Newgate from August 1811 onwards. In these Cobbett deployed his undoubted knowledge of international affairs, international law and American politics to present a prescient if highly unpopular view of the disputes that were dragging Britain and the United States into war.

Britain's blockade, and her policy of stopping American ships in order to search for and seize what were neutral goods carried in neutral shipping had been a cause for violent dispute with the United States ever since the start of the French War. Her impressment of all American sailors of British origin found on those ships greatly exacerbated the dispute, and matters grew worse after 1806 when the blockade was extended to the Baltic ports and when, under Orders in Council, the British Navy began to seize not only the cargoes, but also the ships they were carried in.

If these were matters that had driven many in the United States to a warlike frenzy, there were also, on the American side, policies that created alarm in Britain. The Western States cared little for the damage done to the shipping and trading interests of New England, but they were eager for a war that would allow the British to be chased out of Canada. Jefferson, who had recently retired from the Presidency, had always told Americans that the whole of North America must be theirs and that the occupation of Canada would be 'a mere matter of marching'.

For much the same reason pressure had been mounting in the United States for the Floridas to be occupied in order to prevent the British, as allies of Ferdinand VII of Spain, sending troops there ostensibly to defend Spanish interests. American politicians were still fearful of a British attempt to reverse the verdict of the War of Independence, which they might have been able to achieve by mounting simultaneous attacks from the North and the South and at the same time encouraging the Indians in their attacks on the Western Settlements.

The provocations were, to a certain extent, disproportionate. The blockade was causing actual damage to the United States whilst the threat to Canada and the Floridas, though much discussed, had not as yet been transformed into action. It was commonly believed in Britain, moreover, that the United States would never dare to declare war on the mistress of the seas and the only European power that had demonstrated, in the Peninsula, its ability to defeat the armies of Napoleon. Nevertheless, in November 1810 President Madison had passed the Non-Intercourse Act which closed American ports to British ships and British exports, withdrew his Ambassador from London and sent proposals to Congress for greatly enlarging the army and navy. This caused indignation in London, where fears of a Franco-American alliance were revived and Madison was accused of acting as Napoleon's jackal.

In the first of his *Letters* Cobbett analysed the situation and found that, in her conduct of the blockade, Britain was in breach of international law which did not permit the seizure of neutral goods and neutral shipping any more than it permitted the impressment of American nationals. In the next he warned against underestimating the willingness and ability of the Americans to wage war against Britain, and then proceeded to warn the country that America was well on her way to becoming a great power. Moreover, the blockade had had the effect of turning her into an industrial one no longer dependent on imports from Britain. Indeed, it was now Britain who was dependent on her imports of cotton, timber and other raw materials from the United States, and her new textile factories were being ruined because of the Non-Intercourse Act. The balance of industrial, commercial and even naval power was beginning to change. Thus Cobbett returned to the theme he had so ardently supported as Peter Porcupine, the necessity for an Anglo-American alliance:

> This little Island, cut off, as she will be, from all the world, cannot, I am persuaded, retain her independence, unless she now exerts her energies in something other than expeditions to the continent of Europe, where every creature seems to be arrayed in hostility against her. The mere *colonial* system is no longer suited to her state . . . A system that would combine the powers of England with those of America, and would thus set liberty to war with despotism . . . would give new life to an enslaved world, and would ensure the independence of England for a time beyond calculation.[17]

These were not popular statements. There were those who remembered how Cobbett had been accused, before, of being more of an American than an Englishman. Nevertheless the Government was sufficiently alarmed at the prospect of being forced into a diversionary war to revoke the Orders in Council relating to the seizure of American prizes. But news of this arrived too late in Washington, for on 1 June 1812 Madison sent a state of war proposal to Congress and on 18 June both Houses empowered him to declare war on Britain.

The London papers insisted that this was nothing more than Yankee bluster. Cobbett, who had predicted what would happen, was savagely sarcastic: 'At last, however, America *has dared to go to war*, even against that great warrior George the Third . . . Napoleon is nothing to him as a conqueror; and yet the Americans have dared to declare war against him.'[18]

It would be two years after Cobbett's release from Newgate before the American War came to an end in 1814. Both sides enjoyed victories and endured reverses in what proved to be a futile struggle which produced no material advantage to either beyond a strong disinclination ever to go to war with one another again. Few Englishmen can have rejoiced as publicly as did Cobbett whenever the Americans gained an advantage. When the new American frigates out-fought the British ones in single-ship engagements and successively forced the *Guerrière*, the *Frolic* and the *Macedonian* to strike their colours the nation had been almost as shocked as if Villeneuve had won at Trafalgar. Only Cobbett rejoiced, and poured scorn on those who found an excuse in the fact that the American ships carried heavier guns. 'Something,' Cobbett wrote, 'should be allowed for our superiority in point of experience. Where did Isaac Hull gain his naval experience; and where Mr Decatur? There are two Decaturs, the father and son. They were my neighbours, in the country, in Pennsylvania. They were farmers more than seamen, though the older went to sea occasionally as commander of a merchant ship.'[19]

When Cobbett later published his *Advice to Young Men*, in 1829, he recalled, in a discussion on how to rear children, those American naval victories 'which filled us with shame and the world with astonishment'. The Americans, he wrote, had won, not because they were braver than the British sailors, but because they were bigger. 'From their very birth, they have an *abundance* of *good* food; not only of *food*, but of *rich* food. Even when the child is at the breast, a strip of *beef-steak*, or something of that description, as big and as long as one's finger, is put into his hand.'[20] Has anyone else ever explained the naval strategy of the 1812 war in such basic terms?

The Non-Intercourse Act had had a ruinous effect on Britain's textile industry. Already deprived of its European markets by the Berlin Decrees, it now lost the all-important American market, from which it imported its cotton and to which it exported its finished woollen and cotton cloths. Many mills closed down, and in others the workers had their wages savagely cut. Most of them were former hand-loom weavers who had been forced into the mills because the new machines had made their traditional methods of production uneconomic. Now the machines themselves had betrayed them, and so the more desperate of them formed themselves into gangs, blackened their faces, armed themselves with what they could and engaged in that campaign of machine-smashing, arson and generalised violence that became known as the Luddite Riots. They were, more than anything else, bread riots, the product of hunger rather than of politics, and, having started in Nottingham, they spread to the mill towns of Yorkshire, Lancashire and the West Country.

The Prince Regent sent a message to Parliament suggesting that this was the work of revolutionary conspirators, and that evidence of this was contained in a sealed green bag whose contents should be considered in secret session as a prelude to legislative action. There was no British politician who did not remember how mob violence had heralded in the French Revolution. Many believed that there were plenty of English Jacobins prepared to play at Danton or Robespierre. There was, consequently, little opposition in Parliament when a committee was formed to consider the evidence in secret.

The contents of what Cobbett referred to always as THE BAG* were never publicly disclosed but, when the committee had reported, legislation was rushed through which, amongst other things, made frame-smashing a capital offence and gave the magistrates wide powers to disperse any assembly, to arrest without warrant and to search for arms. This was the beginning of what Radical historians have referred to as the Age of Repression. It could be, and was argued that the ills of the people were the consequences of a war that had to be fought to its end, and that the cure for them did not lie in the hands of any government since they resulted from the actions of their enemies in Europe and America. The supposedly more liberal Whigs, and even such *bien pensants* as Wilberforce, accepted that argument almost unanimously. Only the Radicals, Cobbett now prominent among them, argued that if the war were the cause of their miseries, then the war must be stopped.

Cobbett's first comments on the rioting were, for him, remarkably unpolemical. In an article written in Newgate and published in the *Register* of 23 November 1811, he discussed the Nottingham riots in these terms:

It is stated that the price of *bread* became one of the subjects of discontent amongst the rioters; and it is also stated, that a

* Cobbett used the upper case much as he used italics: to give emphasis to a special point in his argument. However, when he used upper case for the same subject time after time, it was generally evidence that he was indulging in one of his conspiracy theories. Thus THE BAG joined THE BOOK as proof that THE THING, which was the general conspiracy of the borough-mongers, tax-eaters and financiers against the people, was in existence. Needless to say, most of the conspirators involved in THE THING were inhabitants of, or connected with THE WEN, which, of course, was the monstrous growth that was London.

scarcity of work, added to the other causes, first led to the riots. The *military* having been collected together in great force; the riots appear to have been put an end to. – Now, that these riots may be traced to the American non-intervention Act, and to Napoleon's continental system, is very clear . . . It does not follow, [therefore,] that the government are to blame . . . [but] measures ought to be adopted, not so much for the putting an end to the riots, as to prevent the misery out of which they arise.[21]

The measures which he suggested revealed how little he understood the problems and aspirations of the new industrial working class whose cause he was, for the first time, espousing. Napoleon and the Americans, he argued, had now destroyed Britain's main export markets and, by doing so, had also destroyed, for the foreseeable future, any need for a developing factory system. 'It is vain to hope for the return of such a state of things as would return the manufacturers to their *former* state. That state of things will *never* return . . .'

What, then, was to be done? The answer was a simple one, and Cobbett had given it in article after article for the past ten years. The land could provide better employment and more food for the hungry than the factories. The Government must now so reform its taxing and Enclosure policies as to make it possible for the former factory workers to return to the land.

But, if Cobbett had conceded that the Government was not to blame for the riots, he considered it was greatly to be blamed for the remedies it now adopted. He wrote at least two *Register* articles under the title of 'The Luddites or History of The Sealed Bag' in July 1812, just after he was released from Newgate, which demonstrated that imprisonment had done nothing to tame him. The secret committee, he wrote, had been nothing but the instrument of the Government. The sealed bag was its device for passing repressive legislation without ever presenting evidence of the supposed conspiracy to the public. The fact that only Burdett and Whitbread in the Commons, and Lord Byron in the Lords, had spoken against that legislation proved that this was, indeed, a conspiracy, but a conspiracy to magnify what was no more than another bread-riot into an insurrection that justified calling in the Army and ruling by force.

Two of the most culpable of the conspirators, in Cobbett's eyes, were Castlereagh and Perceval himself. The former had defended the emergency legislation in the House, declaring that the Luddites had treason as their object; that they had been moved to violence, not by unemployment and hunger, but by their hatred of an existing form of government which they wished to destroy. Cobbett answered this with an apparently irrelevant but none the less effective sarcasm:

> I do not wish to justify the woman who, according to the newspapers, committed *highway robbery* in taking *some potatoes out of a cart at Manchester*, and who was HANGED FOR IT . . . I allow her to have been guilty of highway robbery . . . and I allow that the law has made *highway robbery* a crime punishable with *death*, if the judges think proper; but I cannot and will not allow, that her forcible taking of some potatoes was any proof of a *treasonable* design and of hatred against the whole form of our government.[22]

But it was Perceval, that prosecuting, fining, imprisoning former Attorney-General, who was the greatest threat to the country's freedoms. 'The press he had extinguished, or had rendered the tool of his absolute will . . . Not content with this, he meditated the complete subjugation of London to the command and control of a military force'. In short, on the evening of 11 May 1812, Perceval had gone to the House with plans in his pocket 'for the establishment of a permanent army, to be stationed in Marybonne Park, for the openly-avowed purpose of *keeping the metropolis in awe* . . .'[23]

It was at this moment that, almost, according to Cobbett, by the grace of Heaven, Perceval was assassinated by John Bellingham, a man quite unassociated with the Luddites, even though the murder was used to furnish extra reasons for their forcible repression. The act, said Cobbett, was loudly applauded by the people. Bellingham, who was undoubtedly deranged, had shot Perceval on the Monday. He was tried on the Friday and hanged the following Monday. Cobbett, standing at a window in Newgate, had watched him being taken to Tyburn, and swore that he had been executed with the crowds calling out 'God Bless You, Bellingham'.[24]

On 9 July 1812 Cobbett was released from Newgate and was entertained to dinner by Burdett at that famous political meeting place, the Crown and Anchor Tavern. Six hundred guests joined in the feast, the celebrations being temporarily marred by the fact that some malicious person had placed a copy of one of the violent articles Cobbett had written in his Tory days against that Jacobinical villain Sir Francis Burdett, under every soup plate. Cobbett swore that he had never written the piece – another example of one of his lapses of memory which, whether genuine or not, were never less than convenient. His denial was accepted by the company and the celebration remained unmarred, though Cobbett must have wondered which of his many enemies had wanted it to be otherwise.

As he travelled back to Botley the following day, the people rang the church bells and presented him with addresses of welcome in many of the villages and towns he passed through. A public breakfast had been arranged for him at Alton, and at Winchester, where Ann waited for him, his friends had arranged a great public dinner which Ann, perhaps wisely, was not allowed to attend. Mr. Baker had locked the doors of Botley church to prevent the bells being rung in Cobbett's honour, but the villagers insisted on taking the horses out of his carriage and pulling him in triumph through the village.

A political journalist, whose trial had in no way redounded to his credit and whose writings had been principally directed to inter-national and economic problems, had gone into Newgate. The man who came out was, for many Englishmen, a public hero who had been unjustly punished for defending the poor and the weak, and who was well on his way to being accepted as the tribune of the people and the scourge of all tyrants.

CHAPTER SIXTEEN

Rancour, Populism and Exile

Quidquid agas, prudenter agas, et respice finem.
(Whatever you do, do cautiously, and look to the end.)
                                      Anon: *Gesta Romanorum*

Cobbett's political career prior to his imprisonment had been so remarkable for its inconsistency that he was perhaps expected to remain consistently inconsistent. But Newgate altered the pattern and persuaded him to devote the remainder of his life to Radicalism and Reform. Nevertheless, since most Radicals are, self-confessedly, progressive and forward-looking, and since the Reformers believed in the equal value of every citizen and believed democracy essential if that value were to be acknowledged, Cobbett lacked at least some of the qualities one would expect of a man who was to lead the Radical Reformers.

Compassion for the underdog is undoubtedly the political virtue Radicals most frequently claim for themselves. But compassion alone is scarcely enough to distinguish one well-meaning politician from another whatever label each wears. Indeed, no politicians believe themselves to be ill-intentioned, which is why each of them can claim to be as compassionate as the next.

What has always seemed to be the most distinctive, and possibly the most effective factor in left-wing radicalism, however, has been that particular form of political rancour we have learnt to refer to as class hatred. Radicals have to have at least as much hatred for the overdog as they have compassion for the under one before the 'left' can become a powerful force in politics. Without class hatred, radicalism is little more than an expression of political velleities everyone can agree with and no one will be forced to act upon.

Cobbett had always been a rancorous politician, but fickly so. As he changed one party for another he had always been able to reverse his rancours in order to attack former allies or support one-time opponents. But the strong vindictive streak in his character made it impossible for him to forget or forgive a personal injury even after he had danced on the graves of those who had injured him. Since he always equated being prosecuted with being persecuted, he was convinced that his imprisonment had been such an injury inflicted on him by the whole of the Establishment – politicians, lawyers, clergy, tax-eaters and all – and he never forgave them. Mere political rancour, as a consequence, developed into something as close to class hatred as an innately conservative man who moved easily in all classes of society was capable of.

Newgate, in short, gave a new focus and a new permanence to his rancours which made it impossible for him to desert the Radicals as he had deserted both Whigs and Tories. Vindictiveness had brought about what even his deep and life-long compassion for the underdog had failed to produce – unswerving allegiance to a single party and a single programme, if not a single goal, for the rest of his life.

Yet being tied to the Radical party and the Reform programme was by no means the same as being tied to all Radicals and all Reformers. There were those on the wilder fringes of English radicalism who applauded violence and desired revolution. Cobbett was far too much of a constitutionalist to want either, even though the threat of them provided him with his most powerful arguments for immediate and peaceful Reform. But Reform itself, which would eventually become as fashionable as motherhood and apple pie, meant different things to different people, so allowing all but the most diehard politicians to accept varying amounts of it as inevitable. It could mean no more than abolishing the patronage that went with the right to buy and sell Parliamentary seats. It could mean the abolition of the rotten boroughs and a slight widening of the franchise. It could mean equalised constituencies, adult male suffrage and annual Parliaments. The first of these almost all politicians were prepared to accept. The second was supported by the 'moderate' Reformers including the Burdettites, most of the Whigs and some of the Tories. The last was the 'radical Reform' that Cobbett demanded.

He rightly suspected that 'moderate' reform would perpetuate the Pitt System by giving political power to the industrial, financial and tax-eating class Pitt himself had done so much to create. It was for this reason that, within a few years, he would quarrel with Burdett, who moved as rapidly towards moderation as Cobbett moved towards radicalism, and so was to earn more abuse from Cobbett than any he ever had heaped on Pitt or Addington.

From now on every political article Cobbett wrote and every political speech he delivered would be more or less predictable. They would all revolve around the immediate and absolute necessity for radical reform as the only alternative to ultimate revolution. They would also, since he was above all a polemicist, contain endless attacks on the Jacobins and Levellers who wanted everything changed, on the diehards who wanted nothing changed, and on the moderates who wanted to delay the process of change by taking no more than a preliminary and cautious peck at the electoral cherry.

This became Cobbett's ultimate political position as spokesman and leader of the Radical Reformers. What he achieved and failed to achieve in that role became part of the history of English Radicalism. But what, at the same time, became lost to posterity was an opportunity to study the fluctuating effect of political ideas on a wholly political animal who was attempting to construct a political system from first principles. The converted, unfortunately, are rarely as interested or as instructive as those who are still struggling with Satan. Cobbett had finally discovered his principles and he ceased to develop or change. He had, as it were, become entombed in his own dogma.

Cobbett's imprisonment had been by far the greatest setback he had experienced in a career that had already been surprisingly successful and one that he confidently expected would bring him as much fortune and fame as Canning or Vansittart, those other one-time pamphleteers with whom he had first set out to make his mark in British politics. But now he was suddenly plunged into a situation of political danger and great financial difficulty. He had lost the largest part of his publishing empire and been separated, at a crucial period, from the farms in which he had invested so much. Did he realise that enemies who had done this to him would do even more if he continued his damaging attacks on them? The Government had, after all, added to its existing wartime powers measures that would allow it to silence anyone thought to be inciting the civilian population to disaffection. Cobbett was certainly aware that to be completely silenced, to be imprisoned with no such access to the *Register* and the ear of the public as he had enjoyed in Newgate, would bring about his political and financial ruin. He was determined that this should not happen, even if it meant withdrawing for a time from the struggle. But he was equally determined not to abate his attacks on the Government or the system. Nor, to judge by the tone of his articles, was he even prepared to attack them in a slightly more moderate manner.

He had, by now, developed a strong sense of mission. He was convinced that he, and perhaps only he, could so mould public opinion as to make the politicians accept the inevitability of Radical Reform. This was, he believed, no time for mealy-mouthed caution. His moment had come. Every sporadic outbreak of Luddite violence, every calling out of the troops, every hanging, imprisoning and transportation convinced him that the crisis was imminent and that England had already entered that pre-revolutionary stage he had written about so often. Were it not for the war, he argued, the Government would even then have been faced with the stark choice between Reform and Revolution. The extraordinary powers it had taken and the large Home Army which allowed it to enforce them might delay the moment of choice, but that moment must come as soon as the war was over.

He was correct in his analysis but out in his timing. That choice would not, in fact, be faced for another twenty years, and even then it would not be so stark a one as he envisaged. His misreading of the situation stemmed, oddly enough, from a failure to understand what was then happening in those areas of politics in which he was supposedly an expert. For he had built his reputation and his readership on his reporting and analysis of foreign rather than domestic affairs, and on his often shrewd comments on the conduct of the war.

The tide of that war had begun to change whilst he was in Newgate, and public opinion in England changed with it. From 1812 onwards people began to believe that an advantageous and durable peace might be achieved. 1812 was the year of Badajoz and Salamanca and of the ruin of the French Grande Armée in the snows of Russia. 1813 was the year in which Wellington's victory at Vittoria and the subsequent storming of the Pyrenean passes made it possible to place a British army on French soil at a time when Prussia and Austria abandoned their roles as Napoleon's satellites and put their armies in the field against him.

By that time most Englishmen had ceased to take much interest in domestic politics and concentrated their attention, instead, on the war. The fact that it was no longer a war to prevent the invasion and conquest of Britain but one that concerned the invasion and conquest of France not only renewed and strengthened the bellicosity of almost every Briton but also revived their interest in what their war aims should be. It had taken twenty years of almost continual fighting, much bloodshed, great expenditure and increasing hardships at home for Britain to arrive at this stage. Such sacrifices would be wasted unless the war ended, not with compromises and a temporary peace, such as had been reached at Amiens, but with a once-and-for-all settlement of the 'French problem'.

Such a settlement, Pitt declared as he went reluctantly to war in 1793, could only be achieved by the destruction of Jacobinism and the restoration of the Bourbons. Britain needed nothing less for her own survival and owed nothing less to her European allies.

When a seemingly invincible Napoleon had replaced the Jacobins there had been several occasions when his successors would have settled for considerably less, and would have abandoned the Bourbons if they could have been assured that Napoleon was willing to leave the seas, the colonies and overseas trade to Britain and to confine his imperial ambitions to Europe. Napoleon's *Weltanschauung* had always made such a compromise improbable, and now that his final defeat seemed only a matter of time, it once again became official policy to continue the war until the Bourbons had been restored and all that had happened in France since 1789 had been reversed, whether that was what the French people now wanted or not.

Public opinion did not, at that time, influence foreign policy as much as it does today. Nevertheless this was a policy most people in Britain were very willing to accept. Yet there were a few who, like Cobbett, had ideological and political reasons for opposing it. For those who called themselves Democrats the restoration of a Bourbon provided reason enough, as even the most well-meaning and inoffensive member of that family had become a symbol of absolutism and reaction. (Bourbon absolutism, which derived, in theory at least, from the divine right of kings, was thought to have far less divinity about it than the absolutism of the Jacobins or of Napoleon, which had been derived, though once again only in theory, from the will of the people.) Cobbett may not have been quite so metaphysical about it, but he had opposed the British war effort in Spain because it had, as one of its objectives, the restoration of a Bourbon king who had never succeeded in winning the trust or allegiance of the majority of his subjects. How, then, could Cobbett support the restoration of a French Bourbon when the French, over the years, had given so many different indications of preferring to be ruled by almost anyone else?

However, the root and purpose of Cobbett's argument lay in England. Since he was convinced that it was only the continuation of the war that stood between England and Reform, then the quicker the war was ended, whether the French had been properly defeated or not, the quicker Reform would come.

That thought alone had turned the former warmonger into a most strident peacemonger who used any and every argument that might bring the war to an immediate end. So it was that he had recently discovered that it had never been either a necessary or a just war so far as Britain was concerned but merely a contrived one embarked upon only in order to preserve the British oligarchy and to perpetuate the Pitt System. If it was humbug to claim that it had been fought to defend Britain's best interests, it was even greater humbug to give it a moral purpose by claiming that it had been fought to save the French from themselves and to restore order, religion and a legitimate monarchy to those unfortunate people. For, given that such things were benefits, they were benefits the French had manifestly enjoyed ever since the day Napoleon had made himself Emperor:

> There is Social Order and Regular Government in plenty in France at this time; and as to the Altar and the Throne, we hear of nothing but their Imperial Majesties, the King of Rome and of Bishops and Masses. Here is Altar and Throne and enough of them if we wanted Altar and Throne. What, then, displeases us now? Will nothing suit us? Will neither *republicans* nor *emperors* do for us?[1]

The poor harvest of 1813 provided him with another argument. Food prices had soared in England and this, surprisingly enough, brought large quantities of cheap corn and cattle flooding into England from France in spite of the war. Such trading with the enemy was encouraged by the French for much the same reason as the Americans today encourage the sale to the Soviets of the grain Russian agriculture seems incapable of producing. The argument in both cases was, and is, that it deprives the enemy of hard currency that might otherwise have been spent on military hardware. To Cobbett, however, this was proof of how much better France had been governed for the past twenty years than England: 'France, in consequence of her happy Revolution, seems to have become a *new country*. She has now an abundance of all the necessaries of life, and her superabundance she is selling to us.'[2]

That 'superabundance' proved the truth, of course, of almost every political point he had made for the past five years. The French peasants, far from being driven off the land, had been given ownership of it free from all tithes, rent and feudal dues. They could undersell English farmers in the English market because there was no French National Debt, no French paper currency and no large pauper population to be kept alive by the Poor Rates. The opponents of Reform had always claimed that the Jacobins and Napoleon had brought France nothing but disaster. Cobbett could only wish to have such disaster inflicted on the English. This could not happen, however, so long as the war continued, but it was being continued merely in order to prevent that happening.

At the same time Cobbett, almost gloating over every success the Americans had gained over the British at sea, on the Great Lakes and at New Orleans, kept pointing out how well this demonstrated the advantages conferred on a nation by free and democratic government: 'There the people understand their rights; they are made acquainted with the acts and real motives of their government; they know what they are at war for; they have real representatives, who speak their voice, and who, if they were so minded, could not delude them.'³

Cobbett, in short, had, in his zeal for Reform, fallen into the habit, dangerous for a man who had to live by his pen, of finding nothing to praise in Britain and everything to praise in the two countries she was at war with. As if this were not enough to irritate and anger the majority of his readers, he was now more than halfway towards being a Bonapartist at a time when Napoleon was almost certainly the most hated man in Europe. He, who had always admired Napoleon's military genius, came close to deploring the consequences of his Russian campaign, and actually declared that the burning of Moscow had been an act of monstrous barbarity on the part of the Czar.

When Napoleon fell and was exiled to Elba, Cobbett wrote a long, almost regretful explanation of what had led to his downfall:

The *immediate* causes of this event were, evidently, the loss of his army in Russia, the subsequent abandonment of him, in the midst of battle, by his German Allies, and the overwhelming force of the combined armies. But the more distant cause, and the only cause, was his *vanity* . . . He lost the hearts of all the best men in France, that is to say of the enlightened friends of freedom, by abolishing the republic, by assuming the title of Emperor, and by acting the despot, but he lost his crown by his vanity. He must needs be, not only a *Royal* personage, but he must be related to the *old* Royal race: he must marry . . . a daughter of the House of Austria . . . He had the power of doing great good; he had the power to give freedom to all of Europe; he did much good to France; he established, or rather, he did not destroy the good laws which the Republicans had made; he did not bring back and replant the curses, which the Republicans had rooted out: France, under him, was much happier than France before the Revolution. But the lovers of freedom put great means into his hands: he had a mind calculated to give effect to those means; he did, for a while, employ them well; but, being seized with the vanity of being a king, and with that most abominable itch of being a *papa* and leaving a son, descended from a mother of the old Royal race, he, from that moment, wholly abandoned the good cause, and laid the foundation for what has now come to pass.⁴

In the next year, when the high drama of the Hundred Days had been played out, when Napoleon had surrendered himself to the British and all of Europe was arguing over what should be done with him, Cobbett produced what was probably the most moving and most dignified of all his eulogia together with the most far-fetched of all his conspiracy theories. The eulogy was contained in a *Letter to Lord Castlereagh* published in the *Register* and started:

My Lord – At last, then, you have Napoleon in your power. That is to say, you have a composition of bones, skin, flesh and blood, warmed and kept alive by the vital principle; but this is all; and whether this vital principle be now to be speedily extinguished, or the whole body be to remain a few years longer above ground, you have not the power, and you never will have the power to efface the memory of his deeds, or to destroy, or even to lessen, the effects of those deeds . . . Do what you will; if you were to thumbscrew him, flog him, and, at last, cut him to mince-meat, you could do away not one jot of his military renown; his battles, his victories, his conquests, his mastership of all the old families of the continent, are recorded in a way never to be forgotten; they form a portion of the knowledge of mankind; they occupy a seat in all men's minds; and, as to his *fall*, why, we all fall at last; only the far greater part of us fall with little more noise than is occasioned by the fall of a bullock, whereas his fall is the subject of conversation amongst . . . *all the people of the civilised world* . . .

Yet even the emotion he so obviously felt when this demi-god fell could not prevent Cobbett attaching a political moral to his lament over that fall. The article was concluded in his most minatory political style:

The COURIER says: '*The play is over; let us go to supper.*' . . . '*The play*' may be over; but, oh! no! we cannot '*go to supper.*' We have *forty-five millions a year for ever to pay for the play*. . . . The *first act* is, perhaps, closed. But, that grand revolution, that bright star, which first burst forth in the year 1789, is still sending forth its light over the world. In that year, feudal and ecclesiastical tyranny, ignorance, superstition, received the first heavy blow; they have since received others; and in spite of all that can now be done in their favour, they are destined to perish.[5]

Cobbett may not have arrived at his conspiracy theory at that time, for it was not published until his *History of the Regency and Reign of King George the Fourth* appeared in 1830. What is known is that when Napoleon escaped from Elba in 1815, Cobbett strongly opposed any renewal of British hostilities against him. If the French people wanted him, he argued, and they had shown that they did by the manner in which they flocked to his eagles, then the French should have him. His was, however, a lonely voice and the war was renewed until Waterloo finally brought it to an end. What Cobbett's conspiracy theory attempted to explain was why all this had happened.

The British Government, so his theory ran, had been dissatisfied with the peace negotiated with France in 1814. It had not reduced the French to such poverty that the benefits derived from the Revolution had been destroyed. So long as the French were left to enjoy such benefits there was a danger that Englishmen would claim equivalent benefits for themselves, so destroying the Pitt System and the landed aristocracy. What would retrieve the situation was another war which would end with a much harsher peace being imposed on the French. The only way of bringing this about was to release Napoleon, once more, on France and on Europe, and it was for this reason that the British government not only allowed, but actually assisted the former Emperor to escape from Elba.

So improbable a theory demonstrated how close to paranoia Cobbett's delusions of conspiracy could take him. When it was published it was so derided that it came close to destroying the reputation he had deservedly won as a shrewd, if prejudiced commentator on foreign affairs. Nevertheless, what he actually wrote between 1812 and 1815 on the subject of war and foreign policy was, for a variety of reasons, of some importance. The admiration he expressed for the benefits that revolution had brought to France and the United States did much to damage him as a politician engaged in domestic politics. He was now constantly accused of being a Jacobin and a revolutionary and people refused to believe him when he claimed, in all honesty, to be a constitutionalist and a monarchist who wanted nothing more than a radical reform of Parliament peacefully achieved.

He did nothing to help his credibility as a monarchist when, in 1816, he launched a somewhat xenophobic attack on the British Royal Family. Although he was in favour of a king in theory, it was always one who, like some mythical member of the Plantagenets whom he idealised, would both reign and rule, and stand between the people and the rapacious barons:

It appears, at first sight, very strange that England should have for its sovereigns a race of *foreigners*; and that the marriages should be so made up as that no king should, supposing nothing illicit go on, ever have a single drop of English blood in his veins. But, if we consider these apparent sovereigns, as we ought, nothing more than mere puppets in the hands of the Borough-mongers, we shall find a very substantial reason for this seemingly strange taste. It is the interest of this body of men, to have upon the throne a person for whom the people have no regard. The English nation have a rooted hatred, or, at best, contempt for all foreigners; yet, be they who or what they may, these foreign princes and princesses always surround themselves with Hanoverians, Brunswickers and other Germans, and care is taken that the race shall never mix with any English race; so that this contempt, on the part of the people, is constantly kept alive.[6]

Radicals usually believe that they voice the opinions of all but a small section of the public, but Cobbett, at this time, was strangely out of touch with public opinion. It was not merely that he had turned the *Register* into a propaganda sheet for the Radicals – the Radicals, the Luddites and the chopsticks no doubt applauded his views but they were not, on the whole, the people who bought his paper. Nor was it only that he had put himself into a position where his enemies could plausibly dismiss him as a Jacobinical agitator. It was rather that his writings were so slanted towards a particular viewpoint – one still far from being popular – that even those who had previously read him only in order to be irritated, now feared that they would be bored.

For the first time the *Register* lost circulation. This had two immediate consequences. The Government and the newspapers supporting the Government, who had once thought it necessary to write Cobbett down or buy and bully him into silence, now began to think it safe to ignore him. More important, however, was that it reduced Cobbett's only assured source of income at a time when he was already struggling with a great burden of debt. His trial, imprisonment and fine* had cost him well over £10,000. He and his two sureties had, in addition, entered into recognisances of £5,000 which stood to be forfeit if he should ever, in the next seven years,

---

* It was said that, before Cobbett left Newgate, the Government had offered to remit his fine if he would agree to stop supporting the Princess Regent in the *Register*. If such an offer was made, it was certainly refused. In her series of public quarrels with her husband, Caroline of Brunswick invariably provided the Radicals with a most useful and almost apolitical weapon to use against the Government. See page 427 passim.

be convicted for a breach of the peace. Since he was so remarkably contentious a man, that was always a possibility, as was clearly shown at a County Meeting held in Winchester in March 1817. There Cobbett engaged in a somewhat heated argument with a certain Mr. Lockhart, who was the local Member of Parliament and who, as a consequence, challenged Cobbett to a duel. Cobbett, although he approved of fisticuffs, had always objected to duelling on principle. He therefore refused the challenge with a certain amount of contempt, which was certainly increased by the fact that Lockhart, who was a lawyer, must have known that a duel was a breach of the peace and that Cobbett, win or lose, would have had to forfeit £5,000 if he engaged in one.

Such future risks apart, Cobbett was still faced with the need to find £10,000, and would have had to sell Botley if his friends had not come to his assistance with various loans or gifts. Burdett alone had given or lent him £3,000, a gesture which, in future years, provided Cobbett with another reason for quarrelling with him. But in spite of this help, Cobbett's trade creditors continued to press him so hard that, in a rare act of financial prudence, he transferred the title to the *Register* to his printers to prevent its being seized for debt.

With the Botley farms now only precariously held, the Fairthorn house closed and a cheaper establishment rented in the village, with a *Register* readership that had shrunk to below 3000 and the ownership of that paper at least nominally lost, Cobbett, with apparent unconcern, jumped immediately back into the political battle. In the same month as he left Newgate he was busily engaged in supporting Henry Hunt when he stood as Radical candidate at Bristol. In October 1816 Cobbett offered himself, also as Radical candidate, to the electors of Southampton. Neither man was elected, but Cobbett swore that the result at Southampton had been rigged. He did not, however, appeal against the poll because even he realised that he could not afford the expense of a petition to Parliament.

Hunt and Cobbett now emerged as the spokesmen and leaders of the Radical Reformers. The two men had much in common. Both had previously been soldiers and were presently farmers. Neither was in favour of 'moderate' reform, which meant that both would soon come to disapprove of Burdett. 'Orator' Hunt was, in his way, as effective an agitator as Cobbett, although he used his tongue where Cobbett still preferred to rely on his pen.

Meanwhile the country was suffering even greater hardships in the peace than it had in the war. The mills and factories that had been pouring out war supplies for the great numbers of men Britain and her allies had under arms now had to switch to much lower levels of peacetime production. British exporters who, as a consequence of the blockade, had enjoyed something approaching a monopoly in overseas markets now met growing competition as industry and trade revived on the Continent. Britain's most important export market was in the United States, and this had been greatly reduced because both the blockade and the War of 1812 had hastened the rate at which that country industrialised and became self-sufficient. American farmers, according to Cobbett, had imported and bred Merino sheep in sufficient numbers to allow American industrialists to establish a large textile industry of their own.

What was more generally damaging to agriculture, as well as to industry in Britain, was that the Government had embarked on a monetary policy which was strongly deflationary. Since none of its policies had been able to prevent a steady depreciation of its paper currency, the Government began to prepare for a return to the gold standard by reducing the amount of paper money it put into circulation. This cut in the money supply – without any reduction in the National Debt, the costs of government or the levels of taxation – produced a sharp fall in capital values and reduced the incomes of everyone who was not a government servant, client or pensioner, or who was not a fund-holder or stock-jobber. Employment and wages had to be cut if the industrialists and farmers were to survive, but food prices rose as a consequence of a series of poor harvests and the protection given to agriculture by successive Corn Bills.

There was a sharp increase in bankruptcies. Some country banks failed. Cobbett, like most other farmers, found that he was farming at a loss which added to his already considerable financial difficulties. Shipping was laid up and long-established landowners had to sell their estates. But the principal and most numerous victims of those times were, of course, the mill hands who had been thrown out of work and the farm labourers who were invited to survive on reduced wages and what they could get from parish relief.

Unemployment, low wages and food hunger inevitably bred anger. Though many people passively accepted their misery, the anger of others erupted into sporadic and almost purposeless mob violence. That violence was violently suppressed by a government which had armed itself with all the powers it might need for the purpose. Even when there was apparent calm in the factory towns and the rural areas the authorities suspected that violence had merely gone underground. The Government, indeed, began to see revolutionary conspiracies almost everywhere: in the rioting of the

Luddites; in the doctrines, destructive of all constitutional and property rights, preached by the Spenceans, a small band of agrarian socialists; in the illegal attempts of the workers to form Combinations for the purpose of wage bargaining; even in the network of Hampden Clubs that Major Cartwright had established for no more sinister purpose than to argue the case for Reform.

Parliament met twice in secret session in the first four years of the peace in order to consider what the Government described as proof of the existence of widespread revolutionary conspiracies. Although that proof was contained in documents that were never published – held in a locked bag that, so far as the public was concerned, was never unlocked – the Government obtained, on each occasion, the additional powers it asked for. If any politicians thought that the Luddites and the Spenceans provided bare justification for such powers, further justification had been manufactured by the small army of spies and *agents provocateurs* employed by the Home Office. All of this was done constitutionally. Britain had not become an absolutist state like pre-revolutionary France, nor even a police one in the modern style. Nevertheless there was enough absolutism, enough police work, enough repression to dismay those who believed in the inevitable progress of liberalism in the Western World.

Cobbett, of course, never believed in liberalism. But neither had he ever believed in the need for revolution or mob violence in Britain where men had long enjoyed the protection afforded them by the Constitution and the Common Law. Once he had felt nothing but anger and contempt when he himself was threatened with mob violence, first in Philadelphia and later in London. Now, however, his sympathies, if not his reason, had to be with the rioters rather than with their victims. He saw them as men whose violence grew out of a natural anger at their poverty and food hunger. Since his politics were directed towards the eradication of such conditions, he saw himself as a man who willed the same ends as the rioters but differed from them only over the means.

Cobbett had, until now, written for, argued with, and attempted to convert to Radical Reform those who might be described as members of the 'political classes'. Apart from the practising politicians, for whom the *Register* had become required reading, these were, for the most part, educated and well-to-do people who took some interest in foreign affairs and the Ins and Outs of domestic politics. They formed a remarkably small proportion of the total population, as the circulation figures of the *Register* revealed. Nevertheless they had to provide almost all the readers there were for the *Register* or any other national newspaper.

The Stamp and Paper Duties made newspapers too expensive to be bought by the working classes. There was, therefore, no economic reason to produce papers for them, and no electoral reason either. Consequently, although Cobbett had come to believe that Radical Reform, and only Radical Reform, would provide a cure-all for their ills, he found it difficult to convert them to that belief since he had no means of communicating with them other than by speeches at election time.

But if Cobbett could not speak to the labourers, he was determined to speak for them, and he devoted many of his *Register* articles to their problems. Those articles, however, were written for his regular readers who, as members of the 'political classes', could reasonably be expected to follow his long, carefully reasoned and fully documented arguments even if they seldom agreed with them. They were not arguments, on the whole, that would be easily understood by Lancashire mill-hands, Hampshire chopsticks or rioting Luddites.

It was not a matter of Cobbett's style, for his writing was as accessible as Defoe's. Like Defoe, he made skilful use of the language, constructions and rhythms of everyday speech and so achieved the effect of conversing with his readers. The vigour and ease this gave to his writing distinguished him from almost all his contemporaries, the majority of whom were still wallowing in Ciceronian orotundities. The difficulty, rather, lay in the complexity of Cobbett's arguments.

It was Lord Cochrane who, towards the end of 1816, first suggested to Cobbett that he should write an article for the working rather than the 'political' classes to read, which would contain a more popular and simplified version of his principal arguments for Reform. It was important to organise the working classes in support of Reform, if only to prevent them being organised in support of revolution. Cobbett was reluctant at first to abandon what seemed to him to be the supremely important economic argument in order to make a simple – and simplified – political appeal to the masses; but Cochrane eventually persuaded him that such an article would do more for the cause of Reform than all his attempts to convert the 'political classes'. He suggested that the problems of distribution could be overcome by republishing the article as a pamphlet which could be sold to working-class readers for a penny or two.

Lord Cochrane, therefore, ought to be remembered whenever the article that Cobbett wrote for the *Register* of 3 November 1816 is discussed. It was called *An Address to the Journeymen and Labourers*, and it can be variously considered as the most important political article he ever wrote, the first symptom of his lapse into Populism, or the start of a movement from which, by apostolic succession from the Reformers and the Chartists, the British Labour Party would eventually emerge. There was nothing intrinsically new in the article which was, as far as Cobbett was concerned, an old song set to a more popular tune and sung to a different audience. All he could have known from the immediate reactions to the article was that he had launched an effective appeal to the British working classes to organise themselves for political action.

He had listened to Cochrane to the extent of so simplifying his favourite arguments that they amounted to little more than slogans. They must, however, have been the right sort of slogans since some of them are still in use although there are few today who know who first coined them. He set out, in the first place, to persuade the workers of their own importance. The whole of the nation's wealth, he told them, had been produced by their labours. The country's security, and its success in the late war had depended on those of them who had carried muskets in the ranks or had crewed the ships of war. They were not, therefore, to be ignored or despised. 'With this correct idea of your own worth in your minds, with what indignation must you hear yourselves called the Populace, the Rabble, the Mob, the Swinish Multitude.'

The politicians, he told his new readers, would try to persuade them that their present miseries were temporary, that they were part of the aftermath of war or the consequences of a temporary period of over-production and a series of poor harvests. They must reject such explanations. Even more scornfully must they reject the theories of those 'feelosofers' who, following Malthus, maintained that the poor were only poor because they would persist in procreating, and that they could always help themselves by practising continence or emigrating.

What the poor actually suffered from, Cobbett insisted, was the product neither of the war nor their loins, but of the monstrous burden of taxes Pitt had imposed on the nation. They were not out of work or attempting to survive on starvation wages because their employers wished to grind them down, but because the employers themselves had been ground down by the tax collectors. Nor should the workers believe that, because they paid no direct taxes, they were not taxed. The indirect taxes levied on most of what they used, consumed or bought, from the windows of their cottages to the malt in their beer, effectively removed almost half of all they earned. They were the indirect victims of direct taxation and the direct victims of indirect taxation and everything that was wrung out of them went to those who were the consumers and not the producers of the nation's wealth. 'As to the cause of our present miseries, it is *the enormous amount of the taxes*, which the government compels us to pay for the support of its army, its placemen, its pensioners, &c., and for the payment of the interest on its debt.'

How markedly, he pointed out, all of this differed from the lot of the working man in the United States, where there was no taxation without representation and 'the whole of the taxes do not amount to more than about *ten shillings* a head upon the whole of the population; while in England they amount to nearly *six pounds* a head'.

Having shown his readers that their miseries had been caused by the greed and corruption of those who governed them, Cobbett went on to guard his other political flank. The workers were warned not to listen to those who would convince them that a revolution and a sweeping away of all that they had inherited from the past offered the only cure for their ills. 'I know of no enemy to the happiness of the country so great as that man, who would persuade you that *all* must be torn to pieces . . . that there is *nothing good* in our *constitution and laws*.'

The Americans, 'who are a very wise people, and who love liberty with all their hearts, and who take care to *enjoy* it too', once again served as an example. For they had taken care 'not to part with any of the great principles and laws which they derived from their forefathers. They . . . preserve Magna Charta, the Bill of Rights, the Habeas Corpus, and not only all the body of the Common Law of England, but most of the rule of our courts, and all our form of jurisprudence'.

It was a strange example to use for the man who had once railed against Chief Justice M'Kean and sworn that there was no justice to be found in the whole of Pennsylvania, but it served to prove the point this innately conservative Radical most insisted upon. 'There is no principle favourable to freedom, which is not to be found in the Laws of England, or in the example of our Ancestors . . . We want *great alteration*, but we want nothing new. Great principles ought to be and must be the same, or else confusion follows.' Which brought him to the core and purpose of this, and all his subsequent Addresses to the workers, which was, of course, the urgent necessity for a radical reform of Parliament. 'We must have *that first*, or we shall have nothing good.'

It was an article in which Cobbett's plain but eloquent prose, his genius for simplification and his single-minded belief in single remedies came together more happily than ever before. As Cochrane had prophesied, it aroused interest, agreement and

383

criticism on such a wide scale that Cobbett found himself, for the first time since he had written his anonymous *Considerations*, speaking to the nation at large. The *Register* article was reprinted as a broadsheet which sold, before the end of 1817, more than 200,000 copies. But by the end of 1816, as soon as he had seen the initial reaction to the broadsheet, Cobbett had decided to supplement his shilling *Register* with another and cheaper version. If it was to be cheap it could not, because of the Stamp Duty, print the news and reports contained in the larger *Register*. But issued as a pamphlet – he abandoned the broadsheet format – containing no more than one of his political articles, it could be sold unstamped and for no more than twopence.

This cheap *Register* – 'Cobbett's twopenny trash' his enemies called it – was immensely successful in more ways than one. At a time when few national or local papers had a circulation of more than 5,000 it rapidly climbed to one of well over 40,000. Since, as he later wrote, he made more than a halfpenny profit on every copy sold, this added considerably to his income which, he claimed, had risen to well over £10,000 a year by 1817. For the first time since the Ely Mutiny case, he might soon be in a position to pay off his creditors and even to redeem the mortgage on Botley.

But the political profit was even more considerable. Cobbett became what he had never been before, a national figure, and acknowledged as one of the leaders, if not the leader, of the Reform movement. Even more important was the fact that he had made himself the accepted spokesman, counsellor and leader of the working classes. His became the voice of the common people of England who, in Chesterton's phrase, 'never have spoken yet'. And there is, for journalists at least, one further aspect of the cheap *Register* to consider. By starting it Cobbett had, almost inadvertently, pioneered, if not actually invented, the popular press.

The political consequences of the cheap *Register* were such as to cause great rejoicing (and a certain amount of jealousy) in the ranks of the Reformers and considerable alarm in Government circles where the view that Cobbett was no longer dangerous had rapidly to be revised. Samuel Bamford, the Lancashire Radical, who was not one of Cobbett's most ardent admirers, wrote many years later in his *Autobiography*:

At this time the writings of William Cobbett suddenly became of great authority. They were read on nearly every cottage hearth in the manufacturing districts [of England and Scotland] . . . Their influence was speedily visible. He directed his readers to the true cause of their sufferings – misgovernment; and to its proper correction – parliamentary reform.[7]

Cobbett himself, with his passion for statistics, was somewhat more specific when, many years later, he felt it necessary to describe how his cheap *Register* had been born:

> From 1801 to 1817, I published the *Weekly Political Register* at a price of a *shilling*; but just before the commencement of the last-mentioned year, I, in order to give my writings a wide spread, laid aside the *stamp*, and sold the *Register* for two-pence; and instead of selling about two or three thousand a week, the sale rose to *sixty or seventy thousand*. The effect was prodigious; the people were everywhere upon the stir in the cause of *parliamentary reform*; petitions came to Parliament early in 1817 from *a million and a half of men*.[8]

The figures may not have been entirely accurate, and Cobbett does not mention that the idea of giving his writings 'a wide spread' came originally from Cochrane. Nor does Cobbett make it clear that he continued the shilling *Register* as well as the twopenny one. He never intended, at that time, to turn the Reform movement into a purely working-class one, but held high hopes of forming a broad alliance of interests – landowners, farmers and manufacturers as well as workers – which would bring pressure on the 'political class' to agree to Reform. To accomplish this he needed the two papers in order to conduct his arguments at different levels of sophistication.

But he had, by now, largely abandoned the idea that even the most fully-reasoned of his arguments for Reform would bring about any mass-conversion of the 'political classes' in or out of Parliament. Whether as practising politicians or beneficiaries of the Pitt System or both, they stood to lose too much from a truly radical Reform ever to accept it until it was forced upon them. In this respect the Whigs, for all their talk in favour of gradual and 'moderate' Reform, were as unconvertible as the Tories. Only 'a million and a half of men' – farmers as well as farmworkers, manufacturers as well as mill hands – all meeting, protesting and petitioning, seemed to Cobbett to offer any constitutional method of persuading them to accept Reform. And only Cobbett, through the *Registers*, could inspire and organise men to that purpose.

Not all Reformers agreed with him. Burdett, who led the handful of Radicals and Reformers inside Parliament, was, according to Cobbett, increasingly jealous of the latter's assumption of leadership in the movement outside Westminster. It was this, Cobbett wrote later, that drove Burdett to moderation until he eventually found his rightful place, as one of the wealthiest landowners in England, amongst the magnificoes of the Whig oligarchy.

Major Cartwright's Hampden Clubs, on the other hand, gave rise to some slight jealousy on Cobbett's part and not a little apprehension. His respect for that veteran Reformer never abated, but he argued that there was nothing that the Clubs could do that Cobbett's *Registers* could not do more effectively and on a far greater scale. A system of private conventicles in which the converted did no more than argue with the equally converted behind closed doors could, given the Government's use of spies and *agents provocateurs*, provide it with an excuse for discovering yet another Jacobinical conspiracy. This Cobbett was determined to prevent. The Reformers, he declared, must always operate in full view of the people, the politicians and the law and claim nothing beyond their constitutional rights of assembly, free speech and petition. 'I advise my countrymen to have nothing to do with any *Political Clubs*, any secret *Cabals*, any Correspondencies, but to trust to *individual exertions and open meetings*.'*[9]

Paradoxically enough, it was not Cartwright with his Clubs but Cobbett with his pen who placed the Reformers most at risk. The Hampdenites were innocuous enough to merit Cobbett's description of their activities. 'Nothing good will ever be done by meeting and *talking* about what they are to *talk* about next time.'[10] But Cobbett, almost single-handedly, or so he claimed, had turned Reform into a mass political movement which the Government could neither ignore as irresponsible nor easily suppress as seditious. In order to move against it under existing laws it would have to prove that it was connected with the undoubtedly illegal violence of the Luddites on the one hand or the vaguely seditious, vaguely conspiratorial activities of the Spenceans on the other.

The Luddites could be dealt with by the military and the magistrates, as rioters always had been in England. The Spenceans, if they ever became anything more than a splinter group arguing rather than conspiring for a republican and Socialist society, could be left to the Attorney-General, the judges and the remarkably elastic laws of sedition and treason. But Cobbett,

---

* The Corresponding Societies established to further the cause of 'democracy' in the early 1790s were declared illegal in 1799 after a series of trials of leading members for sedition or treason. Cobbett naturally feared a similar fate for the Hampden Clubs and for Major Cartwright who had been associated with both.

openly and lawfully producing his *Registers* and, through them, inducing 'a million and a half of men' to petition for Reform, was a different problem.

When Cobbett first began to seem dangerous again, the Government decided that he must be 'written down'. The Government press, accordingly, became full of articles deriding his 'twopenny trash'; scores of anti-Cobbett pamphlets were published and distributed throughout the country; a fake *Register* was even produced containing reprints of the anti-Jacobin, anti-Radical, anti-Reform articles he had written in his Tory days. Cobbett, apparently, minded none of this. He remarked that it was surprising that the editors of *The Times* and other Treasury papers, who had pointedly ignored him ever since he had been put into Newgate, should now have so much time for him, and he gained considerable satisfaction from calculating how many tens of thousands of pounds of taxpayer's money had been wasted on the pamphlets and the counterfeit *Register*.

Meanwhile, in a series of widely-read articles, Cobbett continued to explain and recommend Reform to his fellow countrymen. The most celebrated of those articles was probably his *Letter to the Luddites* which followed his *Letter to the Journeymen* at the end of 1816. This appeared to have two different but related purposes. The first was to make a sharp distinction between the rioters and the Reformers; the second was an attempt to convert the former into the latter. The article placed him in the strange position, for a man who hated industrialisation and took no interest in machines, of arguing in favour of the new technologies. He set out to prove, using many homely illustrations, that it was not machines that threw men out of work, but governments. It was logical, therefore, to stop smashing machines and start changing the government by petitioning for Reform. For he had now proved to them that, 'if Members of Parliament, for the last fifty years, had been *chosen by the people at large*, and *chosen annually*, agreeably to the old laws of the nation',[11] there would have been no war against the French, no additional taxes to pay for that war, and no unemployment and hunger as a consequence of those taxes.

Cobbett claimed, later, that the immediate reaction to his *Letter to the Luddites* had been an end to the rioting. 'I proved to them that the *riots must make matters worse*. And the effect, the wonderful effect was, that all riot and disposition to riot *ceased throughout the kingdom*, though the misery of the people had been increasing all the while.'[12] Bamford seemed to agree with that claim, for he wrote that, as a consequence of Cobbett's articles, 'riots soon became scarce, and from that time they never obtained their ancient vogue with the labourers of this country'. One cannot help wondering, however, whether the cumulative effects of all the hangings and transportations might not also have had something to do with this.

Cobbett's populist arguments were controvertible then and, with the benefit of hindsight, seem even more controvertible today. He had conveniently forgotten that, at the time of the French Revolution, he, and a vast majority of Englishmen, had been hot for war against the French, and a great deal hotter, for that matter, than Pitt ever was. He contrived never to mention the fact that all wars have to be paid for, sooner or later, by the taxpayers. Nor is it easy, a hundred and fifty years later, to support his thesis that universal suffrage necessarily prevents wars and results in less government, fewer taxes, and no corruption.

But when a publicist of Cobbett's genius was at work no government could expect to out-argue him when it came to convincing the common people. Nor, as the law stood, could he be silenced by trying him again for sedition. Cobbett defied the Government to discover anything seditious or illegal in any of his writings, and gleefully quoted Lord Sidmouth's statement in Parliament that 'he had regularly laid all the *mischievous publications* before the Law Officers of the Crown, and he was *sorry* to say that, hitherto, they had been unable to find out any thing which they could *prosecute with any chance of success*'. What the Government needed if Cobbett and the other Reform agitators were to be silenced, were emergency powers such as would only be granted if evidence of a widespread and dangerous conspiracy could be produced.

Cobbett knew this, and taunted them with it. 'They sigh for a PLOT. Oh, how they sigh! They are working and slaving and fretting and stewing; they are sweating all over; they are absolutely pining and dying for a plot.'[13] He was crowing too soon. Although the Luddite rioting had died down, there was considerable talk, if nothing more, of plans for an armed insurrection. If these were perhaps too vague to amount to plausible conspiracies, the Government had secret agents at work attempting to activate them into plausibility.

Events in 1816 and 1817 were working in the Government's favour in this respect. The Society of Spencean Philanthropists (Thomas Spence himself was now dead) organised a great demonstration at Spa Fields in London. At this they presented their somewhat naïve programme for a British Republic, land nationalisation and the 'single tax'. Henry Hunt was invited to address the meeting on behalf of the Reformers but, seeing the danger of being associated with the Spencean programme, he refused to speak to the Spencean theme. Thereupon the crowd split up. One part stayed to listen to Hunt deliver an orthodox and unexceptionable Reform speech. The rest, gulled into believing that the revolution might be at hand, decided to make immediate use of the occasion by engaging in a certain amount of looting.

Government spies had obtained a copy of the Spencean programme which was considered sufficiently treasonable for a few of their leaders to be put on trial. Evidence was given that the plot, if plot it was, had been going on for the past eight years. The idea of a conspiracy that had taken eight years to hatch and then had produced no more than a few looted London shops was too ludicrous for any jury to accept as proof of treason, and the accused were acquitted. No one laughed more heartily over this than Cobbett. 'Now, when your laughing fit is over, let me ask you, whether you ever heard of a *Plot* and *Insurrection* like this before: What, an eight years' Plot! a *good* insurrection.' Nevertheless the Government had moved towards one of its objectives which was to demonstrate that there were at least prima-facie connections between the Spenceans, who openly proposed to overthrow the Constitution, and the Reformers, who had always argued that they wanted nothing more than to have their ancient rights under the Constitution restored to them.

Hunt's presence at Spa Fields had helped the Government, even though he could prove that he had publicly dissociated himself from the Spenceans. What was even more useful was that Cobbett could also be smeared through his association with Hunt. One or two of the Spenceans were later involved in the much more serious Cato Street Conspiracy of 1820, which can, if one wishes, be taken as evidence that a few genuine insurrectionists must have been present at Spa Fields three years previously.

Cobbett, for all his jibes at the Government, now began to fear that it might act as it had acted at the height of the anti-Jacobin campaign of the 1790s; that is, it would take powers to suppress all forms of dissent and, more specifically, take steps to 'put Cobbett down'. The abortive hunger march on London that came to be known in Radical legend as The March of the Blanketeers, fresh violence in Nottingham, a traditional Luddite centre, and the disturbances that were blown up into the so-called Derbyshire Insurrection of 1817 all provided the Government with extra justification and Cobbett with further reason for fear.

Secret Committees sat in the Lords and the Commons to consider evidence of a common purpose underlying all these happenings, and to decide whether or not the Reformers, Cobbett, the *Registers* and the Hampden Clubs were parts of a national conspiracy to overthrow the Government. The Lords' Committee found that 'the leading malcontents had decided, by means of societies or clubs established in all parts of Great Britain under pretence of Parliamentary Reform, to infect the minds of all classes of the community . . . with a spirit of discontent and disaffection, of insubordination and contempt of all law, religion and morality, and to hold out to them the plunder and division of all property as the main object of their efforts . . . and no endeavours are omitted to prepare them to take up arms.'

The Commons Committee came to a similar conclusion, and declared that the aim of the conspiracy was 'a total overthrow of all existing establishments, and a division of the landed, and extinction of the funded, property of the country'. These references to the Reformers, and the mention made of 'funded property' pointed directly at Cobbett, the chief Reform propagandist and the principal advocate of 'an equitable adjustment'.

By March 1817 Parliament was ready to grant the Government the extraordinary powers it asked for. These included suspension of Habeas Corpus and powers for the magistrates to prevent or disperse all public meetings, to arrest any speaker uttering words 'calculated to stir up the people to hatred or contempt of the government', and to close any inns, meeting places, reading rooms or lecture halls where 'immoral, irreligious or seditious literature' of any description was kept. Any resistance to the magistrates would be punishable by death.

This was precisely the situation Cobbett had feared ever since he had been imprisoned in Newgate, and he had no doubt that the measures had been designed for the express purpose of greatly reducing the circulation of the cheap *Register*, or *Cobbett's Weekly Pamphlet* as he had begun to call it. Its largest distribution had been to inns, reading rooms and other meeting places where workers gathered to read and discuss the first newspaper that had ever been specifically addressed to them. Now, as any magistrate could cancel the licence of such meeting places for harbouring such 'seditious' literature, this particular point of sale would disappear. Nor could he, without fear of arrest, continue to travel the country making speeches criticising the Government and advocating Reform.

But, since Cobbett considered himself to be the target the Government was aiming at, the principal danger to himself lay in the suspension of Habeas Corpus and the passing of the Powers of Imprisonment Act. This allowed the Government to operate through what were, in effect, *lettres de cachet*. It no longer mattered whether or not Cobbett took care to stay this side of the laws of libel and sedition. He could now be thrown into prison at any time without cause given or any access to the courts.

Cobbett therefore consulted Lord Holland, even though Holland was one of the Whig grandees he had so recently been blackguarding. According to the account Holland later gave in his *Memoirs*, Cobbett offered to support Whig policies in the *Register* if, in return, the Whigs in Parliament would give him their protection. Holland, apparently, told him that the Whigs could not afford too close an association with such a notorious turncoat and rabble-rouser, but they might be able to work together at arm's length. Cobbett, he wrote, 'was alarmed at the threatened suspension of Habeas Corpus. He very unaffectedly acknowledged his distrust of his own nerves, and a dread of behaving meanly and basely if arrested; he therefore hinted at an intention, which he afterwards executed, of retiring to America . . .'[14]

Cobbett's suspicions of the Government's intentions regarding himself were largely confirmed as soon as Habeas Corpus was suspended on 4 March 1817. Lord Sidmouth, then Home Secretary, apparently sent him a message in which he offered Cobbett £10,000 if he would close the *Registers*, withdraw permanently from politics and retire to Botley. In an article written immediately after this offer, Cobbett wrote that he could not bear 'the horrid idea of being *silenced*; of sneaking to my farm and *quietly* leaving Corruption to trample out the vitals of my country'.[15] On the other hand, the threat was implicit in the offer. If he turned it down out of hand 'I must be blind not to see that a dungeon is my doom'.

He gave the messenger, therefore, neither a Yea nor a Nay but, as soon as he had left, Cobbett made preparations for an immediate and secret flight to the United States. That flight was severely criticised by those who had been his supporters as well as by those who had always been his enemies. He was accused of cowardice in running away when so many of his supporters stood firm and faced persecution and imprisonment as a consequence. People recalled that he had behaved in a similar fashion in 1792 at the time of the court martial. There was also much talk of his being more of a Yankee than an Englishman. Had he not, for the past five years, written articles which almost fulsomely praised America and the Americans? Had he not also sent his nephew, Henry Cobbett, to New York early in 1816, there to bring out an American edition of the *Register*? Although that had failed in a matter of months, had it not contained several articles by Cobbett praising American institutions and criticising the British Press, Parliament, Royal Family and political parties? What could all this mean except that he had been ingratiating himself with the Americans as a preparation for establishing himself in that country permanently, as other disloyal Englishmen, including Priestley and Paine, had done before him? There were even some who alleged that he had fled, not to escape the Government, nor to find better feathers for his nest in America, but merely to escape his English creditors, and that he had done so secretly because he was in imminent danger of being arrested for debt.

The article Cobbett wrote before fleeing the country, which he called *Mr Cobbett's Taking Leave of his Countrymen*, answered some of these criticisms at great length. He was acting prudently, he explained, because it would have been futile to act otherwise, and because he was considering the end, which was to ensure a reform of Parliament in his lifetime. If he stayed in England he could no longer work for that end: he would be confined either to his farms or a dungeon and would, in either case, be silenced. 'But if I remove to a country where I can write with perfect freedom, it is not only *possible*, but very *probable* that I shall, sooner or later, be able to render that cause lasting services.'

And so he gave his readers two assurances. 'Though I shall, if I live, be at a distance from you . . . my readers may depend on it, that it will not be more than *four months* from the *date of this address*, before the publication of the *Weekly Pamphlet* will be resumed in London.' This was followed by his second assurance:

Never will I own as my friend him who is not a friend of the people of England. I will never become a *Subject* or a *Citizen* in any other state, and will always be a *foreigner* in every country but England. Any foible that may belong to your character, I shall always willingly allow to belong to my own. And the celebrity which my writings have obtained, and which they will preserve, long and long after Lords Liverpool and Sidmouth and Castlereagh are rotten and forgotten, I owe less to my talents than to that discernment and that noble spirit in you, which have at once instructed my mind and warmed my heart; and, my beloved Countrymen, be you well assured, that the last beatings of that heart will be love for the people, for the happiness and the renown of England; and hatred of their corrupt, hypocritical, dastardly and merciless foes. Wm. COBBETT.

This was not the 'renegado', furtively sneaking away from England, about whom people would be talking in a day or two. This was Cobbett as, in all honesty, he saw himself. It is difficult to think of another English writer who could, without getting his tongue jammed into his cheek, simultaneously flatter his readers, blackguard his enemies and accuse himself of possessing so much talent and so much nobility of mind.

Mr Cobbett's Taking Leave of his Countrymen was left at the *Register* office, then at No. 8 Catherine Street, The Strand, on 21 March 1817, although it was not published until a fortnight later, after he had left the country. According to his daughter Anne, he then took leave of his wife in the following manner: 'As soon as Mama was in the room, Papa, his two hands on her shoulder, said, "Nancy, I must go to America". She said, "Billy, I'm glad of it." And so they parted for most of the next two and a half years.'[16]

The equanimity with which they parted may have been due to the fact that Cobbett, not knowing whether he would ever return, intended to have his family follow him to America. As it was he took his two oldest sons, William and John Morgan, with him when he set out for Liverpool on the following day. It was typical of him that, in the course of his flight to that port, he noticed and noted what he saw during the journey. The consequence was that the first article he sent back from the United States contained several passages describing the beauty and richness of the English country-side they had passed through as well as the poverty and miseries of so many of its inhabitants. It was as though he was taking a trial run before embarking on his future *Rural Rides*.

The Cobbetts left Liverpool on the American ship, the *Importer*. It was not an entirely enjoyable voyage. 'In all respects that can be named our passage was disagreeable; and, upon one occasion, very perilous from lightning, which struck the ship twice, shivered two of the masts, killed a man, struck several people slightly, between two of whom I was sitting without at all feeling the blow.'[17] Cobbett, of course, quarrelled with the Captain and with the other cabin passengers with the exception of 'a very pretty woman from Manchester, with two small children, going out to her husband' and 'a Mr Astor, son of a respectable Merchant of New York, who had been some years in Europe, who had travelled over the greater part of it, and who was perfectly civil and polite'.

Although Cobbett was met by a crowd of New Yorkers wanting to shake him by the hand, he had made up his mind that, whilst he was in the United States, he would have nothing to do with American politics or American journalism, but would devote his time to farming and authorship. The following day he crossed to Long Island where he stayed at an inn until he was offered the lease of Hyde Park Farm near North Hempstead.

CHAPTER SEVENTEEN

America Regained

'next to of course god america i
love you land of the pilgrims' and so forth . . .'
e.e. cummings: *next to of course god*

When Cobbett landed in the United States in April 1817, announcing that he had no intention of engaging in American politics or American journalism, he in fact, as a refugee, lacked the status for the one and the capital for the other. Moreover, to engage in either would have given substance to his enemies' allegations that he had long been preparing to turn Yankee. Had he done so – and he did at first entertain the idea – it is difficult to believe that his self-denying ordinance would have endured.

His first letters to his wife suggest that he was planning something more than a purely temporary exile on Long Island. She, when he fled, had been in her customary gravid condition, and the letter he sent from Hyde Park to Botley was full of careful instructions about when she should join him and what farm servants and household and farming equipment she should bring with her. She was not, he wrote on 19 May 1817, to attempt to travel before her confinement. On the other hand, she must cross the Atlantic before the autumn gales started in early September.

When she did undertake the crossing she was to bring 'the plate, linen and books' with her. The two Botley farm hands, referred to as 'J' and 'Dorland' who, with their wives and children were to accompany her, would, of course, travel steerage and, therefore, have to take their food with them. 'Tell J to be sure to *board himself*, and to take plenty of *flour*, onions, cheese, butter and potatoes; but especially *flour*.' J's wife could attend on Mrs. Cobbett whilst J and Dorland looked after the 'Dogs, Pigs, Turkeys, guns and other heavy things'.[1]

She was to tell J and Dorland that Cobbett would guarantee to keep them and their families for a period of two years, Cobbett finding them in 'house, lodging, board and everything but *clothes to wear*, they working for me during that time'. Each man would have, in addition, $200. This apparently generous offer was still something less than the going rate. A farm servant's wage in America at that time, as Cobbett himself recorded in his book *A Year's Residence in the United States*, published in 1819* was $1 a day and all found.

Farmers were beginning to emigrate from Britain to the United States in fairly large numbers, and it was not unusual for them to take farm servants, livestock and farm equipment with them in addition to their families. No sensible man, however, would embark on such an expensive and uncertain venture if he intended to return to England in a year or two. One must assume, therefore, that at that moment Cobbett contemplated a prolonged, if not permanent occupation of Hyde Park, which he described to his wife as 'a beautiful place; a fine park, orchards, gardens, fields and woods. A fine house too, but out of repair'.

Nevertheless, only two months later, he had already decided the conditions under which he would, or would not return to England. 'It is impossible that England can remain long in its present state. *More* must be done, or that which is done must be *undone*; and, if the latter take place and I am alive, I shall return. If the former take place: if a *direct Censorship* of the Press be adopted, which it must be very soon, and if it become evident that this sort of Bourbon government is to remain as long as force will uphold it, I shall, of course, not go to live under that government . . .'[2]

His English readers, however, were not to worry about how he would survive in his exile whilst he awaited his recall. 'In the *meanwhile* I must eat and drink say you. Very true, and, though a little serves me and all belonging to me, I have not the least doubt that we shall be able to get plenty of both from the *earth* . . . the *untaxed* earth. It would be idle to pretend that I have not the means of *living* here by my pen; but it is my intention to be a downright farmer, and to depend solely upon what I can get in that way.'

Wholly and solely a farmer was something Cobbett could never be. Less than a year later, whilst he was writing *A Year's Residence*, he felt it essential to reassure his readers that he had in no way deserted politics and the cause of Reform. 'Let not my countrymen suppose that these [farming] pursuits will withdraw my attention from, or slacken my zeal in, that cause which is common to us all. That cause claims, and has, my first attention and best exertion; that is the *business* of my life; these other pursuits are my

* Its sub-title explained, fairly comprehensively, what it was about: 'Treating of the Face of the Country, the Climate, the Soil, the Products, the Mode of Cultivating the Land, the Prices of Land, of Labour, of Food, of Raiment of the Expenses of House-Keeping and of the usual manner of Living; of the Manners and Customs of the People; and of the Institutions of the Country'.

recreation. KING ALFRED allowed eight hours for *recreation,* in the twenty-four, eight for *sleep,* and eight for *business.* I do not take my allowance of the two former.'

Yet, as always with Cobbett, the political and writing itches were stronger than the 'downright farming' one. Indeed, the more he wrote about farming the less time he spent at it:

> I expected to be able to devote more time to my farming than I afterwards found that I could so devote, without neglecting matters which I deem of great importance. I was, indeed, obliged to leave the greater part of my out-door's business wholly to my men, merely telling them what to do.[3]

These matters of greater importance were, of course, his *Register* articles and his books. With the first he hoped to preserve his political position in England, with the others to provide for his family and keep his creditors at bay. His financial situation, as usual, was difficult. He had fled to America on £500 borrowed from Thomas Hulme. The *Register* had resumed publication as soon as articles began to arrive from Long Island, but Sidmouth's measures had reduced its circulation and its profits had to be shared with the publisher who was now its titular owner. Neither his farms at Botley nor the one on Long Island could produce the large sums of money that were now needed. These he could only hope to earn by an increased use of his pen. And so, like another contemporary writer, Sir Walter Scott, he sought his salvation in the unending production of books. Even though he was twice as strong and even more prolific than that despised Scotsman, it was not strange that he found little time for his 'out-door's business'.

A Year's Residence is, amongst other things, an excellent farm diary, but it also gives very convincing accounts of American farming in general. Long Island itself was, to his mind, an example of all that any farming community should be. For there the farms were 'small in extent; no *great riches* amongst the farmers, and not the smallest appearance of want amongst the labourers'.[4] The land was not as good as in the Western Settlements, a region in which he took some interest, since the soil was light and the Island was not well-watered. But as compared with the richer lands then being opened up in Indiana and Illinois, Long Island had its compensations. One was a regular rainfall and free-draining land. 'The rains come down about once in fifteen days; they come in abundance for about twenty-four hours, and then all is fair and all is dry again immediately.' This combination of reliable rains and quick-drying soils was of the greatest importance to travellers as well as farmers in the days when land-drainage was not widely practised and heavy rains could leave fields waterlogged for weeks and turn roads into quagmires. Cobbett, returning from a journey in New Jersey, 'through such *mud* as I never saw before', rejoiced when he landed on Long Island and took 'a little light waggon that *whisked* me home over roads as dry and as smooth as gravel walks in an English Bishop's garden in the month of July'.

Then again, Long Island farmers were well-placed with regards to markets for their produce, a factor that in America of those days could determine whether one engaged in commercial or subsistence farming. The New York markets could be reached 'by a Steam-Boat in a few minutes, and this boat . . . forms the mode of conveyance from the Island to the City, for horses, waggons and everything else'. Farmers in the Western Settlements, on the other hand, might need to be good men at table. Many would be so far from any market for their produce that they might have to eat every scrap of beef, mutton and pork they produced.

Although it contained a park, orchards, woods, and a number of fields and meadows, Hyde Park was no larger than the generality of Long Island Farms. Nevertheless it proved too large for Cobbett to farm in the manner he desired. Farm labour was too scarce and too expensive for that. It was difficult for a man who had grown up in a Surrey hop-garden, who prided himself on the neatness and order of his Hampshire farms, and who had grown used to having a score of farm labourers at his disposal, to adjust to the rougher and readier methods that were needed in a country where there was an abundance of land and a shortage of labour.

Yet, in addition to his farming experiments (described in Chapter 11), he still attempted to maintain Hampshire standards of high farming. Since he liked his fields to be as smooth and as clean as a garden bed, he would plough two or three times to obtain that effect. He raised his roots, cabbages and Indian Corn in a nursery before transplanting them into the field instead of drilling them and chopping them out *in situ* as was the labour-saving custom of the Americans, who did not even know how to transplant properly. When a field grew foul he subjected it to the laborious process of 'paring and burning', and tried, probably in vain, to persuade his Long Island neighbours to do the same.

William and John Morgan, the two sons who had come with him to America, seem not to have been eager to turn farm labourers. Cobbett wrote sadly about this to his daughter Anne. 'The "Boys" are boiling to be *in the great and busy world*. They are eminently endowed for great things; and though I would have preferred them for the plough and the pruning-hook, it is their happiness, and not my taste that is to be considered'.[5]

Although, in the end, neither his wife nor his farmhands settled with him in America, he found and hired a Hampshire couple who were looking for work on Long Island, and who were related to a Botley family. Thomas Churcher suited Cobbett well as a farm servant, for he knew all about hedging and transplanting and other Hampshire farming methods. Mary Ann Churcher, his wife, suited Cobbett even better. Unlike the American woman who preceded her as Cobbett's housekeeper, she could always produce an apple pudding that was to Cobbett's taste. He recorded that fact in *A Year's Residence*. 'I have now got an English-woman-servant, and she makes us famous apple puddings, she knows very well how to get the apples within side of the paste. N.B. No man ought to come here, whose wife and daughters cannot make puddings and pies.'

Although Cobbett found it difficult to get American labour, and jibbed at the cost of it, he had nothing but admiration for the Long Island equivalents of his Hampshire chopsticks. His politics forced him to maintain that, since this was near-Arcadia – and certainly several leagues closer to Arcadia than England could ever be so long as she lay under the heel of the boroughmonger – those who lived and worked there must be at least quasi-Arcadians. But he also entertained a professional farmer's appreciation of their skill and ability. 'They mow four acres in a day . . . Besides the great quantity of work performed by the American labourer, his *skill*, the *versatility* of his talent, is a great thing. Every man can use an *axe*, a *saw*, and a *hammer* . . . Very few, indeed, who cannot kill and dress pigs and sheep, and many of them oxen and calves. This is a great convenience. It makes you so independent as to a main part of the means of housekeeping. All are ploughmen.'

He admired their physique and commended their manners. 'These "Yankees" are of all men I ever saw, the most active and the most hardy. They skip over a fence like a greyhound. They will catch you a pig in the open field by *racing* him down. They are afraid of nothing [and] are never servile, but always *civil*. Neither boobishness nor meanness mark their character.' Their athletic qualities he attributed to the fact that they were all '*tall* and well built. They are *bony* rather than fleshy; and they *live*, as to food, as well as a man can live.'[6] They were, he pointed out with a certain amount of *Schadenfreude*, the men who had crewed the victorious American frigates in the late war, and who had served with Jackson in 1814 when he defeated the British at New Orleans.

When Cobbett found anything to admire he was bound to bring up a political reason for doing so. The virtues of these Long

Islanders he naturally attributed to their 'free institutions of government. A man has a voice *because he is a man*, and not because he is the *possessor of money*. And shall I *never* see our English labourers in this happy state?' – In short, give the English labourers a vote and they will immediately race you down a pig as smartly as any Yankee.

But even these Yankee paragons lacked certain skills their English counterparts possessed. 'The operations necessary in miniature cultivation they are very awkward at. An American labourer uses a *spade* in a very awkward manner. They *poke the earth about* as if they had no eyes; and toil and muck themselves half to death to dig as much ground in a day as a Surrey man would dig in about an hour of hard work. *Banking* and *hedging* they know nothing about. They have no idea of the use of a *bill-hook*. An *axe* is their tool. Set one of these men upon a wood of timber trees and his slaughter will astonish you.'

As it was with the American farmhands, so it was with the American farmsteads – much praise tempered with small criticisms. The crops, in some districts at least, were 'prodigious'. The great, two-storeyed stone barns that housed produce, stock and implements were magnificent. As for the farmhouses, they provided him with the text for a sermon on American filial piety. 'They consist, almost without exception, of a considerably large and a very neat house with sash windows, and of a *small house*, which seems to have been *tacked on* to the large one.' The reason for this was that 'the father, or grandfather, while he was toiling for his children, lived in the small house, constructed chiefly by himself, and consisting of rude materials. The means accumulated in the small house, enabled a son to rear the large one; and, though when *pride* enters the door, the small house is sometimes demolished, few sons in America have the folly or want of feeling to commit such acts of filial ingratitude.'[7]

This evidence of 'the progress of wealth and ease and enjoyment' was attributed, of course, to 'the system of government under which it has taken place. What a contrast with the farmhouses in England! There the *little* farm-houses are falling into ruins, or are actually becoming cattle-sheds, or, at best, *cottages*, as they are called, to contain a miserable labourer, who ought to have been a farmer as his grandfather was.'

Nevertheless there were certain things in America that a Hampshire man might criticise, even though he were a Radical. There were, for instance, no hedges, although both Whitethorn and Blackthorn grew well. 'The fences are of *post and rail*. This arose, in the first place, from the abundance of timber that men knew not

how to dispose of. It is now become an affair of *great expense* . . .'
Cobbett accordingly announced his intention of teaching the
Americans how to plant, grow and maintain a quick-set hedge.

He thought that England scored heavily over America when it
came to the provision of farm cottages and the maintenance of
cottage gardens. 'Instead of the neat and warm little cottage, the
yard, cow-stable, pig-stye, hen-house, all in miniature, and the
garden nicely laid out and the paths bordered with flowers, while
the cottage door is crowned with a garland of roses or honey-
suckle; instead of these we here see the labourer content with a
shell of boards, while all around him is as barren as the sea-beach.'

But, if the American farmhands did nothing to improve their
immediate environment, their neglect could be explained by their
past history and their present attitudes. No labourer in America
expected to remain a labourer for ever. His cottage, therefore, was
never more than a temporary dwelling place. He had inherited this
attitude of mind from the first settlers who had 'found land so
plenty that they treated small plots with contempt'.

Even so, there was a moral to be drawn, and one that unconsciously revealed Cobbett's attachment to the concept of a hierarchical society. 'The example of neatness was wanting. There
were no gentlemen's gardens, kept as clean as a drawing room,
with grass as even as a carpet. From endeavouring to imitate
perfection men arrive at mediocrity; and those who have never
seen, or heard of perfection, in these matters, will naturally be
slovens.'[8] It had, in short, been bred into his peasant bones that the
'gentry' existed in order to set an example of perfection in all
things. It was the refusal of so many of the English landowners to
live up to this requirement that had caused him to attack them as
degenerates.

Since the absence of 'gentry' meant an absence of gardens
Cobbett determined to teach Americans all that he could about
gardening. This he did by writing *The American Gardener*, which
he published in the United States in 1819. (With his characteristic
economy in the use of material he republished it in a slightly
different form as *The English Gardener* ten years later.) In the
Preface to the first and American version he wrote that its purpose
was 'to cause the art of gardening to be better understood and
practised than it now is in America; and very few persons will deny
that there is, in this case, plenty of room for improvement'.

Cobbett could not, of course, avoid describing the American
countryside, which he did with that remarkable ability to read the
land from the underlying rocks to the tops of the trees that was his
particular gift. The trees especially delighted him. The mere

catalogue he gave of those that grew on Long Island suggested that he delighted in their names almost as much as he delighted in their utility and beauty. 'The Walnut of two or three sorts, the Plane, the Hickory, Chestnut, Tulip Tree, Cedar, Sassafras, Wild Cherry (sometimes 60 feet high), more than fifty sorts of Oaks, and many other trees, but especially the Flowering Locust, or Acacia, which, in my opinion, surpasses all other trees . . . The Orchards constitute a feature of great beauty. Every farm has its orchard, and in general, of cherries as well as of apples and pears.'[9]

Nevertheless he found the American countryside wanting in two important particulars:

There were many birds in summer, and some of very beautiful plumage. There were some wild flowers, and some English flowers in the best gardens. But, generally speaking, they were birds without song, and flowers without smell. The linnet, the skylark, the goldfinch, the woodlark, the nightingale, the bullfinch, the blackbird, the thrush, and all the rest of the singing tribe were wanting in these beautiful woods and orchards of garlands. When these latter had dropped their blooms, all was gone in the flowery way. No shepherd's rose, no honey-suckle, no daisies, no primroses, no cowslips, no bluebells, no daffodils, which, as if it were not enough for them to enchant the sight and the smell, must have names, too, to delight the ear.

It usually suited Cobbett's own bluff, John Bull image to ignore or criticise music, poems, plays and buildings in which other men found beauty; but a man who had no poetry in his blood could never have produced such a litany of flower names. Nevertheless, being Cobbett, he had to end his description of American bird life by reverting, with an almost perverse ingenuity, to the subject of Reform. 'There were indeed birds which bore the name of robin, blackbird, thrush and goldfinch; but, alas, the thing at Westminster has, in like manner, the *name* of Parliament, and speaks the voice of the people whom it pretends to represent, in much the same degree that the blackbird spoke with the voice of its namesake in England.'[10]

Cobbett never travelled in the United States in the prolonged and systematic manner in which he later undertook his *Rural Rides* across Britain. Nevertheless, since he was now, for the first time, recording them in a book, such journeys as he did make are of interest, both because of the pictures they give of America at that time, and because one can see clear evidence of the skills he would eventually display in *Rural Rides*.

Business took him frequently to New York. It was perhaps because he never had to live there that he found it more attractive than the 'Great Wen', even though it was already, after London, 'perhaps the first commercial and maritime city in the world'. It was still, in those days, part of a setting of overall natural beauty. 'Man's imagination can fancy nothing so beautiful as its bay and port, from which immense rivers sweep up on the sides of the point of land, on which the city is. Those rivers are continually covered with vessels of various sizes bringing the produce of the land, while the bay is scarcely less covered with ships going in and out from all parts of the world. The city itself is a scene of opulence and industry; riches without insolence, and labour without grudging.'[11]

In spite of its large population of immigrants, sailors and dockers, New York was, according to Cobbett, a remarkably peaceful place: 'Never do we hear of hanging; scarcely ever a robbery; men go to bed with scarcely locking their doors; and never is there seen in the streets what is called in England, a *girl of the town*.'

What particularly impressed Cobbett about New York was that it contained comparatively few paupers and almost no beggars. Those who did answer to either description were generally either freshly arrived immigrants or negroes. 'There is a class of persons here of a description very peculiar; namely, the *free negroes*. Whatever may have been the motives, which led to their emancipation, it is very certain, that it has saddled the white people with a charge. These negroes are a disorderly, improvident set of beings; and the paupers *in the country* consist *almost wholly* of them . . . a pauper who is a white *native American*, is a great rarity.'

Cobbett always placed a high value on cleanliness and he found the Americans, in this respect, less clean than the English. He once remarked that there was more dirt to be found upon the necks and faces of one American family than could be found 'upon the skins of all the people in the three parishes of Guildford'. (Guildford, the local market town of his childhood, was always for him the touchstone of excellence.) He found that most American cities and towns were squalid, though he was honest enough to mention some exceptions. They were cleaner in Pennsylvania, especially among the Quakers, 'and I am told, that, in the New England States, the people are as neat and as cleanly as they are in England. The sweetest flowers, when they become putrid, stink the most; and a nasty woman is the nastiest thing in nature'. But he thought the American custom of turning pigs loose in the streets to act as scavengers entirely sensible and wondered why the New York and Philadelphia corporations prohibited it.

Cobbett made several trips to Pennsylvania, generally to visit old friends of his Peter Porcupine days. One visit, however, which took him to Harrisburgh and Lancaster, was undertaken in order to revive an old grievance rather than to renew an old friendship. 'It had, for its principal object, an appeal to the justice of the Legislature of that state for redress for great loss and injury sustained by me, nearly twenty years ago, in consequence of the tyranny of one M'KEAN, who was then the Chief Justice of that State.' It was a fruitless journey in that respect; he was granted no redress and not a penny of all that he had lost over the Rush case was ever returned to him.

It gave him an opportunity, however, to visit Lancaster, 'the largest inland town in the United States'. It was, he wrote, a good clean place, with 'no beggarly houses. All looks like *ease* and *plenty*. Nothing *splendid* and nothing *beggarly*.' He ended this description with a quotation that came as close as anything could to encapsulating his basic social philosophy: 'The people of this town seem to have had the prayer of HAGAR granted them: "Give me, O Lord, neither *poverty* nor *riches*".'

The longest journey described in *A Year's Residence*, one to the Western Settlements, was one that Cobbett made, as it were, by proxy. The actual traveller was that same Thomas Hulme who had lent Cobbett the £500 with which he fled to America. The *Journal* Hulme kept during his travels was printed in Part Three of *A Year's Residence*, Cobbett adding an Introduction explaining why this had been done. It all had to do with an argument Cobbett was conducting with Morris Birkbeck concerning farming in the Western Settlements.

Birkbeck, a one-time Suffolk farmer had, after extensive travels in America, bought a large tract of land in the newly opened territory between the Wabash Rivers. It was his intention to sell off parcels of it to British immigrants and so establish what would amount to a British farming colony. He had consulted Cobbett about this when he was in London in 1816, and Cobbett had advised against it. When Birkbeck ignored him, went ahead with his project and actually published two books on his schemes, Cobbett had at least two reasons for anger. As a self-confessed expert on America he believed he should be listened to. He also believed that English farmers would never succeed in the Western Settlements. If they had to emigrate to the United States – and he opposed emigration because that was precisely what the Malthusians and the boroughmongers were encouraging – then they ought to emigrate to the Eastern States where they would find cleared land, established farms, and conditions not very different from those they were accustomed to in England. Pioneering the prairies, Cobbett argued, was best left to the native Americans, who had been born, as it were, with an axe in their hand, a gun over their shoulder, and a strong urge to push westwards into the wilderness.

Cobbett pursued his argument with Birkbeck even more vigorously now that he was himself farming in the United States. He very much wanted to visit Birkbeck's settlement himself, if only to find evidence to buttress his argument and proofs of Birkbeck's folly. However, '*I could not go* to the Western Countries; and the accounts of others were seldom to be relied on . . . Yet, it was desirable to make an attempt, at least, towards settling the question: "Whether the Atlantic or the Western Countries were the best for *English farmers* to settle in".'

It was at this stage that Thomas Hulme visited him at Hyde Park and told him that he proposed to tour the Western Countries before deciding where to settle in America. Hulme was a Lancastrian who came from farming stock but had made a considerable fortune in industry. He had been one of the leaders of the Reform Movement in the North of England, he was a close friend of Major Cartwright, and he hated boroughmongers, parsons, establishment politicians and drunkards even more heartily than Cobbett. The Luddite troubles and the repression that had followed them had persuaded him that he must emigrate to America and, after a preliminary reconnaissance in 1815, and after consulting Cobbett on the subject the following year, he had finally transferred himself, his family and his money to the United States in 1818.

Hulme settled, eventually, in Philadelphia, where he became a prominent industrialist and took some part in American politics. Now, however, before deciding where to settle, he proposed to tour the Western Countries in order to study their potential for industrial development. 'When Mr HULME proposed to make a Western Tour, I was very much pleased, seeing that, of all the men I knew, he was the most likely to bring back an *impartial* account of what he should see.'[12]

Hulme's journey took him by raft, skiff, steam-boat, horseback and waggon from Pittsburgh to Louisville and back, with many diversions, including one to look at Birkbeck's colony. His *Journal* is an important historical document, since it constitutes one of the earliest studies ever made by a foreign industrialist of industrial developments and potential in those parts of the United States. However, the fact that he was primarily interested in natural resources, water power, transport, mills and factories meant that he was less interested in the countryside and its inhabitants, although he did indulge in as many political and moralising digressions as Cobbett might have done. On the whole, however, one could wish that it had been Cobbett who had made the journey and had written the Journal. We would have been told rather more about the settlers and their way of life, and the abuse of English politicians and American drunkards would have been more amusing.

Hulme's comments on Birkbeck's colony were not as critical as Cobbett might have wished. Nevertheless they provided him with some of the facts and figures he needed for the detailed attack on that venture he published in Part Three of *A Year's Residence*. Cobbett never abandoned his interest in, or changed his views on, emigration to the United States. He wrote about it in several articles and finally, in 1829, published his *Emigrant's Guide*, a work which, though it might not have lived up to the promise of its title as a practical handbook for the would-be emigrant, remains one of the most delightful of his lesser works.

Cobbett had enjoyed being famous ever since his Peter Porcupine days. On the other hand, as a Radical, he had to commend the egalitarian manners of the Americans, who refused to be deferential to any man, however famous, powerful or rich he might be. They never even, in those days, allowed a man a Mister to his name. 'Men, be they what they may, are generally called by their *two names* without anything prefixed or added.' This he thought admirable,* but he could not help adding, 'I am one of the greatest men in this country at present; for people in general call me "Cobbett", though the Quakers provokingly persevere in putting the *William* before it, and my old friends in Pennsylvania, use even the word *Billy*, which, in the very sound of the letters, is an antidote to every thing like thirst for distinction'. He was always pleased when he was recognised, and delighted when some English traveller or native American made a pilgrimage to Hyde Park to introduce himself to him. There was one English pilgrim, however, who published an account of his pilgrimage which so angered Cobbett that he felt it essential to add a Second Postscript to *A Year's Residence* in order to deal with him. This was a certain Thomas Fearon, who introduced himself to Cobbett as a fellow-Reformer who had been sent to America to prepare the way for other Reformers who were proposing to emigrate. Fearon, after his return to England, published *Sketches of America* which contained an account of his visit to Cobbett in exile. Extracts from that

---

* Cobbett had obviously forgotten how much the American weakness for honorific and largely meaningless titles had amused him when he was Peter Porcupine.

account were republished in the New York papers under the title of *A Visit to Cobbett*.

Fearon began by observing how melancholy it was to see 'this celebrated man leading an isolated life in a foreign land, a path rarely trod, fences in ruins, the gate broken, a house mouldering to decay'. He then went on to suggest that he had enjoyed a long conversation with Cobbett who had given him the impression that he 'thought meanly of the American people'. He ended with a pen portrait and character sketch of the great man. 'His eyes are small, and pleasingly good natured. To a French gentleman present, he was attentive; with his sons, familiar; to his servants, easy; but to all, in his tone and manner, resolute and determined. He feels no hesitation in praising himself, and evidently believes that he is eventually destined to be the Atlas of the British nation . . . My impressions of Mr Cobbett are, that those who know him would like him if they can be content to submit unconditionally to his dictation . . .'[13]

It is difficult to decide which parts of this angered Cobbett most or caused him to take a series of sledge hammers to the buzzings of such a mosquito. Far from the fences being in disrepair and the house neglected, the Second Postscript spluttered, Hyde Park was a better cared-for and more elegant mansion than a whipper-snapper like Fearon had ever put foot in before. He had enjoyed nothing like an intimate conversation with Cobbett, and so could know nothing of what the latter thought of the Americans. Fearon had arrived unannounced and whilst Cobbett was out shooting. Mrs. Churcher, the housekeeper, had so mistrusted the look of him that she had put him in the kitchen where she could keep an eye on him. When Cobbett returned, 'We took him at first for a sort of *spy*. William thinks he is a shopkeeper's clerk; I think he has been a tailor. I observed that he carried his elbows close to his sides, and his arms below the elbow in a horizontal position . . . Is it not monstrous to suppose, that I should *praise myself*, and show that I believed myself destined to be *the Atlas of the British nation*, in my conversations of a few minutes with an utter stranger, and that, too, a blade whom I took for a decent tailor, my son William for a shopkeeper's clerk, and Mrs Churcher, with less charity, for a slippery young man, or at best an Exciseman?'

All Cobbett claimed to remember of Fearon's conversation was that he had complained that American women were reluctant to enter into 'social intercourse' with him, and that he had spent the previous night in a negro woman's hut. It was to be expected, Cobbett commented, showing a pretty regard for American womanhood and the niceties of class distinction, that the only

American women likely to have anything to do with such a man as Fearon should be black ones. 'Such a man can know nothing of the *people of America*. He has *no channel* through which to *get at them*. And, indeed, why should he? Can he go into families of people at home? Not he, indeed, beyond his own low circle. Why should he do it here then? Did he think he was coming here to live at *free quarters*? The black woman's hut, indeed, he might force himself into with impunity: sixpence would insure him a reception there; but it would be a shame, indeed, if *such a man* could be admitted to unreserved intercourse with *American ladies*. *Slippery* as he was, he could not slide into their good graces, and into the possession of their fathers' soul-destroying dollars; and so he is gone home to curse the . . . *Americans*.'

Fearon's comments had not been so critical that they merited such a reply from a man who called himself a Radical and a democrat, professed to despise social snobberies, and had so loudly praised the absence of such snobberies in American society. The postscript illustrates one of the less attractive aspects of his character. Cobbett claimed for himself the right to criticise anyone and everyone, often in a most scurrilous manner, but he was driven into paroxysms of rage if anything even mildly critical of himself was ever spoken or written. Hazlitt remarked on this trait: 'Like an overgrown schoolboy, he is so used to have it all his own way, that he cannot submit to anything like competition. He must lay on all the blows, and take none. He is bullying and cowardly; a Big Ben in politics, who will fall upon others and crush them by his weight, but is not prepared for resistance, and is soon staggered by a few smart blows.'

That Cobbett was a bully can scarcely be doubted: that he was a coward, can. But then it is customary for Radical publicists to be more savagely critical of fellow Radicals than they generally are of others. It has to be added that, unworthy though Cobbett's attack on Fearon was, it was most efficiently conducted, and much may be forgiven him for the 'tailor' passage and for the admirable phrase about 'soul-destroying dollars'.

Birkbeck and Fearon apart, however, most of *A Year's Residence* was devoted to admiration rather than criticism. There was scarcely a single aspect of American life that was not to be admired and favourably compared with what was prevalent in England. This was especially the case in that part of the work which covered the character, economy, laws, religion, sport, food, customs and housekeeping problems of the Americans. All were admirably and admiringly described. If he discussed the price of groceries, they were half as dear and twice as good as any that could be found in

England. American hospitality was a perpetuation of former English standards of hospitality 'which Boroughmonger's taxes have long since driven out of England . . . [where] in fact there is no *law of property* left. The Bishop-begotten and hell-born system of Funding has stripped England of every vestige of what was her ancient character. Her hospitality along with her freedom have crossed the Atlantic . . .'

Thereupon he described how, as the guest of an American farmer in quite a small way, he was surprised to see no less than fourteen fat hogs slaughtered and turned into sausages, hams and pork all in one day and all for domestic consumption. 'This led me to ask, "Why, in God's name, what do you eat in a year?" ' The answer listed more fat hogs, 'four beeves and forty-six fat sheep' not to mention suckling pigs, lambs, 'the produce of *seventy hen fowls* . . . good parcels of geese, ducks and turkeys, but not to forget a garden of three quarters of an acre and the *butter of ten* cows, not one ounce of which is ever sold!' Here, indeed, was that virtuous circle of low taxes and high living, of ample self-sufficiency and open-hearted hospitality Cobbett so longed to re-introduce into England.

He found the American women to be admirable housewives. But they also '*read a great deal*' and were in possession of 'an habitual and even an hereditary *good humour*. These ladies can converse with you upon almost any subject, and the ease and gracefulness of their behaviour are surpassed by those of none of even our best-tempered English women. They fade at an earlier age than in England; but, till then, they are as beautiful as the women in Cornwall, which contains, to my thinking, the prettiest women in our country. However, young or old, blooming or fading, well or ill, rich or poor, they still preserve their *good humour*.'

Cobbett had the habit, irritating, perhaps, to the feminist, of treating women with great respect, indeed, but as though, being quite different creatures, they needed to be differently classified. Just as, in *A Year's Residence*, he generalised about American and Cornish beauty, so, in *Rural Rides*, he used to generalise geographically. Sussex women, for example, were the prettiest in all of the South of England. Those from around High Wycombe, though also pretty, were noticeably large boned, large featured and 'more like the girls of America, and that is saying quite as much as any reasonable woman can expect or wish for'. In much the same way the women of Kent resembled their counterparts across the Channel in the Pays de Caux. The women of North Wales, for their part, were 'just what we see the milk-women in London. Low in stature but strong . . . small round faces; very fresh-coloured; very pretty; but it is all *hard*; it is not *like* the assemblage of softness and sweetness that you see . . . in the girls in Sussex and Kent.' These Welsh women set him off on another hobby-horse, and the nutritionalist must have taken over from the anthropologist, for he added: 'Such appears to be the difference between the effect of rearing cattle and of eating them when fat.'

Sport, so far as Cobbett was concerned, meant either hunting or shooting. Americans did not follow the hounds in the English fashion, but they had much better shooting. Praising it led Cobbett into his celebrated defence of 'blood sports' and he returned to the subject in a letter to Henry Hunt in which he mixed sport and politics in an attempt to persuade the latter to join him on Long Island for the woodcock shooting. 'What say you to a shooting party here? If you were to set out, I should not wonder if the Borough-mongers, to their other suspensions, were to add a suspension of the prayer for those that "travel by water". However, I hope you will not let the fear of this stop you. The wood-cock shooting is just begun here. Anything of a shot will kill *ten or twelve brace a day. You* would kill a hundred brace every day . . . Partridges are very abundant. *Plovers* are shot all round about here in great numbers. Deer-hunting is going on in October and November at about 20 miles distance. And, observe, the county in which I live is more thickly-settled than your part of Hampshire.'

Having set out the sporting attractions of Long Island, Cobbett added the political ones: 'Here *anybody* shoots *anywhere* . . . Think of it! A hundred brace of wood-cocks a day. Think of *that*! And never to see the hang-dog face of a tax-gatherer. Think of *that*! No Alien Acts here. No long-sworded and whiskered Captains. No Judges escorted from town to town and sitting under the guard of dragoons . . . No hangings and rippings up. No Castleses and Olivers. No Stewarts and Perries, No Cannings, Liverpools, Castlereaghs, Eldons, Ellenboroughs or Sidmouths. No Bankers. No squeaking Wynnes. No Wilberforces. Think of *that*! No Wilberforces!'[14]

Here, then, in Cobbett's reading of it, was a country without poverty or paupers, where good living and good sport prevailed, where men treated each other as equals and no man paid deference to wealth. Here religion was free, and those who went to church supported their pastor with their voluntary subscriptions and those who did not were not forced to pay tithes. Here the very worst that could be said about the natives was that they drank too much: 'You can go into hardly any man's house, without being asked to drink wine or spirits, even *in the morning*. They are quick at meals . . .

seem to care little about what they eat and never talk about it. This, which arises out of the universal abundance of good and even fine eatables, is very amiable. You are here disgusted with none of those *eaters by reputation* that are to be found, especially amongst *the Parsons*, in England; fellows that unbutton at it. Nor do the Americans *sit and tope much after dinner*, and talk on till they get into nonsense and *smut* . . . But they tipple . . .'

Tippling was almost the sole un-Arcadian quality Cobbett discovered in his Yankee Arcadians. He found everything else about them so admirable that our credulity would be suspended less than half-way through his account if we did not remember what, as Peter Porcupine, he had written in dispraise of the Americans twenty years earlier. The one is an antidote to the other: the later excess of praise cancels out the earlier excess of abuse. That done, we are left, between Porcupine and Cobbett, with a great body of writings on the subject of America which, taken all in all, has never been equalled by any other English writer. So long as Englishmen retain any interest in Americans, and Americans retain any interest in their past, that particular section of Cobbett's work will continue to provide material for historians of both nations to work on, and a great deal for the lay reader to enjoy.

But Cobbett's admiring contemplation of the American scene was not allowed to interfere with or diminish his concern for the political condition of England. There were still articles to be written, week after week, for the *Register*. Since these had to be written two months and more before they could be published they lacked much of the bite and relevance that had distinguished them when written in England. Also Cobbett's enduring conversion to Radicalism and Reform had made his political articles predictable and considerably less interesting. There were only a certain number of things he could say, and he had condemned himself to saying them again and again. The element of *déjà lu* was already evident in almost every one of the articles he wrote from Long Island. Parliament, with its 'pretended Elections and artificial Debates' was a sham. History had already condemned the boroughmongers to extinction. Reform had become inevitable. Sidmouth had passed his 'Gagging Acts' for the specific purpose of silencing William Cobbett. 'Parson' Malthus was an un-Christian and unnatural monster. Wilberforce was a sanctimonious humbug. And so he went on, pursuing themes he had already made wearisome through repetition.

The sad fact was that he would pursue those same themes throughout the rest of his journalistic career. He had once dazzled his readers with a succession of political somersaults. Even after he had arrived at his ultimate creed he had, for a time, held his readers with the vigour and novelty of his arguments in support of it. From now on, however, it was the style rather than the content of his articles that his readers looked forward to. His opinions, over the last twenty years of his life, could safely be taken as read, but never his eloquence, his invention, his scurrility, or his wit.*

Two of his Long Island articles for the *Register*, however, have to be specially mentioned. The first of these was as much concerned with the state of affairs in the Americas as it was with British politics. It even has a certain present relevance. It dealt with Britain's foreign policy, a subject on which Cobbett could display better judgment than when he immersed himself in domestic and party politics.

The article, which was published in the cheap *Register* of 27 December 1817, took the unusual form of a humble petition to the Prince Regent, a person Cobbett had never before, and never would again approach with any notable degree of humility. In it he begged the Prince to promote government support for the various independence movements that had recently spread throughout Latin America.

These had, for the most part, started as loyalist risings against a king whom Napoleon had placed on the Spanish throne in the ample shape of his brother, Joseph Bonaparte. But when a Bourbon monarch was restored in 1813, many of the Creoles were unwilling to return to their allegiance to Spain, and their resistance movements developed into a series of revolutionary struggles for complete independence. Spain's fight to re-establish her rule in what had been her American colonies continued for several years, with the Creoles proclaiming a number of ultimately fissiparous republics whose independence they found it difficult to maintain, and which those European monarchs who were members of the Holy Alliance refused to recognise.

When Cobbett urged the Prince Regent in 1817 to recognise and support these republics he was, in terms of British foreign policy, some years in advance of his time. It was not until 1822 that

---

* Sir Henry Lytton Bulwer, the diplomat and man of letters, writing thirty years after both Cobbett and the *Register* were dead, remembered how: 'Whatever a man's talents, whatever a man's opinions, he sought the *Register* on the day of its appearance with eagerness and read it with amusement, partly because he was sure to see his friends abused. But partly also because he was certain to find, amidst a great many lies and abundance of impudence, some felicitous nickname, some excellent piece of practical looking argument, some capital expressions, and very often some marvellously fine writing.' (*Historical Characters*: 1867)

411

Canning became Foreign Secretary, and not until 1824 that he evolved a policy, as he put it, of 'calling the New World into existence, to redress the balance of the Old'. If he had said as much in 1817, one almost wonders whether Cobbett would have proposed something so similar in his *Petition*. Canning ranked too high in Cobbett's demonology for him to wish to agree with him on anything.

But in 1817 it was no part of official policy even to recognise the new and the not-yet-born republics of South America, nor was there any great public demand for such a policy, although the 'left' was already stirring in support of the revolutionaries. Reformers who were not advocates of revolution at home were by no means opposed to them abroad, especially if they were against a Bourbon monarch and defied the doctrine of 'legitimacy' on which the hated Holy Alliance was based. Nevertheless, Cobbett's public support in the *Petition* for the revolution in South America made him something of a pioneer. His brother-in-Reform, Lord Cochrane, had not yet left to take command of the infant Chilean Navy, and the flow of British soldiers and sailors of fortune to South America was not yet at its full.

Although he was not a man for abstract political concepts, Cobbett probably believed, as did most other Radicals, that the South American revolutionaries must be fighting for precisely the same things as the Reformers were struggling for in England; namely democracy, freedom, the rule of law and an end to military oppression. But Cobbett always thought of himself as a practical man, and so the principal argument he used with the Prince was that of British self-interest. Recognising and supporting the South American republics would win Britain a position of special advantage throughout that continent, and would do more than restore to her all she had lost when she lost her North American colonies. New and potentially rich markets would, for the first time, be opened to her. Her maritime and trading supremacy would be confirmed in the Pacific as well as the Atlantic. She would be able, as never before, to influence the course of events throughout the Americas.

This, he assured the Prince, was what the various South American leaders he had met in New York had told him, and this, he believed was the prize that only Britain could win. 'No one is, as it appears to your humble petitioner, nearly so deeply interested as England in this grand Revolution . . .' The *Petition,* taken as a whole and in the context of British foreign policy at that particular moment, displayed at least traces of the foresight and breadth of vision that are supposed to distinguish the statesman from the politician and the political journalists. Indeed, Canning's reputation as one of the more successful statesmen of his time would largely be based on his having undertaken a similar *tour d'horizon* and having arrived at similar conclusions some five years later.

When one considers that Cobbett wrote the *Petition* at the same time as he was embarking on a new farm and on a variety of farming experiments, was carrying out his studies of American life, and was writing about such diverse subjects as the environmental advantages of using pigs as scavengers and the electoral laws of each of the States in the Federation, one cannot help being impressed by his complexity and by the far from superficial diversity of his talents, qualities which contradicted the image Cobbett had accepted for himself which, as Carlyle put it, was that of 'the pattern John Bull of his age'.

There was, indeed, a great deal of John Bull in Cobbett. His love of the countryside and country ways, his traditionalism, his undeferential, damn-your-eyes attitude to authority, his fine inheritance of native prejudices, even his physical appearance seemed to have predestined him for that part, which he played with the utmost sincerity and to the top of his bent. Whilst he was playing it England, and only England, occupied his mind, and he disregarded almost anything that happened and almost anyone who had been born north of the Tweed or south of the Channel.

But there was also the other William Cobbett. This was the man who took a deep interest in foreign affairs and who, although not always above using foreign policy to support his own current political arguments, had always had a clear vision of what Britain's position and policies in the world ought to be. This was the Atlanticist who, perhaps more than anyone else at that time, concerned himself with the state of Anglo-American relations. And this was, above all, the experienced but ever curious traveller who spoke and wrote French almost as well as he did English and who could make himself almost as much at home at Fredericton, Tilques or Wilmington as he could at Botley. Few contemporary politicians or writers could have arrived at their opinions on foreign policy by studying the people, language, economies, politics and customs of other countries as thoroughly as he had. But then few had arrived at their opinions through drilling English soldiers in Canada, teaching English grammar to Frenchmen and French grammar to Englishmen, farming on Long Island, instructing the Americans in politics and gardening, and defining the imperatives of British foreign policy to anyone who would listen.

Almost as soon as he settled at Hyde Park Cobbett addressed a series of six Letters to John Goldsmith of Hambledon and Richard

413

Hinxman of Chilling which were published in the *Register* under the general title of *A History of the Last Hundred Days of English Freedom*. Goldsmith and Hinxman had been, respectively, Chairman and Seconder of that 'meeting of the people of Hampshire to Petition for a Reform in the Commons House of Parliament' which Cobbett had done so much to inspire and organise shortly before his flight. In so far as the Letters were concerned with that giant Petition they did little more than repeat the arguments Cobbett had already used in England, though the three thousand miles of the Atlantic gave him the licence to argue more fiercely. But now Cobbett, as the general title suggested, wanted to do more: to present, in narrative form, a history of all those events, from the start of the Luddite riots to the Spa Fields Meeting and the subsequent persecutions and repressions, that had led up to his flight and the imposition, as he saw it, of a 'Bourbon-style' form of government in England.

This was the first indication Cobbett gave of his growing ambition to write that which he was least suited to write – the past and present history of England, and it is because this apprentice effort already demonstrates how ill-equipped he was as an historian that it deserves examination.

If the *Last Hundred Days* failed as a narrative it was because of its constant digressions. Cobbett felt it essential every now and again to interrupt his account of when and how Lord Liverpool (who had become Prime Minister in 1812) had robbed Englishmen of their freedom in order to argue his own case and explain how grossly he had been oppressed and maligned. Each and every attack on him in the Government Press had to be refuted. He had not gone into exile because he owed the Stamp Office £80,000 or his creditors £30,000, or the owner of Sherecroft, the house he had taken in Botley, one year's rent plus dilapidations. He had not cheated his creditors by salting his money away in New York and then disappearing to escape imprisonment for debt. Long passages which should have been devoted to straightforward narrative were devoted, instead, to elaborate rebuttals of such allegations, whilst others were used to provide equally elaborate reassurals to his friends. He was not, as some of them alleged, a deserter from the cause. He was no cock who, having crowed too loudly, then fled the dunghill, as had been insinuated at the time of the court martial and was being insinuated now. Rather he had, like any good soldier, withdrawn to a better position from which he could more effectively fight for a restoration of British freedom and in defence of Reform.

Considered as a history of all that had recently happened in

England, the *Last Hundred Days* had the advantage of having been written by a man who had had some part in the making of that history. But this was also, in his case, a disadvantage. Although he had not stayed in England to suffer under Sidmouth, Cobbett still felt himself to have been Sidmouth's principal victim. His was, therefore, a victim's version of history, which took not the slightest account of his persecutor's side of the story.

What was even more damaging, since he aspired to be an historian, was his attachment to conspiracy theories. He could not see what had happened as the reactions of a government which, remembering how the French Revolution had started, was determined to prevent an English one, and had overreacted as a consequence. For the Government had also been possessed by a conspiracy theory. It had been known for years that there were English Jacobins at work, and that there were as many hungry, desperate and violent men in the factory towns and the countryside as there once had been *sans-culottes* in France. The Reformers were threatening the Government's power-base from within the Constitution. What was more natural, then, than to believe that they were all parts of a revolutionary conspiracy to overthrow the Constitution itself?

Cobbett, of course, preferred his own theory to the Government's, which he did not attempt to consider. It seemed to him self-evident that what had happened was the gradual unfolding of a carefully prepared conspiracy to keep the Tories in power and perpetuate the Pitt System, even if this meant suspending part of the Constitution and governing by force.

It never occurred to Cobbett that his own conspiracy theory was little more than a mirror-image of the Government's, and that each of them was basically untenable. Parliament was no more prepared to surrender its powers to another Cromwell than the Reformers were prepared to produce another Robespierre. However, Cobbett made his conspiracy theory seem somewhat more plausible than the Government's, in spite of all the evidence the latter had collected and manufactured for the Secret Committee – perhaps even because of it. By the time Cobbett had dealt once more with the Sealed Bag, the Government spies and *agents provocateurs*, the giving of special powers to the magistrates, the frequent calling-out of the troops and the rigged trials with their special juries and savage punishments, he indeed made it seem possible that Liverpool and his gang were engaged in a conspiracy to prevent any further advance of democracy, cost what it may.

Yet, for all its one-sidedness and conspiracy theories, *The Last Hundred Days* remains a work of inspirational, if not of historical importance. It was the first attempt made by a writer of any authority to describe what turned out to be the dawn of the heroic age of British Radicalism. The Luddite Riots, the Derbyshire Insurrection, the Spa Fields Meeting, the March of the Blanketeers and the Great Hampshire Reform Petition were all very recent events. The Repression, with its dragoons, hangings, imprisonments and transportations was a part of everyday life. The Peterloo Massacre was less than a year ahead and the Tolpuddle Martyrs no more than fifteen. Whenever the 'Left' in Britain today wishes, in one of its moments of piety, to consider its Founding Fathers, it ought to remember Cobbett's *History of the Last Hundred Days of English Freedom*. In most great movements, hagiography is generally far more important than history, and *The Last Hundred Days* is important to the English left for exactly the same reason as Foxe's *Book of Martyrs* was once important to English Protestants.

But, if that work recorded some of the early heroes and martyrs of the Left, it also recorded one of the first of those schisms that are a product of the Left's pre-occupation with doctrinal purity. Ever since the Government had succeeded in associating the Reformers with violence and sedition, Sir Francis Burdett had been exhibiting symptoms of galloping moderation. These symptoms had at first alarmed, and then angered Cobbett, nor was his anger lessened by his being in the Baronet's debt to the tune of £3,000. Consequently, no less than two of the six Letters developed into attacks on Burdett for what might nowadays be described as the sins of revisionism.

These were carefully listed. Although he nominally led the Radicals in Parliament, Burdett had, at the last moment, failed to present the Hampshire Petition at the Bar of the House, as he had undertaken to do. That task had had to be undertaken by a more recent but less pusillanimous Reformer, the dashing Lord Cochrane. Burdett had done nothing to prevent the Reformers being smeared and lied about before the Secret Committee. He had said not a word in defence of those leaders of the 'Derbyshire Insurrection' who had been so savagely treated. Worst of all, he had split the Radical vote in the two Westminster by-elections of 1818, and so had let in a Whig for the only constituency that had ever returned two Reform candidates.

The Westminster vote had been split because of Burdett's refusal to accept first Major Cartwright and later Henry Hunt as the other Reform candidate. Cobbett, from Long Island, had written strongly in support of both of these, but had not realised, until it was too late, that he had been indirectly responsible for

416

Hunt's rejection. As early as 1808, before Cobbett had met Hunt, and when he was first embarking on what was then a flirtation with Burdett and the Radicals, Cobbett had written to John Wright: 'There is one *Hunt*, the Bristol man. Beware of him! He rides about the country with a whore, the wife of another man, having deserted his own. A sad fellow! Nothing to do with him.'[15]

Wright, by now Cobbett's most obdurate enemy, had kept the letter, which he gave at this moment to Cleary, Secretary of the Hampden Club. The latter put it in front of the Westminster Reform Committee and it was used as an excuse for rejecting Hunt as a candidate. When Cobbett learnt of this he wrote to Hunt denying that he had ever written such a letter, a strange claim from a man rightfully proud of his retentive memory. Hunt accepted his assurance and their friendship continued for some years to come. Indeed, in the second Westminster by-election of that year (Romilly, the Whig Member, had committed suicide) Hunt proposed Cobbett instead of himself as a second candidate. The Committee, however, decided that it wanted neither Hunt nor Cobbett, whichever of them stood and whichever of them supported.

This was the start of Cobbett's feud against Burdett whom he blackguarded as only Cobbett could. However, Hazlitt, who admired Cobbett but still had some harsh things to say about him, had nothing but praise for Burdett – 'one of the few remaining examples of the old English understanding and the old English character'. Hazlitt was also a Radical and a more consistent one, perhaps, than Cobbett, yet he saw nothing of the apostate in Burdett.

There was another and more damaging consequence for Cobbett to come out of the complicated, and in many ways comical Westminster Election affair. When news reached him of what Wright and Cleary had done he attacked each of them in consecutive numbers of the *Register*. As soon as he returned to England again, each of them sued him for libel and each of them won. Cleary was awarded only 40 shillings as the judge ruled he had been no more than mildly abused. The Cobbett family hailed this as almost a victory. They had to think otherwise when Wright's case came up, for he was awarded £1,000 damages.

Fortunately or not, Cobbett had just declared himself bankrupt and so, once again, friends came to his rescue and paid both damages and costs. That such a polemical writer as Cobbett should have had to defend himself so often in a libel case was, perhaps, to be expected. What is surprising is how frequently, the Ely case excepted, he emerged scatheless, having been acquitted, or had nominal damages awarded against him, or had heavy damages paid for him by others.

Meanwhile, on Long Island, Cobbett continued to pursue his new occupation as an author. As if *A Year's Residence* and *The American Gardener* were not enough in two years, he brought out a new and revised edition of that *Maître Anglois* he had written in Philadelphia twenty-two years earlier. Of this he said, in a circular letter sent to his principal creditors in England: 'The *Maître Anglois* has long been the *sole work* of this kind *in vogue* on the Continent of Europe, in England and in America. It was the only book of the sort admitted into the Pryntanean Schools of Bonaparte, where it was adopted by a direct ordinance . . . I am now engaged in making this book *quite complete* under the title of the "English Master".'

He then offered to assign the copyright in this book to his creditors and added, in order to convince them that he was thereby offering them the means to a fortune: 'Its clearness, its simplicity, its wonderful aptitude to its purpose, its engaging and convincing properties make it so unlike all the offspring of pedantry, that it is no wonder that it should have made its way in general esteem.'

This, however, was not all. He proposed to write another grammar, this time a French one for Englishmen, the copyright in which he would also assign. It would be called, naturally enough, 'The French Master'. This was not, in fact, published until 1824, when it was called *A French Grammar, or, Plain Instructions for the Learning of French*. Meanwhile, and to encourage his creditors, he wrote: 'You will easily see that if I could, twenty-two years ago, actually *write a book* in the French language to French persons, how able I must be to write a book in the English language to teach French.'

As if these were not sufficient undertakings, he went on to describe yet another, and ultimately much more famous Grammar he would offer them. 'I am, you will perceive, getting ready a *Grammar of the English Language*. This, which is a work which I have always desired to perform, I have put into the shape of a series of letters addressed to my beloved son *James* . . . In this work, which I have all my life, since I was nineteen, had in my contemplation, I have assembled together the fruits of all my observations on the construction of the English language; and I have given them the form of a book, not merely with a view to profit, but with a view to fair fame, and with the still more agreeable view of instructing, in this foundation of all literary knowledge, the great body of my ill-treated and unjustly condemned countrymen.'[16]

His *Grammar* was published simultaneously in New York and

London in 1818, and it remained in print for most of the next hundred years. It was, and probably still is, unique amongst Grammars, being straightforward, easily understood and even interesting. He was possibly the only grammarian to bring humour and contemporary politics into a study of English grammar. But then Cobbett intended it, as he said in his sub-title, 'For the Use of Schools and of Young Persons in general; but more especially for the Use of Soldiers, Sailors, Apprentices and Ploughboys'.

Cobbett took to writing books for more reasons than money, one of which is suggested by his reference to his 'ill-treated' countrymen. Like most Radicals, he believed in the better education of the masses, either as a good in itself, or else as a potent weapon in the class war. But, like many other self-educated men, he despised all places of formal education. Knowledge, to his mind, was by no means the same thing as being learned. The educated classes proved that, cluttered-up as their minds were with useless burdens of Greek and Latin. Knowledge was an ability to understand the forces that had made men what they were, rather than what they ought to be.

It was very evident to him that he was uniquely equipped to bring knowledge to the working classes. He had taken a first step in that direction when he started the cheap *Register*. That had given the working classes some instruction in politics. Now he proposed to instruct them in a great many other useful things besides politics. Grammar, in this respect, was no more than 'the foundation of knowledge'. If the workers were ever to be their masters' equals, they must acquire a sound understanding of their history, their economy, their institutions, their laws and their religion, and all of these things Cobbett could give them.

What Cobbett had it in his mind to do was to produce a whole library of books on these subjects. They would constitute school and university for those who had attended neither, and would be open to anyone who could read and find the few shillings that would be the price of each book and the entrance fee to each course. Hitherto the 'political classes' had been the workers' only and grudging instructors. All they had given them to read had been religious tracts designed to reconcile them to this world and prepare them for the next. Cobbett proposed to give them books that would educate them for this world and prepare them for the time when they would become the 'political class'.

These matters he discussed in two long and rambling articles published, at the end of 1817 in the *Register*. They took the form of Letters to 'Mr Benbow, One of the English Reformers now imprisoned'. This Benbow, a shoemaker turned bookseller, had made a name for himself as one of the most radical of the Radical Reformers, and had endeared himself to Cobbett as 'the only man, who had the honesty and sincerity to tell Sir Francis Burdett, that the people were no longer to be made the dupes of personal ambition'. He later became, first joint-publisher, and then sole publisher of the *Register*, until he and Cobbett fell out over money, whereafter Cobbett always referred to him as a blackguard.

Benbow, however, was, like Cobbett, an autodidact, and that was probably why, whilst the one was in prison and the other on Long Island and neither had as yet met, Cobbett involved him in this discussion on education. He had previously outlined to him his intention to produce books, not only on Grammar, but also 'A History of the Laws and Constitution of England', a 'History of the Church and of Religion in England', and 'A View of the present state of the Income, Debt and Expenses of the Kingdom; its Population and Paupers; its Causes of Embarrassment and Misery, and the Means of Restoration to ease and Happiness'. The 'good end' these works would achieve would be 'the rendering of great numbers of the people a match, at least, in point of book-learning, to more than the average of "Noble Lords" and "Honourable Gentlemen".'[17]

The legal history and the economic work never, in fact, got written, whilst the history of the Church was only partly dealt with in Cobbett's *History of the Reformation in England*. Almost every book Cobbett wrote, however, had, as its purpose, the instruction of the masses. He had appointed himself, as it were, Grammarian, Historian, Geographer, Social Observer and Moral Philosopher to the people. In later years there would be placed, on the back page of the *Register*, an advertisement for *The Cobbett-Library*, with his various works listed under 'Books for Teaching Language', 'Domestic Management and Duties', 'Books on Rural Affairs', 'Management of National Affairs', 'History', 'Travels', and 'Law'. The man who was, perhaps, the outstanding autodidact of his age was also, in the end, its most determinedly didactic author.

There was one work, however, that Cobbett planned to write whilst he was in America which never got beyond its preliminary stages. This was to be a 'life' of Thomas Paine, which would be written as a preliminary to 'collecting and republishing the whole of his writings complete in a cheap form, and with some explanatory notes to the *Rights of Man* particularly'. When he was Peter Porcupine Cobbett had vilified Paine and republished a most scurrilous account of his life. Now, with an equal if opposite enthusiasm, he referred to him as 'this truly great man, this truly philosophical politician', adding, 'at his expiring flambeau I lighted my taper'. What he proposed, therefore, was as much an act of penance as a work of homage. 'Justice in his memory, justice to the cause of freedom, justice to the country that gave him birth, justice to his friends on both sides of the Atlantic, demanded at my hands an earnest endeavour to perform this task in a manner worthy of the subject.'

There was an odd attempt made to convince Cobbett that, on his deathbed, the author of *The Age of Reason* had recanted his free thinking and sought the blessings of religion. A Quaker called Collins – 'whom I suspected to be a most consummate hypocrite; he had a sodden face, a simper, and manoeuvred his features, precisely like the most perfidious wretch' – offered to introduce him to a servant woman who had been present at the time. She, however, refused to confirm anything and Cobbett's pious belief in Paine's agnosticism remained unshaken.

Cobbett now engaged on the extraordinary enterprise of disinterring Paine's bones from the unhallowed ground in which they lay in order to carry them back to England. There he proposed to organise a subscription fund with which to pay for a suitable mausoleum in which those bones could be laid. On his return to England with the bones, he had difficulties with the Customs and the public, for once, refused to subscribe to one of Cobbett's requirements. The bones lingered, forgotten, in a box and eventually passed into the hands of the Custodian in Bankruptcy. It may be that Cobbett had thought this project would give some wider publicity to the *Life* he never got round to writing. It became, instead, a public joke,* and one he was never allowed to forget. Yet it was, when one considers it, a somewhat endearing act of folly.

The suspension of Habeas Corpus had to be renewed annually. This was done in 1817, but not in the following year. This meant that Cobbett could return to England without having to risk imprisonment without trial on a Minister's warrant. His friends urged him to return, and the Coventry Radicals nominated him as their candidate at the next election. Cobbett was, seemingly, too engrossed in his new role as author to listen to them. In the summer of 1819, however, fire destroyed his house at Hyde Park. Cobbett

---

* Rhymsters and poets made much of this particular absurdity. The best-remembered quatrain on the subject was contained in a letter Byron wrote to Tom Moore:

> In digging up your bones, Tom Paine,
> Will Cobbett has done well;
> You'll visit him on earth again,
> He'll visit you in hell.

was away at the time, but Mrs. Churcher, at some risk to herself, rescued his books and papers. Even then Cobbett delayed returning to England. 'I resolved on making a sort of thatched tent, in which I might enjoy tranquillity, and in which I might labour without intermission.'

A thatched tent, however, was no place in which to pass a Long Island winter, and in September 1819 Cobbett left the United States for England for the last time. In one way, however, he never left America. For some time his son James Paul remained there to look after his publishing and newspaper business. He retained business connections with New York both as a seedsman and a publisher after James Paul's return, corresponded constantly with his American friends, wrote numerous articles on American and Anglo-American subjects, whilst the last book he wrote, or rather compiled, was an adulatory 'life' of Andrew Jackson (President 1828–36), published simultaneously in London and New York. Jackson, far more than Jefferson, seemed to Cobbett to epitomise all that he had come to respect in American democracy. He held what Cobbett considered to be sound views on money, was pugnacious, fearless, a countryman and, to Cobbett's great delight, 'this bravest and greatest man now living in this world, or that ever lived in this world, as far as my knowledge extends' was, he discovered, the son of poor Irish emigrants. Cobbett may well have seen in President Jackson what he might have become if his parents had left Farnham for the United States and he himself had been born to American rather than English politics.

CHAPTER EIGHTEEN

The Climactic Years

C'est un métier que de faire un livre, comme de faire une pendule; il
faut plus que de l'espirit pour être auteur.
(Making a book is a craft, as is making a clock; it takes more than wit to
become an author.)

Jean De La Bruyère: Des Ouvrages de l'Espirit

Cobbett was greeted by a large and enthusiastic crowd of supporters when he landed in Liverpool on 22 November 1819. The
Peterloo Massacre had taken place three months earlier, but that
egregious mishandling of Hunt's great Manchester meeting by the
local magistrates and an undisciplined yeomanry was still a reason
for great anger on the part of the working classes, and of great
alarm on the part of the authorities. On his triumphal progress
from Liverpool to London and, eventually, to Botley, Cobbett was
forbidden to enter Manchester; but he was fêted and dined in
Coventry and was given a public banquet at the Crown and Anchor
Tavern in London in the course of which one of his creditors
attempted to have him arrested for debt. He was bailed out by
Hunt and his publisher. If his supporters were, for the most part,
enthusiastic over his return, the same could not be said of his
enemies. The Press, which was largely hostile to him, divided its
comments between extracting all that it could from the ludicrous
affair of Tom Paine's bones (one American report insisted that
they were not even Tom Paine's bones, but those of an unknown
negro Cobbett had dug up by mistake), and expressing alarm at the
additional mischief such a rabble-rouser might cause in those
violent and troubled times.

Cobbett remained in London for ten days before returning to
Botley. In that time he quarrelled with Cartwright, refused to be
reconciled to Burdett unless the latter guaranteed to bear all the
costs of getting both Cobbett and Hunt elected to Parliament, and
even showed signs of falling out with Hunt, whom he accused of
jealousy. More unexpectedly, he never visited his wife and children who were then in lodgings in Kensington. Their reunion, he
insisted, could only take place at Botley.

George Spater's researches, published in *William Cobbett: The*

Poor Man's Friend, have revealed that Mrs. Cobbett had actually visited her husband on Long Island in 1818. However she soon returned to England, and the shortness of her stay suggests that she had lost some of her former taste for American life, married life, or both. She had, ever since her husband's radicalisation, objected to what she thought of as the low company he kept. She especially disliked Hunt who not only led her husband astray but had also been rude to her. The rift, if it was one, was bridged when the family was reunited at Botley. Anne Cobbett wrote to James Paul, the only absent member, 'You will be delighted to hear that dear Papa and Mama are as happy as ever they were'.[1]

Cobbett soon returned again to London to struggle with his politics, his business and his creditors. His arrival in England had coincided with the passing of the Six Acts by which Sidmouth sought to curb the activities of the Reformers and the Radicals. One of those Acts imposed a Stamp Duty on periodicals which had previously passed as pamphlets and so could be published unstamped. This had made the twopenny *Register*, which was Cobbett's only assured source of large profits, illegal.* He had to raise the price to sixpence and, when this greatly reduced its sales and destroyed its unique position as a popular newspaper, he eventually had to fall back on the shilling *Register,* the title in which he now prudently transferred to his son.

Undaunted as ever, Cobbett turned to two different solutions to his financial problems. Forgetting past failures in this area he started a daily newspaper which he called *Cobbett's Evening Post*. Describing his situation to James in New York, he wrote with his customary optimism: 'You will see that the villains have cut off the cheap *Register*. What I shall now do is this: on the 24th of this month I begin a daily evening paper. We think that this will have a great sale. Everybody thinks this.'[2] Everybody, however, did not buy the paper and it folded in little more than eight weeks.

While the *Evening Post* survived, however, Cobbett used it as an aid towards his second solution. This was to get himself elected to Parliament as soon as possible. Quite apart from believing this to be a political, and even a national necessity, he had not overlooked the fact that being a Member would give him immunity from

---

* Although Cobbett always fought valiantly for the freedom of the press, he was not prepared to break the law by circulating an unstamped *Register*. Other Radical journals, such as Wooler's *Black Dwarf*, Carlile's *The Republican* and Hetherington's *The Poor Man's Guardian* were so circulated until, in the end, the Stamp Duty was defeated. Cobbett may have thought the *Register* was too important for such hole-in-corner methods. Alternatively, he may not have been prepared to risk further and repeated periods of imprisonment.

imprisonment for debt. He used the paper, therefore, to canvass for a seat at a by-election and when, at the end of January 1820, the death of George III precipitated a General Election, he announced his intention of standing for one of the Coventry seats and invited subscriptions to 'Cobbett's Fund for Reform', the proceeds from which would be used, entirely at his discretion, to defray his election expenses.

Coventry had invited him to stand as a Radical candidate as early as 1817. It was a manufacturing centre with an unusually large electorate and so might be won for the Radicals. But it was also an expensive seat to fight. Potential Radical voters had to be brought to the hustings, and since many of them lived in country districts, and some of them as far away as London, the candidate had to be able to pay for their transport and provide sufficient food and drink to sustain them over the period of the election. Cobbett told subscribers to his Fund that he would need £5,000 to cover these costs, but his readers failed to provide anything like that amount.

Polling went on for eight days, during which Cobbett was forced to admit that he could not hope to match his opponents pound for pound, mob for mob, trick for trick or bully-boy for bully-boy. He lost the election, but posterity gained what must surely be one of the best blow-by-blow accounts ever written of life on the hustings in those pre-Reform days. This appeared in the *Register* of 25 March 1820. Its more light-hearted side may have influenced Charles Dickens when, seventeen years later, he involved Mr. Pickwick in the Eatanswill Election. Nevertheless it was an unusually corrupt and violent affair, made more violent, perhaps, by the recent uncovering of the Cato Street Conspiracy and the assassination in Paris of the Duc de Berri, events which revived old anti-Jacobin fervours in England.

Coventry left Cobbett so deeply out of pocket that he had, at last, to file a petition in bankruptcy. His debts were so large and his assets so few that many of his creditors, including Burdett, refused to enter their claims. Botley was more than fully mortgaged, for land values were falling, and although, under Chancery law, all was not lost and he managed to retain a reversionary interest in the farms for several years, Cobbett was never in a position to redeem them. The *Register* was no longer his property and not a penny dividend was ever paid to the creditors. Cobbett actually had to borrow the pound note and the few shillings that, for form's sake, he surrendered to the Commissioners in Bankruptcy. On the other hand, he was now, for the first time since his purchase of Botley, temporarily free from the debts that had crippled him for so long, for his old enemy, Lord Eldon, granted him his discharge on 20 October 1820.

Cobbett's subsequent business enterprises, his seedsman's business in London and New York and his various farming ventures at Kensington, Barn Elm and later, Normandy Farm continued; but the large sums he earned with his books left him little or no profit since, in order to reach the working-class readers he primarily wrote for, he published them in great quantity and at uneconomic prices. His copyrights and his stocks of books were his only real assets, and these, towards the end of his life, he either dispersed amongst his family or used as security for his continual borrowings.

Meanwhile, however, he immersed himself in politics as though there were nothing else in the world to concern him: no family to support, no *Register* to produce every week, no books to write. Before they moved to Kensington, the Cobbetts lived for a while in squalid London lodgings and survived, very largely, on a diet of vegetables. Yet never once did this remarkable man abandon his fight for Reform or show, to the public at least, any falling-off in his belief in himself as leader, philosopher and guide to mankind. By December 1820 he had not only been made bankrupt, but had also had damages and costs awarded against him in the Cleary and Wright libel actions. Yet in the *Register* of 16 December of that year, he wrote: 'They have now, they say, *sunk* me in good earnest! Never was a man so often sunk! This is no *sinking*. This is what the sailors call merely "shipping a sea;" that is to say, taking a wave on board, which only gives the vessel a *"heel"* but by no means prevents her from keeping on her course; and, gentlemen, you will see that this, like every other "sinking" that I have experienced, will be at last a *mounting* in place of a sinking.'

Much that happened in the following decade appeared to justify his defiant optimism. His books, though they left him little profit, turned him into one of the most widely-read authors of his day. At the same time the course of political events made at least some degree of Reform inevitable and turned such a prominent leader of the Reform movement as Cobbett into a leader of the people. As such a 'tribune' Cobbett took advantage, step by step, of current developments; and in three quite different aspects, the tide of opinion and events had begun to run strongly in his favour.

The first of these was the economic situation. What was important here was that the frequently changing cycle of recession and partial recovery appeared to justify all that Cobbett had written and prophesied on the subjects of inflation, taxation and the currency. When, in 1819, Peel presented a Bill for the return, over a three-year period, to the Gold Standard, but did nothing to

426

reduce the National Debt or the burden of taxation, Cobbett issued his famous Gridiron challenge. If Peel succeeded in this without bringing ruin to the country, he, Cobbett, would give Castlereagh leave 'to put me on a gridiron and broil me alive, while Sidmouth stirs the fire, and Canning stands by making a jest of my groans'.

When the Government had to modify Peel's Act and pass a Bill retaining notes of small denominations as legal tender, Cobbett claimed to be justified, and from then on used a gridiron as what would now be called the *Register*'s logo or colophon. The people, if not the 'feelosofers', accepted his economic theories holus-bolus and had good reason for doing so. The 1820s were a period of intermittent but growing distress in the industrial and rural areas, and that distress, skilfully used by Cobbett and his fellow Radicals, provided the necessary discontent, violence and repression to power the Reform movement. It became increasingly difficult for the Government to ignore Cobbett's frequently published alternative of Reform or Revolution.

Organising discontent was by no means as easy in those days as it is today and, without two other developments of national importance, the Reform movement might have languished, for decades, as little more than the voice of limited and sectarian unrest. These developments involved, first, the apparently irrelevant matter of Queen Caroline's divorce, and, second, the perennial problem of the Irish Question.

The English always enjoy anything that humanises their rulers and betters by a public display and discussion of their weaknesses, especially a good sexual scandal. Only if there is a suggestion of perverse or unnatural practices will it fail to endear its victim to the public. The most damaging allegation made against Caroline, for example, was not that she had entertained so many different lovers, from Sir Sidney Smith down to Bergami, her Italian courier, but that she had enjoyed the antics of Leone, another of her Italian servants who, as the Attorney-General delicately put it, 'used to *imitate*, in the most indelicate manner, *sexual intercourse* before the servants and in the presence of the Princess'. A series of wholesome fornications and adulteries would have been easier to explain away. Indeed Cobbett, in his detailed defence of Caroline, was reduced to commenting that as much and more than Leone's antics could be seen at any English country fair.

Cobbett's dilemma was that he was one of the few men in England who refused to believe that Caroline of Brunswick possessed to the full all the lusty appetites of her race. He had sworn to her chastity and her innocence ever since the days of the 'Delicate

Investigation'. The more frequently evidence to the contrary was produced, the more firmly he declared her to be the victim of a conspiracy. That he had sound political reasons for doing so does not mean that he was insincere. It may mean, however, that he had additional reason for humbugging himself and, as his enemies asserted, humbugging the nation.

The nation, however, was somewhat less concerned with chastity than it was with fair play. An increasing number of people felt that, even if Caroline's adulteries were proven, the Bill of Pains and Penalties was a grossly unfair attempt to deny her that licence to fornicate that King George IV, and so many other Guelphs, had considered theirs as of right. Caroline was, after all, as much of a Guelph as any of them, and everyone knew that continence had seldom been a Guelph virtue. The King himself was a bigamist and a notorious womaniser, as were most of his brothers. His behaviour to Caroline, from his wedding night onwards, had been a public scandal, and had given rise, along with much other gossip, to THE BOOK and one of Cobbett's favourite conspiracy theories. All of this the public was prepared to accept, even to the extent of paying for it, but it was less prepared to accept that a Guelph goose should be persecuted for acts that so many Guelph ganders indulged in, largely at the public's expense.

The national sense of fair play has often been a more potent force in British politics than political analysts allow. As a consequence, the attempt to pass the Bill made the King and the Government widely unpopular. The Whigs were, on the whole, less adroit at exploiting this than the Radicals, whose existence as a Party depended on their ability to arouse public opinion. They now found themselves presented, not merely with a weapon with which to attack the Tories, but with a cause that appealed to a far wider public than the cause of Reform itself. Led in this respect by Cobbett, they made the most they could of the situation, and turned themselves, for the first time, into something resembling a national movement as a consequence.

From June 1820, when the Bill of Pains and Penalties was introduced into the Lords, until August of the following year when Caroline, having seen the Bill fail, unexpectedly died, Cobbett was unceasingly active on her behalf at three different levels. As a publicist he devoted almost the whole of every *Register* to her cause. As a populist he won her the support of the people and turned that support into a significant political force. He had always, as a Reformer, encouraged the public to assemble, discuss, petition and march with such frequency and in such growing numbers as to make it dangerous for the Government to ignore them, and he used much the same methods for Caroline. Under his urging the crowds turned out to cheer and escort Caroline whenever she moved through London whilst, for the same reason, they jeered at the King and his Ministers whenever they did the same. He saw that Addresses and Petitions in favour of Caroline were sent from almost every district in England and from such different bodies as 'The Artisans, Mechanics and Labouring Classes of the Town of Manchester', 'The Inhabitants of the Ward of Farringdon Without', 'The Various Lodges of the Order of Odd Fellows', and 'The Male and Female Inhabitants of the Town of Portsmouth and the Island of Portsea'.

At the third level he nominated himself Caroline's unofficial adviser. Her official and legal advisers at that time were Brougham and Denman, with whom Cobbett eventually and inevitably quarrelled. He tendered his advice, initially, by letter, but eventually developed into something of a courtier and attended on the Queen in person. In October 1820 Anne Cobbett wrote to her brother James, in New York:

> Papa has been to Court and kissed the Queen's hand, and a very pretty little hand he says it is. We made the gentleman dress himself very smart, and powder his head . . . The Queen made him a little speech, in which she thanked him for the great services he had rendered her . . . Her Chaplain told us the next day that when Papa left the room she turned round and said in her lively manner, 'well now, if that is Mr C., no wonder such fine writing comes from him, he is the finest man I have seen since I came to England, aye, aye, if there be only a few such men as that to stand by me, I shall not care for the Lords.[3]

In her next letter, dated 17 January 1821, Anne wrote:

> Papa is become mighty fond of dress, and if you had seen him go off to Court to pay his respects to the Queen this morning, you would not have known him, he looked so smart. A *Claret* coloured coat, white waistcoat and silk stockings, dancing pumps and powdered head, are very becoming to him, I assure you – Pray, is it suspected in America who wrote the letter?

The letter referred to was the famous Letter of Remonstrance, outlining the wrongs done her, Caroline sent to the King which, when it was returned to her unopened, she then sent to the Press for publication. It was almost certainly written, in the first instance, by Cobbett, as, indeed, Caroline's Letter to Parliament and her replies to the various Addresses and Petitions probably were.

Although Cobbett and Caroline, those equally impulsive and portly characters, found each other attractive, Cobbett never lost sight of the political advantages to be extracted from the situation. Caroline had, as it were, put the Radicals on the map for reasons that John Morgan Cobbett attempted to explain in a letter to his brother James Paul, who was still in New York: 'In the first place, with one accord, the people, the whole of the people, Church people, Methodists and sectarians of all sorts, Tradesmen, *Farmers*, labourers and *Soldiers* as much as any, had all long ago declared for the Queen, leaving for her enemies the King, Ministers, and all courtiers and all Parsons. This, in the first place, was almost a Revolution; for the Queen is a Radical, and has consequently joined all together against the Government.'[4]

It is difficult to believe in Caroline's Radicalism, but she did, at least, make Radicalism both more fashionable and more popular than it had been before. That coming together of the working and middle classes – what John Morgan had described as 'the whole of the people' – which Cobbett had helped organise in support of the Queen could, in subsequent years, be organised in support of Reform. It was no wonder that John Morgan described the situation as 'delightful', adding: 'The Governor's power is monstrous now, and they all feel it'. As for 'the Governor' himself, he wrote, in one of his *Register* articles, that, so far as the Radicals were concerned, the Caroline case had been 'a capital thing', and one that was 'a perfect "*God's-send*" to us'.[5]

Most of the *Register* articles of that period, however, were more concerned with the legal than with the political details of the Caroline case. Cobbett, in his best barrack-room lawyer style, worked hard to discredit every scrap of evidence brought forward to prove Caroline's adulteries. Many of his arguments were ingenious. One or two of them lapsed pleasantly into the ingenuous.

An important part of the case against Caroline, for example, was concerned with her behaviour whilst on a long cruise in the Mediterranean. She slept on deck every night in a pavilion that had been put up for her and which she invariably shared with Bergami. This, the Solicitor-General argued, was proof presumptive of adultery. Not so, said Cobbett, it was proof of common sense. No sensible female would spend a single night in such an exposed and flimsy bedroom unattended whilst sailors were about. Bergami had obviously been guarding his mistress rather than coupling with her.

It was never, perhaps, a convincing argument, but Cobbett then went on to ruin it by asserting that, on a sea voyage, no one ever coupled with anyone. It was preposterous, therefore, to assert that the Queen had gone to sea 'for the purpose of indulging in amorous delights; when every one that has been at sea knows, that the very situation, besides its necessary exposures, destroys for the time, every propensity of the kind; that it unsettles the stomach; produces a general loathing of all that was pleasant on shore; causes a disrelish for all the ordinary indulgences; creates a temporary debility; and, in short, suspends the functions as well as the desires. *Sea-sick and amorous*! oh! the filthy! oh! the beastly idea!'[6]

The Bill of Pains and Penalties was abandoned. Caroline triumphed, then died. The Reformers emerged from the affair with a national reputation and a nation-wide organisation they might never otherwise have acquired. From then on, as Cobbett over-optimistically put it, there were no longer any Tories. There were only apprehensive politicians attempting to discover what minimal amount of Reform they would have to concede to avoid a revolution. He never, for his part, forgot what the Reform movement owed to Caroline. He dedicated the fourth edition of his *Grammar* to her during her lifetime. After her death he invariably referred to her as the martyred Queen.

Cobbett was brought into close contact with the Irish problem through his support for Catholic Emancipation. This was, for him, a question of franchise rather than religion. Nevertheless his *History of the Reformation*, published in 1824, earned him the reputation of being a crypto-Papist in spite of the fact that he was as staunch a Church of England man as any fundamentally irreligious person can be. He was a poor historian but a convincing writer, and the 'History' made him something of a hero throughout the Catholic world, if only because it was so unusual for an English Protestant to describe the English Reformation from a Catholic viewpoint, and a prejudiced one at that. He was influenced by the Catholic historian Lingard as much as by his own mediaevalism which led him to respect 'the religion of our forefathers'. The Dissolution of the Monasteries was, for him, a continuing part of the land problem and he had for some years been engaged in an attack on the Church of England clergy, whom he classified as tithe-eaters, tax-eaters, Pittites and pluralists almost to a man.

The Catholics, however, welcomed his support without ever questioning his motives, and that support led him into an association with Daniel O'Connell and the Irish problem which proved to be of considerable advantage to Reform. We have come to accept the alliance between English Radicals and Irish Nationalists as an inevitable factor in British politics. Some may think it an alliance that has been damaging to Britain, but since each ally has drawn support and example from the other, it has been of considerable value to both. But, while Radicals in England have, consciously or otherwise, struggled towards some form of Socialism, Irish Nationalists, whether they were aware of it or not, reached towards the theocratic, mildly illiberal and violently *irredentist* state they have finally achieved.

It would be to credit Cobbett with overmuch foresight to say that he pioneered that alliance knowing the benefits it would bring to the English Radicals. Nevertheless, it was not until O'Connell forced the issue and there was an Irish Nationalist vote in the Commons that the few Radicals in the House could exert much influence and the cause of Reform could be pursued by Parliamentary as well as extra-Parliamentary means.

Yet even in the pioneering days of that alliance, Cobbett's relations with O'Connell revealed the strains that were inherent in their divergence of aims. In the struggle for emancipation, O'Connell was prepared to accept the endowment of the Catholic clergy in Ireland and the abolition of the forty-shilling franchise. Cobbett was violently opposed to both. He saw the first as a version of the greatly-hated tithes, and the second as a retreat from that extension of the franchise that was his *raison d'être* as a politician. Their friendship, therefore, was intermittent. Cobbett attacked O'Connell in the *Register* and O'Connell referred to Cobbett as a 'comical miscreant'. The fact that Burdett sided with O'Connell made matters worse, and the attacks continued. O'Connell attempted to point out that they still had much in common, remarking, 'the bed is large enough for both of us – share the blanket, friend Cobbett'.

Cobbett replied by satirising O'Connell and Burdett in the first of the three political comedies he was inordinately proud of, in spite of the fact that not one of them ever has been, or could be, staged. This one he called *Big O and Sir Glory*: O'Connell was a large, heavy-built man and Burdett had once had the misfortune to be described as 'Westminster's pride and England's glory'. This was far from the last time that Cobbett attacked O'Connell, but a friendship of sorts re-emerged in between the arguments. If O'Connell gave his support to the Reformers in England, Cobbett gave his to the Repealers in Ireland and in this way a beginning was made to the alliance of English Radicals and Irish Nationalists. Cobbett, perhaps more than anyone else, realised how much the Reform movement owed to that uneasy alliance, and when he undertook the very last of his 'Rides' in Ireland, he paid tribute to O'Connell, even though he refused to stay with him.

Because we now think it logical that democracy should have triumphed over 'reaction' in Britain, we tend to think of the Great Reform Bill as an inevitable development – something that owed nothing to circumstance and everything to principle. It is perhaps salutary to be reminded that Reform did, in the end, owe something to circumstance in the shape of such things as an economic depression, an amorous Queen and a large number of Irish nationalists.

It was with such circumstances favouring him that Cobbett, over the next decade, fought for Reform, the leadership of the Radical Reformers, and a seat in Parliament. His political arguments were repeated in endless *Register* articles, several of which were later republished in pamphlet form. In 1822 he began that series of journeys which, continuing intermittently throughout the rest of his life, has been immortalised in *Rural Rides*. Out of these journeys there developed, not merely a succession of formal and impromptu political speeches, but also what grew into a professional lecture round from which he drew a not inconsiderable income.

In those days his name was on everyone's lips. To that extent he might be said to have achieved the 'fair fame' for which he so craved. When one looks for motives that will explain why he endured so many hardships and reverses, why he indulged in such an expenditure of spirit when security and ease were, at almost every turn, his for the asking, one has to accept that fame was his spur. He would not, one supposes, have denied that wealth and power were both worth the having, but fame satisfied a fiercer appetite, one as urgent, perhaps, as his hunger for political and social justice. He never ceased fighting for these, but equally he never ceased fighting to be acknowledged as the one man in England capable of obtaining them.

Although these latter years of his, during which Cobbett was accepted as leader of the Radical Reformers and the putative 'Father of Reform', will always be the most important ones for historians and political biographers, they may seem less important to those who remember him as an author and as one of the great 'characters' of English literature.

'England,' George Santayana wrote, 'is the paradise of individuality, eccentricity, heresy, anomalies, hobbies and humours.'[6] He may, in this respect, have loaded too much on to the English, but it is probably true that no other country cherishes its 'characters' as much. We never seem to need to define all the elements of singularity that go to the making of a 'character' for we can recognise one just as soon as we have had a few moments of conversation with him. In this respect Cobbett was as recognisable as, say, John Aubrey or Sir Thomas Browne, Dr. Swift or Dr. Johnson, James Boswell or George Orwell.

However, Cobbett was more enjoyable as a 'character' in his early and middle years than he was in his last ones. This may have been because he felt increasingly obliged to live up to his reputation, and so began to do self-consciously what he had once done instinctively. He had, for all his bluntness and sincerity, always had a theatrical side to him and, if he had not been so obsessed by political argument, might well have succeeded as an actor, a dramatist, or a combination of both. Almost every account (his own included) of his behaviour on the hustings or the lecture platform reveals how carefully and skilfully he presented himself to the public. In later years it almost seemed that he felt obliged to give the audience what they expected of him, and so he gave them the statesman and the jester, John Bull and John Ball in isolated or intermingled periods, even though he was, in the end, in some danger of caricaturing himself.

All this amounted to no more than the routine hamming that comes, in the end, to any man who has to expose himself continually to the public. But there was also some evidence of a more serious falling-off in Cobbett. Although he was a remarkably intelligent man he was one whose emotions generally moved him more powerfully than his intellect. So long as his more amiable emotions prevailed they contributed to his attractions as a 'character'. His compassion, humour, scurrility, even his anger greatly pleased his supporters and seldom added to his enemies. But now it began to seem that less amiable emotions prevailed. His natural good humour diminished, or was overlaid by a growing egotism, jealousy and intolerance, and these, for the first time, began to characterise his domestic life as much as his political one. More than ever before he seemed to justify Fearon's description of him as one who insisted on others submitting 'unconditionally to his dictation'.

He began to see conspiracies everywhere, most of them directed against himself. There was even some evidence of a persecution mania. He found enemies where none existed, even in the bosom of the family that had once been his refuge and his citadel. Macaulay, observing his behaviour, at the end, in Parliament, wrote of Cobbett in his Journal that 'his egotism and his suspicion that everybody was in a plot against him increased and at last attained such a height that he was really as mad as Rousseau'.[7]

More assiduously than ever before he now looked for a seat in Parliament. He increasingly thought of himself as a man who could either lead or help to lead the nation to salvation. It was possibly in a jocular vein that he wrote to the King offering himself as a successor to Goderich (later first Earl of Ripon) when he resigned as Prime Minister in 1828, but there were serious undertones to that joke. Cobbett always thought of himself as a wiser, more experienced, and politically sounder man than, say, Canning or Vansittart, yet had not the one been Prime Minister and the other Chancellor of the Exchequer, although all three of them had started on comparatively level terms as Tory pamphleteers at the turn of the century?

After he had applied for nominations for other constituencies he finally became a candidate at Preston in the 1826 Election and Sir Thomas Beevor organised a fund which attracted subscribers to the tune of £1,600 to support his candidature. Cobbett came bottom of the poll after a fight that was even more corruptly and savagely pursued than that at Coventry, six years previously. In 1831, when the fight for Reform was at its height and victory was in sight he was asked to stand for a Manchester seat. Although he was by then approaching seventy, he agreed and spent some time canvassing and lecturing in Manchester. However, John Fielden, one of Cobbett's staunchest supporters and a leading industrialist, had been asked to stand for one of the two seats in the adjoining constituency, Oldham. He would only do so if Cobbett agreed to stand for the other seat and so, eventually, Cobbett transferred his candidacy to Oldham. He had to cut his Scottish Tour short in order to return, in December 1832, to fight the General Election of that year, and it was then, some twenty-seven years after he first proposed himself as a candidate at Honiton, that he was finally elected and took his seat in the first Reformed Parliament.

The year before his election, however, he had won another sort of victory, this time on a field where he had suffered quite as many defeats as he had on the hustings. He had his last and most triumphant day in court on 7 July 1831 when he most successfully defended himself in a prosecution for seditious libel. The case, suitably enough, arose out of his interest in, and defence of the chopsticks.

1830 and 1831 had been the years in which the peasants of the Southern and South-Eastern counties engaged in what Cobbett called the 'Rural War', generally referred to now as Captain Swing's Rebellion. The failure of the First Reform Bill had brought about urban rioting in Nottingham and Bristol, but the rural rioting was both more dangerous and more difficult to suppress. The new Whig Ministry was no less alarmed by this than the Tories had been at the time of the Luddite Riots, and acted to end the rick-burning and general arson even more savagely than Sidmouth had acted to put an end to the Luddite's frame-breaking.

Cobbett's sympathies were more actively engaged by the rural rioters than they ever had been by the urban ones. Moreover, he had come to hate a Whig even more heartily than he hated a Tory. This 'Rural War' seemed to him to justify all that he had predicted. Parliament had resisted peaceful change. The time for violent change had, therefore, arrived and, as he had always said would happen, the chopsticks would be the instruments of change. Just as they were harder men than the millhands, so also had they been more harshly treated. Now, unless they were given the justice they demanded, they would change the very condition of England.

It was in this attitude of mind that Cobbett reported every incident of rural unrest in the *Register*. Although he took care not to be seen to encourage future violence, he took equal care to explain and justify violence that had occurred. In a Parliament overwhelmingly representative of the landed interest there were many who thought these articles far more dangerous than any he had written in support of the Luddites. There was much talk, in and out of Parliament, of the rioters having been incited by a few well-dressed agitators travelling secretly around the country, and since Cobbett, at that time, frequently addressed meetings in areas where incidents occurred, he was now accused of having instigated them.

The Member for New Romney, Arthur Trevor, asked the Attorney-General to study what was being published in the *Register* and, the following week, moved that the Attorney-General be ordered to proceed against Cobbett for 'exciting the population to disturbance and discontent'. A few days later, a convicted arsonist, one Thomas Goodman of Battle, who was awaiting execution, 'confessed' that he 'never should have thought of douing aney sutch thing if Mr Cobet had never given aney lactures'.

Goodman was reprieved, which gave him an opportunity to enlarge and elaborate his 'confession', taking care each time to incriminate Cobbett more thoroughly, even though, with each added detail, he did something to lessen his credibility. Since fear of the rioters had induced many farmers to increase farm wages, and several parsons to agree to a reduction in tithes, Cobbett wrote, somewhat imprudently, in the *Register* of 11 December 1830 that the burnings had 'produced good, and great good too'. On 17 February an Old Bailey grand jury returned an indictment against Cobbett for seditious libel. His trial took place at the Guildhall before Lord Tenterden on 7 July and Cobbett defended

himself, with his lawyer sons assisting him. He did this so successfully that he managed to turn his own trial into a trial of the Whig
administration. He had, for once, a conspiracy theory that was
plausible.

Cobbett subpoenaed Lord Grey the Prime Minister, Melbourne
and Palmerston the Home and Foreign Secretaries, Brougham the
Lord Chancellor and Durham the Lord Privy Seal and spent much
of his time in court alternatively lecturing and cross-examining
them. He extracted enough from the witnesses to convince most
reasonable men that much of the evidence against him had been
manufactured, including the 'confession'. He used again the argument he had used in the Rush case, which was that he was being
tried for sedition when what he had written was no more seditious
than a hundred articles that went unprosecuted in other papers. He
called a large number of prominent people as character witnesses,
and he even obliged Brougham to admit that only a few months
earlier he had asked Cobbett for permission to reprint the *Letter to
the Luddites* of 1817, because he thought it might induce the rioters
to refrain from further violence. How, Cobbett asked, can the
Government accuse me of inciting violence when they use what I
have written as a warning against violence?

He was at his best when it came to his final address to the jury,
which took four hours. In it he accused the Whigs of having
brought the prosecution only because they wished to destroy him.
'It is their fears which make them attack me, and it is my death they
intend. In that object they will be defeated for, thank Heaven, you
stand between me and destruction. If, however, your verdict
should be – which I do not anticipate – one that will consign me
to death, by sending me to some loathsome dungeon, I will with
my last breath pray God to bless my country and curse the Whigs,
and I leave my revenge to my children and the labourers of
England.'

It was splendid stuff, and it worked. The jury, after deliberating
for fifteen hours, failed to come to a verdict but remained split six
and six. Cobbett was discharged to the great rejoicing of his
supporters and the great discomfiture of all Whigs, who had seen
their leaders accused in court of every crime from starving the
chopsticks to conspiring against Cobbett. Charles Greville recorded in his diary that Cobbett's 'insolence and violence were past
endurance, but he made an able speech. The Chief Justice was very
timid, and favoured and complimented him throughout.' This may
have been because Tenterden, a Tory, was by no means disinclined
to see the Whig magnates humbled.

Over the whole of this period, Cobbett and Hunt, those two

ageing leaders of the Radical Reformers,* sometimes quarrelled and sometimes came together. Although Hunt had sued Cobbett for libel in 1825 they were sufficiently reconciled by 1827 to attend a dinner given by the Westminster Committee to its two Parliamentary Members, Sir Francis Burdett and John Hobhouse, later Lord Broughton. It is not clear that Hunt and Cobbett were invited, but they attended with several of their followers and engaged in what has to be described as a display of hooliganism. Cobbett objected when a toast to Burdett was proposed and then proceeded to insult Hobhouse. The latter was a diminutive man whose association with the tall and emaciated Burdett had led Cobbett to refer to him as the Baronet's 'little Sancho Panza'. Despite his lack of inches, Hobhouse seized a stick and offered to knock Cobbett down. Pandemonium followed. Cobbett jumped on the table, from which he was knocked off 'with the loss of part of my waistcoat'. A general melée resulted. Burdett withdrew with such dignity as he could muster, to be followed, with rather less dignity, by Cobbett, who was hustled out of the tavern by Burdett's supporters.

All of this was gleefully reported in the London newspapers with near-fatal consequences. Mrs. Cobbett was so distressed by the ruffianly consequences of her husband's renewed association with Hunt that she attempted to commit suicide. George Spater, in his biography of Cobbett, has suggested that she might, at that time, have been suffering from menopausal stress. Cobbett, however, attributed that 'violent and tragical deed' to something 'that had never before happened under my roof, a family quarrel'.[8]

Ann Cobbett's attempted suicide showed how greatly her husband's growing political intemperance had distressed her. One may argue that she had always been too simple and too conventional a woman ever to have understood, or to have shared in Cobbett's mounting ambition to change the mould of British politics. But his children were far from simple or unlettered and had been brought up in the odour of Radicalism, yet still they shared their mother's distress. It is true that a domineering father may eventually find his children rejecting all that was forced on them in their early years. It is equally true that one of his sons, John Morgan, died a Conservative Member of Parliament and that the rest, as members of the professional middle class, became rather more respectable and

* Henry Hunt was ten years younger than Cobbett, who was sixty-four at that time. Nevertheless, since Hunt died in the same year as Cobbett, one may assume that he either aged quicker or wore worse, in spite of being, in his time, as vigorous a man and as dedicated a sportsman as Cobbett.

conformist than their father would have wished. There is no evidence, however, to suggest that they rebelled against his politics during his lifetime. It was his behaviour rather than his beliefs that distressed them. And it was he who, in the end, rejected them.

One can find various reasons why politicians so frequently find it difficult to make a success of their domestic lives. It may even be that one of them is the seldom-admitted fact that the practice of politics can coarsen a man. It had become so common for Cobbett's enemies to accuse him of being excessively bitter, violent and coarse in his political speeches and writings that he now felt that he had to make a public explanation of himself. It may be significant that he felt the need to do this in the early months of 1828. The first quarrel and his wife's recent attempt at suicide might have meant that he was attempting to explain himself to his family as much as to the public, and was beginning to suspect that the violence of his politics was beginning to infect his private life.

His explanations were contained in three different *Register* articles. The first, published in January 1828, dealt with his supposed violence: 'When I began to write, I had attacked no writer, I fell foul of nobody in the shape of a "literary gentleman". I was as modest as a maid, and dealt in qualifications and modifications and mitigations to the best of my poor powers in the line of palavering; but when I discovered that it was *envy* that was at work in my assailants . . . I instantly resolved to proceed in the very way in which I have always proceeded, giving three, four or ten blows for one; and never, in any case, ceased to pursue the assailant in some way or other, until he was completely down.'

In April 1828 Cobbett replied in the *Register* to a 'Correspondent' who had urged him to be less bitter, and who had suggested that, if only he were more amiable, there would be no 'impediment to my obtaining that rank and power, for which he is pleased to think my abilities mark me out'. 'I have,' he wrote, 'no reason to think that I am not, and that I have not been, as amiable as most other men. Very pretty girls in two different countries used, when I was young, to be reasonably fond of me. I have never had a servant that did not like his or her master; and, as to my family and friends, I leave them to say, whether there is the company of any person on earth in which they delight more than mine.'

Having established his credentials as the very soul of amiability, he went on to discuss what was really in question. 'By being *amiable*, my Correspondent means, being soft, being mild towards offenders . . . being only partially just; and trying to wheedle people to do that which is criminal in them not to do; in short, to abandon my duty, to creep to those that Truth and Justice bid me set to defiance.' In short, it was not bitterness, but a love of justice that motivated him. But he then, without realising it, contradicted himself, for he asked why his Correspondent could not see 'that I have acquired this power in spite of all that bitterness . . . (and) that there would be danger in losing the weight I at present possess, were I to alter the course of my proceedings'.[10]

In May of that year Cobbett attacked the subject of his supposed coarseness: ' "Coarse!" the sons and daughters of Corruption will exclaim. "Coarse!" will echo back the scoundrel *seat-sellers* . . . "Vary coarse, ma'awm!" will some grinning Scotch sycophant observe to some she-sinecurist or pensioner. "Coarse as neck-beef" will growl out some Englishman, who has filled his bags by oppression of the poor . . . Yes, it is *coarse* indeed, and coarse it ought to be in a case like this. SWIFT has told us not to chop *blocks* with *razors*. Any *edge* tool is too fine for work like this: a pick-axe, that perforates with one end and drags about with the other, is the tool for this sort of business.'[11]

If these, almost his only attempts at self-justification, meant anything, they meant that he thought of himself as a naturally moderate and amiable man who found violence, bitterness and coarseness useful weapons to employ in the political battle. In so far as his private life was concerned, he still thought of himself as the pleasing companion, the loving husband and the kindly father of his earlier days. He would have found it impossible to admit that that man had disappeared, that the weapons he had so deliberately decided to use in the political battle had gradually taken charge until violence, bitterness and coarseness had become part of his character and had been allowed to enter and influence his private life.

Yet all the evidence that George Spater has recently uncovered concerning Cobbett's private life at this time suggests that, having been coarsened by politics, Cobbett had become, in almost every respect, an embittered and intemperate man who saw envy in every least criticism of himself and a conspiracy in every argument. There was much, apart from his public behaviour, for his family to criticise and argue about. His sons, who had all been brought up to take some part in their father's farming, publishing and business ventures, were increasingly worried by the recklessness with which he managed them. His only tangible assets, once Botley had been lost, consisted of the *Register*, which was now losing readers, a seed business which was rarely profitable, his stock of books, which was considerable because of the large print-runs he ordered, and his copyrights. Some of those copyrights he had, in the past, given to his children, largely in order to keep them out of the clutches of his creditors. His sons, who were all lawyers, and who wanted to save what they could of their rapidly disappearing patrimony, now demanded their rights and, in lieu of what he owed them under the copyrights, Cobbett had to assign to them a large part of his book stocks. His remaining copyrights and book stocks he was gradually forced to assign to his creditors, for he was now borrowing more and more heavily and owed Sir Thomas Beevor alone £6,000. He may well have felt that he had been stripped as bare of his possessions as King Lear had been, and partly, at least, by those who ought to have been his debtors in filial gratitude. He referred in a *Register* article to his belief that there was a 'lawyer's conspiracy' against him, and made it fairly plain that he referred to his sons.

Three of those sons had added authorship to their other occupations, and this began to give rise to rumours that Cobbett, in his old age, was using them as ghost writers. This, his enemies explained, accounted for his astonishing prolificacy as well as for what was commonly believed to be a marked falling-off in the quality of the *Register*. The matter was made worse when his sons launched a short-lived periodical of their own under the title of *Cobbett's Magazine*. This use of the name he, and he alone had made famous convinced Cobbett that his sons had started the rumours in order to establish their own reputations as writers, even if it meant damaging their father's. He published an article denying that he had ever used anyone as a ghost writer and suggesting that his sons were now conspiring 'to crush the *Political Register*, and to drive me from my seat in Parliament'. He was coming close, now, to allowing his conspiracy theories and his persecution mania to come between himself and reality.

As early as 1827, at the time of the first family quarrel, Cobbett had embarked on a somewhat irrational 'contest for mastery'. This involved him in retiring to his study and a back bedroom and holding no communication with his family for a period of seventy-five days. He may or may not have re-established mastery by these methods, but the quarrels continued. In 1831, at the time of the 'Goodman' trial, he quarrelled with James Paul, who went off to live by himself, a natural enough thing for most young men to do but not for one coming from such a close-knit family.

The final break-up of the family, however, came in 1833. Cobbett had taken his seat in Parliament and, perhaps as a consequence, was showing signs of increasing physical weakness and irritability. Much as he disliked Parliamentary life, he took his duties seriously and was assiduous in his attendance. The additional work, the long periods that had to be spent in London, and, above all, the late-night sittings were immensely taxing to a man of his age who was used to country, or, at the worst, suburban air, and to rising with the sun and to retiring not long after it had set.

It was one late-night sitting that led to the climax he later described in a letter to Sir Thomas Beevor. He had returned to his home in Crown Street looking for 'the bowl of warm milk with a little tea in it which I always wish for in such a case'. When he found 'neither bowl nor fire, and nobody but a man to let me in, though there was a wife, three daughters, two sons and two maid servants in the house, all in good beds of my providing' his rage was as terrible as Lear's. Nevertheless his powers of humorous description did not desert him entirely for he added: 'Too happy should L have been, however, if this had been *all*. But when I got into that bed which I so much needed . . . that *tongue* which, for more than 20 years has been my great curse, and which would have worried any other man to death, suffered me not to have one moment's sleep . . . and as I saw that this was a mere *beginning* of a month of it, she breakfasting in bed every day, and having the sofa to lounge on, and the park to take exercise in, to provide the strength of lungs and the power of sustaining wakefulness at night, I also saw that I must get out of the house. Therefore, as soon as it was light, I called up my man, and decamped to Bolt Court, and there I remained 'till the day when the king prorogued us'.[12]

Parliament was prorogued in November 1833 and in the subsequent General Election Cobbett was returned again for Oldham. He never returned again, however, to Crown Street or to family life. He divided the rest of his days between his rooms over his offices at Bolt Court, rooms Doctor Johnson had once inhabited, and his Normandy Farm at Ash. He had some intercourse with his oldest son, William, who looked after his farming interests, but except for him his only domestic companions were his servants and his employees. And so it remained until he was on his deathbed.

If it was a sad finish to something that had started so happily, almost fifty years earlier in snowy New Brunswick, when he had fallen in love at first sight with Sergeant Reid's pubescent and beautiful daughter, it was also a less uncommon one than most of us would care to admit. Daphnis and Chloe must, some day, wither into Darby and Joan, and if Darby, by then, has turned into a querulous and quarrelsome tyrant, it may be because Joan has become a nagging and unsympathetic slut – or, of course, vice-versa.

What was uncommon and, perhaps, sad about the decay of Cobbett's family life was that it revealed, once again, the discrepancies between what he wrote about and what actually happened. His enemies had always accused him of contradicting himself, from year to year, in his politics. It is now clear that he did the same with his private life.

Whenever, in all his voluminous writings, Cobbett had thought it necessary to refer to himself and to his domestic circumstances it had always been to hold both up as models to the Gentiles. His wife was the most amiable, the most gentle, the most loving of women, and the *non-pareil* of all housewives. His children were, without exception, accomplished, affectionate and biddable. He himself was the fondest, kindest and most solicitous of husbands and fathers. His home, as a consequence, was a haven in which peace, comfort, love and virtuous endeavour permanently prevailed.

Whether this had always been so or not – and his reference to twenty years of nagging suggests that it was not – the domestic storms that persisted from 1827 onwards had destroyed the peace of his haven. Yet in 1829 Cobbett wrote what is still surely the most famous and authoritative of all guides to domestic happiness, *Advice to Young Men And (Incidentally) To Young Women In The Middle and Higher Ranks of Life.*

It was in this work of his declining years that he so confidently laid down the ground-rules for success in courtship, marriage and parenthood and justified every precept by referring to his own success in each of those roles. Who had been more perceptive and more prudent than he in choosing a mate? Who had been more constant and more caring a husband? Who had been more successful in cherishing and educating his children? Who, as a consequence, had ever reaped a greater reward in his own home, or had a better right to teach others how to achieve happiness in theirs?

We need not accuse Cobbett of hypocrisy for this. Writers, like politicians and preachers, have to be allowed some latitude between precept and practice or no one would ever offer himself to the use of the public; and now, a century and a half after his death, both the public and the private man have become far less important than the author. The reality of Cobbett lies in his books and, perhaps, in no more than a very few of those. The fact that, as a husband and father, he failed to practice what he preached in *Advice to Young Men* is no more relevant to the value and reality of that work than was the fact that Doctor Johnson suffered from scrofula. Biographers have to remark on such discrepancies, but they ought not to make too much of them.

Because Cobbett's most enduring achievement was to turn author at a comparatively late stage in his career, it is, in the end, not his politics nor his journalism nor even his character that we have to examine, but his books. There is more of the real William Cobbett in them than there was in the ageing, failing and increasingly erratic man who finally achieved what contemporaries considered to be his greatest political success at a time when his fortunes and his happiness had most completely failed. His journalism, to a certain extent, reflected both his successes and his failures, but neither, it would seem, influenced his books. They, since he was essentially an Arcadian, reflect the ideal rather than the actual; and they show few or no signs of deterioration.

Between 1818, when he first turned author proper, and 1833, when the *Northern Tour* was published, he produced over twenty works that can properly be described as books rather than pamphlets. Of these, no fewer than six have survived as minor classics.* Those critics who have thought to see a falling-off in his writing towards the end have to be reminded that *Advice to Young Men* was written in 1829 and the *Northern Tour* in 1832. G. D. H. Cole argued that this last failed to equal the earlier *Rides*, being too shrilly polemical. It was, indeed, polemical and contained even more puffs for himself, in the shape of Congratulatory Addresses, than usual. On the other hand, he had converted what had been thought of as a venture into hostile territory into a triumphal progression, and he was entitled to proclaim that fact to his enemies. His descriptions of the Scottish scene, whether in the Lothians or on the banks of the Clyde, were as fresh and as vivid as any of his other pieces of descriptive writing. Nor had he become any less perceptive: his accounts of bothy life and his two *Letters to the Chopsticks* are, in some respects, better than any other of his many socio-political analyses of rural life amongst the poor. The best of him in these last years was contained in his books rather than in his politics.

As his titles accumulated, advertisements for what was called *The Cobbett-Library* began to appear in the *Register* and various others of Cobbett's publications. What Cobbett himself thought of his 'Library' and how he divided it into its various subjects provides, perhaps, the only *catalogue raisonné* that is needed. The advertisement that follows was included in Cobbett's *Two-Penny Trash* of 1 July 1831. It does not, therefore, include later works, such as *Cobbett's Tour in Scotland*, his *Life of Andrew Jackson*, his *Manchester Lectures* or his *Lectures on the French and Belgian*

---

* Although such things must always be a matter of opinion, majority opinion would probably agree that these should include *A Year's Residence*, *Cobbett's Grammar*, *Cottage Economy*, *Advice to Young Men*, *The Emigrant's Guide* and, of course, *Rural Rides*. His contemporaries would have added *A History of the Protestant Reformation in England*, which was, in its day, translated into more languages and read in more countries than any other work apart from the Bible.

Revolutions. It also omits the obvious pot-boilers he published at the end of his career in a desperate attempt to raise money by the making and selling of books. These would include his *Spelling-Book*, the *Geographical Dictionary of England and Wales* and *A New French and English Dictionary*. What it did include is best left to Cobbett to describe:

> When I am asked what books a young man or young woman ought to read, I always answer, Let him or her read *all that I have written*. This does, it will doubtless be said, *smell of the shop*. No matter. It is what I recommended; and experience has taught me that it is my duty to give that recommendation. I am speaking here of books other than THE REGISTER; and even these, that I call my LIBRARY, consist of *twenty-six* distinct books; two of them being TRANSLATIONS; *six* of them being written BY MY SONS; *one* (TULL'S HUSBANDRY) revised and edited, and one published by me and written by the Rev. Mr. O'CALLAGHAN, a most virtuous Catholic Priest. I divide these books into classes, as follows. 1. Books for TEACHING LANGUAGES; 2. On DOMESTIC MANAGEMENT AND DUTIES; 3. RURAL AFFAIRS; 4. On THE MANAGEMENT OF NATIONAL AFFAIRS; 5. HISTORY; 6. TRAVELS; 7. LAWS; 8. MISCELLANEOUS POLITICS. Here is a great variety of subjects; and all of them very *dry*; nevertheless the manner of treating them is, in general, such as to induce the reader to *go through the book*, when he once has begun it . . .

In the list that followed, the puffs he attached to each title are not without interest. Of his *English Grammar*: 'This is a book of *principles* clearly laid down; and when once these are got into the mind they never quit it.' Of his *French Grammar*: 'More young men have, I dare say, learned French from it, than from all the other books that have been published in English for the last fifty years.' Of *Cobbett's Sermons*: 'More of these Sermons have been *sold* than of the Sermons of all the Church-parsons put together since mine were published.' Of *Rural Rides*: 'If the members of the Government had *read* these Rides, only just *read* them, last year, when they were collected and printed in a volume, they *could not have helped* foreseeing all the violences that have now taken place, and especially *in these very counties*; and foreseeing them, they must have been devils in reality, if they had not done something to prevent them.' Of *Cobbett's Poor Man's Friend*: 'This is my *favourite* work. I bestowed more labour upon it than upon any large volume that I ever wrote.'

This somewhat unusual advertisement ended in the following way: 'This is the Library that I have *created*. It really makes a tolerable *shelf of books*; a man who understands the contents of which may be deemed a man of great information. In about every one of these works I have pleaded the cause of the *working people*, and I shall now see that cause triumph, in spite of all that can be done to prevent it.' This political note was followed by a prudently commercial one. 'N.B. A whole *set* of these books at the above prices amounts to 7£.0s.2d.; but if a whole set be taken together, the price is 6£. And here is a stock of knowledge sufficient for any young man in the world.'

Cobbett not only enjoyed the advantage of being able, as a publisher, to recommend himself as an author. He could also, as a newspaper proprietor, advertise both publisher and author for nothing. But what modern publisher would have the honesty to admit that all the books he offered dealt with 'dry' subjects? And for how many of his authors could he honestly claim the ability to make 'dry' subjects readable?

Indeed Cobbett's books, or at the least large parts of them, are still readable, which is somewhat remarkable considering the subjects he chose and the fact that it was always his purpose to be didactic, moralistic or politically partisan. It is not thus that a modern bestseller is produced. And yet Cobbett's books were, and to a limited extent still are, bestsellers. Contemporary readers can still, if they persevere, find in each one of them at least some moments of sudden and unexpected delight. There will, of course, be *longueurs* arising from what Hazlitt described as Cobbett's 'damnable habit of iteration'. There will be political arguments lost or won so long ago that they are now interesting only to historians. There will be scurrilous attacks on people long dead and references to scandals long forgotten that will have to be explained to become amusing.

Yet one cannot go far in any of his books without coming across a fine piece of descriptive writing or a passage in which something complicated has been so lucidly and simply laid out that his interpretation of it seems both convincing and elegant. Every now and again, and generally when it is least expected, his sense of humour, which was both sly and savage, will surface. His polemics always owe something to his appreciation of all that is ridiculous in a situation or an individual and it is often when he is at his most solemn that something truly comical emerges. His overstocked and underdisciplined mind leads him off into digressions that generally seem more interesting than anything he digressed from. When the reader has resigned himself to the tedium of one of his prolonged political or economic diatribes he will suddenly be jolted into attention by a completely unexpected word or phrase which only on second thought seems apposite and difficult to better. If his language seems plainer than that of his contemporaries, his constructions are often daringly complicated, yet he generally emerges from them with both his meaning and his syntax intact. He is not a writer to be read rapidly or skippingly or the best of him, which is his ability to surprise his reader, will be lost.

A writer's skills can only be properly judged by the effect he has on his reader. Cobbett, by that criterion, was amongst the most skilful, for his works still produce the effects he intended. In another writer this would probably be attributed to his style, but we tend to take Cobbett's style somewhat for granted. This may be because his works have provided so much material for politicians, historians, and even biographers to work on that attention has always been focussed on what he had to say rather than on the manner in which he said it.

Hazlitt, that shrewd literary critic, refrained from analysing Cobbett's style, explaining that 'He might be said to have the clearness of Swift, the naturalness of Defoe, the picturesque satirical description of Mandeville,* if all such comparisons were not impertinent. A really great and original writer is like nobody but himself'. He added, however, that Cobbett 'speaks and thinks plain, broad, downright English', and that, perhaps, brought him halfway to the truth. Cobbett was, in fact, too complex a man to *think* 'plain English', but he did *write* it. That in an age when most educated men had been brought up to believe that in order to write English well one must study and imitate the Romans, made him an original.

Such greatness as Cobbett had as a writer arose, however, out of his love of the English language which was, in its turn, the product of his early circumstances. As a self-educated man he had, in so far as that was possible, escaped the influences of a classical education. He had, instead, read a great deal of English literature and, if he had done so indiscriminately, his natural taste exposed him to the influences of the better rather than the lesser writers. Although in later years he turned ostentatiously Philistine and decried all novelists, most poets and all dramatists, his writings are full of quotations from and references to Shakespeare and Milton, Dryden and Pope, Fielding and Goldsmith, Wycherley and Congreve.

* Bernard de Mandeville (?1670–1733). An English author noted for his satire *The Fable of the Bees* (1723).

Even more important, he had turned himself into a more than competent grammarian and had become enough of an etymologist to be able to correct and rebuke his opponents whenever they used a word in a way which revealed that they were ignorant of its origins and true meaning. A man elects to educate himself in that manner only if he delights in words and language, and this Cobbett very obviously did. As for the way in which he made use of that language, it possibly owed something to the years he spent in the orderly room writing out regimental orders. That could have taught him the value of clarity and precision though it did not appear to have taught him anything about being concise.

But the easy, conversational style he eventually evolved was probably never consciously adopted but was rather an inevitable product of his politics. Once he had turned politician, whether as a Tory or a Radical, he saw himself as a demagogue, in the original meaning of that word, which the dictionary gives as 'a leader of the people as against the other parties in the state'. As Peter Porcupine, he set out to persuade ordinary Americans to abandon their almost traditional attachment to the French alliance. As a Radical, he attempted to persuade ordinary Englishmen to reject the political and economic system imposed on them by the Whigs as much as the Tories. In each case he opposed the Establishment and appealed to the commons.

Whoever appeals to the people must do so, if he is to succeed, in the demotic, or at least in something that resembles it, and if the appeal is a written one, it must come as close as the written language will allow to the spoken word. These were the effects Cobbett's conversational style allowed him to achieve. His more artless readers, at least, did not feel that they were reading, but were rather listening to someone who talked to, reasoned with and argued at them in a style they found congenial and in language they could comprehend. But if they were artless enough to believe that they were being addressed by some acquaintance from across a table, the man who created that illusion was far from artless. Indeed, more writing arts have to be deployed to sustain the conversational style than are used by those who, recognising the fundamental differences between the spoken and written languages, accept the limitations involved, even though these mean distancing themselves from their readers.

Cobbett accepted no such limitations, possibly because he had acquired sufficient skills to do otherwise. He could give to his writing some of the pace and rhythms of speech and was able to create the impression that his words came hot from his mouth instead of being prepared and meditated on before ever they were written. Some of this *trompe-l'oeil* effect was achieved through the constructions he used. He varied the length of his sentences so as to make them resemble the hesitations and overflowings of speech. Some were little more than ejaculations that concluded in an exclamation mark. Others seemed interminable and contained the explanations, recapitulations, parentheses and asides of the spoken language, which can never, by its nature, be as well-organised as the written one. The enthusiasm, passion and humour with which he wrote gave some of the spontaneity of speech to his work and, although he used words more exactly and more correctly than they are used in conversation, he seldom used ones that are not commonly used, or misused, when people speak to one another.

His punctuation, which he used in accordance with the old rules of grammar, that is to say immoderately, was an essential part of his style. Commas separated every clause, and this allowed him to construct sentences in which the clauses could accumulate without the thread being lost. He marched semi-colons, colons and exclamation marks across the page in much the same way as he had once marched soldiers across a barrack square and, perhaps another military touch, he numbered his paragraphs, which made for orderly reading but was typographically ugly.

He made lavish use of another typographical device which, because it is now seldom used, can be irritating. He scattered italics across every page in much the same way, and for much the same reason, as a composer places his markings over every few bars of his score. This was, once again, part of his conversational style. The italicised words marked the places where, if he had actually been talking, he would have raised his voice or have given a knowing wink or have banged his fist on the table. Occasionally, when he wanted that bang to be particularly significant, he would substitute upper case for italics, whether it was in the middle of the sentence or not.

He had a remarkably quick eye for the ridiculous. Although it won him more readers than any other of his accomplishments, he was, in his later days, humorous almost in despite of himself. He was enormously proud of his powers of reasoning – which were always suspect – but far less proud, by then, of his undoubted ability to inspire laughter. 'Who, besides myself,' he wrote in the *Register*, 'has, in our day, attempted to gain popularity by dint of fact and of argument, unmixed with anything to amuse the human mind? If, at any time, I have indulged in a sort of jest I have been almost ashamed of the momentary triumph thereby acquired.'[13]

The Cobbett who wrote that passage had clearly lost the delight in humour that had once made Peter Porcupine so proud that he had 'endeavoured to make America laugh'. For the older man, humour had become a more serious business, a cudgel to be taken out and used on wrongdoers rather than the necessary seasoning to all that he thought and all that he wrote. But he could still make the nation laugh. Even his victims grinned as they squirmed under his attacks. Cobbett never developed, however, into the truly comical writer Porcupine might have become if he had been able to keep away from politics. Nor, on the other hand, did he grow into the great satirist he wanted to be. Irony, sarcasm and vituperation can all, in the hands of a man as witty as Cobbett, earn our laughter, but neither severally nor singly do they amount to satire.

True satire starts from that form of self-knowledge that inspires a high and wholesome degree of self-disgust. Cobbett's self-knowledge was woefully limited. What he did know about himself inspired complacency rather than disgust. Swift, the only man Cobbett ever took as his literary model and guide, was a true satirist because what he hated in the Yahoos was what he hated in himself, whilst all that was noble and benign in the Houyhnhnms was all that was most notably lacking in every forked radish calling himself a man, including, of course, Jonathan Swift.

The distinction is, perhaps, best brought out in one of Swift's best-known sayings: 'Principally I hate and detest that animal called man; although I heartily love John, Peter, Thomas and so forth.' Yet Swift, for all his savage satires on society, was deeply loved by all who knew him and by many who did not. Cobbett, on the other hand, frequently expressed his love for mankind or, at least, for sections of it such as his starving and ill-treated chopsticks or the virtuous, freedom-loving and well-fed Americans. This was, however, an abstract and politically based sort of love that inspired no love in return. Cobbett was often admired and sometimes adulated, but he was seldom liked, for he lacked the gift of friendship. After his death his son James, preparing notes for a biography that was never completed, wrote that his father had been 'steady and constant' only in his hatreds. 'He had but little individual attachment. Liked people's company; & they liked his (when he was agreeable). But he formed very little of *friendship*. And wd. break off with any one, however old an acquaintance, on any affront, or being crossed in his will.'[14]

Cobbett, in spite of all his writings and protestations to the contrary, lacked affection. A man without affection finds it difficult to understand others, and without an understanding of men there can be no true satire. His attacks on the follies, vices and crimes of his enemies were often witty and sometimes funny, for few men have ever handled abuse and ridicule more effectively. But, although he thought of himself as one, he was never a satirist. Yet he could have become a memorable one if only he could have seen in himself the folly he so easily saw in others and if he had had more liking for 'John, Peter and Thomas'.

If his character prevented him from being a satirist, circumstance did something to prevent him from being an even better writer than he was. The need to fill the columns of each week's *Register* forced him to write too much, too often and too quickly, and the state of his finances led him to do the same as an author. He was probably the most prolific of all English writers, and much of his work was dictated to a secretary to be sent, unpolished and unrevised, straight to the printer.

Whilst authors can sometimes, if they need to, make a success of journalism, it is more difficult for journalists to succeed as authors. If Cobbett succeeded in crossing the gulf that separates the one from the other, his books, nevertheless, reveal the price he had to pay for having been first, and primarily, a journalist. Some of his books, *Rural Rides* especially, were no more than collections of *Register* articles that had not even been worked over to prepare them for publication in book form. They lacked, therefore, the discipline and the organisation one expects from a book. It is relevant that Cobbett, both as journalist and author, always acted as his own publisher, editor, and, to a large extent, distributor. This meant that he had only himself and his readers to please and be disciplined by and, since he was an undisciplined thinker and a wordy, repetitive writer who had to follow every hare that he started, this shows in his work.

An outside publisher and editors might well have disciplined him into making his books move steadily and logically forwards, and it was his inability to do this that his contemporaries criticised. Hazlitt wrote that 'Cobbett, with vast industry, vast information, and the utmost power of making what he says intelligible, never seems to get at the beginning or come to the end of any question'. Today, when we read him for entertainment rather than to be informed, we enjoy his digressions and meanderings more than we do the subjects he originally set out to deal with. Who, except Cobbett, would insert into a chapter dealing with potato-growing, a large section criticising the works of Shakespeare and Milton and ridiculing all those Bardolators who had made such public fools of themselves over William Ireland's forgeries? Or who, in the same treatise on farming, would have included in a chapter on pig management such a passionate defence of that animal's sagacity, or have ended by asserting that no sow was properly housed unless her winter quarters were so warm that her owner would be prepared to share them with her?

It is delightful that Cobbett should have strayed into such arguments which few other potato-growers or pig-farmers could have thought of. Nevertheless it was, in a writer, a form of self-indulgence, and self-indulgent writing, most publishers would agree, must always be discouraged. It wastes paper and print, slows the pace of the work, and intervenes between the author and what ought to be his purpose. They would, in Cobbett's case, be no more than partially right, for not all of his digressions were as delightful as these. The merest mention of, say, William Pitt, or paper money, or Old Sarum would set him off at a tangent into digressions that were all the more tedious because they had developed into reflex reactions.

It is not fanciful to believe that Cobbett's particular experiences as a journalist had trained him in this self-indulgence. His absolute control over the *Register* allowed him to say anything and everything that he wanted to say at no matter what length. If he was interested in the subject he would not remain content with a 10,000 word article in a single Number of that paper, but he would chase it through subsequent Numbers until he had ended up with a book-length serial in which everything had been said two or three times over. *Register* readers accepted this because it was, in an indirect way, a guarantee of Cobbett's integrity. Other journalists might have to write to length and to order, but Cobbett was proprietor, editor and journalist all in one, and the very length of his articles proved that there was no one who could bribe, bully or cajole him into his opinions. Journalistic independence, however admirable though it was, bred bad habits in the author.

Yet it is where one would have expected Cobbett's work as a journalist to have influenced his work as an author most that it influenced it not at all. Since he had never used 'journalese' as a journalist he had no need to struggle against it as an author. He never elevated or lowered his style as he alternated between authorship and journalism, but always, as Hazlitt put it, 'wrote himself plain William Cobbett'. His avoidance of 'journalese' was a more considerable feat than the laymen will credit. Most journalists, sooner or later, adopt its convenient shorthand, whether they use it in the high mandarin style of a *Times* leader writer, or the cheerfully vulgar one of the gossip columnist. Cobbett was not above using clichés to save having to use language, but they were generally ones of his own inventing, such as 'the Wen', the 'Sons of Corruption', 'the tax-eaters' or 'the half-pay gentry'. He was remarkably ingenious with nicknames, generally choosing to impale his victims on some laudatory phrase from their pasts. The conceit became irritating, however, when used for the hundredth time, however amusing it had been when Pitt was first referred to as 'the Pilot', Wellington as 'the great Captain' and Goderich as 'Prosperity Robinson'.*

Although Cobbett was almost inordinately proud of the books he wrote, he possibly never thought of himself as primarily an author. Indeed, there was a time, when he was farming out much of the *Register* and all of his *Parliamentary History* to Wright, and his *State Trials* to Howell, when he thought it more important to be a publisher. Then, forgetting his early days in Philadelphia when he had raged against Carey and Bradford, he affected, as publishers sometimes do, to despise mere authors. In December 1808 he had written to Wright about Howell saying: 'I know that he is what the French call *un homme à grandes pretensions*, as, indeed, all your authors are . . . Their conceit is so intolerable that I would sooner have dealings with an old lecherous woman that would be tearing open my cod-piece fifty times a day.'

Taking Cobbett all in all, however, as journalist and author, what must impress any professional writer is his complete professionalism. He achieved that most difficult of all feats, writing to please himself and getting well paid for it. He never flattered, or pampered, or even considered his readers, and yet he never wrote anything except *Important Considerations*, that did not earn him money. To that extent he agreed with Doctor Johnson's dictum that 'no man but a blockhead ever wrote, except for money'.

He never wasted a single thought or a single sentence that could be used again in a different context. A speech or a letter would be resurrected as an article, that article would be republished as a pamphlet, and the pamphlet would be used to furnish a book. He was quite extraordinarily versatile, attempted every form apart from fiction, and wrote, with apparent authority, on almost everything. If he could have known little about the subject before he had started, he could create the impression of knowing everything about it before he had finished. And he could do this without allowing either his initial ignorance nor his subsequent researches to show.

As a consequence, he wrote as an expert on economics, foreign affairs, military matters, household matters, travel, farming, gardening and forestry in addition to writing endlessly about

---

* Pitt had been praised by Canning as 'the Pilot who had weathered the storm', Wellington had been lauded as 'the greatest Captain of his age' and Frederick Robinson, Viscount Goderich, had once, in a Budget speech, talked somewhat unwarily about the prosperity of the nation.

politics. He produced sermons, fables, grammars, biographies, histories and dictionaries. He could achieve almost any effect, being alternately moralistic, dogmatic, scientific, picaresque, sentimental, ribald, polemical and scurrilous. He could make his passions seem justified, his prejudices reasonable and his hatreds ordained by the Deity.

Yet, for all his versatility, he never gave the impression of being superficial. His arguments were so well conducted that those who agreed with them were strengthened in their convictions and those who did not were inspired to counter-argument. He was not, in either case, a man to be ignored or lightly dismissed. Since he frequently indulged in argument for argument's sake, he could leave his readers wondering whether white was, indeed, as light as they had thought, and black quite as dark.

It is thought derogatory to refer to any writer as a hack but it is easier to understand the word if one turns to the world of the horse, where a hack can be described as a most useful, all-purpose sort of animal which goes well at all paces and in all gears. It is perhaps in that sense that Cobbett can be described as the greatest hack in the history of English literature.

But he was also, of course, something more. He was a master of English prose. As a political writer he stands level with Paine and a little below Burke. No writer on country subjects has ever shown a better understanding of the life and the nature of the English countryside. He was an outstanding polemicist who has made it seem as if all his successors have been firing off squibs where he fired off siege guns. He was, within his limited range, an excellent humorist. He was, in the truest sense of the word, an original, for he owed nothing to other writers, most of whom he despised, and he has had, more's the pity, no successors. He was a man of the eighteenth century whose arguments still echo in our minds at the end of the twentieth century for he is, in many ways, closer to us than he was to the Victorians. He still offers the best of company to any reader who has the sense to listen to him, the spirit to argue with him, enough humour to be able to laugh both with him and at him, and, above all, a sufficient liking for the language and for singularity to enjoy him.

EPILOGUE

The Brief Career and Death of a Member of Parliament

Non omnis moriar
(I shall not altogether die)
Horace: *Ars Poetica*

The Reform Bill that finally passed through Parliament in 1832 was a watered-down version of the one Cobbett had fought for. Nevertheless, and unlike Hunt, he accepted it. The industrial towns had been enfranchised, and he still hoped that they would return enough Radical Members to force the rest of the Radical Reform programme through the Commons. The Bill, in short, seemed a half-way stage towards that ultimate victory that would surely bring back Arcadia. Consequently when, on 7 June 1832, the Bill became law, Cobbett had at least half of a victory to celebrate.

He chose to celebrate it in familiar Hampshire surroundings, and in the company of his beloved chopsticks, whose feats in the recent 'Rural War' had, he maintained, made that amount of Reform possible. He therefore organised a great Chopstick Festival for 8 July 1832 at Sutton Scotney. The proceedings were joyously reported in the *Register*. It was possibly the last occasion in all Cobbett's long political career in which he had cause to rejoice unreservedly.

There were bands, banners and processions. The refreshments provided were as carefully recorded as at the Lord Mayor's banquet. Cobbett contributed two sheep which, between them, yielded 260 lbs. of excellent mutton as well as two large Nottingham hams (superbly cooked by his wife). Other contributions to the feast included 'three capital rounds of beef', mountains of loaves, ample supplies of bacon, scores of veal pies, and 250 lb. of plum puddings. One rejoicing Reformer roasted a suckling pig and a couple of geese to add to the victuals and another gave 400 pots of beer. Cobbett, after he had taken a post-prandial nap, addressed the assembled chopsticks, Reformers and members of the Winchester Political Union from a waggon drawn up in front of the inn. One cannot read Cobbett's account of all this without rejoicing with the old man in his moment of triumph.

455

The rest of 1832 passed busily for him. He lectured in Manchester, toured Scotland and rushed back to Oldham for the December General Election. The new Parliament met for the first time on 29 January 1833, and the new Member for Oldham, having looked at the seating arrangements in the Commons,* demonstrated his refusal to respect its conventions by seating himself on the Treasury Bench in the place traditionally occupied by the Leader of the House. Parliament was prorogued in July 1834. A month later Cobbett embarked on the last of his *Rides*, which took him to Ireland. This did not, like the Scottish *Ride*, produce a book, but it did result in a series of *Register* articles which took the form of ten *Letters to Charles Marshall*, he being Cobbett's foreman at Normandy Farm. The articles graphically described Cobbett's distress at seeing so much good farmland produce so much misery and famine. Apart from that, there was little by way of descriptive writing and the rest was taken up with Irish politics.

He returned from Ireland in November, and, having been re-elected, was again in the Commons on 19 February 1835 for the first sitting of the new Parliament. By 18 June of that year he was dead. In short, although he spent almost forty years of his life in politics, he only spent ten months actually in the Commons and so had little time in which to make his mark as a Parliamentarian. This, it was generally observed at the time, he signally failed to do. If, by that, it was meant that he failed to influence the course of debate and the flow of legislation, so much was inevitable. Only a handful of Radical Members had been returned at the 1832 Election, and even when O'Connell's Irishmen voted with them, they could put fewer than 30 men through the Lobby as opposed to some 530 Whigs and Tories who generally combined to vote against them.

Cobbett in Parliament was quite as intransigent and as aggressive as Cobbett of the *Register* had ever been. He refused to be civilised into a good House of Commons man, and was as critical of Westminster, in Westminster, as he was in Bolt Court. His first act was to defy Parliamentary conventions by opposing the re-election of the Speaker, and the first words he uttered in the House were 'It appears to me that, since I have been sitting here, I have heard a great deal of unprofitable discussion'.

The House, not surprisingly, was disinclined to listen to him in

---

* With his usual passion for statistics, Cobbett calculated that, if the Chamber were cleared of every scrap of furniture, 'there is not *a foot and a half square* for each of the six hundred and fifty-eight men to stand upon'. What was worse for a man of his width of beam, 'the length of a bench does not, I believe, allow to each man fifteen inches'.

silence. His second speech was devoted to an amendment to the Address which amounted to a complete rejection of the programme outlined and its replacement by his own detailed proposals for the better government of the country. The new Member's impudence brought constant interruptions until, according to Hansard, Cobbett turned on his tormentors: 'I appeal to you, Mr Speaker, if I have not a right to be heard: please be so good as to keep order. (Laughter) You'll not silence me, that I'll assure you. You may rely on it, if you do not hear me, I shall adjourn the House. I was quite prepared for this, and am not to be put down by it . . . You shall hear every word that I have to say . . . and if the House be determined not to hear me tonight, I will certainly bring it forward tomorrow, and if the House will not hear me tomorrow, I will then bring it forward the day after. The statement I have to make I am determined to make.'

It was shortly afterwards that he referred, in a *Register* article to this time-hallowed Commons tradition of heckling. 'What is wanted in the House is this: ten men, who care not a single straw for all the noises that can possibly be raised against them: and who would be just as insensible to the roarings and the scoffings as they would to the noise of a parcel of dogs howling at the moon.'

Cobbett had brought his personal vendettas with him into the Commons and, shortly afterwards, angered the House by presenting a motion for an Address to be presented to the King praying him to dismiss Peel from the Privy Council for his failure, whilst in office, to manage the finances of the country. The motion was rejected by 298 votes to 6 and the Leader of the House successfully moved that it should not even be entered in the Minutes of the House. Peel was loudly cheered, Cobbett was shouted down, and the Commons decided that it had a barbarian in its midst.

The House generally, in the end, takes its rebels, and even its barbarians to its heart, but years have to pass before they come to be accepted as entertaining and almost lovable comics. Cobbett was denied those years and would in any case have refused to be turned into a cross between a mascot and a raree man. He remained brutally outspoken in Parliament, and about Parliament, for so long as he sat there. He publicly and constantly complained about the way in which it went about its business. It kept ridiculous hours. Members never settled down to anything but drifted in and out of the Chamber as though it were no more than an adjunct to the coffee house Bellamy kept on the premises. He decided that the quality of the speeches was poor, the support generally given to Ministers unduly sycophantic, and the heckling of unpopular speakers unduly childish.

457

He was, it can be seen, industriously trampling on the susceptibilities of the House. He did even worse whenever that citadel of the Establishment acted to defend the interests of the Establishment. He was relentless in his questioning of every Money Bill, and untiring in his demands for the abatement of all taxes levied for the benefit of the tax-eaters. He continued to attack the Establishment's 'perks' in a most uncomradely manner and persisted in exposing each single grant, pension and sinecure Members were accustomed to vote one another. He opposed the Irish Coercion Bill and constantly demanded the repeal of the Malt Tax which, by ceding a monopoly over beer to the brewers, cost the nation considerably more than it brought back in tax.

He spoke more than one hundred and sixty times in that first Parliamentary session, but then, and subsequently, his principal concern was the Poor Law Amendment Bill which became law in 1834. This was a measure to ease the crippling burden of the Poor Rates by abolishing outdoor relief, and Cobbett opposed it bitterly whilst it was still a Bill and never ceased demanding its repeal once it had become an Act.

The Poor Rate was, perhaps, the one tax that Cobbett did not wish to see abated. The arguments for its abatement, other than relief for the landowners, were inspired by the theories of Malthus and Bentham, the two most hated 'feelosofers' in the whole of Cobbett's Rogues' Gallery. The Whigs, under Brougham's guidance, had extracted from their theories two simple, and seemingly irrefutable, propositions on which their Bill was based. The first was that if the receipt of relief were made sufficiently unpleasant, the indigent poor would be discouraged from becoming indigent. The second was that if those who nevertheless accepted relief were strictly segregated according to sex, they would be discouraged from producing offspring. The Act accordingly provided that those who claimed relief would no longer be allowed to live in the community, as they had always done. They would, instead, be shut up in large, purposely built Union workhouses. There, in conditions of contrived discomfort, they would be set to work on arduous but not obviously important tasks, and there husbands would be separated from their wives, mothers from their children, and every male from every female.

The mere concept, let alone its execution, was hateful to Cobbett. He had always, though perhaps mistakenly, maintained that the poor in the community had an historic claim to a share of the community's wealth as of right. It all, of course, went back to the land and the produce of the land. In pre-Reformation days the Church had always, according to him, distributed one-third of the tithes, which were taken in produce, to the poor of the parish, deserving and undeserving, able-bodied and sick alike. When tithes became the sole property of the parson or the squire, Elizabeth the First's Poor Laws made relief of the poor a charge on the parish rate, so retaining a tenuous link between the poor and the land, since rates were a tax on real property. To change this destroyed the last rights of the poor to the soil they had been born on, worked on, and sometimes died, defending. Those rights were inalienable and ought not to be replaced by the carefully calculated charity of the 'feelosofers'.

Much of Cobbett's writing at this time, as well as many of his speeches in the House, dealt with this subject. His last *Register* article, dictated in a semi-delirium from his death bed, was an attack on 'Lord Crackskull', i.e. Lord Brougham, for the part he had played in changing the Poor Laws. Scurrilous to the end, Cobbett described 'Crackskull' as 'a very clever man, though addicted to laudanum and brandy, and with features none of the most human'. Cobbett's last effective speech in the Commons was, for similar reasons, devoted to an attack on the Duke of Richmond for having caused some £2,000 to be spent on extending a work-house in order to put an end to 'the horrible system of bastardy'. The noble Duke, Cobbett declared, had forgotten that he was himself sprung from a bastard, and that he was only noble *because* he had sprung from a bastard.

For so long as his health permitted it, Cobbett was an assiduous Parliamentarian although, towards the end, he would no longer stay for a late-night sitting but left the Chamber by ten o'clock. He spoke frequently, presenting his arguments as clearly and deliber-ately as though he were in Bolt Court dictating a *Register* article. He had confessed to feeling nervous the first time he spoke in the House, but after that neither the heckling nor the quality of his audience appeared to affect him. One observer wrote of him at this time:

In speech and delivery he was quite as dogmatical and downright as in his written diatribe, and he had quite as much sarcastic audacity of self-possession as though he were a wealthy patrician member of that tuft-hunting House.[1]

Sarcasm had come to be Cobbett's favourite weapon, and he had seldom used it more effectively than when, in 1834, he spoke to Lord Ashley's motion to reduce from twelve to ten the number of hours persons under eighteen years of age should be permitted to work in a factory. The motion was bitterly opposed by the industrial interests in the House, their principal argument being that such a restriction on the freedom of labour would place the whole of the nation's economy at risk.

When Cobbett rose, he directed the attention of the House to this particular argument. It had generally been held, he said, that the nation's prosperity depended, variously, on her shipping, on her traders, or on the fertility of her farms and the industry of her yeomen. There were even those who said that it depended on the workings of the Bank of England which had, through its management of the National Debt, its provision of credit and its printing of unlimited quantities of paper money so signally succeeded in spreading prosperity amongst the people. 'But, Sir, we have this night discovered, that the shipping, the land, and the Bank and its credit, are all nothing worth compared with the labour of those three hundred thousand little girls in Lancashire! Aye, when compared with only an eighth part of the labour of those three hundred thousand little girls, from whose labour, if we only deduct two hours a day, away goes the wealth, away goes the capital, away go the resources, the power and the glory of England.'

Irrespective of its message, this was sarcasm most skilfully expressed and most suitably employed. The House has generally been capable of appreciating good oratory whether it agreed with what was said or not. When Charles James Fox rose to speak in support of the Jacobins, and, it was said that although those in the House who agreed with him could all have been packed inside a single post-chaise, Members still flocked in to listen to him. Most contemporary evidence suggests that Cobbett's oratory had no such effect. Yet, over the years, he had developed into a most accomplished public speaker.

Creevey had long since fallen out with Cobbett, and so was probably indulging in spleen when he said of him: 'Cobbett's voice and manner of speaking are tiresome, in addition to which his language is blackguardly beyond anything we ever heard.'[2] Brougham, who had even less reason to like Cobbett, was more inclined to be fair in this respect. 'His style,' he wrote, 'was abundantly characteristic and racy; it had great originality – it suits the man – it possessed nearly all the merits of his written productions, and it was set off by a kind of easy, good-humoured, comic delivery, with no little archness both of look and phrase that made it clear he was a speaker calculated to take with a popular assembly out of doors.'[3]

Those references to *out of doors* and to Cobbett's archness of look and phrase may help to explain why Cobbett failed to succeed as a Parliamentary speaker even though he could always attract great crowds when he spoke on the hustings or in a lecture hall or, quite impromptu, from a window or the balcony of some inn or in the market place. For an agitator, which is what Cobbett essentially was, political speaking would always be a form of street theatre. Professional Parliamentarians generally consider political speaking to be an altogether more serious business, and any hint of theatricality makes them suspect that the fellow lacks sincerity. Cobbett was almost certainly more passionately sincere than the majority of them, but his quick changes of mood, his switches from broad humour to heavy sarcasm, the very use he made of his features, the smiles, nods, winks and confidential asides that amounted to what Brougham described as his archness – all of these may well have persuaded his fellow Members to consider him more of a play actor than a politician.

All of that, however, can be no more than surmise. What is more certain is that the state of his health made it increasingly difficult for him to be as successful as he might have been as Member for Oldham. He had been a few months short of seventy when he was first elected, and seemed, at that time, as vigorous as he had always been. His great strength and rude health had always been a source of pride to him and he obstinately refused to accept that these had diminished in any way. Only six years previously he had taken exception to being described as an old man in the normally friendly *Morning Herald*, and had replied with some heat in the *Register*:

It is an '*old man*', recollect, who can travel five hundred miles, make speeches of half an hour long twice a day for a month; put down the saucy, the rich, the tyrannical . . . an '*old man*', let Thwaites of the *Morning Herald* recollect, who could catch him by one of those things that he calls his legs, and toss him over the fence from Piccadilly into the Green Park; an '*old man*' that is not so ungrateful to God, as to ascribe his vigour of body and mind to his own merit; but certainly, who happens to know of no young man able to endure more hardship or to perform more labour than himself.[4]

James Grant, in his *Random Recollections of the House of Commons*, gave a description of Cobbett at the age of seventy which in no way suggested that the years had enfeebled him, even though they had added greatly to his girth:

Mr Cobbett, in personal stature, was tall and athletic. I should think he could not have been less than six feet, while his breadth was proportionately great. He was, indeed, one of the stoutest men in the House. His hair was a milk-white colour, and his complexion ruddy. His features were not strongly marked. What struck you most about his face was his small, sparkling, laughing eyes. When disposed to be humorous himself, you had only to look at his eyes and you were sure to sympathise in his merriment . . . He usually sat with one leg over the other, his head slightly drooping, as if sleeping, on his breast, and his hat down almost to his eyes . . . Cobbett's usual dress was a light grey coat, of a full make, a white waistcoat, and kerseymere breeches of a sandy colour. When he walked about the House, he generally had his hands inserted in his breeches pocket.[5]

Nevertheless age and illness had already begun to overtake him. Like most full-fleshed men he had always had a weak chest. 'I have at times, especially in November and April,' he had written in the *Register* some years previously, 'a constitutional and hereditary cough, which I have had every year that I can remember of my life, and which is always more violent and of longer duration in London than any where else'.[6] What was particularly troublesome to a man who had to speak in public so long and so often, was that the cough frequently caused him to lose his voice completely. There are numerous descriptions in *Rural Rides* of how, after being caught in the rain during the day's journey, he arrived at the town where he was scheduled to lecture, only to find that he had lost his voice or else could not make proper use of it.

There was a certain irony in the fact that he who, as sergeant-major, agitator and Parliamentarian, had lived so much by his voice should now be dying of it, yet such was the case. By March 1835, when he stood up to speak against the Malt Tax, he could not make himself heard and, after a few hoarse and inaudible words, was forced to sit down. He made his last speech – the one that attacked the Duke of Richmond – in the House on 25 May and it is heartening to know that it contained some scurrilities and was connected with those subjects that were dearest to him, for he was speaking to the Marquis of Chandos's motion on Agricultural Distress.

Illness, in fact, pursued him throughout his short Parliamentary career. In 1833 he had complained of being so short of breath that he had been obliged 'to stop, and to stand still in the street, ten times in going from Crown Street to the House of Commons'. He suffered from what was probably some form of phlebitis, for his heels 'were always swelling in the most odious manner'. In the same year he was forced to retire to Normandy Farm for three months in order to recover from influenza and by 1835 was finding it increasingly difficult to drag himself to the House where, for the most part, he refrained from speaking.

On 26 May, after his Duke of Richmond speech, he went down to Normandy Farm to recover his strength. He was still full of plans for the future, one of them being to launch another evening newspaper to be called *Cobbett's Evening Journal*. He had half-intended, ever since entering Parliament, to abandon the *Register* which was no longer very profitable, but had kept it on because it was the only journal he could be sure would report his speeches in full. In November 1832 he had announced in the *Register*, 'If I be returned a member of Parliament, it is my determination to have under my control *a daily evening paper* to be published in London, without which I should be fighting in muffles; I should be under the infernal hatches of the base and villainous *reporters*. Rather than herd with whom I would beg my bread from door to door, and with whom I must herd, and whom I must treat with both guttle and guzzle, and see my statements either garbled and disfigured, or wholly suppressed . . . I had intended to *drop the Register* at the end of the present year, but I shall *not do that*. It is *so efficient!*'[7]

One is glad that this greatest of all English political journalists never got round to 'dropping' the paper with which he will always be associated. He wrote his last *Register* article for the Number which appeared on 13 June 1835. The one that appeared on 20 June had black borders and contained an account of his death written by his oldest son, William, the only one of his family allowed near him so long as he thought he might recover. For Cobbett died refusing to live with, or even speak to his wife or his children, having convinced himself that they had gone over to his enemies and wanted to rob him of the little he had left. Acting on that belief, he had put padlocks on his doors and windows and his once-adored and long-suffering wife gained access to his death-bed only after he had fallen into a coma.[8]

'A great inclination to inflammation of the throat,' William wrote, 'had caused him annoyance from time to time . . . On the voting of supplies on the nights of 15th and 18th May, he exerted himself so much, and sat up so late, that he laid himself up. He determined, nevertheless, to attend the House again on the evening of the 25th of May, and the exertion of speaking and remaining late to vote on that occasion were too much for one already severely unwell. He went down to his farm early on the morning after this last debate, and had resolved to rest himself thoroughly and get rid of his hoarseness and inflammation. On Thursday night last he felt unusually well and imprudently drank tea in the open air, but he went to bed apparently in better health. In the early part of the night he was taken violently ill, and on Friday and Saturday was considered in a dangerous state by the medical attendant.'

He recovered sufficiently to agree to allow other members of the family to visit him, so long as they undertook not to sleep in the house or give orders to the servants. The following day he felt well enough to talk about his crops, and he had himself taken in a wheelbarrow around his fields, 'which, being done, he criticised the work that had been going on in his absence, and detected some little deviation from his orders, with all the quickness that was so remarkable in him'.

Thereafter he sank rapidly, lapsed into delirium and comas from which he momentarily emerged to speak weakly but with considerable clarity to those around him. His last coherent utterance was a joke at his doctor's expense which left the latter looking blank. 'Mr Cobbett added, with one of his arch and laughing winks of the eye – "There, take that my buck".' He died, then, as he had lived, full of plans, passion, and humour, with his mind still on his fields and his crops and his ear still attuned to the dawn songs of the larks and the blackbirds that had always so delighted him.

They buried him next to his father in Farnham churchyard, and all the politicians, publicists and newspapers he had quarrelled with throughout his career buried him also in praise. Not for them the candid vindictiveness with which Cobbett had greeted the death of an enemy. All those, from the 'bloody old Times' to the Edinburgh Reviewers, who had rejoiced at his every setback and written down his every success, united now in lamenting the death of a great Englishman.

The *Times* was almost excessively laudatory but managed, nevertheless, to squeeze in one note of criticism. It started the obituary, 'Take this self-taught peasant for all in all, he was, perhaps, in some respects, a more extraordinary Englishman than any other of his time . . .' It went on, however, 'The House of Commons, into which he ought never to have entered, and where he never made any figure, has, perhaps, hastened his death'.

There is a fairer and better obituary for Cobbett to be found in something he had himself written, with almost prophetic foresight, a year before his death. It served as an introduction to the last but one of what he called his 'little books'. He had called it *Cobbett's Legacy to Labourers* and explained why he had done so in a passage so full of simple pride that it is empty of vanity:

I call it a LEGACY, because I am sure, that, not only long after I shall be laid under the turf; but after you shall be laid there also, this little book will be an inmate of the cottages of England, and will remind the working people . . . that they once had a friend, whom neither the love of gain, nor the fear of loss, could seduce from his duty towards God, towards his country, and towards them; will remind them that that friend was born in a cottage and bred to the plough; that men in mighty power were thirty-four *years* endeavouring to destroy him; that, in spite of this, he became a Member of Parliament, freely chosen by the sensible and virtuous and spirited people of Oldham; and that his name was

Wm. COBBETT.

Cobbett may not 'have made any figure' in the House of Commons, but who, now, remembers the names of even a half-dozen of those backbenchers who sat in the Parliaments of 1833 and 1835? The *Legacy to Labourers* was, like so many of his works, an immediate best-seller. It is still read and referred to, though not, perhaps, as frequently as *Rural Rides*, *Advice to Young Men*, *A Year's Residence* or *Cottage Economy*.

'Take this self-taught peasant for all in all' as the *Times* had it, he had more right than most to claim, with Horace, *non omnis moriar*.

Oldhamstocks–Brussels–Oldhamstocks,
1978–1982

CHRONOLOGY OF COBBETT'S LIFE

NOTE: Most of Cobbett's published works are listed here. His weekly and daily newspapers are designated (J), republished articles or ones of special importance (A), his monthly publications (M), pamphlets (P) and books, whether single works or part-publications (B). The works of other writers published or translated by him, or with Introductions, Appendices written by him have been omitted. The date in each case is that of the first publication.

1763:   William Cobbett born at Jolly Farmer public house, Farnham.

1783:   Runs away to London and finds work in an attorney's office.

1784:   Goes to Chatham and enlists in the 54th of Foot.

1785–90:   Posted to Canada. Promoted Regimental Sergeant-Major. Meets Ann Reid (b. 1774, d. 1844).

1790–91:   54th ordered back to England. Cobbett obtains his discharge. Marries Ann Reid. Fails in his attempt to bring officers of his regiment to a court martial. Writes, or helps to write, *The Soldier's Friend*. (P. pub. 1793). Leaves hurriedly for France. Spends six months at Tilque.

1792–3:   Tuileries stormed and monarchy overthrown. Cobbetts leave for the United States. Land at Philadelphia. Cobbett applies to Jefferson for government employment and is refused. Moves to Wilmington, Delaware. Teaches English to French emigrés. Anthony Cobbett born.

1794:   Moves to Philadelphia. Second child still-born. Anthony Cobbett dies. Cobbett prospers as language teacher. He writes his first pamphlet, *Observations on the Emigration of Dr. Priestley*. Published anonymously by William Bradford.

1795:   Anne Cobbett born (d. 1877). *A Bone to Gnaw for the Democrats* (P. anon.). Cobbett starts to write under the pseudonym of Peter Porcupine. *A Kick for a Bite* (P); *A Bone to Gnaw Pt. 2* (P). Jay negotiates Anglo-American Treaty. *A Little Plain English* (P); *Le Tuteur Anglois* (B). Randolph resigns as Secretary of State.

1796:   Jay Treaty approved. *A New Year's Gift to the Democrats* (P); *A Prospect from the Congress-Gallery* (P); *The Political Censor* (M). Quarrel with Bradford. Cobbett moves to premises at North Second Street and sets up as publisher, printer and bookseller. *The Bloody Buoy* (P). Threat to burn his shop.

The Scare-Crow (P). Spate of anti-Cobbett pamphlets. *The Life and Adventures of Peter Porcupine* (P); *Remarks on the Pamphlet Late Published against Peter Porcupine* (P). Washington retires. *Observations on the Addresses Presented to General Washington on his Resignation* (P); *The Gros Mousqueton Diplomatique* (P).

1797:   Stops *Political Censor* and starts *Porcupine's Gazette* (J). Prosecuted for criminal libel on instigation of Spanish Ambassador. Acquitted. Yellow fever in Philadelphia. Dr. Benjamin Rush initiates proceedings against Cobbett for libel.

1798:   William Cobbett Jr. born (d. 1878). *French Arrogance* (P); *The Cannibal's Progress* (P); *Detection of a Conspiracy* (P); *The Democratic Judge* (P), republished in England as *The Republican Judge*; *Democratic Principles Pts. 1 & 2* (P).

1799:   Because of pending libel action Cobbett leaves Philadelphia for New York. Opens London Bookshop. Rush case tried *in absentia*. Cobbett fined $5,000. His Philadelphia property seized and sold by the sheriff. Starts *The Rush-Light* (J); *Remarks on the Explanation Lately Published by Dr. Priestley* (P).

1800:   Cobbett threatened with new libel actions and forfeiture of his recognisances. Sails for England. Meets Pitt and other Ministers. Offered ownership of the *True Briton* (J) which he refuses. Opens a bookshop at the sign of the Crown & Mitre in Pall Mall and a publishing house in the Strand. Starts *The Porcupine* (J) to further the Tory and anti-Jacobin cause. John Morgan Cobbett born (d. 1877).

1801:   Published *Works of Peter Porcupine* (B) in 12 volumes. Pitt resigns. Succeeded by Addington. Truce with France which is opposed by Cobbett who supports the New Opposition. Friendship with Windham. *Letters to Lord Hawkesbury* (A). *The Porcupine* sold.

1802:   Helped by Windham, starts *Cobbett's Political Register* (J). Peace of Amiens. *Letters to Henry Addington* etc. (B). Lutz affair. Napoleon Consul for Life. *Le Mercure Anglois* (J).

1803–4:   War with France resumed. *Important Considerations* (A); 'Juverna' articles. Cobbett prosecuted for criminal libel and fined. *The Political Proteus* (P). John Wright employed. *Cobbett's Parliamentary Debates* (B). Thinks of acquiring a place in the country. James Paul Cobbett born (d. 1881).

1805:   Buys Botley and Fairthorn. Eleanor Cobbett born (d. 1900). *Cobbett's Spirit of the Public Journals* (J). Melville affair. Start of Cobbett's attacks on the Pitt system.

1806:   Death of Pitt. Ministry of All Talents. Cobbett parts from Windham. First association with Cartwright, Burdett and other Radicals. Honiton by-election. Start of friendship with Lord Cochrane. *Cobbett's Parliamentary History of England* (B). Death of Fox. Westminster by-election. *Letters to the*

Electors of Westminster (A). Second Westminster Election.

1807: General Election. Tories come in under Portland. Burdett and Cochrane elected at Westminster. Susan Cobbett born (d. 1889).

1808–9: Mary Anne Clarke scandal. Duke of York resigns. Portland ill, replaced by Perceval. Cobbett's campaign against corruption. His prosecution considered. The Ely Mutiny. Burdett sent to the Tower. Cobbett's 'flogging' article. Government starts proceedings against him. *Cobbett's State Trials* (B).

1810–12: Cobbett tried and imprisoned for two years in Newgate. Quarrels with Wright. Perceval assassinated and succeeded by Liverpool. War with the United States. *Letters to the Prince Regent* (A); *Paper Against Gold* (A. published in book form in 1815). Luddite Riots. *The Luddites, or The History of the Sealed Bag* (A). Cobbett released finds himself a public hero.

1813–16: Cobbett's worsening financial position. Richard Cobbett born (d. 1875). End of French and American Wars. *Letter to Lord Castlereagh* (A); *Letters on Late War between the United States and Great Britain* (P. pub. New York); *An Address to the Clergy of Massachusetts* (P. published Boston); *The Pride of Britannia Humbled* (P. published New York). Nottingham Riots. *Letter to Journeymen and Labourers* (A and P). Starts cheap *Register*. Sends nephews to New York to start American *Register*. *Letter to the Luddites* (A). Spa Fields Meeting. Arrest and trial of Spencean leaders.

1817: Prince Regent's coach fired at. Secret Committees of Parliament. Suspension of Habeas Corpus. Cobbett offered £10,000 to retire from politics. Refuses and leaves secretly for United States, accompanied by his sons, William and John Morgan. *Mr Cobbett's Taking Leave of his Countrymen* (A). Cobbett leases Hyde Park Farm, Long Island. *History of Last Hundred Days of English Freedom* (A); *Letter to the Regent* (A). Derbyshire Insurrection. Cobbett attacks Burdett. Farming experiments.

1818: Mrs. Cobbett pays a short visit to her husband. Hunt and Cartwright offer themselves as candidates at the Westminster election. Cobbett breaks with Burdett. *A Year's Residence in the United States* (B); *Grammar of the English Language* (B); *The American Gardener* (B).

1819: Peterloo. Hunt arrested. Suspension of Habeas Corpus not renewed. Hyde Park farmhouse burns down. Cobbett digs up Paine's bones and returns to England. The Six Acts. A cheap *Register* discontinued. Peel's Bill for a gradual return to cash payments. Gridiron challenge.

1820: George III dies, succeeded by George IV. General Election. *Cobbett's Evening Post* (J). Cobbett stands at Coventry and is defeated. Arrested for debt. Files petition in bankruptcy.

Botley abandoned, family lives in lodgings in Brompton. Return to England of Queen Caroline. Bill of Pains and Penalties. Cobbett's support for Caroline. Bill dropped. Libel suits against Cobbett by Wright and Cleary. *A Peep at the Peers* (P); *Links of the Lower House* (P).

1821: Quarrels with Benbow. John Morgan takes over as publisher of the *Register*. Office moved to Clement's Inn and family moves to Kensington. Cobbett sets up as seedsman and nurseryman. Price of wheat falls. Farming distress. *A New Year's Gift to Farmers* (A). Agricultural Committee. *Letters to Landlords* (A). Cobbett embarks on the first of his Rural Rides. Addresses farmers and landowners in several counties.

1822: Second Rural Ride. *Cobbett's Sermons* (B); *Cottage Economy* (B); *The Horse-Hoeing Husbandry* (B).

1823: Third Rural Ride. Norwich Meeting and Petition. Small Note Act. Wheat prices rise. Taxes cut. *Surplus Population* (A Comedy in Three Acts).

1824: *A History of the Protestant "Reformation" in England and Ireland* (B); *A French Grammar* (B); *Letter to Cotton-Lords* (A).

1825: Run on the banks. *Gold For Ever!* (P); *The Woodlands* (B). Third Rural Ride. Quarrels with O'Connell. *Big O & Sir Glory* (Comedy).

1826: Feast of the Gridiron. Recovery from banking crisis. Fourth Rural Ride. *Cobbett's Poor Man's Friend* (B). General Election. Cobbett fights Preston and is defeated. Rents Barn Elm Farm. Experiments with maize.

1827: Liverpool retires, succeeded by Canning who dies, succeeded by Goderich who retires, succeeded by Wellington. Cobbett jokingly offers himself to the King as Prime Minister. *Protestant "Reformation" Pt. 2* (B). Cobbett ejected after scuffle at Westminster dinner in honour of Burdett and Hobhouse. Mrs. Cobbett attempts suicide. Growing evidence of family split. Cobbett spends more time at Barn Elm.

1828: Pressure for Catholic Emancipation increases. O'Connell elected for Co. Clare. *A Treatise on Cobbett's Corn* (B).

1829: Peel's Catholic Emancipation Bill becomes law. *Advice to Young Men* (B); *The English Gardener* (B); *The Emigrant's Guide* (B). Fifth Rural Ride. Growing strength of Radical and working-class organisations and increasing pressure for Reform.

1830: Wellington resigns, succeeded by Whig administration under Grey. Distress in rural areas and manufacturing towns. George IV dies, succeeded by William IV. *History of the Regency and Reign of King George the Fourth* (B). Sixth Rural Ride. *Rural Rides* (B); *Good Friday* (P); *Cobbett's Plan of Parliamentary Reform* (P); *Eleven Lectures on the French and Belgian Revolutions* (B). 'Captain Swing' rebellion.

1831:   Cobbett prosecuted for seditious libel on basis of Goodman 'confession' and acquitted. *Cobbett's Two-Penny Trash* (M). First Reform Bill. Dissolution of Parliament. General Election. Second Reform Bill fails in the Lords. Riots. Third Reform Bill.

1832:   Bill rejected by Lords at Third Reading. Grey resigns. Wellington tries to form government and fails. Grey recalled and Reform Bill passed. Cobbett holds a Chopstick Festival and then tours the North and Scotland. Returns for General Election and is elected for Oldham. *Cobbett's Tour in Scotland* (B); *Cobbett's Manchester Lectures* (B); *A Geographical Dictionary of England and Wales* (B). Rents Normandy Farm.

1833:   Cobbett rents house in Westminster and takes his seat in Parliament. Office moved to Bolt Court. *History of the Regency and Reign of George IV Vol. 2* (B); *A New French and English Dictionary* (B). Final quarrel with family. Lives thereafter at Bolt Court and Normandy Farm. Signs of physical deterioration and persecution mania.

1834:   Tours Ireland. *Letters to Charles Marshall* (A); *Cobbett's Legacy to Labourers* (B); *Cobbett's Legacy to Parsons* (B). Increasing debts force him to sell copyrights and stocks of books.

1835:   General Election. Melbourne Prime Minister. Cobbett re-elected at Oldham. Ill. Retires to Normandy Farm and dies.

NOTES ON SOURCES

1   Arcadia Lost   (pp. 9–37)

1. *The Life and Adventures of Peter Porcupine*, 1796.
2. Ibid.
3. *Rural Rides*, 30.10.1825.
4. *Cobbett's Tour in Scotland*, 14.10.1832.
5. *The Life and Adventures of Peter Porcupine*.
6. Ibid.
7. Ibid.
8. Ibid.
9. *William Cobbett's Letters to Edward Thornton*. Edited with an Introduction by G. D. H. Cole, Letter 22 (O.U.P., 1937).
10. *Rural Rides*, 16.11.1821.
11. *Porcupine's Gazette*, 9.1.1797.
12. *Political Register*, 15.3.1826.
13. *The Life and Adventures of Peter Porcupine*.
14. Ibid.
15. *A Year's Residence in the United States*.
16. *The Life and Adventures of Peter Porcupine*.
17. *A Year's Residence in the United States*, 1818.
18. *Rural Rides*, 27.9.1822.
19. Memorandum to Windham, 27.5.1802. Quoted in Lewis Melville, *The Life and Letters of William Cobbett* (London, 1913).
20. Letter to Windham, 2.5.1804. Quoted in Melville, op. cit.
21. Letter to Windham, 6.10.1805. Quoted in Melville, op. cit.
22. *A Year's Residence in the United States*.
23. Mary Russell Mitford, *Recollections of a Literary Life* (London, 1859).
24. *The Life and Adventures of Peter Porcupine*.
25. Ibid.
26. Ibid.
27. Ibid.
28. *Cobbett's Tour in Scotland*, 3.9.1833 (London, 1833).
29. Ibid.
30. *Rural Rides*, 3.9.1823.
31. Ibid.
32. *Cobbett's Tour in Scotland* (London, 1833).
33. Ibid.
34. *Rural Rides*, 4.9.1823.

35. Ibid., 14.11.1821.
36. Ibid., 7.7.1823.
37. Letter to Charles Marshall. Irish Tour. 14.9.1834.
38. *Cobbett's Tour in Scotland*, 19.10.1832.
39. *Cottage Economy*, Introduction.
40. *Rural Rides*, 11.9.1826.
41. Victoria County History of Surrey, 1900.

2   *Exit into the World*   (pp. 38–57)

1. *Political Register*, 19.2.1820.
2. Ibid.
3. Ibid.
4. Ibid.
5. Ibid.
6. *The Life and Adventures of Peter Porcupine*.
7. Ibid.
8. Ibid.
9. Ibid.
10. Ibid.
11. Quoted in Melville, op. cit.
12. *The Life and Adventures of Peter Porcupine*.
13. Ibid.
14. Ibid.
15. Ibid.
16. Ibid.
17. Ibid.
18. *Advice to Young Men*, 1829, p. 70.
19. *The Life and Adventures of Peter Porcupine*.
20. Ibid.
21. For much of the information about Army life contained in this and
    the following chapter I have drawn, variously, on original material in
    the National Army Museum and on the following published works:
    Hon. J. W. Fortescue, *The British Army 1783–1802* (Macmillan,
    1905); Roorkee, *The Records of the 54th, the Norfolk Regiment*
    (1881); Colonel H. de Watteville, *The British Soldier* (Dent, 1954).
22. *The Life and Adventures of Peter Porcupine*.
23. Ibid.
24. Ibid.
25. Ibid.
26. *Cobbett's Weekly Political Pamphlet*, 6.12.1817. Quoted in Melville,
    op. cit.
27. *The Life and Adventures of Peter Porcupine*.
28. *Advice to Young Men*, pa. 44.
29. *The Life and Adventures of Peter Porcupine*.
30. *Political Register*, 1.4.1821.
31. Ibid., 12.5.1821.
32. *Rural Rides*, 18.5.1830.

33. *Advice to Young Men*, p. 44.
34. Ibid.
35. Ibid.
36. *Political Register*, 12.5.1821.
37. Ibid.
38. *Advice to Young Men*, pa. 45.
39. *Rural Rides*, 1.9.1826.
40. *The Life and Adventures of Peter Porcupine*.
41. Ibid.
42. *Rural Rides*, 14.12.1821.

3 Canada, Love and the 54th (pp. 58–78)

1. *The Life and Adventures of Peter Porcupine*.
2. *Rural Rides*, 8.1.1822.
3. *The Life and Adventures of Peter Porcupine*.
4. Ibid.
5. *Political Register*, 17.6.1809.
6. Ibid.
7. Ibid.
8. Ibid.
9. *Advice to Young Men*, pa. 39.
10. Ibid.
11. Ibid.
12. Ibid.
13. Ibid, p. 31.
14. *Political Register*, 19.6.1809.
15. Ibid.
16. *Political Register*, 6.12.1817.
17. Ibid.
18. Ibid.
19. Ibid., 17.6.1809.
20. Ibid., 6.12.1817.
21. Ibid., 12.3.1831.
22. Ibid.
23. Ibid., 17.6.1809.
24. Ibid., 21.1.1829.
25. *Advice to Young Men*, pa. 142.
26. *Political Register*, 17.6.1809.
27. Ibid.
28. Ibid.
29. Ibid., 17.6.1809.
30. Hazlitt, 'Mr. Cobbett' in *Spirit of the Age* (2nd edition, London 1825).
31. *Political Register*, 17.6.1809.
32. *Advice to Young Men*, pa. 94.
33. Letter 22 to Edward Thornton, 11.6.1800, op. cit.
34. Ibid.

35. *Advice to Young Men*, pa. 95.
36. Ibid.
37. Ibid., pa. 96.
38. Ibid., pa. 140.
39. Ibid., pa. 141.
40. Ibid., pa. 145.
41. Ibid., pa. 146.
42. Ibid., pa. 143.
43. Ibid.
44. Ibid., pa. 144.
45. Ibid., pa. 146.
46. Ibid.
47. Ibid.
48. Ibid., pa. 149.
49. Ibid., pa. 147.
50. Ibid., pa. 148.
51. Ibid.
52. Ibid., pa. 151.
53. Ibid.
54. *A Year's Residence in the United States*, part III, letter to Morris Birkbeck.
55. *Advice to Young Men*, p. 150.
56. Ibid., pa. 144.

4   *A Passion for Justice*   (pp. 79–103)

1. *Advice to Young Men*, p. 149.
2. *Political Register*, 6.12.1817.
3. Rudyard Kipling, *Norman and Saxon*, 1911.
4. *Political Register*, 17.6.1809.
5. Ibid.
6. Roorkee; op. cit. (See Note 21 to Chapter 2.)
7. *Advice to Young Men*, pa. 39.
8. *Political Register*, 14.10.1805.
9. 'A Summary View of the Politics of the United States' from *Works of Peter Porcupine*, vol. I (1801).
10. H. E. Egerton, *The American Revolution* (Clarendon Press, 1923).
11. Fortescue, op. cit.
12. *Canada and its Provinces* (Archives Edition, 1914).
13. *Political Register*, 17.6.1809.
14. Ibid.
15. Ibid.
16. Ibid.
17. Ibid.
18. Ibid.
19. Ibid.
20. Ibid.
21. *The Life and Adventures of Peter Porcupine*.

22. *Political Register*, 17.6.1809.
23. *Advice to Young Men*, pa. 96.
24. Ibid., pa. 97, 8.
25. Mary Russell Mitford, op. cit.
26. *Advice to Young Men*, pa. 216.
27. *Political Register*, 17.6.1809.
28. Ibid., 5.10.1805.
29. Ibid., 17.6.1809.
30. Ibid.
31. Quoted in Melville, op. cit.
32. *Political Register*, 17.6.1809.
33. Ibid.
34. Ibid.
35. Ibid.

5   *A Desire to Instruct*   (pp. 104–118)

1. *Political Register*, 17.6.1809.
2. *The Life and Adventures of Peter Porcupine*.
3. Ibid.
4. Ibid.
5. Quoted in W. Reitzel, *Autobiography of William Cobbett: The Progress of a Plough Boy to a Seat in Parliament* (Faber & Faber, 1933).
6. Ibid.
7. *Political Register*, 5.10.1805.
8. Letter to Rachel Smithers from Philadelphia, dated 6.7.1794. Quoted in Melville, op. cit.
9. *The Emigrant's Guide*, letter 5, pa. 65.
10. Ibid., pa. 68.
11. Ibid, letter 6, pa. 70.
12. Ibid.
13. Conway, *Life of Thomas Paine*, 1892. Quoted in Melville, op. cit.
14. *The Life and Adventures of Peter Porcupine*.
15. Ibid.

6   *The Birth of Peter Porcupine*   (pp. 119–142)

1. Susan Cobbett in a letter to John Morgan Cobbett, 30.9.1835. Quoted in Reitzel, op. cit.
2. *Political Censor*, no. 5.
3. Letter to Rachel Smithers, quoted in Melville, op. cit.
4. *Advice to Young Men*, pa. 167.
5. Ibid., pa. 166.
6. Ibid., pa. 167.
7. *Political Censor*, no. 5.
8. Letter to Rachel Smithers, op. cit.
9. Ibid.

10. *Peter Porcupine's Gazette*, 11.3.1797.
11. Ibid.
12. *Political Register*, 19.9.1804.
13. *The Life and Adventures of Peter Porcupine*.
14. Ibid.
15. Ibid.
16. Ibid.
17. *Political Register*, 29.1.1825.
18. *Collected Works of Peter Porcupine*, vol. IV.
19. *William Cobbett's Letters to Edward Thornton*, op. cit.
20. *A Summary View, Collected Works of Peter Porcupine*, vol. I. p. 113.
21. Ibid., Preface.
22. Hazlitt, op. cit.
23. *A Summary View*.
24. Ibid.
25. *A Bone to Gnaw for the Democrats* 1795, part II.
26. Letters to Windham, 28.11.1802 and 23.3.1803. Quoted in Melville, op. cit.
27. *Political Register*, 10.4.1830.
28. Ibid., 12.10.1805.

7   *Porcupine's Progress*   (pp. 143–177)

1. *A French Grammar*, 1824, letter 2, p. 12.
2. *The Life and Adventures of Peter Porcupine*.
3. Ibid.
4. Ibid.
5. *Political Register*, 22.8.1829.
6. *Observations of the Emigration of Dr. Priestley*, 1794.
7. *Remarks on the Pamphlets*, 1796.
8. Ibid.
9. *The Life and Adventures of Peter Porcupine*.
10. *Remarks on the Pamphlets*.
11. *Porcupine's Gazette*, March 1797.
12. *The Scare-Crow*, 1796.
13. Ibid.
14. *The Democratic Judge*, 1798.
15. *Censor I*, Introduction.
16. *Porcupine's Gazette*, February 1798.
17. *Censor VIII*, January 1797.
18. *Collected Works of Peter Porcupine*, Preface.
19. *Dispute With Great Britain, Collected Works of Peter Porcupine*, vol. I.
20. *Observations on the Addresses Presented to General Washington on his Resignation*.
21. *Dispute with Great Britain*.
22. *Censor VII*, March 1797.
23. Ibid.

24. *Congressional Proceedings*, March 1795.
25. *A Bone to Gnaw for the Democrats*, 1795, part I.
26. *Porcupine's Gazette*, June 1797.
27. *Collected Works*, Preface.
28. Ibid.
29. *Porcupine's Gazette*, August 1797.
30. *The Democratic Judge*.
31. *Cobbett to Thornton*, letter no. 18, op. cit.
32. Ibid.
33. Ibid.
34. Ibid.
35. Quoted in Melville, op. cit.

8   The Homecoming: 1800–1802   (pp. 181–200)

1. Cobbett to Thornton, letter 20, Halifax, 11.6.1800, op. cit.
2. Ibid., letter 21, London, 18.7.1800.
3. Ibid.
4. Cobbett to Wright. Falmouth, 8.7.1800. Quoted in Melville, op. cit.
5. *Political Register*, 1.1.1817.
6. Ibid., 17.6.1809.
7. Cobbett to Thornton, letter 22, London, 4.9.1800, op. cit.
8. *Political Register*, 1.1.1817.
9. Cobbett to Thornton, letter 22, op. cit.
10. *Political Register*, 1.4.1830.
11. Ibid.
12. Ibid., 1.1.1817.
13. Ibid., 1.5.1830.
14. Ibid.
15. Ibid., 10.4.1830.
16. Cobbett to Thornton, letter 22, op. cit.
17. *Political Register*, 6.10.1804.
18. *The Porcupine*, 30.10.1800.
19. Letter to Lord Auckland, 15.6.1801, quoted in Melville, op. cit.
20. *Political Register*, 4.1.1817.
21. Lord Rosebery, *Pitt* (Macmillan, 1906).
22. Letter to Windham, 7.10.1801, quoted in Melville, op. cit.
23. *Letters to Addington*, letter 1.
24. Note by Editors of *Cobbett's Political Works* (London, 1835).
25. Auckland, *Journals and Correspondence*, quoted in Melville, op. cit.
26. *A Year's Residence in the United States*, part I, chap. 1, 5.1.1818.
27. Ibid.
28. Cobbett to Windham, 7.10.1801, quoted in Melville, op. cit.
29. Ibid., 10.10.1801.
30. Cobbett to Lord Pelham, 11.10.1801, quoted in Melville, op. cit.
31. Ibid.
32. *Political Register*, 1.5.1802.
33. Ibid.

34. Ibid.
35. Cobbett to Windham, 24.11.1801, quoted in Melville, op. cit.
36. Ibid.

9 *Cobbett of the* Register (pp. 201–227)

1. Hazlitt, op. cit.
2. *Letters to Addington on the Peace of Amiens*, 29.12.1801.
3. *Political Register*, 10.4.1830.
4. Ibid.
5. Cobbett to Windham, 24.11.1801, quoted in Melville, op. cit.
6. *Political Register*, 12.10.1805.
7. Cobbett to Windham, 24.11.1801, quoted in Melville, op. cit.
8. *Political Register*, 12.10.1805.
9. Quoted in R. W. Ketton-Cremer, *A Norfolk Gallery* (Faber and Faber, 1948).
10. Cobbett to Windham, 1.5.1802, quoted in Melville, op. cit.
11. Ibid.
12. Ibid.
13. Ibid., 17.1.1802.
14. Ibid.
15. *Annual Political Register*, vol. VIII, July–December 1805.
16. Cobbett to Windham, 14.8.1802, quoted in Melville, op. cit.
17. *Political Register*, 20.1.1805.
18. Memorandum sent to Windham in May 1802, quoted in Melville, op. cit.
19. *Political Register*, August 1805.
20. Ibid., 29.1.1803.
21. Cobbett to Windham, 19.12.1803, quoted in Melville, op. cit.
22. *Political Register*, July 1803.

10 *The Enemy Discovered* (pp. 228–258)

1. Cobbett to Windham, 27.9.1803, quoted in Melville, op. cit.
2. Windham to Cobbett, 9.10.1803, quoted in Melville, op. cit.
3. 'Third Hampshire Letter', *Political Register*, May 1809.
4. 'Fifth Hampshire Letter', *Political Register*, June 1809.
5. Ibid.
6. G. K. Chesterton's Introduction to *Cottage Economy* (Peter Davies, 1926).
7. 'The Pitt System', *Political Register*, July 1802.
8. *Political Register*, April 1804.
9. 'Second Letter to Pitt', *Political Register*, October 1804.
10. *Political Register*, 19.1.1805.
11. Ibid., 1.8.1823.
12. 'First Letter to Pitt', *Political Register*, September 1804.
13. 'Paper Aristocracy', ibid.
14. Cobbett to Windham, 7.5.1804, quoted in Melville, op. cit.

15. Lord Rosebery, op. cit.
16. 'Honours to Mr Pitt', *Political Register*, February 1806.

11 *Cobbett's Farming Ventures* (pp. 259–273)

1. Cobbett to Wright, August 1805, quoted in Melville, op. cit.
2. Ibid., 30.9.1805.
3. Ibid., 13.5.1808.
4. Ibid., 27.11.1807.
5. Cobbett to Lieutenant Reid, 22.5.1810, quoted in Melville, op. cit.
6. Cobbett to Wright, 1.12.1805, quoted in Melville, op. cit.
7. *Political Register*, 5.4.1817.
8. Ibid., 10.4.1830.
9. Anne Cobbett to J. M. Cobbett, 16.12.1820, quoted in Melville, op. cit.
10. For this, and much other information, I am indebted to four articles by M. L. Pearl, originally published in the *Countryman* and subsequently republished, by permission, in the Cobbett Society's *New Register*.
11. *Political Register*, 18.10.1828.
12. For details of this meal I am indebted to Mrs. Grimwade's article in the Cobbett Society's *New Register*.
13. *Political Register*, 20.10.1827.

12 *Domestic Life and Domestic Theories* (pp. 274–289)

1. Cobbett to Windham, 6.12.1805, quoted in Melville, op. cit.
2. *Advice to Young Men*, p. 290.
3. Ibid., p. 300.
4. Ibid., p. 307.
5. *Political Register*, August 1807.
6. *Advice to Young Men*, p. 130.
7. Ibid., p. 164.
8. *Rural Rides*, 28.8.1826.
9. Ibid., 21.12.1829.
10. M. L. Pearl, op. cit.
11. Ibid.
12. Quoted in Melville, op. cit.
13. *A Year's Residence in the United States*, chap. 14.
14. *Political Register*, 20.5.1809.
15. Cobbett to Windham, 27.8.1805.
16. Hazlitt, op. cit.

13 *The Agrarian* (pp. 290–317)

1. *Rural Rides*, 31.1.1830.
2. *Political Register*, 2.7.1817.
3. *Rural Rides*, 11.10.1826.

4. Ibid., 19.10.1825.
5. *A Treatise on Cobbett's Corn*, 1828.
6. Ibid.
7. Copland, *Agriculture Ancient and Modern*, vol. II (London, 1866).
8. J. Y. Grey of the Cobbett Society put the problem to the Forestry Commission and quoted this answer in his article on the locust tree in the Cobbett Society's *New Register* of October 1979.

14   The Road to Reform: 1805–10   (pp. 318–340)

1. *Political Register*, 1802.
2. *Political Register*, 5.6.1830.
3. Ibid.
4. Ibid.
5. Ibid., 17.4.1830.
6. Cobbett to Windham, 4.2.1806, quoted in Melville, op. cit.
7. Ibid., 10.2.1806.
8. Major Cartwright to Cobbett, October 1805, quoted in Melville, op. cit.
9. Hazlitt, 'Mr. Brougham and Sir Francis Burdett', op. cit.
10. Letter 2 to Electors of Honiton, *Political Register*, May 1806.
11. 'The Honiton Election', *Political Register*, June 1806.
12. *Rural Rides*, 10.10.1832.
13. *Political Register*, March 1806.
14. 'The Honiton Election', *Political Register*, 1806.
15. Cobbett to Wright, 10.4.1807, quoted in Melville, op. cit.

15   Newgate: 1810–1812   (pp. 341–367)

1. Selections from *Cobbett's Political Works*, editorial comment: vol. II, p. 403.
2. Cobbett to Wright, 3.2.1809 and 12.2.1809, quoted in Melville, op. cit.
3. *Political Register*, 10.4.1830.
4. Ibid., 16.3.1811.
5. Ibid., 1.7.1809.
6. Wallas, *Life of Francis Place* (Longman, 1898), quoted in Melville, op. cit.
7. This hitherto unpublished article was published by *The Times*, who had been supplied with a copy by Wright, on 14.11.1816.
8. *Political Register*, July 1810.
9. Carlyle, *William Cobbett* (London, 1904).
10. I am indebted for these quotations from Louis Simond's *Journal of a Tour and Residence in Great Britain during the years 1810 and 1811 by a Native of France with Remarks on the Country, its Arts, Literature, and Politics, and on the Manners and Customs of its Inhabitants* (1815), to an article by Paul Berry in the Cobbett Society's *New Register* (April, 1979).

11. Cobbett to his wife, 19.8.1811, quoted in Melville, op. cit.
12. Cobbett to his wife, 10.2.1812, quoted in Melville, op. cit.
13. Cobbett to Wright, 25.11.1808, quoted in Melville, op. cit.
14. Cobbett to Thomas Creevey, 24.9.1810, quoted in Melville, op. cit.
15. *Political Register*, 1.3.1812.
16. Ibid., 20.7.1822, referring to a conversation of 1811.
17. *Political Register*, letter 3 to Prince Regent, September 1811.
18. Ibid., letter 6.
19. 'The American War', ibid., January 1813.
20. *Advice to Young Men*, p. 275.
21. *Political Register*, 21.11.1811.
22. 'The Luddites', ibid., July 1812.
23. *History of the Regency and Reign of George IV*, 1830, p. 123.
24. *Political Register*, 3.1.1824.

16 Rancour, Populism and Exile   (pp. 368–393)

1. *Political Register*, 1.6.1811.
2. Ibid., September 1814.
3. Ibid., February 1814, reply to Mr. Canning's Liverpool Speech.
4. Ibid., 16.4.1814.
5. Ibid., 29.7.1815, letter 7 to Lord Castlereagh.
6. Ibid., 8.6.1816.
7. Samuel Bamford, *Passages in the Life of a Radical* (1844).
8. *Twopenny Trash*, July 1830.
9. *Political Register*, 27.4.1816.
10. Ibid., 15.2.1817.
11. Ibid., 30.11.1816.
12. Ibid., 11.4.1818.
13. Ibid., 14.12.1816.
14. Lord Holland, *Further Memoirs of the Whig Party* (London, 1852–4).
15. 'Mr. Cobbett's Taking Leave of his Countrymen', *Cobbett's Weekly Pamphlet*, 5.4.1817.
16. I am indebted for this quotation to M. L. Pearl's article on *Cobbett's Family*, reprinted in the Cobbett Society's *New Register*, June 1981.
17. *Political Register*, 12.7.1817.

17 America Regained   (pp. 394–422)

1. Cobbett to Mrs. Cobbett, 19.5.1817, quoted in Melville, op. cit.
2. 'Last Hundred Days of English Freedom', Cobbett's *Weekly Political Pamphlet*, letter 1, 26.7.1817.
3. *A Year's Residence in the United States*, pa. 163.
4. Cobbett's *Weekly Political Pamphlet*, 12.7.1817.
5. Cobbett to Anne Cobbett, 19.6.1818, quoted in Melville, op. cit.
6. *A Year's Residence in the United States*, pa. 318.
7. Ibid., pa. 16.
8. Ibid., pa. 18.

9. Ibid., pa. 14.
10. Ibid., pa. 22.
11. Ibid., pa. 435.
12. Ibid., Part III, Introduction to *Hulme's Journal*.
13. Fearon, *Sketches of America*.
14. *Political Register*, 3.10.1818.
15. Cobbett to John Wright, 10.4.1808, quoted in Melville, op. cit.
16. Cobbett to Mr. Tipper, 20.11.1817.
17. Letter to Benbow. Cobbett's *Weekly Political Pamphlet*, 29.1.1817.

18   *The Climactic Years*   (pp. 423–454)

1. Anne Cobbett to James Cobbett, 24.12.1819, quoted in George Spater, *William Cobbett: The Poor Man's Friend*, vol. II (Cambridge, 1982).
2. William Cobbett to James Cobbett, 7.1.1820, quoted in Melville, op. cit.
3. Anne Cobbett to James Cobbett, 26.10.1820, quoted in Melville, op. cit.
4. John Morgan Cobbett to James Paul Cobbett, 26.11.1820, quoted in Melville, op. cit.
5. 'To the Radicals', *Political Register*, 28.10.1820.
6. George Santayana, *Soliloquies in England* (1922).
7. *Macaulay's Journal*, 15.1.1855. Quoted in Spater, vol. II, op. cit.
8. See Spater, Chap. 24, vol. II, op. cit.
9. *Political Register*, 26.1.1828.
10. 'A Curious Letter', ibid., 19.4.1828.
11. 'To Sir Henry Parnell', ibid., 24.5.1828.
12. Spater, vol. II, p. 454, op. cit.
13. 'To the Female Reformers of the Kingdom', *Political Register*, 29.12.1819.
14. Quoted in Spater, op. cit.

EPILOGUE: *The Brief Career and Death of a Member of Parliament*   (pp. 455–465)

1. John O'Connell, quoted in Melville, op. cit.
2. *Creevey Papers*, quoted in Melville, op. cit.
3. Speeches of Lord Brougham, quoted in Melville, op. cit.
4. *Political Register*, 8.7.1826.
5. Quoted in Melville, op. cit.
6. Quoted in Spater, op. cit.
7. *Political Register*, 17.11.1832.
8. Spater, *op. cit.*

BIBLIOGRAPHICAL NOTE

Most of Cobbett's important works have already been mentioned in the Chronology and in the Notes on Sources. These last also refer the reader to such books about Cobbett as have provided me with quotations. Every one of the many Cobbett biographies has, to a greater or lesser degree, its own viewpoint and its own emphases. It is not entirely fair, therefore, to recommend only those which approximate to one's own concept of Cobbett.

In this century G. D. H. Cole has undoubtedly produced the best political biography of Cobbett the Radical in his *Life of William Cobbett* (London, 1924; republished 1927; revised 1947). He probably came closest to producing a definitive, single-volume biography even though to achieve it he had to sacrifice some of his customary readability.

George Spater's two-volume *William Cobbett: The Poor Man's Friend* (C.U.P., 1982) comes even closer to being definitive and is rather less partisan. There is always something new to be discovered about a man who was as prolific a writer as Cobbett, and Spater, as befits an eminent lawyer, has produced new evidence concerning Cobbett's private life in his later years. He is also, since he is an American, particularly informative about the American background to Peter Porcupine. Spater's comparative lack of interest in Cobbett as a writer and a 'character' is more than compensated for by the fact that he had two volumes at his disposal, that he researched intensively on both sides of the Atlantic and brings his legal expertise to bear on Cobbett's numerous court cases and his complicated finances. His is a biography that every serious student of Cobbett has to read.

William Reitzel succeeded in extracting from Cobbett's own writings a most ingenious paste-and-scissors *Autobiography of William Cobbett: The Progress of a Plough Boy to a Seat in Parliament* (Faber & Faber, 1933). If it is not the Autobiography Cobbett planned but never got round to writing, it is, nevertheless, the best introduction we have to his life and career as he himself would have presented it.

Equally ingenious is M. L. Pearl's *William Cobbett: A*

Bibliographical Account of his Life and Times (London, 1953). A bibliography is normally the merest skeleton of a man. To add as much flesh to it as Pearl did was a considerable, if slightly perverse act of skill. That skill has also been demonstrated in a number of articles about Cobbett Pearl has, from time to time, contributed to various journals.

W. B. Pemberton's *William Cobbett* (Penguin, 1949) is a useful and easily available biography. G. K. Chesterton's *William Cobbett* (London, 1926) is less interesting as a biography than it is for the insights it provides into both Cobbett's and Chesterton's characters. Asa Briggs' *William Cobbett* (London, 1967) is a necessarily very brief account written around a large number of illustrations. I have, unfortunately, been unable to trace a copy in this country of Mary E. Clark's *Peter Porcupine in America: The Career of William Cobbett 1792–1800* (Philadelphia, 1939) which is highly spoken of by those who have read it. James Sambrook's *William Cobbett* (Routledge & Kegan Paul, 1973) which was written for the publisher's 'Author Guides' series is one of the few works on the subject that successfully combines biography and literary appreciation, something that has too often been denied Cobbett. Other modern biographies exist but, since I have not used them, I leave them to the reader to discover for himself.

Cobbett, a voluminous correspondent, is often at his best as a writer when he unbuttons in his private letters. No one has, as yet, undertaken the multi-volumed work that would be needed if all the letters preserved in libraries on both sides of the Atlantic are to be considered. His letter books in the Rare Manuscript Department of the British Museum alone reveal that many of them have not frequently been reopened since they were first written. Lewis Melville's *The Life and Letters of William Cobbett* (2 vols, London, 1913) is by far the most useful work on this aspect of Cobbett. The 'Life' is, perhaps, perfunctory, but the 'Letters' reveal more about the man than many other more detailed biographies. An almost indispensable aid to understanding the last three years of Peter Porcupine's career in the United States is G. D. H. Cole's edition of *William Cobbett's Letters to Edward Thornton* (O.U.P., 1937) which contains excellent Notes and a good biographical Introduction. It should be added that it is almost impossible for the general reader to appreciate *Rural Rides* as it deserves to be appreciated unless he has had access to the three-volume edition edited by G. D. H. and Margaret Cole (Peter Davies, 1930). It is now, unfortunately, a collector's rarity since it was published in a limited edition with illustrations by John Nash. Quite apart from including the otherwise unpublished Irish Ride and the Scottish Tour, which are included in no other edition. Cole's Introduction, Notes and Index of Persons make this a version of *Rural Rides* all students of Cobbett would most gladly see republished.

Earlier Cobbett biographies tend, on the whole, to be more laudatory than analytical, which was natural enough whilst memories of the great man were still green and people still dreamt of a world made safe for Parliamentary democracy. Robert Huish (London, 1836) and Edward Smith (London, 1878) both produced two-volume biographies full of anecdotal material the modern reader may or may not accept. E. I. Carlyle's *William Cobbett: A Study of his Life as Shown in His Writings* (London, 1904) is a largely bibliographical work which has been more than adequately replaced by Pearl's.

There are several 'Collections', 'Extracts' and 'Anthologies' of Cobbett. These range from that act of filial piety, John and James Cobbett's *Selections from Cobbett's Political Works* in six volumes (London, 1837) to *Cobbett's Country Book: an Anthology of William Cobbett's Writings on Country Matters* edited by Richard Ingrams whose *Private Eye* has some right to be thought of as a descendant of the *Political Register* in reduced circumstances (Davis & Charles, undated).

The scope for background reading is seemingly unlimited. Almost every autobiography, memoir, diary, political work and literary essay of that period contains at least some references to Cobbett, quite apart from what was contained in the newspapers, journals and Reviews. The list of 'Other secondary sources' given by Spater is particularly comprehensive and the serious student is referred to it. There is, between those of his contemporaries who approved of him and those who did not, a great variety of opinions on Cobbett to choose from. Among later political writers and historians one finds that those most interested in the early English Radicals are, quite naturally, those who refer to Cobbett most frequently. He will also, almost of necessity, be mentioned by anyone writing about the history of the British or American press, or of agriculture and agricultural politics, or of gardening, forestry or food, or of British sport, British humour or British social conditions, or of British political cartoons and caricatures of that period, as well as by most military, literary and legal historians. A few of these have been named in the Notes, but it would be invidious to direct the reader to all or any of the many works that have to be read by a Cobbett biographer.

One almost forgotten writer, however, should, perhaps be mentioned, if only because of the personal account he gives of life at that time among the rural poor and the private soldiers in the ranks. This was Alexander Somerville, a man who was, in a few respects, a Scottish version of Cobbett and who, in his *Whistler at the Plough* (London, 1852) and *Autobiography of a Working Man* (London, 1848) described from inside and underneath what Cobbett largely wrote about from outside and on top.

Finally, anyone interested in sustaining and adding to his knowledge of Cobbett on a continuing basis should ensure himself access to the Cobbett Society's *Cobbett's New Register*. Membership and copies of that publication will cost him no more in a year than the price of a drinkable but undistinguished bottle of plonk and will provide him with a series of articles by historians, enthusiasts and Cobbett descendants which, where they do not add to his existing knowledge of that great man, will remind him of aspects of his character and incidents in his life he may well have forgotten. It is entirely fitting that the editor of the Society's journal should be a well-known journalist whose name is Donald Cobbett.

Index

Molière, Jean Baptiste Coquelin, 127, 204
Moniteur, Le, 160, 216–17
Moore, General Sir John, 339, 342
Moore, Tom, 421n
More, Hannah, 219–20
Morgan, John, 175, 188, 192, 199, 207
Morning Chronicle, The, 192, 223–4, 305, 340, 344
Morning Herald, The, 196, 461
Morning Post, The, 192, 214n, 231
Muller, Johannes von, 194
Multitude of Laws, A, 241

Napoleon, 109 and n, 137–8, 160–1, 184, 199, 206, 216, 220, 230, 231–2, 238–9, 244–5, 248, 253, 322, 329, 334, 339, 347, 350, 361–2, 365, 371–5, 376, 411, 418
National Debt, 206, 247, 307–8, 373, 379, 427
Nelson, Admiral Lord, 210, 244
New French and English Dictionary, 445
New Brunswick, 64 *passim*
Newgate Prison, 196, 212, 316, 341 *passim*, 369
New Opposition, The, 194, 206, 236 *passim*
New Orleans, 137 *passim*
New York, 172, 393, 402 *passim*
Nootka Sound, 72–3
Norfolk Petition, 307
Norfolk, Duke of, 323
Normandy Farm, 271, 443 *passim*
'Normans', 237 *passim*
Northern Tour, Cobbett's, 444 *passim*; see also *Scottish Tour*
Northumberland, Duke (Smithson) of, 303, 337
Nottingham, 292, Riots, 310, 389

Observations on the Emigration of Doctor Priestley, 124–5, 128, 146
O'Callaghan, Rev., 445
O'Connell, Daniel, 322–3, 431–2, 456 *passim*
Oldden, John, 154–5
Oracle, The, 229
Orme, Martin, 19n
Orwell, George, 293, 434
Otto, Louis-Guillaume, later Comte de Mosloy, 196

Paine, Thomas, 95, 105, 129, 146–7, 164, 247, 392, 420 and n, 421, 423, 454
Paper Against Gold and Glory Against Prosperity, 359 *passim*
Paper Aristocracy, 241
Paris, bastards in, 217; Treaty of, 140
Parliament, 320, 326, 335, 342 *passim*, 348, 364 *passim*, 456 *passim*
Parliamentary Debates, Cobbett's (Hansard's) 144, 217, 355–7
Parliamentary History of England, 34, 335–6, 453
Parliamentary Reform, see Reform
Patronage, 186, 327 *passim*, 369
Paull, James, 303, 330, 337–8
Peel, Sir Robert, 308n, 426–7, 457
Pellew, Mr., 182
Peltier, of *L'Ambigu*, 216
Penn, Mr., 208 and n, 327
Perceval, The Hon. Spencer, 20, 211, 253–4, 342, 344–5, 352, 360, 365–6
Percy, see Northumberland, Duke of
Perish Commerce, 241, 251, 259–60
Perry, James, 340, 344, 409
Peterloo, 'Massacre' of, 310, 423
Peter Porcupine, birth of, 129; *Life and Adventures of*, 9, 12, 107 and n, 109, 119 *passim*; *Works, of*, 172, 189 *passim*, 193n
Peter Porcupine's Gazette, 147–58, 173–4, 266
Peters, Judge, 171
Petition to the Prince Regent, 411–13
Philadelphia, 9, 15–16, 120 *passim*, 141
Pichegru, Charles, 220
Pickering, Timothy, 137, 168–9
Pilot, The, 224 and n, 225
Pinckney, Charles Cotesworth, 137
Pitt, William (the Younger), 37, 72–3, 84, 94, 98, 106, 183, 186–8, 191–6, 206, 211, 214n, 220, 239n, 242–5, 261, 265, 274, 279, 283, 287–8, 291, 306–8, 321, 325, 328–9, 337, 341, 369, 371–2, 376, 382, 385, 388, 415, 452, 453n
'Pittiad', Cobbett's, 228, 240–1, 245, 249, 251–2, 255–6, 259, 281n, 331–2
Place, Francis, 337, 349
Plunket, William, 254

INDEX

South American Republics, 411 *passim*
Spa Fields, 388 *passim*
Spain, 135 *passim*, 339
Spater, George 423–4, 438, 440
Spence, Thomas (Spenceans), 360, 386, 388–9
Staffordshire Regiment, 20
Star, The, 192
State of the Parties, The, 241
State Trials, Complete Collection of, (Howell's), 34, 355–7, 453
Straw Plat, 317
Stuart, General, 222–3
Stuart, Lord Henry, 254, 261
Summary View of the Politics of the U.S.A., 189
Sun, The, 184, 192
Surplus Population, 339n *passim*
Sutherland, Duchess of, 305
Swann, James, 355
Swift, Jonathan, 38, 293, 357, 434, 440, 447, 450

Talleyrand, Charles Maurice de, 140 *passim*
Tartuffe Detected, see *Observations on the Emigration of Doctor Priestley*
Tenterden, Lord, 436–7
Thornton, Edward, 15, 141, 172–3, 175, 182, 184–5, 188–9
'Tickletoby', 152
Tierney, George, M.P., 214 and n
Tilques, 107
Times, The, 192, 271, 352, 360, 387, 452, 464–5
Tithes, 286 *passim*
Tooke, Horne, 331, 348
Tory, Cobbett as, 24, 109, 149, 187–8, 204 *passim*, 237, 385
Tradescant, John, 312
Treatise on Cobbett's Corn, A, 314–17
Trevor, Arthur, M.P., 436 *passim*
True Briton, The, 184–7, 191–2, 202, 207n, 208, 230
Tull, Jethro, 311, 445
Tuteur Anglais, Le, see *Le Maître Anglois*
Twelve Monthly Sermons (Cobbett's Sermons), 286
Two-Penny Trash, 444 *passim*; see also under *Register*

Vansittart, Nicholas, later Baron Bexley, 186–7, 359, 370, 435
Vauban, Sebastien Le Prestre de, 106
Vergennes, Charles Gravier, Comte de, 135
Visit to Cobbett, A, *see* Fearon

Walpole, Sir Robert, later Earl of Orford, 211, 27
Walworth, William, 36
Wardle, Colonel, 255, 342–4
Washington, George, 23, 132, 140, 151, 159, 162
Waterloo, Battle of, 244
Webster, Noah, 148 *passim*
Wellington, Arthur Wellesley, Duke of, 37, 339, 342, 371, 453n
Wentworth, Sir John, 181
Wesley, John (and Wesleyans), 321 *passim*
Western Settlements, 403 *passim*; *see also under* Hulme
Wey Valley, 23, 25–6, 31–2
Whigs, 228, 385, 391, 436 *passim*, 458
Whisky Rising, The, 159
Whitbread, Samuel, M.P., 365
Whitney, 165
Wilberforce, William, 219, 255, 364, 409–10
Wilmington, 117
Wilson, General Sir Robert, 345
Winchester, Bishop of, 34
Winchester, College, 20 *passim*
Windham, William, 21, 84, 138, 141, 183, 192, 194, 196, 198–9, 206–7 and n, 208–18, 220, 222, 231, 236, 239–43, 245, 254, 256, 275, 285, 287, 325–9, 332, 334, 340, 345–6
Woodlands, The, 19, 29, 313
Wright, John, 154, 182–3, 214, 260–1, 263–6, 275, 285, 287, 327–8, 339–40, 342, 344, 347–8, 351–2, 355–6, 417, 426, 453

XYZ Affair, 140

Year's Residence in the United States, A, 123, 195, 251, 285, 311 and n, 395–6, 398, 403, 405, 407, 408, 418, 444n, 465
Yonge, De, 359

495